RESEARCH HANDBOOK ON EU SPORTS LAW AND POLICY

RESEARCH HANDBOOKS IN EUROPEAN LAW

This important series presents a comprehensive analysis of the latest thinking, research and practice across the field of European Law. Organised by theme, the series provides detailed coverage of major topics whilst also creating a focus on emerging areas deserving special attention. Each volume is edited by leading experts and includes specially commissioned chapters from distinguished academics as well as perspectives from practice, providing a rigorous and structured analysis of the area in question. With an international outlook, focus on current issues, and a substantive analysis of the law, these *Handbooks* are intended to contribute to current debate as well as providing authoritative and informative coverage.

Forming a definitive reference work, each *Handbook* will be essential reading for both scholars in European law as well as for practitioners and policymakers who wish to engage with the latest thinking and ongoing debates in the field.

Titles in this series include:

Research Handbook on EU Criminal Law
Edited by Valsamis Mitsilegas, Maria Bergström and Theodore Konstadinides

Research Handbook on EU Public Procurement Law
Edited by Christopher Bovis

Research Handbook on EU Consumer and Contract Law
Edited by Christian Twigg-Flesner

Research Handbook on EU Institutional Law
Edited by Adam Łazowski and Steven Blockmans

Research Handbook on EU Labour Law
Edited by Alan Bogg, Cathryn Costello and A.C.L. Davies

Research Handbook on the Law of the EU's Internal Market
Edited by Panos Koutrakos and Jukka Snell

Research Handbook on EU Administrative Law
Edited by Carol Harlow, Päivi Leino-Sandberg and Giacinto della Cananea

Research Handbook on EU Health Law and Policy
Edited by Tamara K. Hervey, Calum Alasdair Young and Louise E. Bishop

Research Handbook on EU Law and Human Rights
Edited by Sionaidh Douglas-Scott and Nicholas Hatzis

Research Handbook on EU Tort Law
Edited by Paula Giliker

Research Handbook on EU Energy Law and Policy
Edited by Rafael Leal-Arcas and Jan Wouters

Research Handbook on Legal Pluralism and EU Law
Edited by Gareth Davies and Matej Avbelj

Research Handbook on EU Sports Law and Policy
Edited by Jack Anderson, Richard Parrish and Borja García

Research Handbook on EU Sports Law and Policy

Edited by

Jack Anderson

University of Melbourne, Australia

Richard Parrish

Department of Law and Criminology, Edge Hill University, UK

Borja García

School of Sport, Exercise and Health Sciences, Loughborough University, UK

RESEARCH HANDBOOKS IN EUROPEAN LAW

Edward Elgar PUBLISHING

Cheltenham, UK • Northampton, MA, USA

Published by
Edward Elgar Publishing Limited
The Lypiatts
15 Lansdown Road
Cheltenham
Glos GL50 2JA
UK

Edward Elgar Publishing, Inc.
William Pratt House
9 Dewey Court
Northampton
Massachusetts 01060
USA

A catalogue record for this book
is available from the British Library

Library of Congress Control Number: 2018931757

This book is available electronically in the **Elgar**online
Law subject collection
DOI 10.4337/9781784719500

MIX
Paper from
responsible sources
FSC® C013056
FSC
www.fsc.org

ISBN 978 1 78471 949 4 (cased)
ISBN 978 1 78471 950 0 (eBook)

Typeset by Columns Design XML Ltd, Reading
Printed and bound in Great Britain by TJ International Ltd, Padstow

Contents

Contributors

Jack Anderson is Professor and Director of Sports Law Studies at the University of Melbourne.

Wladimir Andreff is Emeritus Professor at the University Paris 1 Panthéon Sorbonne, Honorary President of the International Association of Sports Economists and of the European Sports Economics Association, Incumbent President of the Scientific Council at the Observatory of the Sports Economy, French Ministry of Sports.

Simon Boyes is a Senior Lecturer and Director for the Centre for Sports Law at the Nottingham Law School, Nottingham Trent University.

Andrea Cattaneo is a Lecturer in Law at De Montfort University and holds a PhD in Sports Law from Edge Hill University.

Jean-Loup Chappelet is Professor of Public Management at IDHEAP, Université de Lausanne.

Corinna Coors is an Associate Professor of Law at the University of West London.

Nick De Marco is a barrister at Blackstone Chambers, London.

Mads de Wolff holds a PhD from the School of Sport, Exercise and Health Sciences, Loughborough University.

Borja García is a Senior Lecturer in Sport Management and Policy at Loughborough University.

Jacob Kornbeck is a Policy Officer in the European Commission, Youth Unit. Previously, as a Policy Officer in the Sport Unit (2001–14), he participated in developing the EU's current sport policy framework based on Article 165 TFEU. He was a co-drafter of the 2007 White Paper and the 2011 Communication on Sport and served as secretary to the drafting group which prepared the 2008 EU Guidelines on Physical Activity referred to in Chapter 3. He is also an external lecturer at the German Sport University in Cologne.

Seán Ó'Conaill is a Lecturer at the School of Law at University College Cork.

Leanne O'Leary is a Senior Lecturer in Law at Edge Hill University.

Richard Parrish is a Professor at the Department of Law and Criminology at Edge Hill University where he also serves as Director of the Centre for Sports Law Research. He holds the position of Jean Monnet Chair of EU Sports Law and Policy (2016–19).

Neil Partington is a Lecturer at the School of Law, Politics and Sociology at the University of Sussex.

Katarina Pijetlovic is a Senior Lecturer in Law at Liverpool Hope University.

Sylvia Schenk is a lawyer at Herbert Smith Freehills in Frankfurt am Main, Germany, and she is Chair of the Working Group on Sport at Transparency International Germany.

Erika Szyszczak is a Professor at the School of Law, Politics and Sociology at the University of Sussex.

Anastassia Tsoukala is a tenured Associate Professor at the University of Paris XI, France.

Stefaan Van den Bogaert is Professor in European Law and Director of the Europa Institute at Leiden Law School.

An Vermeersch is a Visiting Professor of Sports Law at the University of Gent.

Stephen Weatherill is the Jacques Delors Professor of European Law at the University of Oxford where he also serves as Deputy Director for European Law in the Institute of European and Comparative Law, and is a Fellow of Somerville College, Oxford.

Foreword

In recent times, sport has been too often associated with scandals linked to doping, match fixing, corruption or governance. We must of course face reality and mobilise the appropriate tools in order to fight against the threats sport is facing. However the Commission's most important added value is after all to promote the positive aspects of sport and to make the best use of the benefits it can bring for Europe and its citizens.

Clearly sport can offer numerous opportunities. The impact of sport on people and society in general – from health and well-being, to social inclusion and integration – is greater and more important than ever. The need for an active society, and the role of sport, cannot be underestimated in a world where physical inactivity is such a leading cause of health issues. Sport can here too play an important part of the response to exclusion and radicalisation, and help integrate societies.

The European Commission, as with all public authorities, is continually challenged with the task of being relevant, with seeking ways to find solutions and respond to both these challenges and opportunities. At EU level there have been many significant developments in the last decade, most notably the introduction of sport as a new competence in the Treaty of Lisbon, followed by the inclusion of sport within the Erasmus+ programme from 2014.

Through the latter, we can provide valuable funding to sport, especially at grassroots level where it can make a real difference on the ground. As the first Erasmus+ projects come to the end of their cycle, and the programme ramps up another level, the impact will become increasingly apparent.

From a legal point of view, of course, the Treaty does not allow any legally binding measures, but rather supplementary and supporting competences. Nevertheless, this provides us with an important basis for extensive policy cooperation in sport and gives legitimacy to some EU initiatives.

But the cross-over between legislation and sport can be wide-reaching, as sport reaches out into other areas of EU law, where the economic dimension of sport and the organisation of sport meet with the freedoms of movement of labour, competition law, digital single market, data protection and so on. EU law has also to be seen in the context of 'the specific nature of sport', the inherent characteristics of sport which set it apart from other economic and social activities.

Legal certainty is important for everyone concerned in the field of sport. A recent study we commissioned on the specificity of sport illustrated this interaction between EU law and sport, updating our 2007 white paper on sport. It is therefore edifying that this book will add further clarity and insight in this area, bringing together the thoughts of leading authorities in a variety of fields, not just legal but business and academia.

EU law will continue to evolve in the field of sport, of course. And while the degree of legal certainty continues to build and expand, the future of sport is unknown. Match-fixing was not on our radar in 2007 when we published the white paper on sport. It is now one of the main challenges facing sport. Who knows what the future will hold? The newly adopted EU work plan for sport lays out some priorities, but we need to be flexible to adapt to changes as they happen, to respond in a timely manner to challenges. The pace of change in sport, as in all aspects of society, will only quicken.

Mr Yves Le Lostecque
Head of the Sport Policy and Programme Unit
Directorate-General for Education, Youth, Sport and Culture
Unit C4 – Sport, European Commission
Brussels, 26 October 2017

Acknowledgements

Thanks to the contributors for their endless patience and courtesy as I delayed and dithered. In Ireland, deadlines, like traffic signposts, are viewed as guidelines only. I am definitely Irish. Thanks to my family. This project coincided with a move to Australia. Teresa, Daniel and Katherine's support throughout was unwavering and humbling but, more importantly, filled with love and fun.

Jack Anderson, Melbourne, 26 October 2017

In addition to thanking my co-editors and the contributors, I would like to acknowledge the support of the EU's Erasmus+ Programme in the production of this *Handbook*.

Richard Parrish, Ormskirk, 26 October 2017

I would like to thank my co-editors for their initiative and effort to put this volume together and for the temerity of including me on the team of a law handbook.

Borja García, Loughborough, 26 October 2017

PART I

INTRODUCTION TO THE *RESEARCH HANDBOOK ON EU SPORTS LAW AND POLICY*

Introduction to the *Research Handbook on EU Sports Law and Policy*

Jack Anderson, Richard Parrish and Borja García

The aim of this *Handbook* is to take a thematic approach to EU sports law and one that broadly reflects the themes used by the EU Commission in the field of sports law and policy and, namely sport's role in society, the economic dimension to sport and the organisation of sport. Individual chapters address sub-themes of the above areas as put into context by two leading chapters on the origins and sources of EU sports law and policy.

The EU's interest in sport appears threefold in nature. First, it approaches sport as a discrete, vibrant industry or economic activity that not only contributes to growth and jobs in the EU but also prompts issue of compliance with the fundamentals of EU law. As this project was being developed in 2014, the Commission sponsored the first meeting of European Sport Industries on 21 January in Brussels. In advance of that meeting, the Commission released figures highlighting sport's importance to the EU economy noting that: sport is an important economic sector in the EU in its own right, with a share in the national economies of member states which is comparable to agriculture, forestry and fisheries combined; that the overall sports sector accounted for 2 per cent of the EU global GDP, while the total employment generated by sports activities was 7.3 million, equivalent to 3.5 per cent of the total EU employment; sport contribute €294bn to EU gross value added; and tourism profits benefit from sport because on average, in 2014, 12 to 15 million international trips were made worldwide for the main purpose of watching sport events. Despite these impressive figures, the Commission acknowledged that the economic impact of sport-related industries is 'often underestimated', as are the legal issues that surround the sector. This collection seeks, in a small way, to give the study of sport's economic value its proper estimation.

The EU also recognises that sport's non-economic nature promotes individual well-being, community cohesion and reflects key social values which the EU seeks to project amongst its member states and abroad. This policy aspect on the social and health benefits of sport has been the thread that binds the key policy initiatives on sport such as the Commission's White Paper on Sport in 2007, from 2009 with the coming into force of Article 165 TFEU giving the EU a new supporting competence for sport, the aforementioned Communication on a European Dimension in Sport in 2011, and the European Council's adoption of a Resolution on an EU Work Plan for Sport 2011–14, since renewed. The initial and renewed Work Plans specifically identified the social values of sport, in particular the promotion of participation in sport and physical activity among the priority themes, as augmented by a specific chapter in Erasmus+, the new EU programme for education, training, youth and sport for the period 2014–20 and complementing the health policy aspects of Europe 2020, the EU's ten-year economic-growth strategy.

A key supporting principle here is to strengthen the evidence base for sport policy-making and for academics to demonstrate how and why sport can make a difference to the socio-economic wellbeing of the EU e.g., by analysing the correlation between the fact that there is a projected 45 per cent increase in the number of people aged 65 and over in the next 20 years in the EU leading to rising healthcare costs and issues of access to a dignified and independent life for such an aging population (Europe 2020); and yet, in contrast, a similar percentage of Europeans (44 per cent) do not even exercise to a 'moderate' amount on a weekly basis (Special Eurobarometer 412 of 2014 on Sport and Physical Activity).

The third area of interest is one where the EU seeks to mitigate aspects of sport that hinder its development – integrity threats such as doping; poor governance structures; gender, age or social barriers to greater participation – by again funding evidenced-based, impactful research projects. The dissemination of such projects is assisted by initiatives such as the EU Sports Forum, a platform for structured dialogue between the European institutions, grant holders and sport stakeholders. A brief look at the agenda for the most recent EU Sports Forum in March 2017 illustrates the diversity of topics now of interest to the EU under the umbrella of sport e.g., gender-based violence in sport; digital technologies in sport; the regulation of agents; the role of volunteering and social inclusivity in sport; the environmental impact of sport; good governance and the European Commission Pledge for sport organisations; and sport diplomacy.

Complementing the above policy-oriented emphasis are various contributions in this collection relating to the development of EU sports law as found in the jurisprudence of the Court of Justice of the EU (CJEU) or in actions of or decisions by the Commission. At the CJEU, three cases are, unsurprisingly, referred to repeatedly in this collection – *Walrave v Koch*,

Bosman and *Meca-Medina*. The three cases reflect the increasing intensity of the EU's gaze at sport – from the initial peek at sport as an economic activity in *Walrave*, to *Bosman's* glare at football's autonomy vis-à-vis the fundamental freedoms and the sharp glance of EU competition law in *Meca-Medina*.

The aim of this collection is to encapsulate all the above and, as editors, we thank the contributors profusely for allowing us to tap into the breadth and depth of their expertise.

Finally, when the idea for, and possible contributors to, this book was being debated in 2014, the very idea of a Brexit referendum remained remote. How will that vote and the subsequent triggering of Article 50 TFEU impact on sport? Will there be, for example, a reversal of the *Bosman* inspired principles governing sports employment given that the UK (and the Premier League) would no longer be subject to an obligation imposed by EU law to treat Austrian or French, etc players in the same way as British players. Equally, will it be the case that British players will no longer be able to rely on EU law as basis for non-discriminatory treatment in other member states.

The answer to that question lies in the classic lawyer equivocation – it depends. Put simply, the extent of change in the sporting landscape of the UK and EU post-Brexit will depend entirely on whatever deal is yet to be negotiated by the parties, if any. What we do know now is that the 'Europeanisation' of most leading sporting organisations in the UK (football, athletics, rugby, etc) pre-dates, and will almost certainly post-date, the Brexit debate and possibly even the EU itself.

1. Sources and origins of EU sports law

Stephen Weatherill

I. INTRODUCTION

There can be only one place to go to discover the source of EU sports law – the first ruling of the Court of Justice which addressed sport, *Walrave and Koch v UCI*[1] in 1974. And yet – that ruling had virtually no practical consequence and, moreover, it is tarnished by its intellectually unhelpful embrace of the 'purely sporting' rule. So we need to look elsewhere for the source of EU sports law, and where better than the ruling in *Bosman*,[2] which, 20 years of slumber after *Walrave*, truly broke the dam and made EU sports law a live discipline with real practical impact in litigation. And yet – *Bosman*, as a case dealing only with free movement law, did not provide a constitutionally secure basis for mediating the relationship between EU law and claims to sporting autonomy and it too, like *Walrave*, was contaminated by persisting adherence to the 'purely sporting' rule. So the source of EU sports law might instead be sought in the Court's ruling in *Meca-Medina*,[3] in which, jettisoning the abstract notion of a 'purely sporting' rule, it finally adopted a realistic approach to the routine capacity of sporting rules also to exert economic effects and, applying EU competition law, insisted on the importance of conducting a case-by-case inspection of the compatibility of sporting practices with EU law. And yet – even *Meca-Medina* could not conceal the gaping hole in the EU's legitimacy as a regulator of sport, which is that its founding Treaties do not even mention sport. This changed only as late as 2009, when on the entry into force of the amending Treaty of Lisbon, the EU was finally granted an explicit competence to address sport, Article 165 TFEU. So it is surely this which is the constitutionally genuine source of EU sports law. And yet – how can Article 165 constitute the source of EU sports law given that it

[1] Case 36/74 *Walrave and Koch v Union Cycliste Internationale* [1974] ECR 1405.

[2] Case C-415/93 *Bosman* [1995] ECR I-4921.

[3] Case C-519/04 P *Meca-Medina and Majcen v Commission* [2006] ECR I-6991.

post-dates a stream of case law stretching over several decades since *Walrave and Koch*?

There are imposters here, or at least there are pretenders. Choices need to be made. Let us pursue a balloon debate. All four candidate sources of EU sports law are flying in a hot-air balloon, but it is losing height and we must choose which is the first to be thrown overboard in order to save the remainder. We may need to do the same once we are down to three candidates and again once there are two. We need to decide which is the most important source of EU Sports Law in order to provide a compelling account of the factors that have promoted the development of the discipline.

II. *WALRAVE AND KOCH*

Article 5(1) TEU declares that 'The limits of Union competences are governed by the principle of conferral'. Article 5(2) TEU explains that this means that 'the Union shall act only within the limits of the competences conferred upon it by the Member States in the Treaties to attain the objectives set out therein'. The EU is tethered to a defined mandate, which is that granted by the Member States in approving the Treaties. So, logically and constitutionally fundamentally, the EU may not act in the absence of authorisation provided by the Treaties. Sport was not mentioned at all in the original Treaties which entered into force in the 1950s and in fact sport would remain unmentioned in the Treaties until as late as 2009, when the amendments effected by the Treaty of Lisbon introduced Article 165 TFEU.

So in May 1974 when the Court was for the very first time asked to address questions about EU law's application to sport in a preliminary reference made by a court in Utrecht it might plausibly have denied that the matter fell within the scope of its jurisdiction at all. And had it done so, it would have stopped, or at least delayed, the emergence of EU sports law. But in *Walrave and Koch* the Court chose to be more forthcoming.[4]

The case concerned a requirement introduced by the UCI, cycling's governing body, that with effect from 1973 the pacemaker in the world championships for paced cycling should hold the same nationality as the cyclist. EU law clearly prohibits any discrimination on the basis of nationality: that prohibition was at the time contained in Article 7 EEC,

---

4 Case 36/74 *Walrave and Koch v Union Cycliste Internationale.*

its successor today is Article 18 TFEU. Walrave and Koch, aggrieved Dutch cyclists, were obviously victims of discrimination on grounds of nationality. The question, however, was whether that discrimination fell within the scope of application of the EU's Treaties. Sport, after all, was not mentioned in the text.

In a formula which is of foundational significance in the emergence of EU sports law the Court declared that: 'Having regard to the objectives of the Community, the practice of sport is subject to Community law only in so far as it constitutes an economic activity within the meaning of Article 2 of the Treaty.'[5]

What is today Union law rather than Community law applies to sport *only* in so far as it constitutes an economic activity, but professional sport is readily found to constitute an economic activity. Sport may not have been explicitly mentioned in the Treaties, but the whole thrust of the Treaties was and is to regulate economic activity and this was enough to provoke the Court into making the constitutionally significant connection between EU law and sport. Here, then, is the source of EU sports law.

However, the finding that EU law applied did not mean that the UCI rule was necessarily unlawful. At this point the Court muddied the waters. The Court rescued the UCI's rule from condemnation pursuant to EU law by stating that EU law's prohibition of nationality-based discrimination 'does not affect the composition of sport teams, in particular national teams, the formation of which is a question of purely sporting interest and as such has nothing to do with economic activity'.[6] This evidently meant that selection on the basis of nationality for a representative team – in football, in rugby, not only in paced cycling – did not offend against EU law. This is a hugely significant step in the development of EU sports law, because it shows how a foundational value of the EU, the prohibition of nationality-based discrimination, may be applied with sensitivity to the special features of sport, which include matches between international teams. But it is analytically a mis-step. To claim that the formation of national teams is 'a question of purely sporting interest and as such has nothing to do with economic activity' is plain wrong. Players enhance their profile and popularity, and therefore their earning potential, as a result of their exposure as international footballers. Restricting selection for national teams has direct and important economic consequences, and indeed the very background to the litigation proved that. Walrave and Koch themselves obviously suffered financially

---

5 Ibid., para 4.
6 Ibid., para 8.

by being restricted to pacing only Dutch cyclists in world championship events. This was precisely why they had brought the matter before a court.[7] Nationality discrimination defines the very character of international team competition and accordingly it should be permitted by EU law, but it is empty to claim it is a purely sporting matter.

EU sports law began with *Walrave and Koch*. The Court emphasised the Treaty's broad material scope, which is dictated by emphasis on economic activity,[8] and this brings sport within its net despite the fact that the Treaty was (until 2009) barren of explicit reference to sport. But groping for rules of 'purely sporting interest' was analytically ill-judged: most sporting rules, including those at stake in the case itself, are *also* economic in their effects. This, then, is to offer a principled objection to the way the Court framed EU sports law in *Walrave and Koch*. But there are also practical reasons why the case is deficient. It did not generate interest in using EU law to challenge the autonomy of governing bodies in sport. Walrave and Koch chose not to pursue their complaint further, reportedly as a result of the UCI's threat to withdraw their event from the schedule.[9] Two years later in 1976 the Court confirmed its approach to nationality-based discrimination in its brief ruling in *Donà v Mantero*.[10] But then the flow of case law stopped. From the mid-1970s until the 1990s EU sports law slipped into the shadows, a matter of idiosyncratic academic interest devoid of practical bite.[11] Sporting autonomy reigned.

III. *BOSMAN*

Bosman by contrast changed (almost) everything.[12] In its preliminary ruling, delivered in response to questions referred by a court in Belgium, the Court of Justice refused to *accept* a string of devices that were aimed

---

[7] See in particular the Opinion of AG Warner in the case.

[8] This was fully appreciated at the time: see G Ubertazzi, 'Le Domaine du Droit Communautaire. A propos de l'arrêt Walrave, Union Cycliste Internationale' (1976) *Revue trimestrielle de droit européen* (RTDE) 635.

[9] G Veth, 'Uitsluiting van buitenlandse Voetballers: Mogelijk Binnen de EEG'? (1978) 53 *Nederlands Juristenblad* 504.

[10] Case 13/76 *Donà v Mantero* [1976] ECR 1333.

[11] The paucity of academic attention is tracked in S Weatherill, 'The *Lex Sportiva* and EU Law: the Academic Lawyer's Path before and after *Bosman*' in A Duval and B Van Rompuy (eds), *The Legacy of Bosman: Revisiting the Relationship between EU Law and Sport* (Asser International Sports Law Series/ Springer 2016), chap 10.

[12] Case C-415/93 *Bosman*.

at excluding the application of EU law to sport,[13] but then it found space *within* EU law for recognition of sport's particular characteristics in judging whether particular rules were justified. *Bosman* is more sophisticated in its detailed reasoning than *Walrave and Koch* but it shares with that case a readiness to treat economic activity as an adequate reason to subject sport to the requirements of EU law even though the Treaties lacked explicit reference to sport. It then builds a sensitivity to the peculiar characteristics of sport into the interpretation and application of EU law. In the vitally important paragraph 106 the Court stated that:

> In view of the considerable social importance of sporting activities and in particular football in the Community, the aims of maintaining a balance between clubs by preserving a certain degree of equality and uncertainty as to results and of encouraging the recruitment and training of young players must be accepted as legitimate.

The Court could not have extracted this perception from the Treaty, because, as has been made clear, the Treaty at the time ignored sport. So this is the Court finding its own way to recognise the particular characteristics of sport in order to embed them into its application of the Treaty rules on free movement. This is foundationally important in the development of EU sports law. Indeed the very nature of EU sports law involves the mediation of the assumptions of EU law – competitive cross-border markets cleansed of nationality discrimination – with the expectations of sporting organisation which include, inter alia, nationally-based league structures. *Bosman* crafts a model of *conditional autonomy* at the heart of EU sports law – sporting autonomy is respected on condition that it is shown how and why chosen practices are needed to govern sport.[14]

In *Bosman* itself the Court concluded that nationality discrimination practised at the time in club football did not carry the same resonance as the nationality discrimination at international level to which it had given the green light in *Walrave and Koch*, and that therefore it had to be abandoned within European football in application to nationals of EU Member States. The Court refused to accept that a link between a club and a player's nationality was in any sense inherent to the structure of club football. It was led in this direction by a flamboyant Opinion prepared by Advocate General Lenz, who asserted that supporters are

---

[13] Ibid., paras 69–104, 115–120.

[14] This theme is developed in S Weatherill, *Principles and Practice in EU Sports Law* (OUP 2017).

primarily attached to their club rather than the background of individual players by recalling footballers who have been especially popular when playing in a country that was not their own.[15] The Court was more prosaic, but the real interest lies in appreciation that the interpretation and application of EU law required the shaping of an EU view of the character of football, in particular club football, against an entirely barren Treaty background. The Court, tasked with judging whether a practice that falls within the scope of EU law is justified, is forced to behave in a creative manner.

The Court also reached the conclusion that the transfer system from which Bosman had suffered, which prevented a player from making a free choice of a new employer even where his contract had come to an end, was in violation of the Treaty rules on the free movement of persons. The system placed footballers in a different position from ordinary employees in other sectors, whose status depends on contract and is not affected by collectively agreed and enforced arrangements that span the global game. Footballers are less constrained in selling their labour today than before *Bosman*, though a renovated and slimmed down transfer system survives.[16]

Bosman provided a vocabulary and an opportunity: in stark contrast to *Walrave* the follow-up was rapid and eager. EU sports law was on the move. But even so *Bosman* cannot count as the source of EU sports law because it suffers from the same intellectual glitch as *Walrave and Koch*.

The Court in *Bosman*, citing and repeating *Donà* and therefore by implication also the parallel reasoning provided in *Walrave and Koch*, stated that:

> the Treaty provisions concerning freedom of movement for persons do not prevent the adoption of rules or practices excluding foreign players from certain matches for reasons which are not of an economic nature, which relate to the particular nature and context of such matches and are thus of sporting

---

[15] Petar Radenkovic, Kevin Keegan, Eric Cantona, and Jürgen Klinsmann.

[16] The governing texts are at http://www.fifa.com/about-fifa/official-documents/ accessed 26 Oct 2017. There remain open questions about the compatibility of the system with EU law: see G Pearson, 'Sporting Justifications under EU Free Movement and Competition Law: The Case of the Football Transfer System' (2015) 21 ELJ 220; R Parrish, 'Article 17 of the FIFA Regulations on the Status and Transfer of Players: Compatibility with EU Law' 22 MJ 2 (2015) 22(2) *Maastricht Journal of European and Comparative Law* 256; and Weatherill (n 14), chap 9.

interest only, such as, for example, matches between national teams from different countries.[17]

This formula remains as intellectually fragile as when it was introduced in *Walrave*. True, the reasons may not be 'of an economic nature', but the rules plainly exert economic effects. It is empty to describe them as 'of sporting interest only'. *Bosman* shares with *Walrave and Koch* a readiness to integrate the notion that (in short) sport is special into the interpretation and application of EU law but it also shares with it a poorly articulated basis for expressing why that is so.

After *Bosman* the field of play moved away from free movement law to competition law. Not completely: in *Deliège v Ligue de Judo* the Court decided that rules governing selection for international competitions had an exclusionary effect on those not chosen but that such a limitation is inherent in the conduct of an international sports event, and so it rebuffed an attempt by a disappointed athlete to rely on EU law governing the free movement for services.[18] This focus on whether a rule is 'inherent' in sporting organisation was a rather better formulation than that used in *Walrave and Koch* and *Bosman*. But in *Deliège* as in *Bosman* the Court preferred not to address questions referred to it concerning competition law. This soon became the area of the most intense activity.

IV. *MECA-MEDINA AND MAJCEN*

The Commission began to deal with sport on the basis of EU competition law at a relatively early stage. In 1992 it adopted a decision concerning the sale of package tours to the 1990 World Cup held in Italy.[19] But this was not of high significance. The Commission's *ENIC/UEFA* decision offers a deeper insight into the Commission's emerging treatment of sporting practices in the light of EU competition law.[20] In 1998 UEFA adopted a rule which stipulated that no two (or more) clubs participating in a UEFA club competition may be directly or indirectly controlled by the same entity or managed by the same person. ENIC considered that the rule distorted competition by restricting investment in football clubs. This offered a pleasingly simple example of friction between the normal

[17] Case C-415/93 *Bosman*, para 127.

[18] Cases C-51/96 and C-191/97 *Deliège v Ligue de Judo* [2000] ECR I-2549.

[19] Dec 92/521/EEC Distribution of package tours during the 1990 World Cup OJ 1992 L326/31.

[20] COMP 37.806 ENIC/UEFA, IP/02/942, 27 June 2002.

assumptions of EU competition law, which would treat this as a restraint on competition in the market for acquisition of clubs, and the sport-specific concern to eliminate any whiff of match-fixing that would subvert the uncertainty of result that is essential to the very nature of competitive sport. The Commission agreed that in principle the UEFA rule was capable of falling within the scope of what was then Article 81(1), now Article 101(1) TFEU, but, referring to the need to guarantee the integrity of affected competitions, it decided not to pursue the matter further and it rejected ENIC's complaint. ENIC did not pursue the matter either. The Commission's approach is rooted in a model of 'conditional autonomy': the practice fell within the scope of EU law because of its effect on the market for clubs (that is, there is no absolute autonomy for sport from EU law), but autonomy was permitted provided it met the conditions set by EU law which here were attuned to the special sensitivity in sport to achieve a rigorous separation of ownership between clubs that are supposed to be rivals on the pitch.

In *ENIC* the Commission built its analysis on the Court's ruling in *Wouters*, delivered in February 2002.[21] The factual background in *Wouters* has nothing to do with sport. But *Wouters* has established itself as centrally important in the evolution of EU sports law. The Court was asked to consider the compatibility with what is now Article 101 TFEU of a Dutch rule forbidding the creation of multi-disciplinary partnerships involving barristers and accountants. This prevented the emergence of partnerships offering a wider range of services and able to benefit from economies of scale apt to generate cost reductions. The Court emphasised that there were effects restrictive of competition[22] but it took the view that they did not go beyond what was necessary in order to ensure the proper functioning of the legal profession in the Netherlands. The rules guaranteed the independence and loyalty to the client of members of the Bar as part of a broader concern to secure the sound administration of justice. There was no breach of EU competition law. In short, the question was: is the practice of the legal profession 'special'? The answer: it was. And in *ENIC* the Commission applied the same model to sport. Asking the same question, it arrived at the same answer. Adopting the language of *Wouters*, the Commission in *ENIC* asked whether the consequential restrictive effects of UEFA's rule were inherent in the pursuit of the very existence of credible European football competitions.

---

21 Case C-309/99 *Wouters* [2002] ECR I-1577.
22 Ibid., paras 94, 109, 110.

They were, and so the UEFA prohibition escaped condemnation pursuant to EU competition law.

It was in *Meca-Medina*[23] that the Court got its teeth into the matter. This is the landmark ruling concerning the application of EU competition law to sport but even more so, and the reason it competes for attention as the source of EU sports law, it finally involves the Court shaking off its misguided concern for rules that are 'purely sporting' and instead, and in more intellectually coherent vein, it insists on a case-by-case examination of rules that are typically not only sporting but also economic in their effects.

The case concerned professional swimmers who had failed a drug test administered by the sport's governing body, FINA. As a result they had been banned from competition for a period of two years. The case reached the Court of Justice as a result of the Commission's refusal to pursue a complaint by the swimmers, which was the subject of review by the Court of First Instance, today the General Court,[24] which, on appeal, reached the Court of Justice.

The Court began by confirming that sport is subject to EU law 'in so far as it constitutes an economic activity'.[25] It cited both *Walrave and Koch* and *Bosman*. The Treaty prohibitions against restrictions on free movement 'do not affect rules concerning questions which are of purely sporting interest and, as such, have nothing to do with economic activity'.[26] But in *Meca-Medina* the Court then moved beyond this inadequate formula.

The Court added that even where one finds such a rule, this 'does not have the effect of removing from the scope of the Treaty the person engaging in the activity governed by that rule or the body which has laid it down'.[27] The Court explained that the compatibility of rules with EU competition law cannot be assessed in the abstract. In applying Article 101(1) TFEU, 'account must first of all be taken of the overall context in which the decision of the association of undertakings was taken or produces its effects and, more specifically, of its objectives'; and it 'has then to be considered whether the consequential effects restrictive of competition are inherent in the pursuit of those objectives ... and are

---

23 Case C-519/04 P *Meca-Medina and Majcen v Commission.*

24 Case T-313/02 *Meca-Medina and Majcen v Commission* [2004] ECR II-3291.

25 Case C-519/04 P *Meca-Medina and Majcen v Commission*, para 22.

26 Ibid., para 25.

27 Ibid., para 27.

proportionate to them'.[28] The Court cited its ruling in *Wouters*.[29] This, then, is to import into EU sports law the appreciation contained in EU competition law generally that finding a restriction of competition does not conclude the investigation under Article 101(1). It is to open up the legal assessment of practices that have the *effect* of restricting competition also to include appraisal of their *objective*. For sport that means to open up the legal assessment of sporting practices that have the effect of restricting competition also to include appraisal of their sporting objective.

The Court decided that anti-doping rules did not necessarily constitute a forbidden restriction of competition within the meaning of (what is now) Article 101 TFEU, since they were 'justified by a legitimate objective'.[30] Detailed appreciation of fair procedure and proportionate sanctions would be required but the Court could see no reason to disturb the judgment of FINA that the suspension of the swimmers was necessary for the organisation of the sport. This is consistent with the ruling in *Wouters* on which the Court placed explicit reliance. It is also comfortably in line with the Court's view in *Bosman* that the transfer system pursued 'legitimate' objectives and it chimes too with the depiction of selection rules as 'inherent' in the conduct of an event in *Deliège v Ligue de Judo*, albeit that both those rulings involved free movement law. *Meca-Medina* nudges free movement and competition law towards convergence in their appreciation that sporting specificity moulds the interpretation and application of the EU's rules.

The transformative significance of *Meca-Medina* lies in its abandonment of the notion that there is utility in searching for 'purely sporting' rules. Anti-doping rules are plainly sporting rules, for they define the outer limits of permitted competition, but they are economic too, both in their purpose (given that 'clean' sport is more attractive to sponsors and broadcasters) and in their effect (on athletes, whose earning capacity is affected). The Court in *Meca-Medina* is astute to this. A practice may be of a sporting nature – and perhaps sometimes 'purely sporting' in *intent* – but it must be tested against the demands of EU law where it exerts economic *effects*. *Meca-Medina* establishes that few rules are sporting but not also economic in nature and/or effect. The majority of rules are both. This gives realistic shape to the intersection of EU law and 'internal' sports law. This does not subvert the principle of conferral found in

---

28 Ibid., para 42.

29 Case C-309/99 *Wouters*.

30 Case C-519/04 P *Meca-Medina and Majcen v Commission*, para 45.

Article 5(1) TEU according to which the EU law operates on the basis of a limited mandate, but rather it is to emphasise how the linkage of that mandate to the economic project of market integration grants the EU legal order a broad scope in practice. But within that broad scope the Court insists on receptivity to the claim that sport is (in short) special, just as in *Wouters* the administration of justice was treated as special, so that the EU's rules are applied with contextual sensitivity. Specificity is not a reason to grant absolute protection of sporting autonomy from EU law, but appreciation of sport's special features is fed into the analysis in the application and interpretation of EU law. This is the heart of the model according to which EU law grants sporting bodies a *conditional* autonomy.

The consequence of this approach is a need for a case-by-case examination of the compatibility of sporting practices with the Treaty.[31] True, this has attracted disquiet from within sport on the basis that it breeds uncertainty and unpredictability.[32] But intellectually the Court's approach in *Meca-Medina* is far superior than the contorted claim that 'purely sporting' rules are a useful conceptual category; and the Court is conscientious in ensuring that EU law is open to assessment of the claims by sporting bodies that their practices should be treated as necessary for the organisation of sport.

Meca-Medina is now central to the shape of EU sports law, having ousted the unhappy notion of the 'purely sporting' rule from prominence among the sources of EU sports law. So the European Commission's White Paper on Sport, issued in July 2007[33] places heavy reliance on the Court's ruling in *Meca-Medina*, and in fact cites no other decision of the

---

[31] This was noted at the time: see eg S. Weatherill, 'Anti-doping Revisited – the Demise of the Rule of 'purely sporting interest'? [2006] *European Competition Law Review* 645; M Wathelet, 'L'arrêt Meca-Medina et Majcen: plus qu'un coup dans l'eau' [2006/41] *Revue de Jurisprudence de Liége, Mons et Bruxelles* 1799; A Rincon, 'EC Competition and Internal Market Law: on the Existence of a Sporting Exemption and its Withdrawal' (2007) 3 *Journal of Contemporary European Research* 224.

[32] See eg G Infantino [at the time Director of Legal Affairs at UEFA, now President of FIFA], *Meca-Medina: A Step Backwards for the European Sports Model and the Specificity of Sport?* UEFA paper 02/10/06, at http://www.uefa.com/MultimediaFiles/Download/uefa/KeyTopics/480391_DOWNLOAD.pdf, accessed 26 Oct 2017; J. Zylberstein, 'Collision entre Idéaux Sportifs et Continges Économiques dans l'arret *Meca-Medina*' (2007) 48 Cahiers de Droit Européen 218.

[33] White Paper on Sport, COM (2007) 391.

Court of Justice in its 20 pages of legal analysis. This treats *Meca-Medina* as the purest source of EU sports law!

V. ARTICLE 165 TFEU

The problem in the three landmark cases examined above is that all are based on EU internal market law and none – explicitly – is based on sports law. In these decisions the EU reaches sport through conferred competences associated with the internal market which do not mention sport. The examination above makes the case that the Court has been attentive to the sporting context in which it is asked to apply free movement and competition law, but this will not satisfy those concerned to maximise the autonomy of sports bodies and sceptical of the Court's expertise.[34] There was no explicit basis in the Treaty for the Court to frame its inquiry into nationality rules, the transfer system and anti-doping. The Court's case law strains the reach and legitimacy of EU law.

However, as a result of the revisions made by the Treaty of Lisbon with effect from December 2009, the constitutional landscape is radically transformed. Article 6 TFEU declares that the Union shall have competence to carry out actions to support, coordinate or supplement the actions of the Member States in several listed areas, one of which is sport, which appears in Article 6(e) TFEU in the company of education, vocational training and youth. Article 165 TFEU supplies more detail on the nature of this competence. Sport is now mentioned in the Treaties: it is now an area where the EU is authorised to act. This, one might suppose, is the source of EU sports law.

Article 165 TFEU, filleted of content pertaining to education in order to bring into focus what it does for sport, reads:

> 1. … The Union shall contribute to the promotion of European sporting issues, while taking account of the specific nature of sport, its structures based on voluntary activity and its social and educational function.
>
> 2. Union action shall be aimed at: … developing the European dimension in sport, by promoting fairness and openness in sporting competitions and cooperation between bodies responsible for sports, and by protecting the

---

[34] See eg R. Subiotto, 'The Adoption and Enforcement of Anti-doping Rules should not be Subject to European Competition Law' [2010] *European Competition Law Review* 323; D Dixon, 'The Long Life of Bosman – a Triumph of Law over Experience' (2008) 6(2): 3 ESLJ, http://www.entsportslawjournal.com/articles/10.16997/eslj.60/, accessed 26 Oct 2017.

> physical and moral integrity of sportsmen and sportswomen, especially the youngest sportsmen and sportswomen.
>
> 3. The Union and the Member States shall foster cooperation with third countries and the competent international organisations in the field of education and sport, in particular the Council of Europe.
>
> 4. In order to contribute to the achievement of the objectives referred to in this Article: the European Parliament and the Council, acting in accordance with the ordinary legislative procedure, after consulting the Economic and Social Committee and the Committee of the Regions, shall adopt incentive measures, excluding any harmonisation of the laws and regulations of the Member States; the Council, on a proposal from the Commission, shall adopt recommendations.

This is the sport-specific competence conferred on the EU. At the level of constitutional principle it is transformative: *at last* the EU's involvement in sport is explicitly recognised. However, Article 165 is self-evidently not a generous grant of competence to the EU. It is carefully confined in its reach, in particular by permitting legislative action only through adoption of 'incentive measures'. The EU is no sense elevated to a primary position of responsibility in the regulation of sport. The story behind the negotiations that that led to Article 165 is built on the grudging acceptance by sporting bodies that it was politically impossible for them to extract a promise of absolute autonomy from the EU and so instead they preferred the next best solution, which is inclusion within the EU system, but on terms which highlight the claim of sport to deserve special treatment.[35] This is the gist of Article 165, captured most of all in its insistence that sport has a 'specific nature'. Article 165 exists largely because sports federations grasped from the case law discussed above that a co-existence with the EU was unavoidable and so they sought to impose terms on the nature of that co-existence – that it shall be 'sports-sensitive'.

It follows that Article 165 is constitutionally radical but in substance less remarkable. It provides an explicit orientation for an EU policy on sport and a small budget is attached to its development. This is handled by the Directorate General for Education and Culture within the Commission.[36] This would have been constitutionally impermissible before 2009. For example, there has existed since 2008 a sectoral committee

[35] The full story is told in B García and S Weatherill, 'Engaging with the EU in order to Minimize its Impact: Sport and the Negotiation of the Treaty of Lisbon' (2012) 19 JEPP 238.

[36] Its website is at http://ec.europa.eu/sport accessed 26 Oct 2017.

covering employment in professional football, but this is a product of the 'social dialogue' foreseen by Articles 154 and 155 TFEU: it reaches sport via EU social policy, not as a sports policy per se.[37] Article 165 opens the door to the EU's direct engagement with sport, but it is calculatedly limited in the scope of its grant of competence. This is manifest in the Commission's report on the implementation of the EU's first Work Plan for Sport, which covered 2011–14.[38] It describes a strengthened cooperation between the EU and the Member States in line with Article 165 in an effort to develop further the European dimension in sport, and treats the EU's supporting competence in the field as a means to provide 'a valuable framework for all actors to cooperate in a coordinated way and in mutual respect of national and EU competences'.[39] The follow-up Work Plan for Sport to cover 2014–17 is founded on a Council Resolution.[40] It is similarly marked by promises to work with sports governing bodies and relevant competent organisations at national, European and international levels such as the Council of Europe and the World Anti-Doping Agency (WADA), rather than to claim pre-eminence for the EU. In similar vein an EU Expert Group on 'Good Governance' held its first meeting in December 2011 and in October 2013 the Group adopted *Recommendations on the Principles for Good Governance of Sport in the EU*.[41] The intention is not to impose such principles – there would in any event be no competence for such an intervention – but rather to induce better practice.

Moreover there is no hint that Article 165 is apt to alter the trajectory of internal market law. The Court treats Article 165 TFEU as a corroboration of its case law.[42] This seems compelling. The 'specific nature' of sport recognised by Article 165 is readily understood as a confirmation of the pre-existing model of 'conditional autonomy' developed by the Court over the extended period lasting until 2009 in which sport was not even mentioned in the EU's governing Treaties. The Court's rulings in the landmark cases – *Walrave and Koch*; *Bosman*; *Deliège*; and *Meca-Medina* – are expressions of Article 165 TFEU's direction that the EU 'shall contribute to the promotion of European sporting issues, while

---

37 http://ec.europa.eu/social/main.jsp?catId=480&intPageId=1848&langId=en, accessed 26 Oct 2017.

38 COM (2014) 22.

39 Ibid., 2.

40 OJ 2014 C183/12.

41 http://ec.europa.eu/sport/policy/organisation_of_sport/good_governance_en.htm, accessed 26 Oct 2017.

42 Case C-325/08 *Olivier Bernard* [2010] ECR I-2177, para 40.

taking account of the specific nature of sport'. Article 165 is not tied to either free movement law or to competition law. It should be understood as applying to both, and it promotes the need to interpret them in a convergent manner. In sum, the 'Lisbon vocabulary' serves to re-frame the legal analysis, but the outcome of scrutiny of sporting practices with economic effects in the light of EU law does not change at all.

The principal significance of Article 165 does not lie at the level of detail. Instead its chief significance is that the EU's role in the field of sport is legitimated. Sporting bodies can no longer claim that sport is none of the EU's business. Their aim instead should be to accept that the EU possesses a legitimate role but to seek to steer the EU towards full recognition of sport's particular characteristics. Absolute sporting autonomy is unfeasible; conditional autonomy is the model. It is therefore wise for sporting bodies to seek to work with the institutions of the EU, most of all the Commission, rather than to seek fruitlessly to keep them at arm's length.

Astute sports governing bodies had already grasped this before 2009, propelled by realisation that a strategy of exclusion had been so consistently exposed as unsuccessful before the Court and the Commission.[43] Since 2009 the patterns of cooperative activity have become more marked. In 2014 the Commission made a Decision adopting an arrangement for co-operation between itself and UEFA.[44] This asserts 'a common goal to promote and safeguard the values of fairness and openness in sport'. A commitment is made to respect all relevant rules, including competition law. There is nothing particularly surprising about the content of the agreement, the content of which is frankly rather anodyne. The interest lies in its very existence. It demonstrates that dialogue is the envisaged way forward to manage the intersection of EU law and practices pursued in sport. Governance in sports has come to involve a complex network of actors and stakeholders.[45]

A helpfully concrete example is provided by UEFA's Financial Fair Play Regulations (FFP).[46] The overall intent of FFP is to impose a

---

[43] See in particular B. García, 'UEFA and the European Union: From Confrontation to Co-Operation' (2007) 3 *Journal of Contemporary European Research* 202.

[44] C(2014) 7378, 14 October 2014.

[45] See A Geeraert, J Scheerder and H Bruyninckx, 'The Governance Network of European Football: Introducing New Governance Approaches to Steer Football at the EU level' (2013) 5 *Intl Journal of Sport Policy and Politics* 113.

[46] Available via http://www.uefa.org/protecting-the-game/club-licensing-and-financial-fair-play/, accessed 26 Oct 2017.

break-even requirement. Clubs must not spend more than they earn over a defined period, according to a detailed set of intricate rules which include the power to impose sanctions on offending clubs. It is in short a means to suppress 'financial doping'. The legal problem is that this smells suspiciously like an anti-competitive arrangement struck 'horizontally' between parties – clubs – that should be competing with each other. FFP locks all clubs into an agreed restraint on spending, which will, inter alia, reduce spending on players' wages. FFP will also cement in place the advantages enjoyed by the currently dominant clubs in European football by placing high barriers in the path of a smaller club wishing to spend its way to success by attracting outside investment.

It is possible that the arrangements could be saved if, according to the analytical logic considered above in *Wouters* and applied in *Meca-Medina*, they are shown to be necessary to address particular problems that arise in professional football, most plausibly perhaps that they stop clubs winning trophies through reckless over-spending rather than sporting merit: a subsequent collapse of such a club into administration is small consolation to the club that spent responsibly only to finish runner-up to the financial doper. The legal status of FFP is unclear.[47] UEFA, however, has shrewdly attempted to avert the need to defend its rules in court. In 2012 a 'Joint Statement' by Commissioner Almunia and Michel Platini, then the President of UEFA, declared that FFP's 'break even' rule is based on sound economic principle and added that its objectives are consistent with EU state aid policy.[48] The 'Joint Statement' is not legally binding and its reasoning is frankly thin. But its very existence reveals that UEFA and the leading football clubs of Europe have succeeded in getting close to the Commission and securing its approval. The settlement does not exclude that an individual may act as a 'new Bosman' and attack FFP as a breach of EU competition law before

---

47 For illuminatingly different views see C Davies, 'Labour Market Controls and Sport in the Light of UEFA's Financial Fair Play Regulations' [2012] ECLR 435 (lawful); C Flanagan, 'A Tricky European Fixture: an Assessment of UEFA's Financial Fair Play Regulations and their Compatibility with EU Law' (2013) 13 *Int Sports Law Jnl* 148 (probably lawful); N Petit, 'Fair Play Financier ou Oligopoleague de Clubs Rentiers?: Eléments d'Analyse en Droit Européen de la Concurrence' (2014), http://papers.ssrn.com/sol3/papers.cfm?abstract_id=2438399, accessed 26 Oct 2017 (unlawful). See also Weatherill (n 14), chap 10.

48 IP/12/264, 21 March 2012. The statement is at http://ec.europa.eu/competition/sectors/sports/joint_statement_en.pdf, accessed 26 Oct 2017.

a national court[49] but UEFA's cooperation with the Commission has for the time being removed its fears of attack by that institution. The negotiation of the true meaning of Article 165 TFEU seems likely to intensify still further such institutional interaction in the development of EU sports law.

VI. CONCLUSION

EU sports law is borne aloft by all four of the landmark sources examined in this chapter. To discard any one of the four would radically re-shape – and impoverish – the quality of EU sports law. *Walrave and Koch* was vital in asserting the broad reach of EU law, catching all practices with economic effects including in sport. *Bosman* took this further by requiring adaptation of existing sporting practices in the light of the demands of EU law, thereby showing that EU sports law has practical transformative vitality. *Meca-Medina* gave intellectual weight to the discipline of EU sports law by shifting attention away from the unhelpful category of 'purely sporting' rules and focusing instead on a case-by-case examination that is appropriately infused by sensitivity to sport's peculiar features, and which recognises that most sporting rules that operate in a professional context are *also* rules that have economic effects. Finally, Article 165 has provided a constitutional foundation for EU sports law, both by providing the vocabulary of the 'specific nature' of sport as a means to package the existing case law concerning the rules of the internal market and to provide a basis for future contribution by the EU to improving sports governance.

These are the sources of EU sports law. Put all four together and there is a developing integrated pattern to EU sports law which, moreover, has real practical significance. This chapter's Introduction suggested a need to decide which is the true source of EU sports law, and to discard from the balloon those that cannot attain the summit. This would harm EU sports law. And happily there is no need to do it. The most remarkable change to the landscape of sport in Europe over the last 30 years has not been caused by the case law of the Court of Justice nor the pattern of EU Treaty amendments. The biggest transformative influence in sport has been the deregulation of the market for rights to broadcast events,

---

[49] An attempt failed in Case C-299/15 *Striani v UEFA, URBSFA* Order of 16 July 2015 (reference inadmissible). See S Bastianon, 'The Striani Challenge to UEFA Financial Fair Play. A New Era after *Bosman* or just a Washout?' (2015) 11 *The Competition Law Review* 7.

coupled to startling technological advances which have opened up an unimaginably wide range of means to provide such services. Rights to show top-level sport are eagerly sought by broadcasters in order to secure large market shares and the prices paid are commensurate with the ferocity of that demand. Money has cascaded into sport. There is no need to throw any of our candidate sources out of the balloon. EU sports law will continue to be inflated by its earning capacity for some time to come. Let the balloon ride continue.

2. Sources and origins of EU sports policy

Richard Parrish

I. INTRODUCTION

EU action in the field of sport is constrained by the constitutional principle, pursuant to Article 5 of the Treaty on the Functioning of the European Union (TFEU), that the Union can only act in accordance with the powers conferred upon it by the Member States. Where the Treaty is silent on a particular policy area, the Member States retain competence over that field. The EU's founding Treaty, the 1957 Treaty of Rome, did not grant the EU a competence to develop a sport policy and so for many years EU involvement in sport was ad hoc, sporadic and constitutionally questionable. This situation was remedied with the entry into force in 2009 of Articles 6 and 165 TFEU. These articles granted the EU institutions the ability to 'support, coordinate and supplement' the actions of the Member States in the field of sport.

The absence of a formal Treaty status for sport in the Treaty between 1957 and 2009 meant that EU action in sport was predominantly guided by the sports-related judgments of the European Court of Justice (CJEU). Although the Rome Treaty was established with political ambitions in mind, the engine of European integration was market integration and the regulation of economic activities. As sport began to practice as an economic activity, a series of court judgments incrementally defined sport's relationship with the EU and some of these judgments attracted criticism from the sports movement. The concern was that without a counterbalancing statement in the Treaty on the autonomy and specificity of sport, the sector would be damaged through the insensitive application of EU single market competences, such as free movement and competition law, to the sport sector. Initially reluctant to engage with the EU through fear of having their autonomy compromised, many sports bodies re-thought their EU relations policy and lobbied for an article on sport to be included in the Treaty as a means of securing full or partial immunity from the reach of EU law.

The lack of Treaty status for sport also suppressed EU ambitions for sport, particularly given that the increasing economic, political and social importance of sport offered the EU potentially rich opportunities to advance its influence and achieve policy outcomes in the sport and related sectors. The EU was also increasingly being asked by sports' stakeholders to provide a coherent response to contemporary challenges in sport, such as match-fixing, doping and hooliganism, yet its ability to do so was seriously limited by its lack of competence in this area. As European integration progressed, and as the significance of sport increased, sport became associated not only with single market competences, but also with a large number of other EU policy areas including, public health, education, training and youth, equal opportunities and disabilities, employment, environmental, media and cultural policies. Prior to 2009, delivering policy outcomes in these areas through the vehicle of sport was constitutionally questionable, and promoting sport as policy field in its own right was constitutionally unthinkable. The result saw a series of well-intentioned, but largely ineffective forays into sports policy, including the somewhat inelegant efforts of the 1984 Adonnino Committee to promote the idea of European integration through sport.[1] Without formal Treaty status, sport would remain the eternal unused substitute of European integration and EU action in the area would lack status and coherence.

The watershed in the EU's approach to sport policy came following the judgment of the European Court in *Bosman*.[2] In this case, the European Court held that parts of the international transfer system for football players and the use of nationality restrictions in club football were incompatible with EU free movement laws. The Court was attacked by some international sports federations for allegedly substituting the expertise of sports bodies with that of the Court.[3] Although that interpretation is contested,[4] *Bosman* did result in a redoubling of the efforts of international sports bodies to secure Treaty recognition for sport. This lobbying yielded modest results in 1997 with a declaration on sport being annexed to the Treaty of Amsterdam and a more comprehensive discussion of sport being published in the Nice Presidency Conclusions of 2000, but the apparent breakthrough came with the convening of the

---

1 *A People's Europe, Reports from the ad hoc Committee*, COM (1984) 446 Final.

2 Case C-415/93 *Bosman* [1995] ECR I-4921.

3 D Dixon, 'The Long Life of Bosman – a Triumph of Law over Experience' (2008) 6(2): 3 ESLJ, http://www.entsportslawjournal.com/articles/10.16997/eslj.60/, accessed 26 Oct 2017.

4 See, e.g., Weatherill's consistent line on the matter which has been published in the form of collected papers: S Weatherill, *European Sports Law: Collected Papers* (TMC Asser Press, 2008).

European Convention on the Future of Europe. The Convention was established by the December 2001 Laeken European Council with a mandate to conduct a review of the activities of the EU with a view to proposing a new Constitutional Treaty for the Union. The Convention's final report of July 2003 proposed the incorporation of sport into the legal framework of the new Treaty Establishing a Constitution for Europe.[5]

Although the Constitutional Treaty did not secure full Member State ratification and ultimately failed, it was significant for sport. The provisions on sport were retained in future negotiations and were eventually agreed as Articles 6 and 165 of the TFEU.[6] The EU's approach to sport also altered from one characterised by ad hoc interventions to one in which the EU institutions could, in anticipation of the Treaty coming into force, prepare a more systematic and coherent policy on sport. The publication of the White Paper on Sport in 2007, the Communication on Sport in 2011 and a series of EU Work Plans for sport reflected this change of approach.

II. ORIGINS OF EUROPEAN SPORTS POLICY: INSTITUTIONAL AND LEGAL FRAMEWORKS

Prior to Article 165 TFEU, although sport was routinely discussed in relation to a significant number of EU competences, the EU institutions struggled both organisationally and constitutionally to present a coherent approach to sport. A 1995 study on 'The Impact of European Union Activities on Sport' conducted on behalf of the European Commission by Coopers and Lybrand revealed the extensive, although uncoordinated, involvement of the EU institutions in sport.[7] Article 165 allows for a much more co-ordinated approach to sport and, in that regard, the EU institutions act with greater coherence in the development of EU sports policy.

---

[5] Treaty establishing a Constitution for Europe OJ 2004 C 310, 16 December 2004.

[6] For comprehensive discussion of how Arts 6 and 165 TFEU came to be agreed see B García and S Weatherill, 'Engaging with the EU in Order to Minimize its Impact: Sport and the Negotiation of the Treaty of Lisbon' (2012) 19 JEPP 238.

[7] Coopers and Lybrand, The Impact of European Union Activities on Sport: Study for DG X of the European Commission (European Commission 1995).

II.i The European Commission

The European Commission now lies at the heart of EU sports policy. The Directorate General for Education and Culture (DG EAC) is responsible for the policy areas of Education, Training, Youth, Sport, Languages, and Culture. At the operational level within DG EAC, sports policy is managed by the Sport Unit. Although the Sport Unit existed prior to the adoption of Article 165 TFEU, its role in sport was constitutionally restricted. Article 165 clarifies these powers by providing the EU with the competence to 'support, coordinate and supplement' the actions of the Member States in the field of sport. This means that sports policy remains the competence of the Member States and the competent sports bodies, but the EU, and specifically the Commission, can take action that supports these actors. This marks out Article 165 as lying at the softer end of the EU's competences when compared to those policy areas in which the EU has exclusive competence to act, such as with competition policy, or where it shares competence with the Member States, as with environmental policy.

Although soft, DG EAC's powers in relation to sport are numerous. Article 165(1) commits the EU to 'contribute to the promotion of European sporting issues, while taking account of the specific nature of sport, its structures based on voluntary activity and its social and educational function'. Article 165(2) states that EU action in sport should aim at 'developing the European dimension in sport, by promoting fairness and openness in sporting competitions and cooperation between bodies responsible for sports, and by protecting the physical and moral integrity of sportsmen and sportswomen, especially the youngest sportsmen and sportswomen'.

In operationalising this mandate, DG EAC has at its disposal two distinct instruments and a number of policy tools. The instruments are the ability to propose Recommendations and Incentive Measures. Paragraph 4 of Article 165 provides that Recommendations are adopted by the Council on a proposal from a Commission. This contrasts with Incentive Measures which are adopted by the Council and the European Parliament in accordance with the ordinary legislative procedure. Recommendations and Incentive Measures do not legally bind the Member States and Article 165(4) specifically rules out the harmonisation of national laws and regulations relevant to sport. This means that DG EAC, or other Commission DG's, cannot propose sports related Directives and Regulations using Article 165 as the adopting legal base. However, this does not rule out the possibility of the European Commission proposing sports related laws on the basis of other legal bases in the Treaty, such as Article

114 TFEU which concerns the adoption of legal measures necessary for the establishment and functioning of the internal market.[8]

A Recommendation is a non-legally binding instrument designed to steer policy. Such measures are directed at Member States, as was the case in 2013, when the Commission proposed a Council Recommendation, subsequently adopted by the Member States, on promoting health-enhancing physical activity across sectors.[9] Incentive Measures include the financial support of sports related projects. These projects are now supported under the EU's Erasmus+ Programme and administered by DG EAC. The appearance of sport within Erasmus+ is due to the adoption of Article 165 which has clarified the legal environment surrounding the EU's funding of sports projects.[10] Prior to the entry into force of Article 165, the EU's funding of sports projects was legally questionable. In *UK v Commission*, the UK successfully applied for annulment of certain grants for European projects seeking to overcome social exclusion on the basis that the Commission lacked the legal base to do so.[11] This rendered vulnerable ongoing support for certain sports projects and resulted in sporting actions having to be either abandoned or connected to policy areas in which the EU was competent, as witnessed in the designation of 2004 as the European Year of Education Through Sport, education policy being a competence of the Union.[12]

These specific instruments available to DG EAC are supplemented by a number of policy tools. Prior to the adoption of Article 165, DG EAC published a number of policy documents on sport including a White

---

[8] For example, both prior to and following the EU acquiring a soft competence over public health, the EU institutions have passed legislation on tobacco advertising using art 114 TFEU. For discussion on the use of art 114 see C Barnard, *The Substantive Law of the EU* (OUP 2016).

[9] Proposal for a Council Recommendation on promoting health-enhancing physical activity across sectors, COM/2013/0603 final – 2013/0291 (NLE).

[10] Regulation (EU) No 1288/2013 of the European Parliament and of the Council of 11 December 2013 establishing 'Erasmus+': the Union programme for education, training, youth and sport and repealing Decisions No 1719/2006/EC, No 1720/2006/EC and No 1298/2008/EC, OJ L 347, 20 December 2013, pp 50–73.

[11] Case C-106/96 *United Kingdom v Commission* [1998] ECR I-2729.

[12] Decision No 291/2003/EC of the European Parliament and of the Council of 6 February 2003 establishing the European Year of Education through Sport 2004 [2003] OJ L043, 1–5.

Paper on Sport[13] and a Communication on Sport[14] and post-165, DG EAC is active in the implementation of the successive Work Plans for Sport agreed by the Council (see below). DG EAC is also responsible for financing sports related studies in order to assist with evidence based policy making,[15] although other DG's have commissioned sports studies that fall within the scope of their own remits.[16] DG EAC also provides secretarial support and expertise to the Council expert groups and in 2015, the Commissioner responsible for sport, on his own initiative, established two High Level Groups on Grassroots Sport and Sport Diplomacy.[17] As mandated by Article 165, DG EAC also promotes co-operation between bodies responsible for sports. In this connection, DG EAC plays an important role in engaging in regular dialogue with sport stakeholders through the so-called structured and social dialogue.

Structured dialogue is a term given to the EU's discussion with the sport movement. It can take many forms at different institutional levels, but for DG EAC it involves organising and financing the annual EU Sport Forum and other sports related conferences such as those taking place within the context of the annual European Week of Sport, bilateral meetings with relevant stakeholders and high-level meetings between its Commissioner and senior representatives of sports bodies. In this regard, the use of a pledge board is a recent innovation by DG EAC. A pledge board allows a sports body to voluntarily pledge its support for a particular initiative or cause, such as its adherence to good governance principles. Structured dialogue is beset with the organisational problem of how to establish an inclusive dialogue while not undermining its effectiveness. The sports movement is diverse and comprises Olympic sports and non-Olympic sports, professional and amateur sports, competitive and recreational sports, grassroots sports and sport for people with disabilities. Organisationally, sport in Europe does not conform to any

---

13 White Paper on Sport, COM(2007) 391 final.

14 Developing the European Dimension in Sport (the Communication on Sport), COM(2011) 12 final.

15 See, for example, *Mapping and Analysis of the Specificity of Sport, A Final Report to the DG Education & Culture of the European Commission* (European Commission 2016) p 46.

16 The DG EAC sports related studies can be accessed on the Sport Unit's website: http://ec.europa.eu/sport/library/index_en.htm accessed 26 Oct 2017.

17 Both reports were submitted to Commissioner Navracsics in June 2016. The report on Grassroots Sport can be accessed at: http://ec.europa.eu/sport/library/policy_documents/hlg-grassroots-final_en.pdf and the report on Sport Diplomacy accessed at: http://ec.europa.eu/sport/library/policy_documents/hlg-sport-diplomacy-final_en.pdf both accessed 26 Oct 2017.

single model, often referred to as the European model of sport, and in terms of the representation of interests, clubs, leagues, athletes and other stakeholders such as supporter groups, agent associations and commercial interests have legitimate claims to access structured dialogue. Very broad multi-lateral dialogue renders effective outcomes unlikely but equally, limited bilateral dialogue undermines the legitimacy of outcomes as stakeholders feel excluded from the process. For example, the Commission attracted criticism for agreeing to a co-operation agreement with UEFA in 2014[18] and prior to that in 2012, the 'Striani' complaint was made to the EU Ombudsman that a joint statement made by the Commission and UEFA regarding UEFA's Financial Fair Play (FFP) regulations was prejudicial to a challenge to the regulations launched by a football agent.[19]

Social dialogue, by contrast, is a tool advocated by DG EAC in its sports related policy papers, but an area falling within the remit of the DG responsible for Employment, Social Affairs and Inclusion (DG EMPL). Located in Articles 152–155 TFEU, social dialogue refers to discussions, consultations, negotiations and joint actions involving organisations representing employers and workers (the social partners). The Commission has advocated social dialogue as a means through which labour related disputes in sport can be resolved. With the support of DG EMPL, a Social Dialogue Committee for European Professional Football was established in 2008 and in 2012 it concluded its first agreement on minimum conditions in player contracts.[20] A European sectoral social dialogue in the sport and active leisure sector is also being established.

---

[18] Commission Decision of 14.10.2014 adopting the Arrangement for Cooperation between the European Commission and the Union of European Football Associations (UEFA), C(2014) 7378 final.

[19] The joint statement was made by Commission Vice President Almunia and UEFA President Platini on 21 March 2012, IP/12/264 and available at http://ec.europa.eu/competition/sectors/sports/joint_statement_en.pdf accessed 26 Oct 2017. The complaint to the EU Ombudsman was issued by Daniel Striani following the Commission's rejection of his challenge to the FFP Regulations, see Case C-299/15 *Striani v UEFA, URBSFA* Order of 16 July 2015 (reference inadmissible) and Decision of the European Ombudsman in case 2086/2014/EIS https://www.ombudsman.europa.eu/en/cases/decision.faces/en/61468/html.bookmark (accessed 26 Oct 2017).

[20] Agreement regarding the minimum requirements for standard player contracts in the professional football sector in the European Union and the rest of the UEFA territory, 19 April 2012, http://www.ecaeurope.com/Documents/Dialogue%20social%20IX%20Final%20Version.pdf accessed 26 Oct 2017.

The involvement of DG EMPL in sporting issues highlights how sport has the potential to cut across a range of EU competences. The activities of a number of DG's has the potential to affect sport. For example, the digital single market and media work of the Directorate General for Communications Networks, Content and Technology (DG CONNECT) has implications for sports media rights. In particular, the Audiovisual and Media Services Directive[21] establishes framework conditions allowing Member States to adopt measures to ensure that broadcasters under its jurisdiction do not broadcast events of major importance for society, such as sporting events, on an exclusive basis, as it would deprive the possibility for a majority of the public to follow them.[22]

Perhaps the most significant impact of Commission activities on sport relates to the Commission's enforcement of EU law. In this connection, the activities of DG Internal Market, Industry, Entrepreneurship and SMEs (DG GROW) and DG Competition (DG COMP) are of particular importance. For example, in July 2016, the Commission referred Austria to the CJEU for alleged infringements of EU law relating to restrictions some Austrian provinces impose on ski instructors coming from other EU countries.[23] The Commission's enforcement of the competition rules in the areas of antitrust and cartels, mergers and state aid has been very significant for the sport sector. As will be discussed in various contributions to this collection, DG COMP has dealt with a large number of competition law complaints and has been instrumental in requiring amendments to be made to sporting rules and practices either by way of formal decisions or informal settlements.

Some of these interventions have been very important, and indeed transformative, for the sports sector. For example, the Commission's line of sports broadcasting cases has been influential in allowing sports bodies to develop business models that have generated very significant incomes for the sector. For example, in *British Satellite Broadcasting (BSB)*, the Commission approved an exclusive five-year agreement for what is now Sky plc to broadcast a number of live English football

---

[21] Directive 2010/13/EU Audiovisual Media Services Directive [2010] OJ L 95/1.

[22] See Cases C-205/11 P and C-204/11 P, *FIFA v Commission*, judgment of 18 July 2013.

[23] Freedom to provide services: Commission refers Austria to Court of Justice of the EU over restrictions on foreign ski instructors, IP/16/2493, 22 July 2016.

matches between 1988 and 1993 to a subscription audience.[24] The decision to exempt the agreement from the competition rules was justified by the Commission on the grounds that as a new operator embracing new satellite technology, as opposed to the traditional terrestrial form, BSB needed a long-term contract to establish its operations. The exemption decision helped establish Sky as a market leader for sports rights and was significant in the transformation of not only English football but also the pan-European media industry.

Although the Commission has subsequently amended its approach to the exploitation of sports rights, its choice in later cases to issue a number of exemption decisions in a line of collective selling of sports rights cases has also been significant.[25] The decision to approve the principle of collective selling has been central to the revenue generating business models of some sports, most notably football. The revenues generated from collective selling have not only allowed for redistributive revenue flows within sport, but also contributed to the transformation in the value of the player market in the sector.

II.ii The European Parliament

Despite the absence of a sports competence in the Treaty, the European Parliament has been an active player in sporting matters and has been a strong advocate of greater EU involvement in sport either by way of advocating greater EU powers in this area[26] or through criticising certain sporting practices as witnessed in the Parliament's 1989 Van Raay Report condemning the use of nationality restrictions and the international transfer system prior to the Court's judgment in *Bosman.*[27]

Successive amendments to the European treaties have strengthened the legislative, budgetary and scrutinising powers of the Parliament. In most

---

[24] Case No. IV/33.245 *BBC, BSB and Football Association* [1993] OJ C94/06.

[25] See, e.g., the Commission's approach to collective selling cases in: UEFA Champions League Decision 2003/778 [2003] OJ L291/25; Bundesliga Decision 2005/396 [2005] OJ L134/46; and Football Association Premier League Decision C(2006) 868 [2008] OJ C7/10.

[26] See, e,g,, J Larive, 'Report of the Committee on Culture, Youth, Education and the Media on the European Community and Sport' (European Parliament, 1994) and D Pack, 'Report on the Role of the European Union in the Field of Sport' (European Parliament, 1997).

[27] J van Raay, 'Report for the Committee on Legal Affairs and Citizen's Rights, on the freedom of movement of professional footballers in the Community' (European Parliament, 1989).

areas, the Parliament is co-legislator, sharing with the Council the ability to adopt and amend EU legislation and the EU budget. This power gives the Parliament the ability to influence legislation that although not specifically directed at sport, can have an impact on it. For example, the Parliament inserted an amendment into the second Television Without Frontiers Directive in 1997 enabling Member States to adopt lists of major events, including sporting events, that should be available to the public on free-to-air television.[28]

In sporting matters, parliamentary approval is required for the adoption of Incentive Measures under Article 165 and in this connection, the Parliament has played a role in the adoption of funding programmes for sport. In addition to this role, the Parliament has adopted opinions, reports and resolutions on sport related matters, asked sports related questions of the Commission, commissioned its own sport related studies and organised hearings on sporting issues, such as the 2016 hearing on the Takkula sport report on 'An Integrated Approach to Sport Policy: Good Governance, Accessibility and Integrity'.[29]

Within the Parliament's committee system, sport is dealt with in the Committee for Culture and Education (CULT), although other committees often discuss sporting matters depending on the context. A Sports Intergroup also operates within the Parliament. The Intergroup is an informal group of Members of the European Parliament (MEPs) interested in sporting matters.

II.iii The Council

The sectoral Council of the European Union (Council) is composed of the relevant Member State Ministers depending on the subject being discussed. It acts as the EU's legislator, a role it shares in most cases with the Parliament. Until the entry into force of the Lisbon Treaty, no formal Sports Council existed and the impact of the Council on sport was limited to situations in which its general legislative output affected sporting rules and practices. Regardless of the lack of competence to pass sports legislation, Sports Ministers or their representatives did meet informally on a number of occasions prior to Lisbon. This reflected the

---

[28] Art 3a Directive 97/36/EC and now Directive 2010/13/EU Audiovisual Media Services Directive [2010] OJ L 95/1.

[29] H Takkula, 'Draft Report on Committee on Culture and Education on an Integrated Approach to Sport Policy: Good Governance, Accessibility and Integrity' (European Parliament, 2016/2143(INI)).

Member States' desire to prepare for possible Treaty reform to incorporate sport into the Treaty. For example, in 2004 the Member States established a rolling agenda for sport in order to define priority themes for discussions on sport and as part of this process a Ministerial Conference was organised jointly by the Commission and the Finnish Presidency in 2006.[30] In 2006, the UK Council Presidency commissioned the 'Independent European Sport Review', also known as the Arnaut Report.[31] The non-binding Arnaut Report strongly recommended the EU respect the autonomy and specificity of sport, but conditioned this view on sports bodies adhering to principles of good governance.

Since 2010, following the adoption of Article 165, Sports Ministers do meet formally in Council as part of the Education, Culture, Youth and Sport Council. Formal Council meetings are held twice a year with Sport Ministers also continuing to meet informally. Much of the work of the Council, such as agenda setting, is undertaken by the Council Working Party on Sport. This group is composed of delegates from national ministries responsible for sport and specialised technical staff from the Member States' permanent representations in Brussels.[32]

As explained above, Article 165 grants the EU the possibility to adopt Recommendations and Incentive Measures. On a proposal from the Commission, the Sport Ministers' Council can adopt Recommendations but the approval of the Parliament is required for the adoption of Incentive Measures, such as funding programmes. The Council's legislative power is seriously constrained by the fourth paragraph of Article 165 which prohibits the harmonisation of the laws and regulations of the Member States.

Given the legislative limitations of the Council, much of the Council's sports related work involves the adoption of Conclusions and Resolutions, which are not intended to have legal effects and are designed to express a political position on a topic. Council Conclusions are adopted following debate in Council as was the case in 2016 with the adoption of Council Conclusions on 'Enhancing integrity, transparency and good

---

30 'The EU and Sport: Matching Expectations; Consultation Conference with the European Sport Movement' Brussels, 27–28 November 2006.

31 J Arnaut, Independent Sport Review (2006) discussed by B García, 'The Independent European Sport Review: Half Full or Half Empty?' (2007) 4(3) ESLJ http://www.entsportslawjournal.com/articles/10.16997/eslj.82/print/ accessed 26 Oct 2017.

32 EOC EU Office, Guide to EU Sport Policy (European Olympic Committee 2011) p 10.

governance in major sport events'[33] and with the conclusions on EU sport diplomacy in 2016.[34] Council Resolutions set out a future plan of action in a specific field, which may entail the Commission proposing future legislation. They are widely employed in areas, such as sport, where the EU only has limited competence. For example, in 2010, the Council adopted a Council Resolution on the EU structured dialogue on sport which called for the convening, on a regular basis, and in the margin of the Council meeting, an informal meeting of leading representatives of the EU public authorities and the sports movement with the aim of exchanging views on sporting issues in the EU.[35] In 2011, the Council, by way of a Resolution, adopted the first European Union Work Plan for Sport which ran until 2014.[36] A second Work Plan was adopted for the period 2014–17[37] and a third was agreed in 2017 running until 2020.[38]

II.iv The Court of Justice of the European Union

The jurisprudence of the CJEU has played a vital role in shaping and constraining the approach to sports policy taken by the EU institutions. For example, in *Bosman*, the Court criticised the Commission's complicity in constructing, with UEFA, discriminatory player quotas in European football. In the judgment, the Court reminded the Commission that it does not possess the power to authorise practices that are contrary to the Treaty.[39] Mindful of this experience, the Commission's 2007 White Paper package and its 2011 Communication on Sport fully endorse

---

[33] Conclusions of the Council of the European Union, Enhancing Integrity, Transparency and Good Governance in Major Sport Events (Council of Europe, Doc.9644/16).

[34] Conclusions of the Council of the European Union, Sport Diplomacy (Council of Europe, Doc. 14279/16).

[35] Resolution of the Council of the European Union, EU Structured Dialogue on Sport at 3046th Education, Youth, Culture and Sport Council meeting Brussels, 18 and 19 November 2010 (Council of Europe, 16500/10 Press304).

[36] Resolution of the Council of the European Union and of the Representatives of the Governments of the Member States, European Union Work Plan for Sport for 2011–2014 [2011] OJ C162.

[37] Resolution of the Council of the European Union and of the Representatives of the Governments of the Member States, European Union Work Plan for Sport for 2014–2017 [2014] OJ C183.

[38] Resolution of the Council of the European Union and of the Representatives of the Governments of the Member States, European Union Work Plan for Sport for 2017–2020 [2017] OJ C189.

[39] Case C-415/93 *Bosman* [1995] ECR I-4921, para 136.

the Court's methodological approach to sports cases enunciated in *Meca-Medina*.[40]

The CJEU can hear sports-related disputes through three key routes. First, the preliminary reference procedure allows national courts to refer cases to the European Court for a preliminary ruling which provides guidance on the interpretation or validity of EU law.[41] Second, infringement proceedings before the Court can be initiated by the Commission against Member States for alleged breaches of EU law.[42] Finally, actions for annulment arise in instances where EU institutions or private individuals seek to challenge an EU act, such as a Commission competition decision.[43] In this regard, Article 256 TFEU establishes that decisions given by the General Court may be subject to a right of appeal to the Court of Justice on points of law.

The court has established that sport is subject to EU law 'only in so far as it constitutes an economic activity'.[44] In the same judgment, the Court also determined that Treaty provisions apply to private parties, such as sports bodies, as well as public bodies[45] and that EU law applies to all legal relationships in so far as these relationships, by reason either of the place where they are entered into or the place where they take effect, can be located within the territory of the EU.[46] The fact that many sports bodies are located outside the territory of the EU does not necessarily inhibit the reach of EU law.

In most of the sports cases heard by the Court, the central question raised has concerned whether sport displays specific characteristics that are worthy of protection under EU law. The Court's approach, which is comprehensively covered elsewhere in this book, has divided opinion. Some academic literature points to the sensitivity with which the Court has treated sporting rules and practices and stressed the extent to which the Court has accepted as compatible with EU law proportionate rules that pursue legitimate objectives such as the need to promote competitive balance in competitions, develop young talent, preserve of the integrity of

40 Case C-519/04 P *Meca-Medina and Majcen v Commission* [2006] ECR I-6991.

41 Art 267 TFEU.

42 Art 258 TFEU. Art 259 TFEU establishes a similar cause of action for Member State to challenge another.

43 Art 263 TFEU.

44 Case 36/74 *Walrave and Koch v Union Cycliste Internationale* [1974] ECR 1405, para 4.

45 Ibid., para 17.

46 Ibid., para 28.

sport and ensure the proper functioning of sport.[47] This view is not widely shared by representatives of the sports movement who regard the Court's jurisprudence as damaging to the autonomy and specificity of sport. For example, the Court's approach to anti-doping measures in sport in *Meca-Medina* attracted criticism from the sports movement for its rejection of the purely sporting rule defence originally outlined in *Walrave* and its focus on the need to assess the proportionality of each contested measure. For many within the sports movement, this invites litigation, propagates legal uncertainty and risks the Court becoming a sports regulator.[48]

The hope that the adoption of Article 165, and its reference to the *specific nature of sport*, will settle these debates has not materialised. Evidence suggests that although the Court makes reference to Article 165 in its jurisprudence, the Lisbon Treaty has not fundamentally altered the manner in which the Court treats sporting disputes.[49] In this regard, the central question concerns whether Article 165 amounts to a horizontal requirement, or a mere invitation, for the Court to take into *the specific nature of sport* when dealing with sports related cases that engage, for example, other Treaty provisions such as free movement and competition laws. A clue can be gleaned by reading the statement in Article 165 preceding the reference to the specific nature of sport. That line reads, the EU is to 'contribute to the promotion of European sporting issues, while taking account of the specific nature of sport'. This is a rather unclear statement as it seems to suggest that the recognition of the specific nature of sport is a duty engaged when the EU institutions are contributing to *the promotion of European sporting issues*. This can be contrasted, and 'compares unfavourably' with genuinely horizontal obligations under the Treaty such as Article 168 TFEU on public health.[50] Similarly to Article 165, the public health provision provides for incentive measures and

---

47 See for instance R Parrish, 'Lex Sportiva and EU Sports Law' (2012) 37 *European Law Review* 716–33.

48 See, e.g., G Infantino [at the time Director of Legal Affairs at UEFA, now President of FIFA], Meca-Medina: A Step Backwards for the European Sports Model and the Specificity of Sport? UEFA paper 02/10/06, http://www.uefa.com/MultimediaFiles/Download/uefa/KeyTopics/480391_DOWNLOAD.pdf, accessed 26 Oct 2017.

49 See S Weatherill, 'Fairness, Openness and the Specific Nature of Sport: Does the Lisbon Treaty Change EU Sports Law', (2010) (3/4) 10 ISLJ 16–17 and Parrish (n 47).

50 R Parrish, B García, S Miettinen and R Siekmann, 'Report for the European Parliament Committee on Culture and Education: The Lisbon Treaty and EU Sports Policy' (European Parliament, 2010) p 20.

expressly excludes harmonisation but unlike Article 165, Article 168(1) requires that: 'A high level of human health protection shall be ensured in the definition and implementation of all Union policies and activities'. Similarly, regarding EU environmental policy, Article 11 TFEU, states that: '[e]nvironmental protection requirements must be integrated into the definition and implementation of the Union's policies and activities ...'

The reach of public health and environmental policies into other Treaty provisions is clear, whereas the corresponding reach of Article 165 is not. Ultimately, the horizontal obligation question may be less significant than at first sight as the approach taken by the Court in judgments pre-dating Article 165 has recognised the specificity of sport. For example, in *Bosman* the Court recognised as legitimate the need in sport for 'maintaining a balance between clubs by preserving a certain degree of equality and uncertainty as to results'.[51] In *Deliège* the Court accepted the sporting need for selection criteria to operate in order to allow for the proper functioning of sporting competitions.[52] In *Lehtonen*, the Court established that late transfers could substantially alter the sporting strength of teams in the course of the championship thus calling into question the proper functioning of sporting competition.[53] In *Meca-Medina* the Court recognised as legitimate the need to combat doping for reasons of promoting fair play, integrity and ethics[54] and in *Bernard* the Court found favour with training compensation schemes in sport that promote the development of young athletes.[55] While sport has not been able to assert its autonomy over EU law, it has been granted a form of supervised autonomy by the court and Article 165 does not appear to adjust the boundaries of this autonomy. What is less clear is how the Court will interpret reference in Article 165 to *fairness and openness in sporting competitions*. Fairness and openness are words that can be used to both defend and attack sporting rules, such as for example, rules on the geographical location of sporting teams.[56]

---

[51] Case C-415/93 *Bosman*, para 106.

[52] Joined Cases C-51/96 and C-191/97 *Deliège v Ligue de Judo* [2000] ECR I-2549.

[53] Case C-176/96 *Lehtonen* [2000] ECR I-2681, para 54.

[54] Case C-519/04 P *Meca-Medina and Majcen v Commission.*

[55] Case C-325/08 *Olivier Bernard* [2010] ECR I-2177.

[56] For discussion on the fairness and openness question see Weatherill (n 49). On the question of geographic location of sports clubs see K Pijetlovic, *EU Sports Law and Breakaway Leagues in Football* (Springer 2015).

II.v European Council

The European Council is composed of the Heads of State or Government of EU countries, the European Commission President and the High Representative for Foreign Affairs and Security Policy. Usually meeting quarterly, the European Council does not legislate but it decides on the EU's overall direction and political priorities and it deals with complex or sensitive issues that have not been resolved at lower levels of intergovernmental cooperation.

The European Council's most prominent function is its role in negotiating Treaty reform. On a number of occasions the European Council has been lobbied by representatives of the sports movement to include an article on sport in the treaties that would offer sporting rules and practices shelter from the application of EU law. This campaign met with limited success until the inclusion of a sports article in the 2004 Treaty establishing a Constitution.[57] Due to the failure to ratify the Treaty, the Treaty remained dormant although the sports article was retained in the form of Article 165 TFEU. Prior to that, the only success the sports movement could claim was the European Council annexing a non-binding Declaration on Sport to the 1997 Treaty of Amsterdam.

In a less formal manner, Heads of State and Government have intervened politically in sport. In 2000, at the time of negotiations between FIFA, UEFA and the European Commission over the reform of the international transfer system, the German Chancellor and British Prime Minister published a joint statement supporting the transfer system.[58]

III. EU SPORTS POLICY POST-LISBON

III.i The White Paper on Sport

The signing of the Lisbon Treaty in 2007 and its entry into force in 2009 marked a new phase in the development of an EU sports policy. The Article 165 competence provides the EU with the competence to 'support, coordinate and supplement' the actions of the Member States in the field of sport and in doing so the EU institutions are invited to 'contribute

---

[57] For a discussion see García and Weatherill (n 6).

[58] Bundesregierung der BRD, 'Der Bundeskanzler teilt mit: Gemeinsame Erklärung von Bundeskanzler Schröder und Premierminister Blair zum Transfersystem im ProfiFußball.' Pressemitteilung, Nr. 425/00, 10 September 2000.

to the promotion of European sporting issues, while taking account of the specific nature of sport'.

In preparation for the adoption of the Lisbon Treaty, the Commission published the White Paper on Sport. The White Paper was not a White Paper in the strict sense as it was not designed to act as the basis for legislation, notwithstanding that possible legislative action was discussed in relation to public disorder at sporting events and the activities of sports agents. The choice to present a White Paper reflected the Commission's desire to give sport a status in the EU that it had previously lacked. In that regards, the White Paper was the Commission's first systematic attempt to articulate a strategic approach to sport and it marked a departure from previous statements on sport in so far as it was a more sober assessment of the place of sport within the EU single market. Previously in the 1998 policy paper 'The European Model of Sport', the Commission appeared to give political support for the protection of the widely observed, but still contested, European sports model.[59] Later in the 1999 Helsinki report on sport, the Commission tried, but largely failed, to establish some measure of legal certainty for sport by defining practices which do not come under the EU's competition rules, those that are, in principle, prohibited by them and practices that are likely to be exempt from competition provisions.[60]

The White Paper abandoned these ambitions by recognising the complexity of European sport and the diversity of its stakeholders and basing its assessment on the relationship between sport and EU law on the judicial guidance provided by the Court of Justice following the *Meca-Medina* case.[61] Rather than defining a European model of sport, the White Paper presented three dimensions of sport: the societal role of sport, the economic dimension of sport and the organisation of sport in Europe.

The chapter on the societal role of sport established priority areas for the EU including sport and public health, doping in sport, the role of sport in education and training, volunteering in sport, sport and social inclusion, combating racism and violence, sport's connection with the EU's external policies and sport and sustainable development. The

---

[59] 'The European Model of Sport: Consultation Document of DG X' (European Commission, 1998).

[60] 'Report from the Commission to the European Council with a view to safeguarding sports structures and maintaining the social significance of sport within the Community framework: The Helsinki Report on Sport', COM (1999) 644.

[61] Case C-519/04 P *Meca-Medina and Majcen v Commission.*

chapter on the economic dimension in sport stressed the importance of evidenced based policy making and putting public support for sport on a more secure footing.

The section on the 'organisation of sport' proved most controversial. Here the Commission stated that 'in view of the diversity and complexities of European sport structures ... it is unrealistic to try to define a unified model of organisation of sport in Europe' and that 'the emergence of new stakeholders (participants outside the organised disciplines, professional sports clubs, etc.) is posing new questions as regards governance, democracy and representation of interests within the sport movement'.[62]

These statements disappointed the governing bodies of sport whose position at the head of the sports organisational pyramid granted them strong regulatory control over their respective sports. The Commission's reluctance to endorse the European model of sport in its entirety implied that the vertical model of sports governance was under strain and that the representation of stakeholder interests within governance structures would result in more horizontal channels of communication between stakeholders and sports governing bodies. The Commission was wisely not prescriptive about how this should be achieved beyond stating that it could help promote dialogue between the stakeholders so that sport could find its own solutions to a range of issues which included problems connected to free movement and nationality, the transfer system, players' agents, the protection of minors, crime and corruption, club licensing and disputes involving media sales. In this connection, the White Paper stated that 'the Commission considers that most challenges can be addressed through self-regulation respectful of good governance principles, provided that EU law is respected, and is ready to play a facilitating role or take action if necessary'.[63] One solution recommended by the Commission was the use of social dialogue in the sports sector as a means of avoiding labour related disputes.

Another disappointment for sports governing bodies was the Commission's reliance on the European Court's judgment in *Meca-Medina*. In the White Paper, the Commission repeated the logic of *Meca-Medina* by stating that 'in respect of the regulatory aspect of sport, the assessment whether a certain sporting rule is compatible with EU competition law

---

62 White Paper on Sport, COM (2007) 391, s 4.
63 Ibid.

can only be made on a case-by-case basis'.[64] This approach was favoured by the Court because applying the test of proportionality requires an assessment of the individual circumstances of each case which precludes a general exemption from EU law or the formulation of general guidelines on the application of competition law to sport. Furthermore, following *Meca-Medina* the assessment on whether a sporting rule is compatible with EU law should no longer make reference to whether the contested rule falls into the 'purely sporting rule' category, as defined in *Walrave*. From this perspective the sports movement considered the White Paper a missed opportunity.[65] This view was supported by the European Parliament. In its Resolution on the White Paper, the Parliament requested that the Commission has 'due respect for the specificity of sports, by not taking a case-by-case approach and to provide more legal certainty by creating clear guidelines on the applicability of European law to sports in Europe'.[66]

III.ii The Communication on Sport and the EU Work Plans for Sport

In order to implement the Lisbon Treaty's sport provisions, in 2011 the Commission published its Communication on Sport.[67] The Communication retained the White Paper's focus on the societal role of sport, the economic dimension of sport and the organisation of sport in Europe. The specific priorities contained within these broad headings were defined following a consultation exercise which included the convening of an Independent Group of Sports Experts.[68] The result largely endorsed the priority themes outlined in the White Paper.

Once again, the section on the 'Organisation of Sport' proved most interesting. Rather than simply repeating the White Paper's rhetoric on the importance on good governance in sport, the Communication stated

---

[64] Ibid., s 4.1.

[65] IOC and sports movement, 'EU White Paper on Sport: much work remains to be done' Press Release of 11 July 2007 available at http://www.fifa.com/governance/news/y=2007/m=7/news=white-paper-sport-much-work-remains-done-550327.html.

[66] European Parliament Resolution of 8 May 2008 on the White Paper on Sport (2007/2261(INI), para 4.

[67] Developing the European Dimension in Sport (the Communication on Sport), COM(2011) final.

[68] Report for European Commission by Group of Independent European Sport Experts on EU Priorities in the Field of Sport (European Commission, 2010).

more forcefully that '[g]ood governance in sport is a *condition* for the autonomy and self-regulation of sport organisations' (emphasis added) and that:

> [w]hile it is not possible to define a single model of governance in European sport across different disciplines and in view of various national differences, the Commission considers that there are inter-linked principles that underpin sport governance at European level, such as autonomy within the limits of the law, democracy, transparency and accountability in decision-making, and inclusiveness in the representation of interested stakeholders.[69]

The Commission did not outline the tools at its disposal to enforce this conditional autonomy, nor did it elaborate on whether, in its view, Article 165 TFEU mandated it to adopt such a position. It contented itself on merely offering to promote good governance, such as through the exchange of good practice, targeted support for specific initiatives and the adoption of the above-mentioned pledge board on good governance. In this connection, the Commission once again endorsed the merits of social dialogue.

The remainder of the section on the organisation of sport addressed some of the key issues facing sport including the definition of the specificity of sport, the question of free movement and nationality discrimination in sport, the transfer system and the activities of sports agents and the wider question of how to safeguard the integrity of sport.

Section 5 of the Communication was dedicated to issue of co-operation with third countries and international organisations. Here the Commission stated that '[i]n view of the continental organisation of sport and the renewed consensus on enlargement, cooperation with European third countries, in particular candidate countries and potential candidates, and the Council of Europe should be a priority'. On assuming office in November 2014, the new Commissioner responsible for sport in the Commission, Tibor Navracsics, actively promoted sport as a soft diplomatic means of securing EU foreign policy goals. In doing so, Navracsics established a High Level Group on Sport Diplomacy. The group reported in June 2016 and made 15 recommendations covering three broad themes: EU external relations, promoting EU value in the context of major sporting events and developing an organisation culture of sport

---

[69] Developing the European Dimension in Sport (the Communication on Sport), COM(2011) final, s 4.1.

diplomacy in the EU.[70] As a follow up, the Commission held a seminar on sport diplomacy in Brussels in December 2016[71] and repeated it in December 2017.

Another follow up to the Communication was the Council's adoption of the first European Union Work Plan for Sport which ran until 2014.[72] A second Work Plan was adopted for the period 2014–17,[73] and a third was agreed running from 2017 to 2020.[74] As part of the 2017–20 Work Plan, the Member States agreed to prioritise three key areas. First, the integrity of sport, in particular the promotion of good governance, the safeguarding of minors, the specificity of sport, combatting corruption and match fixing and the fight against doping. Second, the economic dimension of sport, in particular innovation in sport and the digital single market. Finally, sport and society covering social inclusion, the role of coaches, sport and education, sport and health, sport and the environment, sport and media and sport diplomacy. In order to progress these themes, the Member States asked the Commission to work through a number of channels including establishing expert groups, holding seminars and conferences and commissioning studies. Although the expert groups are creatures of the Member States and are required to represent the views of the States, the Commission provides them with expertise and secretarial support.

The use of expert groups is an increasingly employed working method for elaborating EU sports policy. A review of the 2011–14 EU Work Plan for Sport suggested a general satisfaction across the Member States on the operation of the groups.[75] However, the expert groups were faced with significant challenges in terms of delivering on large remits in relatively short time and some Member States reported difficulties in appointing experts.[76]

---

[70] Report to Commissioner Tibor Navracsics by High Level Group on Sport Diplomacy (European Commission, 2016), p 52 and available at http://ec.europa.eu/assets/eac/sport/library/policy_documents/hlg-sport-diplomacy-final_en.pdf accessed 26 Oct 2017.

[71] European Commission Seminar on Sport Diplomacy Outcomes, 6 December 2016 and available at https://ec.europa.eu/sport/sites/sport/files/seminar-sport-diplomacy.pdf accessed 26 Oct 2017.

[72] Resolution of the Council 2011–14 (n 36).

[73] Resolution of the Council 2014–17 (n 37).

[74] Resolution of the Council 2017–20 (n 36).

[75] Resolution of the Council 2011–14 (n 36), 7–8.

[76] Ibid., 8.

IV. CONCLUSIONS

The EU has had a long engagement with sports policy. Initially constrained by the competence question, EU interventions in sport were sporadic and dependent on the relevant EU institution demonstrating sport's connection with an area in which the EU did have competence. Unfortunately for the sports movement, sport's greatest connection with the Treaty was through the EU's internal market provisions. As a result, EU sports policy was largely guided by the judgments of the European Court. For the sports bodies, the adoption of a more systematic and coherent EU approach to sport, including reference in the Treaty to sport, raises some anxieties. On the one hand, the international federations lobbied for sport to be included in the Treaty as means of safeguarding their autonomy and the specificity of sport. In that connection, reference to *the specific nature of sport* in Article 165 was welcomed. On the other hand, formalising EU involvement in sport gives legitimacy to the EU institutions to develop sports policy beyond the narrow confines hoped for by the sports bodies. As Mataija argues, 'it may well even be the case that Art.165 encourages rather than limits the interventions of EU law in the sporting world'.[77]

[77] M Mataija *Private Regulation and the Internal Market: Sports, Legal Services, and Standard Setting in EU Economic Law* (OUP 2016) p 164.

PART II

SOCIETAL

3. Health-friendly sport policy: an emerging soft law doctrine

Jacob Kornbeck

I. INTRODUCTION

If the study of EU law permits identifying 'a continuum running from non-legal positions to legally binding and judicially controlled commitments with, in between these two opposite types of norms, commitments that can be described as soft law',[1] where precisely would novel policy initiatives of the following kind be located: using a Treaty article as their legal base, albeit one specifically (though unnecessarily) excluding harmonisation and indeed any other kind of legally binding measures; adopting non-binding texts with political and legal relevance using 'only' texts up to the level of Council recommendations; relying on Council-based 'soft' coordination mechanisms, the exchange of information and good practice as well as incentive measures?

> 'Soft' law refers to rules of conduct which in principle have no legally binding effect but which in practise may have a significant impact on policy. Soft law frequently offers guidance as to the interpretation and scope of application of EU law and in some circumstances it has acted to progressively 'harden' policy areas on the margins of the EU's legal remit. The use of soft law has characterised much of the development of sports policy. This reflects a lack of a formal Treaty base to take 'harder' measures.'[2]

But where exactly should such measures be placed within the soft law/hard law continuum, granted that it is a scaled one rather than a simple binary black-and-white juxtaposition of soft law versus hard law?

The aim of this chapter is to critically revisit pre- and post-Lisbon sport policy initiatives leading up to and including current ones using Article 165 of the Treaty on the Functioning of the European Union

---

[1] F Terpan, 'Soft Law in the European Union: the Changing Nature of EU Law' (2015) 21(1) *European Law Journal* 68, 70.

[2] R Parrish, *Sports Law and Policy in the European Union* (Manchester University Press 2003) 75.

(TFEU) to promote health-enhancing physical activity (HEPA),[3] i.e., the embedding and coordination of physical activity-friendly policies, including but not limited to sports, within all public policy areas, both at the level of the European Union (EU) and at that of its Member States (MS), by addressing these specific initiatives as a form of EU soft law. For while not legally binding and certainly not enforceable, the norms laid down in these initiatives have a legal and political life of their own: they become (borrowing a phrase from social psychology) 'real in their consequences'.[4] Just like sports governing bodies (SGBs) appear to have responded to the increasing clout of ECJ/CJEU case-law since *Bosman*[5] by 'engaging with the EU in order to minimise its impact',[6] a strategy which may be interpreted as attempted 'delegalisation',[7] either because it aims at 'the softening of hard law norms (limited delegalisation)', or even embodies an outspoken move 'from soft/hard law to non-legal norms (complete delegalisation)'[8] (whether successful or not), the EU's own initiatives to promote HEPA in spite of MS' maintained intact national sport policy prerogative may be phrased as 'engaging with sport policy to maximise its health impact'.

Soft law seems a natural response to a situation where the EU cannot regulate. As far as SGBs are concerned, 'in the absence of a legal base, soft law is the preferred tactic to limit the application of law to sport',[9] which applies equally when a legal base exists (art. 165 TFEU) but cannot be used for adopting legally binding measures, although it may well even be the case that Article 165 encourages rather than limits the interventions of EU law in the sporting world.[10] Under this scenario, a

---

[3] For a history of the HEPA concept, see E Martin-Diener, S Kahlmeier, A Vuilllemin, W van Mechelen, T Vasankari, F Racioppi and BW Martin, '10 years of HEPA Europe; what made it possible and what is the way into the future?' (2014) 62(2) Schweizerische Zeitschrift fur Sportmedizin und Sporttraumatologie 6–12.

[4] W Thomas and D Thomas, *The Child in America* (Knopf 1928) 571.

[5] Case C-415/93 *Bosman* [1995] ECR I-4921.

[6] B García and S Weatherill, 'Engaging with the EU in order to Minimize its Impact: Sport and the Negotiation of the Treaty of Lisbon' (2012) 19 JEPP 238.

[7] See T Serby, 'The State of EU Sports Law: Lessons from UEFA's Financial Fair Play Regulations' (2016) 16 (3/4) *International Sports Law Journal* 37–51.

[8] Terpan (n 1), 86.

[9] Parrish (n 2) 70.

[10] M Mataija, *Private Regulation and the Internal Market: Sports, Legal Service and Standard Setting in EU Economic Law* (OUP 2016) 164.

'soft' legal base may nevertheless formalise an otherwise largely informal approach and lend a certain measure of quasi-enforcement to otherwise unenforceable initiatives.

II. ARTICLE 165 TFEU AS A SOURCE OF EU HEPA SOFT LAW?

II.i Hard Law and Soft Law Competences of the EU

The EU is not a classic international organisation but rather exhibits a number of unusual 'supranational' features: the direct effect and supremacy of EU law; the fact that rights and duties address not only MS but also regional/local authorities, businesses/organisations and individual citizens, with access to judicial review and redress, usually via national courts but occasionally via a direct route; and finally, that EU law indeed is embedded into the legal order of MS. Thus, even in countries with a Eurosceptic mood in policy circles, national courts contribute to further incorporating EU norms into the national legal orders, such as the English judiciary breaking with precedent (no privacy tort without pecuniary loss) because Article 47 of the EU Charter of Fundamental Rights requires a remedy for every right conferred by the Charter (*in casu*, the protection of personal data under art 8).[11] This is a far cry from international law and because EU norms become national norms, in the UK they might even unfold their effect long after an accomplished UK exit.[12] The effects will be felt in the sports sector, though at present only their contours can be gauged.[13]

Undeniable regulatory power is vested in the EU, power which SGBs have sometimes come to resent, be it in relation to international football (soccer) transfers[14] or in relation to anti-doping rules.[15] Yet these powers are limited to very few, well-delineated areas and, whereas the EU's

---

[11] *Google Inc v Vidall-Hall* [2015] EWCA Civ 311.

[12] G Gee and AL Young, 'Regaining Sovereignty? Brexit, the UK Parliament and the Common Law' (2016) 22(1) *European Public Law* 131, 142.

[13] See, e.g., L Thompson, What Might Brexit Mean for the UK Sports Sector (Sport&Recreation Alliance 2016) and available at http://www.sportandrecreation.org.uk/blogs/leigh-thompson/what-might-brexit-mean-for-the-uk-sports-sect (accessed 26 Oct 2017) and J Kornbeck, 'Brexit et Sport: Un Premier Bilan' (2016) 108 Lettre de L'Officiel Juridique du Sport 1–3.

[14] Case C-415/93 *Bosman* (n 5).

[15] Case C-519/04 P *Meca-Medina and Majcen v Commission* [2006] ECR I-6991.

powers (or 'competences' in EU parlance) are graduated from 'exclusive competence' (e.g., 'the conservation of marine biological resources under the common fisheries policy', art 3(1)(d) TFEU) over 'shared competence' (e.g., 'agriculture and fisheries, excluding the conservation of marine biological resources', art 4(2)(d) TFEU) and the coordination of MS' economic and social policies (art 5 TFEU) down to the 'competence to carry out actions to support, coordinate or supplement the actions of' MS (art 6 TFEU), including in the area of 'education, vocational training, youth and sport' (art 6(e) TFEU) as defined in Article 165 TFEU. The 'indirect sport policy'[16] of the EU consisting of hard law unrelated, yet applicable to the sport sector has earned the respect of SGBs, as epitomised by the ECJ's 1995 *Bosman*[17] ruling, though this was attributable to an effect which political scientists might refer to as 'spillover' in the tradition of Haas[18] or, in legal terms, *ignorantia juris/legis neminem excusat*.

II.ii Article 165 TFEU

Since the Treaty of Lisbon, Article 165 TFEU has provided a legal framework for non-binding Union actions 'contribut[ing] to the promotion of European sporting issues, while taking account of the specific nature of sport, its structures based on voluntary activity and its social and educational functions' (art 165(1)), through incentive measures (art 165(4)), Council recommendations (art 165(4)) as well as 'cooperation with third countries and the competent international organisations in the field of education and sport, in particular the Council of Europe' (art 165(3)). This represents an EU competence to 'support, coordinate or supplement the actions' of MS (art 6 TFEU). Whether 'taking account of the specific nature of sport' imposes any limitations to the applicability of EU rules in other areas to sport remains debatable: the available post-Lisbon case-law found in *Murphy*[19] and *Bernard*[20] does not make it cogently clear that the same result could not have been reached without paying lip service to the language of Article 165(1) TFEU.

---

[16] W Tokarski, D Steinbach, K Petry and B Jesse, *Two Players – One Goal? Sport in the European Union* (Meyer & Meyer 2004) 61.

[17] Case C-415/93 (n 5).

[18] E Haas, *The Uniting of Europe* (Stanford UP 1958).

[19] Joined cases C-403/08 and C-429/08 *Football Association Premier League Ltd and Karen Murphy* [2011] ECR I-09083.

[20] Case C-325/08 *Olympique Lyonnais v Olivier Bernard* [2010] ECR I-2177.

On the other hand, Article 165 has been taken into account in a number of recent Commission state aid decisions:[21] in contrast with antitrust decisions and case law where no such effect can be detected. Interestingly, in state aid decisions the line between aid compatible and aid incompatible with the internal market, in accordance with Article 107 TFEU, appears clearly to correspond to the degree to which facilities and services supported through state aid actually benefit the population at large.[22] If the idea is to focus on exempting specific activities, as opposed to specific legal entities,[23] then these recent developments suggest a convergence between the application of EU competition law (hard law) and the promotion of a HEPA policy agenda (soft law), which justifies speaking of an 'emerging doctrine'. This is significant because SGBs are still asking for exemptions from EU hard law provisions:

> It is significant that after the Lisbon Treaty reforms, sporting bodies can no longer claim that sport is none of the EU's business. Instead one would expect them to claim that it is the EU's business but only to a limited extent, and only insofar as respect is shown for its 'specific nature'. The key to the Lisbon adjustments will be whether they affect the interpretation of the Treaty provisions on free movement and competition which the Court and Commission have applied to sport ever since the *Walrave* ruling in 1974.[24]

While SGBs had hoped to achieve blanket exemptions through a Treaty article,[25] this did not materialise. Instead, the Treaty does provide some margin for the development of EU soft law in the field of sport, such as the 2001 exchange of letters and memorandum of understanding between

---

21 See B García, A Vermeersch, and S Weatherill, 'A New Horizon in European Sports Law: the Application of EU State Aid Rules meets the Specfic Nature of Sport' (2017) 13(1*) European Competition Journal* 28–61.

22 See generally chapter 11 of this collection.

23 See J Kornbeck, 'Le geste sportif: ein alternatives Unterscheidungsmerkmal zu den "besonderen Merkmalen" des Sports nach Artikel 165 AEUV?' (2017) 28(5) Europäische Zeitschrift für Wirtschaftsrecht / *European Journal of Business Law* 603–6.

24 García and Weatherill (n 6), 251.

25 R Blanpain, *Le statut du sportif* (Larcier 2004), 35–73; R Blanpain, *European Labour Law* (14th edn, Wolters Kluwer 2014) 376–81; B García, 'UEFA and the European Union, From Confrontation to Co-operation? (2007) 3(3) *Journal of Contemporary European Research* 202; B García and H Meier, 'Limits of Interest Empowerment in the European Union: The Case of Football' (2012) 34(4) *Journal of European Integration* 359.

the Commission and FIFA-UEFA-FIFPRO over transfers[26] or the encouragement[27] of EU social dialogue (arts 151–155 TFEU) which has led to the establishment of social dialogue committees for professional football[28] and active leisure,[29] and to the signing of an agreement on minimum standards in professional football.[30] In relation to HEPA, rather than the bottom-up approach represented by the FIFA-UEFA-FIFPRO file and the two social dialogue committees, a relatively more top-down approach has been chosen (though one lacking the legally binding effects of agreements signed by social partners under art 155 TFEU) including the adoption of non-binding pre-Lisbon standards, so-called EU Physical Activity Guidelines,[31] and, based on these, a 2013 Council Recommendation on HEPA:[32] to date, the first and only one in the field of sport.

II.iii Health-enhancing Physical Activity (HEPA) as a Soft Law Concept

While EU hard law typically covers the commercial activities of professional sport (with some modifications this has been the Court's doctrine since *Walrave*) sport is a far wider social practice, encompassing activities and structures which may be entirely devoid of professionalism or commercialism, although more often than not, the picture if all but clear-cut. The European Commission therefore, in its 2007 White Paper on Sport,[33] committed itself to the definition followed by the Council of Europe since 1992: '"Sport" means all forms of physical activity which,

---

26 Blanpain, ibid., 379–85.

27 White Paper on Sport, COM(2007) 391 final.

28 See Sectoral social dialogue – Professional football. http://ec.europa.eu/social/main.jsp?catId=480&intPageId=1848&langId=en accessed 26 Oct 2017. For a discussion, see R Parrish, 'Social Dialogue in European Professional Football' (2011) 17(2) *European Law Journal* 213.

29 See http://www.europeactive.eu/blog/supporting-test-phase-european-sectoral-social-dialogue-committee-sport-and-active-leisure (accessed 26 Oct 2017).

30 See http://ec.europa.eu/social/main.jsp?catId=89&langId=en&newsId=1279&furtherNews=yes (accessed 26 Oct 2017).

31 European Commission, 'EU Physical Activity Guidelines: Recommended Policy Actions in Support of Health-Enhancing Physical Activity. Approved by the EU Working Group "Sport & Health" at its meeting on 25 September 2008. Confirmed by EU Member State Sport Ministers at their meeting in Biarritz on 27–28 November 2008' and available at http://ec.europa.eu/sport/library/policy_documents/eu-physical-activity-guidelines-2008_en.pdf (accessed 26 Oct 2017).

32 Council Recommendation of 26 November 2013 on promoting health-enhancing physical activity across sectors [2013] OJ 354, 1–5.

33 White Paper on Sport (n 27), 2.

through casual or organised participation, aim at expressing or improving physical fitness and mental well-being, forming social relationships or obtaining results in competition at all levels.'[34]

As a public policy matter, non-professional sport, which may be competitive (e.g., recreational 'pub' football (soccer)) or not (e.g., gymnastics in the Nordic and German tradition), is hard to capture using standard legal concepts. The HEPA concept championed by the World Health Organisation and some MS of the EU has the potential to fill this gap, for if public authorities wish to promote sport for all, an objective concept is needed to ensure the legitimacy and objectivity of policy measures taken, lest support and funding be given on purely subjective grounds; applying HEPA thus further contributes to ensuring public policy accountability, which is of interest in relation to sport policy, where traditional policy styles are open to criticism (e.g., Olympic bids).[35] This debate has been fuelled by evidence of links between the Athens 2004 Olympics and Greek public budget deficits;[36] HEPA detrimental effects of the UK's preparations for the London 2012 Summer Games (with public funds being absorbed by the Olympics);[37] or reports of the burden borne by certain Portuguese local authorities for having hosted matches of the 2008 UEFA Euro Cup, consuming up to 8 per cent of annual municipal budgets.[38]

Surprisingly, stark evidence of over-generous tax exemptions granted by German authorities to the organisers of the 2006 FIFA World Cup[39]

---

[34] Recommendation No. R (92) 13 REV of the Committee of Ministers to Member States on the Revised European Sports Charter (adopted by the Committee of Ministers on 24 September 1992 at the 480th meeting of the Ministers' Deputies and revised at their 752nd meeting on 16 May 2001.

[35] J Kornbeck, 'Lisbonisation without Regulation: Engaging with Sport Policy to Maximise its Health Impact?' (2015) 15 (1/2) *International Sports Law Journal* 112.

[36] A Pappous, 'Do the Olympic Games Lead to a Sustainable Increase in Grass Roots Sport Participation?' in J Savery and K Gilbert (eds), *Sustainability and Sport* (Common Ground Publishing 2011) 81–9.

[37] M Green, 'From "Sport for All" to Not About "Sport" at All?: Interrogating Sport Policy Interventions in the United Kingdom' (2006) 6(3) *European Sport Management Quarterly* 217.

[38] J Alm, *World Stadium Index* (Danish Institute for Sports Studies/Play the Game 2012) 53.

[39] F Knerr, 'Privilegien für Ausrichter internationaler Sportveranstaltungen. Dargestellt am Beispiel der Körperschaftsteuerbefreiung der FIFA anlässlich der Fußball-Weltmeisterschaft 2006 in Deutschland' in K Vieweg (ed) *Impulse des Sportrechts* (Duncker & Humblot 2015) 91–103.

have attracted less media coverage and popular attention than allegations of bribes linked to the 2006 'summer fairy tale' (*Sommermärchen*): parliamentary control may be exercised less exactingly here than in some other policy areas, possibly because committee membership often seems to coincide with involvement in, and/or affinity with the sports sector.[40] But while it is understandable that bribery-related stories do excite the public (and newspapers) one might wonder why the generous tax exemptions still pass largely unnoticed outside specialist circles, especially in light of the fact that, while the London Organising Committee of the Olympic Games (LOCOG) obtained various fiscal exemptions, the UK VAT scheme continued to apply during the London Olympics.[41]

Yet while HEPA is a conceptually challenging subject matter, it is also a promising one, as recreational sport has the potential to improve individual and public health, foster social networks, provide volunteering opportunities, transmit skills (including skills relevant to the labour market), etc. While HEPA includes competitive as well as non-competitive structures and activities, playing the same sport as well-known sports stars is an undeniable source of inspiration and motivation to many (e.g., recreational football follows the same rules as the game played by Lionel Messi, Cristiano Ronaldo, etc.), and the playful aspect of the game may yield higher health benefits, in some populations at least (e.g., untrained men), than workouts in exercise machines.[42] HEPA funding is usually provided by local authorities (while national ones tend to support elite sports) (in some countries, such as Germany, this distribution of tasks is mandatory under constitutional law) and, to a large extent, by households themselves.[43]

---

[40] See further, HE Meier, 'Stammtisch jubelstarker Spesenurlauber?' (2011) 41 (4) Sportwissenschaft 300–314.

[41] A Yazicioglu, 'Specific Tax Exemption Regulations for Major Sports Events: Example of London Olympics and Paralympic Games' (2012) 12 (1/2) *International Sports Law Journal* 53.

[42] P Krustrup, J Nielsen, B Krustrup, J Christensen, H Pedersen, M Randers, P Aagaard, A Petersen, L Nybo and J Bangsbo, 'Recreational Soccer is an Effective Health-promoting Activity for Untrained Men' (2009) 43 *British Journal of Sports Medicine* 825.

[43] Eurostratégies, Amnyos, Centre de Droit et d'Economie du Sport and Deutsche Sporthochschule Köln, 'Study on the Funding of Grassroots Sports in the EU. With a Focus on the Internal Market Aspects concerning Legislative Frameworks and Systems of Financing'. Final report. Vol. I (Eurostratégies 2011) 46 and available at http://ec.europa.eu/internal_market/top_layer/docs/FinalReportVol1_en.pdf (accessed 26 Oct 2017).

Nevertheless, as the involvement of public authorities tends to diminish the closer one gets to the bottom of sport's pyramid how can the role of the EU in supporting HEPA be justified, including as regards the long-established sport policy role of the Council of Europe[44] whose three international law conventions on anti-doping,[45] spectator violence[46] and match-fixing[47] carry legally binding provisions for MS? Apart from the bona fide aspect of the HEPA Council Recommendation[48] (as part of the 'involvement' of the nation state in the integration project,[49] MS are free to enter into any amount of non-binding policy coordination), the recently taken HEPA initiatives correspond with the EU's role in fostering the sharing of information and good practice, including on matters which may be covered by other Treaty provisions (e.g., art 168 TFEU on public health).

III. HEPA PROMOTION FROM *WALRAVE* TO *BOSMAN* (1974–95)

III.i Policy

Until the 1990s not many seem to have expected the European Communities (EC) or (since 1993) the EU to get specifically involved in sport for all; although by the early 1990s funding programmes in the field of

---

[44] Walfried König and Matthias Gütt, 'Der Europarat und sein Beitrag zur Sportentwicklung', in Walter Tokarski and Karen Petry (eds), *Handbuch Sportpolitik* (Hofmann 2010), 79–96.

[45] Anti-Doping Convention, ETS No.135, Strasbourg, 16 November 1989, available at http://www.coe.int/en/web/conventions/full-list/-/conventions/treaty/135 (accessed 26 Oct 2017).

[46] European Convention on Spectator Violence and Misbehaviour at Sports Events and in particular at Football Matches, ETS No.120, Strasbourg, 19 August 1985, http://conventions.coe.int/Treaty/en/Treaties/Html/120.htm (accessed 26 Oct 2017).

[47] Council of Europe Convention on the Manipulation of Sports Competitions, ETS 215, Magglingen/Macolin, 18. September 2014, http://www.conventions.coe.int/Treaty/EN/Treaties/Html/215.htm (accessed 26 Oct 2017).

[48] Council Recommendation of 26 November 2013 (n 32), 1–5.

[49] R Sturm, 'Was ist Europäisierung? Zur Entgrenzung und Einbindung des Nationalstaats im Prozess der europäischen Integration' in G Schuppert, I Pernice and U von Haltern (eds) *Europawissenschaft* (Nomos 2005) 101–27.

education, training, culture and youth had become a reality.[50] EC/EU Institutions were essentially technocratic, with a focus on economic integration. It was precisely the EC/EU's power to regulate the common (later: single) market that led to litigation before the Court of Justice, beginning in 1974 with *Walrave*[51] and the doctrine that 'the practice of sport is subject to Community law only in so far as it constitutes an economic activity within the meaning of Article 2 of the Treaty' (the common market clause in the then-EEC Treaty),[52] yet this in turn led to a very Cartesian dualism (professional/amateur, commercial/non-profit, 'direct' versus 'indirect' sport policy[53]) which could not fully take into account the heterogeneous realities of sport.[54]

The EC/EU did make some attempts at getting involved in sport for all support and funding, yet these attempts were more directed towards large-scale sporting events with major media coverage (and prospects for making the EC/EU popular) than towards HEPA promotion in the sense of ensuring access to sport and physical activity. The authors of the Adonnino Report 'On a People's Europe'[55] had made such recommendations, and in the early 1990s EC funding and visible EC participation at some major sports events (Olympics, sailing) were a regular feature.[56] However it was the completion of the single market programme on 1 January 1993 which led to an increasing realisation that EU law, at least under the terms defined by the Court in *Walrave*, would need to comply with Community law. Though some academics and some lawyers in private practice had long supported the idea of applicability, SGBs largely counted on achieving exemptions from Community law by political means. Their ambition was not as surprising as it may look in

---

[50] L Pépin, 'The History of EU Cooperation in the Field of Education and Training: How Lifelong Learning became a Strategic Objective' (2007) 42(1) *European Journal of Education* 121.

[51] Case 36/74 *Walrave and Koch v Union Cycliste Internationale* [1974] ECR 1405.

[52] Ibid., 4.

[53] Tokarski, Steinbach, Petry and Jesse (n 16) 70.

[54] A Geeraert and E Drieskens, 'Normative Market Europe: the EU as a Force for Good in International Sports Governance?' (2017) 39 (1) *Journal of European Integration* 79–94.

[55] 'A People's Europe, Reports from the ad hoc Committee', COM (1984) 446 Final.

[56] See J Kornbeck, Sport für alle als Aufgabe der EG/EU? 'Zwischen Entgrenzung und Einbindung der Nationalstaaten um die Mitte der 1990er Jahre' in D Jütting and M Krüger (eds) *Sport für alle – Idee und Wirklichkeit* (Waxmann, fothcoming).

retrospect, given that national SGBs in many MS have obtained rather impressive exemptions: that Germany should have allowed the organisers of the 2006 FIFA World Cup to operate virtually tax-free,[57] or that the UK taxpayer should become the major (though unrecognised) sponsor of the 2012 London Summer Olympics,[58] makes the ambitions then pursued by SGBs seem more plausible than they may emerge with the benefit of hindsight.

The European Commission had indeed commissioned a study aimed at identifying the likely implications of a completed single market in the field of sport.[59] While some EC funding was being made available, the chairman of the *Bundestag* select committee on sport saw only a 'lousy, pale concession' and the national sport umbrella organisation of Germany, DSB (*Deutscher Sportbund*) (now DOSB, *Deutscher Olympischer Sportbund*) argued that for the sport sector to be able to contribute to the 'People's Europe' announced in the Adonnino Report, the EC must formally recognise its autonomy.[60]

The Court's *Bosman*[61] ruling was to have a lasting legacy in rejecting key elements of the 'specificity' defended by SGBs and their lawyers. In the years leading up to this landmark decision, SGBs had had several meetings with Commission representatives aimed at achieving recognition of their 'autonomy' or 'specificity', while some Members of the European Parliament (MEPs) had asked questions to the Commission pointing in the very same direction,[62] yet the judgment seems to have found many of the major players entirely unprepared.[63] SGBs reacted in an entirely predictable fashion: 'UEFA and the football authorities worldwide to the Bosman litigation displayed the classic four stages of

---

57 Knerr (n 39) 91–103.

58 K Tetłak, 'The Taxpayer as the Unofficial Sponsor of the London 2012 Olympic Games' (2013) 13 (1/2) *International Sports Law Journal* 97–103.

59 Coopers & Lybrand, 'Gaming in the Single Market: a Study of the Current Legal and Market Situation' (European Commission 1991) and Coopers & Lybrand, 'The Impact of European Union Activities on Sport: Study for DG X of the European Commission' (European Commission 1995).

60 P Danckert, *Kraftmaschine Parlament: Der Sportausschuss und die Sportpolitik* (Meyer & Meyer 2009) 230.

61 Case C-415/93 *Bosman* (n 5).

62 A Parensen 'Die Fußball-Bundesliga und das Bosman-Urteil' in W Tokarski (ed) *EU-Recht und Sport* (Meyer & Meyer 1998) 70–150.

63 J Mittag, 'Die Europäische Union und der Fußball. Die Europäisierung des Profifussballs zwischen Bosman- und Simutenko-Urteil' in J Mittag and J Nieland (eds) *Das Spiel mit dem Fußball* (Klartext 2005) 214.

grief – denial; then anger; followed by depression; and finally acceptance.'[64] SGBs adapted to the new reality once they had realised that the post-*Bosman* doctrine on the applicability of EC/EU law to sport was there to stay. And while their focus kept being on the economic aspects of sport (as SGBs continued to fight for their sources of income), they too became part of discourses on the non-economic aspects and functions. They even started feeding arguments into these discourses; thus the bases for a more structured EC/EU approach to HEPA were born. But which were the antecedents which policy makers could draw upon?

In the years preceding the *Bosman* ruling, the EC had become more sport-conscious. Since *Walrave* it must have been clear to the initiated that the economic activities of SGBs could not be assumed to fall outside EC law, yet this realisation in turn must have made it plausible to argue, *ex contrario*, that certain 'purely sporting' activities (or aspects of activities) could be assumed, by definition, to fall outside its scope. Quite logically, some EC activities started emerging with a focus on sport-for-all as well as on the wider, more public policy-related aspects of elite sports events. These activities had nevertheless little in common with today's HEPA concept, as they generally aimed to capitalise politically on the popularity of elite sports. In 1991 a Commission Communication had focussed on the use of sport as a communication vehicle, suggesting to 'press ahead with its communication work, inter alia by ensuring there is a Community presence at the forthcoming Albertville and Barcelona Olympics on the theme of frontier-free Community, open to the world'.[65] As a consequence, the 1992 Olympics of Barcelona (summer) and Albertville (winter) included an EC presence complete with grants, stands, flags, logos and balloons, so as to 'create a bottom-up Europhile sense of belonging',[66] which however seems also to have provoked the susceptibilities of some less integration-friendly countries and individuals. At every subsequent edition of the Olympics the Commission has had to answer questions on EU medals legal tables[67] and the like,

---

[64] J Anderson, *Modern Sports Law* (Hart 2010) s8.24.

[65] The European Community and Sport: Communication from the Commission to the Council and the European Parliament, SEC (91) 1438 final, 31 July 1991, s5.

[66] B García, 'The EU and Sport Governance: Between Economic and Social Values' in M Groeneveld, B Houlihan and F Ohl (eds) *Social Capital and Sport Governance in Europe* (Routledge 2011) 24.

[67] See e.g., N Gardiner 'Chariots of Brussels? The EU is dreaming of Olympics glory' *The Telegraph* (London, 23 July 2012).

suggesting an undue instrumentalisation of sports events where MS were otherwise competing in national formations.

III.ii Funding

The early 1990s also saw the EC/EU supporting HEPA-style projects through two funding programmes: 'Eurathlon' and 'Sport for the Disabled?'. Eurathlon seems to have been considered quite innovative in its time, as one contemporaneous German PhD thesis in law quotes extensively from it.[68] In 1997, for instance, 174 projects were selected for funding, many of which were clearly grassroots-based, though others seem to have been selected on account of their avowed affinity with European integration;[69] a certain instrumentalisation (not unlike national sport policies) seem undeniable. The Commission's reply[70] to a parliamentary question asked in 1996 reveals that out of 175 projects selected for funding under Eurathlon, 120 targeted young people and 23 women, while none were specifically linked to ethnic minorities. Disability projects were funded separately. Nevertheless, the first selection process, in 1995, attracted 786 eligible applications of which 82 were selected for EC funding. Of the 786 eligible applications, '58% were for purely sporting projects, 18% for purely training projects, and 22% involved both sporting and training activities',[71] so that Eurathlon clearly qualifies as a HEPA programme, albeit one designed and implemented at a time when the HEPA concept was not part of EC policies.

Crucially, Eurathlon lacked an appropriate Treaty base, which led to its demise as a consequence of the ECJ's ruling in *UK v Commission*.[72] Similar pleas of the UK government were upheld in joint cases 239/96 and 240/96[73] by an Order of the President of the Court of 24 September 1996 where it was noted that 'while no such manifest breach has been

---

[68] F Holzke, 'Der Begriff Sport im deutschen und im europäischen Recht' (PhD thesis, Rechtswissenschaftliche Fakultät der Universität zu Köln) 239–40.

[69] IP/97/347 and available at europa.eu/rapid/press-release_IP-97-347_en.pdf (accessed 26 Oct 2017).

[70] E-1714/1996. Answer given by Mr Oreja on behalf of the Commission and available at http://www.europarl.europa.eu/sides/getAllAnswers.do?reference=E-1996-1714&language=SV (accessed 26 Oct 2017).

[71] IP/95/661 and available at http://europa.eu/rapid/press-release_IP-95-661_en.htm?locale=en (accessed 26 Oct 2017).

[72] Case C-106/96 *United Kingdom v Commission* [1998] ECR I-2729.

[73] Joined cases C-239/96 R and C-240/96 R *United Kingdom v Commission* [1996] ECR I-4475.

established at the present stage in the proceedings, the strength of the applicant's submissions, taken together with the importance of the rules alleged to have been breached, cannot be ignored',[74] the cases being taken off the list of the Court.[75] While the UK had challenged the legal base of the then-Community anti-poverty programme, the trial also invalidated other programmes with shaky (because not sufficiently specific) legal bases, as the ECJ 'held that each budget item must have a legal base,' resulting in the Commission abandoning the Eurathlon programme, inter alia. In the early 2000s the situation thus was that:

> subsequent developments in sports policy requiring a budgetary line have had to navigate within the EU's rigorous budgetary rules. On these grounds, the Commission's 2002 call for proposals concerning the development of a Community policy in the field of sport appears legally fragile.[76]

It would not be before the entry into force of the Lisbon Treaty that this problem would be solved, as Article 165 TFEU was to provide a legal base not only for soft coordination mechanisms, but also for incentive measures. While it cannot be taken for granted that this was the UK's explicit policy aim, its lawsuit was nevertheless instrumental in containing EU soft power on HEPA promotion. In law, the result was indisputable as an outflow of the principle on conferral under Community law, though it did lead to at least one lawsuit with an initially successful applicant suing the Commission for compensation.[77] Unsurprisingly, for years to come the Commission was reluctant to propose new such measures, although occasional funding such as under the European Year of Education through Sport (EYES 2004) were concerned with HEPA promotion.[78]

---

[74] Ibid., 70.

[75] M Grodde, 'Der Einfluss des Europarechts auf die Vertragsfreiheit autonomer Sportverbände in Deutschland: Ausgleich zwischen nationalem Verfassungsrecht und europäischem Freizügigkeitsrecht' (Lit 2007) 74.

[76] Parrish (n 2) 218.

[77] Case T-137/01 *Stadtsportverband Neuss eV v Commission* [2003] ECR II-3103.

[78] See Decision No 291/2003/EC of the European Parliament and of the Council of 6 February 2003 Establishing the European Year of Education Through Sport [2004] OJ L43, 1–5.

IV. HEPA PROMOTION FROM *BOSMAN* TO ERASMUS+ (1995–2014)

IV.i Policy

As the preceding section has shown, when SGBs started accepting the outcome of the *Bosman* ruling and engaging actively in debates about the non-economic aspects and functions of sport, antecedents in the policy work of the EC could be found which provided some degree of soft law guidance on HEPA matters. Though the spending actions of the early 1990s were not especially strong on outreach compared with today's HEPA projects, and although they do not seem ever to have been quoted as soft law sources whenever decisions with hard law implications were made, they did represent a base upon which further soft law discourses could be built. When SGBs started sensitising the EU and its MS to the purportedly unwanted extension of Community law to non-professional sports activities, non-binding texts were adopted at the highest political level: the European Council (Heads of State and Government).

A declaration was annexed to the Amsterdam Treaty, in 1997,[79] with a short yet significant message:

> The Conference emphasises the social significance of sport, in particular its role in forging identity and bringing people together. The Conference therefore calls on the bodies of the European Union to listen to sports associations when important questions affecting sport are at issue. In this connection, special consideration should be given to the particular characteristics of amateur sport.

Although this Amsterdam Declaration did not prevent subsequent litigation before the Court to go against many of the vested financial interests of SGBs, it became a source of soft law and led to a further high-level exploration of policy options. The Commission was mandated to identify the scope for 'safeguarding current sports structures and maintaining the social function of sport within the Community framework', which it did by submitting the so-called Helsinki Report on Sport, in 1999, to the

---

[79] Treaty of Amsterdam amending the Treaty on European Union, the Treaties establishing the European Communities and certain related acts – Declarations adopted by the Conference – Declaration on sport. [1997] OJ C 340, 136.

European Council.[80] The Commission duly played its role as guardian of the Treaties by stressing the need to respect the *acquis communautaire*, while also keeping a door open for legislators to make specific exemptions by law, either nationally or at EU level:

> One way of safeguarding the national federal structures could be to provide for them to be recognised by law in each MS of the Union. Other ways of achieving this objective would be the partnership agreements between the State and the sporting federations and to grant the representative sporting federations a specific status which could be based on that of the professional associations. There is also a need to examine, in legal terms, the legal status of clubs, their purchase or the participation of commercial or financial groups in their equity.[81]

The Commission further 'stressed that the basic freedoms guaranteed by the Treaty do not generally conflict with the regulatory measures of sports associations, provided that these measures are objectively justified, non-discriminatory, necessary and proportional'.[82]

Thus, the Amsterdam Declaration and the Helsinki Report actually did not change an iota as regards the applicability of EU law to the sports sector, yet the Commission had provided MS and SGBs with a vocabulary, including that of partnerships, with which to make it more plausible to regulators and courts that 'specific' arrangements found in the sector could be objectively justified, non-discriminatory, necessary and proportional. This line was later confirmed by the European Council in another declaration, adopted in connection with the Nice Treaty.[83] Though not published in the Official Journal, this Nice Declaration has found its way into subsequent Council soft law texts,[84] a Commission White Paper[85] and two opinions delivered by the Advocates General of the Court: Sharpston in *Bernard*[86] and Kokott in *Murphy*.[87] However, this reference

---

[80] Report from the Commission to the European Council with a view to safeguarding current sports structures and maintaining the social function of sport within the Community framework, COM(99) 644 final.

[81] Ibid., para 4.2.2.

[82] Ibid., para 4.2.3.

[83] See http://eur-lex.europa.eu/legal-content/EN/TXT/?uri=URISERV%3Al35007 (accessed 26 Oct 2017).

[84] E.g. Council conclusions of 18 November 2010 on the role of sport as a source of and a driver for active social inclusion. [2010] OJ C 326, 5–8.

[85] White Paper on Sport (n 27).

[86] Case C-325/08 *Olivier Bernard* (n 20), 47.

[87] Joined cases C-403/08 and C-429/08 *Football Association Premier League Ltd & Karen Murphy* (n 19), AG Kokott, footnote 12.

did not change the outcome and was not quoted by the Court in its judgment, and while quoting the Nice Declaration, A.G. Kokott affirmed that 'whilst European Union law respects the special characteristics of sport, sport does not fall outside the scope of that law'.[88]

The Nice Declaration is still not a piece of HEPA soft law (indeed it appears to have done very little to further the aims of SGBs), yet it provides a fertile template for developing one. Though the European Council's avowed aim (it 'hopes to promote the incorporation of sport into the common policies of the European Community in order to preserve and promote its social functions in particular') seems a bit lame for Heads of State and Government, the 'declaration lays down principles concerning the various aspects of sport, with a view to preserving the cohesion and ties of solidarity that exist in sport at all levels, fair competition, and the moral and material interests and physical integrity of sportsmen and women, especially minors'. These concepts can all be found in the Commission's 2007 White Paper and in today's Article 165 TFEU.

Of more direct relevance to HEPA soft law is that the declaration refers to sport *and* physical activity, *without* reserving a privileged role for the recognised sports organisations in delivering physical activity: 'Sporting activity should be accessible to every man and woman, regardless of his or her abilities or interests,' while physical activity 'is extremely important for disabled people and should be encouraged. It is particularly conducive to rehabilitation, re-education, integration into society and individual development'. SGBs did not achieve exemption from the clout of EU law, and although they and some MS sought to achieve such recognition through a specific Treaty provision (the door held open by the Commission in the Helsinki Report), neither the unsuccessful Constitutional Treaty, nor today's Lisbon Treaty made for such exemptions. Yet the Amsterdam-Helsinki-Nice process had led to an emerging EU HEPA doctrine: one of 'physical activity (including but not limited to sport)'.[89] The ambition of SGBs to have the EU identify and recognise the non-economic aspects and functions of sport had led to the unintended outcome that an EU sport doctrine would emerge under which (in contrast with many MS' long-standing special relationships with SGBs) all civil society organisations (including but not limited to recognised sports organisations) have equal access to EU funding, to EU networks

---

[88] Ibid., AG Kokott, 46.

[89] White Paper on Sport (n 27), section 2.1 'Enhancing public health through physical activity.'

for the exchange of information and good practice, and may feed ideas into EU-level policy debates.

The 'including but not limited to sport' doctrine did not emerge overnight. Indeed the first direct policy outcome of the Nice Declaration seems to have been the European Year of Education through Sport (EYES) 2004: a one-off financial instrument with a rather traditional focus on sports organisations and schools, though non-sporting civil society organisations were not formally excluded from participating.[90] What changed the EU's approach was the realisation, around the year 2004, that decreasing physical activity and ensuing overweight and obesity was also a matter of sport policy, not just one of public health. Building on a ground-breaking consultancy study commissioned by the Commission, which for the first time mapped and compared trends in all (then) 25 MS (the Paderborn-Essen Study),[91] a policy process was set in motion through which policy makers recognised that ensuring HEPA access to all citizens could not be achieved merely by giving more money to sports organisations: public funding had to target specific activities, not recognised structures. At the same time, HEPA became a policy aim in its own right, as empirical research indicated that physical inactivity might represent a bigger problem than energy intake:[92] a paradox similar to that found in connection with sports volunteering, that volunteering levels tend to be higher in regions with high unemployment (where citizens would be expected to have less time available for voluntary activities).[93]

The insights gained through the Paderborn-Essen Study directly informed two Commission White Papers both published in 2007, one addressing sport,[94] the other obesity.[95] From then on, the 'including but not limited to sport' doctrine has been integrated into all relevant EU

[90] Decision No 291/2003/EC of the European Parliament and the Council of 6 February 2003 establishing the European Year of Education through Sport 2004. [2003] OJ L 43, 1–5.

[91] W Brettschneider and R Naul, 'Study on young people's lifestyles and sedentariness and the role of sport in the context of education and as a means of restoring the balance' (European Commission 2005).

[92] Ibid., 55–6.

[93] J Kornbeck, 'The Diversity of Sports Volunteering in the European Union: sharing information and good practice to provide EU added value in a field without EU regulatory powers' in N Rosendal Jensen (ed), *Voluntary Work and Youth Unemployment* (Aarhus Universitet 2015) 99–118.

[94] White Paper on Sport (n 27).

[95] White Paper on A Strategy for Europe on Nutrition, Overweight and Obesity related health issues, COM(2007) 279.

policy initiatives in the field of sport, including the 2008 Physical Activity Guidelines[96] and the 2013 Council Recommendation on HEPA.[97] It also formed the basis for eligibility criteria under the Preparatory Actions in the field of sport (2009–13) which bridged the time between the entry into force of the Lisbon Treaty and that of the Erasmus+ Regulation: again prime examples of EU HEPA soft law, as the EU chose to bind itself legally to respect the 'including but not limited to sport' doctrine, even if it had no power to bind others in this regard. Also, the fact that considerable progress could be made during the years 2004–09, before the entry into force of the Lisbon Treaty, attests to a remarkable *de-facto* effect of the HEPA principles promulgated during these years. MS accepted the creation of an EU HEPA working group which provided direct input into the White Papers on sport and obesity. Guiding principles were developed and promulgated on a *bona fide* basis, owing to a strong consensus among MS: 'Lisbonisation without regulation.'[98]

Since the entry into force of the Lisbon Treaty HEPA promotion has been a cornerstone of EU sport policy *and* funding, as indeed it was a key element of EU sport policy in the years immediately preceding it. Building on the insights from the Paderborn-Essen study[99] which led to comprehensive policy development and funding opportunities from other EU budgets, in particular because growing concern over increasing physical inactivity and overweight/obesity reached the EU policy level. This in turn gave an extra edge to efforts to the Commission's efforts to consolidate specific sport-for-all policies, which were phrased under the HEPA paradigm. The post-Lisbon legal framework firmly shifted the point of gravity towards the Council, whose EU Work Plans for Sport for 2011–14[100] and 2014–17[101]

---

[96] European Commission, EU Physical Activity Guidelines: Recommended Policy Actions in Support of Health-Enhancing Physical Activity. Approved by the EU Working Group 'Sport & Health' at its meeting on 25 September 2008. Confirmed by EU Member State Sport Ministers at their meeting in Biarritz on 27–28 November 2008 and available at http://ec.europa.eu/sport/library/policy_documents/eu-physical-activity-guidelines-2008_en.pdf (accessed 26 Oct 2017).

[97] Council Recommendation of 26 November 2013 (n 32).

[98] Kornbeck (n 35).

[99] Brettschneider and Naul (n 91).

[100] Resolution of the Council and of the Representatives of the Governments of the Member States, meeting within the Council, on a European Union Work Plan for Sport for 2011–2014. [2011] OJ C 162, 1–5.

[101] Resolution of the Council and of the Representatives of the Governments of the Member States, meeting within the Council, of 21 May 2014 on the European Union Work Plan for Sport (2014–2017). [2014] OJ 183, 12–17.

and 2017–20[102] included HEPA policy coordination.[103] The exchange of national data allowed identifying differences and making inferences regarding the causalities of HEPA-friendly public policies[104] as suggested by the Commission in its 2011 Communication on the prospects for implementing the Lisbon Treaty in the field of sport,[105] as well as its report on the results of the first EU Work Plan,[106] all of which included specific HEPA-related proposals, using the 2008 EU Physical Activity Guidelines,[107] as a set of benchmarks.

The Lisbon Treaty further allowed the EU to make connections between its hard law and soft law initiatives. Already under earlier treaties there had been evidence of an 'indirect sport policy',[108] as hard-law competences unrelated to sport revealed their sports law and sports policy relevance. Significantly, the EU was able to use the soft Article 165 TFEU to make legally non-binding, yet legally highly relevant proposals to the World Anti-Doping Agency (WADA), in 2011–13, for the revision of the World Anti-Doping Code (WADC):[109] 'the absence of a hard law competence did not deter MS from using Article 165 TFEU to take a major sports policy initiative'.[110] Similarly, the Council's 2013 HEPA Recommendation,[111] proposed by the Commission in 2011[112] and confirmed by the Council in

[102] Resolution of the Council of the Representatives of the Governments of the Member States meeting within the Council on the European Union Work Plan for Sport (1 July 2017–31 December 2020) [2017] OJ C 189, 5–14.

[103] At the time of writing, the adoption was foreseen for the Council (Education, Youth, Culture and Sport) meeting on 22–23 May 2017.

[104] J Kornbeck 'The European Union, Sport Policy and Health-Enhancing Physical Activity (HEPA): The Case of Exercise by Prescription' (2013) 64(6) *Deutsche Zeitschrift für Sportmedizin* 157.

[105] Developing the European Dimension in Sport (the Communication on Sport), COM(2011) 12 final. And Impact Assessment: Accompanying document to the Communication from the Commission to the European Parliament, the Council, the Economic and Social Committee and the Committee of the Regions: Developing the European Dimension in Sport, SEC(2011) 67 final.

[106] Resolution of the Council (n 100), 1–5.

[107] European Commission, EU Physical Activity Guidelines (n 96).

[108] Tokarski, Steinbach, Petry and Jesse (n 16) 61.

[109] See J Kornbeck, 'The Stamina of the Bosman Legacy: the European Union and the Revision of the World Anti-Doping Code (2011–13)' (2015) 22(2) *Maastricht Journal of European and Comparative Law* 283–304.

[110] See Kornbeck (n 35).

[111] Council Recommendation of 26 November 2013 (n 32).

[112] Developing the European Dimension in Sport (the Communication on Sport), COM(2011) final, 7.

2012,[113] while representing the highest level attainable in EU soft law, nevertheless does not reach the level of hard law in any of its provisions. That the German upper house (*Bundesrat*) opposed it regardless[114] may be taken as evidence that EU soft law may still be perceived as unduly encroaching upon national prerogatives and thus still representing a serious variant of EU regulation.

As the sharing of information and good practice depends on the reliability of the available empirical data, the decades-old and highly trusted Eurobarometer surveys are an invaluable resource of legitimacy.[115] Two such surveys[116] contributed to the HEPA soft law process and inspired independent scholars to publish analyses using the data thus generated.[117] The Paderborn-Essen Study[118] defined types of local HEPA networks which became a reference for later projects,[119] some of which succeeded in attracting EU funding.[120]

---

[113] Conclusions of the Council and of the Representatives of the Governments of the Member States, meeting within the Council, of 27 November 2012 on promoting health-enhancing physical activity (HEPA) [2012] OJ C 393, 22.

[114] Vorschlag für eine Empfehlung des Rates zur sektorübergreifenden Unterstützung gesundheitsfördernder körperlicher Aktivität. COM(2013) 603 final; Ratsdok. 13277/13, http://ec.europa.eu/dgs/secretariat_general/relations/relations_other/npo/docs/germany/2013/com20130603/com20130603_bundesrat_opinion_de.pdf (accessed 26 Oct 2017).

[115] R Bogni, 'The Role of Eurobarometer Surveys in the Communication Policy of the European Union' (2010) 5(3) *Studi sull'integrazione europea* 653–71.

[116] See the survey results at: http://ec.europa.eu/public_opinion/archives/ebs/ebs_197_fr_summ.pdf; http://ec.europa.eu/public_opinion/archives/ebs/ebs_183_6_en.pdf; http://ec.europa.eu/public_opinion/archives/ebs/ebs_213_rapport_fr.pdf; http://ec.europa.eu/public_opinion/archives/ebs/ebs_213_summ_en.pdf;(http://ec.europa.eu/public_opinion/archives/ebs/ebs_334_en.pdf;http://ec.europa.eu/public_opinion/archives/ebs/ebs_412_en.pdf (accessed 26 Oct 2017).

[117] See, e.g., A Rütten and K Abu-Omar 'Prevalence of Physical Activity in the European Union' (2004) 49(4) *Social and Preventive Medicine* 281; J Scheerder and C Van Tuyckom 'Sportparticipatie in de Europese Unie' in J Scheerder, C Van Tuyckom and A Vermeersch (eds), *Europa in beweging* (Ghent Academia 2007) 123–57.

[118] Brettschneider and Naul (n 91).

[119] P Parisi, 'Health, Development and Education in an Integral Perspective' in W Brettschneider and R Naul (eds) *Obesity in Europe* (Peter Lang 2007) 101–18.

[120] W Brettschneider, D Hoffmann, R Naul and A Steinzen, 'Von den Erkenntnissen aus dem EU-Bericht (Young people's lifestyle and sedentariness) zur handlungsorientierten Umsetzung der Empfehlungen im Rahmen von zwei

As defined in Article 6 TFEU, Article 165 TFEU provides the Union with a 'competence to carry out actions to support, coordinate or supplement the actions' of MS. Depending on MS' commitment to the cause in question, this may involve mere sharing of information and good practice, but it may also involve policy coordination whereby soft law becomes unusually committing, such as can be seen from the Bologna process, the method of open coordination (MOC) and the European Semester. Despite having 'only' Article 165 TFEU as its legal base, the 2013 Council Recommendation on HEPA[121] provides for such a framework. As suggested by the Commission in its proposal,[122] this Council-based monitoring mechanism was inspired by a mechanism in place in the field of public health.[123] Aimed at comparing and contrasting national policies with regard to how well they ensure access to and participation in HEPA, 'including but not limited to sport', the HEPA monitoring mechanism launched in 2013 is an evidence-based peer-review exercise drawing on the Paderborn-Essen Study, the two Eurobarometer surveys and the 2008 Physical Activity Guidelines as well as benchmarks specially developed for this exercise.

In its first progress report on the implementation of the 2013 Council recommendation, the Commission identified the data collection and comparison exercise as inherent to all subsequent steps.[124] The Council Recommendation provided Member States with an impetus to address physical inactivity through public policy. Of the total of 152 policies and action plans reported by the MS across all sectors relevant for HEPA promotion, 37 were adopted after the Recommendation was adopted in November 2013.[125] But the exercise remains one based on soft law and

---

lokalen Präventionsstudien' in R Naul, A Krüger and W Schmidt (eds), *Kulturen des Jugendsports* (Meyer & Meyer 2009) 67–104.

[121] Council Recommendation of 26 November 2013 (n 32), 1–5.

[122] Developing the European Dimension in Sport (the Communication on Sport), COM(2011) 12 final, 7.

[123] Council Conclusions on a cooperation mechanism between the Council and the Commission for the implementation of the EU Health Strategy, 2876th Employment, Social Policy, Health and Consumer Affairs Council meeting, Luxembourg, 10 June 2008 and available http://www.eu2008.si/en/News_and_Documents/Council_Conclusions/June/0609_EPSCO-Health_Strategy.pdf (accessed 26 Oct 2017).

[124] Report from the Commission to the European Parliament, the Council, the European Economic and Social Committee and the Committee of the Regions on promoting health-enhancing physical activity across sectors, COM(2016) 768 final, 10.

[125] Ibid., 9.

its success depends, ultimately, on MS' capacity to implement the Council Recommendation effectively across sectors. And to offer citizens a framework that favours an active lifestyle.[126]

One could add that it also depends, as ever, on MS' *willingness* to do so. Yet other policy initiatives within the Education and Culture portfolio have shown that remarkable results can be achieved solely with the help of legally non-binding texts and procedures. The Bologna process is perhaps the most striking example here given that MS often do not have the regulatory power, at national level, to ensure its implementation. The same certainly applies to sports and HEPA-related matters.

This soft law exercise has to further address issues with outspoken hard law implications at national level. Considering that some MS are facing heavy public debt, low sport and HEPA participation levels and high overweight/obesity levels, while having invested heavily in sports infrastructure,[127] this raises the question whether infrastructure investment actually permitted widespread sport or HEPA access or not. In some cases, the 'Olympic legacies' debates come to mind, in that infrastructure built to be able to host international events may have had almost no HEPA effect, while adding to public debt. Another example is provided by sports lotteries and gambling structures enjoying monopoly status in many MS, in spite of empirical evidence indicating that gambling-generated revenue does not benefit HEPA as much as this has been suggested by the protagonists of these monopoly structures. HEPA access appears rather to be rendered possible by municipal budgets (16.9 per cent), and by private households themselves (65.7 per cent), while gambling services appear to contribute only 0.1 per cent to grassroots sports;[128] and again, HEPA provision includes but is not limited to sports structures. The EU is uniquely placed to help MS make an informed judgment about the costly sport policy choices made in response to the bidding procedures organised by SGBs, for example: 'the lack of EU sport teams, EU-level sport competitions and EU-bidding for big sporting

---

126 Ibid., 11.

127 See, e.g., J Kornbeck 'The European Union, Sport Policy and Health-Enhancing Physical Activity (HEPA): The Case of Exercise by Prescription' (2013) 64(6) Deutsche Zeitschrift für Sportmedizin 157.

128 Eurostratégies, Amnyos (n 43).

events make it less vulnerable to SGB reprisals and soft power concerns';[129] moreover, 'SGBs can and do block deviant states from participating in international competitions or withdraw the privilege of hosting sporting events'.[130] The EU is immune to latter sanctions: it simply cannot be reached by them.

Thus, even a soft law mechanism may touch upon national prerogatives, leading to pressure for national hard law in the field of sport policy being used differently, yet it uses soft instruments to achieve its aims. Through its funding streams, the EU has been able to engage directly with actors at the local level (sports clubs, civil society and local authorities), fostering multi-sector strategies[131] where the centrally defined national strategies may rather have a focus on recognised sports organisations, and supporting local, community-based networks.[132] At the EU level, the Council-based monitoring mechanism contributes to the implementation of the Council's third (2017–2020) Work Plan for Sport,[133] another soft-law instrument, having replaced the second Work Plan for Sport (2014–17),[134] another soft-law instrument, replacing the first such Work Plan (2011–14),[135] using the empirical resources referred to above for the work of the Council. These efforts, in turn, have been supported by a major consultancy study with impact from academia and the World Health Organization (WHO) (the Erlangen Study),[136] the

---

[129] A Geeraert and E Drieskens, 'Normative Market Europe: the EU as a Force for Good in International Sports Governance?' (2017) 39 (1) *Journal of European Integration* 79, 80.

[130] Ibid.

[131] R Naul, 'European Union Multisector Strategies to Enhance Health, Physical Education and Physical Activities for Children and Youth' (2012) 1(1) *Global Journal of Health and Physical Education Pedagogy* 22–41.

[132] R Naul, D Schmelt, D Dreiskaemper, D Hoffmann and M l'Hoir, 'Healthy Children in Sound Communities' (HCSC/gkgk): a Dutch–German community-based network project to counteract obesity and physical inactivity' (2012) 29 (suppl)1 *Family Practice* i110–i116.

[133] Resolution of the Council of the Representatives of the Governments of the Member States meeting within the Council on the European Union Work Plan for Sport (1 July 2017–31 December 2020) [2017] OJ C 189, 5–14.

[134] Resolution of the Council (n 101), 12–17.

[135] Resolution of the Council (n 100), 1–5.

[136] P Gelius, A Rütten, L Goodwin, M Marin, K Abu-Omar, S Kahlmeier, E Martin-Diener, M. Murphy, K Ferguson, N Cavill and C Foster, 'Study on the implementation of the European Physical Activity Guidelines. Final Progress Report of Tender EAC-2014-0574' (Publications Office of the European Union 2016).

annual European Week of Sport[137] and a High-Level Group on Grassroots Sport[138] appointed by the Member of the Commission in charge of Sport. In late 2016, the Commission submitted a Progress Report on the implementation of the Council Recommendation on promoting health-enhancing physical activity across sectors to the Council.[139]

IV.ii Funding

The concept 'including but not limited to sport' has been used repeatedly in many calls for proposals for EU funding in the field of sport. By means of an example, the 2017 version of the Erasmus+ Programme Guide defines the eligibility criteria for organisations seeking funding through so-called Collaborative Partnerships:

> Collaborative Partnerships offer the opportunity to develop, transfer and/or implement innovative outputs and/or engage into intensive dissemination and exploitation activities of existing and newly available products or innovative ideas in different areas relating to sport and physical activity. They involve various organisations and actors *in and outside sport*,[140] including in particular public authorities at local, regional, national and European levels, sport organisations, sport-related organisations and educational bodies.[141]

This is a prime example of EU HEPA soft law, as the Programme Guide is legally binding upon the Commission and the Educational, Audiovisual and Culture Executive Agency (EACEA) entrusted with the selection of projects for funding. In replacing several well-known EU programmes in the field of education and culture by a single, streamlined programme, the Commission, in addition to the objective of 'growth and ensuring prosperity',[142] pleaded in favour of the field of sport to 'be treated as a separate activity within the Programme',[143] to be able to support 'transnational collaborative projects; non-commercial European sporting events

137 See http://ec.europa.eu/sport/week/index_en.htm (accessed 26 Oct 2017).

138 See http://ec.europa.eu/sport/news/2016/0404-3rd-high-level-group-grass roots_en.htm (accessed 26 Oct 2017).

139 Report from the Commission (n 124).

140 Emphasis added by author.

141 European Commission, Erasmus+ Programme Guide. Version 1 (2017), 227 and available at http://ec.europa.eu/programmes/erasmus-plus/sites/erasmus plus/files/files/resources/erasmus-plus-programme-guide_en.pdf (accessed 26 Oct 2017).

142 European Commission Communication on Erasmus for All: The EU Programme for Education, Training, Youth and Sport, COM(2011) 787, 2.

143 Ibid., 6.

of major importance; strengthening of the evidence base for policy making in the field of sport; capacity building in sport; dialogue with relevant European stakeholders'.[144]

From a doctrinal perspective, financial instruments are not soft law but hard law; they even represent a considerable volume of legislative proposals.[145] In this case, the Erasmus+ programme, including a sport chapter, is based on an Erasmus+ Regulation,[146] which has been negotiated as part of the ordinary legislative procedure (art 294 TFEU)[147] and, in this case, with considerable political input from various sides.[148] In line with advice received through the external evaluation of preparatory actions (2009–13) having prepared for this programme,[149] Regulation 1288/2013 specifically defines the objectives of EU sports funding as aiming at promoting grassroots sport and volunteering, social inclusion, equal opportunities and HEPA and access to sport for all citizens.[150] While funding is seen as a means to fulfil the EU's mandate for 'developing the European dimension in sport',[151] the activities are understood to be grounded in the three EU Work Plans for Sport. Although funding is not reserved exclusively for grassroots sport, sport is understood broadly as 'organised sport practised at local level by amateur sportspeople, and sport for all'.[152] Funding is provided for 'sport, in particular grassroots sport',[153] with the phrase 'in particular' appearing as many as three times.[154] As the Multiannual Financial Framework (MFF) 2014–20 saw the merger of four historical, well-branded programmes

---

144 Ibid., 13.

145 For the Multiannual Financial Framework (MFF) 2014–20 alone, the Commission tabled about 60 proposals for the legal acts concerning multiannual programmes in all policy areas covered by the MFF. See *European Union Public Finance* (5th edn, European Commission 2014) 99.

146 Regulation (EU) No 1288/2013.

147 *European Union Public Finance* (n 145) 104.

148 For details see Kornbeck (n 35).

149 'It is recommended that the majority of funding for future incentive measures be dedicated to transnational networking projects, as these have shown the greatest potential for achieving EU added value across the range of priorities reflected in EU sport policy.' Economisti Associati *et al.* Framework Contract EAC/50/2009 for Evaluation, Evaluation Related Services and Support for Impact Assessment Specific Contract: Evaluation of Preparatory Actions and Special Events in the Field of Sport, Final Report (European Commission 2011) 11.

150 Recital 24 and art 16(1)(c) Regulation (EU) No 1288/2013.

151 Art 165(1) TFEU; art 4(e) Regulation (EU) No 1288/2013.

152 Art 2(24) Regulation (EU) No 1288/2013.

153 Art 1(3) Regulation (EU) No 1288/2013.

154 Art 1(3), art 4 (e), art 16(1) Regulation (EU) No 1288/2013.

into one,[155] it seems remarkable the 'Erasmus+: Sport' became the *only* chapter with a distinct sectoral identity within Erasmus+.[156]

V. DISCUSSION AND CONCLUSION

V.i HEPA 'Including but not Limited to Sports': An Emerging EU Sports Soft Law Doctrine?

Today's EU is far away from the ambition of 1992 to use big international sports events to 'create a bottom-up Europhile sense of belonging'.[157] With the UK's exit from the EU imminent, the current political context is rather different compared with the years leading up to the completion of the single market (then much appreciated by the UK). EU visibility at big international sports events is not always welcome as it may be seen as a threat to national identities.[158] At the hard law level, there is no problem, as neither the Treaty nor the case law of the Court has changed the distribution of responsibilities between MS and the EU. Big international sports events continue to be arenas for staging national identities, and the selection of national teams constitute a lawful exception from EU law's ban on discrimination based on nationality. Challenges to the EU's role are political and psychological, but not legal in nature. In this context, a focus on soft law may be a useful supplement to an assessment of the relevant hard law. SGBs' rather unsuccessful attempts, post-*Bosman*, to have their economic activities exempted from the EU's regulatory clout may, ironically, have produced the unintended effect of providing a foil on which to develop a sport policy which does not *per se* favour SGBs.

Instead, after *Bosman* the EU developed a HEPA doctrine which is innovative and which supplements the sport policies of MS, though it also has the potential to challenge them, if it leads to the realisation that national policies are not HEPA-friendly. The policy challenges are

---

155 *European Union Public Finance* (n 145) 104.

156 The Lifelong Learning Programme (2007–2013) had still preserved four distinct strands: Comenius for schools, Erasmus for higher education, Leonardo da Vinci for vocational education and training and Grudtvig for adult education. Erasmus+ knows no such sectoral distinctions, expect for sport.

157 B García, 'The EU and Sport Governance: Between Economic and Social Values' in M Groeneveld, B Houlihan and F Ohl (eds) *Social Capital and Sport Governance in Europe* (Routledge 2011) 24.

158 N Gardiner 'Chariots of Brussels? The EU is dreaming of Olympics glory' *The Telegraph* (London, 23 July 2012).

relatively easy to identify: rather than competing against each other, elite sports versus grassroots sports organisations, and sports organisations versus the health system, all relevant actors ought to realise in relation to the societal problems caused by physical inactivity they are facing the same challenges,[159] and it is thus up to public authorities to encourage them to work together. But legal implications are harder to identify, and the fact that the available data can still be challenged in many ways[160] will not make it easier for public authorities to take action, when SGBs appear to have clear goals, strong public support and, in many cases, income of their own.

On balance, the material presented in this chapter makes it plausible to argue that the HEPA concept 'including but not limited to sports' represents an emerging EU sports soft law doctrine, even if it cannot be found in the Treaty and has not yet been quoted by the Court.

V.ii Soft Law *versus* Hard Law, or Soft Law *cum* Hard Law?

This is not to suggest that soft law has taken the place of hard law; 'the shift away from hierarchical governance' actually often obscures the fact that enforceability varies, as do actors with regulatory powers.[161] It is not as if 'command-and-control-type regulation'[162] has vanished, and indeed, it seems more realistic to assume that an actor already equipped with hard law powers may be more effective in using soft law also: this already seemed plausible and probable with regard to the EU's involvement in sport policy before the 2013 Council HEPA Recommendation had become an even remote possibility.[163] As Parrish[164] and

---

[159] H Hartmann 'Gesundheitssysteme und Sportorganisationen im gleichen Boot beim Kampf gegen die gefährliche Zeitbombe Bewegungsmangel' (2016) 67(3) *Deutsche Zeitschrift für Sportmedizin* 51–52.

[160] K Siefken and S Titze 'Das Globale Observatorium für Körperliche Aktivität (GoPA!) präsentiert länderspezifische Bewegungskarten. Ein Überblick über die globale Initiative' (2016) 67(3) *Deutsche Zeitschrift für Sportmedizin* 64–7.

[161] P Craig and G de Búrca, *EU Law: Text, Cases, Materials* (4th edn OUP 2008) 146.

[162] Ibid.

[163] J Kornbeck, 'Governance als Soft Law: Innovation oder Notwendigkeit im sportpolitischen Handeln der EU?' in W Tokarski, K Petry and B Jesse (eds), *Sportpolitik* (Sportverlag Strauß 2006) 31–52.

[164] Parrish (n 2).

Duval[165] have noted, the Commission has often used soft law in areas related to sport where it actually *could have* relied on hard law. There are different reasons why this may have been so. But when soft law has been used to bridge gaps through negotiations between the Commission and SGBs, where it 'allows the Commission to respond to political pressure for a softer touch application of competition law to sport whilst not undermining their commitment to the free market',[166] such solutions must stay within the confines of, and be compatible with EU law: as the executive branch of the EU, the Commission does not have a mandate to overrule the primary and secondary legislators.[167]

In this connection, it will be noted that the chapter has consistently compared advances made by the EU through policy, as opposed to those made through funding initiatives. These two avenues of European integration represent different levels of soft law: financial instruments are actually hard law, even if they generally only bind the EU itself. (They rely on separate legal instruments, such as grant agreements, to bind beneficiaries.) This example also shows that, rather than framing the question discussed in this chapter as one opposing soft law *versus* hard law, it may be more subtly (and more helpfully) phrased as one of soft law *cum* hard law, as these two forms of EU action are complementary. That EU HEPA soft law has not exempted SGBs from the burden of EU regulation is another matter. At the time of finishing this chapter, the Commission's investigation into the International Skating Union's (ISU) eligibility rules,[168] following a complaint lodged by two Dutch ice speed skaters Mark Tuitert and Niels Kerstholt, provided a renewed, powerful demonstration of the relevance of EU antitrust law to the activities of SGBs. Should the investigation and an ensuing trial before the Court[169] produce a *Bosman*-like effect, one may however speculate that this could provide renewed impetus to EU HEPA discourses.

---

165 A Duval, 'La Lex Sportiva face au droit de l'Union Européenne: guerre et paix dans l'espace juridique transnational' (PhD thesis, European University Institute 2015).

166 Parrish (n 2) and Duval, ibid.

167 Y Le Lostecque 'Les transferts de joueurs' (2001–2002) 3 *Revue des affaires européennes* 324, 328.

168 File AT.40208, International Skating Union's Eligibility Rules and available at http://ec.europa.eu/competition/elojade/isef/case_details.cfm?proc_code=1_40208 (accessed 26 Oct 2017).

169 Although a trial might seem risky for the ISU, this SGB recently proved in the *Pechstein* case, heard by German national courts, that it is prepared to run such a risk. While this antitrust case concerning an anti-doping ban had been

V.iii A Politically and Legally Sound Choice

If applied successfully, the emergent soft law doctrine for health-friendly sport policy might become yet another manifestation of how 'the EU reveals itself as a normative market – a sort of hybrid actor – within the world of international sport'.[170] Yet this would depend on the extent to which HEPA norms could be quasi-enforced in conjunction with EU hard law in such public policy provinces as single market regulation and fundamental rights. The post-Brexit EU may decide to develop into different directions, as epitomised by the five scenarios identified in the Commission's 'Future of Europe' 2017 White Paper.[171] This White Paper does not mention sport on even one occasion, while it refers to culture once,[172] to youth unemployment once[173] – and three times to health.[174] Linking future sport policy initiatives to health thus seems well advised. That this choice can also be legally sound, is what this chapter aims to have demonstrated.

---

won by the athlete before the court *(Landgericht)* (LG) and high court *(Oberlandesgericht)* (OLG) of Munich, ISU took many observers by surprise when it decided to appeal the OLG ruling to the federal court (*Bundesgericht*) (BGH) in Karlsruhe. The BGH judgment, of 7 June 2016, again took many by surprise by supporting the ISU, whose strategy had manifestly paid off.

[170] Geeraert and Drieskens (n 129), 89.

[171] White Paper on the Future of Europe: Reflections and Scenarios for the EU27 by 2025, COM(2017)2025.

[172] Ibid., 6

[173] Ibid., 13.

[174] Ibid., 10 and 22 (bis).

4. The EU's role on doping in sport

Jack Anderson

I. INTRODUCTION

Until relatively recently, the EU's interest and role with regard to anti-doping in sport was very much secondary to that taken by the Council of Europe. Since the publication of its White Paper on Sport in 2007, the EU Commission, together with Member States, and in conjunction with the Council of Europe, the World Anti-Doping Agency (WADA), the International Olympic Committee (IOC) and the United Nations Educational, Scientific and Cultural Organisation (UNESCO), has sought ways to better coordinate the various different global actions that are being taken to combat the problem of doping in sport. Moreover, under its Work Plan for Sport 2011–2014, the European Council established an EU Expert Group on Anti-Doping that submitted the EU revisions to consultation process on what is now the World Anti-Doping Code (2015). Both the Council and the Commission have continued to work with Member States to ensure that all rules and procedures, linked with the World Anti-Doping Code, comply both with EU law and the EU's vision of an athlete-friendly anti-doping system.

The EU's vision in this respect is that, as well as being linked to serious health issues amongst individual sports professionals, doping negatively affects the public's perception of sport and demotivates participants, seriously undermining the principles of open and fair competition in the process. Accordingly, and in realising its vision of an athlete-friendly anti-doping system, the EU has acknowledged that although anti-doping has been concerned essentially with testing, sanctions and deterrence – important though they are – there must be an acknowledgement that anti-doping rules and programmes in sport need to be supplemented by wider efforts to prevent the emergence and subsequent perpetuation of a doping culture in sport. To this end, the EU has financially supported anti-doping education and prevention programmes to target wider audiences in recreational, youth and amateur sport and not just top-level competitive athletes.

This chapter reviews, briefly and separately, all five points raised in the above introduction and namely: the seminal role of the Council of Europe with regard to anti-doping policy; the EU's role on doping in sport prior to 2007; the 2007 White Paper on Sport as a catalyst for greater EU interest in anti-doping policy; an assessment of the EU Expert Group on Anti-Doping's contributions to revisions of the WADA Code and including its compliance with EU law; and finally, the EU's policy objective of promoting an athlete-friendly anti-doping system through supporting programmes that educate/prevent against, as opposed to those that merely sanction/deter, a doping culture at all levels of sport.

II. COUNCIL OF EUROPE

In June 1967, the Council of Europe's Committee of Ministers produced the first international legal instrument on doping.[1] The Resolution on the Doping of Athletes was interesting in three regards: it contained one of the first attempts to legally define the term 'doping'; the underlying idea on the prohibition of doping appeared concerned more with the professionalisation of sport than the health of athletes; and the legal instrument was of persuasive effect only and hamstrung by the acute geopolitics of sport in the era, which for much of the 1970s would see a Cold War freeze on anti-doping policy and, indeed, ethics in the Olympic arena.[2]

The Council of Europe's 1967 Resolution defined doping as follows:

> Considering that doping is the administration to or the use by a healthy person, in any manner whatsoever, of agents foreign to the organism, or of physiological substances in excessive quantities or introduced by an abnormal channel, with the sole purpose of affecting artificially and by unfair means the performance of such a person when taking part in a competition.

This quasi-legal definition of doping was not the first; an honour which probably should be claimed by the world governing body of athletics, the IAAF, when at its 1928 Congress it defined doping as 'the use of any

---

[1] Resolution on the Doping of Athletes (67/12) adopted by the Committee of Ministers of the Council of Europe Ministers' Deputies, 29 June 1967, available at http://www.coe.int/t/dg4/sport/Resources/texts/spres67.12_en.asp (accessed on 26 Oct 2017).

[2] See generally I Ritchie, 'Understanding Performance-enhancing Substances and Sanctions Against their Use from the Perspective of History' in V Moller, I Waddington and J Hoberman (eds) *Routledge Handbook of Drugs and Sport* (Routledge 2015) chap 2.

stimulant employed to increase the power of action in athletic competition above the average'.[3] Moreover, the Council of Europe's definition was no doubt influenced by the IOC's definition of doping emanating from its 65th IOC Session held in Tehran in May 1967: '[Doping is] the use of substances or techniques in any form or quantity alien or unnatural to the body with the exclusive aim of obtaining an artificial or unfair increase of performance in competition.'[4]

The underlying motivation for and concern with doping at the time, and certainly at the level of the IOC, appeared to be a view that increased drug taking in, for example, sports such as cycling, was symptomatic both of the 'evils' of professionalism and its corrosive influence on the de Coubertin purity or the spirit of (Olympic) participation in sport – epitomised by the death of Danish cyclist Knut Jensen at the 1960 Rome Olympics.[5] It is in this context that the Council of Europe's 1967 Resolution refers to 'the increasingly evil effects of certain practices known as "doping" which jeopardise the health and dignity of those who resort to it and offend against the spirit of fair play essential to all sports.'

This slightly skewed ethical basis to anti-doping policies – premised on a Corinthian notion of the 'spirit of sport' – remains, for some, a weakness in contemporary anti-doping policy.[6] In any event, the Corinthian ethos was not seen at the elite Olympian level of the sport in the 1970s and 1980s, dominated by Soviet bloc athletes who were driven by both the propaganda value of sporting success and extensive state-sponsored doping programmes. In a practical sense, the IOC, not the well-resourced entity that it is today thanks to broadcasting revenues, could only stand, or at least chose to stand idly, by and little was done by way of an effective anti-doping policy in these decades.[7] Equally, the 1967 Resolution was largely ineffective and there is a significantly plaintive element to the reiteration of much of the 1967 Resolution's

---

[3] Cited in J Gleaves and M Llewellyn, 'Sport, Drugs and Amateurism: Tracing the Real Cultural Origins of Anti-doping Rules in International Sport' (2014) 31(8) *International Journal of the History of Sport* 839, 846.

[4] J Todd and T Todd, 'Significant Events in the History of Drug Testing and the Olympic Movement: 1960–1999' in W Wilson and E Derse (eds) *Doping in Elite Sport: The Politics of Drugs in the Olympic Movement* (Human Kinetics) 68.

[5] See generally J Gleaves, 'Doped Professionals and Clean Amateurs: Amateurism's Influence on the Modern Philosophy of Anti-doping' (2011) 38(2) *Journal of Sports History* 237–54.

[6] See generally P Dimeo, *A History of Drug Use in Sport: 1876–1976: Beyond Good and Evil* (Routledge 2007).

[7] See V McDermott, *The War on Drugs in Sport* (Routledge 2016) chap 2.

substantive elements in the Council of Europe's rather grandly titled 'European Anti-Doping Charter for Sport', adopted by its Committee of Ministers on 25 September 1984.[8]

The Ben Johnson affair at the 1988 Seoul Olympics and the fall of the Berlin Wall were critical junctures in the development of current anti-doping policy and in the decade that followed the Council of Europe would play its part,[9] notably with its Anti-Doping Convention of March 1990 which sought to act as the then international reference instrument for the global coordination of national anti-doping policies,[10] but also contributing to the foundation of the World Anti-Doping Agency at the end of that century.[11]

Prior to 1990, it could be argued that the Council of Europe's role in anti-doping was somewhat overplayed; since then, and certainly since the foundation of WADA, the Council's role has been somewhat under-played. Two recent (2016) Recommendations of the Council's Monitoring Group (established under the terms of Art 11.1.d of the Anti-Doping Convention of 1990) are of interest. The first is of a 'hard' nature and relates to 'Information Sharing between Public Agencies and Anti-Doping Organisations';[12] the second is 'softer' in nature and relates to 'Anti-Doping Education Guidelines for Tertiary Education Institutions'.[13]

On the first Recommendation, the Monitoring Group were guided by Article 22(2) and (3) of the World Anti-Doping Code (WADC 2015):

---

[8] Available at http://www.coe.int/t/dg4/sport/Resources/texts/spchart3_en.asp (accessed 26 Oct 2017). See also Recommendation No R (84) of the Committee of Ministers to the Member States on the 'European Anti-Doping Charter for Sport' adopted on 25 September 1984 available at https://rm.coe.int/CoERMPublicCommonSearchServices/DisplayDCTMContent?documentId=09000016804ef140 (accessed 26 Oct 2017).

[9] B Houlihan, *Dying to Win: Doping in Sport and the Development of Anti-doping Policy* (2nd edn, Council of Europe Publishing 2002).

[10] Anti-Doping Convention, ETS No.135, Strasbourg, 16 November 1989, available at http://www.coe.int/en/web/conventions/full-list/-/conventions/treaty/135 (accessed 26 Oct 2017).

[11] Resolution on the fight against doping (1/2000) and available at http://www.coe.int/t/dg4/sport/Resources/texts/spres00.1_en.asp (accessed 26 Oct 2017).

[12] The Recommendation is available at: http://www.coe.int/t/dg4/sport/Resources/texts/Rec(2016)01_EN_Final_RecInformationsharing.pdf (accessed 26 Oct 2017).

[13] The Recommendation is available at http://www.coe.int/t/dg4/sport/Resources/texts/Rec(2016)02_EN_Final_RecEducationGuidelines_TertiaryEducation.pdf (accessed 26 Oct 2017).

> WADC 22.2 Each government will put in place legislation, regulation, policies or administrative practices for cooperation and sharing of information with Anti-Doping Organizations and sharing of data among Anti-Doping Organizations as provided in the Code.
>
> 22.3 Each government will encourage cooperation between all of its public services or agencies and Anti-Doping Organizations to timely share information with Anti-Doping Organizations which would be useful in the fight against doping and where to do so would not otherwise be legally prohibited.

To facilitate Article 22's objectives, the Council of Europe agreed to focus on anti-trafficking measures such as: (a) the better provision of training to customs bodies, law enforcement authorities, anti-doping agencies and other relevant regulatory agencies (e.g., those tasked with regulating the supply of pharmaceutical products) at national level; and (b) ensuring that such information can, when appropriate under national law, be used to further criminal investigations concerning the production, sale, supply, and distribution of prohibited doping substances.

In addition, this Council of Europe Recommendation on information sharing specifically mentioned two further initiatives in relation to anti-doping policy surrounding the hosting of a major international sporting events i.e., the need for the host country to consider: (a) the implementation of specific regulations in accordance with national rules on protection of personal data to provide for the obtaining of information which would be useful in the fight against doping in the context of such international sporting events; and (b) requirements that the organising bodies for such events facilitate this information sharing in accordance with national rules on protection of personal data as a condition of any hosting or similar agreements.

In relation to the Second Recommendation of 2016 (Anti-Doping Education Guidelines for Tertiary Education Institutions), the Council of Europe working in conjunction with WADA and the Institute of National Anti-Doping Organisations (NADO) produced what in University education terms would be considered a template module on doping education useful for modules in degree programmes relating to Sports Law; Sports Management or Administration; Sports Medicine; Sports Nutrition; Sports Pharmacology; Sports Ethics; Sports Physiology; Sports Science; Physical Education; and Sports Journalism. This incredibly useful resource has been largely unheralded.[14]

---

[14] See also http://antidopinglearninghub.org/ (accessed 26 Oct 2017).

III. EU ROLE ON DOPING IN SPORT PRIOR TO 2007

Prior to the White Paper on Sport in 2007, the EU's policy on doping in sport was sporadically expressed.[15] For instance, in December 1998, prior to the foundation of WADA, the Vienna European Council expressed its concern with the extant scale of doping in sports by emphasising the need for 'mobilisation' at EU level.[16] Within a week, on 17 December 1998, this was followed by a resolution of the European Parliament calling upon the Commission to initiate measures at Community level, with a view to better coordination and complementarity between national and European measures and actions.[17] In September 1999, the Committee of the Regions delivered an opinion on the 'European Model of Sport' which contained a chapter on doping and which supported the Parliament's call for the Commission to present proposals on combating doping and particularly in the area of public health policy.[18]

The Commission responded by way of a 'Community support plan' to combat doping in sport.[19] That plan focussed on three areas: assembly of experts' opinions on the ethical, legal and scientific dimensions of doping; greater collaboration with the Olympic movement to create the World Anti-Doping Agency; mobilisation of Community instruments with a view to supplementing the actions already underway in the

---

15 See, e.g., the brief review by M Kedzior, 'Effects of the EU Anti-Doping Laws and Politics for the International and Domestic Sports Law in Member States' (2007) 7(1/2) *International Sports Law Journal* 111–14.

16 Vienna European Council, 11–12 December 1998, Presidency Conclusions, para 96:

> The European Council underlines its concern at the extent and seriousness of doping in sports, which undermines the sporting ethic and endangers public health. It emphasises the need for mobilisation at European Union level and invites the Member States to examine jointly with the Commission and international sports bodies possible measures to intensify the fight against this danger, in particular through better coordination of existing national measures.

17 Resolution on urgent measures to be taken against doping in sport [1999] OJ C 98, 09/04/1999.

18 Opinion of the Committee of the Regions 37/99 fin, 16 September 1999.

19 Communication from the Commission to the Council, the European Parliament, the Economic and Social Committee and the Committee of the Regions – Community Support Plan to Combat Doping in Sport, COM/99/0643 final. See also section 3.2 of the 'Helsinki Report on Sport', Report from the Commission to the European Council with a view to safeguarding current sports structures and maintaining the social function of sport within the Community framework, COM(1999) 644 final.

Member States and to vesting them with a Community dimension, taking account inter alia of the growing mobility of European sportspersons and the Community's competences relevant to the field of doping.[20]

The first, and arguably the most interesting, was a reference to the European Group on Ethics (EGE), an independent multidisciplinary body which since 1991 has advised the European Commission on ethical aspects of science and new technologies.[21] The EGE delivered an opinion on the ethical aspects arising from doping in sport on 11 November 1999 which was then annexed to the Commission's Community Work Plan. There were three key aspects to the EGE report. The first was the EGE's view that fundamental Euro-centric ethical principles should be taken into consideration in the fight against doping, such as: the protection of the health and safety of citizens, which includes sportsmen and women; integrity and transparency, which requires guaranteeing the honesty of sports events and the outlawing of cheating; the protection of vulnerable persons, especially children; and the dignity of all athletes including their freedom from exploitation. In this the EGE's report remains broadly reflective of the principles still contained in the 'Fundamental Rationale' Preamble to the World Anti-Doping Code (2015).

The second point stated that sportsmen and women have 'rights and obligations' in following an ethical approach to this aspect of their sport as relating principally to: autonomy over their own bodies; information about what kind of substances, methods and risks are involved; competition under fair conditions, based on equality of access to competition; protection from any kind of exploitation linked to economic interests which could seriously limit the autonomy of the sportsman/woman; participation in the implementation of ethical rules in sport and including the decision-making processes in the various sports concerned; and all with the aim of informing the sportsmen/women about risks, advantages, forms of medicalisation and how rules are defined with regard to controls and sanctions.

This athlete-centric view of the ethics of (anti) doping policy in sport remains largely ignored in contemporary debates on doping and is something the EU might consider for future (revived) promotion, as is the range of measures proposed by the EGE's opinion, which included:

- the creation of an efficient health monitoring system for sportspersons, more specifically through the establishing of a specialised

---

20 Community support plan to combat doping in sport, ibid., 5.

21 See https://ec.europa.eu/research/ege/index.cfm (accessed 26 Oct 2017).

service providing sportspersons with medical and psychological assistance and information;

- the adoption of a directive on the protection of young sportspersons, notably those who aspire to become professionals;
- the adoption of specific provisions on the protection of sportspersons, as workers exposed to particular risks;
- promotion of epidemiological research into the health of sportspersons;
- organisation of conferences on doping and the health of sportspersons in collaboration with the sports community;
- sensitisation of education professionals to the problem of sports ethics;
- increased level of police and judicial cooperation;
- inclusion in sportspersons' contracts of references to doping and the fact that it is banned;
- the adoption of a joint declaration equivalent to a code of practice in sport at the end of a European conference on doping in sport.

In 2000, the Commission supported the above with a call for proposals for 'Pilot projects for campaigns to combat doping in sport in Europe',[22] followed by a second call in 2001[23] and a third one in 2002.[24] The auditing of and reaction to the successful proposals under the three calls was positive[25] but it is argued that the holistic ethical analysis of doping in sport hinted at in the EGE report, and also areas of interest such as the ethical and legal aspects relating to health professionals and doping, are areas which the EU might return to with greater interest and advocacy in the future given the interrelation of such topics with existing EU instruments in area of such as public health.[26]

---

[22] Call for proposals No DG EAC C 116 of 26/04/2000.

[23] Call for proposals DG EAC No 20/01 of 01/05/2001 [2001] OJ C 130, 8–13.

[24] Call for proposals DG EAC No 33/02.

[25] The evaluation can be found at https://ec.europa.eu/sport/sites/sport/files/doping-pilot-projects-evaluation-2003_en.pdf (accessed 26 Oct 2017).

[26] See, e.g., the correlation between doping and the competency within Art 168(1) TFEU:

> A high level of human health protection shall be ensured in the definition and implementation of all Union policies and activities. Union action, which shall complement national policies, shall be directed towards improving public health, preventing physical and mental illness and diseases, and obviating sources of danger to physical and mental health. Such action shall cover the fight against the major health scourges, by promoting research into their

IV. THE WHITE PAPER, 2007

As stated in the White Paper on Sport, the initiative was the:

> … first time that the [EU] Commission is addressing sport-related issues in a comprehensive manner. Its overall objective is to give strategic orientation on the role of sport in Europe, to encourage debate on specific problems, to enhance the visibility of sport in EU policy-making and to raise public awareness of the needs and specificities of the sector.[27]

The word 'doping' was mentioned 15 times in the White Paper, primarily in section 2 on 'The Societal Role of Sport' and specifically in section 2.2. On reflection, that section of the White Paper was largely bland and generic in nature reflecting the EU's limited competence at the time with regard to sport. In a broad sense, the White Paper focussed on three aspects of doping in sport – the health and prevention dimension; greater cooperation; and harmonisation.

With regard to health, the accompanying staff working document to the White Paper implicitly acknowledged the state-sponsored doping programmes of the 1970s and 1980s by reference to 'serious long-term degradation of individuals' health in the past and in some documented cases it has entailed serious conditions of permanent ill-health, disability or even death'.[28] It also acknowledged doping at amateur level in sport and that 'a special problem is posed in relation to children and young people as it is known that many start taking doping substances at an increasingly young age'.[29] Regrettably, the staff working document did not support the above by way of referenced evidence and the White Paper merely called on 'sport organisations to develop rules of good practice to ensure that young sportsmen and sportswomen are better informed and

---

causes, their transmission and their prevention, as well as health information and education, and monitoring, early warning of and combating serious cross-border threats to health. The Union shall complement the Member States' action in reducing drugs-related health damage, including information and prevention.

27 White Paper on Sport, COM(2007) 391 final, 2.

28 Commission Staff Working Document – The EU and Sport: Background and Context – Accompanying document to the White Paper on Sport, COM(2007) 391 final, SEC(2007)932, SEC(2007)934, SEC(2007)936, SEC/2007/0935, s 2.2.

29 Ibid.

educated of doping substances, prescription medicines which may contain them, and their health implications'.[30]

The lack of supporting evidence also undermined one of the more arresting claims in the staff working document and namely:

> The Doping practices involving illegal substances pose a serious threat to social order, including criminal justice issues, and to the integrity of the sporting community ... For the criminal community, the trade in doping substances can offer an attractive mixture of low risk and high return on investments. Trade in doping substances is often not subject to severe punishment.[31]

Again, the impact of the above in the staff working document was diluted not only by the lack of supporting evidence but also by the rather sweeping, ill-defined statement in the White Paper recommending 'that trade in illicit doping substances be treated in the same manner as trade in illicit drugs throughout the EU'. The practicalities of such equivalence (between performance enhancing substances and illicit drugs) and how it could be given statutory or regulatory form was not in any way addressed by the Commission, leading to the following, rather weak conclusion:

> Partnerships could be developed between Member State law enforcement agencies (border guards, national and local police, customs etc.), laboratories accredited by the World Anti-Doping Agency (WADA) and INTERPOL to exchange information about new doping substances and practices in a timely manner and in a secure environment. The EU could support such efforts through training courses and networking between training centres for law enforcement officers.[32]

On harmonisation, the Commission simply pointed out the lack of harmonisation in global anti-doping policy, attributing it to the fact that:

> ... responsibilities are distributed unsystematically because sport is organised differently in different Member States, because the degree of autonomy of sport organisations varies, because the problem tends to be defined differently and because bodies at several levels – international, national, regional and local – claim responsibility and authority.[33]

---

[30] White Paper on Sport, (n 27), 5.
[31] Commission Staff Working Document (n 28), s 2.2.
[32] White Paper on Sport, (n 27), 4–5.
[33] Commission Staff Working Document (n 28), s 2.2.

In this, the White Paper called for a more coordinated approach in the fight against doping by defining common positions in relation to the Council of Europe and WADA and including the 'proper implementation' of the UNESCO Convention against Doping in Sport by Member States. Again, this was all very generic, although the Commission did specifically identify for itself 'a facilitating role, for example by supporting a network of national anti-doping organisations of Member States'.[34]

Ironically, the most impactful aspect of the White Paper on sport with regard to doping was the analysis of the ECJ ruling in the *Meca-Medina* case.[35] In that case, two professional long-distance swimmers challenged the compatibility with Articles 81 and 82 EC (now Arts 101 and 102 of TFEU) of the anti-doping rules adopted by the IOC and world governing body for swimming, FINA. The two swimmers argued inter alia that the enforcement of 'scientifically unsound' anti-doping regulation restricted athletes' economic freedoms and in this instance, breached EU competition law. The ECJ (re)confirmed that sport is subject to EU law only insofar as it constitutes an 'economic activity'; but this 'specificity of sport' did not necessarily give certain categories of sporting rules a priori exemption from the application of the EU competition law. In summary:

> ... the recognition of the specificity of sport cannot entail the categorical inapplicability of the EC competition provisions to organisational sporting rules but it has to be included as an element of legal significance within the context of analysing the conformity of such rules with EC competition law.[36]

Meca-Medina also usefully attempted to describe the methodological approach that has to be applied in an examination of the compatibility of sporting rules with Articles 101 and 102 TFEU[37] and as a consequence inspired voluminous academic commentary on the methodology and on EU sports competition law well beyond its application to doping regulation.[38]

The above revisionist perspective on the White Paper's discussion on doping must, in itself, be placed in context given that the White Paper preceded the competency given to the EU in sport by way of Article 165

---

34 White Paper on Sport, (n 27), 5.

35 Case C-519/04 P *Meca-Medina and Majcen v Commission* [2006] ECR I-6991.

36 Commission Staff Working Document (n 28), s 3.4(a).

37 Ibid., section 3.4(b).

38 See seminally S Weatherill, 'Anti-doping Revisited – the Demise of the Rule of "Purely Sporting Interest"?' (2006) 27 *European Competition Law Review* 645.

TFEU. Prior to Article 165, competency in sporting matters was, at best, remote, epitomised by the fact that with regard to doping, the most effective Treaty provision was probably Article 152 of the EC Treaty (subsequently Art 168 TFEU) giving the EU a complementary role in preventing and reducing all drug-related health damage, including information and prevention.

With respect to current anti-doping policies, Article 165 TFEU has five points of interest. First, and to reiterate, the provision conferred, for the first time, an explicit sport policy mandate on the EU. Second, the reference in the final paragraph of Article 165(2) TFEU, to 'promoting fairness and openness in sporting competitions' can be taken to be linked to anti-doping policy as, thirdly, can the reference to 'protecting the physical and moral integrity of sportsmen and sportswomen, especially the youngest sportsmen and sportswomen'. Fourth, Article 165(4)'s reference to 'incentive measures' is generally taken to mean the competitive funding of projects within the competence of Article 165; the outcomes of which can, in turn, be supported by Council recommendations as the primary instrument of related EU action. Finally, Article 165(4)'s reference to 'excluding any harmonisation of the laws and regulations of the Member States' is also of further note with regard to anti-doping policies within the EU.

V. EU EXPERT GROUP ON ANTI-DOPING

As stated, the entry into force of the Lisbon Treaty in December 2009 gave the EU a competency to support and supplement sports policy measures taken by Member States. Within two years, the EU Commission's Communication on sport, 'Developing the European Dimension in Sport', was adopted and set out the Commission's ideas for EU-level action in the field of sport. The Communication proposed actions going for both the Commission and Member States in the area of sports policy until 2015. The European Council subsequently adopted a resolution on an EU Work Plan for Sport (2011–14) in May 2011.[39] The Work Plan set out priority themes for action in various areas of sports policy and

[39] Resolution of the Council and of the Representatives of the Governments of the Member States, meeting within the Council, on a European Union Work Plan for Sport for 2011–2014. [2011] OJ C 162/1, 1–5.

including anti-doping policy under the umbrella term 'integrity of sport' and a specific 'Expert Group on Anti-Doping' was established.[40]

The mandate of the Expert Group quickly extended to focus on two points: (a) preparing formal EU responses and comments to WADA Code Review process until the Fourth World Conference on Doping in Sport (Johannesburg, November 2013);[41] and (b) to ascertain best practices in the fight against doping in recreational sport in EU Member States inter alia in relation to prevention, education, control and related measures as well as recovery from substance abuse.[42]

V.i The EU and the WADA Code Review Process

The revision of the WADA Code of 2009 and related international standards had five phases – issues overlapped in each of the phases and in the EU's contribution to same and thus what follows is a summary of the key matters.

In the first phase, comments were invited by WADA on the then extant Code of 2009. The First EU Contribution on the revision of the World Anti-Doping Code was made on 23 February 2012.[43] The primary concern was with data privacy principles. Taking into account Article 8 of the EU Charter of Fundamental Rights (data must be processed fairly for specified purposes) and also the provisions of Article 25(1) and (2) of Directive 95/46/EC (personal data may only be transferred to a

---

[40] Meetings tended to be attended by representatives of the Member States, the Council of Europe and Norway as permanent observers, while the following organisations were also invited to attend on an ad hoc basis: the European Elite Athletes' Association (EEAA) (EU Athletes), the European Health and Fitness Association (EHFA), the European Olympic Committees (EOC), the International Olympic Committee (IOC) (including a representative of the IOC Athletes' Commission) and the World Anti-Doping Agency (WADA).

[41] See generally the comprehensive review by J Kornbeck, 'The Stamina of the Bosman Legacy: The European Union and the Revision of the World Anti-Doping Code (2011–2013)' (2015) 22 (2) *Maastricht Journal of European and Comparative Law* 283.

[42] Conclusions of the Council and of the Representatives of the Governments of the Member States, meeting within the Council, of 10 May 2012 on combating doping in recreational sport. [2012] OJ C 169, 9–10.

[43] Council Document 6846/12 and available at http://register.consilium.europa.eu/doc/srv?l=EN&f=ST%206846%202012%20INIT (accessed 26 Oct 2017).

third-party country if that country ensures an adequate level of protection), the EU expressed concerns with WADA's anti-doping administration and management system (ADAMS – in essence, the tool by which WADA could fulfil its self-proclaimed role as the global doping control information clearinghouse per Art 14.5 of the 2009 Code) and related registered testing pools/whereabouts requirements on athletes (Art 14.3 of the 2009 Code).

The concern was primarily with the reference in Article 14.5 of the 2009 Code to the ADAMS database reflecting 'emerging data privacy principles'. The EU's view was that, pursuant to the powers given in Article 14.5 of the Code, WADA could engage in 'data sharing on a wide scale, worldwide between public and private actors'.[44] Accordingly, the EU was concerned that the reference to 'emerging' data privacy principles lacked legal certainty and might even lead to practices 'potentially violating athletes' rights as data subjects'.[45] Moreover, the then Article 14.6 of the Code, in obliging compliance with both national data protection laws and the WADA standards, did not set out which should prevail should there be any inconsistency. Thirdly, the EU questioned whether the conditions on the transmission of personal data to third countries set out in Article 25 of Directive 95/46/EC were met under the WADA Code in terms of providing an adequate level of data protection in the country of destination.[46]

Data protection and privacy concerns had been a 'recurrent theme' between the EU and WADA for a number of years prior to the above.[47] In 2008, the EU had established a Working Party under Article 29 of Directive 95/46/EC on the then draft international standard on the protection of privacy prepared by WADA. The Working Party produced

---

44 Ibid., 6.

45 Ibid.

46 The extent to which the EU's concerns were addressed in the next (2015) version of the Code with specific respect to Article 14 can be seen at https://www.wada-ama.org/sites/default/files/resources/files/wada-redline-2015-wadc-to-2009-wadc-en.pdf (accessed 26 Oct 2017).

47 See J Kornbeck, 'The EU, the Revision of the World Anti-Doping Code and the Presumption of Innocence' (2016) 15 *International Sports Law Journal* 172, 185.

two opinions on the draft standard;[48] elements of which were acknowledged and integrated by WADA in its final draft of the standard.[49]

In the second phase of the WADA Code Review process, comments were invited on the first version of the draft WADA Code (2015), which was put to worldwide consultation by WADA on 1 June 2012. The Second EU Contribution to this effect was made on 26 September 2012.[50] One of the key issues here was amendments to the then Article 22 of the Code on the involvement of governments. The EU's contribution here addressed the fact that Article 22 of the then Code (2009) contained only expectations and not actual obligations on governments – given that most governments cannot be parties or signatories to, or be bound by, private non-governmental instruments such as the World Anti-Doping Code.

The proposed solution, which was largely adopted in the current (2015) version of the Code was twofold. First, a restatement of the commitment in Article 22 of the Code to governments' signing the Copenhagen Declaration on Anti-Doping in Sport of 3 March 2003 by ratifying, accepting, approving or acceding to the UNESCO Convention of 2005.[51] The second element of the solution was to elevate the standard of expectation of signatories with respect to governments to include

---

48 Opinion 3/2008 on the World Anti-Doping Code Draft International Standard for the Protection of Privacy, WP 156, 1 August 2008 and available at http://ec.europa.eu/justice/data-protection/article-29/documentation/opinion-recommendation/files/2008/wp156_en.pdf. Opinion 4/2009 on the World Anti-Doping Code Draft International Standard for the Protection of Privacy, WP 156, 6 April 2009 and available at http://ec.europa.eu/justice/data-protection/article-29/documentation/opinion-recommendation/files/2009/wp162_en.pdf (both accessed 26 Oct 2017).

49 See 'World Anti-Doping Agency adopts revised data protection standard and continues successful dialogue with the EU' IP/09/733, 11 May 2009 and available at http://europa.eu/rapid/press-release_IP-09-733_en.htm. For the continuing impact of the EU on WADA International Standard for the Protection of Privacy, see https://www.wada-ama.org/sites/default/files/resources/files/WADA-Redline-2015-ISPPPI-to-2009-ISPPPI-EN.pdf (both accessed 26 Oct 2017).

50 Council Document 14204/12 and available at http://register.consilium.europa.eu/doc/srv?l=EN&f=ST%2014204%202012%20INIT (accessed 26 Oct 2017).

51 See generally http://www.unesco.org/new/en/social-and-human-sciences/themes/anti-doping/international-convention-against-doping-in-sport/ (accessed 26 Oct 2017).

governments putting in place legislation, regulation, policies or administrative practices for cooperation in sharing of information with Anti-Doping Organisations.[52]

In the third phase of the WADA Code Review process, comments were invited on the second version of the draft WADA Code (2015), which was put to worldwide consultation by WADA on 1 December 2012. The Third EU Contribution to this effect was made on 15 February 2013.[53] By this point the EU appeared 'generally satisfied' with progress made by WADA in its reworking of the draft Code 2015 (as compared with v. 1.0). Residually, the EU did, however, have concerns that 'WADA has not taken up the general request by the EU and its Member States to provide written explanations to the proposed changes to the Code', which according to the EU, would:

> … be helpful bearing in mind that, ultimately, the Code finally shall also be recognised by national governments according to their commitments under the UNESCO International Convention against Doping in Sport. If governments are to agree to a final version of the 2015 Code, they should be in a position to explain the proposed changes to their parliaments.[54]

In part, the above request related to the fact that in connection with the first (2003) Code and the 2009 Code, WADA had obtained legal opinion on the enforceability of various aspects of the Code. In January 2013, WADA had however engaged Judge Jean-Paul Costa (formerly President of the European Court of Rights) to review aspects of the Code, as relating to its compliance with the principles of proportionality and human rights.[55] Subsequently, several Code provisions were modified to better accommodate those principles.[56] An interesting feature of the Costa report was that its principal reference point was the European Convention on Human Rights and related jurisprudence at the European Court of Human Rights. The Charter of Fundamental Rights of the

---

52 Article 22.2 of the World Anti-Doping Code (2015).

53 Council Document 6427/13 and available at http://register.consilium.europa.eu/doc/srv?l=EN&f=ST%206427%202013%20INIT (accessed 26 Oct 2017).

54 Ibid., 4.

55 The Costa Report is available at https://www.wada-ama.org/en/resources/legal/legal-opinion-on-the-draft-2015-world-anti-doping-code (accessed 26 Oct 2017).

56 For a summary of the changes see https://www.wada-ama.org/sites/default/files/wadc-2015-draft-version-4.0-significant-changes-to-2009-en.pdf (accessed 26 Oct 2017).

European Union was taken into account insofar as it applied to the EU Member States. The status of EU law (from Treaties to judgment of the Court of Justice) and the Code insofar as they might conflict was not explicitly addressed, and the relationships between EU law and the WADA Code, sometimes played out at the Court of Arbitration for Sport, remains a matter of debate.[57]

V.ii Doping in Recreational Sport

In November 2013, the Expert Group on Anti-Doping published a draft document on Recommendations on Doping in Recreational Sport. It is an interesting and (regrettably) largely forgotten document. Its key premise was as follows:

> Much of the vocabulary for doping in elite sports is of a medical and/or moral nature. Policy discussions focus on fairness, integrity, harm to health and biotechnological consequence on sport. In recreational doping, moral criticism is less obvious. A greater emphasis lies on medical and health-related issues, such as high dose polypharmacy (use of multiple medications), unregulated products, adverse somatic effects (cardiac …), reproductive and anti-social behaviours (such as hyper–aggression) and individual problems such as dependency creation (though these too have social consequences).[58]

The above is an important but underplayed element of current anti-doping policy, given that vast majority who participate in sport do so at a recreational (amateur and youth) level but nevertheless may be exposed to a trickledown effect of doping.[59] Moreover, given the public health aspect to the issue, the EU's competency to act is enhanced by Treaty provisions such as the aforementioned Article 168 TFEU and thus this may be an area of anti-doping policy which uniquely the EU can take (and fund) a lead rather than contributing to or replicating initiatives taken by WADA, the Council of Europe, and UNESCO, etc.

---

[57] M van der Harst, 'The Enforcement of CAS Arbitral Awards by National Courts and the Effective Protection of EU Law' in C Paulussen, T Takács, V Lazić and B Van Rompuy (eds) *Fundamental Rights in International and European Law: Public and Private Law Perspectives* (Asser 2015) 279.

[58] The report is available through http://ec.europa.eu/assets/eac/sport/library/documents/expert-groups/anti-doping_en.pdf (accessed 26 Oct 2017).

[59] See recently M Frenger, W Pitsch, E Emrich, 'Sport-Induced Substance Use—An Empirical Study to the Extent within a German Sports Association' (2016) Plos One, Published Online, 26 October 2016, http://dx.doi.org/10.1371/journal.pone.0165103 (accessed 26 Oct 2017).

Of particular interest here would be further research on the use of prevalence and use of food or nutritional substances in sport; a better understanding of the role, and even suggestions on the better regulation, of the nutritional supplement industry.[60]

The effectiveness of the above Recommendations was, as the report self-acknowledged, hampered somewhat by lack of specific research-generated evidence on the prevalence and use of doping products in recreational sports and thus funding was given to a Study of Doping Prevention which mapped the legal, regulatory and prevention practice provisions in the various Member States, published in December 2014.[61] That report made seven key recommendations but again they were of a generic (better co-operation/further evaluation) nature:

> The European Commission in cooperation with the Member States should:
>
> (a) Establish a process to develop a consistent and agreed understanding of which doping substances are used in the context of recreational sport, and whether these substances might overlap or be consistent with the WADA Prohibited List;
> (b) Develop a robust international, research-driven evidence base to inform future policy, practice, and interventions into the problem of doping in recreational sport;
> (c) Further evaluate the legislation of individual MS to identify the specific strengths and weaknesses of relevant authorities;
> (d) Develop agreed MS responsibilities for the co-ordination of prevention programmes related to doping in recreational sport;
> (e) Develop and co-ordinate educational campaigns, using all forms of relevant media platforms;
> (f) Support and develop initiatives aimed at raising awareness within each MS public health sector in order to make an active contribution to the prevention of doping in recreational sport;
> (g) Develop a platform to share and disseminate a consistent and agreed understanding of legislation, regulations and practice in relation to the prevention of doping in recreational sport and to facilitate effective networks for the exchange of actions, campaigns, data and policies.[62]

---

[60] See here Recommendation 21 of the Expert Group on Anti-Doping's a draft document on Recommendations on Doping in Recreational Sport available through http://ec.europa.eu/assets/eac/sport/library/documents/expert-groups/anti-doping_en.pdf (accessed 26 Oct 2017).

[61] EAC/2013/0617. The Report is available at http://ec.europa.eu/assets/eac/sport/news/2014/docs/doping-prevention-report_en.pdf (accessed 26 Oct 2017).

[62] Ibid., 10.

VI. CONCLUSION

Reflecting on the EU's role on doping in sport, the conclusion is that where the EU's various mechanisms and institutions are focussed on a specific area or competency of EU law that is of relevance to doping; it is an effective and positive contributor to current anti-doping policies globally. The area of data protection is a prime example as, potentially, is the EU's role in terms of the regulation of food supplements. In other areas, the EU's potential to contribute to current anti-doping remains underplayed: for instance, significant research has been carried out in terms of recreational doping but also into the ethical and public health aspect of sports doping. Recommendations emanating from these reports have, as outlined above, been prescient and incisive but, regrettably, remain under-utilised. The EU *has* a greater role to play in current anti-doping debates but first it must itself decide and principally through the Commission, what role it *wants* to play.

5. Volunteering and EU sports law and policy

Neil Partington

The fact that good deeds grow in the wild does not free us from the obligation to cultivate them.[1]

I. INTRODUCTION

Without volunteering, the sport movement in the vast majority of European Union (EU) Member States would cease to exist.[2] Put simply, '[v]olunteering is the backbone of sport'.[3] It is estimated that there are in the region of 92–94 million adults involved in volunteering throughout Europe,[4] with the sport sector representing the largest voluntary activity with the greatest involvement of volunteers.[5] For instance, in Austria, Belgium, the Czech Republic, Denmark, Finland, France, Germany, Hungary, Ireland, Latvia, Luxembourg, Malta, the Netherlands, Slovenia, Sweden and the UK, most volunteers appear to be active in the sport and exercise sector.[6] Since the activities of volunteers may be regarded as a cornerstone of European sport, it appears axiomatic that 'the vast network of sports clubs, associations and federations throughout Europe

[1] S Capeling-Alakija, Executive Coordinator (1998–2003), United Nations Volunteers, cited in *Volunteerism and Legislation: A Guidance Note* (Inter-Parliamentary Union International Federation of Red Cross and Red Crescent Societies and United Nations Volunteers 2004) 6 and available at http://www.ipu.org/PDF/publications/volunteer_en.pdf (accessed 26 Oct 2017).

[2] Report for DG EAC submitted by GHK on Volunteering in the European Union (European Commission 2010) 216 and available at http://ec.europa.eu/citizenship/pdf/doc1018_en.pdf (accessed 26 Oct 2017).

[3] Expert Group on Human Resources Development in Sport: Recommendations to Encourage Volunteering in Sport, including Best Practices in Legal and Fiscal Mechanisms (European Commission 2016) 3 and available at: http://ec.europa.eu/transparency/regexpert/index.cfm?do=groupDetail.groupDetailDoc&id=27407&no=1 (accessed 26 Oct 2017).

[4] Report for DG EAC (n 2) 57.

[5] Ibid., 34.

[6] Ibid., 78.

contributes to making sport the most important area of voluntary activity in Europe and provides a fertile ground for social inclusion'.[7] Framed in this convincing manner, it is little wonder that Member States are increasingly receptive to, and aware of, the benefits derived from volunteering in sport.[8] Since sport is progressively seen in the EU as a medium to achieve social policy objectives, and given the significance of voluntary activity as an integral aspect of the wider sport movement, sports volunteering may be regarded as indispensable in fulfilling certain strategic aims and ambitions of the EU.[9]

In view of this context, this chapter begins by clarifying some of the specificities of voluntary activity in sport in the EU. Consideration of background factors requires the unpacking of terminology frequently employed in this field, including definitions of the term 'volunteering', reference to the so-called 'European Sport Model', and the notion and importance of 'grassroots sport'. Clarification of these terms from the outset allows a deeper analysis and understanding of advancements in this field. Next, a brief historical perspective uncovers fundamental developments in the recognition of sports volunteering within EU Sports Policy. Following this initial overview, the chapter turns to a detailed discussion of the first key EU level document providing a comprehensive consideration of EU sport-related issues, the EU Commission's White Paper on Sport 2007. This signified a strategic positioning of voluntary activity in sport at EU level and was a precursor to the anchoring of sport in the EU Treaties with entry into force of the Lisbon Treaty in 2009. Consideration of this new EU competence for sport, followed by the Commission's Communication on Developing the European Dimension in Sport in 2011, and consecutive Work Plans for Sport (2011–14 and 2014–17), provides a structured and instructive framework for this chapter's detailed examination of relevant developments at EU level. Throughout, this commentary is facilitated by an analytical lens centred on sports volunteering. Importantly, this reveals a number of inherent limitations and barriers to a coordinated EU-wide approach and promotion of sports volunteering. Nonetheless, in scrutinising previous progress, the present position of voluntary activity in sport in the EU, and

---

[7] Commission Staff Working Document – The EU and Sport: Background and Context – Accompanying document to the White Paper on Sport, COM(2007) 391 final, SEC(2007)932, SEC(2007)934, SEC(2007)936, SEC/2007/0935, para 2.

[8] Report for DG EAC (n 2), 216.

[9] N Partington, 'Legal Liability of Coaches: A UK Perspective' (2014) 14(3–4) *International Sports Law Journal* 232, 233.

the apparent future role of EU level initiatives, this chapter concludes by recognising the significant 'added value' to be achieved by EU support, coordination and supplementation of strategic frameworks and actions aimed at promoting sports volunteering.

II. BACKGROUND

Before beginning to consider more fully the context of sports volunteering in the EU, and how the Union has (and might in the future) exercised its competence to carry out actions when supporting, coordinating or supplementing the actions of the Member States, the specific nature of sport in the EU generates a number of important peculiarities that from the outset must be defined. In this field, useful terminology frequently adopted at EU level, and warranting further clarification, includes 'volunteering', the so-termed EU structure or 'model' of sport and 'grassroots sport'. As will be revealed, refinement of definitional distinctions at EU level would appear to emphasise how sport is regarded as an important mechanism in achievement of EU social policy objectives.

II.i Volunteering

Each EU Member State has different notions, definitions and traditions with regard to volunteering.[10] This renders adoption of an EU-wide definition of volunteering problematic. Nonetheless, despite there being no universal EU legal definition of the term 'volunteer', it appears commonly accepted that the term 'volunteering' tends to refer 'to all forms of voluntary activity, whether formal or informal. It is undertaken of a person's own freewill, choice and motivation, and is without concern for financial gain'.[11] Moreover, voluntary service and engagement should be open to all, provides non-formal educational opportunities, and fundamentally, offers 'added social value'.[12] In adopting a more precise definition of volunteering, a number of Member States make more explicit links between the voluntary activity and the competencies, qualifications and/or skills legally required of the volunteer (e.g., Czech

[10] Communication on EU Policies and Volunteering: Recognising and Promoting Crossborder Voluntary Activities in the EU, COM(2011), 568 final, 2.

[11] Report for DG EAC (n 2) 49–50.

[12] See, for instance, European Council (2002), Resolution regarding the framework of European cooperation in the youth field [2002] OJ C 168.

Republic and Poland).[13] However, there appears no overall definition of volunteering drawn specifically for the sport sector, with the majority of countries applying the definition used for volunteering in general should such a definition exist.[14] Alternatively, as is the case in Austria, Bulgaria, Cyprus, Czech Republic, Denmark, Finland, Hungary, Lithuania, Malta and Poland, use may be made of a non-official definition which generally defines volunteers as 'people who donate their time to sport organisations to carry out activities in a field they are passionate about'.[15]

Voluntary activities in the EU are mainly undertaken at the amateur level of sport, with most sport organisations and federations generally being non-profit entities.[16] Where individual European countries provide a legal definition for voluntary organisations, they tend to highlight the non-profit nature of the organisations' activities or, in emphasising the notion of 'added value', reinforce the fact that these same activities should be conducted for the public good.[17] Voluntary organisations in the EU are rooted in 'common values, ideas and interests' and are 'of public character and can be created and disbanded without any government intervention. The organisations are based on voluntary commitment and most often on a personal membership of some sorts, and do not aim for economic profit'.[18] In the context of sport, it is the sports clubs/outdoor activity clubs that represent the predominant voluntary organisations volunteered in,[19] thereby providing vital and affordable activities and services for the local community, with some sports clubs entirely dependent on volunteers.[20] Since voluntary activity in sport in Europe may be regarded as a primarily local or national phenomenon, attempts to promote volunteering, and/or remove potential barriers encountered by volunteers and sports organisations, must account for this specificity.[21]

The above factors speak to the propensity for EU sports volunteering to be frequently performed in support of non-profit organisations or

---

13 Report for DG EAC (n 2) 56.
14 Ibid., 173.
15 Ibid.
16 Ibid., 186–88.
17 Ibid., 81.
18 Ibid., 82.
19 Ibid., 80.
20 Ibid., 216.
21 R Parrish, B Garcia, S Miettinen and R Siekmann, *The Lisbon Treaty and EU Sports Policy* (European Parliament 2010) 46.

community-based initiatives,[22] a factor indicative of what has traditionally been referred to as the 'European Sport Model'.

II.ii European Sport Model

EU-level debate on sport frequently attributes considerable importance to what is termed the 'European Sport Model',[23] with this pyramidal model regarded as a 'success factor' in boosting the numbers of volunteers involved in sport.[24] Traditionally, the organisational structure of the sport sector in the majority of EU countries has been based on such a pyramidal model.[25] Since voluntary activities are principally undertaken at the level of amateur sport, it is the lower tier of the pyramid that comprises of 'smaller legal entities where people in the community can become members and practice their sport'.[26] In providing local opportunities for engagement in sport, these entities can be referred to as 'sport associations' (e.g., Denmark), 'sport societies' (e.g., Slovenia), or most commonly, 'sport clubs' (e.g., Finland and Germany).[27] Such terminological discrepancies point to some of the complexities of European sport structures, perhaps cautioning against overreliance on a presumed single unified EU sport model.[28]

Nevertheless, these sports clubs, associations or societies (hereafter: sports clubs (broadly applied)) underpin the organisational structure of EU sport, and in performing a crucial social function, would fail to function without volunteers.[29] For instance, according to figures published by the European Study on Volunteering in Sport in 2010, although noting variations between different Member States, the sport sector in countries including Austria (86 per cent volunteers), France (almost 80 per cent volunteers), the Netherlands (87 per cent volunteers), and

---

[22] Also see, Council Decision No 37/2010/EC on the European Year of Voluntary Activities Promoting Active Citizenship (2011) [2010] OJ L 17, 43.

[23] White Paper on Sport, COM(2007), 391 final, 12.

[24] Report for DG EAC (n 2) 251. 'Success factors' are discussed more fully in s VIII of this chapter.

[25] Ibid., 184.

[26] Ibid., 251.

[27] Ibid.

[28] White Paper on Sport (n 23), 12. See further, S Weatherill, 'Sport as Culture in EC Law' in R Craufurd Smith (ed) *Culture and European Union Law* (OUP, 2004) 147.

[29] R Parrish, *Sports Law and Policy in the European Union* (Manchester University Press 2003) 181.

Portugal (90 per cent volunteers) were significantly reliant on volunteers.[30] This trend appears characteristic of the pyramidal structure of EU sport, reflecting the fact that as generally non-profit entities, sport organisations are instrumental in facilitating 'communitarianism and voluntarism'.[31] In the context of EU sporting provision, communitarianism and voluntarism are coextensive with 'grassroots sport'.

II.iii Grassroots Sport

Grassroots sport tends to be associated with voluntary structures and the social and educational functions of sport.[32] Moreover, the EU's programme for Education, Training, Youth and Sport in Europe, Erasmus+, regards grassroots sport as 'organised sport practised at local level by amateur sportspeople, and sport for all'.[33] Accordingly, it has previously been highlighted by the Commission that:

> Organised sport in almost all EU Member States is built on specific non-profit making governing structures at grassroots level. These are self-governing independent structures, heavily reliant on the commitment of volunteers, with specific forms of legal personality or status that provide the precondition for a range of financial and fiscal advantages.[34]

More recent recognition of the full scope of the social contribution of grassroots sport in the EU prompted the High Level Group on Grassroots Sport (HLG GS) to adopt a broader definition of grassroots sport, regarding it as 'physical leisure activity, organised and non-organised, practised regularly at non-professional level for health, educational or social purposes'.[35] This builds on the more limited legal definition of grassroots sport provided in the Erasmus+ Regulation above, and appears to strategically strengthen grassroots sport and volunteering as key

---

[30] Report for DG EAC (n 2) 186.

[31] J Nafziger, 'International Sports Law' in J Nafziger and S Ross (eds), *Handbook on International Sports Law* (Edward Elgar 2011) 6.

[32] Parrish, Garcia, Miettinen and Siekmann (n 21) 45.

[33] Regulation (EU) No 1288/2013, Establishing 'Erasmus+': the Union programme for education, training, youth and sport and repealing Decisions No 1719/2006/EC, No 1720/2006/EC and No 1298/2008/EC [2013] OJ L 347/50, Article 2(24).

[34] Commission Staff Working Document (n 7), para 2.4.2.

[35] Report to Commissioner Tibor Navracsics by High Level Group on Sport Diplomacy (European Commission, 2016), 4 and available at http://ec.europa.eu/assets/eac/sport/library/policy_documents/hlg-sport-diplomacy-final_en.pdf accessed 13 April 2017.

drivers in EU Sports Policy. In so doing, greater emphasis is placed on the scope of grassroots sport in making a significant contribution to, for instance, informal learning, the development of transversal skills (i.e., teamwork and leadership), and opportunities for enhancement of information technology, marketing, management and communications skills.[36] This underscores the strong correlation between voluntary activity in sport and achievement of EU strategic objectives.

Having defined volunteering, discussed the peculiarities of the EU's pyramid structure on which sport is typically organised in Europe, and considered the notion of grassroots sport, this chapter next examines the broader context of EU Sports Policy. To support this ensuing commentary, an analytical lens focused on sports volunteering is adopted when subsequently scrutinising key documents produced at EU level in this field.

III. VOLUNTEERING AND EU SPORTS POLICY

The important role of volunteering in sport in the EU was first highlighted in the Nice Declaration (2000) which requested Member States to 'encourage voluntary services in sport by means of measures providing appropriate protection for and acknowledging the economic and social role of volunteers, with the support, where necessary, of the Community'.[37] Two years later, sport and voluntary activities were further reiterated in the Aarhus Declaration on Voluntary Work in Sport, recognising that voluntary sport clubs and voluntary work play a significant role in the social and cultural life of Europe and it is therefore important to ensure that their role be maintained.[38] In laying the foundation of EU Sports Policy regarding volunteering in sport, developments in this area have been shaped by recognition in the Nice Declaration that both sporting organisations and the Member States have a primary responsibility in the conduct of sporting affairs. This is consistent with the EU's principle of subsidiarity which:

> serves to regulate the exercise of the Union's non-exclusive powers. It rules out Union intervention when an issue can be dealt with effectively by Member States at central, regional or local level and means that the

---

[36] Ibid., 19.

[37] Report for DG EAC (n 2) 35.

[38] Ibid., 223.

> Community is justified in exercising its powers when Member States are unable to achieve the objectives of a proposed action satisfactorily.[39]

Indeed, it has been made plain that there is no intention for the Commission to advocate a preferred single model of volunteering, or aim to harmonise volunteering cultures at local and regional level.[40] More generally, the impact of European law on volunteering in sport around the turn of the twenty-first century might best be regarded as being governed by an 'indirect EU sports policy'.[41] In being mindful of not acting beyond its powers, and with no explicit Treaty competence for sport at that stage, the EU was required to link its involvement in the sport sector to existing policies and programmes falling within existing Treaty competences, for instance, education policy.[42] Although not legally binding, the soft law measures adopted during this period at EU level will be confirmed in this chapter as having had a significant impact on policy and legal developments in this area.[43] Notwithstanding the merits and influence of related soft law provisions, the EU's limited competence for sport prior to the Lisbon Treaty (2009) prevented a coherent approach to sport founded on well defined, and evidence based, strategic objectives.[44] A key catalyst in fostering momentum for a more coordinated sports policy, and fundamental to establishment of a new EU competence for sport, was the Commission's White Paper on Sport in 2007.

IV. WHITE PAPER ON SPORT, 2007

The Commission's White Paper on Sport marked the first comprehensive consideration of EU sport-related issues, with an overall objective of providing a 'strategic orientation on the role of sport in Europe, to

---

[39] http://www.europarl.org.uk/en/education/teachingresources/howeuworks/subsidiarity.html (accessed 26 Oct 2017).

[40] Communication on EU Policies and Volunteering (n 10), 11.

[41] W Tokarski, D Steinbach, K Petry and B Jesse (eds) *Two Players, One Goal?* (Meyer and Meyer Sport 2004), cited in Parrish, Garcia, Miettinen and Siekmann (n 21), 45. For a more detailed historical consideration of the development of EU Sports Policy see Parrish (n 29) tracing the birth of an European socio-cultural sporting agenda back to the 1984 Fontainebleau Summit.

[42] Parrish, Garcia, Miettinen and Siekmann, ibid.; Report for DG EAC (n 2) 224.

[43] Parrish (n 29) 17.

[44] Parrish, Garcia, Miettinen and Siekmann (n 21) 45.

encourage debate on specific problems, to enhance the visibility of sport in EU policy-making and to raise public awareness of the needs and specificities of the sector'.[45] As previously highlighted, these specificities of the sport sector are premised on the fact that the vast majority of sporting activity takes place in amateur structures, the White Paper citing a November 2004 Eurobarometer survey revealing that approximately 60 per cent of European citizens participate in sporting activities on a regular basis within or outside some 700,000 clubs.[46] The three themes covered by the White Paper concerned: 'the economic dimension of sport'; 'the organisation of sport'; and of utmost relevance to this chapter's focus, 'the societal role of sport'.

Since sport is a social phenomenon, the White Paper recognised that the considerable societal benefits derived from sport are not necessarily measurable in economic terms but, advance the general policy objectives of the EU in areas including public health, social cohesion, education and training, and active citizenship. Therefore, it is necessary for these benefits to be reflected in European policy-making and associated liaison with sport stakeholders.[47] In short, the Commission was of the view that:

> better use can be made of the potential of sport as an instrument for social inclusion in the policies, actions and programmes of the European Union and of Member States. This includes the contribution of sport to job creation and to economic growth and revitalisation, particularly in disadvantaged areas. Non-profit sport activities contributing to social cohesion and social inclusion of vulnerable groups can be considered as social services of general interest.[48]

Clearly, in seeking to more effectively utilise, further develop, and essentially capitalise on the predominantly amateur structure of sport, and its associated reliance on volunteers, the Commission expressly recognised sport in its White Paper as a medium to achieve social policy objectives.

By reason of the effect, scale and scope for volunteering in sport to 'add value' in terms of societal benefits, it appears axiomatic that a number of policies and programmes focused on volunteering in sport might be implemented more successfully by action at EU level. Not least, in promoting and contributing to the European debate on sport, the central role of the Commission includes provision of a platform for

---

[45] White Paper on Sport (n 23), 2.

[46] Ibid., 3.

[47] White Paper on Sport: Frequently Asked Questions, Memo/07/290, 11 July 2007, 1.

[48] White Paper on Sport (n 23), 8.

dialogue with sport stakeholders.[49] To this end, and within the confines of the principle of subsidiarity, the Commission identified key challenges and support for the voluntary sport sector in the White Paper including: support of grassroots sport through the Europe for Citizens programme; encouragement of young people's volunteering in sport through the Youth in Action programme; further development and exchange of information and best practice on volunteering in sport involving Member States, sport organisations and local authorities; and given the important societal role of sport and its strong local anchoring, the Commission committed itself to defending maintenance of the existing possibilities of reduced VAT rates for sport.[50] Also, in order to understand better the specific demands and needs of the voluntary sport sector in national and European policy making, the Commission committed to launching a European Study on Volunteering in Sport.[51] Without question, voluntary activity in sport had received strategic and resounding endorsement at EU level.

V. A NEW EU COMPETENCE FOR SPORT

Sport became anchored in the EU Treaties for the first time with entry into force of the Lisbon Treaty on 1 December 2009.[52] This new EU competence for sport is enshrined in Article 6 and Article 165 of the Treaty on the Functioning of the European Union (TFEU). Under Article 6, sport is expressly highlighted as an area where '[t]he Union shall have competence to carry out actions to support, coordinate or supplement the actions of the Member States'. Moreover, Article 165(1) provides that in contributing to the promotion of European sporting issues, the Union shall take 'account of the specific nature of sport, its structures based on voluntary activity and its social and educational function'. This appears to further consolidate the paramount importance of volunteering in sport in EU Sports Policy. However, Article 165(4) restricts the EU's supporting, coordinating and supplementing competence for sport to adoption of recommendations and 'incentive measures' (i.e., funding programmes),

---

49 Ibid., 18.

50 Ibid., 6–12.

51 Ibid., 14.

52 EOC EU Office, *Guide to EU Sport Policy* (European Olympic Committee 2011) 6.

thereby expressly excluding any harmonisation of the laws and regulations of the Member States.[53] Put simply, in accordance with the principle of subsidiarity, ultimate responsibility for achievement and prioritisation of sporting objectives, for instance, the promotion of sports volunteering, remains within the jurisdiction of individual Member States and sports federations/governing bodies.[54]

Despite such limitations, by enabling sport to be directly financed by the EU without justificatory reference to other Treaty competencies, its (societal) role appears to have been strengthened.[55] This seems particularly the case when action at EU level can provide significant 'added value'.[56] Most recently, acknowledgment of the specific nature of sport's structures based on voluntary activity, including sport's social and educational functions, was emphasised by the HLG GS in 2016 when highlighting the unique position of the EU in shaping sports policy in Europe:

> Volunteering makes a positive contribution on many levels, from individual wellbeing and development to community solidarity and organisational and national economic health. … the role of volunteering in grassroots sport is a fundamental condition for the provision of nationwide accessible, affordable and qualified grassroots sport activities and events in the majority of Member States. In that majority of states, sport clubs are the traditional sports delivery system, and sport clubs rely heavily on the involvement of volunteers, as do many major sporting events, both in grassroots and elite sport … The HLG noted the EU is in a unique position to influence volunteerism from both a policy and funding position, as well as an awareness position.[57]

This perhaps underscores the 'real innovation' triggered by Article 165 TFEU, allowing the EU to directly support and supplement policy in the sport sector.[58] In exercising this new competence for sport, the EU is ideally positioned to support platforms of exchange and debate,

---

[53] Parrish, Garcia, Miettinen and Siekmann (n 21), 27. Also see, section 3 above.

[54] Developing the European Dimension in Sport, COM(2011) 12 final, 3.

[55] Parrish, Garcia, Miettinen and Siekmann (n 21), 11.

[56] White Paper on Sport (n 23), 11; Developing the European Dimension in Sport (n 54), 3.

[57] Report to Commissioner Tibor Navracsics by High Level Group on Sport Diplomacy (European Commission, 2016), 22.

[58] Parrish, Garcia, Miettinen and Siekmann (n 21), 45.

co-finance various initiatives, and where necessary, provide legal clarity.[59] More particularly, despite there being no specific legislative provision for volunteering as such in the treaties,[60] since Article 165 calls for account is to be taken of the specific context of sport when contributing to the promotion of European sporting issues, it is indisputable that volunteering is both integral, and implicitly linked, to EU Sports Policy.

VI. DEVELOPING THE EUROPEAN DIMENSION IN SPORT 2011

The Commission's Communication on Developing the European Dimension in Sport in 2011 recognised that the White Paper on Sport had provided an appropriate basis for EU level activities in the area of sport, including the promotion of voluntary activity in sport, and that the broad thematic chapter of 'the societal role of sport' remained a widely accepted mechanism for the framing of EU sport-related activities and discussion.[61] Following consultations with Member States, and the non-governmental sport sector, the identified priority topics in the EU agenda for sport included: voluntary activity and non-profit sport organisations; social inclusion in and through sport; sustainable financing of grassroots sport; recognition of voluntary activity; and the need for support for networking and exchange of good practice at European level.[62] More specifically, the Commission reaffirmed the autonomy of sport governing structures relating to the organisation of sport and reiterated the competences of the Member States in this area. Despite such parameters, in championing the significant value to be gained from an EU level or macro approach to the sport sector, the Commission's vision for a European Dimension in Sport recognised that:

> In all of the areas elaborated in this Communication, EU action can serve to provide a platform for exchange and dialogue among sport stakeholders, spreading good practice and promoting the development of European networks in the field of sport. In parallel, EU action contributes to the

---

59 Report for DG EAC (n 2) 17.

60 EOC EU Office, Guide to EU Sport Policy (n 52), 52.

61 Developing the European Dimension in Sport, COM(2011) 12 final, 2. Equally, the other two broad themes of 'the economic dimension of sport' and 'the organisation of sport' were also regarded as useful.

62 Ibid., 3.

dissemination of knowledge about EU law in the sport sector, thus ensuring greater legal certainty for European sport.[63]

In short, the Commission's Communication on Developing the European Dimension in Sport further endorsed the contribution of voluntary activity in sport to employability, social inclusion and higher civic participation.[64] Further, it acknowledged the need for more transparency concerning the validation and recognition of qualifications gained by volunteers,[65] and given concerns about the sustainability of financing for non-profit structures based on voluntary activity, called for reinforcement of financial solidarity between professional and grassroots sport.[66] Following this Communication, consecutive Work Plans for Sport marked the next key documents in the continuance of EU Sports Policy and the corresponding further promotion of sports volunteering in Europe.

VII. WORK PLANS FOR SPORT

VII.i Work Plan for Sport 2011–14

The Council's Resolution on a European Union Work Plan for Sport (2011–14),[67] although not legally binding, opened a new chapter of European cooperation on sports policy. For the first time, Member States, the Presidencies of the Council and the Commission were invited to work together along agreed core principles, in order to focus on the priority themes first articulated in the White Paper on Sport ('the societal role of sport', 'the economic dimension of sport', and 'the organisation of sport') and to implement specific actions. In an area where the EU has a supporting competence this Work Plan provided a valuable framework for all actors to cooperate in a structured way and in mutual respect of national and EU competences.[68] The 2011–14 Work Plan for Sport was governed by guiding principles centred on a cooperative, concerted and coordinated approach in the field of sport at EU level, with an emphasis

---

[63] Ibid.

[64] Ibid., 4.

[65] Ibid., 5. For instance, within the framework of the European Qualifications Framework (EQF).

[66] Ibid., 8.

[67] Council Resolution of 1.6.2011 on a European Union Work Plan for Sport for 2011–2014 [2011] C 162/01.

[68] Report on the Implementation of the European Union Work Plan for Sport 2011–2014, COM(2014) 22 Final, 2.

on delivering 'added value'. As stated in the Commission's subsequent report on the implementation of this initial Work Plan, '[m]any of the competencies in the area of sport lie with the Member States. It is thus important that priorities for a new EU Work Plan focus on actions delivering unambiguous value-added at EU level'.[69]

Once again, the specific nature and contribution of sport to other EU policy domains was a fundamental consideration.[70] Moreover, since the Work Plan embraced, adopted and advocated the utility of the above priority themes, regarding these as providing a general basis for future cooperation, voluntary activity in sport appeared to remain firmly anchored within the priority theme of 'the societal role of sport' for the foreseeable future. Nonetheless, a closer reading of the identified actions based on the more general priority theme of 'Social values of sport, in particular health, social inclusion, education and volunteering',[71] makes no specific mention of volunteering in sport. Arguably, volunteering was somewhat subsumed, perhaps understandably given its obvious connection, within more general priority themes regarding, for instance, health enhancing physical activity (HEPA) and participation in grassroots sport. Curiously, this omission, and lack of express mention of sports volunteering, was echoed in the focus and establishment of the Expert Groups[72] intended to support implementation of the 2011–14 Work Plan.[73] As noted by the European Study on Volunteering in Sport, it is submitted that this is reflective of a fragmented approach at EU level, with key responsibilities for volunteering being assumed by different Directorates of the European Commission.[74] Arguably, this problematises

---

[69] Ibid., 9.

[70] Regulation (EU) No 1288/2013, Establishing 'Erasmus+': the Union programme for education, training, youth and sport and repealing Decisions No 1719/2006/EC, No 1720/2006/EC and No 1298/2008/EC [2013] OJ L 347/50, Article 16(1)(c), a specific aim being to 'promote voluntary activities in sport, together with social inclusion, equal opportunities and awareness of the importance of health-enhancing physical activity through increased participation in, and equal access to, sport for all'.

[71] Report on the Implementation of the European Union Work Plan for Sport 2011–2014 (n 68), 4.

[72] Focused on: (i) anti-doping; (ii) good governance in sport; (iii) education and training in sport; (iv) sport, health and participation; (v) sport statistics; and (vi) sustainable financing of sport.

[73] Report on the Implementation of the European Union Work Plan for Sport 2011–2014 (n 68), 3.

[74] Report for DG EAC (n 2), 92.

attempts to identify a coordinated and coherent EU level strategy intended to promote sports volunteering throughout all Member States.

VII.ii Work Plan for Sport 2014–17

The second three-year Work Plan for Sport (2014–17) aimed to further develop a framework of European cooperation in the field of sport.[75] While the guiding principles for this consecutive Work Plan are largely consistent with the previous ones outlined above, there nonetheless appears an albeit subtle, but greater, prominence afforded to both the specific nature of sport, and the wider social policy agenda, not least, the Europe 2020 Strategy.[76] Once again, the key topics of this amended Work Plan focused on 'Integrity of Sport', 'the Economic Dimension of Sport', and of most direct relevance to volunteering, the priority theme of 'Sport and Society'. Within this slightly differently entitled key topic of 'Sport and Society', express mention was made of HEPA, volunteering, employment in sport, and education and training in sport. Further, in also amending the configuration and focus of the Expert Groups, one of the five Expert Groups established for the period of this second Work Plan for Sport was on Human Resource Management in Sport (XG HR), dealing with education, training, employment and volunteering in sport.[77] In further raising the profile of volunteering as a fundamental aspect of EU Sports Policy, Annex 1 to the 2014–17 Work Plan explicitly tasks this new XG HR, under the Key Topic of 'Education, training, employment and volunteering', with identifying 'recommendations to encourage volunteering in sport, including best practices on legal and fiscal mechanisms'.[78] This marks another significant development in the evolving consolidation and recognition of volunteering in sport at EU level.

As the 2014–17 Work Plan draws to an end, it is pertinent to reflect on the state of sports volunteering in the EU at this present time and identify some of the future challenges likely to be encountered in this field.

---

[75] Council Resolution of 21.5.2014 on a European Union Work Plan for Sport for 2014–2017 [2014] C 183/03.

[76] Ibid., 12. The Europe 2020 Strategy is the EU's growth strategy for the next decade.

[77] See http://ec.europa.eu/sport/policy/cooperation/expert-groups-2014-2017_en.htm accessed 26 Oct 2017.

[78] Council Resolution of 21.5.2014 on a European Union Work Plan for Sport for 2014–2017 (n 75), 16.

VIII. OBSTACLES, BEST PRACTICE AND FUTURE CHALLENGES

Following publication of the White Paper on Sport in 2008, the Commission launched a European Study on Volunteering in Sport aimed at identifying ways to better promote the voluntary sector at EU level, and consider how volunteering might support achievement of the wider strategic objectives of the EU.[79] In providing evidence-based findings from across the entire EU, this detailed report published in 2010, by highlighting possible future policies and actions that might most effectively be implemented at EU level, considered best practices on legal and fiscal mechanisms. The findings from this influential study continue to impact present-day EU strategies aimed at encouraging volunteering in sport.[80]

The importance of volunteering in sport varies significantly between Member States, there appearing to be no specific legal framework addressing volunteering in sport in many EU countries.[81] According to the European Study on Volunteering in Sport, in terms of regulatory frameworks within individual Member States in 2010, three distinct categorisations emerged:

- Member States where a legal framework specifically relating to volunteering was in place (Belgium, Cyprus, Czech Republic, Hungary, Italy, Latvia, Luxembourg, Malta, Poland, Portugal, Romania and Spain);
- Member States that did not have a legal framework but where volunteering was regulated by or implicit within other existing general laws (Austria, Denmark, Estonia, Finland, France, Germany, Greece, Ireland, Lithuania, Netherlands, Slovakia, Sweden and the UK); and
- Member States who were in the process of developing a legal framework for volunteering (Bulgaria and Slovenia).[82]

---

[79] Report for DG EAC (n 2), 6.

[80] See, for instance, Expert Group on Human Resources Development in Sport (n 3), 3–5.

[81] Report for DG EAC (n 2), 10.

[82] Ibid. Since Croatia joined the EU in July 2013, it was not included in this 2010 study. Nonetheless, Croatia appeared to be in the process of developing a legal framework for volunteers. See K Hadzi-Miceva, 'Comparative Analysis of European Legal Systems and Practices Regarding Volunteering' (2007) 9(3) *The International Journal of Not-for-Profit Law* 37, 38.

While further progress may have been made in relation to the development of specific legal frameworks for volunteers in a number of Member States since 2010,[83] significant differences between countries no doubt remain. For instance, Sweden and France have always been resistant to the regulation of voluntary organisations, priority instead being given to the independence and autonomy of the voluntary sector,[84] whereas, in Spain, different legislation has been adopted in different regions.[85] Conversely, it may be the case that in Member States with a weak tradition or culture of volunteering, the development of volunteering may be enhanced by enactment of legislation.[86] This suggests that attempts to identify a consistent strategic vision for volunteering at EU level, and clear policy aims and objectives founded on robust and reliable reporting and monitoring of data, may prove challenging.[87] Put simply, the complexity and diversity of volunteering and the voluntary sector, across Member States, prevents uniform regulation in this area.[88] At first glance, since 'every country should decide whether and how to regulate volunteering based on its social, cultural, and economic conditions',[89] the role of the EU in this context does not appear straightforward.

Irrespective of the individual approach of Member States, should the legal framework create obstacles and impede volunteering, this is problematic.[90] The impact of legislation on volunteerism is considerable, and curiously, while laws may protect and encourage the engagement of volunteers, the detrimental effects of some legal provision on voluntary activity may be largely unintentional.[91] As noted by the European Centre for Not-for-Profit Law, problems may include 'the misapplication of labour laws, the taxation of volunteer time, the loss of unemployment benefits, liability issues, and volunteers performing under dangerous conditions and being unaware of their rights and obligations'.[92] Given the

---

[83] See, for instance, 'Volunteering and Legislative Framework: Good Practices and EU Standards' (Technical Assistance for Civil Society Organisations 2015) available at http://www.tacso.org/doc/p2p20151217_report_mn.pdf (accessed 26 Oct 2017).

[84] Report for DG EAC (n 2), 230.

[85] Report for DG EAC (n 2), 201.

[86] Report for DG EAC (n 2), 263. Interestingly, countries including the UK and Denmark have well developed systems of self-regulation and soft law.

[87] Report for DG EAC (n 2), 92.

[88] Report for DG EAC (n 2), 10.

[89] Report for DG EAC (n 2), 264.

[90] Report for DG EAC (n 2), 238.

[91] S Capeling-Alakija (n 1), 23.

[92] Hadzi-Miceva (n 82) 40.

considerable benefits derived from volunteering in sport, in these scenarios, arguments calling for removal of such legal barriers and impediments, and instead, adoption of incentive measures (i.e., a 'dual approach'),[93] appear convincing.[94] In short, over-regulation of the voluntary sport sector, by imposition of an excessive legislative burden, represents a significant potential pitfall to guard against.[95]

The tensions posed by considerations regarding over/under-regulation of volunteering in sport creates a difficult balancing exercise for the EU and individual Member States. It remains imperative that the policy aims of any proposed legislative provision must be absolutely clear, reflect the social, cultural and economic conditions of the particular European country, and be considered in partnership with voluntary organisations.[96] As succinctly noted by the XG HR:

> The lack of a clear regulatory framework has been identified by a large number of sport organisations as one of the main obstacles to volunteering. However, the establishment or revision of such a framework depends very much on the national context, traditions, and the way sport is organized in the given country. This includes how autonomously the sport sector is accounted for in the legal structure.[97]

Significantly, in addressing this fundamental challenge, this appears fertile ground for exercise of the EU's supporting, coordinating and supplementing competence for sport. The unique vantage point of the EU provides the scope to add considerable value when devising sports policy in this field, not least, by dissemination of best practices on legal and fiscal mechanisms. Simply applied, the EU is ideally positioned to raise awareness and cascade information to Member States, thereby highlighting successful strategies and regulatory frameworks designed to enhance voluntary activity in sport.[98]

The European Study on Volunteering in Sport revealed characteristics or 'success factors' underlying effective promotion of volunteering in sport, including:

- overall long-standing traditions with sport and volunteering in sport;

---

93 Parrish, Garcia, Miettinen and Siekmann (n 21), 46.
94 Ibid. 40–41.
95 Ibid., 17–18.
96 See Hadzi-Miceva (n 82), 42.
97 Expert Group on Human Resources Development in Sport (n 3), 7.
98 Report for DG EAC (n 2), 260.

- policy focus at national level;
- well-defined organisational structures;
- various tax benefits and exemptions for volunteers and sport organisations;
- specific programmes;
- relatively low dependence on public funding; and
- several additional features to support volunteering in sport.[99]

Conversely, the study also revealed a number of key inhibiting factors and obstacles at national level, including:

- lack of policy focus;
- new requirements in relation to background checks, licences and qualifications;
- difficulties in accessing land and infrastructure; and
- tension between government 'social goals' and the autonomy of the sector.[100]

In mapping and disseminating examples of best practice, other pressing challenges for the further development of sports volunteering in Europe also relate to the 'professionalisation' of the sport sector,[101] validation of non-formal and informal learning (VNFIL) to recognise the skills and competencies of volunteers,[102] and limitations in data collection and monitoring resulting in difficulties in displaying the socio-cultural and economic value of volunteering in sport.[103] Some of these contemporary tensions and obstacles can be clearly demonstrated by fuller scrutiny of the role of sports clubs in this context.

Throughout Europe, one of the best illustrations of the role of voluntary organisations in providing vital activities and services at community level, thereby facilitating greater social cohesion, integration, leisure and the strengthening of 'social fabric',[104] are the sports clubs.[105] Some sports clubs are entirely reliant on volunteers, including parents,

---

[99] Report for DG EAC (n 2), 250.
[100] Ibid.
[101] Ibid., 255.
[102] Ibid., 17.
[103] Ibid., 256. Other pertinent challenges concerned gender equality, education and training, scarce information on volunteering, and recruitment and retention of volunteers.
[104] Ibid., 223.
[105] Ibid., 169.

and by frequently operating without any paid staff, are better positioned to remove financial barriers to participation. Interestingly, in being mindful of the above-mentioned 'success factors' with regard to the promotion of volunteering, there would appear to be some confusion in sports clubs regarding applicable tax rules and benefits.[106]

This apparent inconsistency at the local or micro-level, both between and within individual countries, would suggest that an overarching sports policy pertaining to volunteers at the EU macro-level may prove elusive. Indeed, varying approaches to VAT reductions and exemptions in different Member States has led to tension with EU legislation in this area.[107] Legal and financial regulations or procedures in the form of micro-policies tend to concentrate on single issues, are often identified by sport organisations,[108] and therefore negate development of a macro-level policy which encompasses volunteering in sport in the EU. It is submitted that this appears to signify a considerable obstacle in devising policies and strategies aimed at promoting voluntary activity in sport throughout Europe. Nonetheless, it simultaneously provides an important illustration whereby dissemination of best practices on legal and fiscal mechanisms by the EU would be likely to prove welcome, instructive, and by seeking to transcend fragmented approaches underpinned by some confusion and inconsistency at national level, add significant value and clarification. This unique capacity of the EU to 'add value' in the promotion and development of volunteering in sport in Europe signifies an enduring justification and mandate for the continued support, co-ordination and supplementation of the actions of the Member States in this context.

IX. CONCLUSION

At first glance, the considerable benefits to be gleaned from the promotion of voluntary activity in sport in the EU points to convincing arguments in favour of identification and implementation of policies and initiatives designed to encourage more sports volunteering. Such a stance appears difficult to contradict and provides the EU with a strong remit to proactively support, coordinate and supplement developments in this area. Since the publication of the European Study on Volunteering in Sport in 2010, this would appear to suggest that progress in achieving a

---

106 Ibid., 206.

107 Ibid., 205.

108 Expert Group on Human Resources Development in Sport (n 3), 7.

more concerted and coordinated approach towards the advancement of volunteering in sport would be achievable. However, this represents a highly nuanced and challenging aspect of EU Sports Policy, not least, given the varying regulatory frameworks and the importance of national contexts and traditions. In establishing or revising regulatory frameworks focused on enhancing voluntary activity in sport, the XG HR notes that:

> The most important characteristic of any such framework, be it a legal or regulatory one, or one that is not directly inscribed in the legal system, is that it is clear and comprehensive. Additionally it should define all the responsibilities, obligations and advantages of both volunteers and volunteering providers (sport organisations) in a transparent way.[109]

Obstacles in this field also appear to be compounded by contemporary dynamics, whereby volunteers appear less prepared to commit for long periods of time with a single organisation (i.e., as coach, trainer or board member), preferring to contribute on a more ad-hoc basis to roles not demanding high levels of skills and/or commitment.[110]

More generally, the challenges facing the EU, in engaging with the voluntary sport sector in 2016, appear to resonate strongly with those articulated in 2010, and continue to centre around issues including the:

(i) lack of reliable and comparable data;
(ii) engagement of volunteers;
(iii) professionalisation of the volunteer area;
(iv) unclear rules and not always necessary regulations applicable to volunteering;
(v) improvement of the data collection process;
(vi) lack of recognition;
(vii) lack of clear strategy; and
(viii) insufficient funding of grassroots sport.[111]

These are barriers largely influenced by micro-policies adopted within individual Member States and autonomous sports organisations, preventing a 'one size fits all approach'.[112] Advocating a recommended best model of volunteering, or aiming to harmonise the regulation of voluntary activities in sport at local and regional level, is not realistic, feasible

---

[109] Ibid.
[110] Ibid., 6; Report for DG EAC (n 2), 193.
[111] Expert Group on Human Resources Development in Sport (n 3), 8–9.
[112] Report for DG EAC (n 2), 145.

and appears to contravene the legal principle of subsidiarity. The response needs to be more fluid, malleable and context specific. Given the fundamental role of sports volunteering in achieving and fully exploiting a number of EU strategic aims and ambitions, the desire to unlock and raise the profile and awareness of the benefits derived from sports volunteering appears to be gaining momentum at European level.

Consequently, this provides highly appropriate circumstances for engagement of the EU's new competence for sport, enshrined in Article 6 and Article 165 TFEU, the potential 'added value' to be achieved by EU support, coordination and supplementation of strategic actions aimed at better promoting sports volunteering being significant. Although progress in this field may be somewhat elusive and slow, the EU has demonstrated a strong determination and commitment to encouraging environments conducive to the continued enhancement and development of volunteering in sport. At EU level, the identification, sharing, and dissemination of best practices in this field, not least, legal and fiscal mechanisms, acknowledges the centrality of sports volunteering in EU Sports Policy. This creates an influential backdrop, and a means of instructive and authoritative guidance and support, from which bespoke solutions can be found that embrace the differing volunteering cultures and traditions of specific Member States. Moreover, it forcefully reaffirms the fundamental and ongoing role of the EU in cultivating voluntary activity in sport in Europe.

6. Human rights at the intersection of EU law and sport

Simon Boyes

I. INTRODUCTION

The interaction of EU law with sport is a central and familiar plank of any modern understanding of the field of sports law. The principal focus of analyses of the relationship is on the regulation by EU law of the economic restrictions imposed by sport's self-regulatory schemes; little attention has been paid to the role and prominence of other rights, notably human rights, and the role played by EU law in effecting such protections.

This chapter seeks to address that lacuna by exploring the extent to which human rights are recognised in and/or protected by the application of EU law in the context of sport. The chapter begins by exploring the differing nature of the rights protected by EU law, and by human rights instruments – principally the European Convention on Human Rights (ECHR). The direct, explicit application of human rights provisions in the context of the intersection of EU law with sport is then assessed, before the chapter explores the range of human rights values which are protected indirectly by the application of EU law in sports cases.

The focus of the chapter is on the prevalence, or otherwise, of human rights values at the intersection between EU *law* and sport. It is clear that the EU has the potential to effect human rights protections across its areas of activity, notably in sports policy following the introduction of sport as a limited competence in Article 165 TFEU, however here I seek to assess this within the legal context.

II. THE CONTEXT: CONTRASTING LEGAL ORDERS

It is, now, well established that the EU, principally EU law, has been the essential catalyst in the 're-regulation' of sport over the period since the mid-1990s.[1] The key focus of this process has been the identification, enforcement and preservation of economic rights – usually of individuals – through the application of the Union's free movement and competition law provisions. Notably though, there has been no parallel 're-regulating' process emanating from the major human rights instruments of which, in the European context, the ECHR is plainly the most significant. The impact of the world's most successful regional human rights instrument has been notable only for its dearth. Indeed, the Convention's institutions have engaged with sport only fleetingly and, generally, only tangentially. Although, at the time of writing, a number of potentially important cases concerning sport's rules and regulations are due to be considered by the European Court of Human Rights, most of the small number of previous cases can be regarded as being connected with, but not strictly *about*, sport, in stark contrast with the role played by EU law.[2]

The markedly different levels of interaction between sport and the respective systems is, perhaps, unsurprising; human rights protections tend to provide a base line, a safety net providing for minimum acceptable standards and, arguably, are by their very nature less likely to be infringed by sport's regulatory schemes. This is because those human rights protections are principally oriented towards the sort of abuses perpetrated by nation states, rather than sports regulators, and that they are a product of the immediate aftermath of war in Europe. By contrast, the economic regulation of the EU – although also grown in a post-war environment – is designed and deployed as a means of attaining and maintaining the Single Market. As such, it is perhaps no surprise that EU law – aspirational and target driven – has been notable in reforming and reshaping those aspects of sport which present a barrier to these ambitions. As such, there is a distinction between the points at which the respective thresholds of intervention of each system are set.

Any measure which infringes a fundamental human right is likely to need be much more egregious than one which merely engages the economic protections provided under EU law. A case in point is the

---

[1] See generally A Caiger and S Gardiner (eds) *Professional Sport in the European Union – Regulation and Re-Regulation* (Asser 2000); S Gardiner, R Parrish and R Siekmann (eds), *EU, Sport Law and Policy: Regulation, Re-Regulation and Representation* (Springer 2009).

[2] See *Sport and the European Convention on Human Rights* (European Court of Human Rights Press Unit 2017) and available at http://www.echr.coe.int/Documents/FS_Sport_ENG.pdf (accessed 26 Oct 2017).

difference in approach between the now redundant European Commission of Human Rights in *X v Netherlands*,[3] and the Court of Justice in *Bosman*.[4] In *X*, the Commission determined that Article 4 ECHR – freedom from forced or compulsory labour – was not infringed by football's transfer system. The decision was predicated on the basis that professional football players chose to enter the profession freely, in full knowledge of the rules relating to transfers between clubs, and that the requirement that a fee be paid was an 'inconvenience' rather than being oppressive. By contrast, in *Bosman*, Advocate-General Lenz was strident in denying the significance of *X* and saw little difficulty in applying free movement provisions, even when infringement of the rights was merely 'seriously threatened'.[5] This evidences that in materially similar circumstances, EU law is much more easily engaged than a related fundamental human right provision.

The distinction is further explicable, considering the nature of the two systems created on the one hand, by the EU and, on the other, by the ECHR. This is perhaps best demonstrated by a consideration of the respective roles of the courts in each context. The Court of Justice of the European Union (CJEU) is part of, and has contributed substantially to, the development of a necessarily assertive, often interventionist, legal system. By asserting the supremacy of EU law over contrary domestic law and developing principles by which that law can be given effect in Member State courts, the CJEU has maximised that law's 'availability' to would be claimants. Similarly, the CJEU itself is readily accessible to litigants before national courts as a result of the preliminary reference system established in Article 267 TFEU, as was the case in *Bosman*. Legal issues may also enter into the EU legal system through the actions of the Commission, either in its role as the 'watchdog' of the Treaties, or in its function as the competition authority.

By contrast the European Court of Human Rights is not part of a 'legal order' in the same way as is claimed by the CJEU.[6] Protocol 15 to the Convention propounds the principle of subsidiarity, conferring the responsibility for the protection of its rights and freedoms on the signatory states. As a consequence the nature of the European Court of Human Rights' jurisdiction is supervisory. Though signatory states may opt to give effect to Convention rights in domestic law, there is no

---

3 Application 9322/81, *X v Netherlands*, European Commission of Human Rights' Decision of 3 May 1983, (1983) 32 DR 274.

4 Case C-415/93 *Bosman* [1995] ECR I-4921.

5 Ibid., para 66.

6 Case 26/62 *van Gend en Loos* [1963] ECR 1.

obligation that they be directly available in domestic courts, only that the rights are not infringed. Even where states have given effect to the Convention in their domestic systems there may still be instances where a domestic court is unable to protect a right even though it recognises an infringement.[7] Nor is there immediate access to the Court of Human Rights, there is no preliminary reference procedure, indeed victims of any breach must exhaust all available domestic remedies before being allowed to proceed to the Court. Similarly, no 'watchdog' exists which proactively seeks out and challenges purported breaches.

EU law is a significantly more pervasive, proactive and accessible system, as well as having much lower thresholds for the triggering of intervention; this goes a long way to explaining the high levels of interaction with sport relative to those of the ECHR.

The two systems do not operate in total isolation, however, human rights generally, and the Convention more particularly, are important parts of EU law – including in the context of sport. The general principles of law common to the Member States – including fundamental rights such as those contained in the ECHR – have long been held to be a source of EU law.[8] Similarly, even though the EU is not yet a signatory to the ECHR, the CJEU recognises explicitly the ECHR and the decisions of the European Court of Human Rights. Such recognition is now enshrined in the EU treaties, having been overtly referenced for the first time by the Maastricht Treaty, and now – since the amendments made by the Lisbon Treaty – expressly forming part of the general principles of EU law.[9] Further, Article 6(2) TEU now provides a legal basis for the EU's accession to the ECHR.[10] Article 6(1) TEU now also provides formal recognition for the Charter of Fundamental Rights of the European Union, and gives the Charter a status equivalent in EU law to the Treaties. It must be noted, however, that the obligations included in the Charter are addressed only to the EU institutions and, when they act to implement EU measures, to the Member States, providing a limited direct jurisdiction on human rights issues, perhaps even more limited where sport is concerned. This poses an interesting question as to the extent, if at all, to which interactions between EU law and sport have

---

[7] See, e.g., Human Rights Act 1998, s 4 (UK).

[8] Case 29/69 *Stauder v Ulm* [1969] ECR 419; Case 47/3 *Nold v Commission* [1974] ECR 491.

[9] Art 6(3) Treaty on the European Union.

[10] Though see *Opinion 2/13* of the Court of Justice, on accession to the ECHR.

engaged fundamental rights including, but not limited to, the rights established by the ECHR.

In order to address this, in the sections which follow I seek to assess the extent to which human rights have had an effect upon, and been given effect in, the application of EU law in sporting contexts. The CJEU and the Commission – acting principally in its capacity as the EU's competition law authority – have provided the principal interfaces between sport and EU law. Thus, these are the best fora in which to seek out and identify instances of human rights measures having these types of impact in instances where EU law is applied in the context of sport.

As indicated above the approach adopted is twofold. In the first instance, this chapter is concerned with the *effect* given to human rights values in the context of EU sports law. That is the extent to which, in the application of EU law in sports cases, specific human rights values are overtly considered and applied. In the second instance, this chapter seeks to identify and assess the extent to which EU law, as it is deployed in 'sports cases' is *affected* – by indirect or incidental means – by human rights values. By this I mean that human rights values are indirectly protected by the invocation of a parallel, related right in EU law.

III. GIVING EFFECT TO HUMAN RIGHTS AT THE INTERSECTION OF EU LAW AND SPORT

In this section I seek to identify and assess the deployment of human rights values in sport's mainstream interactions with EU law. In doing so I will consider and evaluate the jurisprudence of the CJEU relating to the application of free movement and competition law provisions – beginning with *Walrave and Koch*[11] and running through *Bosman* to *Meca-Medina*[12] and beyond. This section will also seek to locate and assess the prevalence of human rights protections through the activities of the Commission.

[11] Case 36/74 *Walrave and Koch v Union Cycliste Internationale* [1974] ECR 1405.

[12] Case C-519/04 P *Meca-Medina and Majcen v Commission* [2006] ECR I-6991.

III.i Direct Application of Human Rights in the 'Sports Law' Cases before the CJEU

As might be expected from a body of law which is predominantly focussed on the assertion of *economic* rights under free movement and competition law provisions, there is, in the mainstream sports law jurisprudence of the CJEU, only very limited overt allusion to human rights values. Predictably, being the most substantial judgment, it is in *Bosman* that these first arose. As noted above, in his opinion in *Bosman*, Advocate-General Lenz considered the factual background to the dispute and drew parallels with the case of *X v Netherlands* before the now defunct European Commission of Human Rights. In that case it was argued that football's transfer system meant that footballers were effectively subjected to forced labour, contrary to Article 4, paragraph 2 of the ECHR.

In *Bosman* the Court also considered, in its judgment, the applicability of Article 11 ECHR, the right to freedom of association. Article 11 ECHR was also considered by the Advocates-General in both *Deliège*[13] and *Lehtonen.*[14] What is perhaps most notable in each of these instances was that Article 11 ECHR was deployed not by the individuals seeking redress against governing bodies, but by the defendant regulators against which the claim was being made. This might be seen as surprising given that human rights measures are more often invoked by weaker parties, usually individuals or groups of individuals, against the state – the stronger party. It is certainly less usual for such a right to be invoked as a shield to legal action, as in these instances. In each case the CJEU, while recognising the ECHR as being part of the EU legal order, determined that the fundamental right was not infringed by scrutiny of these regulatory schemes.

The right to property – protected by Article 17 of the Universal Declaration of Human Rights (UDHR) and Article 1 Protocol 1 ECHR – has been invoked in the EU law context in a very different aspect of its application. The issue of the right to property has arisen most notably in the litigation regarding the legality of the Commission's decisions to approve the 'listing' of major sports events – including the European Football Championships and the FIFA World Cup. The decisions were challenged as being unlawful on the basis that, to limit the ability of the

---

[13] Cases C-51/96 and C-191/97 *Deliège v Ligue de Judo* [2000] ECR I-2549.

[14] Case C-176/96 *Lehtonen* [2000] ECR I-2681.

rights holder to dispose of those rights freely amounted to a deprivation of their property.[15]

Furthermore, Article 17 of the Charter of Fundamental Rights of the EU states: 'Everyone has the right to own, use, dispose of and bequeath his or her lawfully acquired possessions. ... Intellectual property shall be protected.' This, Advocate-General Jääskinen confirmed, is to be regarded as existing in parallel to the right to property articulated in Article 1, Protocol 1 of the ECHR. Of note is that, in interpreting the extent of this right, and its application in EU law, the Advocate-General deployed the broad conception of property adopted by the European Court of Human Rights, beyond the narrow legal definition. This was important, as the relevant domestic law in both Belgium and the UK did not recognise a legally enforceable property right in a sporting event, as such.

As a consequence the Advocate-General determined that the 'listing' of FIFA and UEFA events amounted to a *prima facie* interference, by the state, with the enjoyment of possessions, contrary to Article 1, Protocol 1. However, in considering whether such an infringement could be justified, Advocate-General Jääskinen determined that other interests, such as the right to information or the public interest in ensuring wide access by the public to television coverage of events of major importance, would legitimise limiting the opportunity to derive the highest possible value for the broadcast rights, particularly given their *de facto*, rather than *de jure* nature.

Perhaps notably, the CJEU did not, in its judgment, deliberate at any great length regarding the right to property as a human right; indeed the Court made no direct reference to either the Charter of Fundamental Rights or to the ECHR. Nonetheless, the Court accepted that some sort of interest in the protection of a property right existed, but shared the view of the Advocate-General that such an interest could be abrogated in the pursuit of the protection of valid, competing interests. At first instance, in each of the cases, the General Court had made plain the relevance of the right to property as a fundamental right protected by the EU legal order as a part of the general principles of law, though it too, regarded that right as having been legitimately limited in pursuit of other recognised interests.

That human-rights-based arguments are invoked only sparingly by claimants before the EU courts is perhaps unsurprising. Cases reach the

---

[15] Cases T-55/08 *UEFA v European Commission* [2011] ECR II-271; Cases T-385/07 and T-68/08 *FIFA v Commission* [2011] ECR II-205; Cases C-201, 204, 205/11 P *UEFA & FIFA v European Commission* [2014] 1 CMLR 18.

EU courts because they raise important issues of EU law and as a consequence of a desire by claimants to assert their claims to rights due to them there under. It is not, therefore, particularly unexpected that any human rights claims will be subsidiary and supporting, rather than central to most cases. In order for a claim to reach the CJEU – whether under as an enforcement action against a Member State under Articles 258 and 259 TFEU; a preliminary reference procedure under Article 267 TFEU; or by way of a judicial review action against an EU institution under Article 263 or 265 TFEU – it will necessarily engage a serious question of EU law. It is likely, therefore, that such a claim will turn on the interpretation and application of, usually, a more extensive and exacting level of protection than would be engaged by the corresponding human rights measure. So, although the rights protected by the ECHR are relevant to the CJEU – as forming part of the law common to Member States and, now, protected under the terms of the Charter of Fundamental Rights – it is not a surprise that these are not at the forefront of claims made.

III.ii Direct Application of Human Rights in the 'Sports Law' Claims Before the Commission

It is more markedly noticeable that the material available concerning the actions of the European Commission in the field of competition law, and in its other areas of responsibility, discloses no overt consideration of human rights matters. That the profile of such considerations is lower even than that within proceedings before the CJEU can be explained by the nature of the activity being undertaken. While the Court is, with its teleological view of EU law, taking a more broad-ranging view of the cases before it, the Commission has a much narrower concern. While it is certainly the case that the Commission will consider a range of justifications for rules or behaviour which might otherwise be regarded as breaching EU competition provisions, or the other aspects of EU law it is charged with protecting, and that these will extend to the 'interests' of individuals, these tend to be relatively limited. It is the economic nature of any restriction which is prohibited and which triggers consideration of justifications. When seeking to outline such justifications, those under investigation tend to point to general benefits – competitive balance, encouraging the development of young athletes and so on – rather than the protection of individual rights.

IV. THE EFFECT OF HUMAN RIGHTS AT THE INTERSECTION OF EU LAW AND SPORT

This might, arguably, suggest a significant limitation on the scope of this chapter, however, it is worth considering that rights may be protected not only directly and explicitly, but also effectively protected as a by-product or externality. Arguably this arises where aspirational rights of the sort propounded by EU law, aimed at securing a more ambitious and demanding result are applied. By contrast with the minimalist, lower threshold approach of human rights protections which are essentially aimed at the provision of minimum standards, a threshold below which no state should drop in its treatment of human beings. While EU law similarly provides minimum standards, these are the product of an international agreement to enhance rights in pursuit of a larger aim. Such an approach may, nonetheless, effect an indirect protection of those fundamental, basic human rights.

As a consequence of this, in this part of the chapter I seek to identify and articulate clear links between fundamental human rights provisions and the rights and freedoms protected in the sporting context through EU law. In doing so, I draw principally upon the major international human rights agreements – embodied by the so-called International Bill of Human Rights, constituted of the UDHR, the International Covenant on Civil and Political Rights (ICCPR), and the International Covenant on Economic, Social and Cultural Rights (ICESCR). I also draw upon the most significant European regional human rights instruments – the ECHR and the European Social Charter (ESC). I do so on the basis that they represent the core of the international and regional human rights protections relevant to the EU.

It is possible to identify eight 'clusters' of fundamental human rights which can be seen as supported and developed through the application of EU law in sport. These broadly cast are: non-discrimination; slavery and servitude; work; education and training; association; property; movement; and private life.

IV.i Non-discrimination

The principle of non-discrimination is set out in each of the five human rights instruments identified – in as much as the principle relates to the other substantive rights set out in them. However, Article 2 of the ICCPR also sets out a free-standing and autonomous general right to non-discrimination in respect of 'race, colour, sex, language, religion, political or other opinion, national or social origin, property, birth or other status'. It is undoubtedly reflected in the jurisprudence of the CJEU in sports cases and in the wider approach to EU law's role in the sporting context. This is most obviously evident in the *Bosman* litigation. Indeed in *Bosman* Advocate-General Lenz described the challenged restrictions on the participation of 'foreign' players as representing a 'classic case' of discrimination. Both the Advocate-General and the Court adopted a robust approach to the justifications which were offered for the discriminatory measure and were dismissive of them. Nonetheless, both agreed that, in addition to matters being purely sporting in nature – such as selection for national teams – and thus outside the scope of EU law, indirect discrimination might be justified. This, however, would only be on the basis of reasons of an economic nature capable of satisfying the requirement of being compelling in the general interest:

> If those rules pursued a legitimate aim [compatible with the Treaty] and were justified by pressing reasons of public interest ... application of those rules would still have to be such as to ensure achievement of the aim in question and not go beyond that necessary for that purpose.[16]

This was similarly emphasised by the subsequent litigation in *Lehtonen*. Here the principle of non-discrimination comes to the fore – with the observation that transfer windows in basketball could be justified in the interests of securing the regularity of competition, even though they might limit free movement, *unless* their impact was a discriminatory one.

Notably, the principle of non-discrimination on the grounds of nationality has been extended, indirectly, by the aborted litigation in *Balog v ASBL Royal Charleroi Sporting Club*.[17] The right to move between clubs without constraint at the end of a professional contract – though not the right to freedom from nationality-based player quotas – was extended to include non-EU nationals as a consequence of litigation which was discontinued shortly before the Advocate-General was due to deliver her opinion, following a capitulation by the football authorities.

Though *Balog* invoked EU competition law in challenging an arguably discriminatory measure, there is limited evidence of the principle of non-discrimination taking effect in the context of the application of competition law more widely. Despite this absence of direct evidence, it is certainly arguable that overt discrimination, along the lines of gender

---

[16] Case C-415/93 *Bosman*, para 103.

[17] Case C-264/98 *Balog v ASBL Royal Charleroi Sporting Club* [1998] OJ C 278, 28.

or race for example, involving the exercise of private economic power, would be regarded as an illegitimate and illegal exercise of such control.[18]

The non-discrimination principle in the context of EU law applied to sport was given extended geographical reach by the decisions in *Kolpak*[19] and *Simutenkov*.[20] The cases considered the application of, respectively, an Association Agreement between the EU and Slovakia – not, then, an EU Member State – and a Partnership Agreement between the Union and Russia. The effect of the judgments of the CJEU in these two cases was to recognise the direct effect of the provisions of the respective agreements in as much as they related to non-discrimination on the grounds of nationality. The consequence was the extension of the non-discrimination element of the *Bosman* ruling – though not the free movement limb – to nationals from a significant number of states with similar agreements with the EU. The practical consequence of this was that such as to prohibit the application of nationality-based quotas or other restrictions to athletes of these nationalities.[21]

Notably, the application of the non-discrimination principle, based on nationality, is extensive. This is evidenced in the sporting context by the intervention, by the Commission, in relation to regulations of the Spanish Football Federation precluding non-Spanish nationals over the age of 23 from participating in high-level amateur football. Though the Spanish authorities argued that the issue was outside the competence of the EU – being related to *amateur* sport and thus not an economic activity subject to EU law as set out in *Walrave* – the Commission took the view that Article 7(2) of Regulation 1612/68 was applicable.[22] Regulation 1612/68 granted the right to equal treatment of workers to tax and social advantages but, applying *Grzelczyk*,[23] the Commission considered that this extended to include all EU citizens legally resident in a Member State; this was particularly pertinent as the individual lodging the complaint was a German student living in Spain. The Commission

---

[18] See S Boyes and S Patel, 'After *Bosman* – the Rise of the Bos(wo)man?' [2006] 14(3) *Sport and the Law Journal* 14.

[19] Case C-438/00 *Kolpak* [2003] ECR I-4135.

[20] Case C-265/03 *Simutenkov* [2005] ECR I-2579.

[21] See R Branco-Martins, 'The *Kolpak* case: *Bosman* times 10?' (2004) 4 (1–2) *International Sports Law Journal* 26; S van den Bogaert, 'And Another Uppercut from the European Court of Justice to Nationality Requirements in Sports Regulations' (2004) 29(2) *European Law Review* 267.

[22] Now replaced by Regulation 492/2011.

[23] Case C-184/99 *Grzelczyk* [2001] I-ECR 6193.

similarly considered that the opportunity to participate in amateur sport amounted to a social advantage under the terms of the Regulation. This being that case, the principle of non-discrimination is given significant depth – extending to aspects of life stretching far beyond a narrow conception of work – and notable breadth – broadening the application of the principle to all EU Citizens lawfully resident in another Member State.[24]

The non-discrimination principle has been given further effect following the CJEU decision in *Accept*.[25] The case concerned Directive 2000/78/EC, which establishes a general framework for equal treatment in employment. The Directive relates to discrimination on the grounds of religion or belief, disability, age or sexual orientation. In the proceedings before the CJEU – a preliminary reference from a Romanian court – the central issue was whether a statement made by a 'patron' of the Romanian football club Steaua Bucharest could, under the terms of the Directive, give rise to presumption that the club had a discriminatory recruitment policy. The individual in question, a Mr Becali, had stated that he would never sign a homosexual player. Following a complaint by a pressure group, Accept, lodged with the National Council for Combating Discrimination (CNCD), Mr Becali was issued with a warning, but no action was taken against the club in respect of its allegedly discriminatory recruitment policy. Accept challenged the interpretation of the Directive before the referring court. The CJEU determined that the Directive required that an employer in such a situation should take positive steps to distance itself from such comments, even where it was not bound by them.

In the context of matters relating to sport and human rights, *Accept* is an important indication of the applicability of wider non-discrimination measures. First, it demonstrates the applicability of rights to non-discrimination beyond those based simply on nationality to the sporting context. Second, in rejecting the assertion that the Directive was inapplicable given the peculiarities in the way in which professional footballers are recruited by clubs, the CJEU demonstrated the relevance of the measure to professional sport.

---

24 See European Parliament Petition 0215/2002 by Rüdiger Hartmann (German), on being refused a player's licence in Spain, PE 326.256 rev. VI.

25 Case C-81/12 *Accept* [2013] 3 CMLR 26.

IV.ii Slavery and Servitude

Freedom from slavery and servitude is found in Article 8 ICCPR, Article 4 UDHR, and Article 4 ECHR. Freedom from slavery and servitude are rights which are not, perhaps, most obviously linked with sport. Nonetheless, these rights are undoubtedly extended by the freedoms engaged under Article 45 TFEU, not least the capacity to move freely at the end of a contract of employment. It is arguable that the application of Article 45 TFEU in *Bosman* represents a significant protection of this right, extending as it does the principle of freedom to contract once a termination has been effected. The obligation to permit movement at the end of a contract has, as noted above, been extended to include non-EU nationals as a consequence of *Balog*. The right has been extended yet further by the amendments made in 2001 to the FIFA Regulations on the Status and Transfer of Players, which limits the length of contracts for professional footballers and introduces a 'protected period' beyond which a player may move without the consent of his club, even though his contract is still ongoing. Though the impact of these changes – effected by negotiation with the Commission has, perhaps, not been as extensive as might have been imagined or, indeed, intended, the initial restrictive interpretation of these provisions has been ameliorated to an extent by the judgment of the Swiss Federal Tribunal in *Matuzalem*.[26]

Notably, we still talk of professional players being 'owned' by clubs – although of course it is the player registrations which are held or 'owned' by the club, not the players themselves – which harks back to the judgment in *Eastham v Newcastle United*, the 'English Bosman', where it was observed by the claimant that players were being treated as 'chattels'.[27]

The Commission will be required to consider relevant aspects of the football transfer system pursuant to a complaint lodged by FIFPro, the global professional football players' union.[28] Notably, the complaint details objections to, among other things, the treatment of professional football players as 'tradable assets'. The essence of this element of the claim is that FIFA's Regulations on the Status and Transfer of Players facilitates a system in which players under contract are, 'traded as assets.

[26] *Francelino da Silva Matuzalem v FIFA*, Case 4A_558/2011, judgment of 27 March 2012, Swiss Federal Tribunal.

[27] *Eastham v Newcastle United Football Club Ltd* [1964] 1 Ch 413, 427.

[28] *FIFPro's EU Competition Law Complaint – Executive Summary* (FIFPro, 18 September 2015) available at www.fifpro.org/attachments/article/6156/FIFPro%20Complaint%20Executive%20Summary.pdf (accessed 26 Oct 2017).

Their labour becomes a commodity, which is bought and sold to make profit'.[29] Notably, the complaint invokes the Charter of Fundamental Rights, arguing that the right to working conditions which respects the right to dignity is infringed by the regulatory scheme.

IV.iii Work

The right to freedom from slavery and servitude underpins a further example of EU law supporting and enhancing a fundamental human right, that of the right to work. This is to be found in Article 6 ICESCR and Article 23 UDHR and is also present in Article 1 ESCR. This right is most obviously protected by the freedom to move and to take up employment in another Member State and – as discussed above – to do so without being the subject of unjustified discrimination. The EU law notion of a 'worker', and its application in the context of sport, is relatively generous. The general EU law requirement to satisfy worker status is that an individual performs services, under the direction of another, for remuneration.[30] This generous approach and its application in the context of sport was made clear in the earlier case of *Donà v Mantero* – to the effect that even a semi-professional footballer must be considered to be a worker for the purposes of EU free movement provisions.[31] An even more generous approach is evident in *Deliège*.[32] In that case, the claimant athlete successfully argued that she was 'providing services' for the purposes of what is now Article 49 TFEU, despite receiving no direct payment for her participation in a sporting event. The effect of her receipt of sponsorship dependent on her participation, and that the event in question was an economic activity – selling tickets, media rights, sponsorship and so on – was sufficient to cross the threshold of the provision of a service. So the definition of what amounts to 'work', whether as an employed person or provider of a service, in the context of sport is generously cast. This is also evident where EU law has had to consider restrictions imposed by professional regulations in sport. In *Heylens*, the CJEU declared illegal a French measure requiring a football coach to hold qualifications likely to be limited to French nationals.[33] Similarly in *Piau*, in a decision later validated by the CJEU,

---

29 FIFPro's EU Competition Law Complaint – Executive Summary (FIFPro, 18 September 2015) 4.

30 Case 66/85 *Lawrie-Blum v Land Baden-Wurttemberg* [1986] ECR 2121.

31 Case 13/76 *Donà v Mantero* [1976] ECR 1333

32 Cases C-51/96 and C-191/97 *Deliège v Ligue de Judo* (n 13).

33 Case 222/86 *Heylens* [1987] ECR 4097.

the Commission recognised the need for regulations relating to the licensing of football agents to impose only proportionate restrictions on access to the profession.[34]

Though EU law does not provide a direct right to be employed, it certainly places significant restrictions on the capacity of sport's regulatory schemes to impose limitations, not just on treatment once in work – as set out above in relation to non-discrimination – but also in respect of pursuit of, and access to, that work. In *Bosman* the CJEU gave significant weight to this principle. The Court determined that restrictions on the capacity of professional footballers to move without restriction at the end of a contract amounted to an obstacle to movement between Member States, contrary to Article 45 TFEU. This finding was made despite the acceptance by the Court that such a restriction was non-discriminatory – it affected players equally, irrespective of whether they were seeking to move within or between Member States – but because the restriction impeded access to the employment market in other Member States by deterring them from seeking or taking up work in another Member State.[35] This has clear parallels with the right established by Article 12(2) ICCPR to leave a territory in pursuit of work.

EU law has also effected the application of this notion of a right to pursue and enter employment free of restriction beyond its formal jurisdiction. From a narrow legal perspective, the immediate implications of this aspect of the *Bosman* judgment were applicable only to out-of-contract players moving between Member States; but such was the impact of the judgment that the right to move freely at the end of a contract was ultimately extended to domestic transfers[36] and, indeed, with the introduction of FIFA's Status and Transfer of Players regulations in 2001, effectively across the globe.[37]

One related aspect of the right to work where EU law has had an impact is in relation to collective bargaining. Article 6 ESCR links

---

[34] Case COMP/37.124; Case T-193/02 *Piau v Commission* [2005] ECR II-209; Case C-171/05 *Piau v Commission* [2006] ECR I-37.

[35] Case C-171/05 *Piau v Commission* [2006] ECR I-37, paras 92–104.

[36] P Morris, P Morrow and P Spink, 'EC Law and Professional Football: Bosman and its Implications' (1996) 59 MLR 893, 902; S Gardiner and R Welch, 'The Contractual Dynamics of Team Stability Versus Player Mobility: Who Rules "The Beautiful Game"' (2007) 5(1) ESLJ (online journal) DOI: http://doi.org/10.16997/eslj.74 (accessed 26 Oct 2017).

[37] See generally S Boyes, 'Law, Regulation and the Europeanization of a Global Game' in J Magee, A Bairner and A Tomlinson (eds) *The Bountiful Game? Football, Identities and Finance* (Meyer & Meyer 2005).

collective bargaining to the right to work. It is plainly arguable that the EU is actively facilitating the process through the social dialogue process.[38]

IV.iv Education and Training

The same article of the ESCR – Article 1 – which protects the right to work, also encompasses the right to access to receive relevant training. This is also identified in Article 10 ESCR which provides a right to vocational training. This is further bolstered by Article 13 ICESCR and Article 26 UDHR which provide for a right to education.

This right poses an interesting challenge in the context of EU law, particularly in relation to the application of free movement of persons' provisions in sport. It is in the context of sport that the values of work and education have come into tension. In particular, the need to train and educate young participants in sport has been deployed as a justification – a pressing reason of public interest – for limiting the free movement of, in particular, young footballers. This was first seen in the aftermath of *Bosman*, with the agreement that the right to move freely at the termination of a contract would only apply to those having attained the age of 24. This was in recognition of the need to encourage clubs to develop young talent. The rationale underlying this is that clubs are less likely to invest in the development and training of young players if they are able to leave subsequently, without the club receiving compensation.

This position was reinforced by the decision in *Olivier Bernard*, in which a French law requiring the payment of compensation where first-year professional players signed with any club other than that which had trained them.[39] In her Opinion Advocate-General Sharpston noted that the European Council had, in its declaration annexed to the Treaty of Nice, emphasised that sport has within it educational functions and that this role should be 'preserved and nurtured'.[40] The Advocate-General also recognised the similar importance given to education by both the European Parliament and the Commission.[41] This importance was recognised by the CJEU, which added that this emphasis had then become

38 See R Parrish, 'Social Dialogue in European Professional Football' (2011) 17(2) ELJ 213.

39 Case C-325/08 *Olivier Bernard* [2010] ECR I-2177.

40 Ibid., para 48.

41 Ibid.

integrated into the Treaty with the introduction of Article 165 TFEU by the amending Lisbon Treaty.[42]

Advocate-General Sharpston further noted that the training of young professional players could 'hardly be questioned' as a legitimate aim which might justify an obstacle to free-movement, a point echoed by the Court.[43] The value and importance of education is emphasised both by the Opinion of the Advocate-General and the judgment of the Court that it predominates over the strict application of EU law as it pertains to the right of free movement. As such this is illustrative of a fundamental right – education and training – overriding, or at least achieving parity with, competing interests in work and free movement, which have been extended beyond a base level.

IV.v Privacy

Private and family life – protected under Article 8 ECHR – has not been impacted directly by either the CJEU or the Commission, but EU law has had a notable impact on the concept in the context, particularly, of anti-doping regulations. 'Working Party 29' – essentially the heads of Member States' data protection authorities has had a significant effect on the reshaping of the International Standard for Protection of Privacy, which informs the operation of the World Anti-Doping Code. The detail of the interactions is beyond the scope of this chapter, however, it is important to note the impact that Working Party 29 has had in requiring the World Anti-Doping Agency to reform its practice in this respect. The Working Party first raised its concerns in the lead up to the revised 2009 version of the Code,[44] concerns which were partially met by WADA.[45] The Working Party continued to engage in detailed interactions with

---

[42] Ibid., para 40.

[43] Ibid., para 45.

[44] Opinion 3/2008 on the World Anti-Doping Code Draft International Standard for the Protection of Privacy, Adopted on 1 August 2008 and available at http://ec.europa.eu/justice/data-protection/article-29/documentation/opinion-recommendation/files/2008/wp156_en.pdf (accessed 26 Oct 2017).

[45] Second opinion 4/2009 on the World Anti-Doping Agency (WADA) International Standard for the Protection of Privacy and Personal Information, on related provisions of the WADA Code and on other privacy issues in the context of the fight against doping in sport by WADA and (national) anti-doping organisations, Adopted on 6 April 2009 and available at http://ec.europa.eu/justice/data-protection/article-29/documentation/opinion-recommendation/files/2009/wp162_en.pdf (accessed 26 Oct 2017).

WADA, contributing substantially to the relevant parts of the revision of the Code which came into effect in 2015.[46]

V. CONCLUSIONS

Direct protection of human rights through EU law, in the context of sport, is relatively limited. Although the ECHR has been invoked on a number of occasions before the CJEU, this has usually been as a means of adducing that an EU law claim was inapplicable, or in defence of a claim as a means of defending a regulatory scheme from scrutiny. Indirect protection – through the application of EU law with 'parallel' provisions in human rights – has been much more notable. As suggested, this is because those EU rights are more exacting, and, as a consequence more easily infringed, with the result that fundamental human rights are rarely directly adduced. This does not mean that they are not protected indirectly. In protecting the 'parallel' right, EU law is effecting indirect support for the relevant human rights provisions.

This protection has not only been through the application of EU law by the CJEU and the Commission but has, also, been notable for the extent to which it pervades the work undertaken by, in particular, the Commission, since the granting of a specific supporting competence in sport in Article 165 TFEU.

Arguably, the manner in which human rights are recognised and protected in the intersection between EU law and sport is somewhat patchy. Protection depends on the existence and application of a parallel right in EU law. As such the coverage is incomplete; perhaps this is unsurprising given the indirect and, indeed – as far as specific human rights protections are concerned – different nature and orientation of EU law provisions.

The prospects for a more complete concord in respect of human rights protections at the intersection of EU law and sport is made increasingly likely by two factors. First, the adoption of the Charter of Fundamental Rights means that direct recourse to human rights values will be more frequent in matters falling before both the Commission and the CJEU. This is already the case in the general jurisprudence, which will have an

---

46 Contribution of the Article 29 Working Party to the 3rd stage of WADA's consultation in the context of the review of the World Anti-Doping Code and its International Standards, 5 March 2013 and available at http://194.242.234.211/documents/10160/2133805/Article+29+Working+Party++WADAs+consultation.pdf (accessed 26 Oct 2017).

almost inevitable consequence for the application of the law in sports cases. Second, the supporting competence in the field of sport granted by Article 165 TFEU has already begun to introduce important human rights values into the sporting context, as highlighted in the above analysis.

In combination, the potential for EU actions taken under Article 165 TFEU to be influenced by, and give effect to, Charter rights is significant. Similarly, should the EU ultimately become a signatory to the ECHR, the opportunities for the application of human rights values at the intersection of EU law and sport will be greatly enhanced. It is unlikely to have the result that the CJEU will become a human rights court but, much like the position with the Human Rights Act 1998 in the UK, human rights consideration would necessarily fall for more overt consideration; such an approach cannot but have an influence upon EU sports law.

7. Violence at sporting events

Anastassia Tsoukala

I. INTRODUCTION

It is often believed that violence at sporting events is only associated with football. Yet, academic research across Europe has regularly shown that sports crowd violence has also been observed at basketball, volleyball, ice hockey and water-polo matches.[1] The issue is still under-explored but it seems plausible to affirm that sports crowd violence is associated with the most popular sports in a given country as popularity implies passionate fandom, expanded practice of the sport across the country and, hence, high mediatization of relevant fixtures. The aforementioned sports may further exert a pull on violent supporters because, due to their collective nature, they constitute an optimal frame for collective identities to be built. To the extent that football meets these criteria in most European countries, football-related violence ranks indeed first among other sports-related violent behaviours and, subsequently, has stirred up an ever-increasing specific regulatory frame both at the European and EU level.[2]

Nonetheless, addressing the issue of football crowd violence is a highly treacherous academic endeavour because, in spite of the profusion

---

[1] G Berger, *Violence and Sports* (Watts 1990); N Courakis, 'Football Violence: Not Only A British Problem' (1998) 6 *European Journal on Criminal Policy and Research* 293–302; T Busset, 'Le Supportérisme Violent en Suisse: un état des lieux' (2002) (LV) Revue internationale de criminologie et de police technique et scientifique 348–57; K Koukouris and S Taxildaridis, 'Aggression against Referees in Greek Basketball. Referees' Perspective on Violent Incidents in Greek Basketball', in D Panagiotopoulos (ed.) *Sports Law* (Sakkoulas 2005) 258–65.

[2] In 2011, the European Commission affirmed, however, that 'there is a need for a European approach comprising measures designed to reduce [spectator violence and disorder]' and specifies that this approach, focused on prevention and law enforcement, should also cover other sports disciplines. See Communication from the Commission to the European Parliament, the Council, the European Economic and Social Committee and the Committee of the Regions 'Developing the European Dimension in Sport', COM (2011) 12 final, para 2.3.

of relevant studies in Europe, this form of violence remains poorly framed due to the evolving nature of its multifactorial origin. From the late 1960s on, scholars who looked into the issue produced many studies covering several academic disciplines but, in the absence of multi-disciplinary and comparative research, they failed to construct any broadly acceptable explanatory frames. The absence of an overarching academic definition of the phenomenon, along with the absence of any legal definition of it, be it at national, European or EU level,[3] provided law enforcers with a disproportionate defining power of what the phenomenon is and, subsequently, of the allegedly optimal ways to deal with it, thereby allowing them to influence (in)directly national, European and EU law makers.

Influence of the police-led perception of the issue is visible in the very prioritizing of values to be protected by law when dealing with football crowd violence. While physical harm, material damages and breach of the peace have always fuelled counter-hooliganism policies, policy makers turned a blind eye to other forms of football-related violence. Throughout the 1970s, 1980s and 1990s, football supporters frequently adopted racist behaviour inside stadia. Yet, at EU level football-related racism was not recognized as an important problem to deal with until 1999, when the European Commission sponsored Football Against Racism in Europe (FARE), the first EU-wide anti-racist football network. The Council of Europe adopted the first Resolution on the prevention of racism and xenophobia in sport only in 2000.[4]

The hegemonic expertise of law enforcers also determined the rationale of European law making to the extent that the first Europe-wide relevant regulation, that is, the 1985 European Convention on Spectator Violence and Misbehaviour at Sporting Events and especially Football Matches, extended its target population to cover potential troublemakers,[5] thus introducing at the European law-making process the then rising proactive risk focused crime control model. As the European Convention was adopted in the aftermath of the 1985 Heysel Stadium disaster that was unanimously attributed to English football supporters, focusing on the dangerousness of 'football hooligans' was seen as a highly necessary rational option. Once legitimized by the seriousness of the security threat

---

[3] A Tsoukala, *Football Hooliganism in Europe. Security and Civil Liberties in the Balance* (Palgrave Macmillan 2009) 2–6.

[4] Council of Europe, Resolution N° 4 on preventing racism, xenophobia and intolerance in sport, May 2000 available at https://www.coe.int/t/dg4/epas/resources/texts/Res(2000)4_en.pdf (accessed 26 Oct 2017).

[5] Council of Europe, CETS n° 120, 19 August 1985, art. 3.

policy makers had to deal with, this framing of the issue was not revised when the Belgian judges eventually established that blame for the disaster was to be put on Belgian law enforcers, Belgian football authorities, and only to a lesser degree on English supporters.[6] Solid establishment of this ill-grounded perception and subsequent management of football-related violence was greatly facilitated by the media representation of the issue. While the image of the dangerous English 'thugs' at the Heysel Stadium was immediately broadcasted on a worldwide scale, the counter-image of split liability stemming from the Belgian court ruling was hardly covered at all. From then on, the prevailing image of a serious security threat that had to be rapidly countered justified the unconditional introduction of any measure presented as necessary to curb this form of violence.

Under the impulse of the European Convention, legislation in all signatory countries became increasingly standardized, as it was mainly structured around risk-focused proactive action and situational prevention. This trend was further consolidated by the fact that all post-Heysel UEFA's binding safety and security instructions have been constantly elaborated in line with the main principles of the European Convention. From 1996 on, when the Council of the EU took specific counter-hooliganism action at football matches with an international dimension, its key options institutionalized and further expanded at the EU level what was already set in motion across Europe. In so doing, EU law makers reflected the rise in power of the proactive risk-oriented model in the broader crime control realm. It is commonplace in academia that implementation of this crime control model has entailed serious jeopardizing of civil rights and liberties in many different fields.[7] Quite

---

[6] F Tulkens, 'La tragédie du Heysel: les responsabilités. Le débat sur le plan juridique', (1988) Revue interdisciplinaire d'études juridiques 71–141. The former secretary-general of the Belgian Football Union was charged with negligence with regard to ticketing arrangements; two Belgian law enforcers were charged with criminal negligence in policing; 14 supporters were found guilty of involuntary manslaughter and given a three-year prison sentence, suspended for 18 months – on appeal, 11 of the sentences were slightly increased.

[7] D Garland, *Punishment and Welfare* (Gower 1985); M Feeley and J Simon, 'The New Penology: Notes on the Emerging Strategy of Corrections and its Implications' (1992) 30(4) *Criminology* 449–74; J Simon, 'Governing through Crime', in L Friedman and G Fisher (eds) *The Crime Connection* (Westview Press 1997) 171–89; R Ericson and K Haggerty, *Policing the Risk Society* (OUP 1997); C Shearing, 'Punishment and the Changing Face of Governance', (2001) 3(2) *Punishment & Society* 203–20; E Silver and L Miller,

unsurprisingly then, counter-hooliganism policies in Europe have often been criticized for their propensity to endanger rule of law and football supporters' rights and liberties.[8]

Prevalence of police-led policies has been moderated since the late 2000s when, following the adoption of the Lisbon Treaty, the EU was enabled to promote sporting issues. In its White Paper on Sport of 11 July 2007, the European Commission addressed sport-related violence as an issue to be dealt with along with racism,[9] thus recognizing that politically grounded symbolic violence was as equally disturbing as physical harm, material damages and breach of the peace. Implicitly calling into question of the efficiency of a single police-grounded management of the issue has further led to the promotion of long term preventive policies,[10] while in 2008 the scope of relevant actions was broadened to recognize football supporters as actors likely to be involved in countering football-related violence.[11] Nonetheless, as will be shown below, this new framing of football crowd management was not meant to

---

'A Cautionary Note on the Use of Actuarial Risk Assessment Tools for Social Control' (2002) 48(1) *Crime & Delinquency* 138–61; L Johnston and C Shearing, *Governing Security* (Routledge 2003); M Feeley, 'Crime, Social Order and the Rise of neo-Conservative politics' (2003) 7(1) *Theoretical Criminology* 111–30; P Carlen (ed.) *Imagined Penalities* (Willan 2008); T Daems, *Making Sense of Penal Change* (OUP 2008); S Hallsworth and J Lea, 'Reconstructing Leviathan: Emerging Contours of the Security State' (2011) 15(2) *Theoretical Criminology* 141–57.

[8] A Tsoukala, *Sport et violence*, (Bruylant 1995); G Pearson, 'Legitimate Targets? The Civil Liberties of Football Fans', (1999) 4(1) *Journal of Civil Liberties* 28–47; G Pearson, 'Qualifying for Europe? The Legitimacy of Football Banning Orders "On Complaint" under the Principle of Proportionality', (2005) 3(1) *Entertainment & Sports Law Journal* 4 https://www.entsportslawjournal.com/articles/10.16997/eslj.122/ (accessed 26 Oct 2017); M James and G Pearson, 'Football Banning Orders: Analysing their use in Court' (2006) 70 (6) *Journal of Criminal Law* 509–25; C Stott and G Pearson, 'Football Banning Orders, Proportionality, and Public Order Policing', (2006) 45(3) *The Howard Journal* 241–54; A Tsoukala, *Security Policies and Human Rights in European Football Stadia*, (Centre for European Policy Studies, Research Paper n° 5, 2007); A Testa, 'Normalization of the Exception: Issues and Controversies of the Italian Counter-hooliganism Legislation', (2013) 16 (2) *Sport in Society* 151–66; A Tsoukala, G Pearson and P Coenen (eds) *Legal Responses to Football 'Hooliganism' in Europe* (Asser 2016).

[9] European Commission, White Paper on Sport, COM(2007) 391 final, para 2.6.

[10] Ibid., para 21.

[11] Council of the EU, Conclusions of the High-level Conference 'Towards an EU strategy against Violence in Sport' (5182/08, ENFOPOL 9).

modify prior police-led patterns of controlling football supporters. Current comprehensive management of the issue relies on solidly established risk-based security measures.

Analysis of the multilevel patterns of EU counter-hooliganism policies will rest upon the span of their approach. First, attention will be drawn to the main features of police-led policies, implemented by law enforcers in collaboration with (inter)national sporting bodies. Secondly, focus will be set on the emerging comprehensive management of the issue to highlight its specific facets and assess the way these may intermingle with prevalent patterns of policing football supporters.

II. PREVALENCE OF POLICE-LED POLICIES (1996–2006)

In full compliance with the key options of the European Convention, the very setting up of EU counter-hooliganism policies has been heavily determined by the risk-focused mindset. Relevant actions have been mainly structured around three axes: surveillance via intelligence gathering/exchange; exclusion via football banning orders; and harmonization of policing via a regularly updated handbook for international police cooperation and measures to prevent and control violence and disturbance in connection with international football matches.

II.i Intelligence

In its Recommendation of 22 April 1996 on guidelines for preventing and restraining disorder connected with football matches,[12] the Council of the EU stressed the importance of gathering intelligence on 'known or suspected groups of troublemakers'.[13] Scholars working on security- and risk-related issues have constantly shown how the shifting target of policing, from the real offender to the potential one, and the ensuing pretension to control the future by anticipating human behaviour and putting people under control because they may commit an offence in the future, jeopardize civil rights and liberties because they dismiss offence-grounded evidence and guilt to focus instead on deviance-grounded

---

[12] [1996] OJ C 131.

[13] Council of the EU, Conclusions of the High-level Conference (n 11), para II.1.

indices and suspicion.[14] Once enacted by law makers, marginalization of evidence and growth of suspicion as justificatory basis of the setting in movement of the criminal justice system generate a genuine institutionalization of the control of deviance.[15]

The introduction of the impersonal group-based profiling criteria at the expense of individual-based control, and the ensuing normalization of such an anticipatory policing pattern, gradually modified the very rationale of supporters' management in that it tended to pay less attention to control devices to be grounded instead on surveillance mechanisms, that is, CCTV cameras and undercover policing inside and outside stadia. The subsequent proliferation of police databases entailed extensive control of deviant behaviour that, once institutionalized, became a key component of football crowd management.

The pivotal role of intelligence in counter-hooliganism was acknowledged in Council Resolution of 21 June 1999 concerning a handbook for international police cooperation and measures to prevent and control violence and disturbance in connection with international football matches.[16] From then on, surveillance-based policing that was initially only aiming at establishing the profile of the 'prototype risk fan',[17] will keep on expanding. Council Resolution of 6 December 2001, which updated the aforementioned handbook,[18] defined in vague terms the target population as 'individuals who represent or may represent a danger to public order or to security in connection with the event or who may have been involved in incidents'.[19] While both the definition and assessment of risk behaviour clearly rest upon subjective criteria, thereby dismissing the principle of legal certainty, law makers did not limit their action to blurring the borders between illegal and deviant behaviour. They further provided that the scope of surveillance should be expanded beyond risk individuals to admittedly ordinary ones as it was specified that national football information points (NFIPs) may supply information

---

[14] U Beck, *World Risk Society* (Polity 1999); R Broadhurst, 'Criminal Careers, Sex Offending and Dangerousness', in M Brown and J Pratt (eds) *Dangerous Offenders* (Routledge 2000) 109–26; P O'Malley, 'Risk Societies and the Government of Crime', in Brown and Pratt, ibid, 17–33; D Lyon, *Surveillance Society* (Open University Press 2001); and R Ericson, *Crime in an Insecure World* (Polity 2007).

[15] Tsoukala (n 3) 63ff.

[16] [1999] OJ C 196.

[17] Ibid., Ch 1.

[18] [2002] OJ C 022.

[19] Ibid., Ch 1, IV.1 (b).

'regarding the movements of normal and risk supporters', and that 'the movements and stays of the fans can be monitored'.[20] Surveillance is thus being turned into a limitless social control tool that targets indistinctively known troublemakers, risk supporters and normal football spectators alike. This worrisome broadening of the field of action of intelligence agents becomes even more liberty threatening as it is provided that NFIPs can, should the need arise, also be used for the exchange of information 'regarding other matters besides sporting events'.[21]

Reactions of certain Member States against this broad and indistinct surveillance of football crowds[22] were curbed in 2002 when EU-wide intelligence gathering and exchange became compulsory,[23] since the Council of the EU decided that Member States should establish NFIPs assigned with the task both to exchange relevant information on high-risk supporters[24] and facilitate international police cooperation in connection with football matches with an international dimension.[25]

The tasks of this EU-wide network of information centres, and the way these should proceed to gather and exchange information before, during and after the event, are provided by Council Resolution of 4 December 2006, which updated the aforementioned 2001 handbook. Detailed lists of operational points to be taken into account go along with a new widening of the intelligence scope, with risk supporters being now defined as persons 'known or not, who can be regarded as posing a possible risk to public order or antisocial behaviour, whether planned or spontaneous'.[26] Yet, while emphasis is put on specific aspects the

---

[20] Ibid., Ch 1, s 1, IV.2.

[21] Ibid., Ch 1, s 2.

[22] While Greece and Austria, for example, were resisting the setting up of information centres, the Netherlands were reluctant to include potential troublemakers in police files and pass on the names of such individuals to their foreign counterparts.

[23] [2002] OJ L 121: 2002/348/JHA: Council Decision of 25 April 2002 Concerning Security in Connection with Football Matches with an International Dimension.

[24] Ibid., art 3, NFIPs exchange three-level information; strategic, operational and tactical.

[25] Ibid., arts 1.3 and 2.2.

[26] [2006] OJ C 322/1: Council Resolution of 4 December 2006 concerning an updated handbook with recommendations for international police cooperation and measures to prevent and control violence and disturbances in connection with football matches with an international dimension, in which at least one Member State is involved. Appendix 1, Art 1(b) further provides that NFIPs

dynamic risk assessment should rest upon, it remains unclear what behaviour may be considered antisocial, thus enhancing the risk of individuals having their personal data entered in police files for an array of loosely defined reasons.

II.ii Football Banning Orders

Normalization of intelligence-led policing of football crowds across the EU did not solely entail institutionalization of the control of deviance and subsequent replacement of the legislative power by the executive, as to defining who should be targeted by law enforcers. In several Member States intelligence has also been used as legitimate basis of various forms of administrative football banning orders (AFBOs) that, in relying solely on reports made by police and/or intelligence officers, circumvent judicial control to impose restrictions on the supporters' freedom of movement that are resting upon suspicion instead of evidence.[27]

This replacement of the judiciary by the executive, and the ensuing punishment of deviance,[28] has not been admitted by EU law makers when they sought to restrict freedom of movement of violent supporters. In 1997, the Council of the EU thus wished 'stadium exclusions imposed under [national] civil law [to be applied] to football matches in a European context'.[29] The issue of imposing a ban on supporters entering and/or leaving a country to attend an international match was discussed again in 2001.[30] In 2003, Member States were invited to examine the possibility of issuing football banning orders against individuals 'previously guilty of violent conduct at football matches',[31] and to ensure that

---

should also produce generic and/or thematic national football disorder assessments.

[27] AFBOs have been introduced in many continental European countries. In the UK, football banning orders on complaint do not circumvent but nonetheless alleviate judicial control.

[28] Tsoukala (n 3) 111ff.

[29] [1997] OJ C 193: Resolution of 9 June 1997 on preventing and restraining football hooliganism through the exchange of experience, exclusion from stadiums and media policy, para 1.

[30] Council of the EU, Draft discussion document for a policy debate on a ban on hooligans entering and/or leaving a country and similar measures (SN 3159/01).

[31] [2003] OJ C 281: Council Resolution of 17 November 2003 on the use by Member States of bans on access to venues of football matches with an international dimension, para 1.

such orders may also be applicable at the international level.[32] It was further provided that details of football banning orders issued domestically should be transmitted to countries staging football matches with an international dimension.[33]

This formally rule-of-law-respectful regulation of football bans has, however, inevitably led to distorted implementation of EU law. As NFIPs have to transmit details of football banning orders issued domestically to countries staging football matches with an international dimension, NFIPs in countries that have introduced AFBOs transmit details of all football bans, be they criminal, civil or administrative, thus creating a legally definable bridge between the control and punishment of deviance.[34] Hence, even if supporters served with an AFBO may not be prevented from leaving their country of origin, they may be deported from the country staging the international event. Moreover, as personal data is stored for several years, the initial punishment can have real consequences well after the period of its formal duration has come to an end. For example, Belgian supporters, who had been served with three-month administrative banning orders in the early 2000s, were turned away at the German border or deported from German territory at the time of the 2006 World Cup.

II.iii Harmonization of Policing

On the adoption of the first handbook dealing with operational matters and international police cooperation in 1999, EU law makers sought to harmonize policing of football crowds. For this purpose, they opted for a twofold approach: framing police action and establishing partnerships between all stakeholders. On the one hand, police strategies, methods and practices of controlling supporters inside and outside stadia, before, during and after the event, were described in detail and specific tasks were being assigned to the police forces of all countries involved in a sporting event. On the other hand, in what is meant as co-policing along the same guidelines across the EU, the 1999 handbook and its subsequent updated versions sought to set up multilevel cooperation networks among (inter)national police forces, and between police forces, stewards and sport authorities. In this respect, liaison officers assumed a pivotal role as they were called to bridge foreign police forces, as well as national and local police coordination centres, if any, in order to cover all operational

32 Ibid., para 3.
33 Ibid., para 5.
34 Tsoukala (n 3) 114.

needs. From 2006 on, harmonization of policing was further sought through the sharing of good policing practice.[35]

III. A COMPREHENSIVE APPROACH (2007 ONWARDS)

As noted above, following the adoption of the Lisbon Treaty EU law makers opted for a comprehensive approach that rejected single police-led policies and instead privileged a multi-facetted management of the issue. The new approach, which is presented as 'preventive, incentive, dissuasive and repressive',[36] consists of a broad array of actions that are seen as part of a 'global long-term endeavour'.[37] Breaking with the past is visible in the definition both of the objectives to be attained and the identity of actors to be involved in relevant policies. Public authorities and sport bodies are now called on not only to tackle violence but also racism and other forms of discrimination, including sexism and homophobia inside and outside stadia.[38] This joint objective was reaffirmed in 2011, when the European Commission makes mention of 'the prevention of and fight against violence and intolerance', and encourages Member States to ensure the implementation of relevant EU law[39] and to 'support activities targeted at fighting against these phenomena'.[40]

As regards the identity of stakeholders, social control agents and sport authorities are invited to undertake many different forms of cooperation with football supporters. It should be noted however that this shift in the perception of the issue aims at strengthening rather than weakening the prior police-led management of football-related violence. In their present configuration, counter-hooliganism policies are still structured around a major proactive/repressive pole and a minor society-driven one, which is essentially seen as auxiliary to the former.

---

35 [2006] OJ C 322/1 (n 26), chap 7.

36 Council of the EU, Conclusions of the High-level Conference (n 11).

37 Ibid.

38 Ibid.

39 [2008] OJ L 328: Council Framework Decision 2008/913/JHA of 28 November 2008 on combating certain forms and expressions of racism and xenophobia by means of criminal law.

40 Communication from the Commission to the European Parliament, the Council, the European Economic and Social Committee and the Committee of the Regions 'Developing the European Dimension in Sport', COM (2011) 12 final, para 2.3. As regards racism, see *Racism, Ethnic Discrimination and Exclusion of Migrants and Minorities in Sport* (EU Fundamental Rights Agency 2010).

III.i Law Enforcement

Acknowledgement of the fact that 'there are no simple or supranational solutions to what is a complex phenomenon', and further acceptance of the 'need for a sophisticated European strategy',[41] do not imply any calling into question of the conceptual and operational grounds of prior police-led policies. Not only are these confirmed but also law enforcers are vested with enhanced powers as regards strategic planning, coordination and harmonization of counter-hooliganism policies.

III.i(a) Intelligence

Council Resolution of 3 June 2010, which updated the aforementioned 2006 handbook,[42] thus confirmed illiberal trends of prior surveillance-based policing in specifying that 'timely and accurate information [should be provided] regarding the movements of risk and non-risk supporters'.[43] Moreover, intelligence is upgraded as EU law makers implicitly admit that the expertise of national law enforcers can no longer guarantee the protection of sport mega-events from serious security threats. Therefore, intelligence agents are called to also consider 'serious and organized crime and terrorism' in collaboration with Europol, if needed.[44]

In fact, the aforementioned provision integrates the new duty of Europol that, as from 1 January 2010, is also assigned with the task of providing intelligence and analytical support to a Member State in connection with a major international event.[45] This regulation finalizes a process that had been at work since the early 2000s. The first time Europol was involved in the security preparations of sporting events goes back to 2004, when they produced threat and risk assessments both for

[41] Draft Council conclusions adopting the Work programme on further measures designed to maximise safety and security in connection with football matches with an international dimension (15615/07, ENFOPOL 198).

[42] [2010] OJ C 165/1.

[43] Ibid., Ch. 1, section 1, III. 2(a).

[44] See further the elaborate plan of action to counter terror attacks at sporting events with an international dimension is proposed in: Council of the EU, Draft Annex to the Handbook for police and security authorities concerning cooperation at major events with an international dimension (16933/1/11, ENFOPOL 402).

[45] [2009] OJ L 121, Council Decision of 6 April 2009 establishing the European Police Office (Europol), art 5.1(e).

the Athens Summer Olympics[46] and the Euro 2004 Football Championship. During the FIFA World Cup 2006, Europol guaranteed the exchange of all information regarding the security of the tournament.[47] At the end of the same year, in a Commission Proposal Europol was assigned with the task 'to provide intelligence and analytical support to a Member State in connection with a major international event with a public order policing impact'.[48]

III.i(b) Football bans

Prior illiberal trends of police-led policies are also confirmed with regard to football bans. While the Council of the EU accepts that Member States have the competence to choose between criminal, administrative and civil bans, it seeks to curb their resistance to introduce AFBOs by recommending them to 'consider mutual recognition of banning orders'.[49] If Member States follow this recommendation, AFBOs will be normalized across the EU in spite of the fact that they are usually imposed with none of the procedural guarantees provided by the criminal justice system. Yet, as the imposition of penalties involving loss of liberty outside the framework of a criminal trial may constitute a breach of the principle of presumption of innocence, the EU-wide implementation of this measure could jeopardize the rule of law. Imposition of AFBOs may further constitute a breach of the principle of proportionality to the extent that, in the absence of any legal assessment of the dangerousness of the behaviour being punished, it is impossible to establish with any certainty that the limitations imposed on individual rights are necessary for the protection of collective interests or that the individual rights being limited are less important than the social values being protected.[50] This uncertainty also calls into question the validity of restricting freedom of movement within the EU, which is only legal if done in response to national security needs and is proportionate to the seriousness of the problem in question.

---

46 M Samatas, *The 'Super-Panopticon' Scandal of the Athens 2004 Olympics and its Legacy* (Pella 2014) 16.

47 A De Moor, 'The "new" principal task for Europol to support Member States in connection with major international events. The blurring of boundaries between law enforcement and public order? (10th Annual Conference of the European Society of Criminology 2010).

48 Proposal for a Council Decision establishing the European Police Office (EUROPOL), COM (2006) 817 final, art 5.1(f).

49 Council of the EU, Conclusions of the High-level Conference (n 11).

50 Tsoukala (n 3) 111ff.

Certainly, the idea that AFBOs challenge certain principles of the rule of law is opposed to relevant national court rulings as national judges have deemed that AFBOs do not constitute a penalty but a preventive security measure.[51] Yet, in practice, supporters who are served with AFBOs have their freedom of movement inside their country of origin or abroad restricted. Given the fact that the European Court of Human Rights (ECtHR) has constantly stipulated that, in order to prevent the disciplinary from encroaching illegally on the criminal justice realm, punitive measures should be defined in law according to their effect,[52] a challenge to the claim that this type of measure is not a penalty could be brought before it. Bringing the case before the ECtHR could further allow us to see whether, and up to what extent, it is still possible to protect civil rights and liberties by evoking offence-grounded procedural guarantees when the social control apparatus has been emancipated from the offence-guilt restrictive legal frame to function in terms of risk and suspicion.

III.i(c) Expertise of law enforcers

At the strategic level, the design of future policies becomes intrinsically associated with the law enforcers' perception and assessment of the issue. Expertise of law enforcers, which had been recognized in 2006 as steady component of counter-hooliganism,[53] is now formally turned into a key element of the decision-making process. In 2007, the Council of the EU affirms that the work of the football experts group provides the appropriate basis for taking forward the work programme and 'for preparing firm proposals for approval by the PCWG[54] and the Justice and Home Affairs Council of Ministers'.[55] The pivotal role played by this group in

---

[51] See, e.g.: Belgian Court of Arbitration, 175/2002, 5 December 2002. This Belgian court ruling is similar to one handed down in the UK on 13 July 2001 by a magistrates' court, which took the view that football banning orders on complaint did not seek to inflict punishment but to protect the public in a preventative way, see *Gough v Chief Constable of Derbyshire* [2001] EWHC Admin 554, endorsed on appeal in *Gough v Chief Constable of Derbyshire* [2002] EWCA Civ 351.

[52] M Delmas-Marty, 'Le paradoxe pénal', in M Delmas-Marty and C Lucas de Leyssac (eds) *Libertés et droits fondamentaux* (Seuil 2000).

[53] [2006] OJ C 322/1: Council Resolution of 4 December 2006 (n 26), chap 7.

[54] Police Cooperation Working Group of the Council of the EU.

[55] Draft Council conclusions adopting the work programme on further measures designed to maximise safety and security in connection with football matches with an international dimension (15615/07, ENFOPOL 198).

designing and implementing counter-hooliganism policies, and coordinating relevant actions, is further confirmed as it is provided that the group will work in cooperation with EU bodies, the Council of Europe Standing Committee on the 1985 European Convention, UEFA and other international football authorities; it will seek to establish working platforms with supporters; it will develop arrangements for training police personnel;[56] and it will advise governments and policing agencies of countries hosting international tournaments.[57]

The increasingly influential position of law enforcers in the planning of counter-hooliganism policies was confirmed in 2013, when the Council of the EU assigned to the EU Law Enforcement Working Party Experts for Major Sports Events the task of seeking financial support to enable the European Think Tank Group of Football Safety and Security Experts to provide, inter alia, expertise and resources according to the 2014–16 work programme.[58] Moreover, law enforcers' expertise is now believed to be sufficiently rich to serve as a model to be also transferred to third countries, especially accession states, EU neighbouring countries, and countries scheduled to host major tournaments. Influencing counter-hooliganism policies of third countries also rests upon delivery of policing training, and advisory visits to these countries to support them in setting up NFIPs and developing relevant legal and regulatory frameworks.

Global-scale export of police expertise that also promotes illiberal security measures is particularly worrisome. Dissemination of a contestable security *dispositif*[59] is liberty-threatening per se because it entails an ever-expanding consensus around its illiberal facets until these are fully normalized. Moreover, when this security *dispositif*, with the added value of its EU-human-rights-respectful origin, is proposed to countries less concerned, if concerned at all, with human rights, it ends up confirming,

---

[56] In 2008, the EU football experts group was called on to contribute to the development of 'an integrated training programme [...] as regards dynamic risk assessment, graduated policing tactics' and other standards included in the handbook on police cooperation: Council of the EU, Conclusions of the High-level Conference 'Towards an EU strategy against Violence in Sport' (5182/08, ENFOPOL 9).

[57] Draft Council conclusions adopting the work programme (n 55).

[58] Council of the EU, Conclusions adopting the 2014–2016 EU work programme on minimizing risks to safety, security and public order in connection with sports events, in particular football matches, with an international dimension, 5–6 December 2013, 16373/13.

[59] In the Foucauldian sense of the term.

if not enhancing, already established trends of undemocratic governance in these countries.

III.ii Active Involvement of the Judiciary

During the former period, repressive policies were mainly relying on law enforcers. From 2008, the field of action of the social control apparatus was extended to include the judiciary. Eurojust and the European Judicial Network are thus called on to become actively involved in the prosecuting of various crimes committed during major sport events.[60] To the extent that decisiveness and effectiveness of dissuasion require it to be swift and visible, it is recommended that a Eurojust representative should be invited to major sport events to guarantee immediate public reaction during the event.[61]

III.iii Society-driven Policies

While affirming their commitment to risk-oriented suspicion-grounded policies, EU law makers seek to build up trust and develop mutual understanding with supporters. Under the assumption that partnership with supporters 'should be seen as part of the solution, not the problem',[62] the Council of the EU thus encourages long-term socio-preventive policies, such as fan coaching, as well as various fan-led initiatives.

III.iii(a) Fan coaching

Introduced in Belgium in 1988, 'fan coaching' is a long-term educational project that seeks to gain the trust of young fans by supporting them with administrative matters, suggesting sporting and cultural activities, obtaining professional advice for them, and so on.[63] Designed and long supported by Belgian academia, in collaboration with sporting bodies and local authorities, fan coaching was welcomed both by fans and law enforcers as it eventually became clear that it contributed to the reduction in football-related violence in the country. At the European level, its capacity to disrupt the generational renewal of violent supporters has

---

60 Council of the EU, Conclusions of the High-level Conference (n 11).

61 Ibid.

62 Ibid.

63 M Comeron, *The Prevention of Violence in Sport* (Council of Europe 2002).

been acknowledged in 1999, when it was promoted for the first time by the Council of Europe.[64]

This option marks a turning point in two respects. Faced with the evidence, that is, the limited impact of proactive and repressive policies on countering football-related violence, EU law makers return to the basics of criminology to complete police-led policies with socio-preventive ones. In so doing, they reconsider the dimension of time when dealing with crime and, departing from the single short-term approach, they admit the importance of long-term work to uproot violence through steady collaboration between football clubs, social workers and supporters.

III.iii(b) Fan-led initiatives

In affirming as a general rule that partnerships between all stakeholders should also include supporter groups, the Council of the EU supports the 'development of a network of fan associations and federations in order to exchange best practice and information about local fan initiatives'.[65] A frame of mutual dialogue between supporters and football clubs should be set up in line with the Supporters' Charter that has been developed by the Council of Europe in 2006, and it is even considered that, in spite of its difficulty, 'dialogue with ultras should also be undertaken'.[66]

Besides, the important role played by supporter 'embassies' in countering violence and disorder at major international events[67] is fully acknowledged as long-standing experience has shown that violent incidents at international tournaments may also be sparked by practical factors, such as faulty infrastructures and lack of information. The development of these embassies is therefore promoted[68] so that they continue to provide travelling fans with structural support, ranging from information and advice to assistance in case of emergency and mediation in conflict situations.

These options clearly upgrade the supporters' role in countering football-related violence. Supporters are being moved from their prior marginal position to a more central one, where they are seen as actors likely to become partners of law enforcers and sport authorities. Most probably, fan-led initiatives will have a positive impact on managing

---

[64] Recommendation 1434 on football hooliganism (Council of Europe 1999).

[65] Council of the EU, Conclusions of the High-level Conference (n 11).

[66] Ibid.

[67] The first Fans' Embassy was set up by the Football Supporters' Association during the 1990 World Cup in Italy.

[68] Council of the EU, Conclusions of the High-level Conference (n 11).

violence inside and outside stadia. This hopeful outcome should not however draw attention away from the fact that supporters are to be embedded in a frame of action that has not managed to maintain law and order without jeopardizing their civil rights and liberties. Turning them into integral parts of law-and-order networks therefore rests upon their consensual acceptance of the frame's rationale that, once legitimized by the very social group it targets, can no longer be contested in its core elements.

IV. CONCLUSION

This overview of the main aspects of EU counter-hooliganism policies brings into light a certain irrationality that lies beneath their rational facade. From the mid-1990s up to 2006, they have been elaborated under the sole influence of law enforcers who, in the absence of any definition of football crowd violence, be they academic or legal, have been turned into key definers and managers of this form of violence. Hence, dangerousness of violent behaviour was being assessed, supporters were being accordingly classified, and security measures were being adopted following proactive risk management guiding principles. Law enforcers thus acquired disproportionate symbolic and effective power for, as Stanley Cohen reminds us, 'the real significance of classification lies in the form, not the content, the enterprise itself and not its end-results. The power to classify is the purest of all deposits of professionalism'.[69]

Quite unsurprisingly, these police-led policies have been of limited efficiency[70] because, by definition, they could not go beyond the stage of engaging an endless struggle against the ever-changing manifestation of the phenomenon. In their attempt to counter football crowd violence without taking into consideration the factors that generate it, while complying with the rising risk-oriented crime control model, EU law makers opted for the implementation of group-focused policing of known troublemakers, potentially threatening and ordinary supporters alike, thereby setting up control mechanisms that were very prejudicial to supporters' civil rights and liberties. In so doing, EU policy makers have

---

[69] S Cohen, *Visions of Social Control*, (Polity 1985) 196.

[70] The European Commission thus admits in 2011 that 'spectator violence and disorder remain a Europe-wide phenomenon'. See Communication from the Commission to the European Parliament, the Council, the European Economic and Social Committee and the Committee of the Regions 'Developing the European Dimension in Sport', COM (2011) 12 final, para 2.3.

been trapped in a vicious circle where institutional violence functioned as substitute for civil violence. The increasing violation of rule of law and supporters' civil rights and liberties came to be seen as the only efficient weapon against violence and disorder inside and outside stadia. Arguably, the ensuing replacement of the legislative power and the judiciary by the executive has been tolerated in the name of a certain professional expertise because, from the late 20th century on, the comforting promise of restoring law and order in an increasingly deregulated political, social and economic environment has turned law enforcers into prime reassuring figures in many different areas, well beyond sporting matters.

The re-founding of EU policies, from 2007 on, marks a turning point in countering football crowd violence due to the introduction of long-term preventive policies and the inclusion of supporters in stakeholder groups. Yet, the adoption of such a comprehensive approach seems obedient to realistic rather than conceptual concerns. Prior policy making had to be reconsidered to address the relative inefficiency of police-led security policies. Its ensuing broadening beyond police-grounded measures did not, however, imply any calling into question of their rationale. Therefore, prior illiberal trends are confirmed, while contestable police expertise is exported at a global scale. Certainly, promotion of partnerships with supporters cannot but have a positive impact on countering violence and disorder. Nonetheless, since long-term preventive policies and fan-led initiatives are embedded in an otherwise solidly established conceptual and operational risk-oriented frame of action, with no genuine involvement of supporters in the decision-making process, it is to be feared that the primary role of these newly introduced actors will consist in remedying the deficiencies of the security *dispositif*, while indirectly legitimizing its illiberal facets.

If we further consider that the security *dispositif* set up to counter football-related violence will probably serve as a model to be applied to other sports disciplines, and that relevant police expertise will also be exported at a global scale, it is plausible to assume that illiberal aspects of policing sports crowds will end up being promoted and eventually normalized both inside and beyond the EU.

8. The autonomy of sport and the EU

Jean-Loup Chappelet

I. INTRODUCTION

Sport's claim for special status within society has led to intense debate between continental and international sports organisations and public authorities such as the European Union (EU). The sports movement's initial focus was to gain recognition for the 'specificity' of sport, a goal it has largely achieved. Thus, in 2009 the EU's core treaty – Treaty on the Functioning of the European Union (TFEU) and specifically article 165 – known as the Treaty of Lisbon, acknowledged 'the specific nature of sport, its structures based on voluntary activity and its social and educational function'. But this was not enough for sports organisations, which were really looking for sport to be given special exemption from EU law. Consequently, international sport began following a new tack to ensure its independence from governmental and intergovernmental authorities, both in Europe and around the world, by advocating the 'autonomy of sport'. These efforts seemed to bear fruit to a certain extent, as documents such as the European Commission's White Paper on Sport in 2007 began to refer to the concept of autonomy without, however, granting exemption from EU law.

This chapter looks at how the autonomy of sport has gradually risen to the top of the agenda in Europe, from the concept's emergence in the decades following the Second World War (section II) to its more recent prominence in the wake of the *Meca-Medina* ruling (section III). It then attempts to provide a more precise definition of a concept whose meaning in declarations by the sports movement and recommendations issued by European intergovernmental organisations is often rather vague (section IV). The final section discusses the viability and limits of the concept within the Rule of Law *(Rechtstaat)*, in Europe and throughout the world, and examines possible arguments for why sport should be granted autonomy (section V).

II. THE EMERGENCE OF THE CONCEPT OF AUTONOMY

The concept of the autonomy of sport can be traced back to the foundations of the modern sports system at the turn of the 20th century. Pierre de Coubertin, for example, alluded to the issue of autonomy in his writings.[1] However, it was not until after the Second World War that the concept began to be used more formally, most notably in the International Olympic Committee's (IOC) Olympic Charter and in recommendations made by European intergovernmental organisations such as the Council of Europe and EU.

The word autonomy first appeared in the Olympic Charter in 1949,[2] when the IOC stipulated that National Olympic Committees (NOCs) 'must be independent and autonomous'. Although this condition was included just two years before the Soviet Union joined the Olympic Movement and appears to have been aimed primarily at countries in the Soviet bloc, it was largely ignored. In fact, all the NOCs in the bloc received or kept IOC recognition despite the strangleholds their governments came to exert over all aspects of life, including sport. Even the Chinese Olympic Committee, based in Beijing, was granted recognition in 1979, opening the way for the People's Republic to take part in the 1984 Los Angeles Olympics (alongside Taiwan, whose NOC was forced to rename itself *Chinese Taipei*). The only time in the 1950s–1960s when the IOC withdrew recognition from an NOC was in 1961, when South Africa lost its Olympic recognition following the introduction of the apartheid policy of racial segregation. At the time these events occurred, the sports movement was still arguing that sport should be kept free of politics and the IOC saw the need to exclude South Africa as a defeat of this belief.

Twenty years later, in 1979, following a recommendation by its Committee of Ministers, the Council of Europe approved the European Sport for All Charter. This charter was later superseded by the European Sports Charter, which states:

---

1 J-L Chappelet, *Autonomy of Sport in Europe* (Council of Europe 2010) 14.
2 Ibid., 89.

> Voluntary sports organisations have the right to establish autonomous decision-making processes within the law. Both governments and sports organisations shall recognise the need for a mutual respect of their decisions.[3]

In 1984, the IOC decided to pre-empt government interference in sporting disputes by creating the Court of Arbitration for Sport (CAS), based in Lausanne and operated under Swiss law. Over the next two decades, all the world's international sport federations (IFs) gradually recognised the CAS in their statutes, the last IF to do so being FIFA (Fédération Internationale de Football Association) in 2002 (in exchange for the drawing up of a closed list of arbitrators specialising in football).

In fact, as early as 1974 the Court of Justice of the EU (CJEU) – then known as the Court of Justice of the European Communities – had begun hearing cases relating to certain sports regulations, thereby threatening the considerable autonomy then enjoyed by the sport movement. In both the *Walrave* (cycling) and *Dona* (football) cases, the court accepted the plaintiffs' arguments that sport was an economic activity and therefore subject to European/Community law.

Nevertheless, it was not until the famous *Bosman* ruling, handed down by the CJEU in 1995, and a number of other football and sport-related rulings (such as the *Kolpak* ruling in 2003), that the sports movement really began to feel that its autonomy was being called into question. Even though the CJEU had made several other rulings in the sport movement's favour (most notably in the *Deliège* and *Lehtonen* cases, both in 2000), the court's rulings were nevertheless seen as threats to sport's autonomy. Consequently, the sports movement decided to lobby Brussels, notably by setting up the Office of European Olympic Committees in 1994 (financed by a few NOCs and then by the European Olympic Committees (EOC), the umbrella organisation for Europe's NOCs), and by affirming the specificity of sport. The issue was considered important enough for the president of the EOC at this time, the Belgian Jacques Rogge, to make obtaining EU recognition for the specificity of sport his 'hobbyhorse'.[4] Rogge also created the European Youth Olympic Days (now known as the European Youth Olympic Festival – EYOF), a competition for young athletes that inspired a new

---

[3] Recommendation No R (92) 13REV of the Committee of Ministers to Member States on the Revised European Sports Charter (Council of Europe 1992) article 3.3.

[4] J Rogge, 'The Olympic Movement and the European Union' (1995) XXV(5) *Olympic Review* 44–5 and J Rogge, 'Recognition of Sport by the European Union' (1997) XXVI (14) *Olympic Review* 15–16.

global event, called the 'Youth Olympic Games', created in 2007 when he was president of the IOC.

The EU reacted favourably to this lobbying and in 2000 it convinced the European Council (of heads of state or government) to issue a declaration on 'the specific characteristics of sport and its social function in Europe, of which account should be taken in implementing common policies'. The 'Nice Declaration', as it became known, went on to state:

> The European Council stresses its support for the independence of sports organisations and their right to organise themselves through appropriate associative structures. It recognises that, with due regard for national and Community legislation and on the basis of a democratic and transparent method of operation, it is the task of sporting organisations to organise and promote their particular sports, particularly as regards the specifically sporting rules applicable and the make-up of national teams, in the way which they think best reflects their objectives.[5]

III. THE REVIVAL OF THE CONCEPT OF THE AUTONOMY OF SPORT

As noted in the preceding section, the Nice Declaration was followed by the adoption of an article (165) of the TFEU recognising the 'specific nature of sport'. Sport had become a centre of interest for the EU.[6] At first, the word 'autonomy' did not appear in any European treaties; its introduction was the result of strenuous lobbying by the IOC, which, in the aftermath of the CJEU's *Meca-Medina* ruling in 2006, hosted two seminars on the autonomy of sport, held in Lausanne in 2006 and 2008. Although the *Meca-Medina* ruling upheld the sanctions the International Swimming Federation and the IOC had imposed on two Romanian swimmers found guilty of doping, the CJEU's judges added: 'If the sporting activity in question falls within the scope of the [TFEU] Treaty, the conditions for engaging in it are then subject to all the obligations which result from the various provisions of the Treaty.'[7] In other words,

---

[5] European Council: Conclusions of the Presidency; Nice, Annex V, 7–10 December, point 7.

[6] B García and S Weatherill, 'Engaging with the EU in order to Minimize its Impact: Sport and the Negotiation of the Treaty of Lisbon' (2012) 19 JEPP 238–56 and R Parrish, 'The Politics of Sports Regulation in the European Union' (2003) 10 *Journal of European Public Policy* 246–62.

[7] Case C-519/04 P *Meca-Medina and Majcen v Commission* [2006] ECR I-6991, para 2.

all sporting rules (including anti-doping rules in the *Meca-Medina* case) were potentially subject to EU laws. UEFA's Legal Director, Gianni Infantino, who would later become FIFA President, reacted very strongly, wondering whether the ruling was a 'step backwards for the European sports model and the specificity of sport'.[8]

A study of the autonomy of European sport commissioned by the Council of Europe's Enlarged Partial Agreement on Sport (EPAS) was presented at the 11th Conference of Ministers responsible for Sport in 2008 and published two years later.[9] This study noted several instances of government intervention in sporting affairs in Europe at the end of the 20th century and put forward a definition of the autonomy of sport (see section IV below).

By the time of its second seminar on the autonomy of sport, in 2008, the IOC had realised that sports organisations could not expect to keep their autonomy unless they were well governed. Consequently, after intense debate, it adopted its Basic Universal Principles for Good Governance of the Olympic and Sport Movement (BUPs). Principle number 7 is entitled 'Harmonious relations with governments while preserving autonomy'. Although the Olympic Charter published in 2011 does not refer directly to the BUPs, it includes a new principle:

> Recognising that sport occurs within the framework of society, sports organisations within the Olympic Movement shall have the rights and obligations of autonomy, which include freely establishing and controlling the rules of sport, determining the structure and governance of their organisations, enjoying the right of elections free from any outside influence and the responsibility for ensuring that principles of good governance be applied.[10]

That same year, a communication issued by the European Commission to the European Parliament and Council noted that good governance in sport is a condition for the autonomy and self-regulation of sports organisations.[11]

---

[8] See e.g., G Infantino [at the time Director of Legal Affairs at UEFA, now President of FIFA], Meca-Medina: A Step Backwards for the European Sports Model and the Specificity of Sport? UEFA paper 02/10/06, at http://www.uefa.com/MultimediaFiles/Download/uefa/KeyTopics/480391_DOWNLOAD.pdf accessed 26 Oct 2017.

[9] Chappelet, (n 1).

[10] *Olympic Charter* (IOC 2016) Fundamental Principle 5.

[11] *Developing the European Dimension in Sport* (European Commission 2011).

Following his election as IOC president in 2013, Thomas Bach reiterated the position he had laid out in his speech to the 2009 Olympic Congress and his election manifesto when he presented his (new) doctrine of 'responsible autonomy' to the United Nations General Assembly:

> Regardless of where in the world we practise sport, the rules are the same. They are recognised worldwide. They are based on a common 'global ethic' of fair play, tolerance and friendship. But to apply this 'universal law' worldwide and spread our values globally, sport has to enjoy responsible autonomy. Politics must respect this sporting autonomy. For only then can sport organisations implement these universal values amidst all the differing laws, customs and traditions. Responsible autonomy does not mean that sport should operate in a law-free environment. It does mean that we respect national laws which are not targeted against sport and its organisations alone, sometimes for chiefly political reasons. In many UN member countries, the fact that sport can hold its international competitions and promote its values only if enjoying autonomy is not always understood or accepted. For this reason, I ask you all to take this message back to your countries. In the mutual interest of both sport and politics, please help to protect and strengthen the autonomy of sport. Only in this way we can create the win-win situation of a fruitful partnership for the benefit of youth and society in general.[12]

That same year, a working group set up by the European Commission in 2011 to prepare the European Union Work Plan for Sport 2011–2014 adopted a set of Recommendations on the Principles for Good Governance of Sport in the EU and presented them to the European Council.[13] These recommendations recognised the risk that 'Sports bodies that do not have in place good governance procedures and practices can expect their autonomy and self-regulatory practices to be curtailed.' As a result of this preparatory work, the EU decided to use the Erasmus+ programme to support projects that would promote these principles and combat cross-border threats to the integrity of sport.

One year after Thomas Bach's speech to the United Nations, the 69th UN General Assembly adopted a resolution entitled 'Sport as a means to promote education, health, development and peace'. Point 8 of the

---

[12] T Bach, 'Statement on the Occasion of the Adoption of the Resolution "Building a peaceful and better world through sport and the Olympic ideal"', 68th Session of the UN General Assembly, New York, 6 November 2013.

[13] Deliverable 2: Principles of Good Governance in Sport, Brussels: EU Work Plan for Sport 2011–2014, Expert Group 'Good Governance', December 2013.

resolution states that the General Assembly '*supports* the independence and autonomy of sport as well as the mission of the International Olympic Committee in leading the Olympic movement'.[14] The IOC was quick to issue a press release proclaiming the resolution a 'historic milestone' for sport.[15] However, in 2015, during deliberations over revisions to UNESCO's 1978 International Charter of Physical Education and Sport, the 38th UNESCO General Conference did not want the revised charter to include the notion of the autonomy of sport.[16] Although preparatory drafts of the charter had included the notion, UNESCO's General Conference felt that 'the term "autonomy of sport" is not yet sufficiently defined and would require further contextualization'.[17]

Despite all the principles of good governance, recommendations and reports published at the beginning of the 21st century, the 2000s were a difficult period for international sport, which was afflicted by a succession of corruption scandals within IFs (e.g., taekwondo, volleyball, judo, boxing, weightlifting, handball and, more recently, football, athletics and shooting) and increasing government interference in the autonomy of national sports organisations (in alphabetical order: in Afghanistan, Egypt, Gambia, Ghana, India, Ireland, Kenya, Kuwait, Mexico, Nigeria, Pakistan, Panama, Poland, Sri Lanka, etc.).

In 2014, the IOC suspended the Indian Olympic Association, thereby preventing Indian athletes taking part in the 2014 Sochi Winter Olympics under their national flag (one Indian athlete took part in the luge competition under the Olympic flag). Similarly, Kuwait's national Olympic committee was suspended in 2015 and was unable to send a team to the 2016 Rio Olympics (which did not prevent a Kuwaiti athlete winning a gold medal as an 'independent' athlete). This suspension led a Kuwaiti governmental body to sue the IOC for US$1 billion in damages, via a legal suit filed in a Lausanne court in 2016.[18] The IOC also criticised

---

[14] Resolution adopted by the General Assembly on 31 October 2014, New York: United Nations, A/RES/69/6, 5.

[15] 'Historic Milestone: United Nations Recognise the Autonomy of Sport' International Olympic Committee Press Release, 3 November 2014.

[16] International Charter of Physical Education, Physical Activity and Sport, Paris (UNESCO 2015).

[17] Final Report of the Intergovernmental Committee for Physical Education and Sport, 29–30 January 2015 (CIGEPS/2015/INF.REV) 8.

[18] N Butler, 'Kuwait Body Lodges $1 billion Lawsuit against IOC' (*Inside the Games*, 9 Nov 2016) http://www.insidethegames.biz/articles/1043517/exclusive-kuwait-body-lodges-1-billion-lawsuit-against-ioc (accessed 26 Oct 2017).

threats to sport's autonomy in a number of other countries, including Hungary, Kenya and Mexico, but without taking further action.

Another threat to sport's independence arose within the IOC itself in the summer of 2016, when the IOC member responsible for autonomy, who was also a member of the IOC's Executive Board and president of both the Olympic Council of Ireland and the European Olympic Committees, was arrested in Brazil during the 2016 Olympic Games and charged with ticket touting (he denies the charges). This event shocked observers and revealed the need to take a fresh look at the arguments justifying sport's autonomy.[19]

In 2015 and 2016 four independent reports published by the World Anti-Doping Agency (WADA) substantiated claims made by whistle-blowers that Russia was running a state-sponsored doping programme. The evidence was convincing enough for the International Association of Athletics Federations (IAAF) to suspend the Russian Athletics Federation, thereby preventing Russian track and field athletes taking part in the 2016 Rio Olympics. Athletes who could prove they had trained outside the Russian anti-doping system would be eligible to compete in Rio, but only one was able to do so.

Although the International Paralympic Committee (IPC) followed the IAAF's lead, when WADA asked the IOC to ban all Russian athletes from the 2016 Olympics because of the non-compliance of Russia's anti-doping agency and laboratory, the IOC refused to do so. Citing the presumption of innocence of individual athletes and invoking rule 40 of the Olympic Charter, the IOC asked the IF for each Olympic sport to decide whether Russian athletes should be allowed to compete (in the end, only two IFs – athletics and weightlifting – imposed total bans on Russian athletes). Some athletes filed cases with the CAS contesting the bans imposed by the IAAF, IPC and some IFs, but without success. Nevertheless, the CAS, like WADA, does restrict the autonomy of sports organisations, as is shown by the number of IF and IOC decisions it has overruled.[20]

In fact, 2016 turned out to be a very eventful year with respect to the autonomy of sport. In June, following a contradictory decision by a

---

[19] N Butler, 'Turmoil of IOC Autonomy Tsar has Struck a Nail in the Coffin of Sport's Crusade for Independence' (*Inside the Games*, 29 Aug 2016) http://www.insidethegames.biz/articles/1041079/nick-butler-turmoil-of-ioc-autonomy-tsar-has-struck-a-nail-into-the-coffin-of-sports-crusade-for-independence (accessed 26 Oct 2017).

[20] J Forster, 'Global Sport Organisations' in I O'Boyle and T Bradbury (eds) *Sport Governance: International Case Studies* (Routledge 2013) 260–73.

Bavarian court, Germany's Federal Court of Justice (the country's supreme court) definitively rejected German speed skater Claudia Pechstein's appeal against a ruling by the CAS upholding the sanction she had been given for blood doping.[21] The Federal Court of Justice's decision also confirmed the CAS's independence or autonomy from sports organisations such as the International Skating Union (ISU) and the IOC. In addition, it found that the clause obliging athletes who wish to take part in competitions held under rules set by the ISU (or, by extrapolation, any IF) to take their case in last resort to the CAS is not an abuse of the ISU's dominant position (which would be against German and European competition law).

One of the main arguments underpinning the judges' ruling was that athletes have the opportunity to challenge the CAS's choice of arbitrators and/or to appeal to Switzerland's Federal Supreme Court (which Pechstein did, unsuccessfully). Because Germany has ratified the European Convention on Human Rights (ECHR), Pechstein has been able to file an appeal with the European Court of Human Rights (ECtHR), but the ECtHR had not yet published its decision by January 2017. On the other hand, in September 2016 the European Commission issued a 'statement of objections' informing the ISU that 'the ISU rules under which athletes face severe penalties for participation in unauthorised speed skating events [such as those organised by the Ice Derby company] are in breach of EU antitrust rules'.[22] In December 2017, the European Commission confirmed that the ISU must change these rules within 90 days.

Also in June 2016, the European Commission published a report on the specificity of sport, which reviews recent decisions made by the EU in this area, most notably with respect to the economic dimension of sport and the organisation of sport in Europe.[23] Twenty years after the CJEU's *Bosman* ruling, which had profound repercussions for European sport, this report clarifies current European jurisprudence in areas such as

---

[21] P Bert, "German Federal Supreme Court on Pechstein: Update, Peter Bert's Blog about Litigation, Arbitration and Mediation in Germany – Art Law, Case Law, News etc." (*Peter Bert's blog*, 4 October 2016) www.disputeresolutiongermany.com/2016/10/german-federal-supreme-court-on-pechstein-update (accessed 26 Oct 2017).

[22] 'Antitrust: Commission sends Statement of Objections to International Skating Union on its Eligibility Rules' European Commission Press Release, 27 September 2016 (IP/16/3201).

[23] *Mapping and Analysis of the Specificity of Sport* (European Commission DG Education & Culture 2016), available at http://ec.europa.eu/assets/eac/sport/library/studies/mapping-analysis-specificity-sport_en.pdf (accessed 26 Oct 2017).

sports subsidies, taxation in sport, the media, the protection of sporting rights, agents, player transfers and issues pertaining to nationality. All these areas are subject to numerous sporting rules adopted in an autonomous fashion by sports organisations.

IV. TOWARDS A DEFINITION OF THE CONCEPT OF AUTONOMY

Surprisingly, none of the documents produced by sports organisations or intergovernmental bodies such as the EU and Council of Europe between the 1970s and early 2010s attempted to define either the concept of autonomy or related notions such as the independence and self-regulation of sports organisations.

In 2008 an ad hoc study conducted by Chappelet for the Council of Europe put forward the following definition:

> The autonomy of sport is, within the framework of national, European and international law, the possibility for non-governmental, non-profit-making sports organisations to:
>
> 1. establish, amend and interpret rules appropriate to their sport freely, without undue political or economic influence;
> 2. choose their leaders democratically, without interference by states or third parties;
> 3. obtain adequate funds from public or other sources, without disproportionate obligations;
> 4. use these funds to achieve objectives and carry on activities chosen without severe external constraints;
> 5. draw up, in consultation with the public authorities, legitimate standards proportionate to the fulfilment of these objectives.[24]

This definition limits the autonomy of non-governmental, non-profit sports organisations to the following rights: to set their own rules (especially statutory rules, the rules of the game and the rules governing competitions); to amend and interpret these rules, to freely select their administrators and to obtain the funds needed to carry out their activities from public bodies, sponsors or broadcasters without having to accept undue constraints.

---

[24] Chappelet, (n 1) 49.

These rights are exerted within the framework of international, European or national law, with, in a modern state, the Rule of Law being considered an environment above any legal or juridical person. In other words, 'sporting rules' must respect fundamental legal principles (to be heard, presumption of innocence, etc.), be proportionate and be justified with respect to their objectives. They may not go against common law by, for example, encouraging breaches of the peace or, in the EU and associated countries, restricting the free movement of people, goods or services (a fundamental element of European law, alongside the law on fair competition).

In fact, this definition is no more than a detailed description of a right outlined in article 20 of the 1948 Universal Declaration of Human Rights, which recognises the right to peaceful assembly and association without compulsion. All modern countries have specific laws guaranteeing the right of peaceful association (e.g., articles 60–79 of the Swiss Civil Code). The fifth Fundamental Principle of the current Olympic Charter, first published in 2011 more or less reprises Chappelet's definition, although it does not include point 4 relating to funding or the possible need to take into account non-excessive demands by the public authorities or other outside stakeholders (see section III).

Chappelet deliberately left this final part of his definition vague, while recognising its necessity in a context of exchanges between sports organisations and commercial (sponsors/broadcasters) and public (subsidies) partners. The formulation chosen was designed to establish the idea of funding linked to the provision of specific services, which is increasingly common in public management. However, the Olympic Charter's fifth Fundamental Principle suggests that, rather than being absolute, this right to autonomy is contingent on 'ensuring that principles of good governance be applied'.

For the IOC, these principles of good governance are set down in the BUPs, which are now included in the IOC's code of ethics (see section III). Applying the BUPs is seen as justifying responsible autonomy. By way of contrast, Geeraert *et al* has used the term 'pragmatic autonomy'[25] and defined four dimensions of autonomy: political, legal, financial and

[25] A Geeraert, M Mrkonjic and J-L Chappelet, 'A Rationalist Perspective on the Autonomy of International Sport Governing Bodies: Towards a Pragmatic Autonomy in the Steering of Sports' (2015) 7(4) *International Journal of Sport Policy and Politics* 473–88.

pyramidal; Chappelet has proposed the term 'negotiated autonomy'[26] whereas Weatherill suggests 'conditional autonomy'.[27]

As noted above, many more-or-less similar lists of governance principles have been drawn up, but there are few lists of indicators that can be used to determine whether or not these principles are being followed.[28] A list of such indicators for IFs was produced by the Association of Summer Olympic International Federations (ASOIF) in 2016 (ASOIF 2016) and endorsed by the IOC and by the 14th Council of Europe Conference of Ministers Responsible for Sport, held in Budapest in November 2016. Australia, the UK and Flanders (Belgium) had already adopted similar lists for their national governing bodies, whose government funding is now linked to compliance with the criteria contained in these lists. However, some sports leaders are claiming that such indicators limit the autonomy of sports organisations.

Chappelet completed his descriptive definition of the domains of autonomy by drawing up a classification of types of autonomy.[29] This classification has three main categories according to whether rules apply to: a) the sports organisation's statutes; b) the rules of the game; or c) the rules of sports competitions controlled by the organisation. Sports organisations have a high degree of autonomy over their statutes (a), which are limited only by the laws governing the legal form (association or other) of sports organisations in the country in which the organisation is based. Switzerland, home to numerous international sports bodies, is known to have more accommodating legislation in this area than many other countries. For example, in Switzerland it is possible to become a legal person, such as an association, without registering as a non-profit association, unlike in France, where, under the Associations Act of 1901, an association must register (at the local prefecture) in order to be considered a legal person.

Autonomy with respect to the rules of the game (b) is also almost total, as sports organisations are free to decide on and apply, within their pyramidal structures, the rules governing the field of play, as long as these rules do not encourage breaches of the peace. For example, boxing would not be allowed to adopt a rule requiring fights to be carried out to

---

26 Chappelet, (n 1).

27 S Weatherill, 'On Overlapping Legal Orders: What is the "purely sporting" rule?' in B Bogusz, A Cygan and E Szyszczak (eds) *The Regulation of Sport in the European Union* (Edward Elgar Publishing 2007) 48–73.

28 J-L Chappelet, *Beyond Governance* (2017) (20) Sport in Society, *forthcoming*.

29 Chappelet, (n 1).

the death (as in the time of the gladiators). On the other hand, commercial partners (sponsors and, especially, broadcasters) can have considerable influence over the rules of the game through their desire to ensure the sporting spectacle is as attractive as possible for the audience. Hence, the decision by the boxing's IF to ban protective headgear, presented as a measure to reduce serious injuries, may have been influenced by the wish to allow television viewers to see the boxers' faces more clearly.

The amount of autonomy a sports organisation has when setting the rules for sports competitions (c) depends on the nature of the event. The larger an event's economic dimension, the greater the constraints imposed by common law, especially in Europe. For example, FIFA had to change its rules on player transfers following the *Bosman* ruling. On the other hand, other rules, for example, eligibility criteria for national team selection or restrictions on transfer periods, have been found to be compatible with European law. In addition, as for rules of the game, competition rules, such as the format and timing of competitions, have been adapted to meet the needs of broadcasters and, occasionally, of sponsors. Hence, the finals of the swimming events at the 2008 Beijing Olympics and 2016 Rio Olympics were held early in the morning (Beijing) or late in the evening (Rio) in order to fit in with the prime time scheduling demands of American television networks.

V. THE VIABILITY OF THE CONCEPT OF AUTONOMY

In his seminal work on the history of moral philosophy, Schneewind showed how Kant and other 17th- and 18th-century philosophers invented the concept of autonomy and justified it with respect to the power of the state and the Church.[30]

More recently, the European Charter for Sport, adopted in 1979 as a recommendation by the Council of Europe, supported the principle of autonomy for volunteer-based sports organisations. In 2000 the CJEU's *Deliège* ruling maintained that national sport federations 'normally have the necessary knowledge and experience' to run their affairs autonomously.[31] The European Commission's 2007 White Paper on Sport noted that sports organisations were capable of addressing most challenges

---

30 J B Schneewind, *The Invention of Autonomy* (CUP 1998).

31 Cases C-51/96 and C-191/97 *Deliège v Ligue de Judo* [2000] ECR I-2549.

'through self-regulation respectful of good governance principles' thereby recognising the principle of autonomy, as long as the organisation is governed correctly.[32]

Nevertheless, ten years after the White Paper and in the light of the numerous examples of 'bad governance' exposed in the media, the case for autonomy is no longer self-evident. In fact, even the IOC now advocates 'responsible autonomy', that is, autonomy only for sports organisations that are well governed. With this in mind, in 2014 the IOC set up an Ethics and Compliance Office within its administration in order to ensure members of the Olympic Movement, especially the IFs and NOCs, apply the BUPs of good governance.

Evidently, under the Rule of Law, people and organisations cannot have absolute freedom of action; national and international laws and the legal system that interprets these laws will always limit their autonomy. As sport often involves competitions between athletes from different countries, IFs and the IOC have gradually drawn up rules to be applied around the globe. In 1984 the IOC created the CAS, a specialist tribunal for settling disputes arising from the application of these rules and whose judgments have led to the formation of what is known as the *lex sportiva*.[33] All IFs now recognise the CAS as sport's supreme arbitrational body.

Nevertheless, difficulties sometimes arise from differences between the *lex sportiva* and national or European laws, as occurred (and as described above) in the *Bosman*, *Meca-Medina* and *Pechstein* cases. This creates legal uncertainty for everyone and encourages litigation based on different interpretations of laws and regulations. Given the supremacy of national and European courts of justice in resolving litigation, one way in which sports organisations could maintain a degree of (responsible) autonomy would be to ensure their governance and their dispute-resolution mechanisms, including the CAS, respect universal principles of justice and human rights.

It is, in fact, in the public authorities' interest for the non-profit sports movement to remain autonomous, rather than being run by the state or by private enterprise, as it performs several useful tasks in areas such as youth education, public health and social integration. What is more, these tasks are largely self-financed, thanks to volunteers and sport's sponsorship and broadcasting revenues. If they were not carried out by the sports

---

32 White Paper on Sport, COM (2007) 391.

33 F Latty, *La Lex Sportiva, Recherche sur le Droit Transnational* (Martinus Nijhoff Publishers 2007).

movement, they would fall to either the public sector or the commercial sector. The public sector would probably be unable to entirely accomplish these tasks due to the state having other priorities and the commercial sector would not be able to undertake them without access to specific revenues, unless it created a system of professional leagues, as in the frequently criticised American model (in which professional leagues are fed by 'amateur' leagues at the high school and university levels).

From this point of view, discussions on whether non-profit sports organisations (most of which are associations) should change their statuses to become limited companies or similar for-profit bodies are misguided. Potentially lucrative sports clubs, such as fitness clubs or golf clubs, are already for-profit legal entities. Most IFs are indeed associations, but their missions are to regulate their sport and to reinvest their revenues in 'grassroots' sport (so their objectives are not purely economic, otherwise they would lose their non-profit status). Furthermore, becoming a limited company, the status adopted by many of Europe's professional sports clubs, does not guarantee good governance, as is shown by the number of such clubs that have gone bankrupt.

On the other hand, it would be interesting to examine the possibility of sports organisations becoming cooperatives, a legal form that exists in many jurisdictions, and thereby forming part of the currently very powerful social and solidarity economy movement.[34] As members of the cooperative, athletes within a sport and/or a country would have a much greater say in the decision-making process than they do via the system of general assemblies currently favoured by national and international sport federations, which are generally bodies over which athletes have little influence.

VI. CONCLUSION

Although the concept of the autonomy of sport, which sports organisations in Europe promoted extensively during the second half of the 20th century, dates back to the birth of modern sport in the 19th century, this autonomy now needs to be justified. Sports organisations can no longer consider autonomy to be a self-evident right, even if they implement appropriate systems of governance. Any justification for

---

[34] J S Marques, *Social and Solidarity Economy, Between Emancipation and Reproduction* (UNIRSD 2013).

autonomy must include a more precise definition of its scope and be based on detailed reflections on the independence, legal form and regulation of sports organisations.

PART III

ECONOMIC

9. EU action on sports statistics

Wladimir Andreff

I. INTRODUCTION

Coherent economic statistics about sports emerged in the late 1970s. Since 2006, producing such statistics in the form of EU and domestic sport satellite accounts is on the European Commission's agenda. Though it was not an easy methodological task, a first harvest of results is now at hand. The chapter ends up listing the merits of, and hindrances to, elaborating on sports economic statistics alongside the chosen methodology.

II. STATISTICAL ACCOUNTING OF THE SPORTS ECONOMY; HISTORICAL AND METHODOLOGICAL BACKGROUND

The very concept of satellite accounts can be attributed to the French statistician André Vanoli.[1] It is not surprising therefore that the first attempt at building up a national account of the sports economy had been undertaken for the French sports economy in 1971.[2] This pioneering statistical work used the technique of a sport satellite account (SSA) which is an extension of the UN System of National Accounts (SNA) which consists in covering a specific area (health, education, etc.) in the economy with some adapted concepts and sub-nomenclatures that cannot be found as such in the standard UN SNA framework.

A SSA encompasses – when standard nomenclature data are missing – all available information about sport-related costs, expenditures, revenues, factors of production, and who uses sports goods and services. All

[1] A Vanoli, 'Le système actuel de comptabilité nationale et la planification' (1969) 15(2) *Review of Income and Wealth* 171–84.

[2] C Malenfant-Dauriac, *L'économie du sport en France. Un compte satellite du sport* (Cujas 1977).

data gathered in a SSA are classified within the national accounting nomenclature, although some non-monetary magnitudes may be registered (when possible translated into monetary units). This is the case where the market price for an item is unknown and when there is no price that can be put on a non-tradable good or factor of production (e.g., voluntary work in sport).

In Malenfant-Dauriac's work, the sports economy's gross value added (GVA) was found to be 0.5 per cent of French GDP, and the consumption of sport-related goods and services was about 0.8 per cent of overall household consumption. The non-monetary section of the SSA was very simplified. For instance, it estimated that the number of voluntary workers involved in sports was nearly 600,000 people. If one were to translate such information into monetary units, some awkward assumptions should be made about the monetary value of (one hour of) voluntary work. However, the major SSA shortcoming appeared to be that setting it up is either time consuming (five years of research) or a financially expensive undertaking, or both.

Another SSA was published in Germany for 1990,[3] where the definition of sport was wider since it encompassed activities such as walking, bathing, keep fit and bowling, and because it considered active and passive (from time to time) as well as self-organised sporting practice. Sport GVA represented 1.4 per cent of GDP in reunified Germany and provided 700,000 jobs (2 per cent of total employment).

Other accounting and statistical techniques were mobilised to assess the economic significance of the sports industry.[4] The Committee for the Development of Sport of the Council of Europe had launched an initiative in 1984 that led to the Jones' report (1989) and thereafter the Andreff et al report (1994).[5] In both reports data were collected and presented in a similar statistical framework that is the standard UN SNA. The second report published accounts relying on ex post macroeconomic accounting balance such as:

---

[3] W Weber, C Schnieder, N Kortlüke and B Horak, *Die wirtschaftliche Bedeutung des Sports* (Hofmann, 1995).

[4] W Andreff, 'Sports Accounting' in W Andreff, S Szymanski (eds), *Handbook on the Economics of Sport*, (Edward Elgar 2006) 11–21.

[5] H Jones, *The Economic Impact and Importance of Sport: A European Study* (Council of Europe, 1989) and W Andreff, J-F Bourg, B Halba and J-F Nys, *The Economic Impact of Sport in Europe: Financing and Economic Impact, Background document, 14th Informal Meeting of European Sports Ministers* (Council of Europe 1994).

$$Y = C + G + I + \Delta S + X - M \tag{9.1}$$

In the above, Y stands for GDP; C for private consumption; G for public consumption; I for gross fixed capital formation; ΔS for stock variation; X for exports; and M for imports, applied to the sports economy. The accounting delineation of the sports economy requires both a definition of sport and an aggregation of all those people and activities participating in it. The Jones and Andreff reports retained the Rodgers (1977) definition,[6] which considered the following as sporting activities: game sports; displacement or fitness sports; survival sports and national (traditional) sports. This definition is not without its limitations since it excludes some popular sports such as darts in England or the so-called 'mind' sports (chess, bridge).

In the second report, the focus was more on how sport expenditures are financed with a calculation of the total Sport Domestic Expenditure (SDE), once it had been assumed that any monetary unit flowing into the sport sector is spent for some sporting purpose (practice, events, federations, and so on) by the government (all ministries spending money for sports), municipalities and other local authorities, enterprises and households. The basic idea was not only to collect existing data, but also to ask each sampled country to 'produce' missing data and integrate them into the standard SNA.

This methodology soon reached its own limits since most sampled countries were not able to provide all requested data. The SDE ratio to GDP in 1990 ranged from 0.6–1.8 per cent in all sampled countries except Switzerland (3.5 per cent). Some EU countries have kept a same methodology for years and France, for instance, has been able to publish SDE economic accounts every year from 1990 until now (Table 9.1).[7]

---

6 B Rodgers, *Rationalising Sports Policies: Sports in its Social Context. International Comparisons* (Council of Europe 1977).

7 W Andreff, 'Los intentos europeos y franceses de elaborar una contabilidad nacional de la economia del deporte (European and French attempts to set up a national accounting of the sports economy)', in J M Otero (ed.) *Incidencia Economica del Deporte* (Instituto Andaluz de Deporte 2001) 23–53.

Table 9.1 *Economic accounting of the sport domestic expenditure and employment, France 2000–12 (current € billion and per cent, employment in thousands)*

Sports economy assessed by:	**2000**	**2006**	**2007**	**2008**	**2009**	**2010**	**2011**	**2012**
Sport Domestic Expen. (SDE)	24.6	31.9	33.1	33.8	33.7	34.3	36.0	36.5
SDE annual rate of growth	5.6%	4.8%	4.0%	2.6%	0,0%	1.7%	5.0%	1.4%
of which:								
Enterprise Sport Expenditure	1.7	3.2	3.2	3.3	3.3	3.3	3.3	3.3
Public Sport Expenditure ***	10.3	13.7	14.4	14.9	15.1	15.1	16.2	16.8
Household Sport Expen (HSE)	12.5	15.0	15.5	15.7	15.3	16.0	16.5	16.3
HSE annual rate of growth	4.2%	3.4%	3.3%	1.3%	–2.5%	4.6%	3.1%	–1.2%
SDE / GDP	1.7%	1.7%	1.7%	1.7%	1.7%	1.7%	1.8%	1.7%
Empl in sporting activities **	*93*	*96*	*101*	*103*	*106*	*108*	*108*	*110*
Upstream activities to sport	*100* *	*72*	*73*	*77*	*74*	*74*	*73*	*74*
Total employment in the sports econ.	*n.s.*	*168*	*174*	*180*	*180*	*182*	*181*	*184*

Notes: *** Government and local authorities SDE.
** French nomenclature NAF 92.6A corresponding to the EU's NACE 92.6.
* Rough estimate at the moment.[8]

Source: *Stat Info*, n° 15-01, février 2015 (and previous issues), Statistical mission at the French Ministry of Sports.

A last technical option is to resort to an input–output table (IOT) that gives a picture of the domestic economy as linking different industries into an overall interdependent system. A vertical row of IOT, say for industry j, describes:

[8] Stat Info, n° 15-01, février 2015 and previous issues (French Ministry of Sports).

$$Xj = \Sigma i\ Xij + Aj + Wj + Tj + Pj \qquad (9.2)$$

where Xj stands for output of industry j, Σi Xij for total intermediary consumption of products from upstream industries i by industry j, Aj for consumption of fixed capital (depreciation), Wj for total wage paid, Tj for taxes, and Pj for producers' profit in industry j, while the value added of industry j is Vj = Wj + Tj + Pj. A horizontal row of IOT describes how the value of an industry i is distributed across the intermediary consumption Xji of all its downstream industries in the economy and final demand:

$$Xi = \Sigma j\ Xji + Ci + Gi + GCFCi + \Delta Si + Ei \qquad (9.3)$$

where Ci stands for private final consumption of product i, Gi for its public consumption, GCFCi for gross fixed capital formation in product i, ΔSi its stock variation, and Ei exports of i, while the final demand of product i is Yi = Ci + Gi + GCFCi + ΔSi + Ei. The IOT not only depicts the overall ex post macroeconomic accounting balance including the equality between total value added and total final demand for all industries – (2) = (3) for a same industry j –, but also a consistent interdependence across all industries.

A simulation model SPORT of the German sports economy was based on IOT technique applied to 1993.[9] A sub-IOT encompassing the sports economy was integrated into the overall IOT set up by the *Statistiches Bundesamt* for the whole German economy. This specific sub-matrix was made up of seven rows, in addition to the 58 rows of overall German IOT: (i) bicycles; (ii) sports equipment; (iii) sports footwear; (iv) sportswear; (v) commercial sports services; (vi) sports services supplied by clubs and associations; and (vii) sports services supplied by public and local authorities (the federal government, *Länder*, municipalities).

The aggregated value added calculated for these seven sports industries in 1998 weighed 1.4 per cent of GDP. The SPORT econometric simulation model relies on the relationships between these seven specific sports industries and the 58 other industries in overall IOT. It was used to calculate that in 1998 2.4 per cent of all those employed in Germany worked in the seven sports industries. Another simulation showed that a reorientation of total household demand for sporting activities from the clubs to commercial sport would trigger, as of 2010, a slight increase in

[9] B Meyer, G. Ahlert and C Schnieder, *Die ökonomischen Perspektiven des Sports: Eine empirische Analyse für die Bundesrepublik Deutschland* (Bundesinstitut für Sportwissenschaft 2000).

GDP due to the substitution of high value added and profitable commercial organisations to lower value added and less efficient clubs relying on voluntary work.[10] Efficient commercial organisations would reduce intermediary consumption, compared to the clubs, thus the demand for inputs would fall and 15,600 jobs would be lost between 2000 and 2010 in the whole German economy. The main problem with the SPORT model is to accurately revise the relationships (the so-called 'Leontief coefficients') between the 65 industries, in so far as inter-industrial interdependencies are changing over time in the mid- and long run.

In EU context, Sport Ministers have regularly asked for more solid data to underpin evidence-based policy making in sport given the absence of comparable and sound information on the economic importance of sport and the macroeconomic potential of the sports industry across Member States (MS). Eventually in 2006, they set up an EU Working Group 'Sport & Economics' (WG), chaired by the European Commission's Sport Unit which held its kick-off meeting in September. In the wake of the European Commission's 2007 White Paper on Sport,[11] the WG started working on a common definition of sport and a statistical method for assessing the sport sector's economic importance.

III. THE METHODOLOGY OF EU SPORT SATELLITE ACCOUNTS

The WG adopted the technique of building up SSAs taking IOT as its foundations and supply and use table (SUT) from which IOT can be derived by a Leontief-transformation.[12] A SSA filters the national accounts of a country for sport-relevant activities to extract all sport-related value added and compile the corresponding data in a specific account, distinct from the remaining original national accounts. A statistical definition was required for the WG to do the job. This is the so-called Vilnius definition of sport[13] adopted at a WG meeting in

[10] G Ahlert, 'Reasons for Modelling Sports in a Complex Economic Model: Two Examples' (2000) 7(1) *European Journal of Sport Management* 31–55.

[11] White Paper on Sport, COM (2007) 391 final.

[12] Sport Satellite Account for the UK, Sport Industry Research Centre, *Sheffield Hallam University* (SIRC 2010); C Gratton and T Kokolakakis, 'Sport Satellite Accounts: The European Project', EU Conference on Sport Statistics, Brussels, 23 March 2011.

[13] SpEA, *The Vilnius Definition* (SportsEconAustria 2007).

October 2007 which in fact replicated the 'Austrian Approach' to define sports as described by Dimitrov and others in 2006.[14]

Referring to the EU's statistical nomenclature NACE (*Nomenclature statistique des Activités économiques dans la Communauté européenne*), the strictest statistical definition of sport is comprised of NACE 92.6 Rev 1.1 ('sporting activities') that is the only part of the sport sector which has its own NACE category. NACE 92.6 Rev 1.1 is a single row in overall IOT of any EU MS. However, NACE categories are still too broad for constructing a SSA, because NACE refers to companies or production units. A better targeted measure, instead of production units, is a classification of products called CPA, Classification of Products by Activity,[15] to identify sport-related goods and services; it directly relates to NACE, the first four digits are identical in both nomenclatures.

Then a narrow definition of sport includes all upstream activities which are inputs to sport, i.e., all goods and services which are required for doing sport in addition to the strict statistical (NACE) definition. Technically, the narrow definition = NACE 92.6 + 222 additional CPA categories. A broad definition of sport adds to the narrow one all downstream activities that require sport as input, i.e., goods and services conditioned by sport to be produced and offered. Technically, the broad definition = narrow definition + 176 CPA categories. Obviously IOT underlies this narrow/broad definition of sport since it encompasses a series of inter-relationships between sport and sport's upstream and downstream activities.

According to statistical definition, sport is located in the centre of the entire sport-related value-added chain. Upstream-related industries are: production of sport equipment, construction of sporting infrastructure, education, retail and wholesale trade, advertising, and financial services; all necessary to do sports. Downstream-related industries are: TV and other media, tourism, sport food, the health system, lotteries and betting, sport-related R&D; factors that require sport in order to use it as input. Performing sport can be an activity in the statistical definition and requires input from upstream sectors according to the narrow definition. Such activity or its outcome may serve as input in other sectors whose output is final consumption of sport.

---

14 D Dimitrov, C Helmenstein, A Kleissner, B Moser and J Schindler, *Macroeconomic Effects of Sports in Europe* (SportsEconAustria 2006).

15 See generally http://ec.europa.eu/eurostat/statistics-explained/index.php/Glossary:Statistical_classification_of_products_by_activity_(CPA) (accessed 26 Oct 2017).

From the standpoint of final consumption, typical upstream goods and services are sport shoes and clothes, sport weapons, racing horses, sport cars, bikes and motorbikes, sailing equipment, school education, fitness centres, dancing schools, watches and clocks. Typical downstream goods and services conditional on doing sport are dietary supplements, health services, veterinarian, hotels and restaurants (sport tourism), TV broadcasts and sport bets.

Initially, the methodology was very ambitious: with a comprehensive approach, 402 CPA categories of products were identified as relevant to sport.[16] The price to pay for such ambition would have been a heavy task of collecting (often non-existing) data to fill in a 402 × 402 rows matrix (161,604 squares of a sport-related IOT). Of course, this never happened and will never happen in any MS. The WG established that a number of goods were not listed, despite being explicitly and directly in demand within the context of sporting activities, namely all those connected with investments in sports infrastructure:

> This is an area in which the Vilnius definition of sport is "blind" as it does not include any products relevant to construction beyond the core activity of construction work. Cleaning and care products of the chemical industry intended for care of sport clothing and equipment are not part of the list of products.[17]

The German SSA has attempted to tackle the issue by enlarging the Vilnius list and taking on board data about construction and renovation of sports facilities, but then the trick is in terms of comparison with SSAs built up in other MS.

For many CPA subcategories, the challenge was to find the share of their sport-related content. This sport-related part was obtained as a percentage of the market through a rather tricky process, as exhibited in SIRC,[18] where some element of enquiries, telephone interviews and guesstimates could not entirely be skipped from overlapping with sharply robust estimations. The difficulty is partly due to various industrial and trade classifications that do not provide any information about the use or destination of goods and services when the nomenclature is based on

---

16 SpEA, *The Vilnius Definition* (SportsEconAustria 2007).

17 G Ahlert, 'The German Sport Satellite Accounts (SSA)', *Gesellschaft für Wirtschaftliche Strukturforschung mbH*, Osnabrück, Discussion Paper 2013/4, July 2013, 5.

18 Sport Satellite Account for the UK (n 12).

supply-side criteria – raw materials used as input, technical production process, etc.[19]

The sixth WG meeting attempted to clarify the issue relying on expert work from the Austrian SSA which had shown a variation in the shares of the value of sport in reaction to a change in the definition of any NACE subcategories. This is exactly what happened indeed with the revision of NACE 1.1 (the old NACE) that resulted in the new NACE Rev 2 to be implemented as of 2010 ('Vilnius 2'). Consequently, those SSAs published for any year before 2010 had to be merely considered as 'training by doing' exercises or first-hand SSA estimates.

Let us now exemplify the outcome of few aforementioned methodological difficulties. The SSA for the UK has been computed making use of a 123 industry/product classification coming from UK IOT and SUT made consistent with NACE through a table of correspondence. The inconvenience of IOTs/SUTs is that they do not provide detailed data (only 123 items instead of the expected 402 or more). Since the construction of a SSA is primarily based on secondary data, it is impossible to present indices of statistical bias.[20]

In the SSA for Poland data were collected for 58 types of activities and 465 product groups; from the latter, 43 product groups were significantly related to sport.[21] The SSA for Germany used the aforementioned 65 × 65 German IOT and domestic final demand in sport-relevant goods in 9-digit numerical code to show the production of sport-related goods; these very detailed sport-related results were classified in an overall matrix with 2,643 lines. Eventually, the publication of the German SSA showed up aggregated in ten products and 11 industries to facilitate understanding the logic of SSA and the interpretation of its results.

The best finalised and most precisely explicit implementation of SSA methodology is the Dutch one so that, since then, it is considered the methodological Manual of EU SSAs.[22] All SSAs published earlier or later should be checked in detail through the lens of this Manual and

---

[19] M and W Andreff, 'Global Trade in Sports Goods: International Specialisation of Major Trading Countries' (2009) 9(3) *European Sport Management Quarterly* 259–94.

[20] Sport Satellite Account for the UK (n 12).

[21] ZB Liberda, L Tomaszewicz and I Swieczewska, 'Sport Satellite Account for Poland: Direct and Indirect Economic Effects of Sport', EU Conference on Sport Statistics, Brussels, 23 March 2011.

[22] *Methodological Manual for a Sport Satellite Account*, Statistics Netherlands & Hogeschool van Arnhem en Nijmegen (HAN University of Applied Sciences 2012).

recomputed accordingly. Furthermore, back-office work for preparing SSAs has been achieved by SportEconAustria, SIRC at Sheffield Hallam University, Statistical Service of the Republic of Cyprus, University of Warsaw, Statistics Netherlands and Hogeschool van Arnhem en Nijmegen at HAN University of Applied Sciences, *Gesellschaft für Wirtschaftliche Strukturforschung mbH Osnabrück*, Department of Physical Education and Sports under the Government of the Republic of Lithuania and Statistics Lithuania, and *Instituto Nacional de Estatistica* Portugal.

Two independent Czech researchers have presented SSA results but without details about computation making sure that the WG methodology has been actually implemented and how.[23] Eurostat is not actively involved in the construction of national SSAs so far while it publishes sport statistics covering sport-related employment – in tune with the Vilnius definition – at EU28 level, international trade in sporting goods of EU28, data on sport participation and private expenditures on sporting goods and services in MS.[24]

The WG was replaced on October 2011 by an Expert Group on 'Sports Statistics' (XG STAT) under the EU Work Plan for Sport for 2011–2014 that recommended promoting data collection to measure the economic benefits of the EU sport sector and evaluate the results. The XG STAT continued the development of SSAs and launched a study on the contribution of sport to economic growth and employment.[25] Then, an Expert Group on the Economic Dimension of Sport (XG ECO) was created by the Council in May 2014 with a wider scope covering three topics: SSAs, legacy of major sport events, investment in sport and EU funding. The XG ECO started up with a first meeting in September 2014.

IV. THE OUTCOME: PUBLISHED EU SPORT SATELLITE ACCOUNTS AND BEYOND

As of 2015, SSAs have been published by the EU for seven MS. One Non-Member State, Switzerland, has published its SSA based on a same methodology. The front runners (pilot countries) in constructing SSAs were Austria, Cyprus and the UK. They were joined by Poland, the

[23] K Vltavska and J Sixta, 'Sport Satellite Account in the Czech Republic', 20th International Input-Output Conference, Bratislava, 26–29 June 2012.

[24] *Sport Statistics* (Eurostat Compact Guides 2016).

[25] *Study on the Contribution of Sport to Economic Growth and Employment in the EU* (SpEA, SIRC, Cystat, Meerverde Sport en Economie, FESI, Ministry of Sport and Tourism of Poland 2012).

Netherlands, Germany, and Lithuania. Portugal has published its SSA in 2016, not yet included in EU publications and leaflets (see Table 9.2). France and Hungary, which were part of a seven 'first wave' MS willing to create a SSA have not delivered it so far. Luxembourg and Romania are assumed to be preparing theirs. France uses a different methodology (Table 9.1 above), so that data will not be perfectly comparable without transformation. Seven countries did not even answer on either the questionnaire or the expert interview sent by the EU in 2015; they were Bulgaria, Denmark, Hungary, Italy, Ireland, Latvia and Slovakia. National Statistics Offices in countries without SSAs made no positive replies.

Table 9.2 National sport satellite accounts published (or unpublished) by the EU

Country	**Report**	**Pub**	**Gross value added**		**H'hold consumption Employment**			
	Year	*in*	*Euro bn.*		*Euro bn.*	*% of total*	*000s*	*% of total*
Austria	2005	2010	10.7	4.9	4.9	3.6	242	6.4
Cyprus	2004	2010	0.3	2.4	0.3	3.7	7.6	2.2
Germany	2008	2013	73.1	3.3	89.1	6.6	1,766	4.4
Lithuania	2008	2014	865µ	0.8	n.a.	1.2	18	1.2
Netherlands	2006	2012	4.7	1.0	6.8	2.7	130	1.5
Poland	2006	2011	5.3	2.0	3.5	1.2	225	1.5
UK*	2006	2010	36.6	2.3	32.0	3.0	630	2.5
Portugal	2010/ 2012	2016	1.8	1.1	1.9	1.7	63	1.4
Czech Rep**	2010	2012	10.0***	0.3	n.a.	1.1	25	0.5
Switzerland	2008	2011	9.1	1.7	n.a.	n.a.	89	2.5

Notes: * Data for the 2008 update.
** Preliminary results for 2004–2010, not explicit WG methodology.[26]
*** Billion Czech crowns.
µ Million litas.[27]

Source: EU Commission (2013) and the author's updates.

26 K Vltavska and J Sixta, 'Sport Satellite Account in the Czech Republic', 20th International Input-Output Conference, Bratislava, 26–29 June 2012.

27 EU Commission, *Sport Satellite Accounts. A European Project: New Results, DG Education and Culture* (Brussels 2013).

Figures in Table 9.2 cover only direct effects. They represent a sort of sport sector's weight in domestic economy or initial impact of sport on overall economic activity. Results are scattered: the share of sport sector in GVA varies from 4.9 per cent in Austria down to 1.1 per cent in Portugal, even 0.8 per cent in Lithuania. Sport goods and services weigh between 1.2 per cent (Poland) and 6.6 per cent (Germany) of household consumption. Sport sector employment makes it for 1.4 per cent of total employment in Portugal up to 6.4 per cent in Austria. Adding indirect effects that result from multi-level business-to-business supplies and induced effects from the consumption of income generated in the sport sector would make a sort of overall multiplier of domestic economic activity triggered by sport. Such data were not published with SSAs but are available upon request to WG experts.

For instance, SIRC has found that sport is significantly related to 53 out of 123 input-output product groups.[28] In the German SSA, the share of sport-related in total GVA is 3.3 per cent while its share in total employment is 4.4 per cent which is interpreted as follows: the gap is due to the much increased proportion of part-time and poorly-paid workers in the service provision areas characteristic of sport (sport organisation and supply of training services for sport). This is not in tune with the conclusion drawn from the UK SSA for 2004 that 'the sports economy has achieved higher-than-average levels of productivity, making it an attractive tool for local and regional regeneration policies'.[29] For 2006, the UK SSA aligns on the German one since the share of the sports economy is slightly higher in total employment than in GDP.

In Portugal, the most recently published SSA shows that sport represents 0.3 per cent of GDP and employment with the statistical definition of sport, 0.9 per cent of GDP and 1.2 per cent of employment with the narrow definition, and 1.1 per cent of GDP and 1.4 per cent of employment with the broad definition, on average in 2010–12. Final consumption of sport products by Portuguese households is distributed across sporting and recreation services (38.9 per cent), leather and related products (25.2 per cent), wearing apparel (8.9 per cent), transport equipment (5.7 per cent), education services (2.8 per cent), telecom services (2.3 per cent), publishing services (2.3 per cent), and other manufacturing products (6.1 per cent).[30]

---

[28] Sport Satellite Account for the UK, (n 12).

[29] Ibid., 24.

[30] More details in 'Sport Satellite Account 2010–2012', Destaque Press Release, *Instituto Nacional de Estatistica* (Statistics Portugal), 5 April 2016.

In the German SSA, GVA of sport-related activities is similar in amount to that of German manufactures of motor vehicles. The contribution of different industries to sport-related goods and activities shows up in Table 9.3 below. Government consumption for sport purposes with €16.4 billion represented 3.6 per cent of state expenditure. Nearly €7 billion were spent on construction and renovation of sports facilities. Total output of the sports economy was €165 billion and GVA €73 billion. Sport-related production activities result in €18.2 billion net taxes transferred from enterprises to the state.

Table 9.3 The sport satellite account for Germany (2008, in %)[31]

Individual industries		**Contribution of individual industries to sport-related:**		
	Gross value added	***Household consumption***	***Production (output)***	***Employment***
Agriculture	0.1	0	0.1	0.1
Manufacturing industry	7.2	37	18.1	5.1
Construction	4.6	0	5.5	4.8
Trade	23.3	11	19.8	28.9
Transport, hotels	13.2	15	13.9	18.2
Information, communication	1.9	5	2.3	1.2
Finance, real estate, business	4.3	8	8.3	2.0
State and person-related services	33.1	24	24.5	31.5
Sport (other)	12.3	0	7.5	8.2

Source: Ahlert (2013).

It is a pity that all detailed data collected in the background of SSAs, and how they have been computed, are not extensively published, more publicised, and even available in open access to anyone. SIRC announced the publication of SSA results for each year from 2005 to 2009 by end of

31 G Ahlert, The German Sport Satellite Accounts (SSA), (n 17).

2011 while similar work would be done in the other pilot countries. This is not exactly what happened even though the XG ECO experts assessed that there is a will to update in countries which have produced SSAs before, except Cyprus. SSA updates have been achieved for the UK 2004–12,[32] the Netherlands 2008 and 2010, and Germany 2010. At the 4th XG ECO (2016) meeting, SSA updates for Austria 2011 and 2013, Netherlands 2012 were announced.[33]

At the time of writing, a budget has been approved in Cyprus to continue the work on SSAs whereas Lithuania informed that from 2016 on there was no budgetary support for working on the national SSA. Poland envisaged updating for 2010 and 2012 but expressed no influence and interest at political level for a new SSA study. No progress in the SSA construction had been noticed at the third XG ECO meeting (2015) either in Belgium, Bulgaria, Czech Republic, Denmark, Estonia, Finland, France, Hungary, Italy, Malta, Slovenia, and Spain while experts from Greece, Slovakia and Sweden were absent.

A windfall benefit of EU SSA project has been a study on sport's contribution to economic growth and employment (SpeA et al., 2012) commissioned by the European Commission in which one reads:

> A complete picture of the economic importance of sport for the EU as a whole through the aggregation of 27 national SSAs can only be expected in the longer term, since this approach is a complex and time-consuming task and therefore faces national budgetary and human resource constraints. Meanwhile a macro-economic approach was developed alongside national efforts to implement SSAs ... [for overcoming the partial scope of national SSAs].[34]

This approach consisted in calculating EU-wide economic effects of sport through enlarging the national IOT with sport-related sectors, thus getting 27 Sport IOTs:S which are connected by intra-EU foreign trade, so that they can be linked together in a Multiregional Input-Output Table, MRIOT:S, with 27-regions, 94 sectors and 59 standard CPA divisions + 34 CPA divisions with sport content, which calls for a number of

---

32 T Kokolakakis, 'UK Sport Satellite Account: 2011 and 2012', SIRC, Sheffield Hallam University, July, 2015.

33 Recommendations to measure the economic benefits of sport on the EU based on the ongoing work to promote the set-up of SSAs in the Member States, Expert Group on the Economic Dimension of Sport, 4th meeting, Brussels, 2016.

34 *Study on the Contribution of Sport to Economic Growth and Employment in the EU* (SpEA, SIRC, Cystat, Meerverde Sport en Economie, FESI, Ministry of Sport and Tourism of Poland 2012).

restrictive assumptions to reduce requirements from millions data, most of which are not available, to a few thousands.

The problem is that only 4 out of 27 IOTs:S were available (Austria, Cyprus, Poland, and UK). For the remaining 23 countries, proxy-IOTs:S had to be computed with calculating a lot of estimates derived from expert interviews, other studies and some guesstimates for the reference year 2005. Therefore the results should not be used on a single country basis. To measure economic growth, there was a need to avail two SSAs in two different points in time for each MS, which was impossible.

To circumvent this issue, instead of calculating (GDP, employment) growth rates, the experts substituted the calculation of Leontief multipliers from IOT:S that capture direct and indirect effects of an increase in final demand on sport-related product markets. Potential growth and not actual growth triggered by the sport sector is what the study is all about. Whether potential equals actual growth of sport-related GVA must be precisely assessed by comparing results in 2005 with those in some further year (in a future study?).

The study showed a 1.13 per cent share of sport-related value added for the EU with the narrow definition of sport, 1.76 per cent with the broad definition and 0.28 per cent with the statistical definition. The direct effect of sport combined with its multiplier (indirect and induced) effects adds up to 2.98 per cent (€294.4 bn) of overall GVA in the EU. The share of sport-related employment for the EU is 1.49 per cent (3,138,350 persons) with the narrow definition of sport, 2.12 per cent (4,460,888) with the broad definition and 0.31 per cent (659,770) with the statistical definition; and 3.51 per cent (7,378,671) when indirect effects are taken into account. Since the shares of sport-related employment exceed those of sport-related GVA (Table 9.4), sport-related activities are more labour intensive than average in other industries. Potential growth in the sport-related economy should lead to above average employment growth. Sport should play an important role in securing employment.[35]

[35] Conclusions of the Council and the Representatives of the Governments of the Member States, meeting within the Council, on strengthening the evidence-base for sport policy making, Council of the European Union, Brussels, 26–27 November 2012.

Table 9.4 Broad definition of sport: sport-related activities in nationwide total, 2005[36]

Member State	Value added in € million	Employment in heads	Share of sport-related activities in:	
			Total value added	Total employment
Austria	10,730	242,968	4.03%	5.38%
Belgium	3,043	71,416	1.13%	1.69%
Bulgaria	223	55,843	1.13%	1.87%
Cyprus	310	7,600	2.34%	2.57%
Czech Republic	1,062	89,119	1.18%	1.87%
Denmark	3,719	69,287	2.12%	2.52%
Estonia	162	15,686	1.64%	2.58%
Finland	2,654	74,209	1.94%	3.09%
France	21,607	416,537	1.40%	1.67%
Germany	46,677	1,146,234	2.31%	3.15%
Greece	2,518	70,878	1.44%	1.63%
Hungary	778	55,577	1.02%	1.43%
Ireland	2,377	40,532	1.66%	2.08%
Italy	15,599	329,86	1.21%	1.47%
Latvia	136	17,077	1.11%	1.65%
Lithuania	161	16,178	0.88%	1.10%
Luxembourg	697	19,331	2.37%	5.63%
Malta	93	3,070	2.24%	2.07%
Netherlands	5,828	141,896	1.28%	1.75%
Poland	5,300	225,500	1.56%	1.94%
Portugal	1,534	72,101	1.19%	1.41%
Romania	790	161,248	1.12%	1.77%
Slovakia	472	49,910	1.08%	2.25%
Slovenia	521	28,576	2.10%	3.01%
Spain	10,407	336,177	1.28%	1.77%
Sweden	2,360	73,266	0.92%	1.69%
United Kingdom	39,860	632,400	2.33%	2.16%

Source: SpEA et al. (2012).

[36] *Study on the Contribution of Sport to Economic Growth and Employment in the EU* (SpEA, SIRC, Cystat, Meerverde Sport en Economie, FESI, Ministry of Sport and Tourism of Poland 2012).

Since Table 9.4 demonstrates that proxy-SSAs can be calculated for any MS relying on the work of experts commissioned by the EU, this must have a double-edge effect: an increased interest in Table 9.4 results from those MS which have not constructed their own SSA and a strong disincentive to construct it since a proxy of their SSA is at hand. Most of the latter MS are likely to free ride in particular those where Table 9.4 shows low rates; would they consider it worth to construct a SSA simply confirming that their sport-related activities are below, say, 1.5 per cent of total GVA (Belgium, Bulgaria, Czech Republic, France, Greece, Hungary, Italy, Latvia, Romania, Slovakia, Sweden)? While it is between 2 and 4 per cent in nine other MS. Paying €0.5 million only for that may appear by far too much expensive. Is it only by chance that Austria is the more pushy MS in the XG ECO as regards SSAs? Or is it somewhat related to its top ratios in Table 9.4?

V. MERITS OF, AND HINDRANCES TO, EU SPORT SATELLITE ACCOUNTS

Published SSAs have a number of merits, several shortcomings that could be dealt with over time, and a few more fundamental hindrances that might be harder to overcome. Starting with the merits, the first of which is the SSAs very existence:

(a) SSAs provide a picture of the sports economy's diversity and importance and of interrelationships with the rest of domestic economy, as well as within the sports economy itself;
(b) SSAs stimulate methodological rigour and coherence across MS and over time;
(c) If regularly updated, SSAs can serve to identify growth segments in the sports economy;
(d) SSAs can serve as a programming device for economic research on the sport sector;
(e) SSAs may serve as a labour market analysis reference point in the sport sector;
(f) SSAs may serve as a 'reality check' (in the WG wording) on claims voiced by sport interest groups;
(g) efforts to create SSAs in a EU-wide harmonised manner would help attain the goals of EU 2020 strategy; still a long way to go four years before the deadline since 18 MS are not engaged yet in preparing their SSA;

(h) the WG expressed the view that SSAs may help policy makers from the European down to local level in formulating sport policies.

Let us turn to (the ten) SSAs' shortcomings that could be overcome.

In the second WG meeting, concerns were raised as regards the costs of producing a SSA which actually were in the range of €500,000–600,000 with the Austrian and German expert work for building up their SSAs. Since a SSA has lower interest if not often updated, further updating costs must be afforded as well. The sixth WG meeting noticed that some MS were experiencing substantial delays due to budgetary reasons. How to overcome such financial bottleneck in which several MS are stuck with SSA construction? An EU dedicated budget would help. Or an EU expert team sent in laggard MS to construct the SSA?

Some MS are simply lagging behind in data collection because SSAs are very data demanding and consequently time consuming.[37] If data collection is not comprehensive and does not cover all MS the target of comparing and benchmarking for policy decision making is missed.

Some MS are experiencing substantial delays in SSA construction due to long periods necessary for the research or lack of political support from governments; some have not collected data on the basis of Vilnius definition, but instead have taken different approaches for the time being and published studies on the sports economy that are not in line with the SSA framework. This problem should have been overcome by more awareness-raising actions and more convincing publications including much more detailed background data and computations of existing SSAs.

The WG stated at its first meeting that 'common statistical definition of sport does not require EU MS to agree upon a definition of sport as such. Different countries can have a different understanding of which activities constitute sport. This is a cultural issue and there is no reason for trying to harmonise it'. Country-specific interpretations of sport are unavoidable, but at the same time they jeopardise international comparability. Only the Dutch SSA attempted to tackle this issue with a 'family resemblance test' across all (physical or not) activities to decide whether they belong to sport.[38] It might be one reason for rather low ratios (in percentage of GDP/employment) obtained in the Dutch as compared to Austrian, German and UK SSAs.

A RAS methodology was used to extend IOT to sport-relevant activities while only partial information was available. RAS keeps

---

[37] W Andreff, 'The Constraint of Data Collection in the Sports Industry', EU Conference on Sport Statistics, Brussels, 23 March 2011.

[38] *Methodological Manual for a Sport Satellite Account* (n 22).

constant the technical coefficients included in IOT as in the underlying static Leontief model. That is why using SSAs for estimating the growth of the sports economy is dubious and results cannot be accepted at face value. Consequently each national SSA should be updated every year to get genuine (actual and variable) technical coefficients. Thus, there is a need to conceive a computerised routine for a quasi-automatic SSA update which is also requested for every year policy decision making.

> The implementation of SSA is a costly and time-consuming project. Such usage of resources should be outweighed by returns generated through additional insight in educational and academic settings as well as the application thereof in the context of evidence-based sports policy formulation.[39]

Have the returns of constructing SSAs actually outweighed the costs so far? Have SSAs actually been used yet to monitor the economic importance of sport? Have SSAs had any effect in MS on a policy of national specialisation in the sports-related industry compared to other countries in view of maximising domestic value added? Have SSAs been useful for studying the outcome of a change in the ownership of football stadia for instance? The issue of SSA building opportunity is raised by such questions. A response without conflict of interests must be obtained through an audit of the WG and XGs work achieved by independent experts, not involved in SSA construction.

EU SSAs did not stake on a major advantage of SSA technique because they did not take on board data about very significant non-monetary economic inputs and outputs of the sports economy, the focal case in point being voluntary work.[40] Whatever the metrics used to monetise voluntary work in sports, the outcome is many times larger than all government expenditures for sport.[41] A Eurostat speaker at the EU Conference on Sport Statistics in 2011 also underlined that a number of important non-market players were active in sport. This major root for underestimation of the sports economy creates a gap between what is accounted for in SSAs and the claimed 'reality check'.

---

[39] 'The Use of Sport Satellite Accounts for Policy Purposes', Barcelona Meeting of Sport Directors Generals, Meerwaarde Sports and Economics and SportsEconAustria, 26 February 2010.

[40] Andreff (n 37).

[41] W Andreff and J-F Nys, 'Le dirigeant sportif bénévole: approche économique' in F Alaphilippe and E Bournazel (eds) *Le Dirigeant Sportif Bénévole* (Dalloz 1984) 16–32.

The Vilnius definition of sport is not without its problems. It might be argued which products actually are inputs of sport and which activities actually require sport as input. Take for instance sport food, it uses sport as an input (without sport no or less need of refreshments, diet foods, etc.) on the one hand and, on the other hand, food is an input of sport when it comes to vitamins, calorific and energetic food and performance-enhancing products since they are fuels for sport practice and performance. In the same vein, the health system is downstream when it cures a sport participant from sport fatigue, injury or accident; it is upstream when it brings ex ante medical assistance and preparation to a sportsman/woman before a sport contest.

Physical education is upstream in that those educated with sport will have some sport practice in their lives; it is downstream since physical education is normally input of any balanced educative programme. The same upstream-downstream duality can be noticed for many sport-related activities and products. Consequently, the delineation between narrow and broad definitions of sport is blurred. However, it can be further clarified with comprehensive publication of all detailed computations which are in the background of published SSAs. Following Manual (2012),[42] clear international guidelines on how to implement the Vilnius definition in the construction of SSAs are missing, furthermore every country needs to be explicit in what has been included in its SSA. Part of the solution is that all MS should recalculate their SSAs with perfectly mimicking the Dutch one. Alternatively, the Vilnius definition could be emended.

Two final, and the most serious of all hindrances, are as follows.

Beyond voluntary work, from the very beginning the EU SSA methodology excluding a number of sport-related services and goods (namely sporting infrastructures) was doomed to underestimate the weight of the sports economy.

Even though the WG decided to focus on the broader definition of sport, as early as the second WG meeting some experts raised the issue that 'a single definition based on the broader level would carry a political risk in that it may be attacked as being excessively extensive'. It does not seem that such political risk has materialised meanwhile; but the major flaw is that the broad definition of sport is highway to overestimation of the sports economy's significance.

From an analytical and logical standpoint, in IOT either one considers that the development of upstream industries trickles down into the

---

42 *Methodological Manual for a Sport Satellite Account* (n 22).

development of downstream industries – then the narrow definition of sport is fine but not the broad definition – or one considers that the development of downstream industries triggers back up the development of upstream industries – then the broad definition is acceptable only once the narrow definition has been subtracted from it. How to demonstrate which are those trickling-down and triggering-up industries in economic development has been well known since Aujac (1960).[43] One cannot have a same industry that is by the same token predominantly trickling-down and triggering-up all other industries, except the most 'core' industry in the economy. Do really the WG experts think that the sports industry is core to the entire domestic economy's development? If they do not, they have introduced from the very beginning an overestimating bias; and if they do, they are slightly naive or lack experimental truth. At the end of the day, underestimation plus overestimation together raise the issue of methodological accuracy in building up EU SSAs.

VI. CONCLUSION

The final objective to develop a harmonised European SSA has a long way to go. The focus has evolved in the recent (third and fourth) XG ECO meetings in 2015 and 2016 toward major sports events, their legacy and sustainability, long-term investment and EU funding in sport. The full economic dimension of sport is considered to be much wider and encompasses topics which SSA/IOT-S cannot cover. The practical application of SSAs has shown that policy makers are often interested in different categorisations like the impact on the economy of football or golf, or putting a figure on the cost of physical inactivity or on the value of non-paid work in grassroots sport which is likely to be greatly underestimated (and is excluded from the Vilnius definition and SSAs). A study by Grohall,[44] exhibited that outside those ten countries which already engaged in computing SSAs, the main reason for not computing was lack of political will. During computation the toughest obstacles were the availability of data on trade of sport-related services and sport-related consumption. Recommendations were derived: make the SSA research visible, e.g., by leaflets sent directly to sport ministries or

---

[43] H Aujac, 'La hiérarchie des industries dans un tableau des échanges industriels', (1960) 11(2) *Revue Economique* 169–238.

[44] G Grohall, C Helmenstein, A Kleissner, K Weyerstrass, T Kokolakakis and W de Boer, 'Study on National Sport Satellite Accounts (SSAs)' in the EU, EU DG Education and Culture, Brussels, October, 2015.

other suitable bodies and institutions; hold four to six intensive workshops per year beginning in Spring 2016.

Eventually, EU SSA is like a wonderful Cadillac car, beautiful, sophisticated, expensive, and very much fuel (work) demanding so that it has stopped after eight stages out of 28 in the race, short of fuel. A cheaper, lower-designed, and less work-demanding project may have ended the race and been used straightforwardly for policy decision making.

Policy makers are in need of swift responses to shocks, events, policy options and trade-offs while academics lean in favour of most scientific methodologies – IOT and SSA. A mid-term solution would be to go on slowly with building up SSAs while swiftly designing a much simpler and operational tool such as a set of indexes (an economic dashboard of sport) representative of the sports economy published and updated with annual frequency, immediately useful for evidence-based policy making.[45] Such a dashboard is enough to provide correct assessment of the sports economy even though it may be less detailed than the evaluation achieved with SSAs. Wonder how much it is important for a policy maker to know whether sport-related activities represent 1.4% of total GVA as to IOTs:S (proxy for France) or SDE represents 1.7 per cent of (French) GDP. Would he/she change his/her mind only due to such difference? Many indexes in the French economic dashboard of sport are more up-to-date and tightly connected to current policy and management decision making than GVA, consumption and employment calculated through SSAs. Long life to the latter anyway!

---

[45] Andreff (n 37).

10. State aid and sport

Andrea Cattaneo

I. INTRODUCTION

In the context of the internal market of the European Union (EU), one of the main objectives is to guarantee fair conditions of competition to the undertakings. In order to achieve this objective, the EU must ensure that the intervention of State and public authorities on the market does not distort the competition in favour of a specific undertaking or sector.

The cultural importance of sport has been already discussed elsewhere in this handbook. However, the connection between public authorities and sporting entities must be highlighted again. A Member State may want to pursue objectives of public interest by funding the development of sport infrastructures.

Nevertheless, the competition authorities of the EU must ensure that the intervention of the State on the market will not distort the competition to an unacceptable extent. This chapter will therefore provide a brief overview of the notion of State aid, and the principles that the authorities apply in the context of an assessment of a measure under State aid provisions. In light of the past and recent decision practice of the EU Commission, it will be particularly assessed to what extent the specific features of sport and of the sporting market have been taken into account in this regard.

II. STATE AID

As already mentioned, the objective of State aid rules is to ensure that the intervention of Member States on the economy, although admissible and even necessary in some circumstances,[1] does not distort the competition

[1] Article 107(2) TFEU establishes that aid with social character, or to make good the damage caused by exceptional circumstances have to be allowed by the European Commission.

within the internal market.[2] The State, and the public authorities connected, are fully entitled to take an active role on the market under certain conditions; however, it is necessary to guarantee that this intervention complies with the need to protect the fairness of the competition on the market itself.[3]

The Treaty provision that regulates State aid is Article 107 TFEU. The first paragraph prohibits any type of measure granted by a Member State or through State resources that is capable of distorting the competition within the internal market, by favouring certain undertakings or the production of certain goods. The provision includes a number of different elements, but the decisive aspect of the assessment is the effect of the measure under examination. Indeed, any kind of measure might fall under the definition provided by the Article, regardless of the form it takes, or the way it is defined by the relevant Member State.[4]

A measure will be comprised under the notion of State aid where there is a transfer of resources from the State to a company, or a relief from charges that normally the company has to bear,[5] whereby the financial advantage is received for free, or without adequate remuneration.[6] As the focus is on the effects arising from public financing, the measure will fall under the scope of the provision even when it has not been directly granted by the State, but from other authorities.[7] Indeed, the measure has to be granted by a Member State, or through State resources: this also includes funds that are available or under the control of the State, irrespective of their origin.[8] Moreover, the concept of State in this regard

---

[2] The original objective of State aid rules was to avoid subsidy races between Member States, each attempting to benefit their own enterprises at the expense of rivals located in other Member States. See K Bacon, *European Union Law of State Aid* (2nd edn, OUP 2013).

[3] See J-D Braun, 'Article 87 EC' in O Castendyk *et al* (eds), *European Media Law* (Kluwer Law International 2008) 207–44.

[4] R Plender, 'Definition of Aid' in A Biondi (ed), *The Law of State Aid in the European Union* (OUP 2003) 3–39.

[5] See Case C-156/98 *Germany v Commission* [2000] ECR I-6857, para 25.

[6] See A Sinnaeve, 'Competition Policy, State Aid and State Enterprises' in B Hawk (ed), *Annual Proceedings of the Fordham Corporate Law Institute: International Antitrust Law and Policy* (Juris Publishing 2001) 75.

[7] See Case T-358/94 *Air France v Commission* [1996] ECR II-2109, para 56.

[8] The decisive element is the control of the funding: EU structural funds that are distributed to Member States, which in turn administer them, will be nevertheless relevant under State aid rules. See Decision in Case N 157/2006 *South Yorkshire Digital Region Broadband Project*, para 29.

comprises also central, regional and local authorities, other public entities and even private bodies insofar as they have been established by the State, or they have been designated to control public funding.[9]

Furthermore, the public measure must confer a selective advantage on the recipient undertaking, which, in light of its specific characteristics, will receive a treatment that differs from the general regime applicable to its competitors. The advantage consists of a form of benefit that the company would have not received under normal market conditions, or that mitigates the charges that the company should have borne.[10] Therefore, the analysis of the Commission has to include an element of comparison between the recipient undertaking(s) and the other operators that are in a similar factual and legal situation.[11]

Finally, a measure will be considered under the State aid analysis only if it produces an effect on trade between Member States, and if it is likely to cause a distortion of the competition within the market. While an aid that has effects limited only to a national dimension will escape the prohibition set by Article 107 TFEU,[12] the same approach may not be used when the recipient of the measure is engaged in inter-Member States trade, if the latter is capable of distorting its competitive position vis-à-vis its competitors.[13] Trade may also be affected when the recipient undertaking is not involved in inter-Member State trade, but the measure strengthens its position and makes it more difficult for operators in other Member States to enter the market.[14]

The second paragraph of Article 107 TFEU provides for an exception from the prohibition for those measures that are aimed at offering support of a social character, where they are granted to individual consumers, or

---

[9] See C-487/06P, *British Aggregates v Commission* [2008] ECR I-10515 and Case 248/84, *Germany v Commission* [1987] ECR 4013 para 17 and, for a comment, L Rubini, 'The Elusive Frontier: "Regulation" Under EC State Aid Law' [2011] ESALQ 277.

[10] A Jones and B Sufrin, *EU Competition Law: Text, Cases and Materials* (4th edn, OUP 2011) State Aid Chapter, 24.

[11] See Case C-487/06 P *British Aggregates v Commission*, para 82.

[12] In its Draft Notion on the notion of State Aid Notice, the Commission explains the common features of cases in which the purely local economic impact of the measure does not affect inter-Member State trade. See Draft Commission Notice on the notion of State aid pursuant to Article 107(1) TFEU, paras 196–197.

[13] See Case C-75/97 *Belgium v Commission ('Maribel I')* [1999] ECR I-3671, para 5.

[14] See e.g., Case C-280/00 *Altmark Trans and Regierungspräsidium Magdeburg* [2003] ECR I-07747, para 78.

they make good damage caused by natural disaster or exceptional circumstances.[15]

The final part of the provision grants the Commission the power to assess the compatibility of a specific measure with EU law, in light of an analysis of the positive and negative effects that this is capable of causing on the internal market. A measure may thus be allowed when it promotes the economic development of areas suffering from severe economic difficulties, or when it pursues the development of certain economic areas or activities, and finally where the aid is aimed at the execution of a project of common European interest.[16] The non-exhaustive list provided by the Article terminates with aid to promote culture and heritage conservation and other categories that may be specifically exempted by a decision of the Council on a proposal of the Commission. Therefore, State aid measures can find justification under non-economic grounds where they are granted with the objective of reducing social disparities.[17] European 'common interest' includes aspects related to economic efficiency, equity dimension and any other political objective of the Commission.[18]

The Commission will find a measure to be compatible with Article 107(3) TFEU when it satisfies a number of requirements:[19] the measure will have to pursue a common objective as previously defined, and it has to be targeted towards situations where the intervention of the State is indispensable, as the market cannot remedy the failure and meet the same objective otherwise. Moreover, the measure must be appropriate to address the objective of common interest, and limited to the minimum amount necessary to induce the market to take action. Where the aid is

---

[15] The provision includes also an exception for aid granted to the economy of certain areas of the Federal Republic of Germany which were negatively affected by the division of Germany. Five years after the entry into force of the Treaty of Lisbon, the Council, acting on a proposal from the Commission, may adopt a decision repealing this point.

[16] In this connection, the objective of general economic interest has to be clearly defined, and the measure enacted to pursue it has to be adequate to attain the objective, and proportionate in the restriction that it creates. See the State Action Plan COM (2005) 107 final, para 20.

[17] P Lowe, 'The Design of Competition Policy Institutions for the 21st Century – the Experience of the European Commission and DG Competition' [2008] CPN 1–6.

[18] Bacon (n 2), 14.

[19] These are inferred from a series of soft law measures part of the new set of Guidelines issued by the Commission in the implementation of the State Aid Modernisation Communication. Jones and Sufrin (n 10), State Aid Chapter, 104.

granted to a specific undertaking, it needs to be capable of modifying its behaviour to make it engage in those activities that it would not carry out without the aid itself. Finally, the measure has to be administered transparently and avoid undue negative effects, so to guarantee that its overall balance results in positive effects.[20]

Elements such as the limited amount of the aid granted, the size of the recipient undertaking and the market share cannot exclude the possibility that trade between Member States will be affected,[21] especially when the competition in the market concerned is particularly strong.[22] Conversely, the set of rules comprising the *de minimis*[23] regulations grants some leniency towards measures that involves the granting of small amounts in specific sectors.[24] Furthermore the Commission, having acquired the power to adopt block exempting regulations (GBERs),[25] has adopted the Regulation 69/2001, setting out thresholds below which aids were exempted from notification.[26] In May 2014, the Commission adopted a further GBER,[27] which has also raised the notification thresholds for a number of measures that have incentive effects and provided for more flexible eligibility conditions.

---

[20] Ibid.

[21] Indeed, there is no threshold or percentage that guarantees that trade between Member States will not be affected. See Case C-280/00 *Altmark*, para 81.

[22] See Case 259/85 *France v Commission* [1987] ECR 4393, para 24. However, seemingly in contrast, the Communication from the Commission Developing the European Dimension in Sport COM/2011/0012 final, that at para 3.3 states that aid involving very small amounts 'may remain outside the scope of Article 107(1) TFEU'.

[23] The Commission has issued a *de minimis* Notice [1992] OJ C 213/2, which has been revised by the Notice [1996] OJ C 68/9. Part of this legislation is also formed by the Guidelines on State aid for small- and medium-sized enterprises (SMEs) [1996] OJ C 213/4.

[24] See Case C-351/98 *Spain v Commission* [2002] ECR I-8031, paras 51 and 52. More precisely, the Commission has stated in its 1996 Notice that aid not amounting to a sum beyond €100,000 over a three-year period would have escaped the application of Article 107(1) TFEU. See Jones and Sufrin, (n 10) State Aid Chapter, 83.

[25] See Council Regulation 994/98 [1998] OJ L 142/1, Art 2 (1).

[26] Regulation of the Commission 69/2001 [2001] OJ L 10/30. The threshold set by the Regulation is an overall amount of €200,000. The Regulation was later replaced from January 2014 by Regulation 1407/2013 [2013] OJ L 352/1.

[27] Commission Regulation (EU) No 651/2014 of 17 June 2014 declaring certain categories of aid compatible with the internal market in application of Articles 107 and 108 of the Treaty, [2014] OJ L 187/1.

Unlawful aid[28] may have to be recovered by the Member State, or the other entity that has granted it.[29] A recovery decision would be binding under Article 288 TFEU, and may be enforced before the Court of Justice, while third parties may even claim compensation in national courts.[30] The recipient may therefore have to pay back the sum received, or an amount equivalent to the sum it should have spent in order to get the same benefits,[31] plus the interests accrued from the moment in which it has received the funding, or in which the measure has been granted.[32]

III. THE IMPORTANCE OF STATE AID IN SPORT

Historically, funding for sport originates from a number of different sources, including wealthy patrons, banks and municipal authorities.[33] In particular, the intervention of the State and public authorities in support

---

[28] Unlawful aid is a measure put in place in contrast with Art 108(3) TFEU, including aid not notified and aid put into effect in contravention of a negative decision of the Commission. See Art 1(f) of Council Regulation No 659/1999 of 22 March 1999 laying down detailed rules for the application of Article 108 TFEU OJ L 83/1, 27.03.1999.

[29] The Treaty does not mention the recovery of the aid, but it is a practice that can be inferred from the case law. See Case 70/72, *Commission v Germany* [1973] ECR 813, para 13.

[30] The procedure will not be imposed where it is impossible to recover the aid, or where by doing so the Commission would act against the general principles of Community Law. See Reg. 659/1999 [1999] OJ 83/1, Art 14. The Court has however considered that the recovery of an aid will be contrary to the general principles of Community law only in exceptional circumstances. See Case C-5/89 *Commission v Germany* [1990] ECR I-3437, para 16.

[31] The power of the Commission to recover the aid is subject to a ten-year limitation from the moment in which the aid has been granted, which will be interrupted by any action taken either by the institution or by the Member State. See Reg 659/1999 [1999] OJ 83/1, Art 15.

[32] The interests should be calculated by the Commission at an appropriate fixed rate. See Reg 659/1999 [1999] OJ 83/1, Art 14.

[33] There is, however, a difference between the source of financing of professional and amateur sports. While the first is usually funded by patrons, or undertakings that are interested in a high level of media exposure, the amateur sector is historically financed by local authorities. See W Andreff, J Dutoya and J Montel, 'A European Model of Sports Financing: Under Threat' [2009] (90) 75 RJES, Online and available at http://www.playthegame.org/news/news-articles/2009/a-european-model-of-sports-financing-under-threat (accessed on 26 Oct 2017).

of sport is in certain circumstances desirable,[34] if not expected,[35] and in any event it constitutes a common practice throughout Europe.[36]

Public authorities may intervene in the sport sector for a number of different reasons:[37] the financing may be merely aiming at the development of local facilities. It may be aimed at the enhancement of the participation of the public to sport, in light of its social value, and its ability to promote education, health and wellness.[38] If these are the objectives of the measure, the benefits of this type of intervention will be enjoyed by the local community, and, provided that its restrictive effects on the market are limited or balanced, it is likely to be approved by the Commission.

On the other hand, public intervention might be aimed at supporting professional sport clubs. In this relation, one of the consequences of the liberalisation of the players' market in Europe occurring through the *Bosman* judgment[39] has been an exponential increase in players' wages.[40] To face the increasing costs, sport clubs had to look for alternative streams of income, including public funding. However, public financing for professional sporting entities can also underlie a political rationale: local sport clubs are often deeply connected with the community, cities, regions and Member States.[41] National and local authorities may then decide to support a club in light of its importance for the community, but also to boost the image of the country, and as a tool to attract the

---

34 See Decision of the Commission in Case C4/2008 Investment of the Municipality of Rotterdam in the Ahoy Complex, point 67.

35 See the European Sport Charter issued by the Council of Europe. Article 12 of the Charter states that 'Appropriate support and resources from public funds, that is, at national, regional and local levels, shall be made available for the fulfilment of the aims and purposes of this Charter.'

36 See Andreff, Dutoya, and Montel (n 33).

37 For an historical analysis of the involvement of public authorities in sport, see B Houlihan, *The Government and Politics of Sport* (Routledge 1991).

38 T Traupel, 'Football and State Aid: Really the Greatest Pastime in the World?' [2014] ESALQ 414.

39 Case C-415/93 *Bosman* [1995] ECR I-04921.

40 According to Lago *et al*, the increase in spending on players is also a result of the increasing amount of income, especially coming from TV deals. See U Lago, R Simmons and S Szymanski, 'The Financial Crisis in European Football: An Introduction', [2006] 7 JSE 3.

41 In this context see the reaction of the Spanish government to the announcement of the opening of an investigation on Barcelona and Real Madrid. 'The government will fight to the last to defend Spanish clubs because they are also part of the Spanish brand.' See 'EU targets Real and Barca over illegal state aid', (*Reuters*, 17 December 2013).

sympathy of the electorate.[42] On the other hand, the aid might also be motivated by economic reasons, connected with the promotion and development of the region where the club is based.

In this regard, when professional sport clubs receive economic support from public authorities, they may gain an advantage against their direct competitors, as they might be able to afford bigger expenditures on the players' market.[43] In turn, if a team is capable of having in the squad the most 'famous' players, this might grant it advantages on related markets as well, and therefore increase its ability to sign sponsorship and media contracts.[44] Furthermore, modern professional clubs are now involved in a range of activities that are not strictly related to the performance on-the-field, and they attach their name to commercial enterprises. Therefore, they might be in competition also with market players that have nothing to do with sport, such as undertakings that operate in the field of hospitality, entertainment and food industries.[45]

Political considerations might also affect the enforcement of State aid provisions at European level, and they render the application of the provisions a delicate matter. The club that has received an unlawful aid might not be able to repay the sum, and it might be driven into financial difficulties and even bankruptcy. On the other hand, if the application of this provision would condemn a club to disappearing, this could represent a political own goal in terms of image and popularity for the European institutions, and in general for the enforcement of EU policy in the area.

The topic related to State aid in sport has only recently gained the attention of European institutions and academics. The reluctance of the institutions to initiate proceedings in this area, however, may be the result

---

[42] See R Craven, 'Football and State Aid: Too Important to Fail?' [2014] 3–4 ISLJ 205 and C Durand and E Bayle, 'Public Assistance in Spectator Sport: A Comparison between Europe and the United States' [2002] (2) 2 EJSS 1.

[43] R Craven 'State Aid and Sports Stadiums: EU Sports Policy or Deference to Professional Football' [2014] 35 (9) ECLR 453, and Traupel (n 38).

[44] The range of effects that the Commission has connected with the granting of State aid measures is therefore wide. See P Nicolaides, 'A Critical Analysis of the Application of State Aid Rules to Sport' [2015] MJECL 2, and, as an example, see Decision of the Commission to open an investigation in the case State aid SA.33584 (2013/C) (ex 2011/NN), para 40.

[45] See the Decision of the Commission to open an investigation in the Real Madrid Case, SA.33754. One of the effects of the measure under investigation was the granting of an area to FC Real Madrid that was going to be used by the club to build a hotel and a shopping mall.

of the lack of complaints received in the past.[46] Pursuant to Regulation 659/99, interested parties can inform the Commission of measures that they believe may constitute unlawful aid.[47] The Commission is obliged to investigate the complaint received,[48] and to conclude this preliminary stage with a Decision.[49] As opposed to antitrust investigations, where the Commission can invoke lack of Community interest for not dealing with a complaint, the Commission has no discretion in the area of State aid.[50] The complainant, on the other hand, must demonstrate that it is an interested party to the procedure, and that there are sufficient grounds to show the existence of an illegal State aid.[51] In any event, the complainant that can prove to be concerned party to the procedure may challenge the Decision of the Commission to close the investigation under Article 263 TFEU.[52]

On the other hand, more recent complaints have in fact come from private citizens, which in times of general economic difficulties are reluctant to accept public expenditure on professional sport clubs.

IV. EU STATE AID AND EU SPORTS POLICY

Well before starting to take an active role in assessing State aid measures, the EU institutions mentioned the topic in a number of policy measures.

---

[46] The right of third parties in the area of State aid are comparatively more limited than in other areas of competition law. See M Heidenhain, *European State Aid Law* (Hart 2010) 682.

[47] See Reg 659/1999, Art 20(2).

[48] See Reg 659/1999, Art 10(1).

[49] See Case C-521/06 P *Athinaïki Techniki v Commission* [2008] ECR I-5829, para 37. As a decision would be a formal act of the Commission, it may be challenged under Art 263 TFEU.

[50] See A Sinnaeve and Piet Jan Slot, 'The New Regulation on State Aid Procedures' [1999] 36 CMLR 1153.

[51] As from the Council Regulation (EU) No 734/2013 of 22 July 2013 amending Regulation (EC) No 659/1999 laying down detailed rules for the application of Article 93 of the EC Treaty. If the party seeking to submit a complaint is not an interested party, the Commission is not under an obligation to act, and can use the information received when it will decide to open an investigation *ex officio*. See Jones and Sufrin (n 10), 220.

[52] E Szyszczak, *Research Handbook on European State Aid Law*, (Edward Elgar 2011), 361. Indeed, this Decision would have final legal consequences and for this reason it can be subject of an action for annulment. See also Heidenhain (n 46), 728.

In the Helsinki Report on Sport,[53] it was recognised that the European Community must ensure that the initiatives taken by authorities of Member States or sporting organisations comply with EU law, and respect competition law and the internal market.[54]

The theme of State aid was further discussed in the Staff Working Document attached to the White Paper on Sport.[55] While acknowledging the general prohibition of State aid contained in the Treaties, and the impossibility of granting an exemption to sport *tout court*,[56] the Commission recognised that government intervention in the sport sector may be necessary under some circumstances.[57] In particular, it distinguished public financing measures used for the construction of public infrastructures, which may be comprised under the notion of public policy,[58] and subsidies granted to professional sport clubs, which might distort the competition. Furthermore, the Commission noted that even measures that fall under the definition of State aid may still be exempted from the general prohibition, especially when they fulfil the conditions set by general block exemptions that apply to any economic sector.[59] Within the accompanying Staff Working Document, the Commission finally distinguished between aid granted to amateur and professional sport clubs.

---

[53] Report from the Commission to the European Council with a View to Safeguarding Current Sports Structures and Maintaining the Social Function of Sport within the Community framework – The Helsinki Report on Sport, COM(1999) 644 final.

[54] Ibid., para 4. Based on the report, the Commission subsequently adopted the Declaration on Sport annexed to the Treaty of Amsterdam amending the Treaty on European Union, the Treaties establishing the European Communities and certain related acts. See R Siekmann, 'Is Sport "Special" in EU Law and Policy?' in R Blanpain (eds.), *The Future of Sports Law in the European Union – Beyond the EU Reform Treaty and the White Paper* (Asser Press 2008) 37.

[55] Commission Staff Working Document – The EU and Sport: Background and Context – Accompanying document to the White Paper on Sport {COM(2007) 391 final} {SEC(2007)932} {SEC(2007)934} {SEC(2007)936}.

[56] Contrary to what was suggested in the European Sport Review. See JL Arnaut 'Independent European Sport Review' (2006).

[57] See Commission Staff Working Document to the White Paper on Sport {COM(2007) 391 final}, para 3.2.2.

[58] See ibid., 73.

[59] Such as the *de minimis* aid, exempting measures when limited to an amount of €200,000 distributed over three fiscal years to a single undertaking; or aid that have been granted to clubs in financial difficulties, provided that the measure is in line with a restructuring plan; or training aid, where they comply with the training aid block exemption, or they are part of the competence of the Member States.

While the first type of measure may not be relevant as long as the recipient club does not carry out an economic activity, professional clubs are immediately considered to be engaged in economic activities. In relation to them the strict application of State aid rules helps protecting the fairness and uncertainty of the competition.[60]

Furthermore, in March 2012 the then Commission Vice President Almunia and UEFA president Platini issued a joint statement on the interaction between the rules of Financial Fair Play (FFP) and State Aid.[61] The statement noted that the poor financial situation of football clubs may tempt Member States and public authorities to intervene and distort competition, both on and off the field.[62] The objective of FFP rules of promoting long-term investments in football, with the aim of pursuing the break-even principle, was thus held to be consistent with State aid policy and goals.

IV.i The General Block Exemption

The last piece of legislation that has to be mentioned is the General Block Exempting Regulation (GBER II) issued in June 2014 by the Commission.[63] Under Article 109 TFEU, the Council can delegate the Commission to make regulations exempting some specific types of aid from the requirement of previous notification, if they are considered not significantly harmful for the competition on the market.

GBER II specifies that many types of aid granted by Member States or public authorities in the sport sector do not entail illegal State aid, as the beneficiary is not carrying out an economic activity, or because the measure does not have an effect on trade between Member States.[64] This

---

[60] See Commission Staff Working Document to the White Paper on Sport (n 57), para 3.2.2.

[61] Commission and UEFA, 'Joint statement by Vice-President Joaquın Almunia and President Michel Platini.' 21 March 2012 http://ec.europa.eu/competition/sectors/sports/joint_statement_en.pdf (accessed 26 Oct 2017).

[62] Joint statement by Vice-President Joaquın Almunia and President Michel Platini. 21 March 2012, para 12. State support in this field might run against the principle of market economy, as it would clearly advantage an undertaking over its competitor. Craven (n 42).

[63] Commission Regulation (EU) No 651/2014 of 17 June 2014 declaring certain categories of aid compatible with the internal market in application of Articles 107 and 108 of the Treaty [2014] OJ L 187, henceforth also 'GBER II'.

[64] For example, see the Case SA.38208, UK alleged State aid to UK member-owned golf clubs, where a tax exemption was granted to a local amateur golf club. The Commission held that these types of club operate only locally and

might be especially true for measures that have local character and are taken in the field of amateur sports,[65] while it might not be the case for any measures involving events where the sport performance is offered in exchange for entrance fees.[66]

In practical terms, GBER II establishes a threshold for investment aid in sport infrastructure,[67] provided that a number of conditions are satisfied, in order to reduce the distortion that these measures are likely to cause. The public authorities must guarantee that the multifunctional facilities grant open and non-discriminatory access to the public,[68] and that a fair and transparent tender process has been undertaken for the assignment of concessions to third parties. Moreover, the sport infrastructure shall not be operated by a single professional club, and it shall be used by other sporting entities for at least 20 per cent of the annual time capacity.[69] In the event that the infrastructure is indeed used by professional sport clubs, the pricing conditions should be made publicly available to ensure transparency and equal treatment of users.[70] However, preferential access and more favourable conditions might be granted to those undertakings that have financed at least 30 per cent of the investments costs. Finally, the Regulation, and the exemption thereof provided, does not apply to measures whose amount exceeds €15 million, or where the total cost of the project is over €50 million. GBER II also exempts operating aid[71] for sport infrastructures for a sum up to €2 million per year.

---

they are not capable of attracting customers or investors from abroad, therefore effectively denying the inter-Member State effect of the measure. See paras 24 *et seq* of the Decision.

[65] The classic example is the funding granted for the renovation of a local swimming pool. See Commission decision of 21.12.2000, N 258/2000 – Germany (Leisure Pool Dorsten), [2001] OJ C 171, 16.

[66] See Traupel (n 38), 419.

[67] The Regulations expressly lists investment aid, including aid for the construction or upgrade of sport and multifunctional recreational infrastructure, and operating aid for sport infrastructure. See GBER II, Art 55(7).

[68] The concept of multifunctional arenas comprises any type of recreational facility that offers, in particular, cultural and recreational services, with the exception of leisure parks and hotel facilities. See GBER II, Art 55(3).

[69] See GBER II Art 55(2).

[70] See GBER II, recital 74.

[71] The notion of operating aid for sport infrastructure includes personnel costs, materials, contracted services, communications, energy, maintenance, rent and so on, but it excludes depreciation charges and the costs of financing the enterprise. See GBER II, recital 39.

There is a close relationship between the approach taken by the Commission in the GBER II and the principles protected by Article 165 TFEU.[72] Indeed, the funding of sport infrastructures that are available to the public and serve more than one purpose of recreation is consistent with the goal of promoting European sporting issues, and in particular the structure based on voluntary activity and the social and educational function of sport. It is therefore possible to infer from this that certain types of investment in sport infrastructure are consistent also with the common European interest, as long as the facilities funded are multifunctional and open to the general public, and provided that there is a high risk of profitability that discourages private operators from investing.[73] This is considered enough to enhance the benefit that the community receives from the measure, and to outweigh the antitrust concerns.[74]

V. THE CASE LAW

Having briefly discussed the policy measures adopted in the area, the decision practice must be examined as well. In the first case ever opened by the Commission, *Public Grants to Professional Clubs*,[75] the French government introduced a number of measures aimed at improving the organisation and promotion of physical and sporting activities. Under the scheme, local authorities were subsidising those professional sports clubs that were equipped with a State-approved youth training centre, or that were committing to build one in the future, for a sum of up to €2.3 million a year per club.[76]

While the measure was clearly distorting the market, as it favoured the selected clubs over other competitors, the aid was held to be justified under the objective of improving and promoting the education and

---

[72] See GBER II, recital 74. This has been furthermore confirmed by the Commission in the approach it has taken in the cases concerning the funding for the construction of multifunctional arenas.

[73] See Traupel (n 38), 414. This is also demonstrated in two cases, *Erfurt* and *Hungary*, where the aim of promoting sport development and public access was considered the basis for the approval of the measure by the Commission.

[74] However, it must be noted that the requirement of multifunctionality of the facility can be easily satisfied where it is used by more than just one professional club. See Craven (n 43).

[75] See SG (2001) D/288165 French Subsidies for Youth Training N118/00, Press Release IP/01/599 of 25/04/2001.

[76] Ibid., para 5.

training of young French athletes.[77] The Commission considered that these were legitimate objectives, capable of outweighing the distortion caused by the measure. Furthermore, the French government ensured that the funding received by each club was used for the specific purpose intended, and in order to reach the objective specified.[78] The Commission concluded that the measure did not constitute illegal State aid, because of the objective pursued throughout, which were connected also with the responsibilities of the State in the field of education,[79] and in light of the role of local authorities, which were confined to distribute the grants and control their use.

The second case concerned the legality of an Italian law regulating the financial reporting rules and methods of professional football clubs. The *Salva Calcio* law[80] allowed clubs to submit accounts that underestimated their true costs and hid real losses.[81] Moreover, the measure granted the clubs the possibility of amortizing the costs of players for a period of ten years, instead of writing off the contract during its real duration, thereby improving the reported financial position of the club and giving a misleading picture to possible investors.[82] Hence, the main consequence was that clubs were able to pay inflated prices and wages for players, even when their financial situation would have not allowed them to do it.

The Commission issued a reasoned opinion formally asking the Italian government to change the law,[83] as the measure granted Italian football clubs a selective advantage over their European competitors, and the measure would have been also capable of distorting competition both on and off the field of play. The subsequent amendments adopted by the

---

[77] Moreover, the measure was not solely focused on aspects related to the physical activity. The aim was to combine the highest level of sport training and a good level of education. See the letter sent by the Commission to the French Government SG (2001) D/ 288165, paras 7 *et seq.*

[78] A Lewis and J Taylor, *Sport: Law and Practice* (Bloomsbury Professional 2014) 476.

[79] See the Letter SG (2001) D/288165, paras 13–16.

[80] Law Decree n. 282, 24th December 2002, amended in Law 27 of 21 February 2003.

[81] See Press Release IP/04/854, Commission asks Italy to change its rules on accounting by professional sports clubs ('Salva calcio').

[82] See S Morrow 'Impression Management in Football Club Financial Reporting' [2006] 1(2) IJSF 96.

[83] This is a preliminary stage that may lead to an infringement procedure under Art 258 TFEU.

Italian government[84] satisfied the Commission, which then concluded the procedure.[85]

As briefly mentioned before, the application of EU State aid rules to sport has progressively intensified in recent years. With the intent of providing a comprehensive overview of the most relevant case law, the following section will be divided in two parts: the first will be focused on cases that have dealt with multifunctional arenas and the promotion of sports participation and development, while the second will discuss the investigations on supporting measures to professional clubs.

V.i Multifunctional Arenas

The promotion of sports participation and development may increase the well-being and health of citizens, but it can also have an economic impact on a local, regional or even national basis.[86] Providing support and funding for related initiatives can sometimes be considered a duty of Member States and local communities. In a number of Decisions, the Commission has accepted the legality of State aid measures, in light of the benefits they provided to the citizens.

In 2011, the Hungarian government notified the Commission its intention to implement a scheme granting tax benefits for undertakings investing in sport. The Hungarian government ascribed the low level of involvement of the population in sport to the lack of well-equipped and modern sports infrastructure.[87] As investments in the sector would not be profitable under market conditions, and private investors were not able to fill the gap effectively, Hungary decided to implement a system capable of channelling funds in sport.[88] It therefore granted to undertakings donating money to the sport sector a 70% tax benefit from the yearly

---

[84] The legislation was repealed through the legislative Decree n°115 of 30 June 2005, confirmed by Law n°168 of 17 August 2005.

[85] See Press Release IP/05/1271, Commission closes case against Italy on accounting rules for professional sports clubs ('Salva-Calcio').

[86] See para 3.4 of the Communication from the Commission to the European Parliament, the Council, the European Economic and Social Committee and the Committee of the Regions, Developing the European Dimension in Sport, {SEC(2011) 66 final} {SEC(2011) 67 final} {SEC(2011) 68 final}.

[87] Developing the European Dimension in Sport, {SEC(2011) 66 final} {SEC(2011) 67 final} {SEC(2011) 68 final}, para 5.

[88] Ibid., para 9.

corporate tax, available in the year of the donation and the following three years.[89]

On the one hand, the direct beneficiaries of the system were sports associations,[90] sports clubs affiliated with those associations[91] and investors benefitting from the exemption. On the other, Hungary put forward that the measure aimed at providing positive effects to a wider number of indirect beneficiaries, from the sportspersons to the general public that would have access to the facilities.[92] Improving the sport structures could also make the population more interested in sport activities, which in turn could have positive effects in term of well-being and grassroots participation of young generations. Finally, local municipalities, which in the vast majority of the cases owned the sport facility, would have benefitted from the value increase of the renovation and upgrading of the structures funded by private undertakings.

As the measure was granting private operators an advantage over their competitors, and it was administered through public funding,[93] the Commission carried out an examination under Article 107(3)(c).[94] The Commission finally exempted the measure in light of its objectives and the number of controls put in place by the authorities to limit the potential distortion to the market.[95] The decisive element was the objective of encouraging the development of sports infrastructures and youth training, where negligence and underinvestment made impossible

---

[89] Hungary estimated that the total support through the tax benefit scheme translate into an amount of €445 million. Ibid., para 15.

[90] The decision makes explicit reference to the five most popular sports in Hungary, i.e., football, basketball, ice hockey, water polo, and handball. Ibid., para 28.

[91] Sport clubs were also among the private undertakings that were likely to invest in the renovation and development of the facilities.

[92] The undertaking recipient of the aid shall specify how the general public will benefit from the measure, and the aid will be granted only if such commitments are proportionate to the amount received. See Decision in the case SA.31722, para 43.

[93] In that case, the public funding was considered in light of the loss of revenues for the State resulting from the tax benefit scheme.

[94] As a reminder, Art 107(3)(c) TFEU states that aid may be compatible when it aims to facilitate the development of certain economic activities or of certain economic areas, where such aid does not adversely affect trading conditions to an extent contrary to the common interest.

[95] Decision in the case SA.31722, C(2011)7287 final (JOCE C/364/2011). A specific authority was set up to monitor the deployment of the aid. The Controlling Authority is a legal entity under the Ministry of National Resources (responsible for sport). See Decision in the case SA.31722, paras 49–51.

for the market to meet the need, given the size of the investment required, its level of risk and its limited profitability.[96] In particular, the Commission placed special emphasis on these goals in relation with Article 165 TFEU. In light of the social, educational and health dimension of sport and its ability to be used to improve the living conditions in disadvantaged areas, the objectives of enhancing mass participation and training of young persons were considered in line with the European common interest.

The rationale justifying the Hungarian tax scheme can be seen in other cases where supporting measures for the construction or renovation of multifunctional arenas were held compatible with EU State aid law. In 2013, the Commission approved a number of State aid measures that were characterised by similar objectives and factual background: in *Erfurt*;[97] *Jena*;[98] *Uppsala*;[99] and *Brussels*,[100] the municipalities notified the Commission with a plan to use public funding to build or renovate local arenas.[101] All the structures were meant to be built, or transformed into multifunctional arenas, capable of hosting different kinds of events, and open for the access and use to the widest population possible.[102] Similar to the argument put forward by the Hungarian government, the municipalities claimed that there was a need for the building or renovation of the arenas, as the existing facilities were not meeting the requirements of the public.[103] Moreover, this need could have not been satisfied by private operators on the market, in light of the size of the investment required and the risks connected to it.[104]

---

[96] See Craven (n 42).

[97] Commission Decision of 20.03.2013 on State aid SA.35135 (2012/N) – Germany Multifunktionsarena der Stadt Erfurt, hereafter 'Erfurt'.

[98] Commission Decision of 20.03.2013 on State aid SA.35440 (2012/N) – Germany Multifunktionsarena der Stadt Jena, hereafter 'Jena'.

[99] Commission Decision of 02.05.2013 on State aid SA.33618 (2012/C) which Sweden is planning to implement for Uppsala arena, hereafter 'Uppsala'.

[100] Commission Decision of 20.11.2013 on State aid SA.37109 (2013/N) – Belgium Football stadiums in Flanders, hereafter 'Brussels'.

[101] In light of the experience gained in this field, the Commission was subsequently able to issue the General Block Exempting Regulation. See B Keane 'The Application of Competition Law in the Entertainment and Sport Sectors' [2014] 5 JECLP 592.

[102] See *Erfurt* recital 2, *Jena* para 2, *Uppsala* para 30, and in part also *Brussels* para. 3.

[103] See *Erfurt* para 15, *Jena* para 17, *Uppsala* paras 11 and 13.

[104] See *Erfurt* para 16, *Jena* para 17, *Brussels* para 5, *Uppsala* paras 14 and 27.

The market for organising sport and other types of public events is open to competition between undertakings operating in different Member States, and these measures could therefore affect the condition of competition on the market. In one case in particular, the plan was to realise a multifunctional football arena that was going to be used by a professional football club and that needed to meet the UEFA standard for European football games.[105] Hence, there was a clear advantage for the club using the arena and for the owners of the facilities.

However, all the measures were exempted under Article 107(3)(c) TFEU,[106] as they were considered necessary, proportionate to the objective they were pursuing and their impact was limited through a number of conditions and restrictions.[107] Among these, the most relevant were the imposition of market prices for those clubs that were renting the arenas, and the assurance that the access would have been open to the public at large.

The Commission made reference to the societal role of sport recognised by both the Amsterdam Declaration on Sport and Article 165 TFEU. Moreover, it defined the construction of venues for sport and other public events as a responsibility of the State towards the general public.[108] The pursuit of a policy objective of common interest and the social, cultural and educational role of these enterprises was acknowledged even in relation to the *Brussels* decision, where the main users of the facilities were professional football clubs.[109]

It can therefore be inferred that, under certain conditions, the financing of sport infrastructures does not fall under the prohibition of State aid.[110] Two aspects have to be stressed in this relation: these structures are considered capable to provide benefits to the community at large, while in the market there would be no private operator willing to take up the

---

105 See *Brussels*, para 3.

106 See *Erfurt*, para 22, *Jena* para 23, *Brussels* para 42.

107 See *Erfurt*, para 21, *Jena*, para 17, *Brussels*, paras 37 and 39, and *Uppsala* para 56.

108 See Decision of the Commission in Case C4/2008 Investment of the Municipality of Rotterdam in the Ahoy Complex, point 67, and *Erfurt* paras 13 and 14, *Jena* paras 15 and 16, and *Uppsala* paras 26 and 48. See also Traupel (n 38).

109 See *Brussels* para 34.

110 The Commission had already pointed this out in its Staff Working Document. See Commission Staff Working Document – The EU and Sport: Background and Context – Accompanying document to the White Paper on Sport {COM(2007) 391 final} {SEC(2007)932} {SEC(2007)934} {SEC(2007)936}, para 3.2.2 and note 73.

financing. When these considerations are linked with the effect of GBER II, the consequence is to accept that financing of sport infrastructures is part of the remit of the State, as it fulfils a public interest.

V.ii State Aid to Host International Events

A similar approach has also been adopted when the aid involved major professional football clubs. In 2013, the Commission approved a set of measures financing the construction and renovation of nine football stadia in France, necessary to host the UEFA Euro Championship in 2016.[111] The aid, granted by local and national authorities, amounted to a total of more than €1 billion, and covered the construction of four new stadia and the renovation of five existing ones.[112] The stadia were mainly destined to be used by professional football clubs, which had not been selected through a public tender, but directly appointed.[113] These clubs were going to pay a rent set at market price,[114] but the facilities could also be used by the municipality or other related organisations for cultural, musical or social events.

The Commission held that the measures were providing an advantage to the private undertakings involved in the construction and renovation of the stadia, and also to the professional clubs as users of the facilities. State resources were involved, and the aid was likely to distort the market for organising and hosting international events within the territory of the EU.[115] The Commission relied again on the importance of sport and its social value to argue that the investments were to be considered in line with objectives of common European policy,[116] and responding to a responsibility of the State towards the population.[117] The renovation and

---

[111] See Decision of the Commission on Aide d'Etat SA 35501 (2013/N) – France Financement de la construction et de la rénovation des stades pour l'EURO, 2016 C(2013) 9103 final.

[112] In Bordeaux, Lille, Lyon, Nice, Paris, Saint-Etienne, Marseille, Toulouse and Lens.

[113] Keane (n 101).

[114] See SA 35501, para 301. However, for Marseille, Lille, Nice and Saint Etienne the rent will be fixed taking into consideration the sporting results of the clubs, which might represent a significant variable in this relation.

[115] See SA 35501, para 262.

[116] The Commission cited again Art 165 TFEU and the Amsterdam Declaration on Sport. See SA 35501, para 269.

[117] See SA 35501, para 273.

construction of these facilities were considered necessary to host international events, sporting, cultural and social events,[118] and the need would have not been satisfied without the intervention of the State.[119] The decision finally exempted the measures under Article 107(3)(c), as the amount granted was considered limited to what was necessary to achieve the objective, and in light of the control system put in place by France over the prices paid by the resident clubs.[120]

In the cases discussed above, the Commission has given consideration to some specific characteristics of the sports market.[121] Moreover, the institution had to make reference to the societal and cultural importance of sport to justify the measures as effectively pursuing an objective of common interest. Although involving professional football clubs, some of which are among the most famous in the world, these measures were considered on equal terms as the one involving amateur clubs. It is therefore apparent that the Commission has devised a sport specific approach in this sector, consistently applied with similar conditions and requirements.

V.iii Sports Clubs in Financial Difficulties

The question may be dealt differently when the financing does not involve infrastructures and multifunctional arenas. The following section will give account of an investigation of the Commission over a number of measures granted by local municipalities to Dutch professional football clubs that were going through economic hardship.[122]

During the period 2007–11, Vitesse Football Club faced financial difficulties. In the ten previous seasons the club accumulated debts for €27.4 million, its main creditor being the local municipality of Arnhem. As it was not able to satisfy its creditors, Vitesse was admitted to a

---

[118] K Daly, 'Sport and State Aid – Reining in the Populist Gesture' [2014] 1 CPIAC 1.

[119] See SA 35501, para 275 where the Commission noticed that historically the facilities are owned by local authorities and municipalities, and that private investors are therefore reluctant to fund these enterprises.

[120] Keane (n 101).

[121] And particularly in relation to the ownership of sporting facilities and the lack of interest by private investors.

[122] See Decision of the Commission to open an investigation in the case State aid SA.33584 (2013/C) (ex 2011/NN). The Commission decided to open one cumulative investigation on the different measures, despite them being granted by a number of local authorities.

temporary suspension of payment.[123] The municipality had to settle as well, and accepted to receive a sum amounting to 10% of its recognised claim.[124] The Commission approved the measure, holding that the municipality behaved as a hypothetical private creditor, thereby not conferring any advantage to the club.[125]

In 2010, the municipality of Nijmegen purchased from the local football club[126] an alleged right to buy the multifunctional sports facilities, which at the time were leased to the club but still owned by the municipality itself. The right to purchase the multifunctional sports facilities was included in the lease contract, and the municipality agreed to buy the said right at a price established through outside property evaluation experts.[127]

Since 2004, Willem II had rented the stadium from the municipality of Tilburg. In 2010, with an outstanding rent of €1 million, the club announced that it was on the brink of bankruptcy and could not pay the rent. The municipality decided to lower the rent with a retroactive effect until 1 July 2004, and to suspend it from 2009 onwards.[128] The municipality argued that the bankruptcy of the club would have prevented the authority from recovering any outstanding rent, and it would have obliged it to demolish the stadium, left without a tenant, not to mention the loss of an attraction for fans and tourists.[129]

In 2010, MVV Maastricht was facing a debt load of €6.5 million, of which €1.7 million was owed to the municipality. The authority, without proceeding to a formal suspension of the payment, waived its claims

---

123 This is a procedure laid down by Dutch insolvency law, permitting a trustee to attempt to find an agreement with the creditors to restructure the debt, providing the company has a prospect of future profitability.

124 See SA.33584 para 22. This sum, however, does not include the contractual fines for not having repaid the debt.

125 See SA.33584 para 43 and 44. Claiming back the sum could have led the club into bankruptcy and prevented the municipality from recovering the credit.

126 Nijmegen Eendracht Combinatie, also known as NEC.

127 See SA.33584 paras 24–28 and 47. The Commission found that the Dutch Authority based its decision solely on one of two discording legal opinions, without giving reasons as to why it chose one and disregard the other.

128 See SA.33584 paras 29 and 30.

129 See SA.33584 para 30. This argument was not accepted by the Commission, which considered that in the event of bankruptcy, a successor club could have been found as user of the stadium. See Commission Decision, SA.40168 – 2015/C (ex SA.33584 – 2013/C (ex 2011/NN)) implemented by the Netherlands in favour of the professional football club Willem II in Tilburg, para 35.

towards the club as part of a creditor's agreement.[130] It also bought the stadium which was owned by a foundation and only used by the club. The behaviour of the municipality departed from the conduct of other creditors, which refused to waive their claims or transformed them into claims for future incomes.[131]

In 2011, the municipality of Eindhoven entered into an agreement with PSV to buy the land under the stadium and the training ground, owned by the club, only to then lease the land back to the club.[132] The municipality alleged that the land sales was expected to be neutral for its budget, and that both the sales price and the annual lease were based on outside expertise. However, rather than avoiding making a loss and settling for a neutral effect, a private investor would have tried to make a profit out of the enterprise.[133]

In 2010, as part of a larger plan involving all the creditors, the municipality of Den Bosch waived the debt of the club by selling it to the organised supporters for a symbolic sum of €1. The supporters would have then transformed the debt into a shareholding of 60% in a new legal structure of the club, leaving the remaining 40% to the creditors. Furthermore, the municipality purchased from the club its training centre for €1,400,000.[134] The Dutch Authority argued that the waiver of the debt could not constitute an advantage for FC Den Bosch, because the sum would have not been repaid anyway. However, the municipality sold his claim for virtually nothing, while other creditors transformed their claim into shareholdings. Moreover, through this decision the club was able to set up a new legal structure with a clean balance sheet.

In all the measures comprised under the investigation, the football clubs received a selective advantage over their competitors through State resources. Indeed, each of them have the potential to participate in European competitions, and their activity is not limited to competing on

---

130 The Dutch authority held that claiming back the debt would have led to the bankruptcy of the club, which would have prevented the municipality from recovering the credit, as a subordinate claim. See Commission Decision SA.41612 – 2015/C (ex SA.33584 (2013/C) (ex 2011/NN)) implemented by the Netherlands in favour of the professional football club MVV in Maastricht, para 16.

131 See SA.33584 para 55.

132 See SA.33584 paras 33 and 34. The sum paid by the municipality and the rent paid by the club were both determined on the basis of an independent land valuation. See Commission Decision on the Measure SA.41613 – 2015/C (ex SA.33584 – 2013/C (ex 2011/NN)), at paras 19–20, and 48–52.

133 See SA.33584 paras 61 and 62.

134 See SA.33584 paras 35 and 36.

the pitch, but it also extends to signing media and sponsoring contracts, operating on the players transfer market, and possibly in the field of hospitality.[135]

However, the Commission cleared all the measures under Article 107(3)(c) TFEU.[136] Indeed, it decided that the transaction involving PSV Eindhoven was carried out under acceptable market conditions.[137] Conversely, although they did not pass the market operator test, in the cases of Den Bosch, MVV, NEC and Willem II the measures were granted following the implementation of a realistic restructuring plan.[138]

The Commission was 'on a roll' and it did not stop there. Indeed, it opened an investigation over measures put in place by Spanish public authorities to support professional football clubs in financial difficulties. The aid was therefore characterised by rationale and objectives similar to the cases seen above. Between 2009 and 2013, the Instituto Valenciano de Finanzas (IVF),[139] provided guarantees for a number of bank loans to Valencia FC, Hercules FC and Elche CF. In all the three instances, IVF received as counter guarantee the pledge on shares of the clubs.[140]

The Commission noticed that, as the guarantees covered 100% of the loans, it appeared that market operators were not willing to bear any risks of insolvency of the clubs. As the clubs did not pay for the guarantee received, the Commission argued that the three clubs received a selective advantage, granted through State resources.[141] However, as opposed to the measures granted in the Netherlands, the Commission maintained that

---

135 See SA.33584 paras 40. In particular, these effects are not strictly dependant on the ability of the clubs to participate in European competitions, but might occur anyway in light of the broad range of activities they undertake.

136 See European Commission, Press Release IP/16/2402, State aid: Commission clears support measures for certain football clubs in the Netherlands, Brussels, 4 July 2016.

137 Factors considered by the Commission in this assessment were the presence of a safety deposit and a guarantee for the payment of the lease. Furthermore, the stadium was located in a very profitable area. See Commission Decision on the Measure SA.41613 – 2015/C (ex SA.33584 – 2013/C (ex 2011/NN)), at paras 57–58.

138 In this relation, the measure was considered to comply with the Community guidelines on State aid for rescuing and restructuring firms in difficulty [2004] OJ C 244.

139 The Instituto Valenciano de Finanzas, IVF hereafter, is a public financing institution under the control of Generalitat Valenciana, the governing authority for the Comunidad Autonoma de Valencia. IVF is attached to the Ministry of Finance and Public Administration.

140 See State aid SA.36387 paras 9–12.

141 SA.36387 para 35.

there was no restructuring plan for the clubs in financial difficulties. The Commission therefore held that the measures were unlawful.[142]

The two sets of investigations presented some similarities. In both the Dutch and the Spanish cases,[143] the clubs were facing financial difficulties.[144] The Commission decided to assess whether the Community Guidelines on State aid for rescuing and restructuring firms in difficulty[145] could apply in these instances, although the national authorities did not try to argue the point. However, the measures granted by the Spanish government lacked some necessary elements in order to qualify as restructuring aid: aid granted to firms in financial difficulty have to be conditional to the implementation of a restructuring plan aiming at restoring the long-term viability of the firm in a reasonable timescale.[146] Furthermore, the granting of restructuring aid is allowed only on a one-time basis, unless ten years have elapsed from the first measure. Finally, the Guidelines mention the need for compensatory measures, which should offset the adverse effect of the aid for the competitors of the recipient.[147] In the sport sector, these may be points deduction, limits on the number of players in the squad, the imposition of a cap between salaries and turnovers and other sporting sanctions.[148] The Commission includes in these possible compensatory measures commitments to increase pro bono activities, which would represent an effective tool for the EU institution to pursue and enhance societal benefits from the role of professional sport clubs within the community.[149] However, neither the

---

142 See European Commission, Press Release IP/16/2401, State aid: Commission decides Spanish professional football clubs have to pay back incompatible aid, Brussels, 4 July 2016.

143 For the Dutch clubs, see State aid SA.33584 para 76 and for the Spanish clubs, see State aid SA.36387 paras 17–25.

144 Although there is no Community definition for it, the Commission regards an undertaking as a firm in difficulty where it is unable to survive without the intervention of public authorities, due to increasing losses, diminishing turnovers, mounting debts and other parameters. See Communication from the Commission—Community guidelines on State aid for rescuing and restructuring firms in difficulty (n 138), para 9 and Craven (n 43).

145 See Communication from the Commission, ibid.

146 Ibid., paras 34–37.

147 However, under the current guidelines, compensatory measures do not apply to small enterprises, as the Dutch clubs were considered. See ibid., para 41.

148 For a discussion on the effectiveness of compensatory measures in sport, see Traupel (n 38).

149 Craven (n 43).

Dutch nor the Spanish authorities have mentioned the imposition of such sanctions to the teams that have received the aid.[150]

While in the Decisions on the funding of sporting facilities the Commission stressed the societal and cultural role of sport, the approach in these cases is much stricter. The societal and cultural role of sport is overlooked against the application of rules that consider professional clubs as any other undertaking carrying out an economic activity.[151] In these cases, the characteristics of the market in the sporting sector, and in particular the lack of private investors, seem to have less importance.

V.iv State Aid to Professional Sport Clubs

The last group of investigations opened by the EU Commission assessed the legality of a tax exemption granted by the Spanish government to four professional football clubs,[152] and the legality of a transfer of land between the municipality of Madrid and Real Madrid CF.[153]

The *Ley del Deporte*[154] adopted by the Spanish government in 1990, obliged all the Spanish professional sport clubs to convert into sport limited companies.[155] Sport clubs are treated as non-profit entities, which qualify for a partial corporate tax exemption according to the Spanish fiscal law.[156] The provision aimed at imposing a model of legal and financial responsibility, as opposed to a situation where neither the members of the clubs, nor their administrators bore financial responsibility for the losses cumulated.[157]

---

150 The Commission, however, identified on its own some compensatory measures in the Dutch cases. See Commission Decision, SA.40168 – 2015/C (ex SA.33584 – 2013/C (ex 2011/NN)) implemented by the Netherlands in favour of the professional football club Willem II in Tilburg, para 51.

151 Craven (n 42).

152 See Decision of the Commission to open an investigation in the case State aid SA.29769 (2013/C) (ex 2013/NN) – Spain State aid to certain Spanish professional sport clubs.

153 See Decision of the Commission to open an investigation in the case State aid SA.33754 (2013/C) (ex 2013/NN) – Spain Real Madrid CF.

154 Ley 10/1990, de 15 de octubre, del Deporte, BOE de 17 de Octubre de 1990.

155 Sociedad anonima deportivas.

156 Art 9(3)a) of the Spanish Corporate Tax Law (Ley del Impuesto sobre Sociedades). As non-profit entities, clubs were allowed to pay corporate tax for their commercial income at a reduced rate of 25 per cent instead of the general rate of 30 per cent. See SA.29769, para 7.

157 See SA.29769, para 4.

However, the Seventh Additional Disposition of the *Ley del deporte* exempted from the obligation those football clubs which had a positive balance in the four seasons preceding the adoption of the measure, as this would have shown good corporate management on their behalf. The only clubs that were allowed to maintain their status as sports clubs were Real Madrid CF, Athletic Club Bilbao, Club Atlético Osasuna (Navarra) and FC Barcelona.

The measure is likely to provide a selective advantage if it departs from the regime generally applicable to other undertakings in a similar factual and legal situation. In this case, the reference system is the Spanish Corporate tax system, and any difference must be justified on the basis of the nature and the objective of the taxation system in question.[158] In this regard, losses are not intrinsically connected to a specific form of organisation, and the business performance cannot be considered as an objective criterion to justify a different treatment or the imposition of a particular structure.[159]

The main issue raised by the Commission was the lack of possible reviews or amendments of the system.[160] The *Ley del deporte* did not include further checks and re-assessment of the financial situation of the clubs, which were allowed to maintain their status indefinitely. Conversely, other clubs were prevented from re-converting to sport clubs, irrespective of the way their financial situation subsequently evolved.

Although the four Spanish clubs were able to maintain their status as non-profit entities, they were clearly carrying out profit-oriented professional activities,[161] in competition with other European football clubs, and with their national competitors subject to the normal taxation regime. The revenues they generate can be used to boost their success on the pitch, which in turn depends on the amount of funds they can use to attract the best players and coaches.[162]

---

[158] See the Commission Notice on the Application of State aid rules to Measures Relating to Direct Business Taxation [1998] OJ C 384, para 25.

[159] Ibid., para 24.

[160] See SA.29769 paras 21–23.

[161] To give an idea, two of the clubs that have received the tax exemption were in the season 2013–14 amongst the top five earners in football. Real Madrid CF had revenues of €594.5m (first in this table) and FC Barcelona had revenues of €484.6m (fourth). See Football Money League (18th edn, Deloitte 2015, https://www2.deloitte.com/na/en/pages/audit/articles/deloitte-football-money-league.html (accessed on 26 Oct 2017).

[162] See SA.29769 para 9. In this regard, UEFA has confirmed the connection between success on the pitch and wage bill of the club. See UEFA Club Licensing Benchmarking Report Financial Year 2012.

The Commission declared the measures in breach of State aid rules, as it provided a selective advantage through State resources, and ordered the Spanish government to recover the aid.[163]

The second investigation concerned the transfer of certain properties between Real Madrid CF and the local municipality.[164] The parties had signed an agreement in 2011, which was the object of the investigation, in order to solve a legal issue concerning a number of agreements signed between 1991 and 1998. In brief, Real Madrid agreed to transfer to the municipality 30,000 m^2 of land (part of the *Ciudad Deportiva*)[165] and in exchange the municipality were to provide the club with a number of plots of land. This included 'Las Tablas', designated for sport use and consisting of 70,815 m^2, at a value estimated of €95,194.[166] The parties agreed that this would have not prevented the transfer, provided that Real Madrid respected the classification.

However, the land was subject to an expropriation procedure, and it could have not been transferred immediately. When the Council of Madrid was finally registered as owner of 'Las Tablas' in February 2003, it argued that due to its classification, the land had to be owned publicly and could have not been the object of transfer to a private entity.[167] Therefore, the Council had to compensate the club for not having transferred 'Las Tablas', with a sum corresponding to the current value of the land. The Council agreed to compensate Real Madrid with the transfer of several other plots of land, for a total estimated value of €22,693,054.44. The deal included also an area of 5,216 m^2 in front of the Santiago Bernabeu stadium, where Real Madrid intended to build a shopping mall and a hotel.[168]

---

[163] See European Commission, Press Release IP/16/2401, State aid: Commission decides Spanish professional football clubs have to pay back incompatible aid, Brussels, 4 July 2016. Interestingly, the Spanish government had already amended the legislation to end the discriminatory tax treatment, before the Commission adopted its Decision.

[164] See Decision of the Commission to open an investigation in the case State aid SA.33754 (2013/C) (ex 2013/NN) – Spain Real Madrid CF.

[165] Real Madrid CF training ground.

[166] See State aid SA.33754, paras 4–7. The valuation was done by the administration of Madrid on the basis of the Real Decreto 1020/1993, which offered parameters to estimate the value of urban real property.

[167] This argument was based on the Law 9/2001 of July 17 of the Land of the Community of Madrid.

[168] The Council of Madrid had to change the Plan General de Ordenación Urbana de Madrid to enable the commercial use of the area by the Club. See State aid SA.33754, para 18.

One central element of the 2011 agreement was the impossibility of transferring 'Las Tablas' to the club, due its classification; however, as part of the final deal the Council of Madrid amended the *Plan General de Ordenación Urbana* in order to allow the club to build on the area in front of the stadium.[169] In so doing, the Council did not however adopt the same procedure in relation to 'Las Tablas'. Furthermore, the Council did not seek any legal advice as to the probability of being found liable to pay compensation to the club.[170]

The Commission therefore argued that Real Madrid CF received an advantage, from the fact that a plot of land, originally valued at €595,194, had its value increased to €22 million, and in light of the doubts on the impossibility of the transfer.[171] This selective advantage was granted by the State in a manner which denied it possible (substantial) revenue and out of line with the objective of common interest. The Commission held that the transaction was overvalued and that the Council did not act per the private market operator principles. As it considered that the aid was not aligned with the objective of common interest, the institution declared the measure in breach of EU State aid rules and ordered the municipality of Madrid to recover it.[172]

It must be noticed that the Commission cited Article 165 TFEU and the need to take into consideration the specific characteristics of sport in all the investigations of this last group. However, this did not suffice to constitute an objective of common interest that could justify a State aid. Indeed, all these measures were supporting strong commercial entities: their survival was not in danger, and the measures did not appear to provide any benefits to the community.

---

[169] This amendment was later annulled by the Tribunal Superior de Justicia de Madrid in its judgment no. 77/2015, as there were no considerations of public interest justifying the urban planning change and the transaction in general. See Commission Decision on State aid, SA.33754 (2013/C) (ex 2013/NN) implemented by Spain for Real Madrid CF, paras 74–77.

[170] See Commission Decision on State aid, SA.33754 (2013/C) (ex 2013/NN) implemented by Spain for Real Madrid CF, paras 93–94.

[171] Craven (n 42).

[172] The Commission quantified the aid to be recovered in the difference between the compensation paid by the municipality of Madrid and the maximum extent of its liability under the 1998 agreement, thereby setting it at €18.418 054.44. See Commission Decision on State aid, SA.33754 (2013/C) (ex 2013/NN) implemented by Spain for Real Madrid CF, para 142.

VI. MARKET OPERATOR PRINCIPLE IN SPORT

An important element that has to be considered in any State aid analysis is the application of the 'market economy operator principle': an undertaking will not obtain any unlawful advantage when the State operates on the market like any other normal private player. Therefore, the question is whether the conduct of the public authority is informed by the same criteria and objectives that would be pursued by a private operator.

It is argued that the conduct of private operators is ultimately focused on obtaining a return from the investment made.[173] In this perspective, non-economic concerns may be considered only when they are functional to pursuing profits.[174] The latter, however, may be a long-term objective, as even private entities might be willing to accept losses in the short term for strategic reasons.[175] When assessing a public measure, the Commission has to consider whether the type of conduct corresponds to a well-established practice amongst the private actors that operate in that specific sector.[176] If it is common for private investors not to expect direct profits from an investment in the sporting sector, the State would not provide any advantage to the recipient if it would adopt a similar approach.

Football is the sporting sector most commonly assessed by the Commission. With the exception of few major clubs, most of the professional football clubs are not profitable entities.[177] Furthermore, in many European countries clubs do not own the stadium in which they play their home matches and they are just users of the facility.[178] In this

---

[173] See Case 234/84 *Commission v Belgium* [1986] ECR 02263, para 14, and further confirmed also in the Commission Decision SA.41612 – 2015/C (ex SA.33584 (2013/C) (ex 2011/NN)) implemented by the Netherlands in favour of the professional football club MVV in Maastricht, para 35.

[174] See Case C-303/88 *Italy v Commission* [1991] ECR I-1433, para 21: '[S]uch decisions may be motivated not solely by the likelihood of an indirect material profit but also by other considerations, such as a desire to protect the group's image or to redirect its activities.'

[175] Traupel (n 38).

[176] See Gian Marco Galletti, 'How Reasonable a Private Investor Can Be Assumed to Be? Corsica Ferries France' [2015] 52 CMLR 1095.

[177] In support of this, see the UEFA European Club Licensing Benchmarking Report Financial Year 2011.

[178] As it has been highlighted by the Commission in the cases discussed above. See the Decision of the Commission to open an investigation on the case Aide d'Etat SA 35501 (2013/N) – France Financement de la construction et de la rénovation des stades pour l'EURO, 2016 C(2013) 9103 final, at para 275, and

scenario, recovering or amortizing the investment costs of building or renovating a stadium may be difficult, and anyway impossible in the short term. If these characteristics were effectively taken into account, it would not be legitimate to require a more profit-oriented strategy if public authorities were funding the enterprise.

Another element to be considered is that a measure produces an advantage for a club only if there is no adequate service in return. However, when local entities provide financial support to the local professional sport clubs, they are motivated by the ability of these entities to attract publicity and tourism.[179] These clubs are not only a source of cultural and societal cohesion, but undertakings that produce revenues. The decision to support local professional clubs may be merely economical, as this would keep them viable and guarantee a steady flow of local taxes. This support may also stimulate activities in neighbouring markets, and contribute to the creation of jobs in the area, an objective in line with Europe 2020 strategy.[180] However, the conduct of a private market operator would not aim at promoting regional, social and sectoral considerations, which are instead factors that would be taken into account only by a public authority.

In the decision practice of the Commission, the participative nature of sporting activities has been considered as an objective and a tool for the pursuit of public policies, as long as benefits were granted to the wider community. In other circumstances, the commercial nature that characterises modern professional clubs has obscured the societal benefits that supporting measures may still bring about. However, there needs to be a clear differentiation between aid that is granted to support and sustain local clubs and measures that merely aim to provide an advantage to entities that are otherwise self-sufficient. In any event and in both instances, the characteristics of the market – whether a private operator would invest in the enterprise, the economic conditions of the clubs involved and the possibility of imposing compensatory measures – should be taken into account.

---

the Decision of the Commission to open an investigation in the case State aid SA.33584 (2013/C) (ex 2011/NN).

[179] Traupel (n 38).

[180] See the Communication from the Commission Europe 2020: A Strategy for Smart, Sustainable and Inclusive Growth, COM(2010) 2020 final.

VII. CONCLUSION

In terms of sports law, the application of State aid to sport is one area of intense debate. Sport represents a tool that public authorities use to achieve a number of different objectives of public policy, and it attracts the interest of a large section of the public. EU institutions have finally recognised that the topic deserves attention, but the task of the Commission, in particular, is not an easy one.

The multiple references to Article 165 TFEU demonstrate that the Commission is prepared to accept that sport has some characteristics that Member States may legitimately seek to protect, in light of the benefits that will be granted to the community and its social and educational function. Furthermore, even when the parties involved have not referred to them, the Commission has decided on its own to assess the legitimacy of measures under the relevant guidelines (for restructuring firms in difficulty). Clearly, there is a sport specific approach in this sector, as clearly demonstrated by the general block exempting regulation specifically for the construction of sporting infrastructures.

In this sense, a difference has to be highlighted between public financing measures used for the construction of infrastructure, encapsulated by the notion of public policy, and aid granted to professional sport. While measures comprised under the latter may be assessed by way of a market operator principle, this chapter has tried to show how the application of this test lacks the necessary flexibility in light of specific characteristics of the sporting industry.

On the other hand, the Commission has on multiple occasions confirmed its intention to work with UEFA in a manner that best reconciles the implementation of State aid rules with UEFA's Financial Fair Play regulations. In this regard, it is suggested that the strict application of State aid rules would better protect the principles of fairness and the uncertainty of the competition, also underpinned by Article 165(2) TFEU.

11. Harmonisation and diversity: trends and challenges in European sports image rights law

Corinna Coors

I. INTRODUCTION

The economic value of image rights of athletes has increased tremendously over the past decades. License fees and royalties are a valuable source of income for many sports personalities and clubs in Europe.[1] With USD58 million from endorsements alone, tennis star Roger Federer topped the list of the Forbes' 2017 ranking of the athletes earning the most from endorsements.[2] Despite the immense value of image rights and an increasing number of international and cross-border transactions, there is currently only piecemeal regulation across the European Union (EU). While there were occasional calls for a more harmonised approach across Member States to facilitate business worldwide, there has been no real attempt at harmonisation as of yet.[3]

---

1 I Blackshaw, *Sports Marketing Agreements: Legal, Fiscal and Practical Aspects* (Asser 2011) 1.

2 The world's highest paid athletes – Forbes 2017 ranking, https://www.forbes.com/athletes/list (accessed 27 Feb 2018).

3 For example, it has been argued that the US and Member States of the EU should recognise a general 'right of persona', see J Pinckaers, 'The Right of Persona: A New Intellectual Property Right for the US and EU' in David Vaver (ed.), *Intellectual Property Rights: Critical Concepts in Law* (Routledge 2006). T Synodinou, 'Image Right and Copyright Law in Europe: Divergences and Convergences' (2014) 3 *Laws* 181, 194 advocates the use of 'the well-established, internationally recognised and EU-harmonised model of copyright law' as a guidance for shaping an image right or broader publicity right. FJ Dougherty, 'Foreword: The Right of Publicity – Towards a Comparative and International Perspective' (1998) 18 *Loy La Ent L Rev* 421, 422–3 argues, however, that 'although there may be benefits to an international proprietary right of publicity, one should be cautious of advocating "transplantation" of the U.S. right into other countries.'

After the UK voted to leave the EU on 23 June 2016 (Brexit), the legal situation has become even more uncertain. This chapter highlights the recent trends and challenges of image rights protection in Europe, including the implications of Brexit on the protection of athletes against false endorsement. It is argued that the similarities between the treatments of image rights (recognising both economic and dignitary interests) may outweigh the existing traditional differences (the nature and justification for image rights) in the long term. It may be assumed that the law will tentatively recognise both economic and moral elements, helping to promote a more workable and enforceable harmonised international standard in this area.

II. IMAGE RIGHT PROTECTION IN EUROPE

Despite the widely recognised commercial value of image rights, there is currently no international standard or harmonised legal concept for recognising an image right. Additional confusion arises from the fact that Member States of the EU often use different terminology to describe the legal protection against commercial exploitation of aspects of one's personality by a third party. Some countries use the term 'image rights' but also terms such as 'personality rights' or 'portrait rights' are used.[4] While certain jurisdictions, such as Germany and France offer statutory protection against the exploitation of an individual's image, English law provides no cause of action for the infringement of image rights as such.[5] Various causes of action, such as breach of confidence, privacy, copyright and trade mark infringement, and passing off/false endorsement, are available when seeking to protect a celebrity's claim for image right protection.[6] The rather fragmented and inconsistent framework of image right protection operating across Europe has so far resulted in legal

---

[4] B van Rompuy *et al.*, 'Study on Sports Organisers' Rights in the European Union: Final Report. European Commission' (EAC 18/2012, Feb 2014) 43 and available at http://www.ivir.nl/publicaties/download/1353 (accessed 26 Oct 2017).

[5] Blackshaw, *supra* note 1, at 267.

[6] See *Wombles Ltd v Wombles Skips Ltd* [1977] RPC 99; *Lyngstad & Ors v Anabas Prods Ltd* [1977] FSR 61; *Mirage Studios v Counter Feat Clothing Co Ltd* [1991] FSR 145; *Elvis Presley Enterprises Inc v Sid Shaw Elvisly Yours* [1999] RPC 567.

uncertainty for persons wanting to invoke their image rights against third parties across the EU.[7]

Some clarification on the issue of jurisdiction and applicable law for infringements of personality rights on the internet was, however, recently provided by the Grand Chamber of the Court of Justice of the European Union (CJEU) in its joined cases of *eDate Advertising v X and Olivier Martinez v MGN*.[8] The cases concerned articles published on the internet that were alleged to infringe the rights of the individuals named in the articles. The second reference, C-161/10, was brought under Article 9 of the French Civil Code, which provides that 'everyone has the right to respect for his private life'. The publisher challenged the jurisdiction of the French court, arguing that there was no sufficiently close connecting factor between the placing online of the information in the UK and the alleged damage in France.

The CJEU rejected that argument and pointed out that a person who claims an infringement of his or her personality rights by means of content placed on an internet website can choose to bring an action before the court of the Member State in which they have their 'centre of interests' in respect of all of the damage caused.[9] The CJEU also held that the provider of an electronic commerce service covered by the E-Commerce Directive cannot be made subject to stricter requirements than those provided for by the law of the Member State in which it is established. The outcome in *eDate Advertising* will be welcomed by those who have their personality rights infringed on the internet. It effectively recognised the protection of personality rights in the digital era which allows for the rapid dissemination of potentially infringing material on the internet and social media, signalling an important step forward to the harmonisation of this area of law.[10]

II.i UK

Although English law does not expressly recognise an image or personality rights, English courts are stretching the boundaries of traditional common law, increasingly recognising the commercial value of celebrity

---

[7] See van Rompuy et al. *supra* note 4, at 43.

[8] Cases C-509/09 and C-161-10, *eDate Advertising GmbH v X, and Oliver Martinez and Robert Martinez v MGN Ltd* [2011] ECR I 10269.

[9] Ibid., 69.

[10] A Savin, *EU Internet Law* (Edward Elgar 2013) 59.

and athlete endorsements.[11] In *Proactive Sports Management Ltd v Rooney & Ors* Lady Justice Arden expressly highlighted the economic value of image rights: 'the endorsement of goods encourages the purchase and consumption of goods, and the court is entitled to assume that it is in the interests of the public that image rights should be fully realisable for this economic purpose'.[12]

One of the first high-profile, false-endorsement cases involving a professional sportsman in the UK was *Irvine v Talksport* in 2002 where the radio station Talksport had sent out promotional material to potential advertising buyers including a brochure featuring a photograph of the F1 racing driver Eddie Irvine.[13] Talksport had manipulated a previous photo of Irvine in which he had been holding a mobile phone by superimposing the Talksport radio onto the image in place of the phone. Irvine successfully sued Talksport Radio for passing off. The *Irvine* case was a significant step towards the development of image right protection in the UK, bringing traditional passing off law in line with modern commercial reality.[14]

In a recent decision of the English Court of Appeal, involving the pop star Rihanna and the fashion chain Topshop, Lord Justice Kitchin confirmed that: 'There is in English law no "image right" or "character right" which allows a celebrity to control the use of his or her name or image.'[15] The court upheld the trial judge's finding that Topshop's unauthorised use of Rihanna's image on a T-shirt was passing off.[16] The Rihanna decision, however, is unlikely to open the floodgates for claims to be brought every time the image of a celebrity or sportsman is used without consent on merchandising. Each case will depend upon the individual circumstances as Judge Birss emphasised that 'the mere sale

---

[11] C Walsh, 'Are Personality Rights Finally on the UK Agenda?' (2013) 35(5) EIPR 253, 260; H Beverly-Smith and L Barrow, 'Talk That Tort … of Passing Off: Rihanna and the Scope of Actionable Misrepresentation: *Fenty v Arcadia Group Brands Ltd (t/a Topshop)*' (2014) 36 (1) EIPR 57.

[12] *Proactive Sports Management Ltd v Rooney and Ors* [2011] EWCA Civ 1444, para 93.

[13] *Edmund Irvine Tidswell Ltd v Talksport Ltd* [2002] EWHC 367 (Ch) and on appeal as *Irvine and Ors v Talksport Ltd* [2003] EWCA Civ 423.

[14] H Hansen (ed.) *Intellectual Property and Policy, Vol 11* (Hart 2010), 502.

[15] *Fenty and Ors v Arcadia Group Brands Ltd and Anor* [2015] EWCA Civ 3, para 29. See also S Fletcher and J Mitchell, 'Court of Appeal Found no Love for Topshop Tank: The Image Right that Dare not Speak its Name' (2015) 37(6) EIPR 394.

[16] *Fenty and Ors v Arcadia Group Brands Ltd (t/a Topshop) and Anor* [2013] EWHC 2310 (Ch) (Birss J).

by a trader of a T-shirt bearing an image of a famous person is not, without more, an act of passing off'.[17]

II.i(a) Privacy

In addition to passing off, privacy rights have received increasing recognition both at UK and European level. The key justification for this change is Article 8(1) of the European Convention on Human Rights (ECHR) which provides a right to respect for a person's private and family life.[18] Two important cases, *Douglas v Hello!*[19] and *Campbell v MGN*[20] reflect the fast-developing area of privacy law in the UK which has been supported and enhanced by the enactment of the Human Rights Act 1998 (HRA).[21] The first case concerned the actors, Michael Douglas and Catherine Zeta-Jones. In 2000, the stars had granted exclusive rights to pictures of their wedding to the OK! magazine but the defendant, the publisher of the Hello! magazine planned to publish its own pictures. The claimants brought an action preventing the defendant from publishing unauthorised photographs of their wedding on the grounds that the pictures were a breach of confidence and an invasion of the individual claimants' privacy. The House of Lords, by a split majority of 3-2, upheld the action for breach of confidence and ruled that the disputed photographs provided information as to how the wedding looked and constituted confidential information.[22]

In *Campbell v MGN* the model Naomi Campbell was photographed leaving a rehabilitation clinic where she attended regularly meetings of Narcotics Anonymous (NA). The photographs were published in a publication run by MG Newspapers. The headline alongside the photograph read: 'Naomi: I'm a drug addict' and the article contained some general information relating to Miss Campbell's treatment for drug addiction, including the number of meetings she had attended in the clinic. Miss Campbell claimed damages under the tort of breach of confidence. On appeal, the House of Lords held in favour of Miss

---

17 Ibid., para 75.

18 See T Aplin, 'The Development of the Action for Breach of Confidence in a post-HRA Era' (2007) 1 IPQ 19–59; A McLean and C Mackey, 'Is there a Law of Privacy in the UK? A Consideration of Recent Legal Developments' (2007) 29(9) EIPR 389.

19 *Douglas v Hello! Ltd* [2001] QB 967.

20 *Campbell v MGN Ltd* [2004] UKHL 22.

21 K Ziegler, E Wicks and L Hodson, *The UK and European Human Rights: A Strained Relationship* (Hart 2015) 4.

22 *Douglas v Hello! Ltd* [2008] 1 AC 1 (HL).

Campbell. While it was acceptable to publish a story about her having lied about taking drugs and her addiction and the fact that she was receiving therapy, publishing the additional information about the treatment with NA, together with details of the treatment and photograph, went too far and were deemed irrelevant for a public course defence.[23] As a result of these decisions the UK courts have recognised that celebrities have a right of privacy during private events on private property and similarly regarded information about a person's health and their treatment for ill health as confidential. The action for breach of confidence interpreted in the light of privacy greatly strengthens the protection available to a private person against unwanted intrusion of his privacy, while at the same time protecting the interests of the rights of freedom of expression.

II.i(b) Brexit

How will Brexit affect the protection of athletes against false merchandising and endorsement in the UK? Is the extension of privacy law in recent years likely to continue after the UK voted to leave the EU on 23 June 2016?

Leaving the EU would, generally, not affect the rights of athletes under the European Convention on Human Rights (ECHR), as this comes from the Council of Europe, not the EU. As it currently stands, the UK will remain signatory to the ECHR when it leaves the EU. In the UK the Human Rights Act 1998 (HRA) gives effect to rights and freedoms guaranteed under the ECHR. Following *Douglas* and *Campbell*, the UK Courts will therefore most likely continue to recognise that the values enshrined in Article 8 and Article 10 of the ECHR are part of the cause of action for breach of confidence.

Although Prime Minister Theresa May was reportedly planning to withdraw from the ECHR, repeal the HRA and replace it with a British Bill of Rights and Responsibilities, this is now unlikely to happen while the process of Brexit is under way.[24] However, fresh consideration might

---

[23] *Campbell v MGN Ltd* [2004] UKHL 22, para 24 per Lord Nicholls of Birkenhead. On whether people engaging in adulterous or casual sex affairs have a reasonable expectation of privacy, see also *Mosley v News Group Newspapers* [2008] EWHC 1777 (QB) and *Mosley v United Kingdom* [2011] 53 EHRR 30.

[24] Samuel Osborne, Conservative manifesto: Theresa May announces UK will remain part of European Convention on Human Rights, 18 May 2017: http://www.independent.co.uk/news/uk/politics/conservative-manifesto-uk-echr-european-convention-human-rights-leave-eu-next-parliament-election-a7742436.html.

be given to the UK's domestic human rights framework once the arrangements for the exit from the EU are known.[25]

In the short term, the current proposed approach of the new flagship Brexit legislation, the EU Withdrawal Bill, is to avoid regulatory gaps by incorporating all EU laws into UK domestic law prior to exit and giving Parliament time later to decide which parts it wishes to retain or repeal.[26] Although the Bill in its current form notably removes the Charter of Fundamental Rights of the European Union, the principal source of essential rights enshrined in the Charter is the ECHR.[27] The substance of many fundamental rights, such as respect for private and family life in Article 7, would therefore most likely be retained in domestic law under the largely corresponding Article 8 of the ECHR, respectively, Article 8 of the HRA.[28]

However, some concerns remain because the charter provides some rights and judicial remedies that have no clear equivalents in UK domestic law.[29] If, after Brexit, a new domestic human rights framework is introduced in the UK, whatever form and configuration it takes, it would most likely be subject to reduced national enforcement.

False endorsement claims like *Irvine* and *Rihanna*, however, will most likely continue to be judged under the traditional requirements of the common law of passing off. Generally, during the transitional period and given the extent of the task reviewing existing EU influenced laws, the UK courts will most likely continue to consider the judgments of the CJEU and the ECtHR in the short term. It remains to be seen, however, how the law will respond to the numerous challenges of the uncertainties following the exit of the UK from the EU in the future.

---

[25] Ibid.

[26] European Union (Withdrawal) Bill 2017-19, available at: https://services.parliament.uk/bills/2017-19/europeanunionwithdrawal.html.

[27] Charter of Fundamental Rights of the European Union (2000/C 364/01).

[28] Charter of Fundamental Rights of the EU Right by Right Analysis of 5 December 2017, https://www.gov.uk/government/uploads/system/uploads/attachment_data/file/664891/05122017_Charter_Analysis_FINAL_VERSION.pdf.

[29] The EU Charter after Brexit, Oxford Human Rights Hub, November 2017, N Bamforth, M Campbell (et al), p. 5, http://ohrh.law.ox.ac.uk/wordpress/wp-content/uploads/2017/11/The-EU-Charter-After-Brexit-.pdf.

III. THE PROTECTION OF IMAGE RIGHTS IN EUROPE

The European view has traditionally focused on protecting the reputations and images of individuals from harm rather than providing economic benefits and incentives to the creator.[30] The personality rights approach derives in particular from Civilian jurisdictions and traditions, such as France and Germany, which recognise a dignitary right to 'personality' as a special legal right closely connected with the human being.[31] In this respect European law has typically focused on protecting the personality of the individual: her human rights, dignitary interests and autonomy.[32] This trend is continuing with the central importance of instruments such as the ECHR. In relation to the protection of one's personal image, the ECtHR, for example, confirmed in the second *Hannover v Germany* judgment that image is:

> one of the chief attributes of (…) personality, as it reveals the person's unique characteristics and distinguishes the person from his or her peers. The right to protection of one's image is thus one of the essential components of personal development. It mainly presupposes the individual's right to control the use of that image including the right to refuse publication thereof.[33]

Many European countries, for example, Germany, Greece, Spain and the Netherlands see image rights as part of personality rights which are fundamentally protected by their constitution in combination with various other laws, such as copyright law and/or trademark law.

III.i France

As for the protection of image rights of athletes, most European courts hold the position that athletes need to give their consent to the use of their images or photos for commercial purposes such as advertisement and merchandising, unless there is a prevailing public interest in the information. For example, in France in 1995 the footballer Eric Cantona

---

[30] S Martuccelli, 'The Right of Publicity under Italian Civil Law' (1998) 18 *Loy LA Ent L Rev* 543, 545.

[31] G Brüggemeier, 'Protection of Personality Rights in the Law of Delict/torts in Europe: Mapping out Paradigms' in G Brüggemeier, A Colombi Ciacchi *et al* (eds) *Personality Rights in European Tort Law* (CUP 2010) 7.

[32] C McCrudden, 'Human Dignity and Judicial Interpretation of Human Rights' (2008) 19 EJIL 655, 664.

[33] *Von Hannover v Germany (no. 2)* (2012) 55 EHRR 15 at 96.

brought a claim against the publishers of the magazine 'But' before the Tribunal of Nanterre.[34] The court ruled that, although the photos of Cantona shown in the magazine were all taken in public places, the purpose of the special edition was not to inform the public but to exploit the image of Cantona for commercial profit.

French courts did not recognise a commercial image right (droit à l'image) independent from privacy rights until the *Papillon*[35] case in 1970. That case concerned the publication of a book that was based on the documents from the files of the court that sentenced Henri Charrière, a.k.a. Papillon, to life imprisonment 40 years earlier. Charrière brought an action against his publisher, claiming a violation of his right to privacy as well as unauthorised use of his photograph on the cover of the book. While the court held that the publication of the book did not amount to an invasion of Papillon's privacy, the unauthorised reproduction of his photograph on the book jacket infringed upon his right of image entitling him to recover damages.

After the recognition of both the right of privacy and a commercial image right by the French Courts, the French Legislature introduced specific statutory protection in Article 9 into the French Civil Code, providing that 'everyone has the right to respect for his private life'.[36] Article 9 paragraph 2 further strengthens the right to privacy by additionally providing that the court in case of emergency may grant an interim order to prevent or put an end to an invasion of personal privacy.

The traditional high value and importance of the right to privacy under French law was recognised in a case involving the unauthorised use of the name and image of the French cyclist, Richard Virenque, by the editors of a book on the cyclist's sporting success. The High Court of Paris found that Mr Virenque's right to privacy and intimacy outweighed the defendant's right to freedom of expression and that, consequently, the use of Mr Virenque's name and image in the book was unlawful and required consent.[37]

---

[34] Tribunal de grande instance de Nanterre, 6 avril 1995, Gazette du Palais, 24–25 mai 1995, 33. See also S Cornelius, 'Image Rights' in J Nafziger and S Ross (eds) *Handbook on International Sports Law* (Edward Elgar 2011) 52.

[35] TGI Paris, ord ref, Feb 27, 1970, JCP 1970, II, 16293.

[36] Law No. 70-643 of July 17, 1970, JO, July 19, 1970, p 6751 (codified in C Civ Art 9 (Fr)).

[37] Tribunal de grande instance de Paris, 25 février 1998, Légipresse,1998, n°152, I-68.

III.ii Germany

The issue of infringement of personality rights in unlicensed merchandise cases has been the subject of much legal activity in Germany over the past 40 years.[38] Famous sports personalities have sought protection against the commercial use of their images without their consent. High-profile cases involved, for example, the former footballer and coach, Franz Beckenbauer, and the three-time Wimbledon Champion, Boris Becker.[39]

In Germany, a general right of personality (Persönlichkeitsrecht) has been recognised in the case law of the German Federal Court of Justice (Bundesgerichtshof) since 1954 as a basic right, constitutionally guaranteed by Articles 1 and 2 of the Basic Law (Grundgesetz) and protected in civil law under Sections 823(1) and 1004 of the German Civil Code (Bürgerliches Gesetzbuch).[40] The fundamental right guarantees the protection of human dignity and the right to free development of the personality, protecting any person against the unauthorised use of specific aspects of their personality.[41]

One recognised aspect of an individual's personality is the right in one's own picture.[42] Section 22(1) of the German Copyright Act (Kunsturhebergesetz, KUG) guarantees the freedom for an individual to determine how he presents himself to the public. The use of the image of a personality for advertising or commercial purpose generally requires consent of the depicted person unless there is an overriding public interest in the information. For example, in a case concerning the

---

38 See, e.g., J Marten, 'Personality Rights and Freedom of Expression: A Journey Through the Development of German Jurisprudence under the Influence of the European Court of Human Rights' (2012) (4) 2 *Journal of Media Law* 333–49; F Hofmann, 'The Right to Publicity in German and English Law' (2010) 3 IPQ 325–40.

39 See OLG Frankfurt, 11 January 1988, NJW 1997, 402 (concerning Boris Becker's action against the publication of a tennis instruction book that depicted his image on the cover. The Frankfurt Court of Appeal argued that even though the use of the claimant's image on the cover was clearly designed to capitalise on his fame, the book also explained and opposed various tennis techniques of famous tennis players); BGH of 29 October 2009, I ZR 65/07, GRUR 2010, 546 (concerning Boris Becker's action against the unauthorised use of his image for a promotional campaign in the German newspaper 'Frankfurter Allgemeine Sonntagszeitung' on their front page).

40 Constant case law since 13 BGHZ 334 [Schacht-Brief] [Schacht-Letter].

41 26 BGHZ 349 [Herrenreiter] [Gentleman-Rider].

42 143 BGHZ 214 [Marlene Dietrich].

unauthorised use of photographs of the former German football icon Franz Beckenbauer taken during a football match against Greece for a wall calendar,[43] the German Federal Court held that the public interest prevailed in this case on the basis that the pictures on the wall calendar showed Mr Beckenbauer 'in action', allowing the public to experience a true match situation as it had happened on the pitch during an important football match.

In contrast, in a case involving the German former goalkeeper of the national team *Oliver Kahn v EA-Sports*, the Hamburg Court of Appeal held that consent by Oliver Kahn was required for the use of his name and image in a computer game, because Mr Kahn's image was used for commercial purposes and there was no public interest in the use of Mr Kahn's name or image.[44] In 2010, the Higher Regional Court Hamburg rejected a claim of Michael Ballack concerning the unauthorised use of his name in an advertising campaign. Mr Ballack played at that time at Chelsea and was a member of the German national football team.[45] In connection with the financial crisis and the financial difficulties that hit the football clubs, the media had discussed whether the owner of Chelsea, Roman Abramovich, should sell Ballack to another club. The defendant, a private bank, then launched the following advertising campaign:

Mr Abramovich, you do not have to sell Ballack!

You better come to a bank with 6% return in 2008.

The court argued that that the public interest in information prevailed over the interest of Mr Ballack not to be named in the advertisement. The ad was a current, ironic-satirical analysis of the influence of money in sport which neither transferred the image value or the advertising value of Mr Ballack to the product nor gave the impression that Mr Ballack recommended the bank.

In the most recent decision concerning the image rights of a sports celebrity a German Higher Regional Court had to balance the constitutionally guaranteed personality rights against the freedom of the art as

---

43 Bundesgerichtshof [BGH] [Federal Court of Justice] 2 February 1979, Neue Juristische Wochenschrift [NJW] 1979, 2203 [Fussballspieler] [Football player].

44 OLG [Higher Regional Court] Hamburg, 13 Jan. 2004, 7 U 41/03, confirmed by the High Court Frankfurt in the *Konami-decision*, LG Frankfurt, 12.12.2008, 6 O 249/06.

45 OLG Hamburg 2.3.2010, 7 U 125/09.

guaranteed in Article 5(3) of the Basic Law.[46] The claimant, the German professional golf player Martin Kaymer, sought an injunction prohibiting the distribution and publication of portraits which the defendant had offered for sale both on his website and on an internet auction platform. The images showed a photo of the claimant which the defendant had turned into pop art portrait by using several colour combination styles. The claimant considered that his right to his own picture and his personality right were violated by the defendant's photos. The defendant claimed that the portrait was covered by artistic freedom under Article 5(3) of the German Basic right, fulfilling a higher interest of the general public in information.

The appeal court found in favour of Mr Kaymer, arguing that the dissemination of the portrait without the claimant's permission violated the claimant's personality rights, namely his right to deal with his portrait.[47] The defendant was not fulfilling any interest of the general public in information, but was mainly using the portrait to satisfy his business interest. The court further considered that rather than being an achievement of fine art, the portrait had mainly decorative character. Consequently, the claimant's interest in the protection of his personality rights prevailed over the defendant's right to freedom of art.

The decision sets forth the tendency of German courts to rule in favour of celebrities and athletes whose personality features are exploited for merchandising products. In an earlier decision the Federal Court had enjoined the defendant from distributing T-shirts, bags, postcards, etc. bearing the image of the famous singer Nena on the rationale that it was the exclusive right of a celebrity to determine who is allowed to exploit his or her personality commercially.[48]

III.iii Italy

Under Italian law, the right to exploit, promote, show and publish an individual's image, with or without his or her consent (diritto all'immagine), is enshrined in Article 10 of the Civil Code and Articles 96 and 97 of the Copyright Law. Italian courts have interpreted Article 10 quite widely, holding that not only the commercial use of an image of a celebrity, but even the unauthorised use of elements that merely evoke him/her, could amount to an infringement under Italian image rights

46 OLG Düsseldorf 23.07.2013 - I-20 U 190/12.

47 See 20 BGHZ 345 ff. [Dahlke].

48 *BGH* 14. Oct. 1986, VI ZR 10/86 [Nena].

law.[49] Such an extensive interpretation of Article 10 of the Civil Code was recently confirmed by the High Court in Milan[50] in a case concerning an advertising campaign, which included the use of a photographic reproduction of an ambience and a character played by a model that according to Hepburn's estate recalled Audrey Hepburn's image and a famous sequence from Breakfast at Tiffany's.

The court held in favour of the estate and ruled that the scope of Article 10 codice civile did extend to elements, such as dressing, accessories and make up, if an observer would associate these elements with the famous personality.

Similarly, the Austrian Supreme Court[51] recently had to decide whether image right protection afforded by Section 78 of the Austrian Copyright Act (Urheberrechtsgesetz) extends to pictures that do not show a person's face.[52] The case concerned the picture of a professional bodybuilder that was published in a newspaper alongside an article about doping. Although a black bar covered his eyes and his face was unrecognisable, the Supreme Court held that a person's face did not necessarily need to be shown clearly to qualify for image right's protection, as long as the person shown on that picture can be recognised. In the stated case, the bodybuilder could be recognised despite the black bar over his eyes, as he was regularly recognised by his body rather than his face.

Returning to Italy, and as a general rule, consent to the use of the image may be legitimately withdrawn in case of uses detrimental to the represented individual's dignity or reputation, and moreover, according to the local Highest Civil Court, it can be revoked at any time and even without just cause.[53] However, as in Germany, athletes may successfully object to the unauthorised use of their images, if the main purpose of the use or publication was for profit and commerce. For example, in 2013 the Court of Naples handed down an order to a petition for a temporary

---

[49] See Pret Roma, 18 aprile 1984, in Giur it, 1985, I, 2, 544 (concerning the protection of some characteristic elements of the appearance of the Italian popstar Lucio Dalla); see also Trib. [Tribunale] [Ordinary court of first instance] Milano 26 ottobre 1992, Diritto dell'informazione e dell'Informatica [Dir. Inf.], 1993, 942 Cass, [Corte di Cassazione] sez. II civile, 12 marzo 1997, n. 2223, Dir. inf., 1997, 542 (concerning the protection of some characteristic elements of the appearance of the Italian actor Toto).

[50] Trib di Milano, 21 gennaio *2015*, n 766.

[51] OGH 14.3.2006, 4 Ob 266/05d [Profi-Bodybuilder].

[52] Section 78 of the Austrian Copyright Act provides that an image of a person must not be published or made accessible by the public if the legitimate interest is infringed.

[53] Corte di Cassazione, 29 gennaio 2016 n 1748.

injunction in a case involving the petitioner, the footballer, Diego Maradona, who complained about the unlawful commercial use of his name and image on a DVD that contained images of goals made by him when he was playing for Naples.[54]

The legendary number 10 applied for an order prohibiting the production and marketing of the DVD. The court considered the use of the image unlawful and rejected the existence of a right of the club to freely use the images of its former player for commercial purposes based on the employment contract between the parties. A similar order to a petition for a temporary injunction was handed down by the Court of Milan[55] in 1999. The petitioner, the former German footballer, Oliver Bierhoff, applied for an order prohibiting the production and marketing of objects bearing his own name and image on the basis of abusive use of his likeness for commercial profit. The court ruled for Mr Bierhoff, arguing that the unauthorised use of his image was merely designed to capitalise on his fame rather than offering any newsworthy or relevant information for the public.

III.iv Spain

With the world's most valuable football clubs Barcelona and Real Madrid, Spain is, arguably, the epicentre of the commercialisation of football. The clubs have also signed the world's most expensive football players Messi, Ronaldo and Suárez, each player being a global brand on his own. As in many European countries, the concept of image right protection in Spain is linked with the right of privacy. It rests on the statutory organic law of 5 May 1982 which provides protection for the fundamental rights to honour personal and family privacy, and one's own image (el derecho a la propia imagen) guaranteed by Article 18 of the Spanish constitution of 1978.[56]

The Spanish Constitution offers protection against use of one's image which may be considered damaging to one's honour. However, in 2009 the Spanish Supreme Court[57] confirmed that a Nike TV advertisement

---

54 Trib di Napoli, sez II, 30 luglio 2013 (ord).

55 See L Ferrari, 'Sports Image Rights under Italian Law', (2004) 1–2 ISLJ 179.

56 *Ley Orgánica 1/1982*, de *5 de mayo* (RCL *1982\1197)* on 'el derecho fundamental al honor, a la intimidad personal y familiar y a la propia imagen' ('fundamental right to honour, personal and family privacy, and one's own image').

57 S.T.S [Sentencia Tribunal Supremo] 613/2009 – ECLI:ES:TS:2009:613.

showing Ronaldo dribbling easily past seven professional footballers of the club Deportivo Compostela did not interfere unlawfully with the image rights of the seven players. The six players had brought an action against Nike in 1998, claiming the unauthorised use of their images had injured their rights to honour and privacy. The court rejected the claim, arguing that the Spanish Premier League ('La Liga') had lawfully assigned the right to Nike to broadcast them from La Liga matches including their sponsored player Ronaldo.[58]

On the issue of damage to the 'honour' of the seven footballers, the court highlighted the difference between the moral and patrimonial element of the protection afforded by the constitution of Spain. Moral rights which are designed to protect privacy and dignity in private life need to be distinguished from commercial exploitation of a person's image. The court concluded that the reproduction of the image did not affect the player's personal or professional dignity. The advertising spot did not injure or lower the reputation of athletes, but showed high-quality football, allowing the public to review the most important moments of the football match.

In addition to constitutional and civil rights, Spain provides for special sports laws and statutes to regulate the use of the image rights of athletes. The most important rule can be found in Royal Decree 26th June 1006/1985, regulating the special employment relations of sports professionals. Article 7.3 of the Royal Decree states that the rule applicable to the image rights of sports professionals shall be that envisaged in the collective agreement applicable, or that agreed between the sportsperson and the employer in the individual work contract.[59] Similar statutes that regulate the exercise of the image rights of sports players also exist, for example, in Portugal (the Sport Labour Act 1998)[60] and Poland (Polish Act on Sport).[61]

III.v The Netherlands

Although the Netherlands does not recognise an image right as an absolute right, several sections in the Dutch Copyright Act and the Dutch Civil code provide protection for persons, including athletes, against the

[58] Ibid.

[59] *See* Yago Vazquez Moraga and A Sarrias, 'Sports Image Rights in Spain' (2010) 3–4 ISLJ 122, 126.

[60] Law No 28/98 of 27 June, as amended by Law No 114/99 of 2 August.

[61] Act of 25 June 2010 on Sport, Official Journal of the Republic of Poland, Dz. U. No. 127 position 857, as amended.

unauthorised commercial use of images of third parties without their consent. Articles 19–21, 25a and 35 of the Dutch Copyright Act specifically protect image rights of sports players when depicted in a portrait. These 'portrait rights' may include photographs, paintings, television and recordings and even include characteristic features of athletes if they are recognisable by the public.[62] For example, in a case concerning the unauthorised use of a photograph of the Dutch marathon skater, Yep Kramer, for gas boilers, a district court held that not only the facial features in the picture but also the characteristic posture of the skater on the ice made him identifiable by people who saw the advertisement.[63] This wide interpretation of the portrait right may support athletes who have not yet achieved extensive fame but can nevertheless protect their distinctive features.

According to Article 21 of the Dutch Copyright Act the portrayed person can object to the unauthorised publication of his portrait if he can prove that he has a 'reasonable interest' in the prevention of publication of his image. Such a reasonable interest could be a privacy interest as enshrined in Article 8 of the ECHR and Article 10 of the Dutch Constitution or, depending on the sportsman's popularity, a commercial interest.[64] Any privacy interest needs to be balanced against other interests such as the freedom of expression and information of Article 10 ECHR. In addition, the Dutch Supreme Court has recognised a commercial 'reasonable interest' in one's image to prevent publication, if the person has gained 'exploitable popularity' (*verzilverbare populariteit*).[65]

Whether the athlete has gained exploitable popularity will be decided on a case-by-case basis but the term does not exclude amateur players from protection per se. Recently the Dutch Supreme Court and the Amsterdam Court of Appeal have clarified the position of the Dutch Courts on whether sports players have an absolute right of self-determination in one's image.[66] In 2003 the publisher Tirion published the photo book 'Johan Cruijff – De Ajacied' which contained a collection of photos of the legendary Ajax football player Johan Cruijff. Tirion offered Cruijff financial compensation before publication but Cruijff

---

62 S Hagen, 'Sports Image Rights in the Netherlands' (2011) 3–4 ISLJ 115.

63 Ktr. [Kantonrechter] [Sub-District Court] Harderwijk, 29 May 1991, Prg. 1991, no 3507.

64 Hagen, *supra* note 62, 119.

65 Hoge Raad der Nederlanden [Supreme Court of the Netherlands] 13 April 1960, NJ 1961, 160 (Teddy Scholten); 19 January 1979, NJ 1979 383 ('t Schaaep met de Viif Pooten).

66 HR 14 June 2013, ECLI:NL:HR:2013:CA2788 (*Cruyff v Tirion*).

declined the offer. Cruijff then brought a claim against Tirion, arguing the publication was unlawful on the basis of his portrait right.

After both lower courts ruled that there was no violation of Cruijff's image rights, the Supreme Court held that the person portrayed can object to his portrait being made public without his consent if he has a reasonable interest therein which outweighs freedom of expression under the circumstances. As for the privacy claim, the court emphasised that the pictures did not show any aspect of his private life and the pictures were not in any way harmful or defamatory. According to the court, Cruijff could also not prevent publication of the photographs based on the argument of 'reasonable interest'. Although Cruijff had '*verzilverbare populariteit*' he could not base his claim on the portrait right since a reasonable financial compensation was offered to him by the publishing company and the existence of an absolute right of consent prior to publication could not be assumed.

The Amsterdam Appeals Court in 2013 confirmed this view in another ruling concerning an action of the association of professional football players against the Dutch football clubs and the Dutch football federation KNVB.[67] The court rejected the view of the players' association that all professional football players in the Dutch leagues have an absolute 'portrait right' based on Article 21 of the Dutch Copyright Act, allowing them to prohibit any image taken during matches without their consent. The court effectively based its argument on economic considerations that the players already earn income for their participation in the matches deriving from broadcasting rights, and they cannot therefore claim additional remuneration for their images shown during the broadcasting of these matches.

IV. CONCLUSION

Although there is currently no European-wide harmonised legal concept for recognising an image right, a widely-held view of the national courts is that, unless there is a prevailing public interest in the information, athletes need to give their consent to the use of their images or photos for commercial purposes. There are still obvious legal differences between the national legal systems, largely based on common law and civil law traditions, but the current degree of difference is not of a fundamental,

---

[67] Gerechtshof Amsterdam [Court of Appeal of Amsterdam], 10 December 2013, ECLI:NL:GHAMS; 2013; 4501 (Centrale spelersraad, Vereniging van contractspelers and Proprof v. (all) KNVB soccer clubs).

practical nature. National courts in many European countries increasingly rely on economic arguments to justify protection against the unauthorised use of image rights or, as in the UK, where image rights are not (yet) recognised, against false endorsements. Two recent Dutch cases show however, that the economic argument can also work the other way round: to limit image right protection where there is a risk that athletes, who already earn income from broadcasting rights, would be remunerated twice. This is a welcome development as it will help to make earnings deriving from image rights more transparent and less open for tax evasion.

As the UK continues to remain a member of the EU even after triggering Article 50 of the Lisbon Treaty, there will be no immediate effects of Brexit on the existing protection scheme against false endorsement and intrusions into privacy in the short term. Even after Brexit, and during a transition period, UK courts will most likely continue to consider the judgments of the CJEU and the ECtHR. It remains to be seen, however, how the courts will respond to the numerous uncertainties following the exit of the UK from the EU in the long term.

12. Sustainable financing in football and the EU

Seán Ó'Conaill

I. INTRODUCTION

The European Union in its Work Plan for Sport (2014–2017) identifies the sustainable financing of sport as a priority for the European Union (EU). Football, being by a considerable distance the highest profile sport in the EU, has always merited special attention. Given that the European football market was projected to exceed €25 billion in the 2016/2017 season,[1] it is clear that the industry makes a significant financial contribution to economic activity within the EU in addition to its social contribution. It is also noted however the industry is reported to have made a combined loss of €487 million,[2] which raises serious questions about the ongoing financial sustainability of the industry.

This chapter will look at the various interventions by the EU into the area of sustainable finance in football. Although the majority of the interventions relate more generally to sport rather than to football specifically an analysis of the various interventions shows that football was clearly to the forefront of the minds of the EU's institutions on many occasions. Much on the EU's focus on sport more generally has been led by football developments such as the *Bosman* ruling, football broadcast rights and the rights of clubs. The EU's focus on sustainable finance in the context of football is not solely on the professional game at the top level. As noted in the Expert Group on Sustainable Financing of Sport,[3] the redistribution of funds from professional sport to grassroots sport

[1] *Reboot: Deloitte Annual Review of Football Finance* (Deloitte Sports Business Group 2016) 6 https://www2.deloitte.com/content/dam/Deloitte/uk/Documents/sports-business-group/deloitte-uk-annual-review-of-football-finance-2016.pdf (accessed 26 Oct 2017).

[2] Ibid., 12.

[3] 'Expert Group on Sustainable Financing of Sport – Strengthening Financial Solidarity Mechanisms within Sport' (December 2012) http://ec.europa.eu/assets/eac/sport/library/documents/xg-fin-201211-deliverable.pdf (accessed 26 Oct 2017).

plays a key role in the sustainable financing of sport with football given as the leading example.[4] To this end, this chapter will commence with an analysis of the various EU interventions which chart the development of an ever-increasing focus on sustainable finance within European football. Furthermore, an analysis of the role played by the Financial Fair Play Regulations (FFP) and the various Transfer Regulations (TR) will be conducted in order to assess their impact on issues of sustainable finance in football with a particular focus on, first, their effectiveness in achieving this and secondly on their compatibility with EU law.

II. THE EU'S COMMITMENT TO SUSTAINABLE FINANCING IN FOOTBALL

Financial instability was recognised as one of the major challenges facing European football in the 'Agreement for Co-Operation between the European Commission and UEFA' in 2014.[5] That being said, the issue of sustainability in sport generally has been a key focus of the EU from a much earlier stage and can be located in the 1997 Amsterdam Declaration, the 1999 Helsinki Report and the 2000 Nice Declaration on Sport. The Amsterdam Declaration was extremely brief in terms of content while being extremely broad in terms of scope. No mention of finances or sustainability were made at all although there was a certain foreshadowing of the future interventions with a mention of the need to 'listen to sports associations when important questions affecting sport are at issue'.[6]

The Helsinki Report, while not directly referencing sustainable finance, did highlight many of the issues and problems sport within the EU faces such as the increased focus on commercial revenue which could pose a challenge to the solidarity mechanisms underpinning the financial

---

[4] Ibid., 4.

[5] Commission Decision of 14 October 2014 C(2014) 7378 adopting the Arrangement for Cooperation between the European Commission and the Union of European Football Associations, para 2.3. http://ec.europa.eu/assets/eac/sport/news/2014/docs/uefa2014_en.pdf (accessed 26 Oct 2017).

[6] Treaty of Amsterdam amending the Treaty on European Union, the Treaties establishing the European Communities and certain related acts – Declarations adopted by the Conference – Declaration on Sport [1997] OJ C 340, P 0136.

sustainability of sport.[7] The Nice Declaration made passing references to the economic dimension of sport with a particular focus on solidarity between various levels of sport. It did however point towards a growing role for the EU in the field of sport noting that, 'the Community must [...] take account of the social, educational and cultural functions inherent in sport and making it special, in order that the code of ethics and the solidarity essential to the preservation of its social role may be respected and nurtured'.[8]

The Nice Declaration also makes specific reference to the role that the distribution of television revenues could make in ensuring an economic benefit and increasing the financial solidarity between all levels of sport.[9] While none of these early interventions can be looked upon as having a dramatic influence on sustainable finance in football, or even in sport more generally, they represent a starting point for EU intervention into the finance of sport and an early tepid recognition of the potential role of solidarity in sustainable finance in a post-*Bosman* world.

The first significant steps from the EU towards a clear recognition of the role to be played by sustainable finance in sport occurred in 2007 with the adoption of the White Paper on Sport and the passing of the 2007 European Parliament resolution on professional football. The White Paper in particular served to drive a new era of EU interaction with sport under a series of different headings which the Commission noted was for the first time 'addressing sport-related issues in a comprehensive manner'.[10]

Although the notion of sustainable finance in sport was not a central theme at this juncture, a number of provisions of the White Paper are of particular interest, for example, where the Commission invited Member States 'to reflect upon how best to maintain and develop a sustainable financing model for giving long-term support to sports organisations'.[11] The White Paper, while recognising the specificity of sport, noted that

---

[7] Report from the Commission to the European Council with a View to Safeguarding Current Sports Structures and Maintaining the Social Function of Sport within the Community Framework – The Helsinki Report on Sport, COM(1999) 644 final, 4.

[8] European Council – Nice, 7–10 December 2000, Conclusions of the Presidency, Annex IV: Declaration on the Specific Characteristics of Sports and Its Social Function in Europe, of which Account should be taken in Implementing Common Policies.

[9] European Council – Nice, 7–10 December 2000, Conclusions of the Presidency, Annex IV, para 15.

[10] White Paper on Sport, COM(2007) 391 final, 1.

[11] Ibid., 12.

EU law does indeed apply to sport as an economic activity. It is submitted that this dual stance is at the very core of the dichotomy in EU law and policy towards sport and football more specifically. While the White Paper recognised that EU law applies to the professional and commercial elements of sport there is also a recognition by the EU that sport has a particular role within society.

The 2008 European Council Declaration on Sport emphasises that policy making and legal structures need to take account of the specific characteristics of sport, over and above its economic dimension. Although earlier declarations, such as the Amsterdam Declaration, note that amateur sport has a special status, the reality of the funding model of football in particular is that professional sport, through various solidarity mechanisms, makes a very significant contribution towards the financial sustainability of amateur football. Any twin-track approach which seeks to adopt a different standard for amateur and professional football would accordingly be somewhat artificial given the symbiotic relationship between both strands of the game. In applying EU law to the economic activity of professional football there are accordingly significant knock-on consequences for amateur football.

The White Paper also examined the funding model of sport and the contribution that such funding makes to the sustainability of sport. Public financial support in principle is allowed and encouraged: 'Investment in and promotion of training of young talented sportsmen and sportswomen in proper conditions is crucial for a sustainable development of sport at all levels.'[12] It should be noted however that this stance does not render football immune from state aid considerations particularly at the professional end of the game.[13]

The White Paper also touched briefly on the issue of taxation when it suggested an investigation as to whether levying of tax on gambling aids to help fund state investment contributes positively to sustainable finance in sport. Finally, the White Paper noted the importance of the exchange of knowledge with a view to promoting sustainable economic growth thus sowing seeds for the later recognition of the need for evidence-based policy and the development of Erasmus+ funding streams to investigate financial sustainability.

Although the White Paper represented a significant development in the EU's relationship with the notion of sustainable financing in sport, it lacked in-depth engagement and specific actions. Moreover, although

---

12 Ibid., 6.

13 See generally Ch 11 of this Handbook.

since Article 165 of the Lisbon Treaty came into force in 2009 the EU has enjoyed a direct competence in sport, positive law engagements on the issue of financial sustainability remain lacking. Instead the EU has focused on a softer approach of working with UEFA (and to a lesser extent FIFA) as a stakeholder and seeking to 'encourage' sustainable financing and financial best practice. This has been accomplished by a series of further reports, resolutions and recommendations coming either directly from the EU institutions often following on from the various EU Work Plans for Sport or via commissioned expert reports or research projects funded through initiatives such as the Erasmus + funding call.

The 2011 Commission Communication 'Developing the European Dimension in Sport'[14] further developed the engagement with the economic dimension of sport including the issue of sustainable finance. The document addressed the societal role of sport, the organisation of sport and co-operation with non-EU countries and institutions. The economic dimension of sport was also addressed with a number of key areas identified for further action. The first action concerning the economic dimension was, not surprisingly, the highlighting of the need for the development of evidence-based policy. The issue of sustainable financing for sport was specifically addressed, although the focus was on the redistribution of funds raised through ventures such as the sale of intellectual property rights, broadcasting deals and redistribution of gambling taxes.[15]

No specific mention was made of football or the mechanisms by which governing bodies could work with the EU in order to ensure that the professional clubs themselves could be encouraged to contribute towards the sustainable financing of sport. Although links were also made between the promotion of good governance, integrity in sport and overall financial health, no specific mention of mechanisms were made aside from a passing reference to club licensing systems.[16] Club licensing systems have indeed been particularly useful tools in the promotion of sustainable financing at the European and domestic levels however it is difficult to gauge what impact, if any, EU interventions rather than UEFA initiatives have had on their development. This stands in contrast when compared with the more overt influence the EU has had in areas such as FFP and TR, discussed below.

---

14 Developing the European Dimension in Sport, COM(2011) 12 final.

15 Ibid., para 3.2.

16 Ibid., paras 4.1–4.5.

An expert report, which arose as part of the 2011–2014 European Union Work Plan for Sport, on sustainable finance in sport made a number of recommendations which built strongly on the various interventions to date. This 2012 expert report on sustainable financing in sport made a series of recommendations. The report called for greater clarity and guidance on how EU law applies to sport, particularly taking into account the 'specificity of sport'. The report made particular reference to rules concerning state aid and VAT and how their applicability to sport can contribute to sustainable financing within sport. The report also noted the importance of grassroots sports to the long-term sustainability of sport and called for increased solidarity mechanisms between the top professional levels of sport and the grassroots levels.[17]

While all of the various interventions by the EU mentioned above were broadly aimed at sport in general and applicable to football in the last ten years, there have been a number of football-specific interventions that have also emerged from the EU. A detailed resolution by the European Parliament in 2007, which covered many aspects of the applicability of EU law to football made only passing reference to sustainable finance noting that it supported the club licensing system 'which aims to ensure a level playing field between clubs and contributes to their financial stability'.[18]

SD Europe, a supporters' organisation which draws most of its funding from UEFA and the EU, made similar recommendations in a 2012 position paper – calling for increased focus on financial sustainability throughout leagues (including club licensing and financial fair play) rather than focusing only on European competitions. The SD Europe paper also echoed many of the EU's interventions calling for an equitable redistribution of finances of the game to all levels to improve financial sustainability.[19] The 2014 European Commission and UEFA agreement for co-operation again made a number of references to issues relating to financial sustainability such as long-term development, financial instability and again referenced solidarity between professional football and the grassroots; for example, some more practical advancements were made

[17] Expert Group on Sustainable Financing of Sport – Strengthening Financial Solidarity Mechanisms within Sport (December 2012).

[18] European Parliament resolution of 29 March 2007 on the future of professional football in Europe (2006/2130(INI)), para 20.

[19] Supporters Direct Europe, 'The Heart of the Game: Why Supporters are Vital to Improving Governance in Football; A Position Paper' (SD Europe 2012) section 2 http://www.sdeurope.eu/wp-content/uploads/2016/03/SDE_Position_Paper_2012_GB.pdf (accessed 26 Oct 2017).

with commitments given towards 'financial stability, transparency and better governance … financial fair play'.[20]

That Commission/UEFA agreement also focused on 'responsible self-regulation' rather than any strict imposition of regulations by the European institutions. Many of the commitments and recommendations made in the agreement for co-operation can be attributed as the manifestations of the prior work of the European institutions and in particular the expert report of 2012 which bears many similarities to the final UEFA/European Commission document. Furthermore in 2014, financial solidarity between professional and grassroots was identified as 'important in maintaining financial viability' with an emphasis on factors such as stability, transparency, a focus on long-term as opposed to short-term and sustainable development.[21]

Finally, a number of references to the importance of sustainable financing and financial solidarity between professional and grass-roots football can be found in the 2017 European Parliament resolution on an integrated approach to sport policy, illustrating that for the Parliament at least sustainable finance is still considered an important factor in EU sports policy.[22] Interestingly however, particularly given the previous focus on the subject, the EU's most recent Work Plan for Sport makes no reference whatsoever to sustainable finance, although it could perhaps be inferred that sustainable finance might be more generally considered under the specificity of sport heading.[23]

III. FINANCIAL FAIR PLAY

The UEFA FFP Regulations and their impact have been widely debated; at the heart of the regulations is the simple break-even principle – a

---

[20] Commission Decision of 14 October 2014 C(2014) 7378 adopting the Arrangement for Cooperation between the European Commission and the Union of European Football Associations, para 2.7.

[21] Expert Group on Sustainable Financing of Sport (n 17), paras 2.6 and 2.7.

[22] European Parliament resolution of 2 February 2017 on an integrated approach to sport policy: good governance, accessibility and integrity (2016/2143(INI)).

[23] Resolution of the Council of the Representatives of the Government of the Member States, meeting within the Council, on the European Union Work Place for Sport (1 July 2017–31 December 2020) adopted by the Council at its 3541st meeting held on 23 May 2017, http://data.consilium.europa.eu/doc/document/ST-9639-2017-INIT/en/pdf) (accessed 26 Oct 2017).

football club should not spend more than it can organically generate.[24] From a sustainable finance point of view, the FFP's aims and objectives are clearly laid out in Article 2 of the FFP Regulations: where there is a focus on sound financial behaviour from football clubs with particular reference made to encouraging responsible spending and to viability and sustainability in the long term.[25]

It is not the focus of this chapter to analyse the effectiveness of these regulations from the point of view of UEFA, the ultimate body responsible for them, but rather to investigate the relationship between the regulations and the EU. It is first noteworthy that the FFP Regulations make no reference whatsoever to the EU. This omission, while no doubt deliberate, is somewhat surprising given that the financial heart of European football is based around large football clubs located within the EU. The connected nature of football and the recognition of the particular status of the EU has been recognised in other similar regulations such as the EU-specific portion of the FIFA Regulations for the Status and Transfer of Players (TRs).

The regulations themselves do however reflect in very real terms many of the interventions made by the EU in football finance, sustainability and long-term viability as well as provisions to enable limited redistribution of monies in a manner consistent with the solidarity goals outlined therein. Some element of care in the drafting of the FFP Regulations was taken by UEFA in an effort to comply with EU law and it is clear that there was consultation throughout the process of drafting and commitments were made for further consultation.[26]

Notwithstanding the EU's initial support for the FFP Regulations, serious questions still arise about FFP's legality and compatibility with

---

24 UEFA Financial Fair Play Regulations, see generally http://www.uefa.com/insideuefa/protecting-the-game/club-licensing-and-financial-fair-play/index.html (accessed 26 Oct 2017).

25 UEFA Club Licensing and Financial Fair Play Regulations (2015), art 2, http://www.uefa.com/MultimediaFiles/Download/Tech/uefaorg/General/02/26/77/91/2267791_DOWNLOAD.pdf (accessed 26 Oct 2017).

26 See the joint statement made by Commission Vice President Almunia and UEFA President Platini on 21 March 2012, IP/12/264 and available at http://ec.europa.eu/competition/sectors/sports/joint_statement_en.pdf (accessed 26 Oct 2017). The complaint to the EU Ombudsman was issued by Daniel Striani following the Commission's rejection of his challenge to the FFP Regulations, see Case C-299/15 *Striani v UEFA, URBSFA* Order of 16 July 2015 (reference inadmissible) and Decision of the European Ombudsman in case 2086/2014/EIS https://www.ombudsman.europa.eu/en/cases/decision.faces/en/61468/html.bookmark (accessed 26 Oct 2017).

EU competition law in particular. The pleadings in the *Striani* case highlighted concerns around a number of issues including: a restriction of investments; the fossilisation of the existing market structure; a reduction in volume and worth of transfers; a restriction on the number of players under contract per club; and the potential deflationary effect on the level of players' salaries.[27]

Although *Striani* encountered issues with admissibility and justiciability, the pleadings did nothing to resolve the serious questions as to whether FFP Regulations were indeed compatible with EU law. While the specificity of sport has often been put forward as a catch-all solution, it is difficult to see how such a position can be defended in professional football which is without doubt an international economic activity with knock-on consequences for employment rights, free trade and free movement. The 2016 document 'Mapping and Analysis of the Specificity of Sport', which was prepared for the European Commission, made no further claims as to the compatibility of the FFP Regulations with EU law and merely noted the outcome of *Striani*.[28] The impact of the FFP Regulations, it is submitted, cannot be simply confined with the body of football's *lex sportiva* and will sooner rather than later require clarification on its compatibility with EU law.

In spite of the existing questions as to the compatibility of the FFP with EU competition law, and Article 101(1) in particular, the EU has demonstrated a commitment to the principles and goals of the regulations. The European Parliament and European Commission have both expressly supported the FFP Regulations although Bastianon has argued that this support is not because the EU institutions are fully convinced as to the legality of the FFP Regulations but rather because they '[do] not want to be the first to clearly say it because of a kind of deference towards UEFA'.[29] Indeed, Geey argues that statements of support from the European Commission were 'so heavily caveated that [they are] of little practical use'.[30]

---

[27] See Case C-299/15 *Striani v UEFA, URBSFA* ibid.

[28] *Mapping and Analysis of the Specificity of Sport* (European Commission DG Education & Culture 2016), para 3.3, available at http://ec.europa.eu/assets/eac/sport/library/studies/mapping-analysis-specificity-sport_en.pdf (accessed 26 Oct 2017).

[29] S Bastianon, 'The *Striani* Challenge to UEFA Financial Fair Play: A New Era after *Bosman* or just a Washout?' (2015) 11(1) *Comp L Rev* 7–39.

[30] D Geey, 'The UEFA Financial Fair Play Rules: A Difficult Balancing Act' (2009) ((1) ESLJ, 5. DOI: http://doi.org/10.16997/eslj.30 (accessed 26 Oct 2017).

IV. THE INTERNATIONAL TRANSFER SYSTEM AND SUSTAINABLE FINANCE

The EU's role in sustainable financing in football is predominantly driven by the factors already outlined. Nevertheless, one of the less obvious ways in which the EU has 'intervened' in this regard is in the FIFA-mandated Regulations on the Status and Transfer of Players (TR), which include significant provisions concerning training compensation and solidarity payments to be made to football clubs involved in the development of young players.

In the post-*Bosman* football world, there was an immediate appreciation that an accommodation needed to be found between EU law on the one hand and FIFA's TRs on the other. Although, as noted above, both FIFA and UEFA are not merely confined to the EU, a significant number of the key power brokers, prominent national federations and the biggest football leagues are domiciled within the EU. Accordingly, any new uniform global transfer regulations would have to be in line with EU law for it to be in any way functional within the world game. It is not the focus of this section to take an overall look at these detailed regulations but rather to look specifically at two particular elements of the regulations which have the potential to contribute greatly to sustainable finance.

FIFA's TRs provide that when a young player under the age of 23 either transfers professionally across a border or signs their first professional contract a fee is payable to the club or clubs responsible for training that player from the age of 12 upwards. An additional and separate solidarity scheme provides that where a player is transferred internationally for a fee, regardless of their age, a proportion of the transfer fee involved is distributed among the clubs who contributed to the development of the player up to the age of 23.

Both these schemes have the potential to contribute greatly to financial stability, particularly with a view to rewarding smaller clubs, amateur and voluntary clubs, who have contributed to the development of the stars of the future. The trickle-down effect from the top levels of the professional game to the lower and grass-roots levels can be felt strongly when such a system operates effectively.[31] In this, FIFA's TRs emerged from the

---

[31] In 2010/2011 1.8 per cent of all transfer indemnity fees (out of a total of 3billion (euros)) related to training compensation and solidarity payments, see KEA – CDES, 'Study on the Economic and Legal Aspects of Transfers of Players, EAC/17/2011' (January 2013) 7 http://www.keanet.eu/docs/full_study_transferofplayers.pdf (accessed 26 Oct 2017).

detailed and protracted involvement by the EU in negotiations with FIFA and UEFA and as such carry to a certain extent the seal of approval of the EU; however, a number of serious questions regarding EU law attach to the operation of such schemes.

From the very earliest discussions on the emergence of a new transfer system in the post-*Bosman* environment, the notions of solidarity and training were prominent recognising the role played by clubs who contribute to the footballing education of players from a young age.[32] When the final scheme was ultimately revealed in 2001, significant changes which contributed to the sustainability of football were included as underpinned by an implicit recognition of the requirement to satisfy the specific demands of EU law. To this end, Annexes 4 and 5 of FIFA's TRs deal with the schemes in place, while Article 6 of Annexe 4 makes special provision for transfers which take place within the EU.

The training compensation and solidarity schemes by their very nature tend to be most beneficial to the clubs with whom young players have trained earlier in their careers. Such clubs are more likely to be amateur or smaller clubs in the player's home locality given that both schemes reward clubs involved in the training of players from the age of 12 upwards. Clubs which sign players on cross-border professional contracts or pay transfer fees for international transfers tend, predominantly, to be much larger clubs with substantial budgets and as such both schemes serve as an indirect method of redistributing capital to lower levels of the game. The operation of these schemes ultimately has the effect of making the development of younger players, and consequently football as whole, a more financially sustainable sport. In doing so however it raises a number of questions relating to how the scheme operates and whether it is wholly consistent with EU law.

The training compensation elements of FIFA's TRs have been tested by the EU courts. In the *Olivier Bernard* case, it was held that the training compensation provisions of FIFA's TRs, while clearly a limitation on the free movement of a worker, were a justified limitation in the sporting context.[33] The European Court further held that the fundamental freedoms guaranteed by EU law did not preclude a scheme that had the objective of encouraging, recruiting and the training of young players and further noted that:

---

[32] Joint statement by Commissioners Monti, Reding and Diamantopoulou and Presidents of FIFA Blatter and of UEFA Johansson, Brussels, 14 February 2001 (IP/01/209) http://europa.eu/rapid/press-release_IP-01-209_en.htm (accessed 26 Oct 2017).

[33] Case C-325/08 *Olivier Bernard* [2010] ECR I-2177.

> the clubs which provided such training could in the future be discouraged from investing in the training of young players if they could not obtain reimbursement of the amounts spent for that purpose where, at the end of his training, a player enters into a professional contract with another club. This would be particularly the case where it was or is a small club providing the training and whose investments at local level in the recruitment and training of young players are likely of considerable importance for the social and educational function of sport.[34]

Having established that such schemes contribute to the sustainability of financing football by rewarding smaller clubs in particular for the role they play in developing players, questions remain however about the operation of the schemes and their continued compatibility with EU law and stated EU policy as outlined above.

FIFA's TRs on training compensation and solidarity have never been fully challenged before the CJEU and as noted by Duval, '[i]ts legally binding nature remains vague and subject to speculation'.[35] Although the training compensation scheme received certain approval in *Bernard*, a fundamental question arises about the drafting and the interpretation of FIFA's TRs within a single market. While prima facie it is accepted that that a requirement to pay such contributions when a young player transfers would normally be considered a violation of EU law, *Bernard* appears authority for the view that such an interference may be justified relative to the scheme's objectives in helping make football finances more sustainable.[36]

FIFA's TRs apply to transfers including training compensation and solidarity payments when a player transfers internationally. National associations are empowered to enact their own regulations for domestic transfers and training compensation, however, the principle of contribution to sustainable finance is again referenced whereby it is noted that such national regulations 'should also provide for a system to reward clubs investing in the training and education of young players.'[37]

---

[34] Ibid., para 44.

[35] A Duval, 'The FIFA Regulations on the Status and Transfer of Players: Transnational Law-Making in the Shadow of Bosman' in A Duval and B Van Rompuy, *The Legacy of Bosman* (TMC Asser Press 2016) 81–116.

[36] Case C-325/08 *Olivier Bernard* (n 33), para 42.

[37] Article 1.2 of the FIFA Regulations on the Status and Transfer of Players (2016) 7 http://resources.fifa.com/mm/document/affederation/administration/02/70/95/52/regulationsonthestatusandtransferofplayersnov2016weben_neutral.pdf (accessed 26 Oct 2017).

Originally when the solidarity payment scheme was first adjudicated upon by the competent FIFA body, it held that where any transfer which attracted a transfer fee took place outside the home jurisdiction of a player, a solidarity payment was due to all the clubs who helped to train the player between the ages of 12 and 23. Such a solidarity payment was due to all training clubs where a player transferred either internationally or within the same national association's jurisdiction. This ruling however was subsequently reversed by a later decision and accordingly a solidarity payment is now only due when a player transfers between the jurisdiction of one national association and another.[38]

The operation of the solidarity scheme as it now stands however raises questions about its compatibility with EU law and whether the scheme currently achieves its aim of contributing to the clubs who have helped train the players in question. Given the existence of a single market within the EU it is difficult to justify why an EU-wide scheme such as the solidarity contribution ought to apply to transactions differently depending on the location of the transaction. It is submitted that a scheme which paid solidarity contributions on all transfers within the EU where a fee was paid, would amount to a more successful scheme for rewarding training clubs while also being more compatible with the notion of a single market.

A further problem with the current solidarity payment system arises when smaller football jurisdictions are considered. Smaller football jurisdictions which border larger jurisdictions are often disproportionately impacted by the existing arrangements. The Republic of Ireland serves as an example. Given the Republic of Ireland's small domestic league, historic ties and proximity to the UK, it is not surprising that virtually all the top level players from the Republic of Ireland play in leagues in the UK (predominantly the English league system). Elite players usually leave Ireland at a young age and sign their first professional contract with an English club or, in rarer circumstances, turn professional with an Irish club and transfer to England at a later stage, usually for a minimal transfer fee. Once established in the English league, elite players tend to transfer only within the English system. When a player transfers within the English system a solidarity payment is not due and thus the training clubs who contributed greatly to the development of the player are not rewarded even when a player is transferred for very significant sums.

---

[38] See generally, F de Weger, *The Jurisprudence of the FIFA Dispute Resolution Chamber* (2nd edn, TMC Asser Press 2016) 331–446.

Although smaller English training clubs also stand to lose out on any solidarity there is at the very least scope for the national association concerned to bring forward solidarity rules for clubs within their own jurisdiction. In this regard and at present, neither FIFA's TRs nor EU law intervenes despite all the aims stated above concerning solidarity and the rewarding of clubs for training players and which would greatly contribute to the sustainable financing of lower level and grassroots football.

V. REFORM

The 2013 Independent Expert Group Report investigated the solidarity payments system as part of a wide-ranging report and noted 'the inadequate role played by the solidarity mechanism in the redistribution of income to clubs involved in the training and education of football players',[39] while also noting the lack of consistency (and sometimes total absence) throughout Europe in how domestic rules applied to the redistribution of transfer fees in order to improve financial sustainability.[40] Although some proponents of reform such as the Independent Expert Group have suggested greater monitoring of the international transfer system and an increase in the level of financial contributions, it is submitted that the best solution would focus on the operation of all transfers within football.

FIFA's TRs do impose regulations for international transfers, however, most international transfers tend to occur between clubs at the top financial end of the game. Although FIFA's TRs do make some small contribution towards acknowledging the role played by grass-roots clubs, the lack of any equivalent uniform system in the domestic transfer systems run by national associations severely undermines the entire stated principle of making finances in football more sustainable across the EU. The European Parliament continues to call for improved financial distribution of funds in professional sport noting for example 'calls for more financial solidarity at all levels'.[41] Now, in 2018, it remains difficult to see how this 'call' can be practically realised given that EU law effectively only influences a certain small constituency of transfers.

---

[39] KEA – CDES, 'Study on the Economic and Legal Aspects of Transfers of Players, EAC/17/2011' (January 2013) 256.

[40] Ibid., 47.

[41] European Parliament resolution of 2 February 2017 on an integrated approach to sport policy: good governance, accessibility and integrity (2016/2143(INI)) para 39.

VI. CONCLUSION

When it comes to collectively analysing the legal rules, regulations and norms impacting on sustainable financing in football, the conclusion at first instance is that the matter remains predominantly one driven by the internal *lex sportiva* of football, rather than one directly influenced by substantive EU law. The influence of, and interventions from, the EU with regard to sustainable financing in football come in a more indirect form – of statements of policy and recommendations; nonetheless, these interventions have had a profound impact in shaping the debate on sustainable finance in football both at the European level *via* UEFA and at a global level *via* FIFA.

As noted by Strezhneva, there is a certain element of encroachment (or perhaps encouragement) by the EU towards football in demanding better governance, including financial sustainability:

> moves towards democratisation and the upgrading of football governance, and measures to increase its transparency and accountability – which are enhancing its legitimacy – are the best means to guarantee against (the unwelcome) intrusions from outside into football's affairs, irrespective of these intrusions' motives.[42]

Ultimately, the EU appears to have recognised, through its policy-based interventions and at times more substantial legal interventions, that the sustainable financing of football is worthy of recognition within the debate on the specificity of sport. Simply put, without sustainable financing football could ultimately consume itself and in this the EU recognises that Europe's favourite sport serves a far greater purpose than simply an economic activity.

---

[42] M Strezhneva, 'The Role of the European Union in Football Governance' (2016) 7(3) *Comparative Politics (Russian)* 45–54, 52 and DOI: 10.18611/2221-3279-2016-7-3(24)-45-54 (accessed 26 Oct 2017).

13. Application of EU competition rules to sport

Erika Szyszczak

I. INTRODUCTION: AN AMBIGUOUS RELATIONSHIP

'Competition and Sport' conjure the idea of a complementary dream team. Not so in EU law. Nothing could prepare the lawyer, or the athlete, for the complexity of unravelling the ambiguous relationship between competition law and sport in EU law. The United States' approach to the regulation of sport creates a stricter divide between professional and amateur activity, allowing for the economic consequences of a sport to be more clearly regulated in commercial law. In contrast, in Europe the idea of a pyramid structure is deployed to explain the organisation of the sport and the economic consequences. This model is useful to explain why the relationship between sport and competition is ambiguous.

The pyramid structure allows for Sports Governing Bodies (SGBs) to take on a monopolist role in the regulation of a particular sport. The SGBs would argue that their activity is purely of a governance nature. But where there are economic consequences of their actions, as a result of increased commercialisation of sport, there is the opening for competition law to treat SGBs as 'undertakings'. This has repercussions for competition law in terms of the regulation of clubs and individual athletes who may find the rules of the SGB restrictive. The rules of the SGBs may lead to market foreclosure: controlling when, where and how a club, or an athlete, may perform prevents a competitive sports market from emerging.

The pyramid model also, and aptly, describes the way in which sport allows individuals to develop as separate economic actors. In this respect athletes' activity becomes 'economic activity' by the desire to exploit their sporting ability: to attract payment for performing in sports events, as well as a host of ancillary activities, sometimes, but not always, associated with their sporting ability, and increasingly more often, using their media familiarity to endorse non-sports, commercial products. In EU competition law, such athletes may also be viewed as 'undertakings' for the purpose of applying the competition provisions to their sporting activities, as well as ancillary commercial activities derived from their sporting skills. The higher up the pyramid an athlete travels, the greater the opportunities for commercial activity. It is only in recent years that this model of sport has come under closer scrutiny from the perspective of EU competition law.

There are some bright lines in sport and competition law. As other chapters in this book demonstrate, where sporting activity has a clear commercial content – for example in the field of broadcasting, merchandising and sponsorship – the susceptibility of sport to the application of EU competition law is not questioned. The difficult legal situation is where individuals seek to exploit their sporting skills in new commercial events or are restricted from competing in official events by regulatory rules and decisions.[1] These rules have economic consequences which may be anti-competitive.

Here EU law has not been able to adopt a rigorous policy and appears to be lagging behind the changing consumer and athlete attitudes towards sport. The EU is also lagging behind the US where litigation and complaints based upon competition (anti-trust) are more commonplace.[2] Further, a tension arises in that challenges to behaviour or rules of sporting bodies throw open to question the role and purposes of competition law and its failure to adapt to changing circumstances where activity which was once shielded from the full force of the application of the economic rules of the EU law is now exposed to scrutiny because of its economic consequences. However, as more challenges are being brought in national courts and before regulatory or competition authorities, the role of EU competition law in curbing private power which has transnational effect is also being viewed in a constitutional light.

---

[1] For example, a ban as a result of a positive doping test, or unacceptable behaviour.

[2] See, e.g., the complaint brought by the North American Soccer League against the US Soccer Federation in a Brooklyn Federal Court. The complaint alleges that the USSF has violated federal antitrust laws through its anti-competitive division structure that divides men's professional soccer for US-based leagues based on arbitrary criteria that the USSF has manipulated to favour MLS, which serves as the commercial business partner of the USSF. See 'US: NASL files federal antitrust lawsuit against US Soccer' (*Competition Policy International*, 20 September 2017) available at https://www.competitionpolicyinternational.com/us-nasl-files-federal-antitrust-lawsuit-against-us-soccer/ (accessed 26 Oct 2017).

II. A TURNING POINT: *BOSMAN*

The *Bosman*[3] ruling of 1995 is taken as a turning point in EU law.[4] Pre-1995 there was little interest in using the EU economic rules to challenge anti-competitive behaviour in sport. SGBs appeared untouchable, yet the private regulation of transnational markets was capable of producing anti-competitive effects since markets were restricted and tightly controlled and competition was deterred, especially through sanctions deployed by SGBs for breaches of 'their' regulatory rules. The principle of the 'sporting exception' in EU law, developed from the ruling in *Walrave and Koch* in 1974,[5] deterred challenges to the rules of SGBs because a wide interpretation would appear to grant an immunity for any action or activity consisting of a purely sporting character, even if the effect or consequences of the application of SGM rules restrained the economic freedom of athletes.

The *Bosman* case is important in recognising that there was a significant shift in sport, from amateurism towards increased professionalism, and the concomitant economic consequences of the increased commercialisation of sport as an economic activity. Prior to *Bosman*, SGBs appeared immune from legal challenge. Most of the central organisational activities were situated outside the EU, usually in Switzerland, making it difficult for any kind of private challenge or enforcement of EU law.

After *Bosman* there was an increase in legal activity concerning sports-related disputes. Van Rompuy makes the point that pre-*Bosman*, the European Commission had adopted only four formal sport-related decisions under Article 101 TFEU. The cases were economic in nature and related to revenue-generating activities. Post-*Bosman*, between 1996 and 1999, there was an exponential increase in notifications and complaints to the European Commission, obliging it to open 60 sports-related

---

[3] Case C-415/93 *Bosman* [1995] ECR I-4921. S Van den Bogaert, 'Bosman: The Genesis of European Sports Law', in M Maduro and L Azoulai (eds) *The Past and Future of EU Law: The Classics of EU Law Revisited on the 50th Anniversary of the Rome Treaty*, (Hart 2010) 488–98 and S Weatherill, '*Bosman* Changed Everything: The Rise of EC Sports Law' in Maduro and Azoulai, ibid., 480–87.

[4] B Van Rompuy, 'The Role of EU Competition Law in Tackling Abuse of Regulatory Power by Sports Associations' (2015) 22(2) *Maastricht Journal of European and Comparative Law* 174–204.

[5] Case 36/74 *Walrave and Koch v Union Cycliste Internationale* [1974] ECR 1405.

competition complaints.[6] The extra territorial effect of EU competition law offered the opportunity to erode the immunity from litigation that had previously protected SGBs.

But when analysing the European Commission's previous attitude we see that sport has been given special treatment in competition law; the European Commission often pleads that there is no *Community interest* in pursuing sports-cases relating to competition. When it does start to investigate, the secrecy and lack of transparency of the decision-making process has made it difficult to discern the European Commission's thinking as to why sport should be given special treatment.

It was not until the *Meca-Medina* case in 2006 that the European Courts came to consider the application of competition law to sport.[7] While the CJEU recognised the economic implications of the rules of sporting bodies, stating that they could be brought within the scope of the EU competition rules, it also recognised a broader basis for the justification to keep sport special when applying the economic rules of EU law. The Court recognised the autonomy of sporting bodies to choose independent forms of arbitration to settle disputes, restricting the possibilities of challenges using EU law through the conventional channels of the European Commission and appeals to the European Courts. The *Meca-Medina* judgment did not follow the usual route of analysing if a restriction on competition could benefit from an exemption under Article 101(3) TFEU but instead adopted the *Wouters* approach of balancing the pro- and anti-competitive of a restriction of competition, allowing for measures to be justified against a standard of necessity and proportionality.[8]

This autonomy of sport is now being challenged, driven by greater commercialisation and intensification of competing sporting activities, allowing new sports markets to emerge. There are two demand drivers to this. First, the increased professionalism of sport, alongside advances in research technology and in physiology and nutrition, has raised the bar in sporting performance. Second, athletes may have shorter time-frames, and with greater and more intensive competition, in which to realise their peak performance. This may create a demand from athletes to have more

---

[6] See generally, Van Rompuy (note 4) and G Georgiev, 'Contagious Efficiency: The Growing Reliance on US-style Antitrust Settlements in EU Law' [2007] (4) *Utah Law Review* 971–1037.

[7] Case T-313/02 *Meca-Medina and Majcen v Commission* [2004] ECR II-3291 and C-519/04 P *Meca-Medina and Majcen v Commission* [2006] ECR I-6991.

[8] Case C-309/99 *Wouters* [2002] ECR I-1577.

opportunities to compete in top-class events. A correlation of this is the increased demand from a global audience to watch live and multi-media platform performances of athletes. As a result, a greater number of sports disputes are being brought before *national* courts and *national* competition authorities, using the EU economic law provisions to challenge any restrictions on activity.

III. REACTING TO THE CHALLENGE OF EU LAW: FROM AUTONOMY TO SPECIFICITY

Following the *Bosman* ruling it is possible to discern a clearer development of EU Sports law, or a *lex sportive*, as the SGBs realised that unless they retained a concept of 'sporting rules', which could be separated from the economic commercial exploitation of sport, inevitably the economic rules of the EU would apply. There was a danger that opportunist litigation would chip away at all regulation which limited an athlete's ability to practise sport in an autonomous manner, as well as dilute the accepted kudos of major sporting events and tournaments, such as the Olympic Games or the World Cup in football.

Having lost the argument that sport was immune from the reach of EU law, SGBs adopted a different discourse, which was translated into EU policy largely through soft law policy documents, as the 'specificity of sport'.[9] This concept refers to the inherent characteristics of sport which set it apart from other economic and social activities and was recognised in Article 165 TEU.

Thus, in EU law, the application of the economic Treaty rules to sport was shrouded in a protectionism derived from the lack of competence for the EU to legislate in sporting matters. This in turn has allowed the European Commission to avoid taking responsibility for certain sport rules which are anti-competitive and would not stand up to scrutiny in applying a proportionality test. A good example of this is seen in the Financial Fair Play regulations where, for political reasons, the European Commission would prefer that football clubs do not break away from the main regulatory body, UEFA.[10]

---

[9] T Serby, 'The State of EU Sports Law: Lessons from UEFA's "Financial Fair Play" Regulations' (2016) 16(1) *International Sports Law Journal* 37–51 and S Weatherill, 'Is There Such a Thing as EU Sports Law?' (2011) 11(1) *International Sports Law Journal* 39.

[10] Discussed by Serby, ibid.

IV. THE USE OF ARBITRATION IN SPORT

One aspect of protecting the specificity of sport, and as an explanation for the lack of case law before the European Commission and the European Courts, was the deliberate policy choice to reduce the opportunities for athletes to use EU law in national courts by the Olympic Federations and SGBs, such as FIFA, inserting arbitration clauses in their statutes. This approach creates the notion of sport as an independent autonomous area of activity, similar to the manner in which commercial law has developed.

In commercial law disputes, arbitration is established as a dispute resolution of choice because of its confidentiality, flexibility and the potential for expeditious and cost-effective determination. It is also viewed as a voluntary act. As Higgs notes: 'the ability to shield disputes, and thus underlying commercial practices and malpractices from public scrutiny remains a real and arguably increasing attraction of arbitration'.[11] The attraction of arbitration for athletes, and for the reputation of the sport involved, is that many disputes are disciplinary, conduct-related disputes or challenges to access and entry of sporting competitions.

The use of arbitration clauses has allowed SGBs to insulate themselves from control by national competition authorities (NCA), national courts, the European Commission and the European Courts. In the *Cañas* decision, the European Commission rejected the argument that compulsory arbitration was anti-competitive.[12] It decided that compulsory arbitration clauses would only constitute a restriction on competition if coupled with anti-competitive restrictions.[13] The European Commission also rejected the argument that compulsory arbitration clauses infringe the access to justice principle.[14] This explains why the Court of Arbitration for Sport (CAS) situated in Lausanne, Switzerland, has developed as the principal legal forum for sport disputes.[15] CAS awards may only be appealed to the Swiss Federal Tribunal (SFT).

It is possible for a national court to be involved in the review of a CAS award where it is enforced in one of the Member States of the EU, and

---

[11] J Higgs, 'Learning the Arbitration Art' (*Counsel*, October 2016) https://www.counselmagazine.co.uk/articles/learning-the-arbitration-art (accessed 26 Oct 2017).

[12] CAS 2005/A/951 *Cañas v ATP*, 23 May 2006.

[13] Ibid., para 40.

[14] Ibid., para 41.

[15] A Duval, 'The Court of Arbitration for Sport and EU Law' (2015) 22(2) *Maastricht Journal of European and Comparative Law* 224–55.

this could open up an opportunity for competition law issues to be considered. In the few cases where athletes have attempted to use EU competition law as either an appeals forum against decisions of the CAS, or to challenge the regulatory rules and decisions of a sport regulator against EU competition rules, the European Commission has been reluctant to adopt this role.

By allowing arbitration to be the major forum for sports dispute resolution negates the impact that EU competition principles may have on sport. If the parties to the arbitration raise EU competition law points, then the arbitration panel must consider the legal points. But, as Duval points out, this does not occur regularly.[16] There has been much academic discussion as to whether an arbitral tribunal has a duty to raise EU law *ex officio*. The lack of influence of EU competition law in cases before the CAS is explained by the insulation of the CAS. The parties before the arbitration tribunal may not have recourse to the European Commission for advice and the CAS is not able to engage in a dialogue with the CJEU through the preliminary reference procedure. This has resulted in a situation described by Duval (2015) where the 'CAS and EU law have been "talking past each other" for a long time'.[17]

In *Eco Swiss*, the CJEU held that a breach of Article 101(1) TFEU must be considered as a breach of public policy in the sense laid down in Article V(2)(b) of the Convention on the Recognition and Enforcement of Foreign Arbitral Awards (the New York Convention) 1958 and:

> where its domestic rules of procedure require a national court to grant an application for annulment of an arbitration award where such an application is founded on failure to observe national rules of public policy, it must also

---

[16] Ibid. A rare example of the CAS applying EU competition law can be found in *AEK Athens and SK Slavia Prague v UEFA CAS* 98/200. More recently in *RFC Seraing v FIFA CAS* 2016/A/4490, the CAS held that EU law was applicable to the dispute because it satisfied the condition that it was a 'mandatory provision of foreign law' under Art 19 of the Swiss Federal Act on Private International Law. Mandatory provisions of foreign law must be taken into account where three cumulative conditions are satisfied: such rules belong to a special category of norms which need to be applied irrespective of the law applicable to the merits of the case; there is a close connection between the subject matter of the dispute and the territory where the mandatory rules are in force; and in view of Swiss legal theory and practice, the mandatory rules must aim to protect legitimate interests and crucial values and their application must lead to a decision which is appropriate.

[17] Duval (note 15), 253.

> grant such an application where it is founded on failure to comply with the prohibition laid down in Article [101(1) TFEU].[18]

In Germany, the Court of Appeal in Bremen found a CAS award unenforceable for non-compliance with EU law and, contrary to the *ordre public* of German law. The court considered that it was the duty of the national court to review a CAS award for compatibility with mandatory German law. The difficultly in denting the immunity of arbitration clauses from scrutiny against other legal norms may be seen in the lengthy litigation brought by Claudia Pechstein, a speed skater who was found guilty of doping offences and banned for two years by the International Skating Union (ISU).[19]

The ban resulted in Pechstein missing the Vancouver Winter Olympics Games. Pechstein was unsuccessful in challenging the ban before the CAS,[20] and was also unsuccessful in two actions brought before the Swiss Federal Tribunal.[21] Pechstein also brought an action before the European Court of Human Rights (ECtHR), alleging a contravention of Article 6 ECHR.[22] Further, Pechstein challenged the validity and enforceability of the CAS before a German court in Munich (Landgericht)

---

[18] Case C-126 *Eco Swiss* [1999] ECR I-03055, para 37. D Geradin, 'Public Policy and Breach of Competition Law in International Arbitration: A Competition Law Practitioner's Viewpoint' 29 May 2016 TILEC Discussion paper No 2016-029 available at SSRN: https://ssrn.com/abstract=2786370 (accessed 26 Oct 2017).

[19] The circumstances of the guilty verdict explain the tenacity of Pechstein in exploring all legal avenues to challenge the finding. At the International Skating Union (ISU) All-round World Speed Skating Championships in Norway in 2009, a blood sample taken from Pechstein showed an abnormal increase in reticulocytes (immature red blood cells) when compared with her biological passport, a blood profile compiled from previous test samples. This suggested potential blood doping and Pechstein was the first athlete to be banned based solely on her blood values having never tested positive.

[20] CAS 2009/A/1912 and 1913 and CAS OG 10/04.

[21] BGer 4A_612/2009 and 4A_144/2010. See generally B Hess and F Kaps, 'Claudia Pechstein and SV Wilhelmshaven: Two German Higher Regional Courts Challenge the Court of Arbitration for Sport' (Conflict of Law.net, 6 February 2015) and available at http://conflictoflaws.net/2015/pechstein-and-sv-wilhelmshaven-two-german-higher-regional-courts-challenge-the-independence-of-the-court-of-arbitration-for-sport/ (accessed 26 Oct 2017).

[22] *Claudia Pechstein v Switzerland* (no. 67474/10) Application communicated to the government in February 2013. In 2009, following positive drugs tests, the skater Claudia Pechstein was given a two-year ban by the Disciplinary Commission of the ISU. The Court of Arbitration for Sport upheld that decision,

claiming damages of EUR 4 million from ISU and the German Skating Federation (DEU) for lost income during her suspension.

The German court found that the arbitration clause in Pechstein's licence with the national and international skating federations was void, because it was compulsory: she could not compete in competitions unless she agreed to the arbitration clause. Furthermore, the CAS arbitration did not satisfy all the requirements of Article 6 ECHR because of the manner in which arbitrators were appointed and the institutional bias in favour of sports federations. However, the court then found that Pechstein was bound by the CAS award, since she had never raised any objections to the arbitration process (including the competence and impartiality of the panel) at the time, and therefore the German court was precluded from reconsidering the decision which was *res judicata*. In addition, the court held that it was obliged to recognise the CAS award in accordance with Article V of the New York Convention on the Recognition and Enforcement of Foreign Arbitral Awards.

On appeal, in March 2015, the Oberlandesgericht Munchen overturned the first instance decision finding that the arbitration agreement in favour of CAS, and the CAS award issued on the basis of that agreement, infringed the abuse of a dominant position provision of German competition law. However, on 7 June 2016, the Federal Court of Justice (Bundesgerichtshof/BGF) reversed the previous decision. It noted that sport governing bodies are in a dominant position and that they dominate the CAS. Nevertheless the German court found that the CAS is a neutral and independent body. The court also noted that necessity of an independent body providing a fast and uniform system of justice for sport. At the time of writing, the outcome of an appeal to the German Constitutional Court and the ECtHR proceedings, remain pending.

V. THE POSSIBILITIES FOR EU COMPETITION LAW TO AFFECT SPORT

The first case where the application of the EU competition rules to sport was considered by the European Courts was *Meca-Medina*. Two international long-distance swimmers challenged the anti-doping rules of the

---

and Pechstein's application to the Swiss Federal Court for judicial review was dismissed in 2010. Pechstein alleges a violation of Article 6(1) (right to a fair hearing) and Article 6(2) (presumption of innocence) of the Convention. See further https://hudoc.echr.coe.int/eng#{"itemid":["001-117166"]} (accessed 26 Oct 2017).

Fédération Internationale de Natation (FINA), implementing the International Olympic Committee anti-doping rules. Two swimmers from Spain and Slovenia had tested positive in an anti-doping test for Nandrolone, a prohibited anabolic steroid and were banned for a period of four years by a decision of FINA's Doping Panel. Meca-Medina and Majcen appealed the decision before the Court of Arbitration for Sport, which first confirmed the suspension but then subsequently reduced it to a period of two years. Meca-Medina and Majcen challenged the ruling, by using the complaint procedure to the European Commission relying upon the EU free movement and competition rules.

The European Commission was evidently uncomfortable in being asked to review the decisions of the SGB, seeing the CAS as the appropriate legal forum for such disputes. The European Commission,[23] the General Court[24] and the CJEU[25] rejected the swimmers' appeal on various grounds. The European Commission and the General Court acknowledged the independence and impartiality of the CAS and indicated that the swimmers should have explored all avenues of appeal under the arbitration system, including the right to appeal to the Swiss Federal Tribunal, before raising the complaint using EU competition law before the European Commission.

At first sight the European Commission and General Court appear to acknowledge that competition law is not the appropriate regulatory tool for sport where disciplinary and regulatory rules for a particular sport are concerned. However, the case created a new precedent in that the CJEU held that the rules of SGBs were not immune from EU competition law; any rules imposed which would restrict the ability of athletes to compete should be subject to scrutiny using the proportionality principle. The Court borrowed from the ruling in *Wouters*[26] in finding that not every agreement, which restricts the freedom of action of the parties, is necessarily caught by the prohibition laid down in Article 101 TFEU, because account must be taken of its objectives. This was insightful because it also meant that sporting rules do not have to go down the conventional route of looking to Article 101(3) TFEU as a means of exempting the rules from the application of competition law.

---

[23] Commission Decision COMP/38158 *Meca-Medina, Majcen v CIO*, 1 August 2002.

[24] Case T-313/02 *Meca-Medina and Majcen v Commission* [2004] ECR II-3291.

[25] C-519/04 P *Meca-Medina and Majcen v Commission* [2006] ECR I-6991.

[26] Case C-309/99 *Wouters* [2002] ECR I-1577.

In *Wouters*, the Court allowed assessment of the need to supervise professional ethics and ensure the sound administration of justice to be balanced against the concerns of EU competition law. This has been categorised as a 'European-style rule of reason'[27] or 'regulatory ancilli-arity'.[28] The judgment in *Meca-Medina* is a clever balance. It recognises the growing commercialisation of sport but continues to respect the validity of SGB to impose regulation on the sport, while offering the opportunity for law to step in and control rules which are not legitimate for the governance of the sport.[29]

From a legal perspective, the use of proportionality to examine SGBs' rules which restrict the application of EU law are more familiar in the application of the free movement provisions, rather than in competition law. But they provide a wider basis of justifications and explanations for the necessity of sporting rules.

In a similar case, *Cañas*, which involved the use of EU competition law to challenge the anti-doping rules adopted by the Association of Tennis Professionals (ATP) in order to implement the World Anti-Doping Code, the European Commission expressed a similar position: that the CAS was the appropriate forum to resolve sports disputes. The ATP had imposed a two-year ban on the Argentinian tennis player, Cañas, after a positive drugs test during a tennis tournament in Mexico.[30] Cañas argued that the positive result was because of a mix up in prescriptions by the tournament doctor. The SFT quashed the CAS decision on procedural grounds. On remittal, the CAS imposed a 15-month ban and this decision

---

[27] See generally G Monti, 'Article 81 and Public Policy' (2002) 39(5) *Common Market Law Review* 1057–99.

[28] R Whish and D Bailey, *Competition Law* (8th edn, OUP 2015) 140.

[29] Not surprisingly the judgment was not received so favourably in the sports' legal community: See e.g., G. Infantino [at the time Director of Legal Affairs at UEFA, now President of FIFA], Meca-Medina: A Step Backwards for the European Sports Model and the Specificity of Sport? UEFA paper 02/10/06, at http://www.uefa.com/MultimediaFiles/Download/uefa/KeyTopics/480391_DOWNLOAD.pdf (accessed 26 Oct 2017). See also R Subiotto, 'The Adoption and Enforcement of Anti-doping Rules should not be subject to European Competition Law' (2010) 31 *European Competition Law Review* 323–30. Cf, E Szyszczak, 'Competition and Sport' (2007) 32(1) *European Law Review* 95–110.

[30] Consequently, Cañas was disqualified from the tournament and had to forfeit any medals, titles, computer ranking points and prize money obtained at the tournament. In addition, he was declared ineligible to participate in tournaments for two years from 11 June 2005, he was disqualified from all the tournaments he had participated in since Mexico and he was also ordered to repay all the prize money he had won during this latter period, some $276,070.

was the subject of the complaint to the European Commission, Cañas arguing that the strict liability of the anti-doping rules was incompatible with EU competition law.

Again, the European Commission was adamant that it did not think that it was the appropriate forum to challenge the regulatory rules of the SGBs. Although the Decision found that the governing body of CAS, the ICAS, was not an undertaking for the purposes of competition law the Commission did note the specialist nature of the CAS as an independent institution for sports disputes and which, accordingly, was one comparable to that of a national court. Furthermore, even though the European Commission did not find that EU competition law was captured in the case it nevertheless decided to consider the application of the rules, finding that they were proportionate.

The CJEU ruling in *MOTOE*[31] confirmed that a SGB that mixes regulatory functions with economic activities should be subject to the application of EU competition law. The CJEU confirmed that organisations such as sports federations that regulate sporting events and have a direct commercial interest in the events (e.g., entering into sponsorship, advertising and insurance contracts) can lead to exclusive rights. The CJEU clarified that the procedures and criteria for selection used by SGBs should be transparent when responding to other organisations that are applying to organise events. The fact that the SGB (the Greek Automobile and Touring Association) was operating a virtual monopoly in organising motorcycle events was not, per se, a breach of Article 102 TFEU but rather, the fact that there was no legal recourse for appeal or review for undertakings refused consent, could be seen as an abuse of the SGB's dominant position.

It is surprising that Article 102 TFEU has not been used more frequently to challenge SGBs. The use of Article 9 of Regulation 1/2003 to enter into a dialogue with the European Commission and to offer commitments to alter anti-competitive rules would be a diplomatic solution to complaints.

Together with the *Meca-Medina* ruling, the *MOTOE* judgment destroyed the notion that 'purely sporting rules' have an automatic exemption from the scope of EU competition law. However, there is still some ambiguity in the relationship between sport and competition. The judgment confirms that the specific features of sport should be considered in assessing the compatibility of organisational sporting rules with EU competition law. In particular *MOTOE* clarifies that EU law expects

---

[31] Case C-49/07 *MOTOE* [2008] ECR I-4863.

that the organisation of sports events should be subject to stringent regulations by governing bodies.

VI. NATIONAL COMPETITION AUTHORITIES AND NATIONAL COURTS

A new forum for sport and competition law complaints is emerging. Certain sports now appear to be the focus of NCA investigations. For example, the motor racing industry has been the subject of investigation at the national level. The Italian NCA started a competition investigation in 2008 into the regulations and conduct of the national motor sports federation (ACI) under Articles 101 and 102 TFEU. The investigation focused on regulatory and statutory provisions intended to limit access to the market for the organisation of motor sport events for competitors. In 2009, that NCA adopted a commitment decision after the ACI undertook to, inter alia, allow its members to participate in events not organised by the federation.

The above investigation was followed in 2011 when the Swedish NCA found a breach of national competition law against the Swedish Automobile Sports Federation, ordering it to amend its rules preventing its members from participating in unauthorised events.[32] The offending rules concerned the excessive sanctions of a fine and/or withdrawal of the licence to participate in SBF events. This decision was upheld by the Swedish Market Court.[33] This court also applied Article 101 TFEU. The court held that the mere existence of the Automobile Association rules distorted competition to a significant degree because an absolute ban on participating in external evens would affect trade between the Member States. The court held that an absolute ban on an external activity could not satisfy the proportionality test imposed by EU law in the *Meca-Medina* judgment. Interestingly, the Swedish court also considered if the rules of the Automobile Association could benefit from an Article 101(3) TFEU (and the equivalent national law) exemption but found that these

---

[32] Swedish Competition Authority (Konkurrensverket) *Swedish Automobile Sports Federation*, Decision dnr. 709/2009 (13 May 2011) and available at http://www.konkurrensverket.se/en/news/more-should-be-able-to-organise-motor-racing-events/ (accessed 26 Oct 2017).

[33] Case A 5/11, *Svenska Bilsportförbundet v Konkurrensverket* (20 December 2012) and available at http://www.konkurrensverket.se/en/news/good-for-competitors-spectators-and-the-development-of-automobile-sports/ (accessed 26 Oct 2017).

conditions were not satisfied. The Automobile Association was obliged to amend its rules and drop the sanctions. The case illustrates a willingness of a NCA and a national court to treat sports activity as on a par with ordinary commercial activity.

Following this precedent, another challenge, to a different sport was made before the Swedish NCA in October 2013 by BMR Sport Nutrition AB against the rules of the SKKF, the Swedish Bodybuilding and Fitness Federation. The SKKF enjoyed a monopoly position as the only national member of the International Bodybuilding Federation (IFBB). Athletes and officials must be members of the SKKF in order to participate in IFBB international competitions. The SKKF incorporated the IFBB rules into the Swedish national statutes. One rule, which was the matter under challenge, was a loyalty clause: it imposed a fine or suspension on athletes who competed and participated in contests not approved by the SKKF or the IFBB. An additional deterrent from participating in outside events was the rule that athletes who participated in an external event had to undergo a doping test at their own expense before they could be admitted to SKKF and IFBB events in the future.

BMR Sport Nutrition was a manufacturer of bodybuilding supplements and other foodstuffs and it had started to organise bodybuilding and other fitness events in Sweden outside of the SKKF. Its complaint was based upon Article 101 TFEU,[34] arguing that the SKKF rules prevented organisers of competing events from being able to enter the market and compete with the SKKF. Furthermore, the sanctions of the SKKF were so stringent that athletes were deterred from contemplating alternative events. The Swedish NCA closed the case in 2014 when the SKKF agreed to amend its practice and no longer fine or suspend athletes participating in external events.[35]

Equestrian sport is another example where the national competition authority has been the forum for a complaint. An investigation by the Belgian NCA was upheld by the Brussels Court of Appeal in 2016. In June 2015, Global Champions League (GCL) complained to the BCA that the Federation Equestre Internationale (FEI) abuses its regulatory powers as the SGB to protect FEI-promoted commercial events against

---

[34] Using the corresponding Swedish national competition law: Chapter 2, Article 1 Swedish Competition Act.

[35] Swedish Competition Authority (Konkurrensverket), *Bodybuilding and Fitness Competitions*, Decision dnr. 590/2013 (28 May 2014) and available (in Swedish) at http://www.konkurrensverket.se/beslut/13-0590.pdf (accessed 26 Oct 2017).

competition from independent organisers.[36] This was implemented by a new exclusivity clause, suspending riders, horses and officials from participating in FEI-promoted events if they participated in events not approved by the FEI.

The FEI refused to approve the GCL events and GCL requested the Belgian NCA to suspend the exclusivity clause. In July 2015, the BCA agreed with GCL that a preliminary assessment confirmed that the FEI exclusivity clause breaches competition law and granted interim relief to GCL, thus allowing the GCL to launch events in 2016 with riders and horses under the protection of interim measures. In August 2015, the FEI appealed the decision of the BCA, asking for the suspension of the interim measures and for their annulment. The Court of Appeal rejected the FEI's request for the suspension of the interim measures and upheld the BCA decision giving riders and horses the freedom to choose to compete in the GCL.

The court held that the FEI had failed to demonstrate that the interim measures inflicted serious and irreparable harm on the federation. The FEI had managed for more than a century without the clause and failed to show why it was indispensable. The court held that any undermining of the credibility of the FEI as the sport's governing body as a consequence of the Belgian NCA decision was not a challenge to its autonomy to govern the sport, but rather it was a risk to which the FEI has exposed itself by engaging in the marketing of equestrian competitions. The court rejected the FEI's request for the annulment of the interim measures, finding that the FEI exclusivity clause was in breach of competition law in respect to the GCL.

In Ireland, the NCA had also opened an investigation into a rule of Show Jumping Ireland (SJI) that prevented members of the SJI to compete at unaffiliated show jumping events. The case was closed after the SJI agreed to amend the rule. The new rule allows SJI to penalise its members where they participate in events not covered by the specified

---

[36] The global league for show-jumping was designed to replicate the success of motor racing's Formula 1 franchise and was backed by Frank McCourt, the billionaire sports investor and former owner of the Los Angeles Dodgers baseball team.

Health and Safety Standards and where the SJI has not been provided with evidence that the event is covered by adequate insurance.[37]

In October 2015, the Spanish National Commission of Markets and Competition opened an investigation into the financial conditions set by the Spanish Basketball Clubs Association (Law Asociation de Clubes de Baloncesto ACB) for clubs being promoted to the ACB's national league. The Spanish NCA investigated whether the conditions were discriminatory and against fair sporting competition. The investigation was initiated following the complaint by the Club Baloncesto Tizona, relating to conditions requiring payment of 3.2 million euros within three months of joining the ACB, and 1.8 million euros in a fund for promotion and relegation purposes, as well as a 270,000 euros contribution to a wage guarantee fund.

Issues relating to the regulation of football are also emerging before national competition authorities. In Belgium, the White Star Woluwe Football Club had been refused a licence to compete in the premier division by the Licences Commission of the Union Royale Belge des Sociétés de Foootball Association. This decision was upheld by the Cour Belge d'Arbitrage pour le Sport. The Belgian Competition Authority accepted that it could review an arbitral award against EU competition law but refused to grant provisional measures.[38]

The regulation of football agents and other intermediaries has been subjected to assessment against EU competition and free movement law. In 1998 a French football agent, Piau, brought a complaint to the European Commission alleging that the rules of FIFA governing football agents were discriminatory and contrary to Article 101 TFEU. Following negotiations with FIFA, the rules were amended, and the European Commission closed the case. Piau appealed against the European Commission Decision to the CFI (now the General Court). The Court acknowledged the regulatory power of private sporting bodies and the restrictive effect their rules could have on economic freedoms. The CFI

---

[37] Competition and Consumer Protection Commission of Ireland, 'Show Jumping Ireland Amend Allegedly Restrictive Rule' (1 May 2012), case summary available at https://www.ccpc.ie/business/enforcement/civil-competition-enforcement/closed-investigations/show-jumping-ireland-restrictive-rule/ (accessed 26 Oct 2017).

[38] M Montejo, 'Sports arbitration and EU Competition law: the Belgian competition authority enters the arena' (*Asser International Sports Law Blog*, 7 September 2016) and available at http://www.asser.nl/SportsLaw/Blog/post/sports-arbitration-and-eu-competition-law-the-belgian-competition-authority-enters-the-arena-by-marine-montejo (accessed 26 Oct 2017).

held that regulations adopted by a private organisation were subject to EU competition law but the Court did not find the FIFA regulations were incompatible with EU competition law and that Article 101(3) TFEU could be used to exempt any anti-competitive effects. The CFI also supported the European Commission in finding that Article 102 TFEU could also apply to FIFA, but concluded that because there was the possibility of an exemption under Article 101(3) TFEU an abuse of a dominant position had not been established.[39]

In April 2015, FIFA adopted a new set of regulations governing the role of agents and intermediaries and these were implemented by the German Football Association in the form of the Reglement für Spielervermittlung (DFB).[40] The Landgericht Frankfurt am Main found that parts of the regulations infringed Article 101 TFEU and issued an injunction. On appeal, the Oberlandesgericht Frankfurt am Main found that the parts of the regulations subjecting agents and intermediaries to be subject to the jurisdiction of the DFB, UEFA and FIFA and the rule imposing a duty to provide an extended certificate of good conduct usually reserved for professions involving a risk to the integrity of minors were not proportionate to attain the stated objectives and contrary to Article 101 TFEU.[41]

VII. ESCALATION OF COMPLAINTS TO THE EUROPEAN COMMISSION

The European Commission is also receiving an escalation of complaints.[42] For example, a complaint was made by two Formula 1 teams,

---

[39] Case T-193/02 *Piau v Commission* [2005] ECR II-209; Case C-171/05 *Piau v Commission* [2006] ECR I-37.

[40] Available (in German) at https://www.dfb.de/fileadmin/_dfbdam/61514-DFB-Reglement_fuer_Spielervermittlung_120515.pdf (accessed 26 Oct 2017).

[41] See further, A Duval and K Mekenkamp, 'De- or Re-Regulating the Middle Men? The DFB's regulation of intermediaries under EU law scrutiny at the OLG Frankfurt' (*Asser International Sports Law Blog*, 6 October 2016) and available at http://www.asser.nl/SportsLaw/Blog/post/de-or-re-regulating-the-middlemen-the-dfb-s-regulation-of-intermediaries-under-eu-law-scrutiny-at-the-olg-frankfurt-by-antoine-duval-and-kester-mekenkamp (accessed 26 Oct 2017).

[42] Useful sources of up-to-date information include: http://www.lawinsport.com/articles/competition-law; and http://www.asser.nl/Spo.rtsLaw/Blog/

Force India and Sauber, making an allegation that the organising body, Formula One Group, was infringing Article 102 TFEU (abuse of a dominant position) relating to funding and governance issues by favouring the position of the five largest motor racing teams[43] and thereby discriminating against smaller racing teams.

Another complaint concerned an allegation from the football players' union, FIFPro, that FIFA's transfer rules are anti-competitive and prevent football clubs from competing against each other to buy the best players. This is an attempt to argue that rules, previously negotiated as compatible with EU law, no longer achieve the aims of guaranteeing their intended purpose of guaranteeing the stability of contracts, the competitive balance between football clubs and a fair distribution of revenue. Indeed, it is argued that the rules have skewed the economic balance between football clubs, with the clubs with significant financial backing dominating the transfer market.[44]

The difficulty of involving NCA and national courts is that a claimant may find that he falls between various jurisdictions and competences, with each forum reluctant to take on the competition law matter. One example is the challenge brought before the Brussels Court of First Instance by Daniele Striani, a football agent licensed by the Belgian Football Association, complaining that UEFA's 'break even' rule distorted competition between clubs by imposing a limit on the level of investment in players. He argued that the rule negatively affects the salaries and mobility of players because of the restrictions it placed on clubs' transfer budgets. Under the 'break even' requirement, the relevant income of clubs must at least match their relevant expenses, subject to permitted deviations.

The CJEU rejected the request from the Belgian Court of First Instance for a preliminary ruling under Article 269 TFEU. The order from the CJEU stated that the Belgian court's request did not meet the necessary requirements of admissibility; it was insufficiently clear and precise to enable the CJEU to rule on a point of EU law and did not show that the

---

43 Mercedes, Red Bull, Ferrari, Williams and McLaren.

44 Serby (note 9) and B Van Rompuy, 'The Brussels Court Judgment on Financial Fair Play: a Futile Attempt to pull off a Bosman' (*Asser Sports Law Blog*, 6 July 2015) http://www.asser.nl/SportsLaw/Blog/post/the-brussels-court-judgment-on-financial-fair-play-a-futile-attempt-to-pull-off-a-bosman-by-ben-van-rompuy (accessed 26 Oct 2017).

answers to the questions were necessary for the solution of a dispute to be settled in the main proceedings.[45]

In February 2016, Euroleague Properties, a subsidiary company of Euroleague filed a complaint against the International Basketball Federation (FIBA) and FIBA Europe to the European Commission, stating that FIBA had put clubs under pressure to join its Basketball Champions League. In response, FIBA submitted a complaint to the European Commission against Euroleague based on a similar basis – allegations of anti-competitive behaviour in order to gain a competitive advantage.

The Euroleague complaint to the European Commission against FIBA, alleged that FIBA had infringed competition rules by making illegal threats and applying unfair pressure on clubs, players and referees, in order to coerce them into participating in FIBA competitions. FIBA's response to this 'conflict of interest' allegation was directed against a subsidiary of Euroleague Commercial Assets (ECA) for breaching similar competition rules, including putting pressure on clubs, players and referees to take part in a Euroleague competition or face expulsion from their other events, as well as unfair discrimination against certain clubs.

In an unusual, and significant step, the European Commission sent a 'Statement of Objections' to the International Skating Union (ISU) on 27 September 2016, indicating that it will undertake an in-depth investigation into the rules of the ISU which limit the availability of ice skaters to compete in new events which compete with established ice skating events.[46] The thrust of the dispute is that the commercial freedom of skaters to compete is restricted, and markets are foreclosed by the ISU, by limiting potential competitors' ability to stage new events. The issues are very similar to the issues raised at the national level in the IEF/Global Champions League dispute.

Thus, at the time of writing, this may be a pivotal turning point in the relationship between EU competition law and sport.

---

[45] Case C-299/15 *Striani v UEFA, URBSFA* Order of 16 July 2015 (reference inadmissible) and Decision of the European Ombudsman in case 2086/2014/EIS https://www.ombudsman.europa.eu/en/cases/decision.faces/en/61468/html.bookmark (accessed 26 Oct 2017).

[46] Case AT.40208. See E Szyszczak, 'Eligibility Rules, Sport and Competition: Is the ISU Skating on Thin Ice?' (*Littleton Chambers*, 7 October 2016) http://www.littletonchambers.com/eligibility-rules-sport-and-competition-is-the-isu-skating-on-thin-ice-by-prof-erika-szyszczak-1026/ (accessed 26 Oct 2017); 'Competition and Sport: No Longer *So* Special' (2018) JeClap forthcoming.

VIII. WHY SPORT AND COMPETITION?

The final part of this chapter addresses the question of whether and why competition law should apply to sport. From the discussion so far it is evident that there is an increase in sports-related competition complaints. These appear to be generated at the individual level as well as by competitors wishing to break up the monopoly created by SGBs in the organisation of official events. We see a preference for using Article 101 TFEU to attack restraints of competition, rather than, at first sight, the more obvious use of Article 102 TFEU to claim that SBGs are abusing a dominant position.

From the growing number of complaints at the national level, competition law has shown that it can intervene and grant remedial action to alter rules of a SGB that are anti-competitive. This interferes with the governance and democratic structure of SGBs requiring the adjustment of certain rules, without an outright challenge to its legitimacy. But, the crucial point, is that SGBs are no longer immune from scrutiny and are accountable for their actions, especially where individual fundamental interests are at stake such as access to justice and the right to engage in an economic activity. Additionally, it exposes the SGBs to transparency and accountability. The question arises as to what is the aim of involving competition law in this way? And, further, can it be used to regulate sport in the future?

One answer is that EU competition law is being used as a constitutional tool in two dimensions. First, it is being used to protect, and to exploit, individual freedoms to participate in sport and to earn an economic living, either through state-sponsored or professional payments, or through ancillary economic advantages such as commercial endorsements. Secondly, it is being used as a tool to curb, restrain and make accountable private power. Indeed, the CFI in *Piau* stated that the legitimacy of a body like FIFA was questionable, given that FIFA had not received a mandate from a public authority:

> The very principle of regulation of an economic activity concerning neither the specific nature of sport nor the freedom of internal organisation of sports associations by a private-law body, like FIFA, which has not been delegated any such power by a public authority, cannot from the outset be regarded as compatible with Community law, in particular with regard to respect for civil and economic liberties.
>
> In principle, such regulation, which constitutes policing of an economic activity and touches on fundamental freedoms, falls within the competence of the public authorities. Nevertheless, in the present dispute, the rule-making

> power exercised by FIFA, in the almost complete absence of national rules, can be examined only in so far as it affects the rules on competition, in the light of which the lawfulness of the contested decision must be assessed, while considerations relating to the legal basis that allows FIFA to carry on regulatory activity, however important they may be, are not the subject of judicial review in this case.[47]

The official aims and purposes of EU competition law are not widely contested.[48] They can be distilled down to two: the protection of consumer welfare and market integration. In relation to the latter, the complaints challenge the national protection offered by SGBs to develop local markets free from competition and thus it is easy to see why cross-border interference with trade might occur. With regard to consumer welfare, the question arises as to 'who' is the consumer when addressing the role competition should play with sport. Most of the cases so far have concerned the interests of athletes who want to be unshackled from restrictive participation rules of the SGBs, or in the case of individual disciplinary actions, want to challenge their inability to participate in a sport where there are economic consequences of a ban/restriction.

These are the direct 'consumers' gaining the benefit from the challenges to sporting restrictions but underlying the individual nature of the claims is a nod towards the wider consumer market of sports activities. EU competition law is notoriously lacking in a legislative definition of a 'consumer'. Indeed, case law is also rather scarce when compared with other areas of EU law.[49] The European Commission takes a position that the overarching objective of the application of the competition rules is to protect competition on the market as a means of enhancing consumer welfare and of ensuring an efficient allocation of resources.

The effects of internationalisation and globalisation have created new opportunities for athletes to participate in sporting events across the globe

---

47 Case T-193/02 *Piau v Commission* [2005] ECR II-209 paras 77–78.

48 See generally P Akman, 'Searching for the Long-Lost Soul of Article 82 EC' (2009) (29) (2) OJLS 267–303; O Andriychuk, 'Rediscovering the Spirit of Competition: On the Normative Value of the Competitive Process' (2010) 6(3) *European Competition Journal* 575–610; O Odudu, 'The Wider Concerns of Competition Law' (2010) 30(3) OJLS 599–613; and D Zimmer (eds), *The Goals of Competition Law* (Edward Elgar 2010).

49 A Jones and A Albors-Llorens, 'The Images of the "Consumer" in EU Competition Law' in D Leczykiewicz and S. Weatherill (eds) *The Images of the 'Consumer' in EU Competition Law: Legislation, Free Movement and Competition Law* (Hart 2016), 43–92.

and to have their performance relayed in a virtual internet and broadcasting world. In terms of promoting consumer welfare, access and choice to these events may provide greater opportunities to see athletes performing live, and in different digital environments.

But there are countervailing pulls against the introduction of competition into a sports market. And this is the ambiguity. These countervailing pulls may be for public policy reasons, or social reasons, and even economic (commercial) reasons. It is a fine balance to decide what kind of restrictions imposed by a SGB or by individual business organisations (such as football clubs) are credible sporting concerns, and of a public policy nature, and what restrictions may be holding back the development of competitive markets in sport.

There may be good public policy, ethical, as well as commercial reasons, why a SGB or a private body may justify imposing restrictions on competition. For instance, and for social and public reasons, an athlete may need protection (both physical and mental) from too many opportunities to display her talents. But, on the other hand, curbing her ability to exploit her skills, especially in a sport with a very short period when an athlete is at 'peak' performance (e.g., female swimming competition) could restrict her capacity to exploit her capabilities and popularity.

Sports bodies, national and international, also have an interest in the over-exploitation of athletes, wanting the leading athletes to compete and 'peak' at the major international and regional events of that sport. This again is not solely born out of altruism: seats have to be sold, especially where a major event such as the Olympic Games has involved investment in new stadia and other facilities, as well as the commercial spin offs: broadcasting rights, memorabilia.

Revisiting *Meca-Medina* and *MOTOE*, the approach taken by the CJEU, allowing a balance between scrutiny of sporting rules and the proportionality of the justification, while recognising the competence for SGBs to develop governance rules, appears to be a sound approach. Competition law is not yet overwhelmed by sports-related complaints, but from the recent trend it may be that, as more commercial sponsors come forward, SGBs will be obliged to justify exclusivity clauses. As NCAs take on the complaints, the main challenge is to ensure consistency from the outcomes of decisions. Where several national complaints emerge relating to similar national SGB rules implementing underlying *international* SGB regulatory rules, there is a Community interest in the European Commission intervening of its own volition to ensure consistency in rules across the EU. EU competition processes provide some pathways for a dialogue, through Article 15 of Regulation 1/2003;[50] further, NCAs could take advantage of the European Competition Network to provide a vehicle for exchanging information and best practice.

[50] This provision is under-used, but a national court may contact the European Commission to ask it to transmit any information in its possession or to give its opinion on questions concerning the application of EU competition rules.

PART IV

ORGANISATION

14. European law and the governance of sport

Borja García and Mads de Wolff

I. INTRODUCTION

Arguably, the aspect of European sport[1] most affected by the application of EU law is that of governance. This has, however, been a rather long, protracted and indirect process. One will not find the EU directly regulating sport as it has done in other markets, such as the audio-visual industry or the air travel industry. No European directive on the governance of sport exists and yet the cumulative effect of EU policies, court judgments, Commission competition policy decisions and, lastly, the nascent EU sports policy under Article 165 of the Treaty on the Functioning of the European Union (TFEU) have contributed to the transformation of European sports governance.

Walrave,[2] the first sport-related ruling of the European Courts, was, in essence, a governance conflict. The case was about two sportspersons challenging the rules adopted by the International Cycling Union (UCI). There was a conflict about the power to regulate access to competitions between the governing body and the athletes. And that is what governance is about: having robust, reliable and accountable processes by which an organisation takes decisions. As Tricker excellently puts it, 'management is about running an organisation, good governance is about ensuring and demonstrating that it is properly run'.[3]

What the ECJ (now the CJEU) did in *Walrave*[4] and two decades after in *Bosman*[5] was just to ensure that the governing bodies respected the basic rights of the athletes and, in doing so, it reminded those federations of the need to take into account the rights and opinions of their most

---

[1] B García and H Meier, 'Global Sport Power Europe? The Efficacy of the European Union in Global Sport Regulation' (2016) 55(4) JCMS 50–70.

[2] Case C-36/74 *Walrave and Koch v Union Cycliste Internationale* [1974] ECR 01405.

[3] R Tricker, *Corporate Governance, History of Management Thought* (Ashgate 2000).

[4] Case C-36/74 (n 2).

[5] Case C-415/93 *Bosman* [1995] ECR I-4921.

fundamental stakeholders. The term governance does not appear much in Court rulings or Commission decisions, though. It is actually much easier to find it in policy documents. In order to understand the reciprocal importance of governance and EU sports law, it is necessary to note a number of key points for the correct understanding of this chapter.

First, it is essential to underline that the impact of EU sports law on governance is the aggregated result of the indirect (and to some extent also unforeseen) consequences of a large list of decisions and rulings in single cases. So, for example, *Bosman*[6] fundamentally transformed the balance of power in the relationship between football players, clubs and governing bodies.

Second, it is important to understand that many EU decisions in the area of sport governance are as much political as they are legal. Whereas this chapter contributes to a research handbook of law, it will invariably refer to policy and politics as well. Sports governance, at its very core, deals with the distribution of power and authority in sport, and that is a profoundly political reality as much as it may also be a legal debate. Thus, after years of court judgments and other decisions, the Council of the European Union in 2011 incorporated governance as one of the priority areas within the Work Plan for Sport[7] and thus giving strategic direction to the nascent EU Sports Policy.

Third, for the sake of clarity and to facilitate analysis, this chapter makes a conscious choice to stay at a general level to explain EU sports law's relevance to shaping European sport governance. Given the tight space constraints, particular references are made at some points in the chapter to individual decisions but the intention is to provide an overview of how EU sports law and regulations have altered, over time, the power relations amongst stakeholders in European sport.

This chapter, therefore, aims to discuss and evaluate the implications of EU sports law for sports governance. It adopts a historical approach, although a major focus on most recent developments is preserved. The chapter is structured around a conceptual definition of governance, which comprise two different (yet complementary) dimensions.

The chapter, therefore, proceeds in four steps. First, a definition of what we understand by sports governance is provided. Second, the impact of EU sports law and policies on systemic governance is

---

[6] Ibid.

[7] Council of the European Union, Resolution of the Council and of the Representatives of the Governments of the Member States, meeting within the Council, on a European Union Work Plan for Sport for 2011–2014 [2011] OJ C 162/01.

discussed. In other words, this section will deal with the changes in European sport's power structures that have an origin in EU law. Third, recent policy initiatives in the area of good governance principles are discussed – focusing on the more normative approach to sports governance adopted by EU institutions. Finally, the chapter concludes with a reflection on the role of EU law and policies in the transformation of European sports governance.

II. SPORTS GOVERNANCE: WHAT ARE WE TALKING ABOUT?

Roderick Rhodes pointed out that the term governance is perhaps used in too many contexts and with different meanings.[8] Yet, in the field of sport it is possible to narrow down our understanding of governance to a number of basic dimensions. Henry and Lee, for instance, argue that sports governance can be encapsulated under three headings: systemic governance; political governance; and good governance.[9] The first one refers to the structures that facilitate power and authority relations of stakeholders within the sports system. The latter refers to the normative principles that should define those relationships within the management of sport organisations. Political governance, for these authors, refers to the specific role of the state and public authorities in regulating sport and their relationship with sport non-governmental organisations. It is, however, possible to subsume political governance as one specific element of the wider systemic governance, which would then reduce the conceptual dimensions to just two useful heuristic devices to build our analysis upon.

This chapter refers to: (i) governance as a systemic structure that makes sense of the relationships among a large number of stakeholders;[10] and (ii) governance as 'good governance', which is defined as involving the principles of effective, transparent and democratic management.[11] As Holt points out, these definitions of governance can be seen as both

---

[8] R Rhodes, *Understanding Governance: Policy Networks, Governance, Reflexivity and Accountability* (Open University Press 1997).

[9] I Henry and P Lee, 'Governance and Ethics in Sport' in S Chadwick and J Beech (eds) *The Business of Sport Management* (Pearson Education 2004).

[10] Rhodes (n 8), 53.

[11] Ibid., 49–50.

analytical (or descriptive) and normative.[12] Applied to sport, this means that we can use the concept of governance to analyse how sport is governed systemically and to comment on how well it is or should be governed.

Therefore, in this chapter we will first explore the relevance of EU sports law for the systemic governance of European sport in order to continue, afterwards, analysing the normative vision of EU sports law and policy on how European sport should be governed through the principles of good governance. Before getting to that, this section needs to finish with a deeper look to the definition of these two dimensions of governance.

II.i Systemic Governance

Systemic governance is an analytical concept. This dimension of governance refers to the management of a structure with a large number of stakeholders where power, authority and resources are diffused and distributed across the system.[13] In the area of sport, Chaker defined governance as 'the creation of effective networks of sport-related state agencies, sport non-governmental organisations and processes that operate jointly and independently under specific legislation, policies and private regulations to promote ethical, democratic, efficient and accountable sports activities.'[14] Chaker's understanding of governance in the field of sport is, therefore, quite similar to Rhodes' abstract and general definition.

In both cases there are three important components: a systemic structure, the role of non-governmental organisations with a degree of self-regulation, and the participation of public authorities in the networks. Thus, this chapter uses systemic governance as a concept to bind together, in one section, our discussion of the relevant EU law provisions that have facilitated an evolution of European sport's governance structures. This relates mainly to questions about the role and responsibilities of governing bodies (e.g., the IOC, European sports federations); the

---

[12] M Holt, *UEFA, Governance and the Control of Club Competition in European Football* (Football Governance Research Centre, Birkbeck College, University of London 2006) 4.

[13] Rhodes (n 8), 53.

[14] A Chaker, *Good Governance in Sport, a European Survey* (Council of Europe Publishing 2004) 5.

level of power and representation of stakeholders (e.g., athletes, supporters or professional clubs); and the regulatory relations between public authorities and all those other sports non-governmental actors.

II.ii Good Governance

Those who study governance are also interested in the notion of good governance. Rhodes describes good governance as involving the principles of effective, transparent and democratic management, and we can certainly examine these in the context of sport.[15] Good governance refers to the extent to which organisations observe principles of good management, transparency, democracy and/or accountability. Certainly, the notions of good governance and systemic governance are complementary, as one would expect those involved in the system of governance to observe good governance principles. In the case of sport, the necessity to observe good governance principles is applied to governing bodies and their policies· but it is also applicable to other stakeholders, such as clubs in their management of economic and human resources.[16]

III. SYSTEMIC GOVERNANCE: EU SPORTS LAW AND THE EUROPEAN MODEL OF SPORT

For a long time, the governance of European sport remained unchanged with a pyramidal structure that reinforced the vertical authority of international, European and national governing bodies over other stakeholders.[17] The European Commission labelled this systemic structure in 1998, somehow accidentally, as the 'European Model of Sport'.[18] Years later, the same institution, the European Commission, had to acknowledge that it was 'unrealistic to try to define a unified model of organisation of sport in Europe'.[19] One of the reasons behind the Commission's rectification was the transformation of the traditional

---

15 Rhodes (n 8), 53.

16 See, e.g., S Hamil, M Holt, J Michie, C Oughton, and L Shailer, 'The Corporate Governance of Professional Football Clubs' (2004) 4(2) *Corporate Governance* 44–51.

17 B García, 'Sport Governance After the White Paper: The Demise of the European Model?' (2009) 3 (1) IJSPP 267.

18 Ibid.

19 *White Paper on Sport* COM(2007) 391 final, 12.

European sport pyramid in the years after the *Bosman* ruling.[20] The commercialisation and professionalisation of European sport was the origin of many conflicts between governing bodies and stakeholders who wanted to reap the economic benefits of the growing sports industry.

Much of that was also due to the liberalisation of the audio-visual market on the continent, whose impact on sport cannot be overestimated, for it created numerous frictions among those who wanted to benefit from the booming TV and marketing contracts. This section explains the role that European sports law and policy had in shaping the evolving nature of that elusive European Model of Sport. The section covers three main points. First, a reflection on the rulings and decisions that shaped the balance of power amongst stakeholders, with special focus on the governing bodies. Second, a particular reference to the social dialogue as an alternative forum outside traditional sports governance structures. Finally, the section looks at the structured dialogue, as a platform of cooperation between EU institutions and sports organisations.

III.i From Pyramids to Networks

When European law first entered the territory of sport in 1974, it was a major surprise for many of those in the industry. Even when the ECJ ruled in *Bosman*, it was also unexpected for those in the governing bodies of the sport. This is perhaps best explained by the organisational autonomy that the sporting movement had historically enjoyed. Sport has been for the most part a self-governing industry, which has perceived any external regulation as unnecessary, unless it is related to funding. The traditional pyramidal structure of sport governance put governing bodies firmly at the top, whereas athletes were relegated mostly to the bottom of the structure, without a major say in strategic decisions. However, this has been slowly overturned by the application of EU sports law over the years.

The *Bosman* judgment of 1995 was the first major blow for sport's established powers, for it allowed team sport players to break free from the tight control of transfer regulations and nationality quotas – further extended in *Kolpak*[21] to nationals of countries with an association agreement containing non-discrimination clauses. In *Bosman*, the Belgian footballer had to bring the governing bodies to court, as European law

[20] García (n 17).

[21] Case C-438/00 *Kolpak* [2003] ECR I-4135.

was the only tool available to him given the reluctance of the football federations to consider the necessary reforms of the transfer system.[22]

The clear tensions in the relationship between athletes and governing bodies are seen in the fact that a number of other legal challenges ensued, such as *Deliège*,[23] *Lehtonen*[24] and *Meca-Medina*.[25] Perhaps with less wide-ranging consequences in governance terms than *Bosman*, these cases were interesting nonetheless. First and foremost because they institutionalise clear tensions in the power and authority relations between governing bodies and athletes. Second, because they demonstrate an erosion of the former's legitimacy in the eyes of the latter. In *Lehtonen*, for instance, the CJEU took the view that yet another typical regulation of sport (the so-called transfer windows) was not entirely in line with EU law, although the practical consequences of the case were relatively minor. Yet, it was once again the presence of EU law that reminded sport federations that there is another layer of accountability with which they need to comply. In governance terms, EU law provided an avenue for dissatisfied stakeholders in the governance of European sport to challenge the power of the governing bodies.

This was not limited to rulings of the Court of Justice. Competition policy investigations by the European Commission provide a more cost-effective mechanism for those who, perhaps, could not afford a fully-fledged legal challenge. Moreover, competition investigations can also be opened by the Commission at its own initiative. Whereas the court cases referred to above have mostly featured athletes challenging the governing bodies, in the case of competition policy it has frequently been the clubs arguing that federations were behaving un-competitively and closing their access to the market.

The most representative of these cases is the European Commission investigation into the collective selling of broadcasting rights for the UEFA Champions League,[26] for it summarises perfectly the dynamics at play. In that case, the dossier was opened by UEFA communicating its selling arrangements to the Commission, and thus no direct challenge by

---

[22] B García 'He was not Alone: Bosman in ontext' in A Duval and B Van Rompuy (eds) *The Legacy of Bosman: Revisiting the Relationship between EU Law and Sport* (Asser 2016) 13–30.

[23] Cases C-51/96 and C-191/97 *Deliège v Ligue de Judo* [2000] ECR I-2549.

[24] Case C-176/96 *Lehtonen* [2000] ECR I-2681.

[25] Case C-519/04 P *Meca-Medina and Majcen v Commission* [2006] ECR I-6991.

[26] Case COMP/ AT.37398 Joint selling of commercial rights of the UEFA Champions League [2003] OJ L 291/25.

the clubs. However, given their status as interested parties, the clubs could nevertheless avail themselves of the opportunity to submit their views to the Commission. It is not necessary to enter into the details of the case here, more so due to space restrictions. But one of the important decisions that the Commission had to make was to ascertain whether the broadcasting rights of the Champions League belong to UEFA as competition organiser or to the clubs participating. At play were the commercial rights of the most prestigious, most lucrative, professional competition in Europe and to the victor the economic and political hegemony over these rights. As it happens, the Commission took a Solomonic decision, for it considered that the rights belonged to both clubs and UEFA. Once again, what the *Champions League* case reminded was that EU law offers an opportunity to challenge the decisions of the governing bodies. Similar to the manner in which players were 'liberated' by *Bosman*, competition policy provided clubs with the necessary impetus to question the decisions, regulations and commercial strategies of the governing bodies.

In football, the governing bodies have however managed, after some reforms, to maintain their governance role. In other sports, such as basketball, this order has been heavily altered in Europe, as demonstrated by the creation of the semi-closed Euroleague, a breakaway European club competition featuring the top teams of the continent.[27] This tournament is managed and commercially exploited by the clubs themselves, not the sport's governing body (FIBA).

Thus, EU law needs to be seen as a facilitator, and perhaps accelerator, in the transformation of governance and power structures in European sport. This refers especially to the way in which EU institutions offered stakeholders alternative avenues to challenge the power of the governing bodies. Such transformations differ greatly among different sports, as the cases of football and basketball clearly demonstrate. It is also true that the core regulatory nature of the governing bodies has not been fundamentally challenged, but perhaps moderated.

In *Meca-Medina*[28] the CJEU recognised that it was for the IOC and other sport bodies to adopt anti-doping regulations. Similarly, in *Piau*[29] both the Court of First Instance and the CJEU also conceded FIFA's

---

[27] M Long 'Euroleague basketball in rude health as the Euroleague turns 15', (*Sports Pro*, 12 May 2015) available online at http://www.sportspromedia.com/notes_and_insights/european_basketball_in_rude_health_as_the_euroleague_turns_15 (accessed 26 Oct 2017).

[28] Case C-519/04 (n 25).

[29] Case C-171/05 *Piau v Commission* [2006] ECR I-37.

legitimacy to regulate the profession of football agents. In the competition investigation about the involvement of the International Motorsport Federation (FIA) in commercialising Formula One,[30] the Commission questioned the dual role of FIA as both the regulator and commercial agent of the competition, for it could be a case of dominant position. However, the Commission did not fundamentally challenge the authority of FIA as a governing body, but the way in which it managed the business side of the sport. Despite the legal challenges, sport governing bodies have proved resilient due to the firm grip they hold on the transnational regulation of sport.[31]

The legal route, via legal challenges under EU law, has not been the only opportunity for sport stakeholders to affect change in European sport systemic governance. A more political process has been also possible through the so-called social dialogue (between employers and employees in the industry) and, more recently, the structured dialogue (between EU institutions and sports organisations). These are processes that rely on negotiation and dialogue, therefore need to be seen as more political than legal.

III.ii The Social Dialogue

The European social dialogue is considered by the Commission as 'a unique and indispensable component of the European social model'.[32] It is an opportunity for management and labour to achieve collective bargaining agreements to regulate their employment conditions under the umbrella of the Commission and EU law. Professional football was the first sport to explore the possibilities of the social dialogue. This is not surprising given the proactive work of players' trade unions such as FIFPro in demanding a reform of footballers' working conditions and the empowering effect of *Bosman*.

Moreover, the European Commission encouraged clubs and players to pursue a social dialogue initiative in order to settle the problems arising

---

[30] COMP/36.638 Notification by FIA/FOA of agreements relating to the FIA Formula One World Championship [2001] OJ C 169, 5.

[31] H Meier and B García 'Protecting Private Transnational Authority against Public Intervention: FIFA's Power over National Governments' (2015) 93(4) *Public Administration* 890–906.

[32] Commission Staff Working Document – The EU and Sport: Background and Context – Accompanying document to the White Paper on Sport, COM(2007) 391 final, SEC(2007)932, SEC(2007)934, SEC(2007)936, SEC/2007/0935, 59.

from the disputes that prompted *Bosman* and all the subsequent reforms of football's international transfer system.[33] Following years of studies, the social dialogue in football was launched on 1 July 2008 with a first meeting, in Paris, attended by the then commissioners for Employment, Social Affairs and Equal Opportunities, Vladimid Spidla, and Education, Training, Culture and Youth (responsible for sport) Jan Figel.

The social dialogue committee was composed by representatives of FIFPro (as employees) and the European Professional Football Leagues (EPFL, as employers), but importantly there was also representation from UEFA (the governing body), whose president was elected to chair the committee. The decision to allow UEFA to be part of the committee is testimony to the power that the governing body still maintains over the game's stakeholders. Legally speaking, UEFA is not required on that committee, as it is neither an employer nor an employee. The Commission has justified the presence of governing bodies in sport social dialogue on two grounds: first as a decision of the social partners and, second, as an expression of the so-called specificity of sport.

The social dialogue process can address issues such as stability of contracts, transfer systems or the release of players for national teams, among others. This could certainly lead to improved governance in professional sport. Social dialogue offers a venue for players and clubs to negotiate their employment conditions without the need to resort to the courts. It is an institutionalised EU procedure, which gives legal certainty to any agreement facilitated by it. In terms of governance, social dialogue raises two important issues. First, the institutionalisation of a sectoral committee where athletes and clubs (or leagues) are the main actors, reinforces the idea of sports governance as a horizontal network of stakeholders departing from the traditional vertical structures of the pyramid. Moreover, it could be seen as yet another example of sport stakeholders using EU (political) venues to challenge the legitimacy of governing bodies (UEFA in the case of football).

Whereas social dialogue is an avenue open to any industry, the real results in the case of sport are best seen as modest, if not disappointing. The football social dialogue committee has only managed to reach agreement on minimum contract standards for football players, but it has not addressed more fundamental issues such as contract termination or player mobility.[34] The transformative effects of the social dialogue after

---

[33] Ibid., 60.

[34] R Parrish 'Social Dialogue in European Professional Football' (2011) 17(2) *European Law Journal* 213–29.

nine years of work are nowhere near to what *Bosman* or other legal cases achieved.

Similarly, clubs are able to force more change through threats of break-away competitions than in the social dialogue committee thus far. If anything, the case of the social dialogue in the football sector has demonstrated the ability of UEFA to control the governance agenda even when the stakeholders resort to an external political/regulatory venue. Football is not the only sport that has considered the European social dialogue process, but results have been similar elsewhere. There were also attempts in cycling and more generically in the sport (as recreation) industry. None of these have had major results to date.

Whereas social dialogue brings together sport stakeholders, the so-called structured dialogue process provides an opportunity for sports organisations to enter into dialogue with EU institutions involved in the design of EU sports policy. This is, again, a political avenue whose objective is to inform EU policy-making. It is of interest because it provides an opportunity to analyse the extent to which sport organisations have conditioned EU decisions in this area. It is also relevant because it is one of the pillars of the now formal EU sports policy under Article 165 TFEU.

III.iii Structured Dialogue

One of the few explicit goals stated in Article 165 TFEU is to promote 'cooperation between bodies responsible for sports', hence carrying the implication that the EU should engage with the sports movement going forward when developing this new policy area. In essence, structured dialogue refers to a mechanism of bi-annual meetings between the EU institutions and sporting stakeholders.

The concept of 'structured dialogue' was initially introduced in the White Paper on Sport, where the European Commission argued that one added value of EU action in sport was to provide a platform for dialogue on sport. It thus proposed organising 'Thematic discussions with limited participants.'[35] Shortly after the White Paper on Sport, the EU's political leaders meeting in the European Council decided that there was a need 'for the strengthening of [the] dialogue with the International Olympic Committee and representatives of the world of sport'.[36] The Commission was therefore invited to implement this idea coming from the very top,

---

35 White Paper on Sport COM(2007) 391 final, 12.

36 European Council, Presidency Conclusions – Brussels, 11 and 12 December 2008 [2009] Council Document 17271/08 REV 1.

the result being two meetings between representatives of the IOC[37] and the Commission[38] during 2009. Thus, in this definition of structured dialogue, the 'sports movement' was practically equated with the Olympic Movement; and the EU was equally equated with the European Commission.

Upon ratification of the Lisbon Treaty the Member States immediately started discussing the Council's role in facilitating 'structured dialogue'. The Spanish Presidency of the Council of the European Union in the first part of 2010 put the issue on the Council's agenda, although it did not transmit any concrete proposals. The Council's Working Party on Sport supported the Spanish Presidency's initiative but requested further technical details, deciding it should be dealt with at a later time.[39]

The succeeding Belgian Presidency constructed the Council's proposal. In designing procedures for structured dialogue, the Member States looked at arrangements in similar policy areas, in particular those in youth policy. In youth policy's structured dialogue, participants are explicitly defined and convened in a 'European Steering Committee', in which one pan-European organisation, the European Youth Forum, is the only designated civil society organisation.[40] However, the Belgian Presidency felt the model from the Youth field was not directly transferable, due to the 'complexity' of the sports movement:

> [R]egarding the sport movement's participation, the situation is less clear, given the complexity of European sport structures. The Presidency considers that, while the number of participants should be limited, the aim should be to achieve representative, broad and balanced participation.[41]

Thus, the Belgian Presidency argued for a broad representation – implicitly, that the IOC would not be representative of the entire sports

---

[37] International Olympic Committee, 'Meeting between Rogge and Figel on European Council Declaration' (*IOC Press Release*, 29 Jan 2009) https://www.olympic.org/news/meeting-between-rogge-and-figel-on-european-council-declaration / (accessed 26 Oct 2017).

[38] European Commission, Commission holds second high-level meeting with Olympic movement (IP/09/888, 8 June 2009) http://europa.eu/rapid/press-release_IP-09-888_en.htm (accessed 26 Oct 2017).

[39] Council of the European Union, Preparations for the EYC Council in the field of sport [2010] Council Document 8251/10.

[40] Council of the European Union, Council Resolution of 27 November 2009 on a renewed framework for European cooperation in the youth field *(2010–2018)* [2009] OJ C 311/01.

[41] Council of the European Union, *The EU Structured Dialogue on Sport – Background paper* [2010] Council Document 11954/10.

movement. Two main options were outlined. First, the Council could designate a list of stakeholders to be invited for every meeting, invoking practices from the youth field. Second, that the incumbent Presidency be given a mandate 'to invite participants at its discretion' depending on the specific agenda items and particular Presidency priorities.[42]

During consultations, representatives of the Olympic Movement professed to the Belgian Presidency a preference for continuing the procedure at place during the 'high-level' meetings organised with the Commission. However, both the European Commission and the Member States now agreed that representation of the sports movement should not be handed over purely to the IOC in the new structured dialogue.[43]

An adopted resolution[44] saw the Council settling on the latter option as recommended by the Belgian Presidency. Thus, structured dialogue meetings would be ad hoc in nature, with topics chosen and stakeholders invited at the discretion of the incumbent Council Presidency.

In practice, structured dialogue refers to a one hour 'working lunch' held before the convening of the last ministerial Council meeting in Brussels of a Presidency term.[45] The Council of the European Union is represented by the so-called 'trio Presidency' and accompanied by a member of the incoming trio. The EU is also represented by the Commissioner responsible for sport, the Council Secretariat, and occasionally a member of the European Parliament. The lunch directly precedes the convening of the formal Council meeting which, after formal procedures, is followed by a policy debate between Ministers, generally on the same topic that has been discussed during the structured dialogue meeting.

Sport stakeholders are invited according to the topic of the day. Topics are generally, if not exclusively, linked to issues on the Council formal agenda. Thus, structured dialogue has been implemented in two main ways. First, as an opportunity to discuss specific topical issues which *may* require further action in the future, with an example being how the Hungarian Presidency in 2011 organised its meeting on match-fixing and

---

42 Ibid.

43 Mads de Wolff, 'Playing for the Same Team? The Trio Presidency and Agenda-management in European Union Sport Policy' [2016] Doctoral Dissertation, Loughborough University and available at https://dspace.lboro.ac.uk/dspace-jspui/handle/2134/21470 (accessed 26 Oct 2017).

44 Council of the European Union, Council Resolution of 18 November on the EU structured dialogue on sport [2010] OJ C 322/01.

45 For an extended analysis, see de Wolff (n 43), Chap 5.

'sport-related aspects of on-line betting'.[46] Second, to facilitate input on topics already set to move forward in the EU in the near future, with an example being how the Cypriot Presidency organised its structured dialogue meeting on the topic of the European Week of Sport.[47]

Given the timing of the meeting – just before Council ministerial meetings, rather than at the beginning of a Presidency term – it is clear that structured dialogue has mainly been designed with a focus on debriefing the sports movement of Council outcomes and plans, thus strongly limiting the potential of stakeholders to influence EU sports policy in this mechanism. In this, structured dialogue is decidedly 'top down' in direction. Given the scarce time allocated to these meetings, it may be seen, at best, as an 'exchange of impressions' to inform the Council.

Indeed, no actors in EU sports policy are able to point to any concrete actions or results deriving from the mechanism.[48] However, even if the mechanism has since been subject to much criticism from both stakeholders[49] and the European Commission,[50] the Member States have so far been unwilling to change how structured dialogue meetings are organised.

Summing up, it was shown how the Olympic Movement initially pursued a role as exclusive partner in the structured dialogue in sport. However, the Member States have been insistent on not giving any sporting stakeholders 'special' status in structured dialogue, similar to how the Member States have been unwilling to grant the international

---

[46] Participating stakeholders: International Olympic Committee, European Olympic Committee, European Lotteries, Union of European Football Associations, European Non-Governmental Sports Organisation, Fédération Internationale de Football Association. See also de Wolff ibid, 91.

[47] Participating stakeholders: European Health and Fitness Association, Union of European Football Associations, European Physical Education Association, Federation of the European Sporting Goods Industry, International Sport and Culture Association. See also de Wolff ibid.

[48] See de Wolff ibid, 93.

[49] European Non-Governmental Sports Organisation , 'EU Ministers of Sport adopt New Work Plan for Sport 2014–2017 and Council Conclusions on Gender Equality' (*ENGSO Newsletter*, 4 June 2014) https://docs.wixstatic.com/ugd/d2e761_e9dda63d08f54bba910b2c0df9839b3d.pdf (accessed 26 Oct 2017).

[50] European Commission, Report from the Commission to the European Parliament, the Council, the European Economic and Social Committee and the Committee of the Regions on the implementation of the European Union Work Plan for Sport 2011–2014 [2014] COM(2014) 22 final.

governing bodies any special legal exemption in terms of EU law.[51] By design, structured dialogue is informal; while intended to promote dialogue with the sports movement, it also seems to have been designed this way so as to keep the sports movement at arm's length from the Council's decision-making. Thus, as predicted by Meier and García,[52] politics has seen the Member States not concede any particular status to the Olympic Movement in structured dialogue.

The impact of structured dialogue is superficially negligible. However, it needs to be understood as an initial stage in the policy process. It also needs to be emphasised that consultations and dialogue between public authorities and stakeholders takes place in many other settings. This is evident in the next section which explores how the EU has endeavoured to develop and disseminate principles of good governance.

IV. EU LAW AND THE QUEST FOR GOOD GOVERNANCE IN SPORT

The EU has had a longstanding interest in furthering good governance in sports organisations; as evident in this chapter highlighting that the early 'sports law' decisions of the European Courts were essentially governance conflicts. That good governance has risen to such a prominent position on the EU sports agenda during this time is not unexpected, considering how scandals suggesting deeply entrenched cultures of corruption within the governing bodies of sport seem to appear in a constant stream.[53]

Accordingly, recent years have seen EU institutions adopt numerous decisions explicitly touching on good governance in sport. These include

---

[51] B García and S Weatherill, 'Engaging with the EU in Order to Minimize its Impact: Sport and the Negotiation of the Treaty of Lisbon' (2012) 19 (2) JEPP 238–56.

[52] H Meier and B García, 'Abandoning Hopes for Veto Power: Institutional Options for Sport Governing Bodies in the European Union' (2013) 5(3) *International Journal of Sport Policy and Politics* 421–43.

[53] See, e.g., 'Sepp Blatter and Michel Platini lose Fifa Appeals but Bans Reduced' (*BBC Sport Online*, 24 February 2016) http://www.bbc.com/sport/football/35655454 (accessed 26 Oct 2017); C Mortimer, 'Panama Papers: New Fifa boss Gianni Infantino Linked to Corruption Scandal' (*Independent.co.uk*, 5 April 2016) http://www.independent.co.uk/sport/football/news-and-comment/panama-papers-new-fifa-boss-gianni-infantino-linked-to-corruption-scandal-a6970381.html (accessed 26 Oct 2017).

the European Commission's 2007 White Paper[54] and the 2011 communication on 'Developing the European dimension of sport.'[55] To generalise, these documents can be said to define the relationship between public authorities and sports organisations as one of 'supervised autonomy'. As described by Ken Foster, 'supervised autonomy' implies that 'self-regulation should only be permitted subject to a proper rule of law system of governance'.[56]

This has been the position taken by the European Commission, which has consistently described good governance as:

> a condition for the autonomy and self-regulation of sport organisations [...] there are inter-linked principles that underpin sport governance at European level, such as autonomy within the limits of the law, democracy, transparency and accountability in decision-making, and inclusiveness in the representation of interested stakeholders.[57]

Those are rather generic and strategic documents that relate to the power balance between public authorities and sport organisations. In this section, however, we intend to look more closely at the concrete level of policy making, more specifically on the EU's quest for developing and spreading principles of good governance in sport through a variety of measures adopted by the institutions. Notably, this effort has been longstanding. For instance, among the European Commission's preparatory actions in the field of sport (2009–13), eight projects were focused on promoting good governance.[58]

More recently, the Council of the European Union has become the key actor in this endeavour. In the 2011–2014 EU Work Plan in the field of sport, the Council specified 'good governance' as one of the key priorities in EU sports policy. To that end, the Council established an Expert Group on 'Good Governance in Sport', which was tasked with

---

54 White Paper on Sport (n 19), 12.

55 European Commission, Developing the European Dimension in Sport [2011] COM(2011) 12 final.

56 K Foster, 'Can Sport Be Regulated by Europe? An Analysis of Alternative Models' in A Caiger and S Gardiner (eds) *Professional Sport in the European Union: Regulation and Re-Regulation* (Asser Press 2000) 64.

57 European Commission (n 55), 10.

58 European Commission, Towards an EU Funding Stream for Sport: Preparatory Actions and Special Events 2009–2011 (Publications Office of the European Union 2012).

developing 'principles of transparency concerning good governance' by mid-2012.[59]

The Expert Group on good governance released its deliverable in September 2013 in the form of a lengthy text defining 'Principles for the good governance of sport in the EU'.[60] These principles are underpinned, again, by the idea of 'supervised autonomy', stating that 'sports bodies that do not have in place good governance procedures and practices can expect their autonomy and self-regulatory practices to be curtailed'.[61]

While intended for universal use, the recommendations are also limited: they represent minimum standards that can be flexibly implemented at various levels. The principles are addressed to governments and to the sports movement at three different levels: grassroots sport organisations; national sports governing bodies; and European/international federations. Among the recommendations is the principle that all organisations should adopt a 'code of ethics' and that the respective roles, responsibilities and objectives of sports bodies and their stakeholders should be codified.

Importantly, the Member States have recognised the need to actively develop and disseminate these principles. This is evident in a number of ways, not least in how 'good governance' was highlighted as a specific priority in Erasmus+, the 2014–2020 EU programme for education, training youth sport.[62] Accordingly, numerous projects have already been funded on promoting good governance.[63]

At the same time, the EU Member States have actively sought to disseminate these principles of good governance. The key development in this regard is the adoption of the second EU Work Plan on sport for

---

59 Council of the European Union (n 7), 4.

60 Expert Group Good Governance, 'Deliverable 2: Principles of good governance in sport' (European Commission, September 2013) http://ec.europa.eu/assets/eac/sport/library/policy_documents/xg-gg-201307-dlvrbl2-sept2013.pdf (accessed 26 Oct 2017).

61 Ibid., 3.

62 European Parliament and the Council of the European Union, Regulation (EU) No 1288/2013 of the European Parliament and of the Council of 11 December 2013 establishing 'Erasmus+': the Union programme for education, training, youth and sport and repealing Decisions No 1719/2006/EC, No 1720/2006/EC and No 1298/2008/EC [2013] OJ L 347/50.

63 For example, see 'Erasmus+: Sport 2015 – Round 2 – Collaborative Partnerships (Other topics)' (European Commission 2015) https://eacea.ec.europa.eu/sites/eacea-site/files/sport_2015_round_2_collaborative_partnerships_other_topics.pdf (accessed 26 Oct 2017).

2014–2017.[64] Here, the Council of the EU again identified good governance as one of its main priorities in the field of sport. This decision includes a proposal for a new mechanism in EU sports policy, namely the establishment of so-called 'pledge boards'. A pledge board is defined as an 'instrument where mainly sport organisations can voluntarily make public their commitment to certain issues.'[65] Importantly, in the 2014–2017 Work Plan, the Council agreed to continue the promotion of the good governance principles, 'possibly followed by a pledge board'.[66]

Indeed, the EU has already had some success in this regard. Thus, as reported by the European Commission in 2016, so far 31 sports organisations have signed onto a pledge board on good governance, a list which includes numerous national Olympic committees and sports federations, most notably perhaps UEFA.[67]

Thus far, neither the European Commission nor the Council have published any clear explanations on the functioning of these pledge boards. However, it is clear that they represent a desire among European public authorities to normatively define and monitor the activities of sports organisations. The EU has also proposed pledge boards on related issues such as gender equality[68] and the organisation of major sport events.[69] In proposing a pledge board for the latter, the Council makes it clear that while pledge boards are voluntary, they still constitute 'a light monitoring system'.[70] Accordingly, such soft law initiatives need to be understood as the EU not only re-affirming its commitment to supervised autonomy, but a desire to spread normative principles and to enhance its ability to monitor how sports organisations actually govern themselves, based on said normative principles.

---

[64] Council of the European Union, Resolution of the Council and of the Representatives of the Governments of the Member States, meeting within the Council, of 21 May 2014 on the European Union Work Plan for Sport (2014–2017) [2014] OJ C 183/12.

[65] Ibid., 13.

[66] Ibid., 15.

[67] 'A Pledge to Implement Good Governance in European Sport' (European Commission September 2016) https://ec.europa.eu/sport/policy/organisation-of-sport/pledge_en (accessed 26 Oct 2017).

[68] Council of the European Union, Council Conclusions of 21 May 2014 on Gender Equality in Sport [2014] OJ C 183/39.

[69] Council of the European Union, Conclusions of the Council and of the Representatives of the Governments of the Member States, meeting within the Council, on enhancing integrity, transparency and good governance in major sport events [2016] OJ C 212/14.

[70] Ibid.

As pledge boards are entirely voluntary their impact, if any, would result from peer pressure and public shaming. In other words, pledge boards could, in theory, induce pressure to reform based on a mixture of 'peer accountability' and 'public reputational accountability'; that is, pressure mechanisms that have traditionally not proven particularly effective.[71] Nonetheless, pledge boards may still prove influential.

Pledge boards do not directly represent a curtailment of the autonomy of sport organisations. Rather, they represent an implementation of the logic of 'sincere cooperation' between European public authorities and the sports movement as enshrined in the Treaties. While the effects are likely to be limited, pledge boards nonetheless represent a new stage in systemic European sport governance, namely, a phase whereby European public authorities not only see their roles as providing normative guidance, but also expect a role in monitoring compliance.

V. CONCLUSION

This chapter has analysed different ways in which European Union sports law and policy have transformed or helped to transform the governance structures of European sport. From a systemic governance perspective, the most visible consequence is the weakening of the traditional pyramid of governance in European sport, the so-called European Model of Sport. The result is a much more horizontal network of stakeholders where power and authority are shared and diffused. Whereas this is true as a generic analysis, the intensity of these transformations is highly variable from sport to sport. Furthermore, it is fair to affirm that governing bodies still remain very central to European sports governance, even if their power has been eroded.

It is now more than 20 years since the well-known *Bosman* judgment, but it is clear that legal challenges through the court are the most powerful and effective tools to induce change in European sport governance. The rest of the avenues, even under the nascent and direct EU sports policy have, at best, reinforced the finite and supervised nature of the autonomy of sport.

EU sports law remains a powerful and important element to understand the structures of sport in Europe. It is sometimes the threat of a legal challenge that may generate changes. It could be argued that the EU has lacked the political will to enforce more direct regulation of sports

---

71 R Pielke Jr, 'How can FIFA be held Accountable?' (2013) 16(3) *Sport Management Review* 255–67.

governance structures. It is equally true that EU sports law has provided stakeholders with an opportunity that was not present before. What is clear is that the intervention of the EU, both legally and politically, has controlled the behaviour of sport governing bodies to a level that no other public institution in the world has been able to achieve to date.

15. Specificity of sport

An Vermeersch

I. INTRODUCTION

The 2009 Lisbon Treaty endorsed the constitutional recognition of the specificity of sport. Despite its wide recognition, both from a political and a legal perspective, the concept of the specificity of sport remains enfolded by a number of questions. This chapter analyses the origin of the concept and its legal implications. The main contention is that sport is special to a certain extent. The case law of the European Court of Justice and the decision practice of the European Commission take into consideration the peculiarities of sport and provide for sufficient guidance in assessing sporting rules or sporting practices under EU law.

II. THE SPECIFICITY OF SPORT: ITS EARLY ORIGINS AND LEGAL IMPLICATIONS

The idea that sport is 'special' and that its specific characteristics can influence the application of EU law, goes back to the early 'sports case law' of the European Court of Justice, in particular the Court's attempt to explain why the EU free movement provisions do not interfere with the composition of national teams. In *Walrave*, the Court stated that the prohibition on the discrimination based on nationality: 'does not affect the composition of sport teams, in particular national teams, the formation of which is a question of purely sporting interest and as such has nothing to do with economic activity'.[1] Similarly, but with some extra nuance, the Court in *Donà*, declared that the freedom of movement of persons and of provision of services does 'not prevent the adoption of rules or of a practice excluding foreign players from participation in certain matches for reasons which are not of an economic nature, which relate to the particular nature and context of such matches …'.[2]

[1] Case 36/74 *Walrave and Koch v Union Cycliste Internationale* [1974] ECR 1405, para 8.

[2] Case 13/76 *Donà v Mantero* [1976] ECR 1333, para 14.

The Court's assumption that competitions between national teams fall outside the economic activity is not correct. Already in the seventies, this was – at least for certain sports and certainly football – questionable. Today, the economic interests in sport, and football in particular, are immense and still mounting. Whereas the legal basis of the Court's reasoning was questionable, the approach in the early case law corresponds to the general feeling that the composition of national teams was a matter of 'national pride and identity'.[3] European law should not 'interfere' with a key responsibility of sporting federations.

Even if the Courts' formulation was inaccurate, its early case law illustrates that sport was considered to be somehow 'special' and could – at some point – escape from the application of EU law. It became apparent from *Bosman* that a general exemption status for sport was not to be accepted. Equally, the Court introduced a justification test for sporting practices or rules falling within the scope of EU free movement provisions. Sporting rules or practices that constitute a restriction under internal market law can be justified under the objective justification framework as set out in *Kraus* and *Gebhard*:[4] if the sporting rules or practices (i) pursue a legitimate aim compatible with the Treaty and were justified by pressing reasons of public interest and (i) are compatible with the principle of proportionality, they can be justified.[5]

The Court in *Bosman* widened the justification under free movement law to cover private interests.[6] In applying this justification test, the distinct characteristics of sport were fully taken into account,[7] as the Court recognized:

> the considerable social importance of sporting activities and in particular football [...], the aims of maintaining a balance between clubs by preserving

---

[3] S Weatherill, 'Discrimination on Grounds of Nationality in Sport', in A Barav and J Wyatt (eds), *Yearbook of European Law 1989* (Clarendon Press 1990) 60.

[4] Case C-19/92 *Kraus v Land Baden-Württemberg* [1993] ECR I-1663, para 32; Case C-55/94 *Gebhard v Consiglio dell'Ordine degli Avvocati e Procuratori di Milano* [1995] ECR I-4165, para 37; K Pijetlovic, 'EU Competition Law and Organisational Rules', in A Duval and B Van Rompuy (eds), *The Legacy of Bosman. Revisiting the Relationship between EU Law and Sport* (Springer 2016) 122.

[5] Case C-415/93 *Bosman* [1995] ECR I-4921, para 104.

[6] S Weatherill, 'The *Lex Sportiva* and EU Law: The Academic Lawyer's Path Before and after *Bosman*', in Duval and Van Rompuy (n 4), 238.

[7] Ibid., 247.

a certain degree of equality and uncertainty as to results and of encouraging the recruitment and training of young players must be accepted as legitimate.[8]

The final judgment was negative as transfer fees for expired contracts were found unsuitable for the achievement of the said objectives and justifications for player quotas at club level were not accepted. Subsequently, 'the specific nature' or 'the particular characteristics' were all acknowledged in several policy documents.[9] However, none of these documents provide a clear definition of these 'hollow' concepts. According to Miège this explains why at the end of the nineties both the president of FIFA and the French minister for sport proclaimed the sporting exception, or 'l'exception sportive'.[10]

As there is no clear-cut definition of the specificity of sport, reference can be made to a number of arguments and elements that have been mentioned in this respect. A first element relates to a non-economic or an *a contrario* reasoning. This approach was followed by the Belgian football federation in *Bosman*. The URBSFA argued that only the major

---

8 Case C-415/93 *Bosman* (n 5), para 106.

9 For instance: Resolution of the European Parliament on the role of the European Union in the field of sport, [1997] OJ C 200/252: 'the specific nature of sport and the autonomy of the sports movement, it being understood that the economic activity generated by professional sport cannot be exempt from the provisions of Community law'; Declaration (No.29) on Sport, annexed to the final act of the Treaty of Amsterdam, [1997] OJ C 340/136: 'Special consideration should be given to the particular characteristics of amateur sport'; Communication from the European Commission (COM (1999) 644), Report from the European Commission to the European Council with a view to safeguarding the current sport structures and maintaining the social function of sport within the Community framework (Helsinki Report on Sport): 'must take account of the specific characteristics of sport, especially the interdependence between sporting activity and the economic activity that it generates, the principle of equal opportunities and the uncertainty of the results'; Presidency Conclusions, Santa Maria de Feira European Council, Bulletin EU 6-2000: 'The European Council requests the Commission and the Council to take account of the specific characteristics of sport in Europe and its social function in managing common policies'; Declaration on the specific characteristics of sport and its social function in Europe, of which account should be taken in implementing common policies, annexed to the Conclusions of the Nice European Council, Bulletin EU 12-2000.

10 C Miège, 'Le sport dans l'Union Européenne: entre spécificité et exception?' (Etudes Européennes 2006) 2 http://www.etudes-europeennes.eu/images/stories/Archives/9-11_Sport_et_UE_C_Miege.pdf (accessed 26 Oct 2017). On the sporting exception see R Parrish and S Miettinen, *The Sporting Exception in European Union Law* (Asser 2008).

European clubs may be regarded as undertakings, whereas clubs such as RC Liège – playing at the first national division in Belgium – 'carry on an economic activity only to a negligible extent'.[11]

In the same case, UEFA stated that the economic aspects of football cannot easily be distinguished from its sporting aspects, proclaiming that a European Court of Justice decision on professional football 'might call in question the organization of football as a whole'.[12] The German government argued that 'in most cases a sport such as football is not an economic activity'.[13] On the same line, the judo federations emphasized the amateur status of a judoka in the *Deliège* case.[14] More recently, in *Meca-Medina and Majcen*, the Finnish government made a distinction between 'sporting activity properly so called' and 'economic activity which attaches itself to sport'. According to the Finnish government, 'the sporting activity properly so called and the rules inherent in that activity, among which are the anti-doping rules, fall outside the scope of Community competition law'.[15]

The European Court of Justice strongly opposed this approach and stressed that a restriction on the scope of the Treaty provisions based on the particular nature and context of certain sporting events cannot be relied upon to exclude the whole of a sporting activity from the scope of the Treaty.[16] The *a contrario* approach became less applicable. On the one hand, sport became an important economic sector. On the other hand, the competences of the EU evolved over the years and include these days a broad range of less-economic or non-economic subjects. The Court in *Meca-Medina and Majcen* acknowledged the difficulty of severing the economic aspects from the sporting aspects of a sport[17] and convincingly stated that:

> the mere fact that a rule is purely sporting in nature does not have the effect of removing from the scope of the Treaty the person engaging in the activity governed by that rule or the body which has laid it down.[18]

---

[11] Case C-415/93 *Bosman* (n 5), para 70.

[12] Ibid., para 71.

[13] Ibid., para 72.

[14] Joint cases C-51/96 and C-191/97 *Deliège v Ligue de Judo* [2000] ECR I-2549, para 45.

[15] Case T-313/02 *Meca-Medina and Majcen v Commission* [2004] ECR II-3291, para 34.

[16] Case C-519/04P *Meca-Medina and Majcen v Commission* [2006] ECR I-6991, para 26.

[17] Ibid., para 26.

[18] Ibid., para 27.

Beside the non-economic dimension of sport, various specific characteristics have been linked to sport. A distinction can be made between two approaches: a theoretical, sociological and political approach on the one hand, and a more pragmatic approach view where concrete specificities of sport are taken into consideration when assessing the compatibility of certain sporting activities or sporting rules with European law on the other hand.[19]

The sociological and political approach can be found in various policy documents of the European Commission, the European Parliament and the Member States, promoting the multifunctional aspect of sport, with its social, educational, cultural, public health and recreational dimensions.[20] A more pragmatic approach can be perceived in the case law of the European Court of Justice and a number of Commission decisions.[21] Next to the training of young sportsmen, key considerations relate to the competitive balance or the need to ensure uncertainty concerning outcomes. This is closely linked to the mutual interdependence between competitors and the recognition of the difference 'between the way competition works in sport and in economic sectors'.[22]

Similarly, the primary responsibility of sporting federations to ensure the regularity and proper functioning of competitions has been recognized. In *Lehtonen*, the Court acknowledged that the setting of deadlines for transfers of players may meet the objective of ensuring the regularity of sporting competitions.[23] In *Deliège* the Court considered the limiting

---

19 Miège (n 10), 1.

20 Resolution on the role of the European Union in the field of sport [1997] OJ C 200; Commission Staff Working Document – The EU and Sport: Background and Context – Accompanying document to the White Paper on Sport, COM(2007) 391 final, SEC(2007)932, SEC(2007)934, SEC(2007)936, SEC/2007/0935.

21 A Husting, 'Quelle reconnaissance pour l'"exception" ou pour la "spécificité" sportive dans la nouvelle Constitution européenne?' [2004] RMCUE 515–19. In its White Paper, the European Commission declared that the specificity of European sport can be approached through two prisms: the specificity of sporting activities and of sporting rules and the specificity of the sport structure, White Paper on Sport (COM(2007) 391 final).

22 M Monti, European Commissioner for Competition, 'Speech/01/84 "Competition and Sport: the Rules of the Game" at a Conference on "Governance in Sport" – European Olympic Committee – FIA – Féderation Internationale de l'Automobile – Herbert Smith, Swissotel Brussels, 26 February 2001', available at http://europa.eu/rapid/press-release_SPEECH-01-84_en.htm (accessed 26 Oct 2017).

23 Case C-176/96 *Lehtonen* [2000] ECR I-2681 para 53.

effects of selection criteria as 'inherent in the conduct of an international high-level sports event'.[24] With regard to anti-doping regulations, the Court referred to the 'organisation and proper conduct of competitive sport' and the purpose to ensure healthy rivalry between athletes.[25]

Even without a clear definition, the concept of the specificity of sport is fully endorsed in the case law of the European Court of Justice. As explained above, the Court in *Bosman* applied a justification test in relation to free movement law. In *Meca-Medina and Majcen*, the Court followed a similar approach in relation to competition law but focused even more on the objectives pursued by a specific sport measure. Importantly, the compatibility with EU competition law cannot be assessed in the abstract.[26] Applying the *Wouters* test,[27] the Court emphasized that for the application of Article 81(1) TFEU, account must be taken of the overall context in which the concrete sporting rule was construed and, more specifically, of its objectives. It has then to be considered whether the consequential restrictive effects are inherent in the pursuit of those objectives and are proportionate to them.[28]

This case-by-case analysis does not provide the ultimate exemption – or 'legal certainty' as some sporting bodies would call it – but leaves sufficient room for the particularities of sport in the overall assessment. In reality, this may lead – as Weatherill states convincingly – to the acceptance of practices under EU law that would not be tolerated in other sectors.[29] Sporting rules and practices which are justified and proportionate are accepted under EU law. More generally, the acceptance and the legal implications of the specificity of sport is succinctly described by Miège: 'Si l'exception sportive n'a pas été acceptée, en revanche l'idée de prendre davantage en compte les spécificités du sport a connu un meilleur succès.'[30]

---

24 Joint cases C-51/96 and C-191/97 *Deliège v Ligue de Judo* (n 14), para 64.

25 Case C-519/04P *Meca-Medina and Majcen v Commission* (n 16), paras 45–46.

26 Ibid., para 42.

27 Case C-309/99 *Wouters* [2002] ECR I-1577.

28 Case C-519/04P *Meca-Medina and Majcen v Commission* (n 16), para 42. It is to be noted that the Court introduced the concept of inherent rules in *Deliège*, which was a free movement case.

29 Weatherill (n 6), 243.

30 Miège (n 10), 1.

III. CONSTITUTIONAL RECOGNITION OF THE SPECIFICITY OF SPORT

The inclusion of sport as a supporting, coordinating or supplementing EU competence and the recognition of its specific nature in the Treaty on the Functioning of the European Union (TFEU) marks an important step in the relationship between the world of sport and the EU.[31] Yet, the question emerged to what extent Article 165 TFEU would change this relation. Essentially, Article 165 TFEU provides the necessary legal and financial basis for the further development of a direct sports policy.[32] From a legal point of view, Article 165 TFEU was not expected to bring a change in the application of EU law to sport. It was clear from the outset that its importance would be of a purely symbolic nature.

It should be recalled that Article 165 TFEU merely mentions that the Union shall take 'account of the specific nature of sport, its structures based on voluntary activity and its social and educational function' while contributing to the promotion of European sporting issues. Contrary to what the sport governing bodies may have wished, this clause was not integrated to alter the application of EU law to sport.[33] In this regard it is rather paradoxical that the 'sport debate' in the EU, which originated from the question – and at some point the claim – of the sport governing bodies to exempt sport from EU law, resulted in a – admittedly limited – formal EU competence in the field of sport.[34]

Compared to Article 165 TFEU, the Nice Declaration was more far reaching, declaring in a more general way: 'the Community must, in its action under the various Treaty provisions, take account of the social, educational and cultural functions inherent in sport and making it special ...'.[35] The decision not to reassert this phrase in Article 165

---

[31] Consolidated version of the Treaty on the functioning of the European Union [2012] OJ 326/47. An identical provision was included in Art III-282 of Treaty establishing a Constitution for Europe [2004] OJ 310/1.

[32] S Van den Bogaert and An Vermeersch, 'Sport and the European Union: A Tale of Uneasy Bedfellows?' (2006) 31(6) ELRev 821–40.

[33] Ibid.

[34] An Vermeersch, *Europese spelregels voor sport – Overzicht van het Europees sportbeleid in wording en de toepassing van het Europees recht op sport* (Maklu 2008).

[35] 'The European Council requests the Commission and the Council to take account of the specific characteristics of sport in Europe and its social function in managing common policies'; Declaration on the specific characteristics of sport and its social function in Europe, of which account should be taken in

TFEU is to be welcomed. Even if it would not provide a general exemption for sport, it could give rise to a lot of controversy and misinterpretation. A general exemption clause was no option. First, because it seems improbable that consensus at Member State level can be found in order to introduce such a drastic change.[36] Second, and more importantly, because the sporting world fails to come up with convincing arguments which would justify such a radical measure.[37]

Still, sport governing bodies and academics awaited a concrete Court case in order to appraise the impact of Article 165 TFEU in practice. The *Bernard* case provided the first occasion for the Court to articulate its view on the new 'sports Article'.[38] Not surprisingly, when assessing the French Football Charter under EU free movement law, the Court referred extensively to its own jurisprudence in *Bosman*. After the Court found that a rule that obliged a young player to sign his first professional contract with the club which trained him or alternatively to pay a compensation to this club constituted a restriction on freedom of movement for workers,[39] the Court applied the objective justification test.[40]

With explicit reference to the infamous paragraph 106 of *Bosman*, the Court confirmed that the objective of encouraging the recruitment and training of young players must be accepted as legitimate.[41] In assessing the proportionality of the measure at stake, the Court held that:

> account must be taken … of the specific characteristics of sport in general, and football in particular, and of their social and educational function. The relevance of those factors is also corroborated by their being mentioned in the second subparagraph of Article 165(1) TFEU.

This formulation leaves no doubt: the Court was fully capable of assessing the French Football Charter on the basis of its own pre-Lisbon case law. The Court embraced the specificity of sport long before the Lisbon Treaty. In *Bernard*, the Court indicated that Article 165 TFEU merely confirms this case law. At the same time the reference to the

---

implementing common policies, annexed to the Conclusions of the Nice European Council, Bulletin EU 12-2000.

[36] P Van Nuffel, 'Case law: Bosman' [1996] 2 *Columbia Journal of European Law* 345.

[37] S Weatherill, 'Do Sporting Associations make Law or are they merely Subject to it?' (1998) 9 (7/8) *European Business Law Review* 217–20.

[38] Case C-325/08 *Olivier Bernard* [2010] ECR I-2177.

[39] Ibid, paras 35–37.

[40] Ibid., para 38.

[41] Ibid., para 39.

'sporting Article' illustrates that, although Article 165 TFEU and the constitutional acceptance of the specific characteristics of sport are not explicitly linked to the EU free movement or competition law provisions, the Court is willing to use Article 165 TFEU in applying EU law to sport. However, here again, this is not new, but simply a confirmation of the Court's approach.[42] As in *Bosman*, the final 'verdict' of the Court was negative because the French system did not pass the proportionality test. The Court did accept a payment of training compensation.[43] However, the French system involved the payment of damages unrelated to the actual costs of training. This, according to the Court, is not necessary to ensure the attainment of the objective of training and therefore not compatible with EU law.[44]

IV. STATE AID AND SPORT: WHAT ROLE FOR THE SPECIFICITY OF SPORT?

Bosman, *Meca-Medina and Majcen*, and Article 165 TFEU provide a clear framework for sport under EU law: its specificity is fully recognized and guides the EU institutions when assessing sporting practices and rules being challenged as restrictions on free movement or as an anticompetitive practice or as an abuse of dominant position. Conversely, the state aid granted to the sports sector remains relatively underexposed. Only recently, an influx of state aid cases in the field of sport emerged. The year 2011 marked a turning point.[45] Since then, the Commission has taken a decision in more than 20 cases.[46] This chapter will focus on the question to what extent the specificity of sport has been taken into account in these cases and what influence of it emerged.

Articles 107–109 TFEU set out the constitutional framework for the EU's state aid policy. Article 107(1) TFEU entails a definition of 'prohibited' state aid and two sets of exceptions (Arts 107(2) and 107(3)

---

42 See also Stephen Weatherill, 'Fairness, Openness and the Specific Nature of Sport: Does the Lisbon Treaty Change EU Sports Law?' [2010] (3/4) *The International Sports Law Journal* 11–17.

43 Case C-325/08 *Olivier Bernard* (n 38), para 45.

44 Ibid., para 50.

45 B Van Rompuy and O van Maren, 'EU Control of State Aid to Professional Sport: Why Now?' in Duval and Van Rompuy (n 4), 153–85.

46 B Garcia, An Vermeersch and S Weatherill, 'A New Horizon in European Sports Law: The Application of the EU State Aid Rules meets the Specific Nature of Sport' (2017) 13(1) *European Competition Journal* 28–61.

TFEU). The sport state aid cases of the last five years can be divided into two clusters.[47] The first cluster involves support for sports infrastructure. Generally, the Commission found the aid lawful. All aid was notified to the Commission. The second cluster involves financial aid for sports clubs. Here the support was not notified by the respective Member States and the Commission was more cautious to find the aid compatible with EU state aid law.

The Commission's approach in relation to support for sports infrastructure will be analyzed based on *Flanders Football Stadiums* case.[48] The reasoning and final outcome in the other sports infrastructure cases,[49] is very similar to this case.

In July 2013, Belgium notified the plan of the Flemish government to subsidize, by way of an aid scheme, the renovation and the construction of multifunctional football stadiums in Flanders. In order to qualify for funding, applicants had to demonstrate that the new or renovated stadium fulfilled UEFA criteria and that it would contribute to broader societal goals.[50] In assessing the measure, the Commission followed its classic two-step approach. The Commission first assessed if the four cumulative conditions of Article 107(1) TFEU were met in order for the measure to be qualified as state aid: (1) the measure has to be granted out of state resources; (2) it has to confer an economic advantage to undertakings; (3) the advantage has to be selective and distort or threaten to distort competition; (4) the measure has to affect intra-Community trade.

As regards the first condition, the Commission simply noted that the aid to be granted under the scheme was fully financed from the budget of the Flemish government. Subsequently, the Commission considered the Flemish subsidies as an economic advantage to undertakings. Evidently first and second league football clubs qualified as undertakings. Referring to the Court's case law,[51] the Commission confirmed that not only the operation and management of an infrastructure constitutes an economic

---

[47] Ibid.

[48] Commission decision of 20 November 2013, Case SA.37109, Belgium – football stadiums in Flanders.

[49] Garcia, Vermeersch and Weatherill (n 46).

[50] European Commission, 'State aid: Commission clears Belgian support scheme for football stadiums' (IP/13/1120, 20 November 2013).

[51] Case 41/90 *Klaus Höfner and Fritz Elser v Macroton GmbH* [1991] ECR I-1979, para 21. See for instance Case C-82/01P *Aéroports de Paris v Commission* [2002] ECR I-9297; Case T-196/04 *Ryanair Ltd v Commission* [2008] ECR II-3643; Joint Cases T-443/08 and T-455/08 *Flughafen Leipzig-Halle GmbH and Mitteldeutsche Flughafen AG v Commission and Freistaat Sachsen and Land Sachsen-Anhalt v Commission* [2011] ECR II-1311.

activity but also the construction of infrastructure, which cannot be separated from its later (commercial) operation. Clubs that own their stadium clearly enjoy an economic advantage when receiving subsidies for the construction or renovation of their facilities. Clubs not being owners may enjoy an advantage if the fee they pay for the use of the stadium does not correspond to the market price for such use.

In addition, the requirement of selectivity was easily met: the measure targeted only stadiums used by first and second league football clubs located in Flanders. In this, the stadiums that qualified for support benefited from a selective advantage compared to other stadiums which did not qualify for support. Similarly, the Commission simply stated that the measure of the Flemish government distorted competition by altering existing market conditions. Finally, the Commission confirmed without doubt that the measure could have an effect on intra-EU trade as competitions between professional football clubs clearly have an international dimension and a key goal of the measure was to adapt the stadiums to UEFA criteria for European football games.

On this basis, the Commission found that the measure of the Flemish government constituted state aid.[52] Therefore, the compatibility of the aid had to be assessed. The Commission relied on Article 107(3)(c) TFEU, according to which aid to facilitate the development of certain economic activities may be considered to be compatible with the common market. In order to assess whether a measure is compatible under Article 107(3)(c) TFEU, the Commission balanced the positive and negative effects of the aid. In applying the balancing test, the Commission assessed the following questions:

(i) Is the aid measure aimed at a well-defined objective of common interest?
(ii) Is the aid well designed to deliver the objective of common interest?
(iii) Are the distortions of competition and the effect on trade limited, so that the overall balance is positive?

The specificity of sport comes to the fore when answering the first question. In the *Flanders Football Stadiums* case, the Commission highlighted both the responsibility of the state with regard to the construction of sports infrastructures and the social significance of sport,

---

[52] Commission decision of 20 November 2013, Case SA.37109, (n 48), paras 18–27.

following from its educational role, as well as its social, cultural and health dimension. In doing so, the Commission relied upon and referred to the Amsterdam Declaration on Sport, Article 165 TFEU and its own staff working document accompanying the White Paper on Sport. As the Flemish government's measure had the double aim of realizing multi-functional football stadiums with a high social return, while at the same time improving the quality of stadiums used for professional football, it was regarded as satisfying the policy objectives of 'common interest'.[53]

When assessing the appropriateness, the incentive effect and the proportionality of the measure, the Commission accepted the claim that most of the football stadiums in Flanders were by then outdated and that they could not be renovated without financial support of the government. These points, combined with the social return of the stadiums, were key elements for aid applicants to prove in the application dossier. In addition, the Commission stated that the aid was limited and that the necessary transparency requirements and control mechanisms comprised.

The Commission also answered the third question in a positive way: the aid did not affect trade and competition between Member States to an extent contrary to the common interest. Again reference was made to a high degree of transparency and to the requirement for applicants to prove the need for the stadium. In addition, the 'benchmarking' assurances – setting prices for the use of the infrastructure by clubs that are not owners of the infrastructure – was seen to facilitate a limitation in the distortion of competition compared to privately owned and funded football infrastructures.

The Commission's approach in *Flanders Football Stadiums* is therefore informative for a great number of similar cases. Indeed, the tone was set in 2011 in the case of the Hungarian tax benefit scheme.[54] The Hungarian aid scheme was designed with the aim to channel additional funds to the sport sector by granting tax benefits to undertakings to contribute to sport development. In its assessment of the compatibility of the Hungarian aid measure, the Commission relied on Article 107(3)(c) and Article 165 TFEU.

Again, the starting point of the Commission's assessment was the 'special characteristics of sport'. The Commission cited its staff working document and its Communication on Developing the European Dimension in Sport when highlighting the enormous potential of sport for

---

[53] Ibid, paras 29–34.

[54] Commission decision of 9 November 2011, Case SA.317220, Hungary – Supporting the Hungarian sport sector via tax benefit scheme.

bringing the citizens of Europe together. On the same basis, the educational role of sport, as well as its social, cultural and health dimension were lauded.[55] The Hungarian aid measure was considered to be in line with the common interest because its primary objective was to increase participation of the general public in sport activities and because it provided a remedy for a well-defined market failure.[56]

With the exception of the aid for the German Nürburgring,[57] all subsequent state aid cases involving sports infrastructure were based on the same reasoning, all having a positive outcome, and all referencing to Article 165 TFEU.[58] In addition to Article 165 TFEU, most cases also refer to the Amsterdam Declaration on Sport.[59]

When the sports infrastructure was announced to be used for cultural events, the Commission also relied upon Article 167(4) TFEU promoting cultural diversity.[60] In these cases, the specificity of sport is linked to the state responsibility with regard to the construction or renovation of sports infrastructures and supporting different types of activities which benefit the general public. Further, one could argue that:

> sport is special because of its social significance and therefore the state is responsible for providing infrastructure in this area of life to citizens just as it

---

55 Ibid., paras 86–87.

56 Ibid., paras 88–90.

57 Commission decision of 7 August 2012, Case SA.34890 and SA.51550, Germany – Nürburgring.

58 Commission decision of 20 March 2013, Case SA.35440, Germany – Multifunktionsarena der Stadt Jena, para 15; Commission decision of 20 March 2013, Case SA.35135, Germany – Multifunktionsarena der Stadt Erfurt, para 14; Commission decision of 2 May 2013, Sweden – Case SA.33618, para 48; Commission decision of 15 May 2013, Case SA.33728, Denmark – Multiarena in Copenhagen, para 51; Commission decision of 2 October 2013, Case SA.36105, Germany – Fussballstadion Chemnitz, para 19; Commission decision of 20 November 2013, Case SA.37109, Belgium – football stadiums in Flanders, para 30; Décision de la Commission de 18 Décembre 2013, Case SA.35501, France – Financement de la construction et de la rénovation des stades pour l'EURO 2016, para 269; Commission decision of 9 April 2014, Case SA.37342, United Kingdom – Regional Stadia Development in Northern Ireland, para 91; Commission decision of 22 July 2016, Case SA.44439, Ireland – Sporting arena Cork, para 44.

59 Case SA.35440, para 15; Case SA.35135, para 14; Case SA.33728, para 51; Case SA.33618, para 48; Case SA.36105, para 19; Case SA.37109, para 30; Case SA.35501, para 269; Case SA.37342, para 91.

60 Case SA.35440, para 15; Case SA.35135, para 14; Case SA.33728, para 52; Case SA.36105, para 21; para 270; Case SA.44439, para 46.

> is, for example, responsible for building roads to improve transport or communication.[61]

This is an important role addressed to sport, with important legal implications, especially if one considers that a great part of this state aid benefits (professional) sports bodies and clubs.[62] The Hungarian case mentioned the significance of support for sport infrastructure in general.[63] In subsequent cases, the Commission debated the idea of 'state responsibility' with regard to sport infrastructure. Some of these cases refer to the Commission decision in the Dutch *Ahoy* case.[64] However, the origin of the state responsibility with regard to sport infrastructure goes back to the German *Hanover* case.

The Commission mentioned this case in its staff working document to substantiate the statement that public financing related to the construction of sport infrastructure can be considered not to constitute state aid.[65] The Commission referred to some general principles that were laid down in a letter from the European Commission's Directorate-General for Competition to Germany regarding state funding for the Hanover football stadium. That case dates back to the year 2000 when the organization of the 2006 World Championship was assigned to Germany.

According to the Commission, aid for sport infrastructure could be argued not to constitute state aid on the meeting of three criteria:

> (1) the type of infrastructure involved is generally unlikely to be provided by the market because it is not economically viable; (2) it is not apt to selectively favour a specific undertaking [...]; (3) it is a facility needed to provide a service that is considered as being part of the typical responsibility of the public authority to the general public.[66]

---

61 Garcia, Vermeersch and Weatherill (n 46).

62 Ibid.

63 Case SA.317220, para 89.

64 Case SA.35440; Case SA.35135; Case SA.37109; Case SA.36105; Case SA.37342; Case SA.35501. See also the Commission decision of 21 October 2008, State aid measure C 4/08, The Netherlands – Investment by the municipality of Rotterdam in the Ahoy complex, para 67. The Commission stated:

> the investment in the Arena is intended to provide a venue at which activities will take place that are aimed at the general public. The provision of a sports venue of this type can be regarded as a matter for which the authorities are responsible to the general public, provided its multifunctional character is maintained.

65 Commission Staff Working Document (n 20), 28.

66 Ibid.

It should be noted that both *Ahoy* and *Hanover* were not state aid cases. The support was considered not to constitute state aid because of the absence of a selective advantage. These cases illustrate that long before the inclusion of Article 165 in the TFEU, the Commission put forward the concept of 'state responsibility' with regard to sport infrastructure. Long before Article 165 TFEU, the Commission took into consideration that sport was somewhat special.

The influx of state aid decisions on sport infrastructure provided sufficient case experience for the Commission to include aid for sport and multifunctional recreational infrastructures as a new category in its 2014 Block Exemption Regulation (Article 1(1)(k)).[67] Not surprisingly, the Block Exemption Regulation is a mere confirmation and codification of the Commission's decision practice. Recital 74 gives some background in relation to sport. Interestingly, the recital addresses possible state measures that might not constitute state aid. This might be the case for measures which have a purely local character or which are taken in the field of amateur sport.

After a simple reference to Article 165 TFEU, the recital lists some general starting points for the block exemption in the field of sport infrastructure. Again, transparency and non-discrimination are key elements. Article 55 of the Regulation outlines the concrete conditions under which aid for sport infrastructures must be compatible with the internal market. Central elements relate to the fact that there must be no single professional sport user; access, pricing and use must be based on transparent and non-discriminatory arrangements; investment aid must not exceed the difference between the eligible costs and the operating profit of the investment; operating aid must not exceed the operating losses over the relevant period. Article 4(bb) of the Regulation entails notification limits for sport infrastructures: for investment aid a maximum of 15 million euro or the total costs not exceeding 50 million euro per project; for operating aid a maximum of 2 million euro per infrastructure per year. Larger projects, such as the Irish support to the Cork sporting arena,[68] need to be notified to the Commission and will be assessed on an individual basis.

The Commission's decisions on financial aid for sports clubs can be divided into two groups. The first group revolves around measures granted by several Dutch municipalities to five professional football

---

[67] Commission Regulation (EU) No 651/2014 of 17 June 2014 declaring certain categories of aid compatible with the internal market in application of Articles 107 and 108 of the Treaty, [2014] OJ L 187/1.

[68] Case SA.44439.

clubs. After an in-depth investigation, the Commission found that the support was in line with the EU's state aid provisions.[69] In the case concerning PSV Eindhoven, the Commission considered that no aid was involved as the land transaction took place on market terms.[70] The four other cases concerned professional football clubs (FC Den Bosch, MVV Maastricht, NEC Nijmegen and Willem II Tilburg) in financial difficulties. Here, the Commission found that the clubs received aid. Consequently, the Commission assessed the compatibility of the aid in the light of the 2004 Guidelines on state aid for rescuing and restructuring firms in difficulty.[71]

The Commission asserted that a realistic restructuring plan had been implemented for the football clubs. Moreover the clubs took significant measures, such as reducing the number of employees, the number of registered players and players' wages. On this basis, the Commission found the aid in these four cases was compatible with the internal market. The Commission did not rely on the specificity of sport to come to this positive outcome. In the cases of *Den Bosch*[72] and *Willem II*[73] neither Article 165 TFEU nor the specificity of sport were mentioned. In the case of *MVV*, the Commission made a brief reference to Article 165 TFEU when answering the state's argument that it should be taken into account when assessing the derogations in Article 107(3)(c) TFEU and Article 107(3)(d) TFEU respectively.

In response, the Commission simply stated that in its assessment of the notion of development of economic activities in the sports sector, due account of Article 165 was taken. In relation to the cultural derogation, the Commission declared that this Treaty provision could not be considered in a sport case as the Treaty distinguishes between the notions of sport and culture.[74] In the case of *NEC*, the Commission merely

---

[69] European Commission, 'State aid: Commission clears support measures for certain football clubs in the Netherlands' (IP/16/2402, 4 July 2016).

[70] Commission decision of 4 July 2016, Case SA.41613, The Netherlands – professional football club PSV in Eindhoven.

[71] Communication from the European Commission, 'Community guidelines on State Aid for rescuing and restructuring firms in difficulty' [2004] OJ C 244/2.

[72] Commission decision of 4 July 2016, Case SA.41614, The Netherlands – professional football club FC Den Bosch in 's-Hertogenbosch.

[73] Commission decision of 4 July 2016, Case SA.40168, The Netherlands – professional football club Willem II in Tilburg.

[74] Commission decision of 4 July 2016, Case SA.41612, The Netherlands – professional football club MVV in Maastricht, paras 45–46.

confirmed that its assessment of the notion of 'development of economic activities' in the sport takes due account of Article 165.[75]

A second group of Commission decisions in relation to financial support for clubs concerned seven Spanish professional football clubs. Following three separate in-depth investigations, the Commission concluded that the public support measures granted by Spain gave the clubs an unfair advantage over other clubs in breach of EU state aid rules. As a result, Spain had to recover the illegal state aid.[76] A first investigation involved guarantees given by the state-owned Valencia Institute of Finance for loans granted to three Valencia football clubs. At the time, those clubs were in financial difficulties. Unlike the Dutch cases, the aid was not linked to any restructuring plan to make the clubs viable and none of them implemented compensatory measures. Therefore, the support was deemed not to be in line with the guidelines on state aid for rescuing and restructuring firms in difficulty.[77] The Commission merely mentioned Article 165 TFEU but did not rely on the sports article in its legal analysis.[78]

A second investigation concerned tax privileges for four professional football clubs (Athletic Club Bilbao, Club Atlético Osasuna, FC Barcelona and Real Madrid CF). Whereas professional football clubs in Spain were considered as limited liability companies for tax purposes, these four clubs were treated as non-profit organizations. On this basis, these four clubs payed a 5 per cent lower tax rate for over 20 years. The Commission found that that this selective tax system constituted state aid.[79] In assessing whether the aid was compatible with EU law, the Commission briefly mentioned Article 165 TFEU and the promotion of sport as a potential objective of common interest. However, the Commission asserted that neither Spain nor the beneficiaries had claimed that any of the exceptions provided for in Article 107 TFEU applied.[80]

---

[75] Commission decision of 4 July 2016, Case SA.41617, The Netherlands – professional football club NEC in Nijmegen, para 68.

[76] European Commission, 'State aid: Commission decides Spanish professional football clubs have to pay back incompatible aid' (IP 16/2401, 4 July 2016)

[77] Commission decision of 4 July 2016, Case SA.36387, Spain – Valencia Club de Fútbol Sociedad Anónima Deportiva, Hércules Club de Fútbol Sociedad Anónima Deportiva and Elche Club de Fútbol Sociedad Anónima Deportiva.

[78] Ibid., para 101.

[79] Commission decision of 4 July 2016, Case SA.29769, Spain – State aid for certain football clubs.

[80] Ibid., paras 84–89.

The third Spanish case related to a land transfer between Real Madrid and the City of Madrid. An independent study revealed that the transaction was overvalued by €18.4 million.[81] The Commission concluded that Real Madrid benefited from state aid which was not compatible with the internal market. Article 165 TFEU, nor the specificity of sport were mentioned.

In the Dutch and Spanish cases, sport was not treated in a special way. The – brief – references to Article 165 TFEU illustrate that the specificity of sport was not completely neglected. The support measures for the professional football clubs in The Netherlands and Spain were assessed within the normal economic logic. As Commissioner Margrethe Vestager, in charge of competition policy, rightly pointed out: 'Professional football is a commercial activity with significant money involved and public money must comply with fair competition rules.'[82] Several appeals have been lodged against the Commission decisions in the Spanish cases.[83] This provides the European judges with the opportunity of elaborating their view on the state aid provisions in relation to sport. However, it is not to be expected that the judges will substantially diverge from the Commission's analysis.

V. CONCLUSION: WHAT FUTURE FOR THE SPECIFICITY OF SPORT?

The specificity of sport is abundantly recognized, both from a legal and a political point of view. Article 165 TFEU can be regarded as the constitutional culmination of a long and lively debate after the *Bosman* judgment on the relationship between sport and the EU.[84] Even if there is no plain definition of the concept, a number of elements have repeatedly been put forward in relation to the specificity of sport. On the whole, a certain balance has been reached: sport cannot escape the application of

---

[81] Commission decision of 4 July 2016, Case SA.33754, Spain – Real Madrid CF.

[82] European Commission, 'State aid: Commission decides Spanish professional football clubs have to pay back incompatible aid' (IP 16/2401, 4 July 2016).

[83] Case T-679/16R *Athletic Club v Commission*; Case T-766/16R *Hércules Club de Fútbol v Commission*.

[84] B García and S Weatherill, 'Engaging with the EU in order to Minimize its Impact: Sport and the Negotiation of the Treaty of Lisbon' (2012) 19 JEPP 238–56 and Weatherill (n 6).

EU law and its specificity is duly taken into account when assessing the compatibility of sport rules and practices with EU law. Whereas this assessment is based on a case-by-case analysis, the case law of the European Court of Justice and the decision practice of the European Commission provide sufficient guidance. From a legal point of view, this is fairly reasonable. From a political point of view, a certain uneasiness seems to remain. A recent study commissioned by the European Commission refers to the 'growing interest of Member States'[85] and France tabled a document at the November 2016 Council meeting calling for a 'clear and watertight definition of the specific characteristics of sport'.[86] These developments illustrate that politics, or at least some in politics, remain eager to match the world of sport's expectations on the concept of the specificity of sport.

---

[85] Mapping and Analysis of the Specificity of Sport (European Commission DG Education & Culture 2016), available at http://ec.europa.eu/assets/eac/sport/library/studies/mapping-analysis-specificity-sport_en.pdf (accessed 26 Oct 2017). The study merely reviews all new cases and decisions relevant to sport since the White Paper on Sport in 2007.

[86] General Secretariat of the Council, 'Developments and specific features of the organisation of European sport – *Information from the French delegation*' (14173/16, 9 November 2016) and available at http://data.consilium.europa.eu/doc/document/ST-14173-2016-INIT/en/pdf (accessed 26 Oct 2017).

16. European model of sport: alternative structures

Katarina Pijetlovic

I. INTRODUCTION

The European model of sport is traditionally described as a monopolistic pyramid, with one federation per sport and per country. In this system, national federations organise competitions, promote and regulate their sport at their respective national levels. They operate under the umbrella of a single European and a single global federation that sits at the apex of the pyramid. Amateur, semi-professional and professional athletes and clubs are at the bottom of the pyramid. They are members of their respective national federations and participate in various leagues according to their sporting achievements. It must, however, be emphasised that, although there is no uniform organisational structure of European sports, the architecture of different sports corresponds to this broad pyramid description to various degrees.

Sports governing bodies have an extensive mandate to regulate their discipline. They pass the rules concerning the access to competitions, take care of disciplinary and integrity matters, guarantee the uniform rules of the game, ensure the rules relating to safety at events are in place and promote their sport at all levels, etc. At the same time, they are also commercial actors with economic interests in the sport they regulate. In their role as organisers of competitions, they enter into a number of business deals to sell merchandise, tickets, hospitality packages, media and other commercial rights in sporting events.

This intermingling of regulatory and commercial functions in a single body inevitably leads to a conflict of interests, and often causes a detriment to actual or potential competitors in the relevant market. For example, sports federations strive to maintain monopoly via the market restrictions in their statutes and other rulebooks designed to prevent the operation or even emergence of a rival, competing league or other organisational market for 'their' sporting events. In doing so, they can commit antitrust infringements under Articles 101 and 102 TFEU.

It is an interesting time to be writing about the legal issues involved in such restrictions. In 2016 the EU Commission issued a Statement of Objections relating to the International Skating Union ('ISU case'), the first case after *Meca-Medina* that addresses this question, and cross-complaints have filed between the international and European basketball federations, and private promoter of basketball competitions.

A wave of recent decisions by national enforcers of EU competition law had sought to clarify the TFEU requirements applicable to the regulation of organisational markets by sporting associations. The general principle that emerged was that any clause preventing a possibility of entry and expansion in the market for the organisation of sporting events would be considered restrictive of competition, unless it could be justified by reference to regulatory or commercial ancillarity.

These 'ancillary' labels imply that a reason for restriction can be legitimately attributed to either public interest objectives or to legitimate commercial goals, and that in imposing such restrictions the principle of proportionality is respected. As a matter of law, if a restriction designation cannot be avoided under ancillary restraints doctrine, in some cases a respondent might yet be able to rely on economic efficiency arguments. Before moving on to provide details of this legal framework and the applicable case-law, this chapter will outline policy changes towards the traditional pyramid structure in European sports and argue that this model is not a part of 'specificity of sport' with regard to organisational aspects.

II. EU POLICY AND THE EUROPEAN MODEL OF SPORT

In 1998 the European Commission published a consultation document that said: 'there is a European model of sport with its own characteristics … Sport in Europe has a unique structure. For the future development of sport in Europe these special features should be taken into account'.[1] This document rejected the free market model for the future of European sport, resisting the pressures of 'Americanisation' which is seen as the ultimate evil of excessive commercialism leading to destruction of European sporting values, the only true sporting values.[2] In the Opinion

---

[1] The European Model of Sport: Consultation Document of DG X (European Commission, 1998) para 1.3.

[2] L Halgreen, *European Sports Law: A Comparative Analysis of the European and American Models of Sport* (Forlaget Thomson 2004) 64.

given by the Committee of Regions on 'The European Model of Sport', the American model is centred too much on a business- and market-oriented approach to sport making a clear distinction between professional and amateur sport and giving them totally separate structures. The Committee of Regions retained its faith in, and asserted its preference for, the European socio-cultural model. It further emphasised the special characteristics of the European model and said that the inclusion of an economic factor should not be allowed to jeopardise traditional values.[3]

A political consensus regarding the need to preserve the structures of sport in Europe was apparent also in other policy documents, notably in the 1999 Commission Helsinki Report. That Report also considered that the inclination of certain sporting operators and large clubs to leave the federations in order to reap the maximum economic benefit from the sport for themselves alone was symptomatic of several phenomena, and notably: the rise in popularity and internationalisation of sport and the unprecedented development in the economic dimension of sport.[4] The Nice Declaration noted similar developments in the world of sport, but considered that federations must continue to be the key feature by providing a guarantee of sporting cohesion and participatory democracy, and by way of the ties of solidarity binding the practice of sport at every level.[5]

The 2007 Parliament Report on the future of professional football in Europe (Committee on Culture and Education) noted in a similar spirit that:

> European sport, and football in particular, is an inalienable part of the European identity, European culture and citizenship, and the European Football Model, characterised by open sports competitions within a pyramid structure in which several hundred thousand amateur clubs and millions of volunteers and players form the base for the top professional clubs … .[6]

---

[3] The European Model of Sport: Opinion of the Committee of the Regions (1999/C 374/14).

[4] Report from the Commission to the European Council with a view to safeguarding sports structures and maintaining the social significance of sport within the Community framework: The Helsinki Report on Sport, COM (1999) 644, section 2.

[5] European Council – Nice, 7–10 December 2000, Conclusions of the Presidency, Annex IV, para 15.

[6] European Parliament resolution of 29 March 2007 on the future of professional football in Europe (2006/2130(INI)), para B.

The Report also identified the growing concentration of economic wealth and sports power as a threat to the future of professional football in Europe. It stressed 'its attachment to the European Football Model, with its symbiotic relationship between amateur and professional football'.[7]

Finally, the Amsterdam Declaration on Sport[8] similarly centred on the social significance of sport. These policy statements are based on the desire to preserve fundamental values such as the societal role of 'sport for all', self-regulation, and solidarity between professional and amateur levels, as well as the highly beneficial effects that sports have on youth, health and social inclusion policies.[9]

In 2001, the Commissioner responsible for EU competition policy addressed the question of a single federation per sport, acknowledging that: 'while the existence of a single federation overseeing both the regulatory and organisational aspects of a sport is common in Europe … other scenarios exist or can be envisaged'.[10] This signalled a move in the articulation of sports policy away from the prevalent socio-cultural approach towards a more economic-based approach, to be set out in the Commission's 2007 White Paper on Sport.[11] The Commission Staff Working Paper annexed to the White Paper saw the relevance of the pyramid structure for both the organisation of competitions and sport in general as 'greatly reduced'.[12]

In that Staff Working Document, the Commission repeated the previous policy statements on the pyramid structure and labelled certain values and traditions of European sport as worthy of support. But then it went

---

[7] Ibid., para 1.

[8] Treaty of Amsterdam amending the Treaty on European Union, the Treaties establishing the European Communities and certain related acts – Declarations adopted by the Conference – Declaration on sport. [1997] OJ C 340, 136.

[9] L Halgreen (n 2), 64

[10] M Monti, European Commissioner for Competition, 'Speech/01/84 "Competition and Sport: the Rules of the Game" at a Conference on "Governance in Sport" – European Olympic Committee – FIA – Féderation Internationale de l'Automobile – Herbert Smith, Swissotel Brussels, 26 February 2001', available at http://europa.eu/rapid/press-release_SPEECH-01-84_en.htm (accessed 26 Oct 2017).

[11] White Paper on Sport, COM(2007) 391 final.

[12] Commission Staff Working Document – The EU and Sport: Background and Context – Accompanying document to the White Paper on Sport, COM(2007) 391 final, SEC(2007)932, SEC(2007)934, SEC(2007)936, SEC/2007/0935, para 4.1.

on to recognise the diversity and complexities of European sport structures which make it unrealistic to try and define a single organisational model of sport in Europe.[13] Garcia saw this as the Commission's withdrawal of an important element of the political debate, which it did partly because the pyramid model has been politicised and used in arguments by governing bodies, such as IOC, UEFA and FIFA, to further their own agenda, and avoid the legal intervention by public authorities and legitimacy challenges by other stakeholders, such as clubs and athletes.[14]

The White Paper further acknowledged that 'new tendencies are challenging the traditional vision of a unified "European Sport Model"'.[15] These challenges to the organisational structures are the increasing commercialisation and the emergence of new stakeholders outside the sports (such as aspiring private promoters) and inside the sports (such as FIFPro, ECA, and EPFL in football). This supplied another reason for the shift from policy that strongly supported vertical pyramid model to the appreciation of the necessity for a decentralised model that might be more appropriate given the prevailing empirical reality.

III. THE EUROPEAN SPORTS MODEL, THE SPECIFICITY OF SPORT AND ARTICLE 165(1) TFEU

The 'specificity of sport' is the concept that refers to the inherent characteristics of sport which set it apart from other economic and social activities.[16] It has never been set in absolute terms by the Court as its original creator and, as emphasised in the Commission Staff Working Document, its application is always assessed on a case-by-case basis.[17] The Lisbon Treaty amendments that entered into force on 1 December 2009 provided constitutional basis to the concept of 'specificity of sport'. Article 165(1) TFEU states that: 'The Union shall contribute to the

---

[13] White Paper on Sport (n 11), para 4.

[14] B Garcia, 'Sports Governance after the White Paper: The Demise of the European Model?' (2009) 1(3) *International Journal of Sports Policy* 267–84.

[15] White Paper on Sport (n 11), para 4.

[16] Mapping and Analysis of the Specificity of Sport (European Commission DG Education & Culture 2016), available at http://ec.europa.eu/assets/eac/sport/library/studies/mapping-analysis-specificity-sport_en.pdf (accessed 26 Oct 2017).

[17] Commission Staff Working Document (n 12), para 4.1.

promotion of European sporting issues, while taking account of the specific nature of sport, its structures based on voluntary activity and its social and educational function.' A study on the Lisbon Treaty and European Union Sports Policy commissioned by the European Parliament concluded that Article 165(1) TFEU will add little further protection for contested sports rules beyond those already provided by the Court and the Commission because the two institutions have already been highly receptive to the 'specific nature of sport' concept.[18]

The 2011 Commission Communication on Developing European Dimension in Sport interprets the 'specificity of sport' referred to in Article 165 TFEU as the concept encompassing 'all the characteristics that make sport special, such as for instance the interdependence between competing adversaries or the pyramid structure of open competitions'.[19] This quote does not say anything about organisational model or governance of sport, as it is perfectly possible to have vertical structures of competition with central regulatory authority without the vertical structures of an organisational market.

What it does imply is that league structures predicated on promotion and relegation and overseen by a single European champion per sport can be seen as part of the 'specificity of sport' concept in Article 165 TFEU. In economic theory, it is a peculiarity of professional sport production that championships must possess a monopoly status to achieve consistent ranking and increase their value for consumers.[20] In overview then, all that the Communication emphasised is the need to take this into account in the application of the EU economic provisions. Aspects of 'specificity of sport' concept thus taken into account will not necessarily prevail in the balancing act against economic aspects in a potential dispute. The quote also suggests that closed leagues could not be reconciled with the specific nature of European sport within the meaning of Article 165(1) TFEU and would not be able to benefit from it. However, the EU will not

---

[18] Directorate-General for Internal Policies, Study on the Lisbon Treaty and EU Sports Policy (European Parliament 2010), 10–11 and available at http://www.europarl.europa.eu/meetdocs/2009_2014/documents/cult/dv/esstudyeusportspolicy/esstudyeusportspolicyen.pdf (accessed 26 Oct 2017).

[19] European Commission, Developing the European Dimension in Sport COM(2011) 12 final, para 4.2.

[20] H Dietl *et al*, 'Organisational Differences between U.S. Major Leagues and European Leagues: Implications for Salary Cap' (International Association of Sports Economists, Working Paper Series, Paper No 11-05, March 2011) 3 and available at http://college.holycross.edu/RePEc/spe/Dietletal_OrganizationalDifferences.pdf (accessed 26 Oct 2017).

directly impose any particular organisational model on any sport, because each sport has its specificities and deserves to be treated accordingly.[21]

IV. RESTRICTIONS ON ALTERNATIVE SPORTS ORGANISERS: ANALYSIS UNDER EU COMPETITION LAW

Generally, the relevant market for provision of organisational services is attractive for prospective entrants because it automatically enables access to one of the connected markets: the downstream market for commercial exploitation. In application to sport, this primarily includes sales of broadcasting and other media rights, but also product licensing, ticketing, sponsorship, merchandising, etc. In *MOTOE* the Court defined the relevant market as consisting in 'first, the organisation of motorcycling events and, second, in their commercial exploitation'.[22] Those two types of activities were seen as functionally complementary. Being the sole organiser enables governing bodies to have exclusivity over commercial exploitation. The market for services of athletes and/or clubs represents the upstream market. Governing bodies regulate the labour market and player mobility, they engage in club licensing and control other factors of production of the sporting product: the game.

There are three main ways that sports governing bodies restrict or prevent the emergence of a new competitor on the market for organisational services. The first way is to insert clauses in their statutes and other rulebooks that render the access to that market a subject to prior authorisation, but in practice make it excessively difficult to obtain such authorisation. This has thus far been the case in many sports, including European football. Article 49(1) and (3) of the UEFA Statutes, for instance, confer the sole jurisdiction on UEFA to organise or abolish international competitions in Europe in which Member Associations and/or their clubs participate. Any international matches, competitions or tournaments which are not organised by UEFA, but are played on UEFA territory, require the prior approval of FIFA and/or UEFA and/or the relevant Member Association(s).[23]

---

[21] White Paper on Sport (n 11), para 4.1.

[22] Case C-49/07 *MOTOE* [2008] ECR I-4863, para 33.

[23] UEFA Statutes, (May 2016 edition) http://www.uefa.com/MultimediaFiles/Download/OfficialDocument/uefaorg/WhatUEFAis/02/36/36/14/2363614_DOWNLOAD.pdf (accessed 26 Oct 2017).

This means of controlling access to market and making it subject to prior authorisation is not objectionable per se. It is after all a legitimate mandate of the governing bodies to act on behalf of the entire sporting community and protect public interests in their respective disciplines. Not exercising the necessary degree of supervision and leaving regulation of sport to multiple private operators would clearly not be in the interest of sport. In internal market cases the systems subjecting the marketing of goods and services to a prior authorisation procedure are justified if they pursue a public interest objective and comply with the principle of proportionality.[24]

In *Canal Satélite Digital*, the Court specified that in determining whether a system of *ex ante* control complies with the principle of proportionality, it is important to consider: whether a system is based on objective, non-discriminatory criteria which are known in advance so that the regulatory power is not used arbitrarily; whether a system duplicates the control already carried out; whether a subsequent control system would be too late to be genuinely effective to attain the aim pursued, and; whether on account of its duration and the disproportionate cost it deters the operators concerned from pursuing their business plan.[25]

Similar considerations apply in competition law: transparent, objective, fair, non-discriminatory and proportionate criteria directed at pursuing public interest goals will be accepted as legitimate.[26] In *Metro*, the restrictions in a selective distribution scheme were held to fall outside Article 101(1) TFEU where they satisfy objective qualitative criteria and are applied in non-discriminatory manner.[27] This is an example of ancillary restraint doctrine based on legitimate commercial objectives. So, it is not the existence of the system of prior approval that can breach the competition provisions, but the precise drafting of the criteria and the way it is applied in practice.

The second way that governing bodies restrict the emergence of a new competitor on the market for organisational services is to control factors of production needed to stage a competition, such as imposing sanctions

---

[24] See, e.g., Case C-432/03 *Commission v Portugal* [2005] ECR I-9665 and Case C-390/99 *Canal Satélite Digital SL v Adminstración General del Estado, and Distribuidora de Televisión Digital SA (DTS)* [2002] ECR I-607.

[25] Case C-390/99 *Canal Satélite Digital SL* ibid., para 43.

[26] See Commission Notice Guidelines on Vertical Restraints, SEC(2010) 411 final, para 175 and the case law cited therein. It is submitted that when these principles are applied to regulatory bodies pursuing public interest objectives, their market shares do not matter.

[27] Case 26/76 *Metro (I)* [1977] ECR 1875.

on athletes, clubs, and leagues for taking part in the rival event. For example, in the ISU case, the ISU had threatened their athletes with a lifetime ban if they took part in any non-sanctioned event. Clauses such as this successfully prevent any private promoter entering or otherwise expanding the market for the organisation of events that compete with that of a governing body. A recent study that included 19 sports disciplines outlined sanctions faced by athletes for participating in events not authorised by their international sports federation.[28]

The third way that governing bodies restrict the emergence of a new competitor on the market for organisational services is to draft their contract with broadcasters and sponsors in such way as to block the competitor in the exploitation market or make that market commercially unattractive, as was the case in *FIA/Formula One* (discussed anon). The private promoters of grand prix had a clause in their contracts preventing circuits used for Formula One races from being used for races which might compete with Formula One, while the agreements with broadcasters contained a financial penalty of up to 50 per cent of the price paid, if they televised anything deemed to be a competitive threat to Formula One.

The core of the methodological approach, in assessing whether a regulatory rule adopted by a sports association for protection of public interest objectives, infringes Articles 101 and/or 102 TFEU can be found in the analytical framework provided by *Meca-Medina*.[29] According to that ruling:

> not every agreement between undertakings or every decision of an association of undertakings which restricts the freedom of action of the parties or of one of them necessarily falls within the prohibition laid down in Article [101(1) TFEU]. For the purposes of application of that provision to a particular case, account must first of all be taken of the overall context in which the decision of the association of undertakings was taken or produces its effects and, more specifically, of its objectives. It has then to be considered whether the

[28] B Van Rompuy, 'European Commission's ISU Antitrust Investigation Explained' (The Asser *International Sports Law Blog*, 5 October 2015). Available at http://www.asser.nl/SportsLaw/Blog/post/the-european-commission-s-isu-antitrust-investigation-explained-by-ben-van-rompuy#_ftnref7 (accessed 26 Oct 2017).

[29] Commission Staff Working Document (n 12), para 2.1.2.

> consequential effects restrictive of competition are inherent in the pursuit of those objectives (*Wouters and Others*, paragraph 97) and are proportionate to them.[30]

A rule that passes this test will be considered an ancillary restraint, i.e., a restriction on competition that is directly related and objectively necessary for the implementation of the main non-restrictive transaction and is proportionate to it. As such, it will fall outside of the scope of Article 101(1) TFEU.[31] Regulatory ancillarity[32] of this kind was first introduced by the CJEU in *Wouters*[33] and repeated in *Meca-Medina* and has so far applied only in cases of regulatory restrictions imposed by collective private bodies in the public interest.

The *Meca-Medina* analytical framework does not apply to the restrictive rules of associations adopted for the protection of their private commercial interests. However, provided that such restrictive rules are directly related and objectively necessary for the implementation of the main, non-restrictive transaction and are proportionate to it, the rule would be considered legitimate under analytically very similar 'commercial ancillarity' doctrine under Article 101(1) TFEU. Restraints on competition that were ancillary to a legitimate commercial purpose were exemplified in the *DLG* case discussed anon. The exemption would have to be sought under Article 101(3) TFEU and the efficiency defence under Article 102 TFEU.

In contrast to the above, proportionate rules conferring monopolistic powers on sports federations are arguably better left to the governing bodies who can legitimately insist that provisions pertaining to, for example, refereeing, disciplinary matters, independence of clubs, integrity and anti-doping must be included in the regulation of alternative competitions. The Commission acknowledged that consistency of sporting regulations and rules of the game can be achieved only by applicability of uniform, centrally drafted rules.[34] Matters of integrity, such as

---

30 Case C-519/04 *Meca-Medina and Majcen v Commission* [2006] ECR I-6991, para 42.

31 European Commission, Guidelines on the Application of Article 81(3) of the Treaty [2004] OJ C 101/97, paras 28–31.

32 See I Wendt, *EU Competition Law and Liberal Professions: an Uneasy Relationship?* (Martinus Nijhoff 2012); R Whish, *Competition Law* (6th edn, OUP 2009) 126 and; G Monti, 'Article 81 and Public Policy' (2002) 39(5) Common Market Law Review 1087–8.

33 Case C-309/99 *Wouters* [2002] ECR I-1577, para 97.

34 European Commission, Developing the European Dimension in Sport (n 19), para 4.2.

anti-corruption codes, anti-doping policies, or disciplinary matters are likely to constitute inherent rules in EU sports law and are therefore best left to the competence of governing bodies in charge of their sport, subject to the proportionality principle. They should not be entrusted to clubs and private promoters as undertakings interested in private gain as opposed to safeguarding public interest.

In *MOTOE*, Advocate-General Kokott similarly saw the uniformity of these rules as enabling participants to compare their performances, which would not be so easy if rules varied greatly from one organiser to another. Without them, in her Opinion, the public's interest and the recognition of the sport might suffer.[35] The licensing system for clubs in general was listed as an example of a sporting rule unlikely to infringe the EU competition provisions in the Commission Staff Working Document.[36] Ensuring the financial stability of sport clubs/teams is also seen as one of the objective justifications, as it relates to the organisation and proper conduct of competitive sport.[37]

According to the Commission, licensing systems generally aim to ensure that all clubs respect the same basic rules on financial management and transparency, but could also include provisions regarding discrimination, violence, protection of minors and training. In *Piau*, the General Court accepted that FIFA regulations on a mandatory licensing system for football agents could contribute to economic progress by protecting football players, members of a sporting profession with short playing careers.[38]

In its draft preliminary guidelines on the 'Application of Competition Rules to Sport of 15 February 1999', the European Commission agreed with the then International Rugby Board (now World Rugby) that control over the official match calendar by a governing body is necessary for the good of the game, ensuring solidarity and development of sport at the grassroots level, matters which individual clubs, if allowed to act in their own self-interest, are unlikely to take into account.[39] Control over the official event calendar is not only necessary to ensure regulatory integrity and a proper balance between different events. It also ensures that certain revenues are generated not just for the elite at the top of the pyramid but

---

35 Opinion of A-G Kokott in Case C-49/07 *MOTOE* (n 22), para 92.

36 Commission Staff Working Document (n 12), para 2.2.1.7.

37 Ibid., para 2.1.5.

38 Case T-193/02 *Piau v Commission* [2005] ECR II-209, paras 100–106.

39 J Taylor and A Lewis 'Governing Body Restraint on Breakaways' (British Association of Sport and the Law Conference Paper, London, 31 March 2011).

also for the benefit of football as a whole, as the competitive playing base of the pyramid would shrink without such solidarity.[40]

The situation is more difficult when it comes to governing bodies' attempts to maintain monopoly over other issues, such as the organisation and commercial exploitation of sporting events. Conflation of regulatory and commercial functions in one body necessarily leads to conflict of interest and as such will always be carefully scrutinised. The Commission considered rules shielding sports associations from competition as a prime example of sporting rules that may infringe completion provision.[41] Thus, when a sporting federation adopts rules that lead to foreclosure in the organisational market, or that make it excessively difficult to enter or operate in that market, it will always amount to, at the very least, prima facie restriction on competition under the *Meca-Medina* test (the examples of three main ways that this may occur was outlined above in this section). That test provides that when a public interest accepted as legitimate is at the heart of the reason for restriction on commercial activity, the challenged rule will be further examined for its proportionality. The rules placing restrictions on alternative organisers that are not backed up by public interest objectives, that rely on them only as a mask for private commercial goals, or that are not connected to 'specificity of sport', are to be assessed under the standard competition law framework, and *Meca-Medina* will not be applicable. These rules may be exempted on the basis of commercial ancillarity under Article 101(1) TFEU, or economic efficiency exemption under Articles 101(3) and 102 TFEU.

The Commission in its Staff Working Document specified that the legitimate objectives of sporting rules will normally relate to the 'organisation and proper conduct of competitive sport'.[42] It lists a number of public interest goals that have so far been accepted as legitimate in the sports-related jurisprudence of the Court and Commission decisional practice. These include the ensuring of fair sport competitions with equal chances for all athletes, the ensuring of uncertainty of results, the protection of the athletes' health and the safety of spectators, the encouragement of training of young athletes, the ensuring of financial stability of sport clubs/teams or the ensuring of a uniform and consistent exercise of a given sport.[43] The Commission also emphasised that the

---

40 Ibid.

41 Commission Staff Working Document (n 12), para 2.2.2.1.

42 Ibid., para 2.1.5.

43 Ibid.

'specificity of sport' will be taken into consideration when assessing the existence of a legitimate objective.

Accordingly, in sports where lower tiers of competition and grassroots are reliant on the mechanisms of financial solidarity, the governing bodies of such sports can legitimately require a part of the profits from the alternative events to be transferred for the benefit of lower tiers of the game. Richer clubs participating in prestigious competitions usually depend on harvesting young talents and players developed by the less well-off clubs and leagues. Keeping those lower tiers financially afloat is important both for the game and to preserve their socio-cultural contribution, and it would not be sustainable to have private promoters free-ride on their developmental efforts. Financial solidarity can also be used as a mechanism of competitive balance, the maintenance of which was held as a legitimate objective in *Bosman*.[44]

Additionally, financial solidarity is one of those public policy objectives that can be repackaged as an economic efficiency argument under Article 101(3) TFEU. When UEFA notified its joint selling (TV broadcasting) arrangements to the Commission, it relied on financial solidarity as a justification for exemption under Article 101(3) TFEU. It submitted, and the Commission accepted, that its financial solidarity model supports the development of European football by ensuring a fairer distribution of revenues. The Commission considered, on the basis of well-established case law, that a solidarity model improves production and stimulates the development of the sport and emphasised that it is in favour of the financial solidarity principle.[45]

Whether or not particular financial contributions required from the alternative organisers will pass the competition test ultimately depends on their proportionality. This is the very core of the *Meca-Medina* analytical framework that usually determines the outcome and requires a case-by-case approach. It is important to remember when carrying out proportionality assessment that sometimes rules that are not restrictive enough can be a cause for infringement, as much as rules that are overly restrictive.[46] The cases discussed below in this chapter will highlight the approach of the courts and the competition authorities at both EU and the Member State level in various factual contexts pertaining to restrictions on alternative competitions.

---

[44] Case C-415/93 *Bosman* [1995] ECR I-4921, para 106.

[45] COMP/37.398—Joint Selling of Commercial Rights (UEFA Champions League) [2003] OJ L 291/25, paras 164 and 165.

[46] See, e.g., S Hornsby, 'The Harder the Cap, the Softer the Law?' (2002) 10(2) *Sport and the Law Journal* 142.

V. COMPETITION LAW BREACHES BY ALTERNATIVE STRUCTURES

The issue of breakaway and alternative structures is usually approached from the point of view of restrictions on rival organisers by one of the three methods outlined above. But it should not be assumed that rival organisers are free from claims under Articles 101 and 102 TFEU. While tendering the media rights, drafting contracts with investors and broadcasters, designing the league structure, or running already established alternative competition, they are susceptible to committing as many competition law infringements as the governing body itself. The FIBA case against Euroleague Commercial Assets (ECA) testifies to this.

Access to the alternative league for clubs and athletes should be based on objective, clearly defined, non-discriminatory and transparent criteria. It would be hard to legally defend any closed league structure if challenged by the aspiring entrant or the federations concerned.[47] The league that consists of all European elite clubs will likely give a rise to a collectively dominant position held by those clubs, and a dominant position as regards the organiser of such league.[48] As such, these undertakings should not allow their conduct to impede the inherent competitive structure of the market. It should be kept in mind that every assessment of competition issues is very dependent on the facts of the case, structure of the market and characteristics of the sport concerned.

V.i *MOTOE*

So far, only three cases exist that raise related issues to, and provided limited guidance for, evaluating clauses in sports governing bodies' rulebooks preventing or restricting the establishment of rival structures. *MOTOE*[49] concerned Articles 102 and 106(1) TFEU in the context of the organisation and regulation of motorcycling in Greece. Addressed to the EU Member States, Article 106(1) TFEU applies to state measures of a regulatory nature which are directed at activities of an economic nature. It does not have an independent application because it is a reference provision which can be applied only in conjunction with other TFEU articles. The rationale behind Article 106(1) TFEU is that a Member

---

47 R Parrish and S Miettinen, *Sporting Exception in European Union Law* (Asser 2008) 213.

48 K Pijetlovic, *EU Sports Law and Breakaway Leagues in Football* (Asser 2015) 303–8.

49 Case C-49/07 *MOTOE* (n 22).

State may be held liable for the breaches of the Treaty by undertakings when the monopoly held by an undertaking is statutory.

The dispute arose over Article 49 of the Greek Road Traffic Code that conferred exclusive power on ELPA (the Automobile and Touring Club of Greece) to grant consents for the organisation of motorcycling events in Greece, necessary to get license from the competent ministry. ELPA was itself organising the same kinds of events in Greece. MOTOE (Greek Motorcycling Federation) was refused the consent from ELPA for no apparent reason and therefore failed to obtain license. According to MOTOE, this refusal by ELPA amounted to abuse of its monopolistic position.

The mere creation or reinforcement of a dominant position through the grant of special or exclusive rights within the meaning of Article 106(1) TFEU was not in itself considered incompatible with Article 102 TFEU. The key question was the discretion that a Member State left for the regulatory bodies to 'abuse' the conferred powers. Should an undertaking be under an obligation to engage in abusive practices, the Member State is responsible for the abuses that take place, and conversely, if an undertaking has discretion not to abuse its special powers the Member State will not be held responsible for the committed abuses.[50]

The general approach appears to be that a Court will consider Article 106(1), in conjunction with Article 102, breached when the dominant position creates the mere possibility and circumstances which can lead the undertaking to commit an abuse. The concept of abuse in this context is interpreted expansively to include creating 'a risk of an abuse of a dominant position'. This is more reminiscent of the approach to oligopolistic markets, or to substantive assessment of concentrations, than it is to the well-established approach to violations of Article 102 TFEU. On the facts of the case, ELPA was itself organising and commercially exploiting motorcycling events, and in addition was in charge of giving consent to other undertakings to organise and commercially exploit motorcycling events. These different powers placed ELPA in apparent advantage over its competitors whereby it could restrict access to the relevant market for the other operators.[51] The final word of the Court on the conflict of

[50] For analytical comment on *MOTOE* that details this point see S Miettinen, 'Policing the Boundaries between Regulation and Commercial Exploitation: Lessons from the *MOTOE* Case' in S Gardiner, R Parrish and R Siekmann (eds), *EU, Sport, Law and Policy* (Asser 2009) 137–49.

[51] Case C 49/07 *MOTOE* (n 22), para 51. In Case C-41/90 *Höfner and Elser v Macrotron* [1991] ERC I-1979 it was held that the state measure within the meaning of Art 106(1) would be unlawful where it facilitated a situation such

interests between regulatory and commercial functions created by the state was that a combination of Articles 106(1) and 102 TFEU precludes:

> a national rule which confers on a legal person, which organises motorcycling events and enters, in that connection, into sponsorship, advertising and insurance contracts, the power to give consent to applications for authorisation to organise such competitions, without that power being made subject to restrictions, obligations and review.[52]

On the facts of this case there was no such control placed upon ELPA. Miettinen concludes that *MOTOE* provides a basis to argue that all undertakings endowed with regulatory powers, and thus potentially in a dominant position, must be subject to 'restrictions, obligations and review'.[53] Weatherill suggests, with more nuance, that giving exclusive rights which lead to conflict of interests is not a problem in itself; so long as sporting federations thus endowed have 'transparent, objectively justified, and non-discriminatory procedures and criteria for selection which are followed faithfully and openly', and the applicant promoter is afforded a right to a hearing and given reasons for decisions taken, which should be reviewable by an independent body.[54]

Interestingly, long before *MOTOE*, the competition authority in Finland (*Kilpailuvirasto*) cautioned the Finnish Basketball Association that it had to exercise its market position and influence over the sport responsibly, and that its decisions had to be clearly reasoned and made in a transparent and timely manner.[55]

---

that, by exercising exclusive rights conferred on it, an undertaking cannot avoid abusing dominant position. Similarly, in Case C-203/96 *Dusseldorf* [1998] ECR I-4075 the Court held that Art 106(1) in conjunction with Art 102 will be breached where the Member State 'adopts any law, regulation or administrative provision which enables an undertaking on which it has conferred rights to abuse its dominant position'.

52 Case C 49/07 *MOTOE* (n 22), paras 51–52.

53 Miettinen (n 50), 147.

54 S Weatherill, 'Article 82 EC and Sporting "Conflict of Interest": The Judgment in *MOTOE*' (2009) 9 (1–2) *International Sports Law Journal* 3–7.

55 Decision of 5 August 1995 in Case 511/61/1994, *Suomen Koripalloliitto* (*Finnish Basketball Association*).

V.ii Commission Investigation in *FIA/Formula One* Case

Another case concerning the conflict of interest between the regulatory and commercial functions of a sport association involved the *Fédération Internationale d'Automobile* (FIA), the international association for motor sport. FIA was the organiser and promoter of motor sport championships, including Formula One.[56] It issued licences to any party wishing to take part in international motor sport events authorised by FIA, including track owners, vehicle manufacturers, organisers of motor sport events and drivers. License holders were allowed to organise or enter only those events authorised by FIA. Entering or organising events not authorised by FIA meant loss of license and the virtual end of any commercial activity in motor sport.

The Commission found evidence that a competing organisation (GTR) was, in effect, forced out of the market by these rules, and its GTR series replaced by a FIA GT Championship. Further, FIA claimed the television rights to all events incorporating the FIA name into their title, which were then transferred to International Sportsworld Communicators (ISC). It also forced the Formula One teams by the terms of tripartite Concorde Agreement to assign to it all broadcasting rights in the Formula One championship, which it then transferred to Formula One Administration Ltd (FOA), a commercial rights holder. The same agreement also prevented Formula One teams from racing in any other series comparable to Formula One for a very long period of time.

The promoters' rights were taken directly by FOA which had been given the power by the FIA to determine who could and could not be a promoter of a grand prix. The promoters' contracts prevented circuits used for Formula One races from being used for races which could compete with Formula One, while the agreements with broadcasters placed a massive financial penalty, ranging from between 33–50 per cent of the price paid, if they televised anything deemed by FOA to be a competitive threat to Formula One.[57]

In 1999, the Commission issued a Statement of Objections. It came to the preliminary conclusion that the rules described were contrary to

---

[56] Notice published pursuant to Article 19(3) of Council Regulation No 17 concerning Cases COMP/35.163 – Notification of FIA Regulations, COMP/36.638 – Notification by FIA/FOA of agreements relating to the FIA Formula One World Championship, COMP/36.776 – GTR/FIA and others (2001/C 169/03).

[57] 'Commission opens formal proceedings into Formula One and other international motor racing series' (IP/99/434, 30 June 1999).

Articles 101(1) and 102 TFEU as they gave FIA the control to block the organisation of races which competed with the events FIA promoted or organised. The Commission also objected to certain terms of the contracts between the FOA and broadcasters because they made it possible to block the organisation of motor sport events that would compete with Formula One races. Finally, the Commission objected to FIA rules according to which FIA automatically acquired TV rights to all the motor sport events it authorised even if these were promoted by a different promoter. The core of all of the objections was the conflict between FIA's legitimate role as the regulator of international motor sport and its interests in the commercial side of motor sport.[58]

In 2001 the Commission closed the case[59] after reaching a settlement with FIA's president, Max Mosley, and the CEO of FOA, Bernie Ecclestone. The settlement provided that: (i) FIA would remove certain conflicts of interest by limiting itself to the role of sport regulator without influence over the commercial exploitation; (ii) enable access to the market and factors of production (teams and circuit owners) to rival organisations provided they meet safety standards; (iii) waive its TV rights or transfer them to the promoters concerned; and (iv) remove the anti-competitive clauses from the agreements between FOA and broadcasters.[60] In 2003, the Commission ended the monitoring of compliance with the 2001 settlement.[61]

Unlike *MOTOE*, in *FIA/Formula One* there was no element of state involvement, as the powers which enabled it to control the relevant markets were not endowed by an act of public authority but by its own rules and web of private agreements. The safeguard against unjustified refusal of licenses in the *FIA/Formula One* case was the obligation to insert a new clause ensuring that legal challenge against FIA decisions would be available not only within their structure but also before national courts. In sum, both *MOTOE* and *FIA/Formula One* involved sporting bodies protecting private interests, rather than acting on behalf of public interests in general. Neither of the cases involved 'specificity of sport' in any form. This made them imperfect precedents for the standard type of restrictive rules on alternative establishments.

---

[58] 'Commission welcomes progress towards resolving the long-running FIA/Formula One case' (IP/01/120, 26 January 2001).

[59] 'Commission closes its investigation into Formula One and other four-wheel motor sports' (IP/01/1523, 30 October 2001).

[60] Commission Staff Working Document (n 12), para 2.2.2.1.

[61] 'Commission ends monitoring of FIA/Formula One compliance with 2001 settlement' (IP/03/1491, 31 October 2003).

V.iii Case C-250/92 *DLG*

The closest analogy for alternative structures is supplied by the *DLG* case decided in 1994 in the context of agriculture.[62] DLG was a cooperative purchasing association established to pursue common commercial objectives for its members, as opposed to public interest objectives relied on by sporting federations under the *Meca-Medina* test. It held only 36 per cent of the relevant market share, which is to be contrasted with the virtual monopolies held by sports governing bodies. DLG was permitted to place a restriction on their members' participation in alternative agricultural cooperatives, on the basis that the restriction in fact benefited competition and was necessary to protect legitimate goals necessary for the functioning of the cooperative. The Court said that in a market where product prices vary according to the volume of orders, the activities of cooperative purchasing associations may, relative to the size of their membership, constitute a significant counterweight to the contractual power of large producers and bring about more effective competition in some markets.[63]

A dual membership in competing cooperatives was seen to jeopardise both the proper functioning of the cooperative and its contractual power in relation to producers making each association less capable to pursue its objectives. In this sense, prohibition of dual membership did not necessarily constitute a restriction of competition and may even have had beneficial effects on competition.[64] On the other hand, the prohibition also had adverse effects on competition because it restricted the opportunity for members to join other types of competing cooperatives and thus discouraged them from obtaining supplies elsewhere.[65]

The Court held that the statutes of a cooperative purchasing association, forbidding its members to participate in other forms of organised cooperation which are in direct competition with it, was not captured by the prohibition in Article 101(1) TFEU and did not amount to abuse of a dominant position under Article 102 TFEU, so long as the restrictions were necessary to ensure the achievement of legitimate commercial objectives. In *DLG*, this meant the proper functioning of the cooperative and ensuring its contractual power in relation to producers.[66]

---

[62] Case C-250/92 *DLG* [1994] ECR I-5641.
[63] Ibid., para 32.
[64] Ibid., paras 33–34.
[65] Ibid., para 35.
[66] Ibid., paras 35, 45 and 52.

On the facts of the case it did not appear that prohibition on dual membership went beyond what was necessary to ensure that the said objectives were met. First, the restrictions covered only the farm supplies in respect of which there existed a direct relationship between sales volume and price.[67] Second, non-members of DLG, including the plaintiffs, were free to make any purchases from it on the same commercial terms and at the same prices as members, except that 'non-members' were not entitled to annual discount on the amount of the transactions carried out.[68] Finally, DLG's statutes authorised its members to buy fertilizers and plant protection products without using DLG as an intermediary, provided that such transactions were carried out otherwise than through an organised consortium.[69]

In *DLG*, much like in the subsequent *Wouters* and *Meca-Medina* judgments, the Court made it clear that a restriction on commercial freedom is not the same as a restriction on commercial freedom that restricts competition. The aims of EU competition law and policy are centred on the preservation of free competition and do not contain guarantees on unfettered commercial conduct of all the parties. In fact, the success of many pro-competitive agreements depends on the ability to restrict conduct of some of the parties. The judgment in *DLG* is often referred to as a precursor to *Wouters*, a case that supplied the core analytical framework to *Meca-Medina.* This means that even those restrictive rules on alternative leagues that do not have public policy objectives might be able to benefit from similar analysis in Article 101(1) TFEU provided that the restrictions are necessary for the attainment of legitimate commercial goals.

V.iv *ISU* Case Before the European Commission

The first time that the EU institutions have had an opportunity to deal directly with sports governing bodies' clauses restricting the participation in alternative sporting events is in the *ISU* case – currently awaiting final decision before the EU Commission.[70] ISU is recognised as a governing body and a sole regulator of the sports of figure skating and speed skating on ice by the International Olympic Committee (IOC). The facts of the case go back to December 2011 when a private promoter, Icederby

---

[67] Ibid., para 37.
[68] Ibid., para 38.
[69] Ibid., para 39.
[70] Relevant case documents available at http://ec.europa.eu/competition/elojade/isef/case_details.cfm?proc_code=1_40208 (accessed 26 Oct 2017).

International, informed ISU that it intended to organise an alternative international speed skating event with innovative competition format that combined short- and long-track skating. The ISU reacted by revising its Code of Ethics in January 2012 to include an Article 4(h), a clause forbidding participation 'in all forms of betting or support betting or gambling related to any event/activity under the jurisdiction of the ISU'.

As per ISU Communication No. 1717, the Code of Ethics, including its Article 4(h), applied to the widest range of individuals. In addition to the customary list of covered persons such as ISU officials, skaters, coaches, doctors, employees, consultants, members and their members, also volunteers at ISU events and ISU-sanctioned Member events, and all other persons who engage in any activity in relation to the ISU that is prohibited by the Code of Ethics, were covered.[71] On the basis of this article ISU refused to sanction the Icederby event that was to take place in October 2014 in Dubai, even though it was a jurisdiction in which betting activities were strictly prohibited.[72]

The Dubai event had a dedicated sum of EUR 1.4 million in prize money and it would have paid a minimum of US$37,650 and a maximum of US$130,000 to any skater merely taking part in it. This compared very well to the (typical) annual (ISU) season earnings of a long-track speed skater (US$109,000 and a short-track skater (US$31,900).[73] However, ice speed skaters were subject to two rules that made the prize money at the Dubai event (and any other non-sanctioned competition) unattainable: Rule 102(2)(ii) of the ISU's General Regulations held that any person skating or officiating in a non-sanctioned event would be ineligible to participate in events organised by ISU. Similarly, Rule 102(7) provided for the possibility of a lifetime ban from all ISU competitions, including the Winter Olympics and the World and European Championships (Rule

---

[71] See ISU Communications No. 1717 and No. 1853 available at http://www.isuresults.com/seminars/1717&1784&1853_CodeOfEthics.pdf (accessed 26 Oct 2017).

[72] B Van Rompuy, 'Dutch Speed Skating Duo Files Antitrust Complaint Against the International Skating Union' (*Lawinsport.com*, 19 November 2014) and available at https://www.lawinsport.com/articles/item/dutch-speed-skating-duo-files-eu-antitrust-complaint-against-the-international-skating-union (accessed 26 Oct 2017).

[73] D Rossingh 'Skater's Lawsuit May End Sports Bodies' Grip on Competition' (*Bloomberg*, 2 December 2014) and available at http://www.bloomberg.com/news/articles/2014-12-02/skater-s-lawsuit-may-end-sports-bodies-grip-on-competion (accessed 26 Oct 2017).

102(3)). ISU reiterated in its Communication No 1853 that these eligibility rules would be enforced against any skaters or officials that took part in the Dubai event.

Under the threat of a lifetime ban, no skater, unsurprisingly, would agree to participate in any of the non-sanctioned events. As a consequence of this, the alternative organiser, such as Icederby International, was thwarted in its attempts to enter or expand in the market for organisation of ice speed-skating events. Top athletes represent the main factor for staging commercially viable competition and the ISU eligibility rules made it virtually impossible to acquire them.

Nevertheless, two Dutch ice speed skaters, Mark Tuitert and Niels Kerstholt, saw these rules as a restriction on their professional opportunities and filed a competition complaint with the EU Commission in June 2014. They alleged that the ISU eligibility rules were in breach of Articles 101 and 102 TFEU on the grounds that a lifelong ban for participation in alternative competition was not inherent and proportionate to the pursuit of any legitimate objective and thus in violation of the *Meca-Medina* formula. In addition, the skaters highlighted that the barriers to entry and expansion on the market for the organisation of international speed-skating events, had a direct and manifest impact on their commercial interests.[74]

On the basis of this complaint the EU Commission opened formal proceedings against ISU on 5 October 2015 to test the disputed clauses against the EU competition law parameters.[75] As a response to this legal challenge the ISU amended its eligibility rules at its Congress in June 2016.[76] The new Rule 102(2) of ISU Constitution and General Regulations 2016[77] provides that 'a person becomes ineligible to participate in ISU activities and competitions by skating or officiating in an International Competition not sanctioned by the ISU'. ISU Rule 102(7)(d)

---

[74] B Van Rompuy, 'European Commission's ISU Antitrust Investigation Explained' (*Asser International Sports Law Blog*, 5 October 2015) and available at http://www.asser.nl/SportsLaw/Blog/post/the-european-commission-s-isu-antitrust-investigation-explained-by-ben-van-rompuy#_ftnref7 (accessed 26 Oct 2017).

[75] 'Antitrust: Commission opens formal investigation into International Skating Union's eligibility rules' (IP/15/5771, 5 October 2015).

[76] ISU Communication No. 2004, Agenda of the 56th Ordinary Congress, Dubrovnik, June 2016., available at http://www.isu.org/inside-synchronized-skating/synchronized-skating-rules/communications-sys/464-isu-communication-2004/file (accessed 26 Oct 2017).

[77] Available at http://www.isu.org/isu-statutes-constitution-regulations-technical (accessed 26 Oct 2017).

provides for a sliding scale of sanctions ranging from warning to ineligibility for a lifetime. Specifically, it provides that:

> ISU Council shall i) issue a warning in case of minor, first time violations; ii) impose an ineligibility period for up to five years in case of medium heavy violations and in case of repeated minor violations; iii) impose an ineligibility period for up to ten years in case of serious violations; iv) impose an ineligibility period up to life time in case of very serious violations, especially intentional violations which endanger the integrity and jurisdiction of the ISU.

Further, the applicable sanctions are to be determined in accordance with the principle of proportionality, meaning that each case will be considered on its own merits. In particular, 'the degree of fault of the offender, his previous record and the seriousness of the violation with regard to the objectives of the ISU ... the integrity of the ISU's sports and *other legitimate interests* of the ISU', play a role in determining the sanctions.[78] When taken together with the nuanced set of sanctions, it appears that the principle of proportionality is invoked only when the offence has already been classified as minor, medium, serious, or very serious and prescribed one of the applicable range of sanctions.

There is, however, little guidance provided in the ISU's regulations as to what constitutes minor, medium and serious offences. Only the category of 'very serious offence' is broadly defined in Rule 102(7)(d)(iv) and it refers to 'intentional violations which endanger the integrity and jurisdiction of the ISU'. This can be interpreted to indicate that a very long ban or a lifetime ban will be imposed in cases of participation in non-sanctioned events, as they are the very activities that directly compromise the integrity and jurisdiction of the ISU. As such, the amendments to the ISU eligibility rules appear largely cosmetic and do not deal in any way with the issue of disproportionate sanctions for the skaters taking part in unauthorised events. This is surprising given that the reason for which they were introduced was to address the concerns raised by the EU Commission when it opened formal proceedings in the case.

The Commission implicitly recognised that the amendments to the eligibility rules were insufficient in this regard when it issued a Statement

---

[78] Rule 102(3) has remained unchanged and provides that only eligible persons are permitted to take part in ISU Events, including the Olympic Winter Games and other International Competitions. Rule 103(2) provides for reinstatement of ineligible persons upon their application once they have served half of the period of ineligibility determined, or 15 years in case of ineligibility for life-time.

of Objections on 27 September 2016.[79] This is a formal step in antitrust investigation that sets out the position of the Commission and gives the respondent an opportunity to be heard before the adoption of a binding decision. The Commissioner in charge of the EU competition policy, Margrethe Vestager, stated that, in its preliminary view, the Commission considered that the ISU's approach restricted both the commercial freedom of athletes and the entry to the market for the new organisers of international speed skating events. It also indicated that the restrictive clauses in the ISU's regulations would be tested under the *Meca-Medina* framework.[80]

In its response to the Statement of Objections, the ISU emphasised that independent organisers are in fact able to stage international tournaments on the ISU international calendar. In support of this claim, they cited a recently authorised event in the Netherlands co-organised by Icederby International, the private entity which initiated the competition investigation via the two Dutch complainants. According to ISU, this furnished a proof rendering unfounded the Commission's claim that alternative organisers are foreclosed from the market.[81]

If ISU can indeed prove that the entry to the organisational market of this sport is practically possible and that any refusal to sanction rival entities is only for ethical and integrity purposes, and/or to ensure that health and safety of the skaters are adequately safeguarded, they would be one step closer to successfully defending their rules. It will be the proportionality of the chosen methods to attain such legitimate objectives that will be integral to the assessment of the validity of its eligibility rules under the TFEU competition provisions. Having said that, it is extremely unlikely that a lifetime ban for participating in an unsanctioned event would be considered proportionate and as would any other sanction or rule that could effectively put an end to athletes' careers.

---

[79] 'Antitrust: Commission sends Statement of Objections to International Skating Union on its eligibility rules' (IP/16/3201, 27 September 2016).

[80] Ibid. As a matter of update, the Commission issued (still unpublished) decision in *ISU* case on 8 December 2017 confirming its position in the Statement of Objections (see http://europa.eu/rapid/press-release_IP-17-5184_en.htm). The ISU appealed the Commission decision before General Court on 22 February 2018 (Case T-93/18).

[81] 'ISU believes that the European Commission's antitrust allegations are unfounded' (*ISU Press Release*, 27 September 2016) and available at http://www.isu.org/press-releases/2016/2076-press-release-ec-antitrust2/file (accessed 26 Oct 2017).

The decision in this case is widely projected to alter the classic landscape of the European model of sport. It will supply an important precedent that will sooner or later affect the structure of organisational markets in all other sports in Europe, so the influence of the decision extends far beyond skating. For example, in the near future, football will likely see the emergence of alternative European cross-border league and the above will provide guidance on how that league might be properly and proportionately sanctioned by both the UEFA and the relevant national associations.

VI. ALTERNATIVE LEAGUES IN NCA'S AND MS NATIONAL COURTS' DECISIONS

It must be noted that the Commission's position in the ISU Statement of Objections comes as no surprise given the outcomes in the series of cases that took place before the Member States' national courts and national competition authorities in the past few years. The cases discussed in this section involve similar restrictions on competition as presented by the *ISU* case, and they replay, in various forms, the underlying issues of conflation of regulatory and commercial functions in a single governing body. All of the national enforcers took the same line of approach in assessing the legality of the restrictive rules in cases decided after *Meca-Medina*, providing inter alia an indication of the effectiveness of mechanisms for preserving uniformity in the decentralised system of EU competition law enforcement.

VI.i Sweden: *SBF v KKV* and *IFBB* Cases

In 2012 and 2014, the Swedish enforcers had an opportunity to rule on two sports cases on alternative events under EU competition law. In *SBF v KKV*,[82] the Swedish Automobile Sports Federation (SBF, *Svenska Bilsportförbundet*) responsible for organising automotive sport in Sweden challenged the decision of the Swedish Competition Authority (KKV, *Konkurrensverket*)[83] according to which SBF Common Rules forbidding

---

[82] Case A 5/11, *Svenska Bilsportförbundet v Konkurrensverket* (20 December 2012) and available at http://www.konkurrensverket.se/en/news/good-for-competitors-spectators-and-the-development-of-automobile-sports/ (accessed 26 Oct 2017).

[83] Swedish Competition Authority (Konkurrensverket) Swedish Automobile Sports Federation, Decision dnr. 709/2009 (13 May 2011) and available at

its members from participating as drivers and event staff in races not sanctioned by the SBF are contrary to EU competition law.

In its decision KKV found that the clauses were obviously aimed at preserving the SBF's monopoly, while being harmful to drivers and other interested parties, restricting competition and inhibiting the development of the automotive sport.[84] The Swedish Market Court (*Marknadsdomstolen*) confirmed the decision of KKV, and decided on the case without making a preliminary reference to the Court of Justice of the EU.[85] It mirrored the approach by the KKV and accepted as legitimate the socio-cultural and educational objectives of sport, as well as the need to ensure safe competition but considered the restrictions a disproportionate means of attaining those objectives.[86]

In particular, the SBF failed to convince the Market Court that less restrictive means were not available and that the objectives could only be safeguarded by the challenged measures which constituted an absolute ban on competition. After the court pronounced its judgment, SBF was required to amend its Common Rules and remove the clauses preventing their members taking part in 'unsanctioned' automotive events.

Commenting on the case, Lindholm correctly noted that the Market Court was not willing to rule on the organisational model of sport as such.[87] This approach is consistent with the EU policy discussed above emphasising the autonomy of sport to organise itself and refusing to be prescriptive as regards any structural model of sport.

It took only a couple of years before another private promoter relied on the *SBF v KKV* precedent before the Swedish Competition Authority. In 2014, BMR Sport Nutrition AB submitted a complaint under Article 101 TFEU against the Swedish Bodybuilding and Fitness Federation (SKKF), the only national member of International Bodybuilding Federation

---

http://www.konkurrensverket.se/en/news/more-should-be-able-to-organise-motor-racing-events/ (accessed 26 Oct 2017).

[84] Swedish Competition Authority (Konkurrensverket) Swedish Automobile Sports Federation, Decision dnr. 709/2009 (13 May 2011) para 69.

[85] Case A 5/11, *Svenska Bilsportförbundet v Konkurrensverket* (20 December 2012) paras 15 and 107 in which the Market Court refused the request by SBF to make preliminary reference to CJEU.

[86] Ibid., paras 144–146.

[87] J Lindholm, 'The Impact of SBF v KKV on Sport: Swedish Fender-Bender or European Pileup?' (2013) 34(7) *European Competition Law Review* 367–72, 370.

(IFBB).[88] More specifically, the complaint targeted the so-called 'loyalty clause' in SKFF by-laws that provided for fines and suspensions for the members (athletes, coaches, officials and judges) who participate in contests that are not sanctioned by the SKFF or IFBB. The Swedish Competition Authority closed the investigation into this case after SKFF committed to amending the 'loyalty clause' and removing the threat of fining or sanctioning their members for participation in unsanctioned events.[89] It can safely be assumed that had the decision been reached, it would have mirrored the outcome in the *SBF v KKV* case.[90]

VI.ii *Show Jumping Ireland* case

In May 2012, the Irish Competition and Consumer Protection Commission (ICCPC) closed their investigation into Article 299N of the Show Jumping Ireland (SJI) Rulebook that prevented their members from competing at unaffiliated show jumping events where the prize fund exceeded €50/£50.[91] Any breach of this rule had entailed penalties for members. ICCPC considered that the rule likely breached Irish and EU

---

[88] Swedish Competition Authority (Konkurrensverket), Bodybuilding and Fitness Competitions, Decision dnr. 590/2013 (28 May 2014) and available (in Swedish) at http://www.konkurrensverket.se/beslut/13-0590.pdf (accessed 26 Oct 2017).

[89] Konkurrensverket (Swedish Competition Authority) news item 'Svenska Kroppskulturförbundet ändrar tillämpning av lojalitetsregel' (translation: Swedish Bodybuilding Association changes its application of loyalty clause) 2 June 2014, available at http://www.konkurrensverket.se/nyheter/svenska-kroppskultur forbundet-andrar-tillampning-av-lojalitetsregel. See also Swedish Competition Authority Annual Report 2014 available at http://www.konkurrensverket.se/globalassets/english/publications-and-decisions/annual-report-2014.pdf (accessed 26 Oct 2017).

[90] For more on the case 'Swedish Bodybuilders' (*Competition Law Insight*, 10 June 2014) and available at http://www.competitionlawinsight.com/region/europe/swedish-bodybuilders-100584.htm (accessed 26 Oct 2017) and B Van Rompuy, 'Sport and EU Competition Law: Uncharted Territories – (I) The Swedish Bodybuilding Case' (*Asser International Law Blog*, 12 September 2014) and available at http://www.asser.nl/SportsLaw/Blog/post/sport-and-eu-competition-law-uncharted-territories-i-the-swedish-bodybuilding-case-by-ben-van-rompuy#_ftnref7 (accessed 26 Oct 2017).

[91] Competition and Consumer Protection Commission of Ireland, 'Show Jumping Ireland Amend Allegedly Restrictive Rule' (1 May 2012), case summary available at https://www.ccpc.ie/business/enforcement/civil-competition-enforcement/closed-investigations/show-jumping-ireland-restrictive-rule/ (accessed 26 Oct 2017).

competition law because it not only prevented SJI members from participating in unaffiliated events but it also and simultaneously prevented third parties from organising and hosting such unaffiliated events.

The SJI committed to amend the rule to address the competition concerns. Members of SJI who enter into an unaffiliated show can now be penalised only if the show (i) has not signed up to the specified Health and Safety Standards; and, (ii) has not provided the SJI with evidence of adequate insurance.[92]

Equivalent competition law decisions against restrictive clauses of national sports governing bodies could be seen in decisions of Italian[93] and Finnish[94] competition authorities.

VI.iii Belgium: *Global Champions League* case

In July 2015 in the so-called *Global Champions League* case,[95] the Belgian Competition Authority (BCA) examined a clause in the International Equestrian Federation (FEI, *Federation Equestre Internationale*) General Regulations according to which FEI had exclusive rights to accredit international equestrian competitions. To receive FEI accreditation organisers were required to waive intellectual property rights even when their events did not bear the FEI name, and to comply with all FEI rules, regulations and requirements even when their contests and series did not count towards the Official FEI classification.[96]

---

[92] Compecon (*Competition & Regulatory e-zine No 9*, July 2012, 9–10) and available at http://www.compecon.ie/attachments/File/EZ9.pdf (accessed 26 Oct 2017).

[93] See Italian Competition Authority (*Autorità Garante della Concorrenza e del Mercato*) decisions in Case A378 *Italian Equestrian Sports Federation*, decision no 18285 of 28 July 2008, Bollettino no 19/2008, available at http://www.agcm.it/component/joomdoc/bollettini/19-081.pdf/download.html (accessed 26 Oct 2017); and Case A396 *Gargono Racing*, decision no. 19946 of 11 June 2009, Bollettino no. 23/2009, available at http://www.agcm.it/concorrenza/concorrenza-delibere/open/41256297003874BD/5764581408C13D8EC12575E60039872C.html (accessed 26 Oct 2017).

[94] The Finnish Competition Authority (*Kilpailuvirasto*) decision of 18 December 2002 in Case 625/61/2002, *AKK – Motorsport ry*, and decision of 5 August 1995 in Case 511/61/1994, *Suomen Koripalloliitto* (*Finnish Basketball Association*).

[95] Autorité belge de la Concurrence (Belgian Competition Authority) [2015] Décision no. ABC-2015-V/M-23 of 27 July 2015, available at https://www.bma-abc.be/sites/default/files/content/download/files/2015vm23-abc-pub.pdf (accessed 26 Oct 2017).

[96] Ibid., para 75.

The 'exclusivity clause' further included a six-month suspension from FEI accredited events for athletes, horses, and officials, who participated in events and/or competitions not accredited by the FEI.[97] The governing body claimed that the exclusivity clause was adopted in order to protect the welfare of horses and integrity of competitions.[98]

When Global Champions League (GCL) applied for authorisation of a new league alongside its existing competitions, FEI declined to approve it mostly on the basis that its own Nations Cup series was sufficient to meet the demands of the sport and its participants. This reason for blocking the new GCL league became apparent from the transcripts of the long negotiations that lasted for more than a year. It was clear that without FEI authorisation, the Global Champions League that was scheduled for April 2016, would not be organised and the project would have to be abandoned. GCL therefore applied to BCA for interim measures to suspend the application of the exclusivity clause. This request was held admissible and well-founded by the BCA who ordered the FEI to suspend Article 113(4)–(6) of the General Regulations with respect to the participation of athletes and horses in the Global Champions League until the final decision in the case. In addition, the FEI was to indicate unambiguously in its news section that 'no athlete or horse may be suspended or sanctioned as a result of participating in a competition organized under the Global Champions League'.[99]

On 28 April 2016, the BCA refused the FEI request for annulment of the BCA interim measure. Instead, it confirmed its validity and also upheld BCA's prima facie assessment of infringement of Belgian and EU competition laws.[100]

In deciding on the temporary measure, the BCA doubted the real motivation behind the exclusivity clause and noted that the approval process lacked transparency and clarity, which should have been the case given the conflict of interest between FEI regulatory and commercial functions. Moreover, the BCA considered that the approval process was not based on the sporting aspect (because GCL already complied with all of them). The BCA also took into account a range of factors surrounding the approval process and including the fact that: it was not applied without any discrimination and not proportionate to the sporting objectives; that it was accompanied by strict deadlines; that even if a contest

[97] Arts 113 (4)–(6) and 156 (9) of the FEI General Regulations.

[98] Autorité belge de la Concurrence (n 95), para 58.

[99] Ibid., Operating part of the decision, p 159.

[100] Brussels Court of Appeal, Case 2015/MR/1, *Fédération Equestre Internationale/Autorité Belge de la Concurrence*, 28 April 2016.

or series complied with all the rules and regulations of the FEI (as the Global Champions League did) the FEI could still refuse to give its consent for arbitrary and commercial reasons in its sole discretion; and, finally, the BCA had highlighted that in 2012 and 2013, when the contested clause was introduced, the FEI's revenues immediately doubled.

Consequently, the BCA concluded that the FEI's exclusivity clause prevented an independent organiser or promoter from accessing the 'raw materials' of equestrian sports (i.e., athletes, horses and officials) as no internationally competing athlete would participate in a non-accredited competition given that such participation would prevent him/her from participating in any national and international competition accredited by the FEI for six months. On the basis of these factors, the BCA concluded that the FEI approval process, applied in the context of the FEI's exclusivity clause, allowed the FEI to abuse its position as a sports regulator in order to promote its own commercial interests at the expense of alternative organisers and independent promoters, such as the Global Champions League.[101]

VI.iv Germany: *Euroleague Basketball* and *NRWTV Triathlon* cases

Interim measures were also granted in June 2016 by the Munich Regional Court in *Euroleague Basketball v FIBA and FIBA Europe*.[102] The background of the dispute is interesting and procedurally unique. In February 2016, Euroleague Basketball filed a complaint on the basis of Article 102 TFEU before the EU Commission against FIBA and FIBA Europe for putting pressure on clubs, players and referees to force them to abandon the Euroleague and the Eurocup organised by Euroleague Commercial Assets (ECA) and only participate in FIBA competitions.

National federations that took no steps to discipline their clubs and domestic leagues in this regard would lose their national team rights to participate in 2016 Rio Olympic Games and EuroBasket 2017 organised by the respondents.[103] Two months later, FIBA launched an equivalent

---

[101] Autorité belge de la Concurrence (n 95), paras 61–80. For more on the case see A Haffner and K Mistry, 'The Law on Banning Athletes from Competing in Rival Sports Leagues' (*Lawinsport.com*, 5 October 2016) and available at https://www.lawinsport.com/blog/snr-denton-blog/item/the-law-on-banning-athletes-from-competing-in-rival-sports-leagues (accessed 26 Oct 2017).

[102] Munich Regional Court I, Case no.: 1 HK 0 8126/16.

[103] 'Euroleague Basketball presents a complaint before the European Commission against FIBA and FIBA Europe' (*Euroleague Basketball News Item*,

counter-complaint before the EU Commission against ECA for breaches of Article 102 TFEU, referring to the legal action against itself and FIBA Europe as a 'smokescreen' intended to mask ECA's own anti-competitive behaviour. Specifically, FIBA's complaint related to: (i) abusive compliance by ECA that imposed undue pressure on leagues and clubs and threatened them with exclusion from Euroleague; (ii) the undermining of any commercial and sporting value of domestic leagues and the competitive balance in European basketball by arbitrarily cherry-picking clubs for Euroleague and Eurocup, and; (iii) abusively discriminating against financially weaker clubs, thereby placing them at a further competitive disadvantage. In sum, and according to FIBA: 'ECA wished to reap the benefits of the basketball ecosystem developed by national federations (players, coaches, referees, thousands of other clubs) without contributing to the foundations of the sport's pyramid and holding the national teams hostage to serve the interests of six commercially powerful clubs.'[104]

In May 2016, a group of Euroleague and Eurocup clubs, domestic leagues and Euroleague Basketball petitioned the Munich Regional Court for interim relief in an attempt to avoid irreversible damage to national teams before the EU Commission could rule on the complaint by Euroleague Basketball.[105] A temporary measure was granted on 2 June 2016. The judge in the case prohibited FIBA Europe and FIBA from sanctioning or threatening to sanction, directly or indirectly, the applicants (the basketball clubs, National Basketball Federations, or national or supra-national basketball leagues in the geographic area of FIBA Europe) because of their decision or intention to cooperate with ECA and its subsidiaries.[106]

---

22 February 2016) available at http://www.euroleaguebasketball.net/euroleague-basketball/news/i/6p8c54yjk66qsitp/euroleague-basketball-presents-a-complaint-before-the-european-commission-against-fiba-and-fiba-europe (accessed 26 Oct 2017).

[104] 'FIBA files complaint against Euroleague' (*FIBA Press Release*, 5 April 2016) available at http://www.fiba.com/news/fiba-files-complaint-against-euroleague (accessed 26 Oct 2017).

[105] 'Munich Regional Court Rules against FIBA and FIBA Europe' (*Euroleague Basketball News Item*, 3 June 2016) available at http://www.euroleaguebasketball.net/euroleague-basketball/news/i/6xfdyb9eg4ex5ioa/munich-regional-court-rules-against-fiba-and-fiba-europe-sanctions (accessed 26 Oct 2017).

[106] Munich Regional Court (Landgericht München I), AZ.: 1 HK O 8126/16, *Euroleague and others v FIBA Europe and FIBA*, available (in German) at http://www.euroleague.net/rs/6xk9t4qutjtn5uf4/84bd1f8d-134d-42a0-a8ee-cd688d29aaa2/f03/filename/munich-court-decision-german.PDF (accessed 26 Oct 2017).

The EU Commission now has an option to open a formal investigation into this dispute(s), or to reject the complaint(s) on the basis of there being no sufficient EU interest.[107] As far as predicting the outcome of the potential investigation, both complaints have merit. ECA would be forced to revamp the rules on access to their competitions (to become open, transparent and non-discriminatory), and release the clubs from obligation to play in both Euroleague and Eurocup. At the same time, FIBA would be required to remove the threat of sanctions against any of the parties taking part in ECA organised competitions. However, if FIBA can prove that the manner in which ECA competitions are organised jeopardises domestic leagues, and that the chosen sanctions are the least restrictive method capable of protecting domestic leagues, it is not inconceivable that it might prevail in both cases.

The EU Commission will hopefully join the two cases and open the full investigation leading to a formal decision and it is hoped, provide clarification on an acceptable way to organise an alternative sporting structure.[108]

Finally, a less complicated scenario was presented in another German case.[109] In April 2013, the Higher Regional Court of Dusseldorf held valid the fees that North Rhine-Westphalia Federation (NRWTV) was charging to private organisers of triathlon competitions in exchange for benefits, such as providing advertising space in their newsletter and website. The fact that the federation itself was active on the organisational market and had a conflict of interests in regulating and commercially exploiting the sport, and that there existed an actual restriction on competition, did not affect the outcome of the case. The fees charged in the case were not disproportionate to the actual benefits received.[110] Therefore, in the circumstances when a private entity did not

---

107 'Commission Notice on the handling of complaints by the Commission under Articles 81 and 82 of the EC Treaty (Text with EEA relevance)' [2004] OJ C 101, 65–77.

108 For more on the case see M Montejo, 'FIBA/Euroleague: Basketball's EU Competition Law Champions League- first leg in the Landgericht München' (Asser International Sports Law Blog, 15 June 2016) and available at http://www.asser.nl/SportsLaw/Blog/post/fiba-euroleague-basketball-s-eu-competition-law-champions-league-first-leg-in-the-landgericht-munchen-by-marine-montejo (accessed 26 Oct 2017).

109 Higher Regional Court of Dusseldorf (Oberlandesgericht Düsseldorf) Beschluss vom 2. April 2013 · Az. VI – U (Kart) 9/13, available at https://openjur.de/u/633726.html (accessed 26 Oct 2017).

110 The defendant charges an authorisation fee of € 30.00 for association members and € 100.00 for non-association organisers as well as a so-called event

pay proportionate fees, the refusal by the NRWTV to authorise their event was held not to have infringed EU and German competition laws on the abuse of dominant position.

VII. CONCLUSION

A recent wave of cases discussed in this chapter illustrate the kind of assessment of restrictions on alternative organisers that will be carried out by the enforcers of EU competition law at both European and national level. Even though EU law refuses to be prescriptive as regards a structural model for European sports, it would be wrong to think that it cannot and will not force changes in those models indirectly via other routes.

Cases such as *SBF v KKV* show that inconsistency with the competition law of certain governing bodies' rules leads to modifications that indirectly open up previously non-existent possibilities in the organisational market. This in turn causes a change in the structure of that market. Indeed, there is no legally justified reason for sports governing bodies to insist on being a single undertaking in a market for the organisational services or on being the owner of the commercial rights in all of the sporting events under their regulatory competence.

Conversely, the vertical pyramid structure of regulatory authority in sport has a good chance of survival under the EU competition law, provided that the principle of proportionality is respected. Even though there is a good degree of fluidity in application of the economic provisions in sports industry and which requires a case-by-case analysis, what makes a decisive difference in the outcome of the cases is whether a specific regulatory rule protects public or private interests, and whether the 'specificity of sport' is involved. Those regulatory rules that serve private gains and do not benefit from the notion of 'specificity of sport' are likely not to pass the *Meca-Medina* test. As a matter of law, such rules may nevertheless benefit from similar commercial ancillarity analysis, Article 101(3) exemption and/or the equivalent economic efficiency defence under Article 102 TFEU.

Sporting federations that maintain clauses in their rulebooks designed to block competing organisers will be forced to make necessary amendments and comply with the newly clarified legal environment if and when

tax. This amounted to a uniform 10 per cent of the start-up funds received by 2011 and amounts to € 2.00–10.00 for each participant at an approved event, depending on the competition distance.

challenged. The possibilities of entry into the organisational market for potential competitors, as well as the possibility of expansion for the existing market, must exist. This is bound to bring about a re-characterisation of the sports industry making it even more attractive for potential investors and opening even more commercial opportunities.

17. Sport, free movement and nationality

Stefaan Van den Bogaert

I. INTRODUCTION

In the seminal case of *Walrave and Koch v UCI* in 1974, the Court of Justice of the European Union issued the principled statement that sport is part of EU law insofar as it constitutes an economic activity within the meaning of the Treaty.[1] This resulted in the first application of the Treaty rules on free movement to the rules of a sporting federation. Two years later, in *Donà v Mantero*, the Court would reiterate this position, again in the context of a dispute concerning the conformity of a sporting rule with the fundamental freedoms.[2] The Court rendered these judgments in spite of the absence of a clear EU competence in the field of sport.

Originally, sport did not figure in the European Treaties. Only with the entry into force of the Lisbon Treaty in 2009 would sport become an official – albeit merely supportive, coordinating or supplementing – EU policy.[3] This however did not prevent the European institutions, in the first place the Court of Justice, from exerting a considerable indirect influence on sporting affairs, when assessing the compatibility with EU law of contested sporting rules.[4] Initially, when the opportunity presented itself, the Court invariably opted for settling a dispute on the basis of the free movement provisions (Arts 45 and 56 TFEU). Most of these cases dealt with instances of discrimination on grounds of nationality. Only at a later stage, would it also start ruling on the lawfulness of contested sporting rules under the Treaty rules on competition law.[5]

---

[1] Case 36/74 *Walrave and Koch v UCI* [1974] ECR 1405, para 4.

[2] Case 13/76 *Donà v Mantero* [1976] ECR 1333 para 12.

[3] Article 165 TFEU.

[4] See e.g., S Weatherill, '"Fair Play Please": Recent Developments in the Application of EC Law to Sport' (2003) 40 *Common Market Law Review* 51; S Van den Bogaert and A Vermeersch, 'Sport and the EC Treaty: A Tale of Uneasy Bedfellows?' (2006) 31 *European Law Review* 821.

[5] See e.g., E Szyszczak, 'Competition and Sport' (2007) 32 *European Law Review* 95; S Weatherill, 'Anti-doping Revisited – the Demise of the Rule of "purely sporting interest"?' (2006) 27 *European Competition Law Review* 645.

This contribution first provides a general overview of the main rules and principles concerning the Treaty free movement provisions. The focus is primarily on the free movement of workers and the freedom to provide services. Secondly, it specifically analyses the case law of the Court of Justice as regards nationality discrimination in sport.

II. SPORT AND FREEDOM OF MOVEMENT

Essentially, the right to free movement entails the right for EU citizens to move to another Member State, reside in the host Member State, and work there under the same conditions as the host State's nationals.[6] Articles 45 and 56 TFEU are the specific expression of the cardinal Treaty prohibition of discrimination on grounds of nationality laid down in Article 18 TFEU. Articles 45 and 56 TFEU have direct effect.

In *Walrave*, the European Court of Justice (now CJEU) had held that these provisions could also be relied upon before national courts in proceedings against rules of a sporting federation. The prohibition of discrimination 'does not only apply to the action of public authorities, but extends likewise to rules of any other nature aimed at regulating in a collective manner gainful employment and the provision of services'.[7] The fundamental Treaty objective to remove restrictions to freedom of movement would be compromised if the abolition of national barriers could be neutralised by obstacles resulting from private associations' exercise of their legal autonomy.[8] Moreover, limiting the prohibition of discrimination to acts of a public authority 'would risk creating inequality in their application'.[9]

The examination of the compatibility of a contested sports rule with the free movement provisions entails three steps: first, it needs to be assessed whether, and if so, which Treaty provision is actually applicable to the situation at hand; secondly, it must be examined whether the applicable right to freedom of movement has been infringed or not; before finally, the attention turns to the issue of justification.

---

[6] For more information, see e.g., P Craig and G de Búrca, *EU Law. Text, Cases and Materials* (6th edn OUP 2015).

[7] Case 36/74 *Walrave and Koch v UCI* [1974] ECR 1405, para 17.

[8] Ibid., para 18.

[9] Ibid., para 19.

II.i The Application of Articles 45 and 56 TFEU

To trigger the application of Articles 45 and 56 TFEU, a set of criteria must be met: first, the athlete concerned must be a national of an EU Member State; secondly, he must perform an economic activity, i.e., be considered as a 'worker' or as a 'service provider'; and thirdly, a cross-border element must be present in the situation.

The first condition is straightforward: in principle, only nationals of the currently 28 Member States of the EU are entitled to invoke the Treaty free movement rights before national courts. A Belgian football player can rely on Article 45 TFEU before an Italian judge, a South-African football player cannot. Nationals of non-EU countries cannot directly derive free movement rights from the Treaty. This does not mean they do not enjoy any free movement protection whatsoever under EU law.[10] The precise content and extent of their rights must be assessed on a case-by-case basis.

The second condition entails that the athlete must be engaged in an economic activity. The concepts of 'worker' or 'provision of services' not having been defined in the Treaties, the Court has almost consistently interpreted them widely. In relation to the concept of 'worker', the Court stated that the 'essential feature of an employment relationship is that for a certain period of time a person performs services for and under the direction of another person in return for which he receives remuneration'.[11] A part-timer worker enjoys full free movement protection, even if the pay is below the minimum level of subsistence.[12] The economic activity must be 'genuine and effective, and not merely marginal and ancillary'.[13]

The distinguishing feature between a worker and a self-employed service provider is the element of subordination, which is absent in the provision of services. Previously in *Walrave*, the Court had little difficulty in holding that when the practice of sport has the character of gainful employment or remunerated service it comes within the scope of

---

[10] S Van den Bogaert, *Practical Regulation of the Mobility of Sportsmen in the EU Post Bosman* (European Monographs 48, Kluwer Law International 2005), 79–108.

[11] Case 66/85 *Lawrie Blum v Land Baden-Württemberg* [1986] ECR 2135, para 17; Case 139/85 *Kempf v Staatssecretaris van Justitie* [1986] ECR 1741, para 14.

[12] Case 53/81 *Levin v Staatssecretaris van Justitie* [1982] ECR 1035, para 15.

[13] Ibid., para 17.

Articles 45 or 56 of the Treaty.[14] Later, in *Bosman* and *Lehtonen*, the Court unequivocally stated that football players and basketball players are workers for the purposes of the Treaty.[15]

In practice, this second hurdle to the application of the free movement provisions is often relatively easily taken. The Court's decision in *Deliège* nicely illustrates this.[16] Deliège was a Belgian judoka who challenged her federation's refusal to select her to participate in an international judo tournament. She claimed this refusal constituted a violation of her right to freedom to provide services. Conversely, the judo federation was of the opinion that the case concerned a matter – amateur sport – not subject to EU law. It argued that sports associations are entitled freely to determine the conditions governing access to competitions which concern only amateur sportsmen.

In that regard, the Court observed that 'the mere fact that a sports association unilaterally classifies its members as amateur athletes does not in itself mean that those members do not engage in economic activities within the meaning of the Treaty'.[17] It proceeded to state that sporting activities and, in particular, a high-ranking athlete's participation in an international competition, are 'capable of involving the provision of a number of separate, but closely related, services' which may fall within the scope of the Treaty, even if some of those services are not paid for by those for whom they are performed.[18] It illustrated this with the example that an organiser of such a competition may offer athletes an opportunity of engaging in their sporting activity in competition with others; while at the same time, the athletes' participation in the competition enables the organiser to put on a sports event which the public may attend, which television broadcasters may retransmit and which may be of interest to advertisers and sponsors. Moreover, the athletes provide their sponsors with publicity the basis for which is the sporting activity itself.[19]

Ultimately, the Court left it to the national court to determine whether Deliège's sporting activities constituted an economic activity, but, by subtly referring to grants awarded to her on the basis of sporting results

---

[14] Case 36/74 *Walrave and Koch* (n 7), para 5.

[15] Case C-415/93 *Bosman* [1995] ECR I-4921; Case C-176/96 *Lehtonen* [2000] ECR I-2681.

[16] Cases C-51/96 and C-191/97 *Deliège v Ligue de Judo* [2000] ECR I-2549.

[17] Ibid., para 46.

[18] Ibid., para 56.

[19] Ibid., para 57.

and to sponsorship contracts directly linked to the results she achieved,[20] it left little doubt as to its stance on this issue.

At the outset, it was more or less generally assumed that amateur sport – which does not qualify as an economic activity – did not come under the scope of the Treaty. However, it has become clear now that EU law also grants free movement rights to amateur sportsmen.[21] First, the practice of sport can be considered as a 'social advantage' within the meaning of Article 7(2) Regulation 492/2011.[22] EU nationals who exercise their free movement rights to work in another Member State also have the right to practise sport at amateur level in the host Member State, without being discriminated vis-à-vis the host State's nationals. The underlying thought is that sports practice is conducive to facilitate the integration of migrant workers and their families in their new environment.

Secondly, the introduction of the concept of European citizenship has considerably strengthened the position of non-economically active nationals of an EU Member State who want to practise sports at amateur level in another EU Member State.[23] An EU national legally residing in a host Member State can invoke the Treaty citizenship provisions to challenge discriminatory practices in amateur sports.

The third criterion requires the presence of a trans-frontier element in the situation. EU law does not apply to 'wholly internal' situations.[24] In *Bosman*, the European football association UEFA considered that the dispute precisely for that reason fell outside the ambit of the Treaty, as it concerned a Belgian player whose transfer fell through because of the conduct of a Belgian club and a Belgian association. However, the Court pointed to the fact that Bosman had entered into a contract of employment with a club in another Member State and held that this constituted the factor bringing the player's situation under the scope of EU law. In general, the Court is willing to readily accept the presence of a

20 Ibid., para 51.

21 Van den Bogaert (n 10), 66–74.

22 Regulation (EU) No 492/2011 of the European Parliament and of the Council of 5 April 2011 on freedom of movement for workers within the Union [2011] OJ L 141/1.

23 Part Two TFEU.

24 Case 175/178 *R v Saunders* [1979] ECR 1129, para 11.

cross-border element to trigger to application of EU law.[25] This third condition does not often pose problems in practice.

II.ii The Establishment of a Restriction to Articles 45 and 56 TFEU

Once it has been determined that the conditions for the application of Articles 45 or 56 TFEU have been fulfilled, it must be examined whether the free movement rights of the athletes have been infringed in a given situation. Article 45(2) TFEU stipulates that the freedom of movement for workers entails the 'abolition of any discrimination based on nationality between workers of the Member States as regards employment, remuneration and other conditions of work and employment'. Article 56 TFEU prohibits 'restrictions on freedom to provide services within the Union in respect of nationals of Member States who are established in a Member State other than that of the person for whom the services are intended'.

Concretely, the Treaty provisions exclude, in the first place, discriminatory treatment of migrating EU nationals as regards nationals of the host Member States. Both direct and indirect discrimination are in principle prohibited. Direct discrimination occurs when the explicit ground for the differential treatment of foreign EU nationals in a comparable situation is nationality. Indirect discrimination implies different treatment of persons in a comparable situation on an apparently neutral ground, such as language or residence, which actually or potentially puts foreigners in a disadvantageous position.[26] Unsurprisingly, therefore, the Court ruled in *Donà* that rules of a sporting organisation, which limit the right to take part in football matches as professional or semi-professional players solely to the nationals of the State in question, are incompatible with Articles 48 or 56 of the Treaty.

In addition, the Court in *Bosman* has also held that the free movement provisions are intended to facilitate the pursuit by EU citizens of occupational activities of all kinds throughout the Union, and hence preclude measures which might place EU citizens at a disadvantage when they wish to pursue an economic activity in the territory of another Member State.[27]

---

[25] See e.g., N Nic Shuibhne, 'Free Movement of Persons and the Wholly Internal Rule: Time to Move on?' (2002) 39 (4) *Common Market Law Review* 731.

[26] Case C-237/94 *O'Flynn v Adjudication officer* [1996] ECR I-2617.

[27] Case C-415/93 *Bosman* (n 15), para 94.

> Rules which preclude or deter an EU national from leaving his country of origin in order to exercise his right to freedom of movement therefore constitute an obstacle to that freedom, even if they apply without regard to the nationality of the workers concerned.[28]

The transfer rules in issue were considered to directly affect players' access to the employment market in other Member States and were thus capable of impeding freedom of movement for workers.[29] Likewise, in the case of *Olivier Bernard*, the Court held that rules requiring a young football player, at the end of his training period, to sign a professional contract with the club which trained him, under pain of being sued for damages, are likely to discourage this player from exercising his right of free movement. Even if such rules do not formally prevent the player from signing a professional contract with a club in another Member State, they nevertheless make the exercise of that right less attractive and constitute therefore a restriction on the freedom of movement for workers.[30]

The wide interpretation of the concept of restriction notwithstanding, the Court in *Deliège* also ruled that the contested selection rules in themselves could not be regarded as restriction on the freedom to provide services prohibited by Article 56 TFEU. Even though selection rules inevitably have the effect of limiting the number of participants in a tournament, such a limitation is viewed as inherent in the conduct of an international high-level sports event, which necessarily involves certain selection criteria.[31] The concept of 'restriction' is thus not all-encompassing. Moreover, the Court also established that certain effects ensuing from the application of a particular rule may simply be 'too uncertain and indirect' a possibility for particular rules to be capable of being regarded as liable to hinder freedom of movement for workers.[32]

II.iii The Existence of a Justification

A measure which constitutes an obstacle to freedom of movement can be accepted only if it pursues a legitimate aim compatible with the Treaty and complies with the requirements of the principle of proportionality.

A restrictive measure may be allowed as a derogation expressly provided for by the Treaty. The Treaty stipulates that limitations may be

---

28 Ibid., para 96.
29 Ibid., para 103.
30 Case C-325/08 *Olivier Bernard* [2010] ECR I-2177, paras 35–37.
31 Cases C-51/96 and C-191/97 *Deliège* (n 16), para 64.
32 Case C-190/98 *Graf v Filzmoser Maschinenbau GmbH* [2000] ECR I-493.

justified on grounds of public policy, public security or public health.[33] It also states that the free movement provisions do not apply to employment in the public service or the exercise of official authority.[34] This list of Treaty derogations is exhaustive. Alternatively, restrictions may also be justified, in accordance with the case law of the Court, by overriding requirements in the public interest.[35] Especially this latter category of objective justifications has already played an important role in the Court's case law concerning sports. In particular, in *Bosman*, the Court – importantly – accepted the aims of maintaining a balance between clubs by preserving a certain degree of equality and uncertainty as to results and of encouraging the recruitment and training of young players as legitimate, 'in view of the considerable social importance of sporting activities and in particular football in the European Union'.[36]

In *Lehtonen*, the Court further acknowledged that the setting of transfer deadlines may meet the legitimate objective of ensuring the regularity and proper functioning of sporting competitions.[37] Clearly, the Court is receptive to the argument that 'sport is special'.[38] In *Bernard*, the Court explicitly confirmed this, stating that in ascertaining whether a restrictive measure may be justified, 'account must be taken of the specific characteristics of sport in general, and football in particular, and of their social and educational function. The relevance of those factors is also corroborated by their being mentioned in the Article 165(1) TFEU'.[39]

Evidently, even if a restrictive measure does indeed pursue a legitimate objective, its application still has to be such as to ensure achievement of the objective in question and not go beyond what is necessary for that purpose.[40] Otherwise the measure is incompatible with the Treaty free movement provisions. The Court in *Lehtonen* ultimately left it up to the

33 Articles 45(3) and 52 TFEU.

34 Articles 45(4) and 51 TFEU.

35 This was accepted for the first time by the Court in the *Cassis de Dijon* in the context of free movement of goods: Case 120/78 *Rewe-Zentrale AG v Bundesmonopolverwaltung für Branntwein* [1979] ECR 649.

36 Case C-415/93 *Bosman* (n 15), para 106.

37 Case C-176/96 *Lehtonen* (n 15), para 53.

38 See e.g., R Parrish and S Miettinen, *The Sporting Exception in European Union Law* (Asser 2007); E Szyszczak, 'Is Sport Special?' in in B Bogusz, A Cygan and E Szyszczak (eds) *The Regulation of Sport in the European Union* (Edward Elgar Publishing 2007) 3.

39 Case C-325/08 *Olivier Bernard* (n 30), para 40.

40 See e.g., T Tridimas, 'Proportionality in Community Law: Searching for the Appropriate Standard of Scrutiny', in E Ellis (ed.) *The Principle of Proportionality in the Laws of Europe* (Hart 1999) 65.

national court to decide whether the differential treatment between basketball players from a federation in the European zone and that of players from a federation not in that zone could be justified, in *Bosman* and *Bernard* the Court reached the conclusion that the restrictive measures at issue did not comply with the requirements of proportionality and could thus not be maintained.

III. DISCRIMINATION ON GROUNDS OF NATIONALITY IN SPORT

As the Treaty free movement rules are in essence a specific expression of the general prohibition of discrimination on grounds of nationality laid down in Article 18 TFEU, it does not come as a surprise that a substantial part of the Court's case law relating to free movement and sport concerns instances of nationality discrimination.[41] Discrimination on grounds of nationality frequently occurs in sports. Usually, nationality clauses take two different forms: either they exclude athletes from playing for a certain team or from taking part in a sporting competition on grounds of their (foreign) nationality; or they consist of quantitative restrictions for clubs to contractually engage and/or field foreign players in official contests.

III.i Nationality Clauses at Club Level

First, so far the Court of Justice of the EU has firmly and consistently rejected all discriminatory measures at club level as incompatible with European law.[42] The first time the Court had to deal with this issue was in the case of *Donà v Mantero*. The Court was asked to scrutinise a number of rules of the Italian Football Federation, according to which only professional or semi-professional football players who were affiliated to the federation were entitled to take part in official matches, membership in that capacity being open only to players of Italian nationality.

[41] See e.g., S. Weatherill, 'Discrimination on Grounds of Nationality in Sport' (1989) 9 *Yearbook of European Law* 55; S Van den Bogaert, 'From Bosman to Bernard C-415/93; [1995] ECR I-4921 to C-325/08; [2010] ECR I-2177' in J Anderson (ed.), *Leading Cases in Sports Law* (Asser 2013) 91–106.

[42] S Van den Bogaert, *Practical Regulation of the Mobility of Sportsmen in the EU Post Bosman* (European Monographs 48, Kluwer Law International 2005), chap 6.

Having confirmed its principled statement from two years earlier in *Walrave* that sports comes within the scope of EU law insofar as it constitutes an economic activity, the Court proceeded to hold that this applied to the activities of professional or semi-professional football players, which are in the nature of gainful employment or remunerated service. Where such players are nationals of a Member State, they benefit in all the other Member States from the Treaty provisions on freedom of movement of persons and freedom to provide services. Finally, the Court concluded that the rules allowing only nationals to take part in matches organised by the responsible national federation amounted to discrimination and were thus contrary to Articles 18, 45 and 56 TFEU.

As a result, sporting federations were no longer entitled to completely exclude foreign EU sportsmen from participating in official matches at club level. That did not mean however, that federations set the door wide open for foreigners. To the contrary, many, if not all federations, continued to set limitations on the number of foreigners to be recruited and/or fielded in official matches. These restrictions varied from one federation to another, from one sport to another, from one season to another, from one level to another, etc.

The Court's subsequent dismissal of the UEFA '3+2' nationality clause in *Bosman* appears to have shut the door for sporting federations' more favourable treatment of domestic players over foreign players with the nationality of a country belonging to the EU or the European Economic Area. According to this '3+2' rule, national associations were permitted to limit to three the number of foreign players whom a club could field in any first division match in their national championships, plus two players who had played in the country of the relevant national association for an uninterrupted period of five years, including three years as a junior. The same '3+2' limitation also applied to matches in UEFA's European Cup competitions for club teams.

The Court had little difficulty in establishing the existence of an obstacle to the freedom of movement, holding that 'in so far as participation in matches is the essential purpose of a professional player's activity, a rule which restricts that participation obviously also restricts the chances of employment of the player concerned'.[43] Subsequently, the '3+2' rule also failed to pass the justification hurdle.[44]

None of the arguments put forward by the sporting associations and by the intervening governments succeeded in detracting the Court from its

---

43 Case C-415/93 *Bosman* (n 15), para 120.

44 Ibid., paras 121–137.

finding of a violation. First, the Court unequivocally quashed the argument, based on the role served by the nationality clauses, in maintaining a traditional link between a club and country. According to the Court, a football club's links with the Member State in which it is established cannot be regarded as any more inherent in its sporting activity than its links with its locality, town or region. It pointed out that there exists no such rule restricting the right of clubs to field players from other regions, towns or localities in official matches either.

Secondly, the Court also failed to be convinced by the supposed indispensability of the nationality clauses for the good of the national team. It observed that although the right to freedom of movement:

> by opening up the employment market in one Member State to nationals of the other Member States, has the effect of reducing workers' chances of finding employment within the Member State of which they are nationals, it also, by the same token, offers them new prospects of employment in other Member States.[45]

In addition, football clubs must release their foreign players for official matches of their national team.

Thirdly, the Court also ruled that the nationality clauses are not an appropriate means to preserve a certain competitive equilibrium between clubs: these clauses may prevent the richest clubs from engaging the best foreign players, but there are no rules limiting the possibility for such clubs to recruit the best national players, 'thus undermining that balance to the same extent'.[46]

Finally, in reply to the argument that the '3+2' rule had been drawn up in collaboration with the European Commission, the Court categorically answered that the Commission could not give guarantees concerning the compatibility of specific practices with the Treaty and that in no circumstances does it have the power to authorise practices which are contrary to the Treaty. In the light of the discriminatory nature of these nationality clauses, this strict approach of the Court is rather unobjectionable.

The *Bosman* decision forced the sporting associations to fully liberalise the EU sports employment market for sportsmen from EU/EEA countries. English football club Manchester United is now, for instance, entitled to play with 11 Dutchmen. In the wake of the *Bosman* ruling, masses of EU/EEA athletes have made use of their free movement rights.

---

[45] Ibid., para 134.
[46] Ibid., para 135.

In football, foreign players nowadays take up a significant portion of the total number of players in any given league in Europe. Sport can be considered as a paradigm of migration in Europe. As a result, a typical team squad in many a sporting discipline is nowadays composed of a mixture of national players, EU citizens and also third-country nationals.

Be that as it may, to be perfectly clear, the Court's ruling in *Bosman* did not signal the end of nationality clauses at club level. The judgment only concerned the Treaty rights of EU/EEA citizens. Many sporting associations decided to cling to quota with regard to third-country nationals. In 2003, the Court was invited for the first time to express its opinion on the legality of such nationality requirements. The case of *Kolpak* involved a professional handball goalkeeper of Slovak nationality who played in the German second division and who challenged the rule of the German handball federation, stipulating that clubs were entitled to field only two non-EU/EEA nationals in official matches.[47]

Importantly, at the material time, Slovakia was not a EU Member State yet. The Court concluded that Kolpak, who was legally employed in Germany, could legitimately invoke Article 38(1) of the Association Agreement concluded between the European Communities and Slovakia, which confers the right to equal treatment to Slovak nationals as regards working conditions, remuneration and dismissal in the EU in relation to the host Member State's nationals. Again, the Court showed no inclination to accept the arguments to justify the contested rule, which were grossly the same as in *Bosman.*[48]

Admittedly, the dispute in Kolpak concerned a national from a country which was, at the time of the proceedings, at the verge of becoming an EU Member State. The impression could therefore not entirely be discarded that the final outcome, in particular the Court's stance on the justification issue, might have been different had the case involved a sportsman from a non-accession country. After *Kolpak*, the situation was still not completely clarified. An excellent occasion to settle the issue presented itself two years later. In the case of *Simutenkov*, a Russian footballer playing for Tenerife complained that the Spanish football federation had issued a license as a non-EU player, subjecting him to the quota for non-EU/EEA nationals.[49] Russia has no plans to join the EU.

---

[47] Case C-438/00 *Kolpak* [2003] ECR I-4135.

[48] For more information, see J-P Dubey, 'Case Note on *Kolpak*' (2005) 42 *Common Market Law Review* 499; S Van den Bogaert, '... And Another Uppercut from the Court of Justice to Nationality Requirements in Sports Regulations' (2004) 29 *European Law Review* 267.

[49] Case C-265/03 *Simutenkov* [2005] ECR I-2579.

Notwithstanding this, in its judgment, the Court followed exactly the same line of reasoning as in *Kolpak*, enabling Simutenkov to base his claim for an EU license directly on Article 23(1) of the Partnership Agreement concluded between the European Communities and Russia. The Court refrained from entering into an in-depth analysis of the justification issue, seemingly conveying the message that the hard line it had previously adopted with regard to nationality discrimination of EU/EEA nationals is to be extended to nationality clauses concerning certain 'privileged' third-country nationals.

The potential impact of the *Kolpak* and *Simutenkov* decisions is far-reaching. For non-EU/EEA sportsmen to be able to successfully challenge nationality clauses, four cumulative criteria must be met: (i) they must be legally employed in a host EU Member State; (ii) an international agreement establishing a partnership or association must be concluded between the EU and its Member States and the country of origin of the non-EU/EEA athletes concerned; (iii) the international agreement must contain an equal treatment provision as regards working conditions, remuneration and dismissal in the host EU Member State; and (iv) that provision must be directly effective. The EU has concluded international agreements containing a similar equal treatment clause with a large number of third countries.[50]

To give but one example: in 2000, the EU and its Member States have concluded the Treaty of Cotonou, a partnership agreement between the EU and 78 ACP (Africa – Caribbean – Pacific) countries. And arguably, several of these equal treatment clauses in these international agreements may fulfil the criteria for direct effect, enabling legally employed third-country national sportsmen to rely on them before the courts of the host Member State, so as to render the nationality clauses inapplicable to them.[51]

---

50 C. Hillion, 'Case Note on *Simutenkov*' (2008) 45 *Common Market Law Review* 815; S Van den Bogaert, 'Free Movement for Workers and the Nationality Requirement', in H Schneider (ed.) *Migration, Integration and Citizenship: A Challenge for Europe's Future, Vol. I* (Forum Maastricht 2005), 55.

51 Art 13(3) of the Cotonou Treaty stipulates that:

> the treatment accorded by each Member State to workers of ACP countries legally employed in its territory, shall be free from any discrimination based on nationality, as regards working conditions, remuneration and dismissal, relative to its own nationals.

The Court of Justice, however, has not yet ruled on the possible direct effect of this provision.

Leaving the requirement of legal employment in the host Member State out of the equation for a moment – after all this primarily belongs to the competence of the Member States – at EU level the lifeline of nationality clauses at club level in sport appears now thinner than ever. This is all the more so taking into consideration the nationality legislation of some (mainly Southern) European countries, allowing third-country nationals (especially South-Americans) to obtain a national passport and thus also EU citizenship status relatively easily, through a quick naturalisation procedure. While playing for Real Madrid, former Brazilian football stars Ronaldo or Roberto Carlos acquired Spanish nationality, allowing the most successful European football club to practically circumvent the prohibition from the Spanish federation to field more than three third-country nationals in official matches. And at the same time, they could hold on to their Brazilian nationality and continue to play for the national team of Brazil.

In view of the foregoing, the practical relevance or effectiveness of nationality clauses has inevitably diminished from a legal point of view. Many 'foreigners' enjoy some form of free movement protection. Notwithstanding this, many sporting federations still have not abandoned the idea of nationality clauses altogether. To the contrary, and for years, the world's football governing body FIFA continues to promote versions of its so-called '6+5' rule, according to which clubs must start official matches with six players eligible to play for the national team of the club's country.

The main identified aims of the rule are the improvement of sporting competition in European football, the promotion of junior players and the protection of national identity and the national teams.[52] The '6+5' rule received strong backing in football circles but met with fierce opposition in European circles. Both the European Commission and the European Parliament expressed negative opinions about the rule as it is clearly at odds with the *Bosman* judgment. The proposed '6+5' rule is in essence virtually identical to the '3+2' rule, which the Court in *Bosman* considered to be an unjustifiable restriction to the right to the freedom of movement for workers: whereas the former prescribes that six players eligible to play for a club's country must feature in the club's starting line-up, the latter holds that a maximum of five foreign players may be fielded during matches.

52 See INEA, Expert Opinion on the Compatibility of the '6+5 Rule' with European Community Law, available at: http://inea-online.com/download/regel/gutachten_eng.pdf (accessed 26 Oct 2017).

Almost the same rule, almost the same objectives, only new clothes. Introducing the '6+5' rule would therefore boil down to a return to the pre-*Bosman* era. This would necessitate a radical reversal of the Court's approach with regard to nationality requirements. This appears unlikely; since it concerns the sacrosanct prohibition of discrimination on grounds of nationality. And a Treaty change introducing an exemption for sport from the normal application of the Treaty free movement (and competition) rules seems equally improbable, given the unanimity requirement. Hence, so far FIFA has – wisely – refrained from introducing the '6+5' rule, backing away from an open confrontation with the EU institutions.

Within Europe, the European football association UEFA has also had its say in the debate, adopting the home-grown rule providing that each club must have a certain number of domestically trained players under contract. This rule applies only for matches in the Europa and Champions League, but UEFA encourages the national federations to apply it also domestically. According to this '4+4' rule, a minimum eight players out of a squad of maximum 25 must be 'domestically trained': a minimum of four players must have received their training at the club itself; the remaining of these (minimum eight) players must have been trained by other clubs from the same country. A player is qualified as 'domestically trained' when he has received three years of training at a club between the age of 15 and 21.

Again, the question arises whether the '4+4' rule is in conformity with EU free movement law.[53] At first sight, UEFA's home-grown rule appears to be favouring local players, nationals of the club's country, and therefore inevitably runs the risk of being qualified as indirectly discriminatory. This prompts the question whether the measure can nevertheless be justified. The training of young players has been recognised by the Court as a legitimate objective. The first requirement that a number of players must be trained locally at club level seems therefore acceptable. Whether that is also the case with the additional requirement that a number of players must have received their training in the same country is less straightforward. Here the underlying objective also seems to be the desire to ensure a sufficiently large reservoir of talent available for the national team.

---

[53] S Miettinen and R Parrish, 'Nationality Discrimination in Community Law: An Assessment of UEFA Regulations Governing Player Eligibility for European Club Competitions (The Home-Grown Player Rule)' (2007) 5(2) Entertainment and Sports Law Journal, Online: https://www.entsportslawjournal.com/articles/10.16997/eslj.68/print/ (accessed 26 Oct 2017).

The CJEU has however rejected this as a justification ground in *Bosman*. In any event, ultimately, the '4+4' rule must also withstand the test of proportionality: is the measure appropriate and necessary to achieve its objectives? The outcome of this balancing act hinges on the level of scrutiny by the CJEU. On the one hand, the home-grown rule only directly concerns a limited number of players and leaves the clubs a large room for manoeuvring: the '4+4' rule has no impact whatsoever on 17 out of the 25 available places in the team squad. In practice, this means it does not exert any direct influence on the starting 11 for an official match. On the other hand, a rule simply stipulating that clubs are obliged to include a number of junior players in their squad appears to be a plausible and less restrictive alternative to achieve the goal of ensuring the training of young players. The age limit could, for example, be set at 21, as the FIFA Regulations on the Status and Transfer of Players deem training to be completed at that age, or at 23, as training compensation needs to be paid for transfers until that age.[54]

Consequently, it is not certain whether UEFA's home-grown rule would survive (unscathed) a challenge before the Court of Justice. The European Commission has first chosen to carefully monitor the implementation of the home-grown rule. A 2012 study it commissioned to study its impact reached inconclusive results, and recommended that a further study be conducted on whether alternative measures, that do not carry discriminatory effects, can deliver more substantial benefits for European football.[55] In a 2014 reasoned opinion however, the Commission requested Spain to change its rules on the composition of basketball teams, indicating that the applicable quotas for locally trained players, which resulted in reserving for these players between 40 and 88 per cent of the available jobs in the basketball teams, amounted to indirect indiscrimination of players from other Member States. The UEFA home-grown rule (32 per cent of the posts in each team) was referred to as an example of a quota seemingly proportionate in pursuing the

---

[54] FIFA Regulations on the Status and Transfer of Players (2016), available at http://resources.fifa.com/mm/document/affederation/administration/02/70/95/52/regulationsonthestatusandtransferofplayersnov2016weben_neutral.pdf (accessed 26 Oct 2017).

[55] Study on the Assessment of UEFA's 'Home Grown Player Rule': Negotiated procedure EAC/07/2012 (University of Liverpool and Edge Hill University, 30 April 2013) and available at http://ec.europa.eu/assets/eac/sport/library/studies/final-rpt-april2013-homegrownplayer.pdf (accessed 26 Oct 2017).

legitimate aims of promoting the training of young players and maintaining a fair competition between clubs.[56]

The European Parliament, for its part, has been more explicit in its support for the home-grown rule.[57] This stance is probably to be perceived as a predominantly political choice: the home-grown rule is less intrusive in the composition of a team and hence probably also less effective to pursue the stated objectives, but it is arguably less problematic from the point of view of European law. A choice for the possibly legally acceptable UEFA home-grown rule above the in all likelihood legally unacceptable FIFA '6+5' rule?

Apart from the '6+5' rule or the '4+4' rule, there has been some speculation about a joint proposal from FIFA and UEFA to introduce the '9+9' rule. Supposedly, this would entail that clubs could list 18 players on the official match sheet during European Cup competitions, nine of which would have to be trained in the country of the club. A minimum of two of these locally trained players would also need to start the match. Clearly, this proposal seeks the middle of the road between the home-grown rule and the '6+5' rule. Until now, the European institutions have not expressed themselves on this proposal. Clearly, this story is not over yet …

III.ii The Composition of Representative National Teams

Although the Court of Justice invariably condemns nationality clauses at club level as a violation of EU law; it so far has been equally consistent in refusing to interfere with instances of nationality discrimination concerning matches between national teams. In the early cases of *Walrave* and *Donà*, the Court established that the free movement provisions 'do not prevent the adoption of rules or of a practice excluding foreign players from participation in certain matches for reasons which are not of an economic nature, which relate to the particular nature and context of such matches and are thus of sporting interest only'.[58] This hands-off approach of the Court in relation to national teams has not met

---

[56] European Commission, 'April Infringements Package: Main Decisions' (Memo 14/293, 16 April 2014) available at: http://europa.eu/rapid/press-release_MEMO-14-293_en.htm (accessed 26 Oct 2017).

[57] European Parliament resolution of 8 May 2008 on the White Paper on Sport (2007/2261(INI)).

[58] Case 36/74 *Walrave and Koch* (n 1), para 8; Case 13/76 *Donà v Mantero* [1976] ECR 1333, para 14.

with substantive criticism; for instance, in his opinion on *Bosman*, A-G Lenz stated that it appears 'obvious and convincing'.

This may very well still be the case, but it must be acknowledged that in contemporary society, the Court's explanation for this 'restriction on the scope of EU law'[59] often simply does no longer reflect reality. In many sports, matches between national teams are no longer of 'purely sporting interest'. Nowadays, sports and business have become inextricably linked during competitions between national teams. Global events such as the Olympic Games or the World Cup in football have an enormous economic impact, not only for the organising country, but also for the participating teams and federations and last, but certainly not least, also for the individual athletes.

The Court of Justice has realised this very well. In *Meca-Medina*, it effectively dismantled this concept of 'rules of purely sporting interest', that was continuously invoked to justify an exemption from the application of the Treaty rules, virtually stripping it of any legal significance.[60] It also appears to have fine-tuned its position towards sporting rules such as, in particular, rules concerning the composition of national teams: these rules now come under the scope of the Treaty, but can in principle be tolerated, in view of the objectives they pursue and the overall context in which the rules produce their effects, provided the restrictive effects they produce are inherent in the pursuit of these objectives and are furthermore proportionate to them.[61]

This underpinning of the Court's attitude towards national teams under EU law is much more satisfactory: on the one hand, it reflects the assumption that in encounters between national teams, matters such as national pride and identity still play an important role and, in principle, outweigh the economic and financial interests at stake. As a result, these matches, in principle, deserve shelter from the application of EU law. On the other hand, it does not turn a blind eye to the reality that matches between national teams often become huge commercial events. Therefore, when the restrictive effects of these particular nationality clauses go beyond what is deemed necessary and inherent to organise matches between national teams, the Treaty provisions come into play.

In its 2007 White Paper on Sport, the European Commission explicitly stipulated that the right to select national athletes for national team

---

59 Case 36/74 *Walrave and Koch* (n 1), para 9.

60 Case C-519/04 P *Meca-Medina and Majcen v Commission* [2006] ECR I-6991. See also Weatherill (n 5).

61 Case C-519/04 P *Meca-Medina and Majcen* ibid., para 42. See also Case C-309/99 *Wouters* [2002] ECR I-1577, para 77.

competitions constitutes a limited and proportionate restriction to the principle of free movement.[62] It is indeed not to be expected that this legal fine-tuning of the Court in *Meca-Medina* will bring about major changes in practice. When Germany defends its title at the 2018 World Cup in Russia, all players of 'the Mannschaft' will in all likelihood still have the German nationality. However, contrary to the Commission's unequivocal assertion, it is advocated that it cannot entirely be excluded that the Court – if confronted with the issue – might nevertheless impose some small modifications to the rules on the composition of national teams, specifically with regard to the situations of naturalised athletes and of sportsmen with a dual nationality.[63]

In most sports, participating in the Olympics or the World Championships is the ultimate challenge. Most athletes are prepared to do just about anything to be able to compete in these international competitions. Nationality changes are becoming increasingly frequent. However, not all federations have a uniform position in this respect. Some allow an athlete to compete for a country when s/he has acquired the nationality of the country, regardless of whether s/he has previously already competed for another country, whereas others prohibit a sportsperson wearing the shirt of two different countries during their career. There are also federations which make the permission to compete for another country conditional upon fulfilment of a number of conditions, such as a waiting period.

A priori, it would appear reasonable that EU law accepts as inherent in the organisation of a sporting competition, and therefore unproblematic, the rule that only nationals of a given country may represent that country during international competitions between national teams. However, it is much less evident that a rule which stipulates that one national may be selected to appear for the national team of his country whereas the other national is not eligible for that same team, for the simple fact that he has already worn the shirt of another national team, is really necessary. This is all the more so because of the diverging positions of sporting federations on this particular issue. If such a rule were deemed to go beyond what is necessary, it would come under the Court's scrutiny.

It is a generally accepted principle of international law that each country determines under which conditions it confers its nationality on

---

[62] White Paper on Sport, COM(2007) 391 final.

[63] S Van den Bogaert, 'Discriminatie op grond van nationaliteit in de sport: de saga duurt voort' in M Olfers (ed.) *Discriminatie op grond van nationaliteit in de sport* (Sport en Recht nr. 19, Arko Sports Media 2012) 7.

someone.[64] Whoever meets these criteria, should in principle also be entitled to represent the national sports team of that country, regardless of whether he has already played for another national team. In order to avoid possible abuses – some countries try to lure athletes with money to compete for them and adopt flexible nationality laws – additional rules concerning limited waiting periods or to ensure the existence of a genuine link between an athlete and a country, appear legitimate.

Ultimately, everything will hinge upon the level of scrutiny the Court is willing to exercise. In view of the limited competences of the EU in sport and the often-tense relationship between sport and EU law, this review is expected to be marginal. A more fundamental overhaul of the rules, possibly allowing also long-term (foreign) residents with a permanent residence status to compete for the national team, appears for now improbable.

III.iii Nationality Discrimination in Individual Sports

Interestingly, so far the Court of Justice never has had to deal with nationality discrimination in individual sports. Further to the Pierre de Coubertin Action Plan accompanying its White Paper on Sport, the European Commission launched a study on the equal treatment of non-nationals in individual sport competitions.[65] The study was completed in 2010 and charts the situation in 26 Olympic disciplines in the then 27 Member States of the EU. The issues under examination were whether non-nationals are entitled to participate in: (i) official competitions and (ii) national championships; and whether they are excluded from (iii) winning the national title and (iv) the winning of medals during the national championships or the setting of national records?

The study yielded a number of interesting and important findings. Often, it appeared difficult or even impossible to obtain appropriate information about the relevant regulations within a given sports in a certain Member State. Astonishingly, there is still a lot of ignorance about the requirements EU law imposes on the right to equal treatment of non-nationals. As a result, discrimination against foreign athletes is still a

---

[64] Case C-369/90 *Micheletti v Delegación del Gobierno en Cantabria* [1992] ECR I-4239.

[65] 'Study on the Equal Treatment of Non-Nationals in Individual Sports Competitions: EAC/19/2009' (Asser Institute, Edge Hill University and Leiden University, December 2010) available at http://ec.europa.eu/assets/eac/sport/library/studies/study_equal_treatment_non_nationals_final_rpt_dec_2010_en.pdf (accessed 26 Oct 2017).

widespread phenomenon in many sports. Many of the grounds invoked to justify discriminatory treatment of foreign athletes are also inadequate. Conspicuously, there appears to be little or no coherence or consistency between the various sports in one Member State nor between the various countries in relation to one sports discipline.

In Austria, for example, widely varying periods of residence are imposed on non-nationals in different sports: whereas there are no conditions of residence required from non-nationals before they can participate in athletics meetings, they must be resident in Austria for a minimum two years before they can take part in weightlifting competitions. The required period of stay is three years in swimming and archery and amounts to even five years in shooting!

To be able to participate in rowing competitions during a given year, non-nationals must be resident in the country on January 1 of that year in Belgium and Finland; in Estonia all competitions are open to all; in Sweden there is a residence requirement of one year; and in Austria one of three years. The cardinal Treaty rule of prohibition of discrimination on grounds of nationality unmistakably applies equally to individual sports. Consequently, to ban all instances of nationality discrimination in individual sports within the EU, a lot of sporting associations' regulations will have to be amended. A crucial role in this will be reserved to the European Commission to make sporting federations and Member States aware of this important need.[66]

By the same token, it also needs to be observed that several sports are characterised by a surprising openness: national championships in swimming and gymnastics are open to participation for foreign athletes in 11 countries, in archery in 12 and in athletics in no less than 13 Member States. Nationality discrimination certainly is thus not an omnipresent feature of individual sports. Then again, only in a very limited number of sports, such as, in particular, biathlon in Cyprus or gymnastics in France, can non-nationals effectively be crowned national champions.

---

[66] Similarly, see e.g., the recent formal request from the Commission to Croatia to stop discriminatory practices in the area of annual sport and recreational fishing licenses. European Commission, 'September Infringements Package: Key Decisions' (Memo 16/3125, 29 September 2016) available at http://europa.eu/rapid/press-release_MEMO-16-3125_en.htm pdf (accessed 26 Oct 2017).

IV. CONCLUSION

Despite the absence of a clear EU competence in the field of sport until the Lisbon Treaty, since its *Walrave* ruling, the Court of Justice of the EU has consistently adopted the same conceptual approach in cases concerning the mobility of sportsmen within the EU. The Court's search for a solution, taking into consideration the specific claims of the sporting authorities, while at the same time ensuring compliance with the exigencies of EU law, is effectuated on a case-by-case basis and is thus influenced by the circumstances of each case. In sporting circles, the Court is often criticised for over-accentuating the importance of the migration rights of the individual athletes, thereby infringing the freedom of association of the sporting associations and failing to take sufficient account of the specific needs of sport. This criticism is unfounded. In particular, the needs to ensure the training of young players, to maintain a sporting equilibrium or to preserve the regularity of sporting competitions have all been recognised as legitimate objectives capable of justifying proportionate restrictions to athletes' rights of free movement.

Several of the free movement cases concerned instances of nationality discrimination in sport. The Court has invariably brandished discriminatory measures at club level as incompatible with European law. As the law stands now, this firm position is unlikely to change. Conversely, the Court has never dealt with nationality discrimination in individual sports. In view of the cardinal importance of the principle of non-discrimination in the Treaty, there is an important task ahead for the EU institutions to address this particular issue. Nationality discrimination should not be allowed to persist in individual sports. Finally, as regards the composition of national teams, so far the Court has left this issue essentially untouched, while nevertheless refining the legal ground for this position in *Meca-Medina*. This could possibly lead to the modification of some federations' regulations vis-à-vis naturalized athletes and athletes with a dual nationality.

While the legal setting for determining the conformity of sporting rules with the EU's free movement rules seems thus sufficiently crystallised, clearly some work needs to be done with regard to nationality discrimination in sport.

18. Transfers, agents and minors

Nick De Marco

I. INTRODUCTION

This chapter considers the regulation of transfers, agents and minors in sport within the EU. Each of those topics is discussed individually in turn—with the relevant section setting out the regulatory framework and then discussing its efficacy. Where appropriate, connections between the three sections are highlighted and cross-referred. While the chapter aims to consider all regulated sports, its focus is on football, which has the most sophisticated and developed regulatory regimes in relation to these areas. Further, where national regulations are looked at in any detail, the discussion will centre on English law and regulation, reflecting the expertise of the author.

II. TRANSFERS

The EU is the largest transfer market in the world.[1] In football in the last 20 years, the number of player transfers, and the fees attached to those transfers, have increased exponentially. In 1995, the highest transfer fee paid for one player was £13m (which AC Milan paid Torino for Gianluigi Lentini).[2] By 2016, the highest transfer fee paid for one player was over six times that sum, at £89m (which Manchester United recently paid Juventus for Paul Pogba). The number of player transfers in the EU more than tripled between 1995 and 2011, and the total value of transfers in that same time has multiplied by 7.4 (in 1995 the total value of transfers

---

[1] KEA—CDES, 'Study on the Economic and Legal Aspects of Transfers of Players, EAC/17/2011' (January 2013) 6 http://www.keanet.eu/docs/full_study_transferofplayers.pdf (accessed 26 Oct 2017).

[2] A Bret, 'Analysis of the Legal Arguments in FIFPro's Challenge to FIFA's Football Transfer System' (*Lawinsport.com*, 10 March 2016) available at http://www.lawinsport.com/articles/item/analysis-of-the-legal-arguments-in-fifpro-s-challenge-to-fifa-s-football-transfer-system (accessed 26 Oct 2017).

in the EU was €402m, by 2011 it was €3bn).[3] The regulation of transfers is, therefore, of central and particular importance.

The details of player transfers in the EU differ for each sport. In essence, player transfers are changes of employment (the employers being the clubs and the employees the players). However, the frameworks of rules regulating transfers make the system quite different from general employment practice. Most notably, those rules impose significant limitations on players' freedom of movement. Further, transfer rules usually require registration by a national sports association, and prohibit players from being registered with more than one club at a time. That registration does not end when a player's employment contract ends. Instead, the club is required to separately release the player's registration before the player can transfer. Fees are often paid upon transfer, but generally only in two circumstances: first, if the player is transferred before the expiry of his contract; second, in certain defined circumstances (such as if the contract concerns a young player).

There are limitations upon when transfers are permitted, the relevant periods usually referred to as a 'transfer window'. Further, many national federations draft rules designed to defeat sham transfers, to prevent fraud and money-laundering, to limit the geographic scope of transfers, to regulate temporary transfers/loans, to regulate the negotiation of transfers.[4]

Throughout the EU member states and across different sports, player transfers are regulated by different means. All national football federations must, as a minimum standard, conform to FIFA's rules on the transfers of players. Some countries, such as Bulgaria, Greece, Hungary and Lithuania, have national Sports Acts that specifically regulate player transfers; others, such as Belgium, Italy, Portugal and Spain, govern transfers through more general legislation (such as laws on the employment of sports professionals);[5] and in yet others, like England and Wales, transfers are regulated by the national federations and the transfer rules they impose on players and clubs—parties to a transfer will agree contractually to the provisions in the national federation's rules.

As well as being regulated by national law and the rules of national and international federations, transfers within (and to) the EU are governed by Community law. Of particular relevance (unsurprisingly) are those rules surrounding free movement of workers, a principle enshrined

---

[3] KEA—CDES (n 1), 4.

[4] See A Lewis and J Taylor, *Sport: Law and Practice* (3rd edn, Bloomsbury 2014) 1480–85.

[5] KEA—CDES, (n 1), 2.

at Article 45 of the Treaty on the Functioning of the European Union (TFEU), which provides as follows:[6]

> 1. Freedom of movement for workers shall be secured within the Union.
> 2. Such freedom of movement shall entail the abolition of any discrimination based on nationality between workers of the Member States as regards employment, remuneration and other conditions of work and employment.
> 3. It shall entail the right, subject to limitations justified on grounds of public policy, public security or public health:
>   a. to accept offers of employment actually made;
>   b. to move freely within the territory of Member States for this purpose;
>   c. to stay in a Member State for the purpose of employment in accordance with the provisions governing the employment of nationals of that State laid down by law, regulation or administrative action;
>   d. to remain in the territory of a Member State after having been employed in that State, subject to conditions which shall be embodied in regulations to be drawn up by the Commission.
> 4. The provisions of this Article shall not apply to employment in the public service.

Prima facie the registration requirements of transfers are a restriction on freedom of movement, amounting to either an administrative hurdle (with an associated delay) or sometimes even a bar on free movement (in circumstances where a club refuses to register or release the registration of a player). Similarly, rules requiring the payment of a transfer fee—which may in effect deter free movement of nationals of EU/EEA member states—are potentially in violation of Article 45. Registration requirements and transfer fees will only be valid and enforceable, therefore, if objectively justified and proportionate to a legitimate aim.

Transfer rules may also, potentially, infringe Articles 101 and 102 TFEU. Article 101 prohibits as incompatible with the common market:

> all agreements between undertakings, decisions by associations of undertakings and concerted practices which may affect trade between member states and which have as their object or effect the prevention, restriction or distortion of competition within the internal market.[7]

However, the provisions of Article 101(1) may be declared inapplicable if the prohibited agreement (under art 101(3)) 'contributes to the production

---

[6] See also M Beloff, T Kerr, M Demetriou and R Beloff, *Sports Law* (2nd edn, Hart 2012) 94 for a discussion of EU free movement rules and their application to sport and transfer rules.

[7] Art 101(1) TFEU.

or distribution of goods or to promoting technical or economic progress, while allowing consumers a fair share of the resulting benefit' and does *not* 'impose on the undertakings concerned restrictions which are not indispensable to the attainment of these objectives' or 'afford such undertakings the possibility of eliminating competition in respect of a substantial part of the products in question'.[8] Article 102 TFEU prohibits 'any abuse by one or more undertakings of a dominant position within the internal market or in a substantial part of it ... in so far as it may affect trade between Member States'.

II.i Transfers and CJEU

The European Court of Justice (CJEU) considered the application of EC law to the sport sector in *Meca-Medina*.[9] The CJEU's judgment in that matter definitively sets the rules and scope for the assessment of the validity of transfer rules in relation to EU law principles on free movement and competition[10] and is therefore of paramount importance.

First, the decision established that the fact that a rule can be defined as 'purely sporting' does not exclude it from the scope of EU law. Instead, whenever a sport becomes an economic activity it falls within the scope of the TFEU (as it now is). The CJEU held, at [23]:

> Thus, where a sporting activity takes the form of gainful employment or the provision of services for remuneration, which is true of the activities of semi-professional or professional sportsmen ... it falls, more specifically, within the scope of [article 45 TFEU] ... .

And at [27]:

> In light of these considerations, it is apparent that the mere fact that a rule is purely sporting in nature does not have the effect of removing from the scope of the Treaty the person engaging in the activity governed by that rule or the body which has laid it down.

---

[8] Art 101(3) TFEU.

[9] Case C-519/04 P *Meca-Medina and Majcen v Commission* [2006] ECR I-6991, paras 22–34.

[10] See KEA—CDES (n 1), 3 and Commission Staff Working Document—The EU and Sport: Background and Context—Accompanying document to the White Paper on Sport, COM(2007) 391 final, SEC(2007)932, SEC(2007)934, SEC(2007)936, SEC/2007/0935, 35.

Second, the decision established a methodological framework for assessing whether sporting rules are compatible with EC law. It provides that account must be taken of the overall context in which the rule was adopted (particularly its objective), whether the restrictions are inherent to the pursuit of the objective, whether the restrictions are proportionate to the pursuit of the objective.[11] In any event, as pointed out by the learned authors of *Sport: Law and Practice*, transfer rules are not purely sporting rules but rules that directly regulate and impact upon the market for the services of players. Further, 'professional sports clubs are "undertakings" and professional sports associations are "associations of undertakings" ... Transfer rules are [therefore] "decisions of associations of undertakings" ... .'[12]

Domestic and international transfers and the manner in which they are regulated may affect trade within member states. Those rules also prima facie restrict competition.[13] However, even if the rules are in breach of Article 101(1), they may be justified and proportionate under Article 101(3) and therefore remain valid and enforceable.[14]

Some of the legitimate aims that transfer rules may seek to further (and thereby remain lawful under either art 101 or art 45 TFEU) can be summarised as follows. First, competitive balance: maintaining a broad competitive balance between clubs is important for the development of most sports and if unrestricted transfers of players would put that balance at risk, rules can lawfully be imposed that may restrict freedom of movement in order to mitigate the risk—transfer fees, rules prohibiting players being transferred outside a certain geographical area and financial fair play regulations can potentially be justified on this basis.

Second, 'trickle down' benefits: the smaller, low-level clubs can be rewarded for bringing on young players with promise by the payment of a transfer fee from the larger, high-level clubs to whom those young players may transfer. Third, team, contractual and seasonal stability: as

---

[11] Case C-519/04 P *Meca-Medina and Majcen v Commission* (n 9), para 42 and see Commission Staff Working Document, ibid., 36–8 for a discussion of *Meca-Medina*.

[12] See Lewis and Taylor (n 4), 1507 and Commission Staff Working Document, ibid., 66–7.

[13] In *Bosman* case, cited below, the CJEU did not come to any conclusion as to the application of art 101 TFEU to transfer rules but the Advocate General concluded that art 101 TFEU did apply, and his arguments are referred to as 'persuasive' by Lewis and Taylor, ibid., 1509.

[14] For further discussion of the application of arts 101 and 102 TFEU to sport generally see Beloff, et al (n 6), 162–70, and for the application of art 101 TFEU to transfer rules see ibid., 102ff and Lewis and Taylor, ibid., 1507–9.

sports are generally seasonal, and team performance over that season has to be planned, it is essential that the composition of teams is stable throughout a season and that the stability of contracts is also protected (which both allows clubs to plan their teams, and players to have employment security if they are injured)—the imposition of transfer windows is often justified on this basis, as are restrictions on players on loan playing for the team they are loaned to and harsh penalties for breach of contract.

Fourth, the prevention of sham agreements—obligations that transfers must be conducted in good faith, that transfer terms must be notified to the national federation and prohibitions of third party ownership are often justified on this basis. Fifth, training compensation and youth development.[15] The European Commission attaches great importance, in particular, to transfer rules that seek to promote youth development.[16]

In 1995, in the famous *Bosman*[17] ruling, the ECJ considered the application of Article 45 to transfer rules. Bosman was a player registered with Liege in Belgium, who wanted to transfer to Dunkerque in France. Although Bosman was out of contract, the rules at the time permitted Liege to refuse the transfer unless Dunkerque met their transfer fee demand. Dunkerque did not make the payment and the transfer did not take place. Bosman claimed (before the Belgian courts, who referred the matter to the CJEU) that the transfer fee request was an unjustified fetter upon his fundamental freedom to move across member states' borders for the purposes of work. He also argued that the restriction on his movement was anti-competitive and thereby in violation of Articles 101 and 102 TFEU.

The Advocate General found that 'competitive balance' was a justifiable aim but that the transfer rules in question did not foster competitive balance, nor were they the least restrictive means of fostering competitive balance.[18] The CJEU agreed with the Advocate General and held that the transfer fee in those circumstances constituted a prohibited restriction on the free movement of workers in the EU—that is, that fees cannot be demanded for international transfers for out of contract players.[19] One key consequence of this decision is that a player can now transfer for free

---

[15] For further discussion of the aims that may justify a restriction on freedom of movement see Lewis and Taylor, ibid., 1486–95.

[16] See KEA—CDES (n 1), 3.

[17] C-415/93 *Bosman* [1995] ECR I-4921 and for detailed discussion see Beloff et al (n 6), 98ff.

[18] C-415/93 *Bosman*, ibid., 5016.

[19] Ibid., 5072, para 107.

at the end of their contract, often known as a 'Bosman transfer'.[20] This feature of the modern transfer rules is an important factor in the way values in the transfer market are calculated today. Players may also use the threat of running down their contract and thus reducing their transfer value as a means of leveraging their club for a new contract and salary increase.

Following *Bosman*, the European Commission warned FIFA that many of its transfer provisions were likely to be incompatible with Article 101 TFEU. Challenges to the transfer system began to increase.[21] In July 1997, the Employees, Technicians and Executives Union of the General Federation of Belgian Employees filed a complaint with the Commission against the transfer rules.[22] In 1998, complaints were made by AC Perugia, AC Reggiana and FC Palermo. In December 1998, the Commission then issued a statement of objections in relation to FIFA's transfer system, which focused in particular on criticism of four rules.

First, the rule which provided that a player who unilaterally terminated his contract would not be able to play for a new club even if he paid whatever damages were due for breach of contract. Second, the rule that the agreed upon transfer fee need not bear any relation to the actual costs that the transferring club had incurred in relation to developing or training the player. Third, the rule that obliged national associations to organize their domestic transfer regimes in accordance with the principles set out in the FIFA rules. Fourth, the provision in the FIFA statutes that prevented parties taking disputes concerning transfers to the civil courts.[23]

A major challenge to the imposition of transfer windows—something common to the regulation of transfers in many sports—was brought by the Finnish basketball player, Lehtonen, in 2000. In the *Lehtonen* case,[24] the CJEU considered the legality of transfer windows under Article 45 TFEU and ultimately upheld the imposition of transfer windows as justified and proportionate. Lehtonen was a Finnish basketball player who played in the Finnish basketball league. He sought to transfer into the Belgian basketball league, which would require re-registration with

---

20 For further discussion of the consequences of the *Bosman* decision see Beloff et al (n 6), 98–101.

21 Lewis and Taylor (n 4), 1510.

22 Case IV/36 583 European Commission, Rejection Decision, Case IV/36 583, SETCA & FGTB v FIFA, 28 May 2002, available at http://ec.europa.eu/competition/elojade/isef/index.cfm (accessed 26 Oct 2017).

23 Beloff et al (n 6), 103.

24 C-176/96 *Lehtonen* [2000] ECR I-2681.

the Belgian national league. The Belgian league rules prohibited that transfer after a certain date. Lehtonen transferred after that date, notwithstanding the rule. The club he transferred to was fined by the national association and effectively forced to resile its relationship with Lehtonen.

The matter was referred to the CJEU who held that there could be valid reasons for enforcing a transfer window, despite the effect of those rules on free movement of workers, stating as a general principle that:

> late transfers might be able to change substantially the sporting strength of one or other team in the course of the championship, thus calling into question the comparability of results between the teams taking part in that championship, and consequently the proper functioning of the championship as a whole.[25]

The ECJ left it to the national court to decide whether or not the particular Belgian rules were objectively justified and proportionate.[26]

II.ii Transfers and RSTP

In 2001—as a result of *Bosman*, the subsequent challenges and the European Commission's statement of objections—FIFA introduced a new transfer regime entitled FIFA's Regulations on the Status and Transfer of Players ('the RSTP'). The Commission announced, in March 2001, that it was satisfied that the RSTP ameliorated its concerns about the old transfer regime.[27] As presently established (the RSTP were amended in 2005, 2008, 2009, 2010 and 2012),[28] the RSTP provide that contracts may only be a maximum of five years in length, or three years for players aged 18 or under (art 18(2)). They may only be terminated for just cause or by mutual agreement (arts 13 and 14)—hence, the transfer of a player under contract may not take place without the agreement of the player and both clubs.

A player out of contract may transfer clubs without any transfer fee being payable, but an agreement to sign for another club may only be entered into in the last six months of a contract or after its expiry (art 18(3)). However, perhaps most critically, a player who terminates an existing contract without just cause is liable to pay compensation (art 17(1)), jointly with any new club for whom the player has signed

---

25 Ibid., para 54.

26 Lewis and Taylor (n 4), 1500–501 and Beloff et al (n 6) 101 for a discussion of this case.

27 Beloff et al, ibid., 103.

28 Lewis and Taylor (n 4), 1512.

(art 17(2)), and will also be subject to sporting sanctions (including a ban on playing for any team) if the wrongful termination occurs in the first two or three years of the contract, depending on the age of the player (art 17(3)). FIFA guidelines suggest that a failure to pay a player would only be just cause for that player to terminate the contract if payment was not made for a period of more than three months. If an 'established professional' plays in fewer than 10 per cent of the official matches for their club during the course of a season, there is also the possibility for that player to terminate their contract for 'sporting just cause' (art 15).

II.iii Transfers and CAS

The amount of compensation payable if a player terminates a contract without just cause has been a controversial question.[29] The Court of Arbitration for Sport ('the CAS') in *Webster*[30] rejected the argument that the player should be liable for their full market value, holding that: 'giving clubs a regulatory right to the market value of players and allowing lost profits to be claimed in such manner would in effect bring the system partially back to the pre-Bosman days'.[31] The damages were instead calculated based on the 'outstanding remuneration due until expiry of the term of the contract'.[32]

Webster caused something of an outcry from many clubs, as it was felt that it would enable players effectively to buy themselves out of their

---

[29] The cases in which the CAS considered and applied art 17 include *Phillipe Mexes & AS Roma v FIFA & AJ Auxerre* CAS 2004/A/708, 709, 713 and 2005/A/902, 903, 916; *Webster* (see discussion and citation below); *FC Pyunik Yerevan v L., AFC Rapid Bucaresti and FIFA* CAS 2007/A/1358; *Elkin Soto Jaramillo and FSV Mainz 05 v CD Once Caldas and FIFA*, CAS 2008/A/1453 and 2008/A/1469; *Matuzalem* (see discussion and citation below); *Fenerbahçe Spor Kutubu v Stephen Appiah, Stephen Appiah v Fenerbahçe Spor Kutubu*, CAS 2009/A/1856 and CAS 2009/A/1857; *FC Sion and El-Hadary v FIFA and Al-Ahly Sporting Club* CAS 2009/A/1880 and 2009/A/1881; *FC Shakhtar Donetsk v Ilson Pereira Dias Junior*, CAS 2010/O/2132; *Sevilla FC SAD and Morgan De Sanctis v Udinese Calcio S.p.A*, CAS 2010/A/2145, 2010/A/2146 and 2010/A/2147. For further discussion of these cases and the application of art 17 see P A Czarnota 'FIFA Transfer Rules and Unilateral Termination Without "Just Cause"' (2013) (1) *Berkeley Journal of Entertainment and Sports Law* 3 Online: http://scholarship.law.berkeley.edu/bjesl/vol2/iss1/3 (accessed 26 Oct 2017).

[30] *Webster* CAS 2007/A/1298/1299/1300.

[31] Ibid., at para 81.

[32] Ibid., at para 86.

contracts too easily. In *Matuzalem*,[33] however, the CAS held that a player who had terminated his contract unilaterally without cause was liable for an amount based on his replacement value on the transfer market (more than €11m). Matuzalem was unable to pay this amount and he was consequently subject to a worldwide playing ban. The decision to prohibit him from playing was later annulled by the Swiss courts for violation of public policy (essentially because he could never make payment if he could never work), but the case nevertheless established that the cost to a player of unilaterally terminating their contract without just cause would be strongly connected to the player's value in the transfer fee market. This finding was based on consideration of the Swiss law principle of 'positive interest'; that is, that the party in breach must return the injured party to the position he would have been in had the contract been performed properly.[34]

Following *Matuzalem*, the CAS considered a number of other cases relating to the alleged unlawful termination of employment contracts by players. The first of these was the *FC Sion*[35] case in which a player, El-Hadary, sought to terminate his contract with an Egyptian club to transfer to FC Sion. The Egyptian club disputed the player's right to terminate and issued proceedings against the player and FC Sion. FIFA's Dispute Resolution Chamber (the DRC) found that the player had breached his contract and that FC Sion had induced that breach—they ordered that the player pay €900,000 in compensation. On appeal, the CAS upheld the decision of the DRC on liability but disagreed with the DRC's compensation calculations and instead applied the positive interest principle as in *Matuzalem* (that is, assessing the compensation by reference to the amount that the club would have to pay to replace the player with someone of similar value). Applying that principle, the CAS reduced the compensation payable to the club.

In the *Appiah*[36] case, Appiah, the player, sought to terminate his contract with Fenerbahce. Two years into his contract with Fenerbahce, Appiah underwent surgery on his knee and claimed that the club had exposed him to medical mistreatment. He claimed that this entitled him to terminate his contract and he left the club (although he did not play for another team owing to his injury). Fenerbahce demanded Appiah's return and issued proceedings against Appiah before the DRC, claiming compensation of c. €12m. The DRC ordered Appiah to pay Fenerbahce

---

33 *Matuzalem* CAS 2008/A/159.

34 Ibid., at para 86 and 88.

35 *FC Sion v FIFA and Al-Ahly Sporting Club* CAS/A/1880 & 1881.

36 *Fenerbahçe Spor Kulubu v Stephen Appiah* CAS 2009/A/1856 & 1857.

€2.2m in compensation. Both Appiah and Fenerbahce appealed to the CAS; Fenerbahce argued that the compensation should be higher; Appiah argued that compensation was due to him as a consequence of his medical mistreatment, or that if compensation was due to Fenerbahce then it should be €0 because the club's saving (through not paying Appiah's salary for the remainder of the contract) outweighed the losses incurred by Appiah's termination.

Applying the 'positive interest' approach of *Matuzalem*, the CAS held that Appiah should not have to pay compensation: Appiah was of no value to any club during the remainder of his contract (owing to his injury) and as such could not be liable for the club's failure to receive a transfer fee, or the costs of replacing Appiah (which they would have had to do anyway owing to his injury).

In the *Morgan De Sanctis*[37] case, the player (De Sanctis) unilaterally terminated his contract with Udinese prior to the contract's expiration date. The DRC ordered the player to pay over €3m in compensation to Udinese. On appeal, the CAS reduced this amount to €2.25m—the sum of Udinese's costs in obtaining replacement services, less the salary expense that the club had saved by way of the termination, plus an additional sum of compensation owing to the 'specificity of sport'. Although the CAS calculated the compensation by reference to the player's replacement costs, rather than his estimated value, the court emphasized that there was no single method for calculating compensation but that 'each case must be assessed in the light of the elements and evidence available to each CAS panel'.[38] The CAS confirmed that the remuneration and other benefits under the terminated contract should be deducted from the sum payable in compensation.[39]

[37] *Sevilla FC SAD and Morgan De Sanctis v Udinese Calcio S.p.A*, CAS 2010/A/2145, 2010/A/2146 and 2010/A/2147 and for further detailed discussion of this case see PA Czarnota 'FIFA Transfer Rules and Unilateral Termination Without "Just Cause"' (2013) (1) *Berkeley Journal of Entertainment and Sports Law* 3 Online: http://scholarship.law.berkeley.edu/bjesl/vol2/iss1/3 (accessed 26 Oct 2017) 19ff.

[38] *Sevilla FC SAD and Morgan De Sanctis*, ibid., para 86.

[39] Ibid., para 87.

II.iv Transfers and FIFPro

There has been much criticism of, and opposition to, the RSTP and the new transfer system—with that criticism largely focused on the complaint that the RSTP does not go far enough in protecting the fundamental principle of free movement for players. In September 2015, FIFPro (the worldwide union for professional footballers, which represents more than 65,000 players around the world) lodged a formal complaint with the Directorate General for Competition of the European Commission against FIFA and its member associations that challenged the global transfer market system for football. The complaint claimed that the transfer system was a violation of Articles 101 and 102 TFEU. FIFPro's complaint highlighted three features of the RSTP which operate as restrictions on the labour market.

First, the calculation of compensation if the player terminates their contract without cause. Second, the imposition of a playing ban for the wrongful termination of a contract by a player during the first two or three years of a contract. Third, the rule that a contract with a different club may only be entered into in the final six months of a contract or after it has expired. FIFPro's argument was that these provisions were a disproportionate means of furthering the legitimate aim of contractual stability. FIFPro also argued that the scale of transfer fees meant that the less wealthy clubs were unable to compete for the best players and that competition in the market was thereby reduced. This complaint is still pending.

While the European Commission has recognized the RSTP as 'an example of good practice that ensures a competitive equilibrium between sport clubs while taking into account the requirements of EU law',[40] it has expressed concerns over the 'legality of the financial flows' involved with transfers and has recommended the implementation of a system that would increase financial transparency.[41] In order to explore this possibility, the Commission launched a study on the economic and legal aspects of transfers, that was published in January 2013 by KEA and CDES—'The economic and legal aspects of transfers of players'.[42] The study concluded that the transfer market suffers from a lack of transparency; that the system of transfer fees 'essentially benefits clubs and intermediaries' (implying that the system does not benefit players); that the

---

40 White Paper on Sport, COM(2007) 391 final, para 4.3, p15.

41 Ibid.

42 KEA—CDES (n 1), 'Study on the Economic and Legal Aspects of Transfers of Players, EAC/17/2011' (January 2013).

current transfer rules in Europe do not fight effectively against competitive imbalance, with there being a *de facto* closed league system rather than the true promotion of excellence through a working system of promotion and relegation; that redistribution and solidarity compensation derived from transfers have a limited impact on competitive balance; that solidarity schemes managed by international federations (such as FIFA and UEFA) do not adequately address competitive imbalance.[43]

The study recommended that the transfer system be reformed along the following five 'action lines': (i) improve fair and balanced competition through increased redistribution between clubs as well as control over financial transactions and accounting linked to transfers; (ii) limit transfer fees; (iii) support youth development and protection of minors; (iv) improve governance through transparency and fair dispute resolution mechanisms; (v) develop cooperation with public authorities for better law and transfer rules' enforcement.[44]

Given the concerns of the Commission, the inconsistent case law of the CAS, the FIFPro complaint and the general public interest in a fair and transparent transfer system it is most likely that the regulation of player transfers shall undergo further radical reform and development in future years.

III. THE REGULATION OF AGENTS

There are currently between 5,695 and 6,140 sports agents—including both official and unofficial agents—operating in the territory of the EU. Football is the sport with by far the largest number of official agents (and football, taken together with rugby, basketball and athletics, the three sports with the next highest number of agents, accounts for 95 per cent of the total number of official sports agents in Europe).[45] The commissions earned by player agents on transfers of players in European football are estimated at €200m per year.[46] As to the regulation of those agents, five EU countries (Bulgaria, France, Greece, Hungary and Portugal) and four international federations (FIBA, FIFA, IAAF and World Rugby (all defined below)) have developed specific regulations for sports agents.[47]

[43] See KEA—CDES, 'Study on the Economic and Legal Aspects of Transfers of Players, EAC/17/2011' (January 2013) 6–7.

[44] See KEA—CDES, 8–9.

[45] Ibid., 4.

[46] Ibid.

[47] Ibid.

More generally, agents working in the EU are also governed by EU and national law. The European Commission has concluded that acting as a sports agent in Europe is generally compatible with Community law, although in regulating the profession care must be taken to comply with competition law, freedom to provide services and freedom of establishment.[48] Given that the vast majority of sports agents work in football, the following discussion will focus on the regulation of football agents, although referring to other sports where relevant.

III.i Agents and FIFA

FIFA's Regulations on Working with Intermediaries ('RWI') came into force on 1 April 2015. The RWI define an intermediary as a 'natural or legal person who, for a fee or free of charge, represents players and/or clubs in negotiations with a view to concluding an employment contract or represents clubs in negotiations with a view to concluding a transfer agreement'.[49] That is, the new RWI expands the old category of 'player's agent' and regulates a far broader class of persons, none of whom are now required to be licenced as intermediaries (as agents were required to be). The only qualification for acting as an intermediary is an 'impeccable reputation' and 'no contractual relationship with leagues, associations, confederation or FIFA that could lead to a potential conflict of interest'.[50]

Intermediaries must be registered in the manner and circumstances set out at Article 3 of the RWI; in particular, this requires those intermediaries to sign a declaration confirming adherence to the FIFA statutes. Under Article 5 of the RWI, the intermediary must also complete a representation contract setting out the legal relationship between the player/club and intermediary and the minimum details listed at Article 5(2). The representation contract and the declaration must be deposited with the relevant association when the intermediary is registered. Under Article 6, the RWI require players and clubs to disclose to their

---

48 Ibid., 6.

49 FIFA Regulations on Working with Intermediaries (RWI 2015) 4 and available here: http://resources.fifa.com/mm/document/affederation/administration/02/36/77/63/regulationsonworkingwithintermediariesii_neutral.pdf (accessed 26 Oct 2017).

50 Arts 4(1) and 4(3) of the RWI.

associations all payments made to an intermediary[51] and require the member associations to publish that information annually.[52]

Under Article 7, the RWI set out a recommended limit of 3 per cent of the player's income/transfer fee to be earned by the agent as a commission.[53] Further, where a player/club are negotiating the employment contract/transfer agreement of a minor no payments may be made to the intermediary.[54] However, intermediaries are permitted to enter into contracts with minors and those contracts may last beyond the minor's 18th birthday, after which the intermediary may be able to earn a fee under the contract.[55] This gives rise to some concerns about the protection of minors, addressed in more detail in the section of this chapter that deals with minors. Further, with regard to the benchmark fee cap, Article 7(3) makes clear that the 3 per cent figure is merely a recommendation, to be considered in the light of national regulations and international and national laws.

Under Article 8, the RWI stipulates that prior to engaging an intermediary, players/clubs must ensure that there are no conflicts of interest[56] but the player and club may engage the same intermediary on the same transaction provided that both give their express written consent.[57] Under Article 9, the member associations have responsibility for sanctioning breaches of the RWI—further, the association must publish and inform FIFA of any disciplinary sanctions against intermediaries; FIFA will then consider whether the sanction should have world-wide effect. The RWI also state that they are minimum requirements that must be implemented by national associations, although those national associations can add further requirements.[58]

---

[51] See art 6(1) and 6(2) of the RWI.

[52] See art 6(3) of the RWI.

[53] See art 7(3) of the RWI.

[54] see art 7(8) of the RWI.

[55] For discussion as to whether the intermediary would be entitled to a fee in such a situation see N De Marco 'The new FA Football Intermediaries Regulations and the disputes likely to arise' (*Blackstone Chambers Blog*, 27 April 2015) para 26, available at http://www.blackstonechambers.com/news/publications/the_new_fa_football.html (accessed 26 Oct 2017).

[56] See art 8(1) and 8(2) of the RWI.

[57] See art 8(3) of the RWI.

[58] See the preamble to the RWI.

III.ii Agents and the FA

The English Football Association ('The FA') implemented a version of the RWI ('The FA RWI') which also came into force on 1 April 2015. The FA RWI are not identical to the RWI but do contain the same provision with regard to a proposed cap of 3 per cent on the fees of intermediaries (see regulation C.11 of The FA RWI). When the draft regulations were published, there was a great deal of concern surrounding this provision as it was feared by many agents that a limit of 3 per cent, which was significantly below the commission rates paid at that time (which were on average between 5–10 per cent),[59] would depress the commission of agents to such a degree that it would be uneconomical for them to continue work as an agent, which would ultimately be detrimental to players. Shortly before the RWI and FA RWI came into force, therefore, England's Association of Football Agents ('AFA') made a complaint to the European Commission challenging the RWI as incompatible with EU law.

The basis of this claim was that the 3 per cent benchmark cap on agents' remuneration (particularly arts 7(1) and 7(8) of the RWI) is an anti-competitive price-fixing provision and/or an abuse of a dominant position and thereby an infringement of Article 101(1) and/or Article 102 TFEU. The AFA also considered making an application for interim relief under Rule K of The FA Rules to prevent the FA from implementing those parts of The FA RWI/RWI under challenge. Ultimately, the AFA was able to withdraw this complaint since national federations in Europe did not require parties to agree the 3 per cent cap. The FA's standard representation contract, for example, does not include a template form suggesting that the parties limit remuneration to 3 per cent commission.

In sum, the RWI has not had the effect of limiting fees and the complaint was no longer necessary. Nonetheless, the act of bringing the complaint, and the active lobbying on the part of the AFA as well as the European Association of Football Agents on this matter, was perhaps partly responsible for ensuring that the RWI recommendation was not enforced by the national associations. In France, for example, the maximum sum has been set at 10 per cent. In Portugal, 3 per cent is set as a minimum commission fee. In the Netherlands, 5 per cent has been set as the maximum fee. In England, the author's experience is that most

[59] D Lowen, 'A Guide to the FA's Regulations on Working with Intermediaries' (*Lawinsport.com*, 17 February 2015) and available at http://www.lawinsport.com/articles/item/a-guide-to-the-fa-s-regulations-on-working-with-intermediaries (accessed 26 Oct 2017).

Intermediary Representation Contracts, at least at the higher levels in football, continue to provide agents with a 5 per cent commission and those that don't tend to allow for a higher rate (up to 10 per cent).

The recommended commission cap is not the only aspect of the RWI to come under criticism. Other contentious provisions are as follows. First, the fact that a company can act as an intermediary means that a player may only have the right to representation by the company, not by a designated individual and could, indeed, face a situation where a number of different individuals (all registered as intermediaries themselves, and carrying out work on behalf of a company registered as an intermediary) would be able to carry out work on the same transaction. As the player may have only agreed to the contract because of a relationship with a specific individual he then cannot be represented by, this can cause conflict, and lead to an increased number of disputes between clubs, players and intermediaries.

Second, the RWI do not provide for any maximum duration of the representation contract between a player and an intermediary (this is in contrast to the old system whereby no contract could continue for a term beyond two years unless a new contract was agreed). This is of some concern as young and inexperienced players would be better served by a regulatory system that protected them from being bound for long periods of time to terms that they would be able to substantially improve if able to negotiate a new contract (this is particularly true as football players have relatively short careers and their earning power can dramatically increase from one season to the next).[60]

Third, intermediaries are not able to earn any fee from a representation contract with a minor. As a result, if an intermediary choses to represent a minor, they must do so for free. As a means of protecting minors from exploitation, this is laudable. However, it potentially exposes minors to other risks—for example, if a minor is unable to pay an agent to negotiate a high-value contract, the minor will likely not be as well

[60] National federations can, of course, impose a limit on the duration of the representation contract. The FA only permits contracts for a period of two years. It is submitted that this strikes a sensible balance between the commercial interests of the agent, who must invest time and work with a player, and the right of the player to change his agent as his career develops. Two years is a reasonable period given it is most likely that a player will have to renegotiate his contract, or negotiate a new one, on average every two years. However, the fact that some European countries may limit the permitted period for a contract to two years while others do not (because the FIFA RWI do not) creates an obvious tension.

represented as they could be, and may as a result not be in a position to negotiate the most advantageous deal. A more sensible provision would be to allow those players aged between 16 and 18 to enter into representation agreements under which the intermediary can receive a fee, but the term of which is limited to two years.

Fourth, the RWI contain no regulatory provision prohibiting intermediaries from approaching players already under contract with another intermediary (that is, 'poaching' that player) or approaching players already under contract with one club and attempting to induce them to join another club ('tapping up'). Although, of course, such conduct is likely to be unlawful under national law.[61]

Fifth, there is no requirement that intermediaries take out professional liability insurance—such requirement is important for disincentivizing dishonest or disreputable persons from registering as intermediaries and thereby protecting players. It would also protect those who deal with intermediaries from bringing claims against impecunious persons. Such protection is particularly necessary with the abolition of licences.

III.iii Agents and the General Law

The activities of agents (or intermediaries) are further regulated by domestic law in each of the countries in the EU. In England and Wales, for example, agency is defined at common law as the 'fiduciary relationship which exists between two persons, one of whom expressly or impliedly manifests assent that the other should act on his behalf as to affect his relations with third parties'.[62] This would include those persons defined as an 'intermediary' under the RWI. Accordingly, there are a number of common law duties that an agent is subject to when carrying out activities on a player's behalf.

---

[61] See, e.g., *McGill v Sports and Entertainment Media Group and Ors* [2016] EWCA Civ 1063 concerning, among other things, civil liability for inducement to breach a football agent's representation contract.

[62] P Watts (ed.) *Bowstead and Reynolds on Agency* (20th edn, Thomson Reuters 2014) para 1-001. See also discussions of the regulation of agents at English common law and in legislation in Lewis and Taylor (n 4), 1421–35 and D Lowen 'The English FA's Regulations on Working with Intermediaries' in M Colucci (ed.) *The FIFA Regulations on Working with Intermediaries* (Sportslaw & Policy Centre 2016) 271–86 and available at http://football intermediary.co.uk/wp-content/uploads/2016/02/Chapter-for-book-final.pdf (accessed 26 Oct 2017).

It is not possible to list them all,[63] but generally speaking an agent cannot exceed his authority as agent and must, with reasonable diligence, obey all lawful and reasonable instructions given by the player.[64] In doing so, the agent must employ the skill and care necessary in the profession or reasonably necessary for the proper performance of the agent's duties.[65] The agent must make full disclosure of conflicts of interest.[66] Further, as an agent owes a player a duty of loyalty under English common law, the agent is also subject to fiduciary duties towards the player—that is, the agent must act in good faith, must not make a profit out of his trust, must not act for his own benefit or the benefit of a third person without the informed consent of the player.[67]

In *Imageview Management Ltd v Jack*,[68] the Court of Appeal in England and Wales considered the scope of the fiduciary duties owed by an agent to a player. The case concerned an agent who had made a secret deal for his own benefit, upon knowledge of which the player had ceased to pay the agency fee. The Court observed that:

> the law imposes on agents high standards. Footballers' agents are not exempt from these. An agent's own personal interests come entirely second to the interest of his client ... An undisclosed but realistic possibility of a conflict of interest is a breach of [an agent's] duty of good faith to [his] client.[69]

Accordingly, the Court ordered that the undisclosed side deal was a breach of the agent's fiduciary duties and that the player could therefore recover agency fees and a portion of the secret profit received by the agent for doing the side deal.[70]

Many countries in the EU also have domestic legislation that regulates the activities of agents. In France, for example, the 'Sports Code'

---

[63] Neither Lewis and Taylor (n 4), 1422 nor P Watts (ed.) *Bowstead and Reynolds on Agency* (20th edn, Thomson Reuters 2014) attempts to do so.

[64] Watts, ibid., paras 6-002, 6-008 and 6-012 and Lewis and Taylor, ibid., 1422.

[65] Watts, ibid., at para 6-017 and Lewis and Taylor, ibid.

[66] Lewis and Taylor, ibid.

[67] Watts (n 62), para 6-033 and *Bristol and West BS v Mothew* [1998] 1 Ch 1 at 18 per Millett LJ.

[68] *Imageview Management Ltd v Jack* [2009] EWCA Civ 62.

[69] Ibid., para 6.

[70] Ibid., paras 44–50 per Jacob LJ and Lewis and Taylor (n 4), 1423–4.

specifically regulates the activities of sports agents.[71] The US also has legislation that specifically regulates the activities of sports agents.[72] In the UK, there is no such specific legislation but a number of statutes are relevant to the activities of agents, these include the Employment Agencies Act 1973 and the Conduct of Employment Agencies and Employment Business Regulations 2003 (which, together, set minimum standards of conduct for employment agencies and employment businesses, although no intermediary or licenced agent has yet been charged under either the Act or the Regulations),[73] the Bribery Act 2010 (which created the criminal offences or bribing another person or being bribed by another person—therefore, if an intermediary offers payments to a third party in relation to duties he carries out for a player, he could be charged with one of these offences, for which the maximum sentence is ten years' imprisonment),[74] the Fraud Act 2006, the Theft Act 1968.[75]

III.iv Agents and International Governing Bodies

Players' agents are also internationally regulated in rugby, athletics and basketball. World Rugby provides that national associations are responsible for the regulation of players' agents, but that those national regulations must contain, at a minimum, the following general principles: that World Rugby has jurisdiction to adjudicate on players' agent issues of an international nature; a prohibition on a players' agent acting for more than one party in a transaction; an obligation of disclosure by the agent to the player with regard to any current or previous relationship with any parties to the transaction; a prohibition on players' agents inducing players to breach their contracts; a general obligation on agents to behave ethically and fairly; an obligation on agents to have appropriate insurance; a prohibition on transferring players' agent accreditation from one person to another; an obligation on agents to keep and make available accounting records; a maximum two-year term for written representation

---

[71] The key features of the French legislation are detailed at Lewis and Taylor, ibid., 1456, although it should be noted that the RWI have come into force since this book was published.

[72] See Lewis and Taylor, ibid., 1452ff for an overview of the US legislation, but note that this book was drafted before the RWI came into force.

[73] Lowen (n 62), section 2.2.

[74] Ibid.

[75] For a full discussion of these statutes in relation to sports agents, see Lewis and Taylor (n 4), 1425ff.

agreements; a requirement that the agent only be paid by the party by whom he was engaged.[76]

In athletics, athletes may use an Athletes' Representative ('AR') to assist them in the negotiation of their athletics program and other matters, there are also Authorised Athletes Representatives ('AAR') on whom those athletes ranked in the top 30 of the International Association of Athletics Federations ('the IAAF') world list must rely. ARs and AARs are regulated by the IAAF Athletes' Representatives Regulations 2012 (amended in April 2014).[77] In Basketball, players' agents are regulated under the amended Internal Regulations of the Federation of International Basketball Associations ('FIBA'), which came into force in September 2006.[78]

IV. REGULATING THE TRANSFER OF MINORS

The protection of minors is an issue that concerns all sports within the EU. However, as with the other sections of this chapter, football—because of the large amounts of money concerned, the high numbers of transfers and the increasing recruitment of younger players[79]—is the sport focused on in most detail in the following discussion. The health and welfare of young players has long been a concern in international football and regulations have sought to protect against the risk of overtraining and exploitation, missed education opportunities, use of doping substances, sexual abuse and harassment. There is also particular concern over human trafficking and the risk that intermediaries and clubs will target and exploit minors from countries outside the EU.[80] It is, therefore, an area that is increasingly carefully regulated.

---

[76] World Rugby Handbook, Regulation 5: Agents, available at https://www.worldrugby.org/handbook/regulations/reg-5 (accessed 26 Oct 2017).

[77] IAAF Athletes' Representatives Regulations, available at https://www.iaaf.org/athletes/athlete-representatives (accessed 26 Oct 2017).

[78] FIBA Internal Regulations, Book 3, Chapter 9, Regulations Governing Players Agents, available at http://www.fiba.basketball/agent/become-fiba-agent (accessed 26 Oct 2017).

[79] For some years, there has been a shift in the core recruits by major European clubs from the 16–17 age group to the 12–13 age group: see KEA—CDES—EOSE: 'Study on Sports Agents in the European Union', (European Commission, November 2009) available at http://ec.europa.eu/assets/eac/sport/library/studies/study-sports-agents-in-eu.pdf (accessed 26 Oct 2017) fn 232.

[80] White Paper on Sport, COM(2007) 391 final, 16 and KEA—CDES—EOSE, ibid., 130.

IV.i Transfer of Minors and the General Law

Minors in professional sport in the EU are generally protected by Directive 94/33/EC of the Council, which governs the protection of young people at work.[81] In each member state, they are further protected by the provisions of domestic labour law and contract law. In England and Wales, for example, it is an established principle of contract law that apart from contracts for necessities and contracts of apprenticeship, education and service, contracts with persons under the age of 18 will be voidable at the minor's option.[82]

In *Proform Management Ltd v Proactive Management Ltd*,[83] the High Court considered whether an agency agreement, which had been agreed with Wayne Rooney when he was aged 15 and already contracted to Everton FC, was a voidable contract. The High Court found, at [paras 39–40] per Judge Hodge QC, that because the player was already signed with a club, from which he did not want to move, and because the agency agreement was not the means by which the player earned his living, the agency agreement was not for his benefit and was voidable.[84]

In some EU countries domestic law provides specifically for the relationship between young sports players and agents. In Portugal and Greece, for example, sports agents are banned from entering into contracts with minors[85] and in France, although sports agents can agree contracts with minors, those contracts will be void if they give rise to any payment or advantage for the sports agent.[86]

---

81 Discussed in KEA—CDES—EOSE: ibid., 126–7.

82 *Chitty on Contracts* (32nd edn, Thomson Reuters 2015) para 9-007 and Beloff et al (n 6), 108.

83 *Proform Management Ltd v Proactive Management Ltd* [2006] EWHC 2903 (Ch). See also the discussion of this case at Lewis and Taylor (n 4), 1471–4.

84 It is also worth noting that this judgment was given on a summary judgment application. Judge Hodge QC was therefore satisfied that there was 'no real prospect' of the claimant's successfully arguing that the agency agreement was enforceable, see *Proform Management Ltd*, ibid., para 39 per Judge Hodge QC.

85 See Portugal's Law 5/2007, art 37 and Greece's Ministerial Decision No. 23788/2002 and discussion at KEA—CDES—EOSE: 'Study on Sports Agents in the European Union', (European Commission, November 2009) 127.

86 Article L 222-5 of the Code of Sport and discussion in KEA—CDES—EOSE (n 79), 127.

IV.ii Transfer of Minors and FIFA

International transfers of minors in football are regulated by the FIFA Regulations on the Status and Transfer of Players (defined above as the RSTP). The RSTP, at Article 19(1), prohibits the international transfer of players under the age of 18. There are, however, three exceptions to this prohibition (listed at art 19(2)). They are as follows:

(a) The player's parents move to the country in which the new club is located for reasons not linked to football.
(b) The transfer takes place within the territory of the European Union (EU) or European Economic Area (EEA) and the player is aged between 16 and 18. In this case, the new club must fulfil the following minimum obligations:
    (i) It shall provide the player with an adequate football education and/or training in line with the highest national standards.
    (ii) It shall guarantee the player an academic and/or school and/or vocational education and/or training, in addition to his football education and/or training, which will allow the player to pursue a career other than in football should he cease playing professional football.
    (iii) It shall make all necessary arrangements to ensure that the player is looked after in the best possible way (optimum living standards with a host family or in club accommodation, appointment of a mentor at the club, etc.).
    (iv) It shall, on registration of such a player, provide the relevant association with proof that it is complying with the aforementioned obligations.
(c) The player lives no further than 50km from a national border and the club with which the player wishes to be registered in the neighbouring association is also within 50km of that border. The maximum distance between the player's domicile and the club's headquarters shall be 100km. In such cases, the player must continue to live at home and the two associations concerned must give their explicit consent.

If a player is eligible for transfer under one of the exceptions at Article 19(2), Article 19(4) provides that that transfer must be approved by the sub-committee appointed by the Player's Status Committee before it can be effective. The application for approval must be submitted by the association that wishes to register the player and the former association will be entitled to make representations on that application. An association cannot request an International Transfer Certificate unless the sub-committee has approved the transfer. Breaches of article 19 will be sanctioned by the FIFA Disciplinary Committee but the FIFA Disciplinary Code and the RSTP are silent as to the specific sanctions that may be applied upon a finding of a breach of Article 19.

Article 19—in only allowing the international transfer of minors in certain, exceptional circumstances—is potentially in violation of Article 45 TFEU, which (as set out above) guarantees freedom of movement for workers within the EU (art 45(1)) and prohibits discrimination on the basis of nationality (art 45(2)). However, the relationship between EU law and Article 19 has been considered by the CAS in a number of cases, where the CAS upheld sanctions imposed by FIFA for violation of Article 19 and confirmed that Article 19 was a valid, proportionate restriction on freedom of movement.

A case brought by FC Cadiz and the Spanish Football Association was the first time that a transfer was rejected for violating Article 19. In 2005, the Paraguayan player Carlos Javier Acuna Caballero (then aged 16) signed a contract with FC Cadiz, to transfer from Club Olympia de Paraguay. The Paraguayan Football Association refused to issue an International Transfer Certificate on the grounds that the transfer contravened Article 19. The Spanish Football Association appealed to FIFA's Player's Status Committee, relying on the exception at Article 19(2)(a)—they argued that because Caballero's mother had recently got a job in a Spanish restaurant, the family had moved to Spain for reasons not linked to football. The Player's Status Committee held that Article 19(2)(a) did not apply.

FC Cadiz appealed to the CAS on the basis, inter alia, that Article 19 was an impermissible restriction on a player's freedom of movement. The CAS dismissed the appeal, holding that Article 19 did not violate any mandatory principle of public policy under Swiss law or any other national or international law because it was in pursuit of a legitimate objective, and proportionate to that objective.[87] The CAS also held that the exception at Article 19(2)(a) was not engaged in these circumstances.[88]

Shortly after the *FC Cadiz* decision, the Danish club FC Midtjylland brought a case before the CAS. In 2006, FC Midtjylland and the Danish Football Association registered three minor players from Nigeria as amateurs. The FIFA Player's Status Committee investigated the matter

---

[87] R Simons, 'Protection of Minors vs European Law' (2010) (1) *Eur Sports Law Bulletin* 165–83, 172 and *Carlos Javier Acuna Caballero v FIFA and Asociacion Paraguaya de Futbol* CAS 2005/A/956, para 7.2.2.

[88] See *Cadiz CF and Caballero v FIFA & Asociacion Paraguaya de Futbol* CAS 2005 /A / 955 and CAS 2005 /A /956 (not published on the CAS database).

and found a breach of Article 19, which it held applied equally to amateurs and professionals. Both FC Midtjylland and the Danish Football Association were sanctioned with a strong warning. FC Midtjylland appealed the decision to the CAS on the grounds, inter alia, that Article 19 did not apply as the players were mainly in Denmark as students (the players had been granted a residence permit by the Danish Immigration Service as students and had been given upper secondary school educations in Denmark); and that the exception at Article 19(2)(b) should be interpreted to benefit citizens from third countries which have made a bilateral agreement with the EU to protect citizens of those third countries from discrimination on the basis of nationality.[89]

The CAS dismissed the appeal:

> after taking into due consideration all evidence produced and all arguments made, the Panel finds that the Appellant (FC Midtjylland) has breached Article 19 of the [RSTP] and that it was justified to impose a sanction for the registration of the Players. Further, the Panel is of the opinion that the nature and the level of sanction imposed on the Appellant is totally appropriate.[90]

The CAS dismissed FC Midtjylland's arguments based on EU law and discrimination of workers, holding that the relevant EU provisions protecting against discrimination on the basis of nationality only apply to 'workers', not to students or persons who intend to enter the employment market in a European Community Member State.[91]

In 2012, FC Girondins Bordeaux also appealed FIFA's refusal to approve a transfer of a minor under Article 19.[92] In early 2011, Valentin Vada joined FC Girondins Bordeaux. He was then 15 years old and was an Italian national (although he had been born and grown up in Argentina). The French Football Association applied to the sub-committee of the Player's Status Committee to approve the international transfer. Approval was refused as the transfer did not satisfy any of the exceptions in Article 19(2). FC Girondins Bordeaux, however, ultimately appealed the matter to the CAS who held that the intention behind Article 19(2)(b) was to protect the freedom of movement of workers in the EU/EEA and found that there was unwritten exception to the Article 19

---

[89] See Simons (n 87), 170 and *FC Midtjylland* CAS 2008/A/1485, paras 2.3–2.6 and 3.3.

[90] *FC Midtjylland*, ibid., para 8.1.

[91] Ibid., paras 7.4.5–7.4.16.

[92] This judgment is only available in French: *FC Girondins de Bordeaux c FIFA* TAS 2012/A/2862.

prohibition allowing the transfer of minors from outside the EU, provided that the minor is an EU national.

Finally, in 2014, the CAS also considered the application of Article 19 to the registration of ten minors with FC Barcelona. FC Barcelona had completed the transfer of the ten players and the Real Federacion Espaniola de Futbol (RFEF) had registered them without obtaining approval from the FIFA sub-committee. FIFA sanctioned FC Barcelona with a national and international level transfer ban for two consecutive seasons, a fine of CHF 450,000 and a reprimand; FIFA sanctioned the RFEF with a fine of CHF 500,000.[93]

FC Barcelona argued that the sanction was disproportionate and incongruous in that it banned the transfer of all players, not merely minors. FC Barcelona also argued that they complied with the spirit of the RSTP as their academy incorporated educational training programs, accommodation, meals, medical care, attention to the needs of children and sports development plans. On this basis, FC Barcelona appealed the decision but their appeal was dismissed by the FIFA Appeal Committee and the CAS.

The CAS considered the core issue of the case to be whether the sanction was proportionate and defined three main elements for assessing the proportionality of the sanction: (i) the gravity of the illegal act; (ii) the power to dissuade the offender from repeating the same infringement in future; (iii) the importance of the rule of law that is being protected. The CAS found, applying those principles, that because the protection of minors was such a serious issue, it was important that FIFA sent a strong signal to other clubs and the sanction was proportionate to that aim.[94]

Aside from Article 19, the RSTP contain a number of other provisions designed to protect minors. These include, Article 19bis which governs the registration and reporting of minors at academies, annexe 4 which outlines how training compensation is to be paid, and annexe 2 which involves minors in the FIFA Transfer Matching System. Further, as discussed above in the section of this chapter that addresses the regulation of agents, under the RWI no agent can receive remuneration under

---

93 'Spanish FA, FC Barcelona sanctioned for international transfers of minors' (*FIFA Press Release*, 2 April 2014) and available at http://www.fifa.com/governance/news/y=2014/m=4/news=spanish-barcelona-sanctioned-for-international-transfers-minors-2313003.html (accessed 26 Oct 2017).

94 The Court of Arbitration for Sport (CAS) dismisses Barcelona's Transfer Ban Appeal (CAS Media Release, 30 December 2014) available at http://www.tas-cas.org/fileadmin/user_upload/CAS_Media_Release_BarcelonaFIFA.pdf.

a representation agreement with a minor (however, although this provision is aimed at protecting the minor, it may disadvantage them in forcing them to rely on *pro bono* representation—possible reforms to this rule are discussed above).

IV.iii Transfer of Minors and UEFA

UEFA has also taken measures to protect minors. In 2006, UEFA introduced a 'home-grown rule'. This applies to all clubs entering European club competitions and provides that by the 2009 season the final eight places in a team's 'A' list squad (of 25) must be reserved for locally trained players—that is, players who (regardless of their nationality) have either been registered with their current club (or another club in the same association) for three entire seasons (continuous or non-continuous) or 36 months while aged 15–21.[95]

UEFA argued that this rule is necessary to promote competitive balance, encourage the education and training of young players and protect national teams. However, it led to some concern that it would lead to an increase in international transfers of minors which would, in turn, increase the risk of child trafficking and encourage clubs giving contracts to very young players.[96] In response to that concern, in 2009, UEFA ratified a resolution that:

> no international transfers (or first registration of non-nationals) of players under 18 into Europe or within Europe should be permitted. This means in particular that the third exception foreseen today in article 19, paragraph 2 b), of the FIFA Regulations for the Status and Transfer of Players, and which relates only to the EU/EEA, should be reviewed in order to guarantee that the same system regarding transfer bans of under-18 year old players applies both within and outside Europe and that this system is strictly monitored.[97]

---

[95] As a result of UEFA implementing these regulations, since 2009/10 the Football League has operated a home-grown player rule requiring a minimum of four of the club's 16-person matchday squad to be registered domestically, for a minimum of three seasons prior to their 21st birthday; and since 2010/11 the Premier League has introduced a squad cap of 25 and a domestic home-grown player quota of eight of those 25 players. See generally P Minderhoud and H Oosterom-Staples, 'Obstacles to Free Movement of Young Workers', (European network on free movement of workers, Jan 2011) 9.

[96] See Minderhoud and Oosterom-Staples, ibid., 9–10.

[97] Simons (n 87), 177. See also KEA—CDES—EOSE (n 79), 132 and UEFA, 'Protection of young players and encouragement of youth development, Resolution of the Professional Football Strategy Council' (UEFA, 9 March 2009)

IV.iv Transfer of Minors and International Governing Bodies

With regard to other sports, the international sports federations of basketball (FIBA), rugby (World Rugby) and athletics (IAAF) also specifically regulate the international transfers of minors. The FIBA Internal Regulations 2010,[98] provide (similar to art 19 of the RSTP) that 'an international transfer is not permitted before a player's eighteenth (18) birthday, except in special cases as decided by the Secretary General after examination of the matter with the member federations and, if necessary, with the clubs and the player concerned'. Article 51 of the FIBA Internal Regulations provides that if the proposed transfer is not linked to basketball, it may be authorised; Article 52 provides that academic and training facilities should be taken into account by the Secretary General when considering whether to authorise the transfer. World Rugby and IAAF mandate that national federations regulate the international transfer of minors, so its regulatory provisions on the transfer of minors are minimal.

---

and available at http://www.uefa.com/MultimediaFiles/Download/uefa/KeyTopics/80/81/02/808102_DOWNLOAD.pdf (accessed 26 Oct 2017).

[98] FIBA Internal Regulations, Book 3, Chapter 2, arts 50–65, available at http://www.fiba.basketball/internal-regulations/book3/players-and-officials.pdf (accessed 26 Oct 2017).

19. Professional team sports and collective labour law in the European Union

Leanne O'Leary

I. INTRODUCTION

The employment arrangements of athletes in a professional team sport competition in the European Union (EU) are determined at a national level by the Member States. A player will have a contract with a club or federation and his or her legal status will be determined under national law. A player may provide services as an employee or an independent contractor. The players in some professional leagues have unionised and a collective agreement may also regulate the employment relationship in accordance with national labour relations law. In the Premier League, for example, a club employs a professional player under the standard terms of a contract that is collectively negotiated by the Professional Footballers' Association and the clubs. A professional rugby union player in Ireland is employed by the national federation, the Irish Rugby Football Union (IRFU) to provide services to professional teams managed by the Irish provinces of Connaght, Munster, Leinster and Ulster. The IRFU and the Irish Rugby Players' Association collectively negotiate the standard terms of a player's contract. In France, a rugby league player is an employee of a club in the Super League competition, a transnational professional rugby league competition that is organised by rugby league clubs in England and the south of France. The standard terms of a player's contract are approved by the national federation in England, the Rugby Football League, and also governed by a national collective agreement in France. These are arrangements that arise under national law and are specific to the organisation of the respective leagues in each country.

National laws are influenced by the EU in areas where the Union has the power or competence to act under the European Treaties and the employment and social sphere is one of those areas. European employment law can influence the employment arrangements of a professional athlete through the rights provided under the Treaty of Lisbon and other European legislation and through the decisions of the Court of Justice of the European Union (CJEU). Some professional athletes are employed on terms and conditions that far exceed those minimum labour rights that European employment law may direct Member States to provide in national law. Other individual rights such as the right of free movement and the freedom to provide services are Treaty rights that extend to those athletes who are employees or workers.

The free movement rights have provided an additional mode of legal challenge for athletes against overly restrictive working conditions implemented in a professional team sports competition. *Bosman*[1] and the less well-known case of *Kolpak*[2] are just two important examples of European law influencing the employment arrangements of professional athletes in a team sports competition. Opportunities to move without migration obstacles can remove restrictions on employment opportunities in competitions abroad and make it easier for a club to recruit players into a competition in another Member State. Increased competition for a player's services can lead to improved working conditions. Establishing a rival professional league within a country is often difficult so competition from employers in an established competition in another Member State can be beneficial for a player.

The EU has a more limited competence to act in the area of collective labour rights; it is excluded from acting in relation to the right to strike, lockout and freedom of association.[3] The collective labour relations law at a European level has generally related to a right to receive information and to be consulted in the workplace.[4] There have been, however, a number of CJEU decisions that have considered the interplay between national labour relations law and internal market law (as the area of law encompassing competition law and free movement is known). In the United States of America (US) the interplay between labour relations law and antitrust law (as competition law is known in that country) has played an important role in determining the employment arrangements of athletes in a professional league.

Federal labour law requires an employer to engage in collective bargaining with a trade union on the mandatory subjects of wages, hours and other terms and conditions of employment.[5] Federal labour relations law and US Supreme Court case law shield many of the measures that a

---

1 Case C-415/93 *Bosman* [1995] ECR I-4921.

2 Case C-438/00 *Kolpak* [2003] ECR I-4135.

3 Art 153(5) TFEU.

4 See Council Directive (97/74/EC) and the European Works Council Directive (2009/38/ EC).

5 National Labor Relations Act of 1935, 29 USC §158(d).

professional league may introduce from a claim under antitrust law. The legal framework provides an incentive for the teams in a league to collectively bargain and agree with the players those employment measures that are anti-competitive. Resolving the tension between national labour relations law and internal market law is more problematic at a European level because of the EU's limited competence to act in the industrial relations sphere, an absence of political consensus and CJEU decisions which resolve the conflict between national labour relations law and internal market law in different ways.

This chapter will discuss the influence of European employment law, on the working arrangements in a professional team sports competition, specifically whether exemptions similar to the statutory and non-statutory labour exemption in the USA exist in the European legal order. It will commence with a discussion of European employment law and the EU's competence or power to regulate employment and labour relations law. It will consider the conflict between national collective labour rights and internal market law and discuss how the conflict has been resolved at a European level. It will conclude with a discussion regarding the legality of measures such as a salary cap and consider whether European employment law could enable measures that are commonplace in a professional team sports competition in the US to apply in a professional league in the EU.

II. EUROPEAN EMPLOYMENT LAW

National laws are influenced by the EU in areas where the Union has the power or competence to act under the European treaties. The founding treaty of the EU, the Treaty of Rome, was originally conceived as an economic treaty with the purpose of facilitating economic prosperity, peace and political stability through the formation of a common market.[6] To enable the common market to function, the factors of production pivotal to the production process needed to be able to move without obstacle between the EU's Member States. The Treaty outlined the four fundamental freedoms of free movement of workers, goods, services and capital, and contained provisions prohibiting the restraint of competition in the common market and discrimination.

As originally conceived, the Treaty did not provide the EU with a broad competence to legislate in the area of labour law and policy. It was

---

[6] See generally G Conway, *EU Law* (Routledge 2016) and P Craig and G de Búrca, *EU Law Texts, Cases and Materials* (6th edn, OUP 2015).

widely viewed that a free market economy would ensure the optimal allocation of resources, remove obstacles to free movement and provide economic growth with a consequential positive effect for full employment and a high standard of living.[7] There were some social objectives in the Treaty, such as equal pay and non-discrimination, but social policy objectives were to be achieved primarily through the design of a common market. Over time, however, the Member States have recognised the importance of a social policy at a European level and have provided the EU with an expanded competence in the area. Title X on Employment and Title XI on Social Policy are the key parts of the Treaty, which provide the EU with the power to enact measures which regulate. The objective of establishing a highly competitive social market economy that aims for full employment and social progress is now recorded in Article 3 TFEU.[8]

Labour law and policy in a Member State is principally determined by that State,[9] but the EU has introduced some legislation and uses soft law processes like the Open Method of Coordination and social dialogue to regulate employment throughout the Union. Legislative initiatives have generally taken the form of a Directive and have arisen in the areas of equal treatment and equality, flexible working, health and safety, the transfer of an undertaking, collective redundancies and information and consultation with workers.[10] The Open Method of Coordination is a process of policy-making that involves the EU establishing guidelines

---

[7] C Barnard, *EU Employment Law* (4th edn, OUP 2012) 5.

[8] Art 9 TFEU further provides that:

> In defining and implementing its policies and actions, the Union shall take into account requirements linked to the promotion of a high level of employment, the guarantee of adequate social protection, the fight against social exclusion, and a high level of education, training and protection of human health.

[9] Article 147 TFEU.

[10] See, e.g. Council Directive 2000/78/EC of 27 November 2000 establishing a general framework for equal treatment in employment and occupation; Council Directive 2010/18/EU of 8 March 2010 implementing the revised framework agreement on parental leave; Council Directive 89/391/EEC of 12 June 1989 on the introduction of measures to encourage improvements in the safety and health of workers at work; Council Directive 2001/23/EC of 21 March 2001 relating to the safeguarding of employees' rights in the event of transfers of undertakings, businesses or parts of undertakings or businesses; Council Directive 98/59/EC of 20 July 1998 on the approximation of the laws of the Member States Relating to Collective Redundancies; and Council Directive 2002/14/EC of 11 March 2002 establishing a general framework for informing and consulting employees.

and fixing goals or specific targets for each Member State to achieve in the employment sphere, taking into account national differences. A Member State's performance is benchmarked against other Member States and a Member State is encouraged to exchange best practices. The European Commission monitors the process. It is not legally binding and it does not result in legislation, but there is the expectation that Member States will conform and engage in the process.[11]

Social dialogue has been equated with transnational collective bargaining but it encompasses a more flexible relationship between the social partners at all levels, the EU and national institutions.[12] The social partners are the representatives of management and labour and the European Commission defines social dialogue as 'discussions, consultations, negotiations and joint actions involving organisations representing the two sides of industry (employer and workers)'.[13] It is promoted by the European Commission as a prerequisite for the functioning of Europe's social economy and 'crucial to promote competitiveness and fairness and enhance economic prosperity and social well-being'.[14] It is unsupported at a European level by the mechanisms that are ordinarily used to apply economic pressure during collective bargaining; those mechanisms, such as strike action or lockouts, may still be available at a national level for employees who are collectively organised. Social dialogue relies on the parties' voluntary engagement with the process to be effective and occurs in the sports sector at a European level.[15] So far, the social dialogue process in professional football has established the minimum requirements for a professional player's employment contract,[16] and in the sports sector

---

[11] Barnard (n 7) 61–7.

[12] B Bercusson, *EU Labour Law* (2nd edn, CUP 2009) 127.

[13] European Commission Social Dialogue, see generally the resources at http://ec.europa.eu/social/main.jsp?catId=329&langId=en (accessed 28 Feb 2018).

[14] See Conference on a 'New Start For Social Dialogue', European Commission Employment, Social Affairs & Inclusion (Brussels 5 March 2013) and available at http://ec.europa.eu/social/main.jsp?langId=en&catId=329&eventsId=1028&furtherEvents=yes (accessed 28 Feb 2018).

[15] See generally M Colucci and A Geeraert, 'Social Dialogue in European Professional Football' (2012) 33(1) *Comparative Labor Law and Policy Journal* 202–34 and R Parrish 'Social Dialogue in European Professional Football' (2011) 17(2) *European Law Journal* 213–29.

[16] 'Agreement regarding the minimum requirements for standard player contracts in the professional football sector in the European Union and in the rest of the UEFA territory' (UEFA, 19 April 2012) and available at http://

generally has resulted in guidelines on working time and on health and safety.[17]

Employment and labour relations systems and cultures differ between the Member States.[18] In the Scandinavian countries, for example, labour relations are generally characterised by a high level of unionisation, industry-level collective bargaining, limited State intervention and a series of labour market collective agreements, with almost all workers covered by a collective agreement. In Anglo-Saxon countries, there is also limited State intervention, but a low density of union membership and voluntary collective agreements are not legally binding. In some other Member States the State may play an active role, protecting workers' rights through a constitution and a collective agreement may be extended to all workers and employers through an administrative act. Employment and labour relations is also an area of important political importance and obtaining political consensus for regulation in the area at a European level can be difficult. At a European level, the Open Method of Coordination and social dialogue are viewed as the principal mechanisms through which European employment law and policy can be achieved.

There is no European employment legislation that applies solely to the professional sports industry at a European level. Insofar as a professional athlete falls within the definition of 'worker' or 'employee' as that term is defined in European law, then the employment rights and protections that exist under European law apply to professional athletes in the Member States. An essential characteristic of a working relationship under European law is subordination. Under Article 45 TFEU, which extends the right of free movement to a worker, the term 'worker' is defined as a person who, for a certain period of time, performs services for and under the direction of another person in return for remuneration, which the person may receive directly or indirectly.[19]

A person classified de jure as self-employed under national law but de facto is in an employment relationship or relationship of subordination

---

www.ecaeurope.com/Documents/Dialogue%20social%20IX%20Final%20Version.pdf (accessed 28 Feb 2018).

[17] 'EASE Guidelines on Health and Safety' (EASE, 10 October 2013) and available at http://www.easesport.org/pdf/EASE%20Guidelines%20on%20working%20hours.pdf (accessed 28 Feb 2018).

[18] Barnard (n 7), 59.

[19] Case 66/85 *Lawrie-Blum v Land Baden-Wurttemberg* [1986] ECR 2121, para 17 and Case C-337 *Meeusen v Hoofddirectie van de Informatie Beheer Groep* [1999] ECR I-3289, para 15.

with the person who receives the services, may, nonetheless, be a worker under European law.[20] Self-employed workers who are not engaged in a relationship of subordination will ordinarily fall outside the definition of worker.[21] If a professional athlete can demonstrate that he or she is performing services for another person in return for remuneration, irrespective of the legal status of the athlete under national law and for the purposes of European law, the athlete may be a worker. It is already well established that a professional handball player, football player and basketball player fall within the definition of worker under European law.[22]

A club, league or federation is not permitted to introduce working conditions that unlawfully restrict an athlete's right of free movement under Article 45 TFEU. The free movement of athletes is an enduring concern of employers in a professional team sports competition. It purportedly affects competitive balance, destabilises team dynamics, limits a coach's capacity to build a successful team and may affect detrimentally supporter loyalty. On the other hand, a player's capacity to move to another employer can increase competition for services with consequential flow on benefits for the player of improved working conditions. In a career of short duration, a player's desire to follow better working conditions is understandable. Achieving a balance between the employer and employee's interests in a professional league can be difficult.

Insofar as collective labour laws are concerned, there is recognition of the right to organise and to other social rights outlined in the Charter of Fundamental Rights of the European Union and the use of social dialogue between management and labour organised at a European level. The EU is expressly excluded from passing legislation on the right to strike or impose a lockout and freedom of association. Its influence in the labour relations sphere has related primarily to extending rights of

---

20 *See* Case C-256/01 *Allonby v Accrington and Rossendale College and Others* [2004] ECR I-873, paras 69–72, a case decided under the Treaty provisions concerning equal pay.

21 C-268/99 *Jany and Others v Staatssecretaris van Justitie* [2001] ECR I-8615, paras 32–34.

22 Case C-415/93 *Bosman* [1995] ECR I-4921; Case C-176/96 *Lehtonen* [2000] ECR I-2681; Case C-325/08 *Olivier Bernard* [2010] ECR I-2177; Case C-438/00 *Kolpak* [2003] ECR I-4135; and Case C-265/03 *Simutenkov* [2005] ECR I-2579.

information and consultation to employees,[23] and the CJEU decisions which have endeavoured to reconcile the conflict between internal market law and national labour relations law. The jurisprudence has been influential in two important areas of industrial relations: the legality of anti-competitive provisions that form part of a collective agreement and the capacity of a trade union to take industrial action which may affect an employer's economic rights under the Treaty. The following section deals with the legal principles established by the Court in the first of these areas: the legality of collective agreements.

III. THE CONFLICT BETWEEN INTERNAL MARKET LAW AND LABOUR RELATIONS LAW

There is an inherent conflict between industrial action, collective bargaining and collective agreements that protect the rights of workers at a national level and the Treaty objective of establishing an internal market through recognition of the fundamental freedoms and a system of undistorted competition. Trade union activities are potentially an obstacle to an employer's freedom to establish or provide services in another country; the terms of a collective agreement may also conflict with competition law.

In the US, the conflict between federal antitrust law and federal labour law that promotes collective bargaining and recognises a right to engage in collective action, has been resolved through the statutory and non-statutory labour exemptions for trade union activities and collective agreements. Political agreement in favour of a labour policy that promotes and encourages collective bargaining enabled the statutory exemption to be adopted. The statutory labour exemption is contained in the Clayton Act of 1914 and the Norris-LaGuardia Act of 1932.[24] The exemption excludes trade union activities (such as boycotts, picketing or strike action) from challenge under antitrust law and removes the jurisdiction of the federal courts from certain labour disputes. In circumstances of a conflict with antitrust law not covered by the statutory exemption, the US Supreme Court created the non-statutory labour exemption to give effect to federal labour law and policy.

---

23 See Council Directive (97/74/EC) and the European Works Council Directive (2009/38/ EC).

24 Clayton Act of 1914 15 USC §17, § 52 and Norris-LaGuardia Act of 1932 29 USC §101.

The non-statutory labour exemption excludes the terms of a collective agreement from a claim under the Sherman Act of 1890,[25] provided the term relates to wages, hours and working conditions and is obtained through bona fide, arm's length bargaining in pursuit of a union's own interests and not in the interests of a non-labour organisation.[26] Crucial factors are not the form of the agreement but its impact on the product market – as opposed to the labour market – and the interests of union members.[27] The conflict between labour law and antitrust law is often highlighted through well-publicised legal proceedings in the sports industry.[28] The exemptions can provide an incentive for collective agreement on working conditions, which may otherwise be subject to antitrust liability if implemented unilaterally.

Resolving the conflict in the European legal system is more problematic. There is political disunity and an absence of legislative competence at a European level to regulate collective labour relations. There are no express legal provisions in the Treaty or other legislation that are equivalent to the statutory exemption that applies in the US. Also, conflicts between national labour law and the Treaty provisions are not easily resolved in the CJEU's jurisprudence. The resolution of the conflict in one area does not automatically resolve the conflict in the other area.[29] If a conflict arises between the terms of a collective agreement and European competition law, then the agreement may fall outside the scope of Article 101 TFEU, which prohibits anti-competitive agreements.[30] If the conflict arises between strike action and an employer's freedom to establish or provide services, the trade union activity is not exempt from legal scrutiny under Articles 49 and 56 TFEU.[31] Instead the Court applies a proportionality test to determine whether the strike

---

[25] *Local Union No 189 Amalgamated Meat Cutters and Butcher Workmen of North America v Jewel Tea Company* 381 US 676 (1965). See also *United Mineworkers of America v Pennington* 381 US 657 (1965); *Connell Construction Company v Plumbers and Steamfitters Local Union No 100* 421 US 616 (1975); and *Brown v Professional Football Incorporated* 518 US 231 (1996).

[26] *Jewel Tea Company* 381 US 676 (1965) 689–90.

[27] Ibid., 690.

[28] See *Brown v Professional Football Incorporated* 518 US 231 (1996); *Powell v NFL* 930 F.2d 1293 (8th Cir 1989); *Mackey v NFL* 543 F. 2d 606 (8th Cir 1976); and *Brady v NFL* 644 F.3d 661 (C.A.8 (Minn) 2011).

[29] C-438/05 *International Transport Workers' Federation & Anor v Viking Line ABP and Anor* [2007] ECR I-10779.

[30] C-67/96 *Albany International BV v Stichting Bedrijfspensioenfonds Textielindustrie* [1999] ECR I-5751.

[31] C-438/05 *Viking Line ABP* [2007] ECR I-10779.

action is a permissible infringement of an employer's fundamental freedom.

The labour market in professional sport is a market in which the conflict between employment law and competition law can arise. Professional clubs must act together to produce the entertainment product; a club cannot produce the entertainment for consumers on its own. The nature of the entertainment product requires agreement between the clubs regarding the rules under which the product will be produced. Some of those rules organise the competition in a uniform manner; others enable the competition to compete effectively with other entertainment products. Some of the uniform rules, standard terms or practices apply to the labour market in which an employment relationship under national law is formed and in some sports professional players have unionised. Collective agreements may regulate a player's employment and industrial disputes may result in strike action. In some circumstances, in a professional team sports competition, European law may be engaged or may influence the resolution of the conflict between labour relations law and competition law at a national level. The following section considers how the CJEU has resolved the conflict between collective agreements and competition law.

III.i Collective Agreements

Article 101 TFEU prohibits agreements between undertakings, decisions of associations of undertakings and concerted practices that affect trade between the Member States and which have the object or effect of preventing, restricting or distorting competition in the internal market. It is well established in the CJEU case law that agreements entered into within the framework of collective bargaining between employers and employees and which are intended to improve employment and working conditions are excluded from the scope of Article 101 TFEU.

The exemption was established in the case of *Albany International BV v Stichting Bedrijfspensionenfonds Textiekindustrie*,[32] which considered questions referred by the Dutch courts during proceedings between Albany International, an employer in the textile industry, and a Pension Fund. An industry-wide collective agreement in the textile industry required all employers to be affiliated to the Pension Fund. Albany International had been a member of the Pension Fund since 1975 but in the early 1980s had entered into a supplementary pension scheme with an

---

[32] C-67/96 *Albany International BV* (n 30).

insurance company to provide additional benefits for its employees. The Pension Fund introduced a new scheme and Albany International sought an exemption from the new scheme on the basis that the pension arrangements already in place for its workers were more beneficial than those provided under the new scheme. Albany International also believed that the cost of joining the new scheme was too onerous. The exemption was refused and Albany International challenged the compulsory affiliation requirement under European competition law in the Dutch courts. In the course of proceedings, the question of whether a collective agreement between employers and employees fell within the scope of European competition law was referred to the CJEU.

The Advocate General examined the treatment of collective agreements in the Member States and also in the US and noted that any exemption provided for collective agreements in other jurisdictions was not without limitation.[33] The Advocate General suggested that collective agreements should be immune from competition law claims provided three conditions were met: first, the agreement must be made within the formal framework of collective bargaining; secondly, the agreement should be concluded in good faith; and thirdly, the agreement must relate to the core subjects of collective bargaining, such as wages and working conditions, and not directly affect third parties or third markets.[34] The Advocate General's suggested approach was broadly in-line with the non-statutory exemption developed by the US Supreme Court.

The CJEU did not expressly endorse the Advocate General's approach but took a broader view. It concluded that collective agreements were exempt from European competition law provided two conditions were met: first, the agreement must be the outcome of collective negotiations between organisations representing workers and employers; and secondly, the agreement must contribute to the improvement of working conditions.[35] The Court considered that the collective agreement at issue in the proceedings satisfied those conditions and fell outside the scope of Article 101 TFEU.[36]

The CJEU focused its analysis on the nature and purpose of the agreement rather than considering whether a collective agreement was an agreement between undertakings (which may also have led to the same conclusion because a worker is not considered to be an undertaking and a trade union representing workers during collective negotiations for an

---

[33] Ibid., para 189, AG Opinion.
[34] Ibid., para 190–192, AG Opinion.
[35] Ibid., paras 62–63.
[36] Ibid., para 64.

agreement is not considered to be an association of undertakings). The test laid down by the CJEU is extremely broad and provides a blanket exemption for collective agreements that are agreed within the framework of collective bargaining and which aim to improve working conditions. There is no indication from the CJEU of any limitation to the scope of the exemption, which creates uncertainty regarding the type of terms that may be included in a collective agreement, particularly in the sport sector where the employment terms agreed can very often have anti-competitive effects in the labour market.

Albany has been followed in a number of subsequent decisions.[37] The *Albany* principle has also been extended to exclude from the scope of Article 101 TFEU an agreement that is negotiated by a trade union on behalf of self-employed workers in certain circumstances. In *FNV Kunsten Informatie en Media v Staat der Nederlanden*,[38] two Dutch trade unions that represented musicians entered a collective agreement with an employers' association regarding the working conditions of substitute musicians who were hired to fill in for members of an orchestra. The agreement prescribed minimum fees for those substitutes who were hired under an employment contract and those who were hired on a self-employed basis. The self-employed musicians and the employee musicians performed the same work; the only difference was the musicians' legal status under Dutch law. The Dutch competition authority concluded that the agreement fell within the purview of Article 101 TFEU because the self-employed musicians were undertakings and the trade union was an association of undertakings which brought the agreement within the scope of competition law. The trade unions sought a declaration, from the Dutch courts, that the agreement did not contravene competition law and in the course of proceedings, the question was referred to the CJEU.

---

[37] See, e.g.: C-180/98 *Pavlov v Stichting Pensioenfonds Medische Specialisten* [2000] ECR I-64511, para 67; C-222/98 *Van der Woude v Stichting Beatrixoord* [2000] ECR I-7111, para 22; and Case C-413/13 *FNV Kunsten Informatie en Media v Staat der Nederlanden* [2015] 4 CMLR 1, paras 29–30. See also a decision of the EFTA Court in Case E-8/00 *Norwegian Federation of Trade Unions v Norwegian Association of Local and Regional Authorities* [2002] 5 CMLR 160. The EFTA Court is the judicial body that interprets the Agreement on the European Economic Area (EEA). The EEA includes the European Union countries and Norway, Liechtenstein and Iceland and enables the latter countries to be a part of the internal market. The EFTA Court's jurisdiction applies to those countries that are members of the EEA but are not European Union countries and runs in parallel to the CJEU's jurisdiction.

[38] Case C-413/13 *FNV* [2015] 4 CMLR 1.

The CJEU considered that the self-employed musicians were, on the face of it, 'undertakings' as that term is defined for the purposes of competition law. A self-employed musician offered his or her services on the labour market for remuneration and performed the activities as an independent operator in relation to the orchestra for whom the services were provided.[39] A trade union negotiating on behalf of a group of undertakings was classified as an 'association of undertakings' and not a social partner.[40] On that basis the provision of the agreement that was negotiated and agreed on behalf of the self-employed musicians, was not an agreement negotiated by the social partners for labour and management and fell within the scope of Article 101 TFEU.[41]

The Court went on to say, however, that even though the self-employed musicians were 'undertakings', a collective labour agreement negotiated on their behalf would be excluded from challenge under Article 101 TFEU if the musicians were 'false self-employed' or in a comparable position to the employer's employees.[42] The Court concluded that if a person has been hired as self-employed under national law, a person's status as a worker under European law is not affected, provided:

> the person acts under the direction of the employer as regards his freedom to choose the time, place and content of work and does not share in the employer's commercial risks, and for the duration of the relationship, forms an integral part of the employer's undertaking so that it forms an economic unit with that undertaking.[43]

This is consistent with established case law that a person's legal status under national law does not preclude a finding that the person is an employee or worker under European law.[44] The status of a self-employed worker as false self-employed was a matter for the national Court to determine. Any provision of a collective labour agreement for a false self-employed service provider falls outside the scope of Article 101 TFEU.[45]

Not all collective agreements have withstood a challenge under European competition law. In *Federation Nationale de la Coop Betail et*

---

39 Ibid., para 27.
40 Ibid., para 28.
41 Ibid., para 30.
42 Ibid., para 42.
43 Ibid., para 42.
44 Ibid., para 36.
45 Ibid., para 42.

Viande (FNCBV) v Commission of the European Communities,[46] a case that arose in the wake of an outbreak of 'mad cow' disease in some Member States and a 'foot and mouth' epidemic in the UK, several federations of farmers' unions and slaughterers in France entered an agreement to suspend meat imports and to fix the minimum purchase price paid for beef by slaughterhouses. In the circumstances of that case, the Court concluded that the farmers were undertakings and that the agreement was not a collective agreement concluded by organisations representing employers and workers but an inter-trade agreement between two links in a production chain in the beef sector. The agreement did not relate to the improvement of terms and conditions of employment but had the object of restricting competition in the internal market.[47]

The CJEU has consistently held that a collective agreement, entered into within the framework of collective bargaining between employers and employees or false self-employed service providers at a national level, and which intends to improve employment and working conditions, does not fall within the purview of Article 101 TFEU.[48] The exemption is broad and the parameters unclear which leaves the scope of the exemption subject to further development. The issue is relevant to the sports industry because of the potential for terms and conditions of employment or employment-related regulatory rules being excluded from scrutiny under European competition law through inclusion in a collective agreement. Collective bargaining in a league is usually characterised as multi-employer, with the clubs represented through the league as a single bargaining unit and the players represented by a trade union.

A salary cap, for example, is a form of wage payment model; it relates to a player's remuneration – which is a core term and condition of employment – and can improve the working conditions and employment of professional athletes, particularly those less high-profile athletes. It spreads wages more evenly between the players, having a solidarity effect for those players who are generally less well paid than a 'superstar'. If negotiated between the players and the clubs within the framework of collective bargaining, a wage payment model that includes a cap on wages may fall outside the scope of European competition law.

---

46 Case T-217/03 *Federation Nationale de la Coop Betail et Viande (FNCBV) v Commission of the European Communities* [2008] 5 CMLR 5.

47 Ibid., paras 97–98.

48 C-67/96 *Albany International BV* (n 30), para 60.

Salary caps have not been the subject of CJEU scrutiny although in *Bosman*[49] it was noted – but not expressly endorsed – by Advocate General Lenz that a collective wage agreement could be an alternative to the then existing transfer rules in football as a mechanism for achieving 'financial and sporting equilibrium'.[50] The important point is that it is negotiated collectively with players in the context of collective bargaining and not unilaterally implemented by the clubs or a federation as a regulatory rule, which can occur in leagues organised within the pyramidal structure of sports regulation in the EU. Rules that regulate wage levels or club spending on player wages have usually been agreed by the professional clubs and/or a federation only.[51] In those circumstances a professional club, league or a federation is an undertaking or association of undertakings as those terms are defined under European competition law.[52] An agreement between undertakings or a decision of an association of undertakings that restricts competition in the internal market is subject to challenge under Article 101 TFEU.

The case of *Meca-Medina and Majcen*[53] establishes the approach that the Court will adopt when considering the legality under Article 101 TFEU of anti-competitive measures arising in the context of a professional sports competition. The Court will take into account the context in which an agreement is made and its nature and purpose as part of the overall factual matrix that is considered under Article 101 TFEU. It will also assess whether 'the consequential effects restrictive of competition are inherent in the pursuit of those objectives and are proportionate'.[54] Arguments and evidence of whether the cap is required to encourage fiscal prudence among the clubs or to increase the competitiveness of the competition in the entertainment product market become important under the *Meca-Medina* analysis.

Collective bargaining changes the context in which a salary cap is agreed. It becomes an agreement that pursues a social policy objective,

---

49 Case C-415/93 *Bosman* (n 1).

50 Ibid., para 226.

51 See L O'Leary, 'Price-Fixing Between Horizontal Competitors in the English Super League' (2008) (8) 3–4 *International Sports Law Journal* 77–85 and J Lindholm, 'The Problem With Salary Caps Under EU Law' (2011) 12(2) *Texas Review of Entertainment and Sports Law* 189–213.

52 See, e.g., Case T-193/02 *Piau v Commission* [2005] ECR II-209, Case C-519/04 P *Meca-Medina and Majcen v Commission* [2006] ECR I-6991 and Case C-49/07 *Motosykletistiki Omospondia Ellados NPID v Elliniko Dimosio* [2008] 5 CMLR 11.

53 Case C-519/04 P *Meca-Medina and Majcen* ibid.

54 Ibid., para 42.

which benefits the employment relationship and may be excluded from a claim under Article 101 TFEU. Subjecting a collective agreement to a competition law analysis places the Court in the position of determining terms and conditions of employment, which may have been collectively negotiated, agreed voluntarily by the parties and contribute to stable labour relations in the industry. The unique characteristics of a professional team sports competition that are taken into consideration under European competition law are usually reflected in work practices and employment terms that differ from other industries.

The CJEU has not addressed specifically the issue of whether a collective agreement in a professional league is exempt from Article 101 TFEU. The Court has recognised elsewhere that the Member States and the social partners enjoy a broad discretion not only in their choice of aims to pursue in the field of social and employment policy but also in their choice of measures which are capable of achieving that objective.[55] If and when a claim arises, recognition of the 'specificity of sport' must also extend to an appreciation of the unique industrial relations practices and terms that may be included in a collective agreement in a professional sports league and which fulfil an important social policy objective.

The issue has great practical benefit for professional sport in the EU. Agreements reached within the framework of social dialogue at a European level between a federation, players' association and representative of clubs, which are implemented voluntarily through national affiliates may be exempt from Article 101 TFEU. Also, an agreement reached at a national level between a league, players' association and federation may also be exempt. It has practical application for the globalisation of a sports league that wishes to establish a franchise in the EU and which includes such measures in their respective agreements. The parameters of the *Albany* exemption are still very uncertain but there is potential for the *Albany* exemption to be developed further in relation to collective agreements in a professional league, in much the same way as has occurred in the US.

III.ii Strike Action

The conflict between an employee's right to take strike action as provided in national labour law and the freedom to establish and provide services in another Member State was the subject for consideration in the

---

[55] Case C–144/04 *Mangold v Helm* [2005] ECR I–9981, para 63 and C-411/05 *Palacious de la villa v Cortefiel Servicios SA* [2007] ECR I-8531, para 68.

landmark cases of *International Transport Workers' Federation v Viking Line ABP*[56] and *Laval un Partneri Ltd v Svenska Byggnadsarbetareforbundet.*[57] In both cases the CJEU confirmed that the employer's exercise of economic rights may be limited by industrial action undertaken by a trade union provided the strike action does not go beyond what is necessary to attain the legitimate objective of protecting the rights of workers.

International Transport Workers' Federation & Anor v Viking Line ABP and Anor,[58] concerned a Finnish passenger ferry, the 'Rosella', which was registered in Finland and whose workers were paid in accordance with a Finnish collective agreement and Finnish labour law. The passenger ferry was operating at a loss on a route between Estonia and Finland and the owners of the vessel sought to re-register the ship in Estonia to take advantage of lower wages applicable in that country by entering a collective agreement with an Estonian Union. The Finnish Seamen's Union (FSU), which was an affiliate of the International Transport Workers' Federation (ITWF), opposed the plan. It informed the ITWF, which in turn issued a circular to its affiliates in Estonia instructing the affiliates not to enter into negotiations with Viking.

Viking commenced proceedings in the High Court in London. It sought an injunction against ITWF that required it to withdraw the circular and an injunction against FSU to prevent the FSU from engaging in collective action. In the course of the injunction proceedings, a question concerning the lawfulness of the strike action under Article 49 TFEU was referred to the CJEU. While recognising that the right to take collective action, including the right to strike, is a fundamental right that forms 'an integral part of the general principles of community law'[59] the Court determined that the right was not absolute and could be subject to restriction. It held that collective action – such as strike action or the ITWF's circular – was a restriction on Viking's freedom of establishment.

A restriction on the freedom of establishment is permissible provided it pursues a legitimate aim, is justified by reasons of public interest, and does not go beyond what is necessary to attain the legitimate aim (in other words, the restriction must be proportionate).[60] In *Viking* the CJEU did not offer a conclusion on whether the strike action was proportionate – that issue was for a national court to determine – although it did offer

---

[56] Case C-438/05 *Viking Line ABP* [2007] ECR I-10779.
[57] Case C-341/05 *Laval* [2007] ECR I-11767.
[58] Case C -438/05 *Viking Line ABP* (n 56).
[59] Ibid., para 44.
[60] Case C-415/93 *Bosman* (n 1), para 104.

guidance. It indicated that the national court was required to consider whether FSU had other means at its disposal to achieve the aim sought and whether it had exhausted those means.[61] Regarding ITWF's policy, the Court gave a strong indication that the policy was not justified because it required ITWF to initiate solidarity action irrespective of whether Viking's exercise of a fundamental economic right had a detrimental effect on employment terms and conditions or not.[62]

A week after the decision in *Viking*, the CJEU came to a similar conclusion in *Laval un Partneri Ltd v Svenska Byggnadsarbetareforbundet*,[63] albeit on different facts. *Laval* involved a Latvian construction company that successfully tendered for renovation work at a school, close to Stockholm in Sweden. The work was undertaken by a subsidiary company of Laval and workers were posted from Latvia to Sweden to carry out the renovation work. The Swedish builders' union entered into negotiations with the subsidiary company, which aimed to secure the application of a sectoral collective agreement to the posted Latvian workers and to negotiate the workers' wages. The sectoral collective agreement contained provisions that were more favourable than those provided under national law. The wage levels sought were based on an average hourly wage for the sector in the region rather than the minimum wage. When negotiations failed, the Swedish trade union organised a blockade of the building site which prevented materials being delivered, established pickets and prevented Latvian workers and vehicles entering the site. It also encouraged secondary action by an electricians' union. The collective action was lawful under national law and aimed at encouraging Laval to enter into a collective agreement. It eventually led to the construction contract being terminated and Laval's Swedish subsidiary going bankrupt.

Prior to the contract termination, Laval commenced legal proceeding in the Swedish Courts seeking a declaration that the collective action was unlawful, an order that the action cease, and compensation from the trade union for damages. In the course of those proceedings, the Swedish Courts referred a number of questions to the CJEU, including a question regarding the interpretation of the Posted Workers' Directive, which applied to the case at hand, and the question of whether collective action that prevented an entity from providing services on a temporary basis in Sweden, infringed Article 49 TFEU. The CJEU again confirmed that the

---

61 Case C-438/05 *Viking Line ABP* (n 56), para 75.

62 Ibid., para 89.

63 Case C-341/05 *Laval* (n 57). See also Case C-346/06 *Ruffert v Land Niedersachsen* [2008] ECR I-01989.

right to take collective action was a fundamental principle in the European legal order which did not fall outside the scope of the free movement provisions but was subject to a proportionality test similar to that applied in cases that reconciled fundamental rights, such as freedom of expression, with the free movement of goods.[64]

The CJEU held that collective action was a restriction of Article 56 TFEU and was only permissible if it pursued a legitimate objective compatible with the Treaty and justified by overriding reasons of public interest.[65] The Court accepted that collective action adopted to protect posted workers could constitute an overriding reason of public interest which could justify a restriction of one of the freedoms guaranteed by the Treaty, provided it was proportionate.[66] In *Viking*, the CJEU had left it for the national court to determine the proportionality of strike action; in *Laval*, it went one step further and held that the restriction could not be justified.[67] The collective action was aimed at securing more favourable conditions than those prescribed in the Posted Workers' Directive and national law and rendered the exercise of the free movement right less attractive thereby infringing Article 56 TFEU.

The decisions in *Viking* and *Laval* have been heavily criticised.[68] Despite the CJEU's recognition of the right to strike as a fundamental principle of European law, the decision to adopt a proportionality test rather than an exemption potentially renders strike action, in certain circumstances, ineffective as a mode of exerting economic pressure on an employer. It requires the trade union to demonstrate the legitimacy of the strike action's aim, that jobs or terms and conditions of employment are under serious threat and that the action is effectively a measure of last resort; what constitutes a 'serious threat' is not clear.

As one academic has highlighted, the more effective the strike action in bringing pressure to bear on an employer, the more difficult it may be for the trade union to justify the action.[69] The approach does not take into account the inherent nature of strike action which is to intentionally inflict economic harm on the employer (and occasionally to third parties)

---

64 See, e.g., Case C-112/00 *Eugen Schmidberger Internationale Transporte Planzuge v Austria* [2003] ECR I-5659 and Case C-36/02 *Omega Spielhallen- und Automatenaufstellungs GmbH v Bundesstadt Bonn* [2004] ECR I-9609.

65 Case C-341/05 *Laval* (n 57), para 101.

66 Ibid., paras 103–105.

67 Ibid., para 108.

68 See, e.g., A Davies, 'One Step Forward, Two Steps Back? The Viking and Laval Cases in the ECJ' (2008) 37(2) *Industrial Law Journal* 126–148.

69 Ibid., 142–143.

as a way of supporting demands for better terms and conditions of employment. Subordinating the right to strike to the economic freedoms outlined in the Treaty may also put the CJEU decisions into conflict with standards prescribed by the International Labour Organisation (ILO) and in conflict with the decisions of the European Court of Human Rights.[70]

Industrial action is not regulated at a European level; national law will apply to action that is taken in a professional team sports competition in support of demands for improved working conditions. If, however, industrial action in some way prevents a professional league from exercising a fundamental freedom that is guaranteed under the Treaty then the industrial action will not be excluded from European law, though it is difficult to envisage such a situation arising in professional sport.

IV. CONCLUSION

The employment arrangements of athletes in a professional team sports competition in the EU are determined at a national level. The competition's organisation, regulatory arrangements, the economic conditions, legal framework and the bargaining power of the player, team, union or league will determine the final form of those arrangements. The influence of European employment law on working conditions in a professional league has so far been seen through development of the rights of free movement and establishment. These rights have been invoked successfully by athletes to challenge overly restrictive working conditions that have limited opportunities for a player to take up employment in a competition in another Member State.[71] The social dialogue process has also had some success with establishing minimum contractual requirements for football players and guidelines on working time and health and safety.

---

[70] See *Enerji Yapi-Yol Sen v Turkey* unreported, Application No 68959/01 (ECtHR, 21 April 2009) and *National Union of Rail, Maritime and Transport Workers v United Kingdom* (2015) 60 EHRR 10. For a detailed discussion, see A Bogg, 'Viking and Laval: The International Labour Law Perspective', in M Freedland and J Prassl (eds), *Viking, Laval and Beyond* (Hart 2014) 41–74.

[71] Case 13/76 *Donà v Mantero* [1976] ECR 1333; Case 36/74 *Walrave and Koch v Union Cycliste Internationale* [1974] ECR 1405; Case C-415/93 *Bosman* (n 1); Case C-438/00 *Kolpak* (n 2); Case C-265/03 *Simutenkov* [2005] ECR I-2579; Case C-176/96 *Lehtonen* [2000] ECR I-2681; and C-325/08 Case C-325/08 *Olivier Bernard* [2010] ECR I-2177.

Measures that are challenged are frequently included in the rules of a federation with whom the player does not have an employment relationship and have been implemented without taking into account the views of professional players in a meaningful way.[72] Some of the measures relate to important terms and conditions of employment, such as wages, contract termination or duration, which could also be the subject of collective bargaining. At a European level, there is a very broad exemption for collective agreements from the scrutiny of Article 101 TFEU, which could incentivise a professional league in the European Union to agree measures, such as a salary cap, that do not incur liability under Article 101 TFEU. There may be no desire to introduce a salary cap or other similar measures in a professional league because of economic conditions in the relevant labour market. But if introduced through collective bargaining, then certain measures may withstand challenge under European competition law or even prevent these from occurring in the first place through consultation and agreement with the players.

---

[72] See, e.g., 'FIFPRO's challenge against FIFA's international transfer system' (FIFPRO Press Release, 18 September 2015) and available at https://www.fifpro.org/news/fifpro-takes-legal-action-against-fifa-transfer-system/en/ (accessed 28 Feb 2018). The FIFPRO proceeding was subsequently settled by the parties: 'FIFA & FIFPRO sign landmark agreement & announce measures to enhance pro football' (Joint FIFA/FIFPRO Media Release, 6 November 2017) and available at http://www.fifa.com/governance/news/y=2017/m=11/news=fifa-and-fifpro-sign-landmark-agreement-and-announce-measures-to-enhan-2918747.html (accessed 28 Feb 2018). See also the European Commission's investigation into the International Skating Union's athlete eligibility rules and the subsequent decision that those rules infringed European competition law: European Commission Case No AT.40208; and European Commission Press Release (8 December 2017) 'Antitrust: ISU's restrictive penalties on athletes breach EU competition rules' (IP/17/5184, 8 December 2017).

20. Integrity of sport

Sylvia Schenk

I. INTRODUCTION

Integrity, as implied in Fundamental Principle Number 1 of the Olympic Charter is at the heart of sport and Olympism: 'Blending sport with culture and education, Olympism seeks to create a way of life based on the joy of effort, the educational value of good example and respect for universal fundamental ethical principles.'[1] Similarly, and despite substantive evidence of corruption and unethical behaviour at the highest level, the (relaunched) mission of the Fédération Internationale de Football Association (FIFA) promises to be guided by the principles of transparency, accountability, inclusivity and cooperation.[2]

While sport for decades has always automatically been linked to fair play, the gap between (self-)perception and reality has grown over the years – the reputation of international sport organizations now being at an all-time low.[3] This is the case 'on the pitch' with regard to doping[4] and the manipulation of sport competitions ('match-fixing'),[5] especially linked to internet betting; as well as 'off the pitch' with greed and

---

[1] International Olympic Committee, *Olympic Charter* (in force 15 September 2017) available at https://www.olympic.org/documents/olympic-charter (accessed 26 Oct 2017).

[2] FIFA, *FIFA 2.0: The Vision for the Future* (13 October 2016) available at http://resources.fifa.com/mm/document/affederation/generic/02/84/35/01/fifa_2.0_vision_e_neutral.pdf (accessed 26 Oct 2017).

[3] K Radnedge, 'Reputation of all sport is tainted by Fifa scandal, says Olympic chief' (*World Soccer*, 10 December 2015) and available at http://www.worldsoccer.com/columnists/keir-radnedge/reputation-of-all-sport-is-tainted-by-fifa-scandal-says-olympic-chief-366368 (accessed 26 Oct 2017).

[4] 'Doping in sport: What is it and how is it being tackled?' (*BBC Sport Online*, 20 August 2015) and available at http://www.bbc.co.uk/sport/athletics/33997246 (accessed 26 Oct 2017).

[5] Interpol, *Integrity in Sport*, http://www.interpol.int/Crime-areas/Crimes-in-sport/Integrity-in-sport (accessed 26 Oct 2017).

corruption[6] by officials on the one hand and alleged human rights abuses[7] and exploitation of workers[8] in connection with major sport events on the other hand.

In this environment the European Union (EU) defines its role with regard to the integrity of sport as follows:

> A key action in the Sport sector is to ensure that proper governance is in place to maintain transparency and fairness for all sportspeople and athletic organisations. Cross-border concerns such as doping and match-fixing are addressed alongside policies regulating team transfers, which must adhere to EU principles of equal treatment and free movement.[9]

Given the values of the EU (respect for human dignity and human rights, freedom, democracy, equality and the rule of law)[10] and the importance of sport in modern societies, the EU can and should be a key factor in changing the game fundamentally in order to restore trust in sports organizations worldwide.

II. INTEGRITY TODAY

As a concept or principle, integrity does not abide by a fixed set of rules; rather it is an attitude. It is above all to live to one's values, to be honest and transparent with strong moral and transparently ethical principles. Integrity's content may differ over time. It may develop in light of new insights or societal benchmarks as to what might be considered morally right or wrong, or between societies and groups with different traditions and culture. If we talk about the integrity of sport, the scope spans from

---

6 Transparency International, *Sport*, https://www.transparency.org/topic/detail/sport/ (accessed 26 Oct 2017).

7 Amnesty International (Netherlands), *Sport and Human Rights*, http://www.sportandhumanrights.org/wordpress/ (accessed 26 Oct 2017).

8 E Margolin, 'Migrant workers at Sochi faced unpaid wages, deportations', (*MSNBC Online*, 16 October 2017), http://www.msnbc.com/msnbc/the-human-cost-sochi (accessed 26 Oct 2017), and S McBain, '400 Nepalese construction workers have died since Qatar won the World Cup bid', (*NewStatesman*, 17 February 2014) http://www.newstatesman.com/global-issues/2014/02/400-nepalese-construction-workers-have-died-qatar-won-world-cup-bid (accessed 26 Oct 2017).

9 European Commission, *Organisation of Sport*, http://ec.europa.eu/sport/policy/organisation_of_sport/index_en.htm (accessed 26 Oct 2017).

10 European Parliament, *Values*, http://europarlamentti.info/en/values-and-objectives/values/ (accessed 26 Oct 2017).

individual behaviour of athletes, officials, supporters and others involved, to the governance and policies of sport organizations.

The latter are facing expectations of institutional responsibility similar to those in the corporate world – or, arguably, even higher expectations, taking into consideration, as quoted above, the International Olympic Committee's (IOC) and FIFA's self-imposed and onerous duties in promoting universal ethical principles and fairness. This has 'raised the bar' for the integrity of sport and concomitantly in terms of public scrutiny.

The yardstick for integrity can be found in globally acknowledged provisions such as the Universal Declaration of Human Rights (UDHR), the Convention on the Rights of the Child (UNCRC), the International Labour Standards (ILO), and the United Nations Convention against Corruption (UNCAC). While these international conventions apply directly only to states, their use has been extended in recent years to business as a benchmark for the corporate world's social and ethical responsibilities in terms of human rights and anti-corruption standards. Most notably, from the United Nations Global Compact to the UN Guiding Principles on Human Rights and Business, a wide range of instruments and guidelines have been developed and applied in the corporate world, influencing everything from core business values to supply chain management.

It follows that international sport organizations and their principal asset (major sport events) must also be viewed differently in this contemporary legal landscape. In terms of anti-corruption measures and approaches, international sports organizations and administrators must, for example, be cognizance of the provisions within the OECD Anti-Bribery Convention, the UNCAC, and the tenth principle on anti-corruption added to the UN Global Compact in 2004 – Businesses should work against corruption in all its forms, including extortion and bribery.[11] This global legal landscape now sets the frame for the integrity of sport – and the EU.

III. THE HISTORY OF GOOD GOVERNANCE AS A GLOBAL ISSUE

About 30 years ago, an understanding of the influential role of 'governance' as the source, or symptom or even the solution to organizational

---

[11] UN Global Compact, *The Ten Principles*, https://www.unglobalcompact.org/what-is-gc/mission/principles/principle-10 (accessed 26 Oct 2017).

challenges in the political and corporate worlds, began to emerge. In international development aid for example, experts realized that without the rule of law no progress could be achieved and in 1996, the International Monetary Fund (IMF) approved a Partnership for Sustainable Global Growth: 'promoting Good Governance in all its aspects including by ensuring the rule of law, improving the efficiency and accountability of the public sector, and tackling corruption, as essential elements of a framework within which economies can prosper'.[12] Two years later, then UN Secretary-General Kofi Annan in his report to the General Assembly stated: 'Good governance is perhaps the single most important factor in eradicating poverty and promoting development', adding that 'support for it has become an increasingly important element in the development-related work of the United Nations'.[13]

In 2003, the EU Commission issued a Communication on 'Governance and Development'[14] naming 'Good Governance' as 'one of the basic tools of the EU's development aid instruments' and one that 'has become an integral part of the Commission's cooperation programmes'. That which applied to international development aid could apply elsewhere both at a policy and institutional level and including sport.

In 2005, the Council of Europe started with Recommendation REC(2005)8 on 'Good Governance in Sport'.[15] The Council asked its Member States to:

> Adopt effective policies and measures of good governance in sport, which include as a minimum requirement:
>
> democratic structures for non-governmental sports organisations based on clear and regular electoral procedures open to the whole membership;

---

[12] International Monetary Fund, *Partnership for Sustainable Global Growth, Interim Committee Declaration* (29 September 1996) available at https://www.imf.org/external/np/exr/dec.pdf (accessed 26 Oct 2017).

[13] UN Press Release, United Nations indispensable instrument for achieving common goals, says Secretary General in Report to General Assembly' (SG/2048, GA/9443, 21 September 1998) and available at http://www.un.org/press/en/1998/19980921.sg2048.html (accessed 26 Oct 2017).

[14] Communication from the Commission to the Council, the European Parliament and the European Economic and Social Committee of 20 October 2003: Governance and development, COM(2003) 615 final.

[15] Council of Europe Committee of Ministers, Recommendation Rec(2005)8 of the Committee of Ministers to member states on the principles of good governance in sport (Adopted by the Committee of Ministers on 20 April 2005 at the 924th meeting of the Ministers' Deputies) and available at https://www.coe.int/t/dg4/epas/resources/texts/Rec(2005)8_en.pdf (accessed 26 Oct 2017).

organisation and management of a professional standard, with an appropriate code of ethics and procedures for dealing with conflicts of interest;

accountability and transparency in decision-making and financial operations, including the open publication of yearly financial accounts duly audited;

fairness in dealing with membership, including gender equality and solidarity.

The EU followed in 2007 with its White Paper on Sport,[16] with its take on the principles of Good Governance in sport:

> The Commission can play a role in encouraging the sharing of best practice in sport governance. It can also help to develop a common set of principles for good governance in sport, such as transparency, democracy, accountability and representation of stakeholders (associations, federations, players, clubs, leagues, supporters, etc.).[17]

In 2009, the IOC adopted its 'Basic Universal Principles of Good Governance of the Olympic and Sports Movement'.[18] That document listed 'Themes' and 'Elements to be considered' but did not lead to significant practical results within the sports movement.

In 2011, the European Commission in its Communication on 'Developing the European Dimension in Sport' noted that: 'Good governance in sport is a condition for the autonomy and self-regulation of sport organisations.'[19]

Finally, in May 2013, the Fifth International Conference of Ministers and Senior Officials Responsible for Physical Education and Sport (MINEPS V) in Berlin approved the so-called Berlin Declaration, section 3.3 of which declares that: 'the autonomy of sport organizations is closely linked to their primary responsibility for the integrity of sport and the compliance with the general principles and international standards of good governance'.[20]

---

16 White Paper on Sport, COM(2007) 391 final.

17 Ibid., 12–13.

18 International Olympic Committee, *Good Governance*, available at https://www.olympic.org/good-governance (accessed 26 Oct 2017).

19 Developing the European Dimension in Sport, COM (2011) 12 final, s 4.1.

20 Available at http://unesdoc.unesco.org/images/0022/002211/221114e.pdf (accessed 26 Oct 2017).

IV. BRINGING THE GOVERNANCE OF SPORT ONTO THE AGENDA

The theory or grand declarations of 'Good Governance' apart, the principles of transparency and accountability remained lacking in application in sport. At the international level, a number of sports federations established 'ethics committees' but generally they were seen as 'nice to have', and not meant to interfere in any substantive way with the common behaviour of serving one's own (or one's federation's) interest. Conflicts of interest were rarely addressed, close links and mixed roles between sport, politics, media and business added to the risk of corrupt practices. Above all sport organizations were reluctant to involve stakeholders from other areas of society and heavily rejected any external criticism or scrutiny. Even the IOC's Basic Universal Principles from 2009 had no, or only little, practical impact.

The establishment of the World Anti-Doping-Agency (WADA) in 1999 and the subsequently approval of the WADA-Code in 2004, was undoubtedly an achievement in harmonizing the fight against doping, but at the same time misled the public with regard to its effect. Prominent doping cases such as those of Marion Jones and Lance Armstrong, were not revealed by drug-testing agencies; indeed, those caught by that anti-doping system could be seen to be those not sophisticated enough to dodge the system.

Match-fixing was still ignored as an area of concern by many sport officials, even when Declan Hill published his famous book 'The Fix' in May 2008.[21] The fact that sports betting markets (and increasingly online) left sport vulnerable to manipulation by organized crime in order to make or launder money, was again largely ignored. This finally changed in autumn 2009 with the so-called Bochum case.[22] Almost overnight, football officials realized that their sport was under threat of losing not just credibility but its most important asset: the uncertainty of competition.

Only one year later, in autumn 2010, the awarding of the FIFA World Cups 2018 and 2022 took place amid a worldwide discussion and swirl

---

[21] D Hill, 'Match-fixing in football' (*The Daily Telegraph*, 9 November 2008) http://www.telegraph.co.uk/sport/football/world-cup/3407747/Match-fixing-in-football.html (accessed 26 Oct 2017).

[22] O Gibson, 'Europe hit by biggest-ever match-fixing scandal' (*The Guardian*, 20 November 2009) https://www.theguardian.com/sport/2009/nov/20/uefa-match-fixing-germany (accessed 26 Oct 2017).

of scandal and corruption allegations.[23] Ever since, the governance of sport organizations has been high on the global agenda.

V. GOOD GOVERNANCE IN SPORT: OBSTACLES AND CHALLENGES

When discussing integrity issues in sport the specific structure of sport organizations – usually private non-profit organizations, mainly structured bottom-up with the annual membership meeting as its principal body – is blamed in first instance to be at the root of all negative incidents. As the academic Roger Pielke Jr has noted in his writing on obstacles to accountability in international sports governance:

> Because most international sports bodies are incorporated as associations – that is, voluntary membership organisations – and are legally characterised as non-profits, in general they are not subject to national or international laws or norms that govern business practices.[24]

The historical, loosely self-regulatory, organizational structure or governance of most sports has struggled to deal with the enormous increases in income that have suffused many sports in recent years because of sponsorship and broadcasting rights deals. But it is not just about structure, it is about attitude, too.

Officials, who started as volunteers at lower, local administrative levels of the sport, and continue quite often as volunteers also on national level, are bringing a specific approach to the leadership role, never really perceiving themselves as 'managers'. Moreover, the insularity of sports administration means that some officials quite often think that the end – i.e., supporting their club, federation, sport – justifies the means. Tax evasion and other breaches of rules and even laws are happening at all levels of sport organizations often with no, or only limited, feelings of any wrongdoing.

Additionally, the culture of gifts and invitations is spoiling the independence of sport officials. Understanding corruption in a traditional way – money paid to a public officer to receive an undue advantage, for

---

[23] B Phillips, 'Corruption, Murder and the Beautiful Game' (*Grantland*, 23 August 2011) http://grantland.com/features/corruption-murder-beautiful-game/ (accessed 26 Oct 2017).

[24] R Pielke Jr, 'Obstacles to Accountability in International Sports Governance' in Transparency International (ed.), *Global Corruption Report: Sport* (Routledge 2016), s 1.4.

example a planning application outside the rules – even expensive watches might be seen as a deserved or earned favour for the 'volunteer's' engagement in 'their' sport.[25] In sum, the broad definition of corruption, used, for example by Transparency International, as 'abuse of entrusted power for private gain' is still not common knowledge in sport.

This does not only lead to a lack of individual and organizational integrity but, exacerbated by the low qualifications of many sport officials (some even without basic language skills to follow the discussion in meetings) appointed to international bodies, has opened the opportunity for 'men of action' to seize senior positions in sport and use it for their own interests, be it power, money or both. By distributing favours – for example travel opportunities or even simple tasks like a victory ceremony – jobs, positions and money, a president of an international federation can easily influence everything, perpetuate their fiefdom and escape any meaningful scrutiny of their activities.

And again it is not just the structure that limits accountability. It is common practice in international sport – or at least has been for long time – to rely always on one's own people or 'constituency' – put simply, footballers elect footballers onto the board of a club or federation, swimmers elect swimmers and so on, justified with the argument that outsiders could never truly 'understand our sport'. When those responsible in sport are bound by a former shared activity – in active sport or during a lasting career as official – the 'familial'[26] atmosphere engendered means that any criticism is seen as a blasphemy. It is much more difficult to act against a 'family member', especially when fellowship and solidarity among peers is seen as a specific value within the group. In order to protect the 'family' it is preferred to deny problems and/or to sweep them under the carpet. Sports organizations tend therefore 'to circle the wagons' when attacked – and for many years used this tactic successfully to avert further public scrutiny.

In addition, it sometimes happened that those who ought to have addressed deficiencies in the governance of sport organizations, in fact helped them to circle the wagons. The conflicts of interests between

---

[25] M Ziegler, 'FIFA orders its executives to return £16,000 watches given as gifts by Brazilian FA' (*The Daily Mail*, 19 September 2014) http://www.dailymail.co.uk/sport/football/article-2761023/FIFA-orders-representatives-World-Cup-nations-return-16-000-watches.html (accessed 26 Oct 2017).

[26] A Selliaas, 'Sepp Blatter's football family' (*Play the Game.org*, 19 May 2014) http://www.playthegame.org/news/news-articles/2014/sepp-blatter%E2%80%99s-football-family (accessed 26 Oct 2017).

many journalists, businesses (sponsors and TV companies alike), politicians and sport organizations was used by sports officials to their own advantage e.g., the crossover between politicians as sports officials;[27] sponsor representatives taking up a supervisory function in a sport club;[28] as well as journalists accepting expensive invitations to events in order to 'report' about it. In a more nefarious way, some sports have long attracted an element of criminality or what Declan Hill has called the phenomenon of 'image laundering through sport'.[29]

Given the above, it is no wonder that whistle-blowers in sport have been isolated and have seldom been successful as could be seen exemplarily with regard to doping.[30] In the fight against doping one can as well observe the integrity challenges faced by sport. All efforts taken in the last 15 years, with millions of dollars being spent and nearly 300,000 samples taken per year, have not 'cleaned' sport. The use of performance enhancing substances is endemic in several sports and countries, as shown by the McLaren Report published in July 2016 – the responsibility is not just limited to the athletes. Over decades many officials as well as journalists, sponsors and politicians have shut their eyes or – worse – been complicit to doping athletes – in Russia and beyond. In May 2015 the German Minister for the Interior Thomas de Maizère, also in charge of sport, linked Olympic medal targets to financial governmental support, putting pressure on athletes and their entourage to bring success without addressing the doping-dilemma. Such

---

27 S Walker, 'Vitaly Mutko promoted to newly created Russian deputy prime minister role' (*The Guardian*, 19 October 2016) https://www.theguardian.com/football/2016/oct/19/vitaly-mutko-promoted-russia-deputy-prime-minister-sport-vladimir-putin (accessed 26 Oct 2017).

28 'Adidas boss Hainer to take over from Hoeness at FC Bayern Munich' (*Reuters*, 14 March 2014) http://in.reuters.com/article/us-germany-tax-hoeness-board-idINBREA2D0R920140314 (accessed 26 Oct 2017).

29 D Hill, 'Dead catting, image laundering and why you should have nothing to do with the ICSS' (*Declan Hill Blog*, Undated) http://declanhill.com/dead-catting-image-laundering-and-why-you-should-have-nothing-to-do-with-the-icss/ (accessed 26 Oct 2017).

30 F Lowe, 'Should cycling's bad apples blow the whistle?' (*Eurosport Online*, 9 August 2013) http://www.eurosport.com/cycling/should-cyclings-bad-apples-blow-the-whistle_sto4706210/story.shtml (accessed 26 Oct 2017) and N Butler, 'IOC provide Stepanovs with consultancy work and training grant following meeting with Bach' (*Inside the Games*, 24 October 2016) http://www.insidethegames.biz/articles/1042950/exclusive-ioc-provide-stepanovs-with-consultancy-work-and-training-grant-following-meeting-with-bach (accessed 26 Oct 2017).

a contradictory approach increases the risks and adds to the notion that far too many do not really want to know in detail how medals and medallists are truly made and cleanly earned.

The biggest threat that sport is facing, match-fixing, did not start with organized crime placing a bet on a manipulated game but has a long tradition for sporting reasons as seen in the Bundesliga scandal 1971.[31] The specific 'end of season situation', where a team with nothing to lose or win in the ranking throws a match deliberately for money (or just a crate of beer, depending on the league) to help another team winning the championship or avoiding relegation can be observed in all leagues. Given this cultural background athletes, referees, and other officials may fall prey to criminals looking for accomplices in a match-fixing scheme. This underlines the huge educational effort that is needed to make sports people immune against all kinds of temptation. Ethics is now a supranational agenda item for sport.

VI. WHY GOVERNANCE IN SPORT MATTERS

Grassroots sport, high-performance sport, the hosting of major sport events are all subsidised to some extent by governmental money and thus any doubt about the integrity of sport and its positive impact on society undermines taxpayers' will to continue that support. The number of European cities withdrawing an Olympic bid, mainly due to a 'No' by its citizens, has increased alarmingly in recent years – Hamburg,[32] Krakow, St. Moritz, Munich, Oslo, Stockholm[33] – with Rome being just the last one to drop out for the Summer Games 2024 because its newly elected Mayor wished to spend money in a 'better' way.[34]

Public money aside, the business of sport depends on private investments by sponsors and broadcasters – and these companies, too, rely not

---

[31] J Rainbow, 'Kickers Offenbach and the infamous Bundesliga scandal of 1971' (*World Soccer*, 4 January 2014) http://www.worldsoccer.com/blogs/kickers-offenbach-344286 (accessed 26 Oct 2017).

[32] 'UPDATE 3-Olympics-Hamburg 2024 Games bid collapses in referendum defeat' (*Reuters*, 30 November 2015) http://www.reuters.com/article/olympics-hamburg-idUSL3N13O0BF20151129 (accessed 26 Oct 2017).

[33] M Masnick, 'Almost no one wants to host the Olympics, because it's a costly, corrupt mess' (*Techdirt*, 3 October 2014) https://www.techdirt.com/articles/20141002/15535528705/no-one-wants-to-host-olympics-because-its-costly-corrupt-mess.shtml (accessed 26 Oct 2017).

[34] J de Menezes, 'Italy withdraws Rome 2024 Olympic bid as mayor says money would be better spent on rubbish collection' (*The Independent*,

just on the emotions of sport competitions and the outreach but also on the positive image of sport. When, for example the doping scandals in cycling reached a peak in 2011, German TV-stations dropped their broadcasts of the Tour de France;[35] while serious sponsors had already left the sport some years before.[36] The same happened with Adidas and the International Athletics Associations Federation (IAAF) in 2016;[37] while FIFA sponsors uttered their concerns on ongoing corruption scandals publicly in May 2015.[38]

And it is not just about doping – other misbehaviour of athletes can destroy a sponsoring strategy as happened with regard to the French national team at the FIFA World Cup 2010 in South Africa.[39]

Principles of good governance are closely linked to the fight against doping, match-fixing and any kind of breaching of the rules by individuals. As known from compliance programmes in business the 'tone at the top' as well as 'leading by example' are key to an institution's culture.[40] All efforts to prevent athletes from wrongdoing are more or less in vain if not accompanied by ethical leadership. It follows that sport nowadays needs Good Governance in order to fulfil its mission and not to lose its reputation and above all its income. The specificity of sport,

---

12 October 2016) http://www.independent.co.uk/sport/olympics/rome-2024-olympic-bid-italy-mayor-withdraws-mayor-rubbish-collection-corruption-a7357046.html (accessed 26 Oct 2017).

[35] 'German television preparing to pull the plug on Tour de France coverage?' (*Cycling News*, 2 February 2011) http://www.cyclingnews.com/news/german-television-preparing-to-pull-the-plug-on-tour-de-france-coverage/ (accessed 26 Oct 2017).

[36] I Austen, 'Cycling's drug problem leads T-Mobile to end sponsorship' (*The New York Times*, 28 November 2007) http://www.nytimes.com/2007/11/28/sports/othersports/28cycling.html (accessed 26 Oct 2017).

[37] M Daly, 'Adidas to end IAAF sponsorship deal early in wake of doping crisis' (*BBC Sport Online*, 25 January 2016) http://www.bbc.co.uk/sport/athletics/35385415 (accessed 26 Oct 2017).

[38] P Pylas, 'Coca-Cola, Visa and Adidas are responding to the FIFA corruption scandal' (*Business Insider UK*, 28 May 2015) http://uk.businessinsider.com/coca-cola-visa-and-adidas-are-responding-to-the-fifa-corruption-scandal-2015-5?r=US&IR=T (accessed 26 Oct 2017).

[39] 'World Cup 2010: Sponsors start to shun France team in turmoil' (*The Daily Telegraph*, 21 June 2010) http://www.telegraph.co.uk/sport/football/teams/france/7843775/World-Cup-2010-Sponsors-start-to-shun-France-team-in-turmoil.html (accessed 26 Oct 2017).

[40] See, e.g., Deloitte's ethics and compliance programme at: http://www2.deloitte.com/us/en/pages/risk/articles/tone-at-the-top-the-first-ingredient-in-a-world-class-ethics-and-compliance-program.html (accessed 26 Oct 2017).

founding on being a force for the good and a role model especially for the young, can only be upheld as a reason to distinguish sport federations from 'normal' companies if sport leaders close the gap between ethical ambitions and reality.

VII. THE APPROACH OF THE EU ON GOOD GOVERNANCE IN SPORT: AN OVERVIEW

When, finally, the Lisbon Treaty (TFEU) in December 2009 mentioned sport as part of the EU's competence by way of Article 165 TFEU, it opened the way for the EU to develop a coherent sports policy with a focus on integrity 'whilst taking account of the specific nature of sport'. In a study to shape this policy, it was stated that the EU has to ensure, 'that sporting autonomy is conditioned on the implementation of good governance in sport'.[41] In the EU Work Plan for Sport for 2011–2014[42] as well in the following one for 2014–2017[43] the Council of the EU and the Member States agreed:

> that the following themes and key topics should be given priority by Member States and the Commission for the period covered by the present Work Plan. They could be complemented by each Presidency in the light of any possible new developments:
>
> 1) Integrity of sport, in particular anti-doping, the fight against match-fixing, protection of minors, good governance and gender equality;
> 2) The economic dimension of sport, in particular sustainable financing of sport, the legacy of major sport events, economic benefits of sport and innovation;
> 3) Sport and society, in particular HEPA, volunteering, employment in sport as well as education and training in sport.[44]

---

[41] R Parrish, B Garcia, S Miettinen and R Siekmann, *The Lisbon Treaty and EU Sports Policy* (European Parliament 2010) 7 and available at http://www.europarl.europa.eu/meetdocs/2009_2014/documents/cult/dv/esstudyeusportspolicy/esstudyeusportspolicyen.pdf (accessed 26 Oct 2017).

[42] Resolution of the Council and of the Representatives of the Governments of the Member States, meeting within the Council, on a European Union Work Plan for Sport for 2011–2014 [2011] OJ C 162/01.

[43] Resolution of the Council and of the Representatives of the Governments of the Member States, meeting within the Council, of 21 May 2014 on the European Union Work Plan for Sport (2014–2017) [2014] OJ C 183/03.

[44] Ibid., para 11.

The EU also included Good Governance in sport in the accompanying Preparatory Actions[45] to the above, giving financial support to 20 projects (mainly on Good Governance and Prevention of Match-Fixing) and further established an EU Expert Group on Good Governance.[46] In September 2013, this Expert Group adopted 'Principles for the Good Governance for Sport in the EU'.[47] In January 2016, the Expert Group further adopted 'Guiding Principles relating to democracy, human rights and labour rights, in particular in the context of the awarding procedure of major sport events',[48] which in turn led to Conclusions of the Council of the EU and the Representatives of the Member States in a meeting on 31 May 2016 on 'Enhancing integrity, transparency and good governance in major sport events.'[49]

Finally, on 23 May 2017, the Council and the Representatives of the Governments of the Member States in a joint meeting adopted a Resolution on the European Union Work Plan for Sport (1 July 2017–31 December 2020).[50] Integrity in sport remains an ongoing issue and one in which the EU is committed to developing new analytical methodologies in order to make the solutions and responses to integrity threats more effective and coherent.

---

[45] For details see http://ec.europa.eu/sport/policy/preparatory-actions/preparatory-actions_en.htm (accessed 26 Oct 2017).

[46] For details see https://ec.europa.eu/sport/policy/organisation-of-sport/good-governance (accessed 26 Oct 2017).

[47] EU Work Plan Sport (2011–2014) 'Expert Group, "Good Governance", Deliverable 2, Principles of good governance in sport' (EU Commission, September 2013) and available at http://ec.europa.eu/sport/library/policy_documents/xg-gg-201307-dlvrbl2-sept2013.pdf (accessed 26 Oct 2017).

[48] EU Work Plan Sport (2014–2017) 'Expert Group on Good Governance, Guiding Principles relating to democracy, human rights and labour rights, in particular in the context of the awarding procedure of major sport events' (EU Commission, 13 January 2016) and available at http://ec.europa.eu/sport/library/policy_documents/expert-group-major-sport-events_en.pdf (accessed 26 Oct 2017).

[49] 'Enhancing integrity, transparency and good governance in major sport events – Conclusions of the Council and of the Representatives of the Governments of the Member States, meeting within the Council, 31 May 2016' (Council of Europe, 9644/16) and available at http://data.consilium.europa.eu/doc/document/ST-9644-2016-INIT/en/pdf (accessed 26 Oct 2017).

[50] 'Resolution of the Council and of the Representatives of the Governments of the Member States, meeting within the Council, on the European Union Work Plan for Sport (1 July 2017–31 December 2020) – Council Resolution, 23 May 2017' (Council of Europe, 9639/17) http://data.consilium.europa.eu/doc/document/ST-9639-2017-INIT/en/pdf (accessed 26 Oct 2017).

VIII. FUTURE PERSPECTIVES

All efforts on new structures, governance or ethics commissions, ethic-codes, guidelines and even comprehensive compliance management systems, will not be successful unless combined with a profound cultural change. To improve its governance, sport above all needs an approach based on good values and a comprehensive assessment of the risks that may lead to violations of these values. More positively, it must not be forgotten that for most of us our initial attraction to or engagement with sport – usually at a young age – is based on sports as an inclusive, safe, healthy and value-driven activity.

Fair play, respect for other competitors, acceptance of rules are basics when practising a sport. But it is common knowledge that the stronger the competition, the bigger the temptation to bend the rules and, finally, to cheat. Therefore, a highly competitive sector like sport – on and off the pitch – needs appropriate prevention measures in place. Endemic doping in sport does not necessarily mean that athletes are endemically deviant in their social behaviour; rather the environment – for example an administrative lassitude to doping practices within the sport – is an endemically aggravating factor and thus 'attitudinal doping' as well as that of a performance enhancing nature must be addressed equally in any governance-led reforms.

The values-based approach was stressed by IOC President Thomas Bach in his speech on the occasion of the Opening Ceremony of the 127th IOC Session in December 2014, on the IOC Agenda 2020 when he stated that 'Progress for' the IOC 'means strengthening sport in society by virtue of' its 'values'.[51] The 2016 FIFA Reform Committee, chaired by Dr François Carrard, in its report dated 3 December 2016, went even further. Under the headline 'Principles of Leadership to Effect Cultural Change at FIFA' it noted:

> While changes to FIFA's Statutes and operations are necessary to ensure compliance and adherence to governance best practices, cultural and behavioural changes within FIFA's leadership are the lubricating oil to effect true and lasting changes in order to restore FIFA's reputation.[52]

---

[51] International Olympic Committee, *Olympic Agenda 2020*, 3 and available at https://stillmed.olympic.org/media/Document%20Library/OlympicOrg/Documents/Olympic-Agenda-2020/Olympic-Agenda-2020-20-20-Recommendations.pdf (accessed 26 Oct 2017).

[52] FIFA, *2016 FIFA Reform Committee Report* (2 December 2015) 3 and available at https://resources.fifa.com/mm/document/affederation/football

Taking this into account the EU, besides supporting projects, fostering best practice and developing recommendations, needs to focus on the cultural and behavioural aspects of change management and leadership by example. And yet, what impact do the 'Guiding Principles relating to democracy, human rights and labour rights, in particular in the context of the awarding procedure of major sport events'[53] really have? For example, what action might have been expected from the EU after the European Olympic Committee awarded the European Games 2019 to Minsk in Belarus 'despite criticism of the country's human rights record'?[54]

In 2015 EU law-makers criticized the government of Azerbaijan ahead of the European Games in Baku for putting critics in jail[55] but it now looks like the effect of such criticism as well as of any other deliverable on Good Governance is limited. The EU – like its member countries – has still not found the right balance between respecting the autonomy of sport on the one hand and ensuring Good Governance and the protection of fundamental rights on the other hand.

governance/02/74/17/54/2015.11.27finalreport_forpublication_neutral.pdf (accessed 26 Oct 2017).

[53] EU Work Plan Sport (2014–2017) 'Expert Group on Good Governance, Guiding Principles relating to democracy, human rights and labour rights, in particular in the context of the awarding procedure of major sport events' (EU Commission, 13 January 2016).

[54] J Ellingworth, 'Belarusian capital Mink selected to host 2019 European Games' (*AP*, 21 October 2016) http://summergames.ap.org/article/belarusian-capital-mink-selected-host-2019-european-games (accessed 26 Oct 2017).

[55] R Jozwiak, 'EU lawmakers call on Baku to free critics ahead of European Games' (*Rferl*, 12 May 2015) http://www.rferl.org/a/azerbaijan-european-games-human-rights-european-union/27012189.html (accessed 26 Oct 2017).

Index